Parent Guide

Glenda Lappan
James T. Fey
William M. Fitzgerald
Susan Friel
Elizabeth Difanis Phillips

PEARSON

Prentice
Hall

Boston, Massachusetts
Upper Saddle River, New Jersey

Connected Mathematics™ Project was developed at Michigan State University with financial support from the Michigan State University Office of the Provost, Computing and Technology, and the College of Natural Science.

Connected Mathematics™ is based upon work supported by the National Science Foundation under Grant No. MDR 9150217 and Grant No. ESI 9986372. Opinions expressed are those of the authors and not necessarily those of the Foundation.

The Michigan State University authors and administration have agreed that all MSU royalties arising from this publication will be devoted to purposes supported by the Department of Mathematics and the MSU Mathematics Enrichment Fund.

Acknowledgments The people who made up the *Connected Mathematics 2* team—representing editorial, editorial services, design services, and production services—are listed below. Bold type denotes core team members.

Leora Adler, Judith Buice, Kerry Cashman, Patrick Culleton, Sheila DeFazio, Katie Hallahan, Richard Heater, **Barbara Holllingdale, Jayne Holman,** Karen Holtzman, **Etta Jacobs,** Christine Lee, Carolyn Lock, Catherine Maglio, **Dotti Marshall,** Rich McMahon, Eve Melnechuk, Terri Mitchell, **Marsha Novak,** Irene Rubin, Donna Russo, Robin Samper, Siri Schwartzman, **Nancy Smith,** Emily Soltanoff, **Mark Tricca,** Paula Vergith, Roberta Warshaw, Helen Young.

ISBN 0-13-165856-5

7 8 9 10   10 09 08

Table of Contents

Connected Mathematics 2

Suggestions for

Helping Your Child Succeed

The goals of *Connected Mathematics 2* (CMP2) are to help students:

- Develop mathematical knowledge, understanding, and skill

- Develop the capacity to define and solve problems with reason, insight, inventiveness, and technical proficiency

- Build on and make connections among mathematical ideas and concepts

- See the connections between mathematics and other disciplines

....

In CMP2, the instructional practices of the teacher and the ways in which students engage in mathematics support these goals. Teaching, learning, and assessing are aligned with each other as integral parts of *Connected Mathematics 2*.

....

For more information, please visit the CMP Parent Web Site: http://www.math.msu.edu/cmp/parents Or the Prentice Hall CMP2 Web Site: http://www.PHSchool.com/cmp2

PEARSON
Prentice Hall

What Are the Strengths of *Connected Mathematics 2?*

....

As a complete mathematics curriculum for grades 6–8, *Connected Mathematics 2:*

- Is organized around important mathematical ideas and processes

- Is a problem-centered curriculum that uses an inquiry-based instructional model

- Develops deep understanding of key mathematical ideas, reasoning, and skills

- Substantially raises the level of mathematical thinking and reasoning of students

- Promotes long-term retention of mathematical concepts, processes, and skills

- Connects mathematical ideas within a unit, across units, and across grade levels

- Provides homework that emphasizes practice with skills and problem solving

- Incorporates technology throughout the curriculum

- Offers multidimensional assessment tasks

- Is based on three decades of experience and research

Authors

....

Glenda T. Lappan, Michigan State University

James T. Fey, University of Maryland

William M. Fitzgerald, Michigan State University (Deceased)

Susan N. Friel, University of North Carolina

Elizabeth Difanis Phillips, Michigan State University

Awards

....

The American Association for the Advancement of Science (AAAS) rated CMP the highest of twelve middle school mathematics curricula stating that it "contains both in-depth mathematics content and excellent instructional support."
— January 22, 1999

The United States Department of Education's Expert Panel designated *Connected Mathematics* as an exemplary mathematics curriculum. Only five K–12 mathematics curricula received this designation. CMP was the only exemplary middle school curriculum.
— U.S. Department of Education, 1999

Royalties

....

The authors receive no royalties from the sale of the *Connected Mathematics* books. The Michigan State University authors and administration have agreed that all MSU royalties arising from the publication of CMP books will be put into a mathematics education fund to support projects related to CMP and mathematics education.

Funding

....

The National Science Foundation and the Michigan State University Office of the Provost, Computing and Technology, and the College of Natural Science provided funding for the development of CMP.

Research and Evaluation Summary

....

A CMP Research and Evaluation Summary is available from the publisher, Prentice Hall.
http://www.phschool.com/math/cmp/research_evaluation

In helping your child learn, one goal is to assist them in figuring out as much as they can for themselves. Good questions and good listening will help make sense of mathematics, build self-confidence, and encourage mathematical thinking and communication. Here are some questions you can use to guide your child's thinking:

Getting Started . . . .
- What do you need to find out?
- What do you know?
- What terms do you understand or not understand?
- Have you solved similar problems that would help? Let's look at your notebook.

Working on the Problem . . . . .
- How can you organize the information?
- Do you see any patterns or relationships that will help solve this?
- Can you describe a strategy you can use to solve this?
- Can you make a drawing to explain your thinking?
- What would happen if . . . ?

Reflecting On a Solution . . . .
- Has the question been answered?
- How do you know your solution is reasonable?
- How can you convince me your answer makes sense?
- What mathematical skills and ideas did you use to solve the problem?
- What did you try that did not work?

Clarifying and Extending Thinking . . . .
- Help me understand this part. . .
- Can you explain it in a different way?
- Is there another possibility or strategy that would work?
- How is this connected to other ideas that you have learned?

Find a Study Place If possible, arrange for a quiet area. Have available materials such as graph paper, notebook paper, a ruler with both metric and standard units, a calculator (graphing for 7th–12th grade), and a dictionary.

Develop a System Help your child develop a system for writing down assignments and keeping track of progress. Check to make sure your child does so consistently.

Develop Note Taking Skills Help your child develop a system for taking meaningful notes. Frequently, note taking is taught during class, so it may just be a matter of seeing if your child is properly taking notes.

Organize Your Notebook Many children need assistance in organizing and maintaining a notebook. Routinely check to see if your child is correctly following the program's guidelines for keeping notebooks.

Foster Time Management Skills Encourage and expect your child to get work done on time, to stay caught up, to get help in a timely manner, and to correct errors in work. You may want to help your child go over incorrect or incomplete work and talk about how the work could be improved.

Master the Needed Skills It is generally expected that middle school students know whole number addition, subtraction, multiplication, and division. If your child is not proficient with these basic skills, help them master the needed skills.

Find Study Buddies Encourage your child to identify study buddies or another student they can call to work with on assignments, get clarification, or find out about makeup work.

Two important goals for all students are that they learn to value mathematics and become confident in their ability to do mathematics. Parents can help them develop a "can do" disposition toward math, by nurturing their curiosity and providing support and encouragement.

Point Out Real-World Mathematics Mathematics is everywhere, yet many children don't see it. Point out and reinforce mathematics skills at home. For example:
- Talk about how you use math at work or home.
- Involve your child in tasks that require computing, measuring, estimating, building, problem solving, and reasoning.
- Look for activities that require your child to use their mathematical skills such as building scale models, cooking, planning trips, and playing logic games.

Have Your Child Explain What They Learned Invite your child to explain what was learned in class. It gives them an opportunity to clarify their thinking, to practice new skills, and to communicate mathematically.

Look for Games Using games and activities is an another way of teaching and/or reinforcing mathematics skills and thinking.

Look for Articles Many articles have data that might interest your child (e.g., sports statistics, data on teenage smoking, facts about natural disasters). Share them and talk about what the numbers mean.

Share Strategies Have your child share their strategies for problem solving, mental computation, and estimation. Share your strategies with them.

Look for Software If your child has access to a computer, look for software that reinforces and teaches mathematical concepts.

Dear Family,

The first unit in your child's mathematics class this year is ***Prime Time: Factors and Multiples.*** This is the first unit of the number strand in *Connected Mathematics.*

UNIT GOALS

Prime Time focuses on the properties of whole numbers, especially those related to multiplication and division. Students will learn about factors, multiples, divisors, products, prime numbers, composite numbers, common factors and multiples, and many other ideas about numbers. Students will participate in a series of activities that reflect many of the key properties of numbers and learn how to use these properties to solve problems.

HELPING WITH HOMEWORK

The goal of *Connected Mathematics* is to help students develop sound mathematical habits. You can help with homework and at the same time encourage sound mathematical habits by asking questions such as:

- Will finding factors or multiples help you solve the problem?
- What relationships will factors or multiples help you see?
- What do the factors and multiples of numbers tell you about the situation?
- How can you find the factors of a number?
- How can you find the multiples of a number?
- What common factors and common multiples do two numbers have?

In your child's notebook, you can find worked-out examples from problems done in class, notes on the unit's mathematics, and descriptions of the vocabulary words.

In this unit, your child will be asked to do a project called "My Special Number." It is introduced at the beginning of the unit, when each student is asked to choose a number and write several things about it. As students work through the unit, they apply what they have learned to write new information about their numbers. At the end of the unit, students create projects that include everything they have learned about their numbers.

HAVING CONVERSATIONS ABOUT THE MATHEMATICS IN *PRIME TIME*

You can help your child in several ways:

- Have your child share his or her mathematics notebook with you, showing you what has been recorded about factors and multiples. Ask your child to explain why these ideas are important.
- Have your child show you the boards for playing the Factor Game and the Product Game. Ask your child to explain the rules, and, if you have time, offer to play a game.
- Have your child explain something that he or she learned from playing the game.
- Look over your child's homework and make sure all questions are answered and that explanations are clear.

A few important mathematical ideas that your child will learn in *Prime Time* are given on the back. As always, if you have any questions or concerns about this unit or your child's progress in the class, please feel free to call.

Sincerely,

Important Concepts	Examples
Factors One of two or more numbers that are multiplied to get a product.	All the factors of 12 are 1, 2, 3, 4, 6, 12 because $1 \times 12 = 12$, $2 \times 6 = 12$, $3 \times 4 = 12$.
Multiples The product of a given whole number and another whole number.	Some multiples of 12 include 12, 24, 36, 48, 60 because $12 \times 1 = 12$, $12 \times 2 = 24$, $12 \times 3 = 36$, $12 \times 4 = 48$, and $12 \times 5 = 60$. Note that any number has an infinite number of multiples. If a number is a multiple of 12, then 12 is a factor of that number. For example, 36 is a multiple of 12 and 12 is a factor of 36.
Prime A number with exactly two different factors, 1 and the number itself.	Examples of primes are 11, 17, 53, and 101. The number 1 is not a prime number, since it has only one factor. All the factors of 11 are 1 and 11. All the factors of 17 are 1 and 17.
Composite A whole number with factors other than itself and 1 or a whole number that is not prime.	Some composite numbers are 6, 12, 20, and 1,001. Each of these numbers has more than two factors. All the factors of 6 are 1, 2, 3, 6. All the factors of 1,001 are 1, 7, 11, 13, 77, 91, 143, 1001.
Common Multiples A multiple that two or more numbers share.	Some multiples of 5 are 5, 10, 15, 20, 25, 30, <u>35</u>, 40, 45, 50, 55, 60, 65, and <u>70</u>. Some multiples of 7 are 7, 14, 21, 28, <u>35</u>, 42, 49, 56, 63, <u>70</u>, and 77. From these lists we can see that two common multiples of 5 and 7 are 35 and 70. There are more common multiples that can be found.
Common Factors A factor that two or more numbers share.	7 is a common factor of 14 and 35 because 7 is a factor of 14 ($14 = 7 \times 2$) and 7 is a factor of 35 ($35 = 7 \times 5$).
Prime Factorization A product of prime numbers, resulting in the desired number. The prime factorization of a number is unique except for the order of the factors. This is the **Fundamental Theorem of Arithmetic.**	360 15 × 24 3 × 5 × 24 3 × 5 × 4 × 6 3 × 5 × 2 × 2 × 2 × 3 The prime factorization of 360 is $2 \times 2 \times 2 \times 3 \times 3 \times 5$. Although you can switch the order of the factors, every prime product string for 360 will have three 2s, two 3s, and one 5.

On the **CMP Parent Web Site**, you can learn more about the mathematical goals of each unit, see an illustrated vocabulary list, and examine solutions of selected ACE problems. **http://PHSchool.com/cmp2parents**

Dear Family,

The next unit in your child's mathematics class this year is ***Bits and Pieces I: Understanding Fractions, Decimals, and Percents***. It is the first of three units to develop understanding of fractions, decimals, and percents. Computation with fractions, decimals and percents will be the focus of *Bits and Pieces II and III*.

UNIT GOALS

Bits and Pieces I focuses on developing a deep understanding of rational numbers. In this unit, your child will learn the meanings of fractions, decimals, and percents, and will become comfortable moving among these three representations of rational numbers. Your child will work on problems that reflect different contexts and that involve writing, comparing, and ordering fractions and decimals.

This unit makes use of models, such as fraction strips, number lines, and grids. Skill with estimating and comparing is developed through a set of benchmark fractions and their decimal equivalents. Benchmark fractions are those that occur often in real-world situations. Some examples are $\frac{1}{4}$, $\frac{1}{3}$, $\frac{1}{2}$, $\frac{2}{3}$, $\frac{3}{4}$, and $1\frac{1}{2}$.

HELPING WITH HOMEWORK

You can help with homework and encourage sound mathematical habits as your child studies this unit by asking questions such as:

- Why do we need to consider amounts that do not represent whole numbers?
- Why can there be different fraction names for the same quantity?
- How can you tell when two fractions are equivalent?
- How can we tell which of two fractions is greater?
- In what situations is a decimal name for a fractional quantity useful?
- How can we change a fractional name to the equivalent decimal or percent name?
- Why are fractions with a denominator of 100 useful?

In your child's notebook, you can find worked-out examples from problems done in class, notes on the unit's mathematics, and descriptions of the vocabulary words.

HAVING CONVERSATIONS ABOUT THE MATHEMATICS IN *BITS AND PIECES I*

You can help your child with his or her work for this unit in several ways:

- With your child, find examples of how fractions, decimals, and percents are used in newspapers, magazines, radio, and television.
- Look over your child's homework and make sure all questions are answered and that explanations are clear.
- Have your child pick a question that was interesting to him or her and explain it to you.

A few important mathematical ideas that your child will learn in *Bits and Pieces I* are given on the back. As always, if you have any questions or concerns about this unit or your child's progress in class, please feel free to call.

Sincerely,

Important Concepts	Examples
Fractions as Parts of a Whole In the part-whole interpretation of fractions, students must: • determine what the whole is; • subdivide the whole into equal-size parts—not necessarily equal shape, but equal size; • recognize how many parts are needed to represent the situation; and • form the fraction by placing the parts needed over the number of parts into which the whole has been divided.	If there are 24 students in the class and 16 are girls, the part of the whole that is girls can be represented as $\frac{16}{24}$. The shaded portion above can also be represented as $\frac{2}{3}$. The **denominator** of 3 tells into how many equal-size parts the whole has been divided, and the **numerator** of 2 tells how many of the equal-size parts have been shaded.
Fractions as Measures or Quantities In this interpretation, a fraction is thought of as a number.	A fraction can be a measurement that is "in between" two whole measures. Students meet this every day in such references as $2\frac{1}{2}$ brownies, 11.5 million people, or $7\frac{1}{2}$ inches.
Fractions as Indicated Divisions To move with flexibility between fraction and decimal representations of rational numbers, students need to understand that fractions can be thought of as indicated divisions.	Sharing 36 apples among 6 people calls for division ($36 \div 6 = 6$ apples each), so sharing 3 apples among 8 people calls for dividing 3 by 8 to find out how many each person receives ($\frac{3}{8}$ of an apple).
Fractions as Decimals Students need to understand decimals in two ways: as special fractions with denominators of 10 and powers of 10, and as a natural extension of the place-value system for representing quantities less than 1.	For the fraction $\frac{2}{5}$, for example, we can find the decimal representation by rewriting as the equivalent fraction $\frac{4}{10}$ or by dividing 2 by 5. This uses the division interpretation of fractions to find the decimal representation of the same quantity. $\frac{2}{5} = 2 \div 5 = 0.4$ 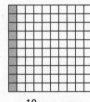
Fractions as Percents This builds the connection between and among fractions, decimals, and percents. Percents are introduced as special names for hundredths, $\frac{1}{100}$.	Ten percent, 10%, is simply another way to represent 0.10 or 0.1, which is another way to represent $\frac{10}{100}$ or $\frac{1}{10}$. 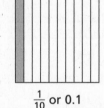 $\frac{10}{100}$ or 0.10 $\frac{1}{10}$ or 0.1
Equivalent Fractions Partitioning and then partitioning again is an important skill that contributes to understanding equivalence. Equivalent fractions have the same value.	If a bar is marked into fourths (the first partition) and then each fourth is marked into thirds (the second partition), each original fourth has three parts (or three-twelfths) in it. This one-fourth is equivalent to three-twelfths. $\frac{1}{4} = \frac{1 \times 3}{4 \times 3} = \frac{3}{12}$ 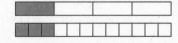

On the **CMP Parent Web Site,** you can learn more about the mathematical goals of each unit, see an illustrated vocabulary list, and examine solutions of selected ACE problems.
http://PHSchool.com/cmp2parents

Dear Family,

The next unit in your child's mathematics class this year is ***Shapes and Designs: Two-Dimensional Geometry***. It is the first unit in the *Connected Mathematics* geometry strand. Students will recognize, analyze, measure, and reason about the shapes and visual patterns that are important features of our world. It builds on students' previous exposure to simple shapes by analyzing the properties that make certain shapes special and useful.

UNIT GOALS

The goal of *Shapes and Designs* is to have students discover and analyze many of the key properties of polygonal shapes that make them useful and attractive. This unit focuses on polygons and develops these two themes:

- How do the measures of angles in a polygon determine its shapes and uses?
- How do the lengths of edges in a polygon determine its shapes and uses?

Each investigation focuses on some key properties of figures and the importance of those properties in applications. Students are periodically asked to identify differences among particular classifications of polygons. Students are also asked to find and describe places where they see different polygons and to think about why those shapes are used.

HELPING WITH HOMEWORK

You can help with homework and encourage sound mathematical habits as your child studies this unit by asking questions such as:

- What kinds of shapes/polygons will cover a flat surface?
- What do these shapes have in common?
- How can angle measures be estimated?
- How can angles be measured with more accuracy?

In your child's notebook, you can find worked-out examples from problems done in class, notes on the unit's mathematics, and descriptions of the vocabulary words.

HAVING CONVERSATIONS ABOUT THE MATHEMATICS IN *SHAPES AND DESIGNS*

You can help your child see how this aspect of geometry is important in everyday life in several ways:

- Whenever you notice an interesting shape in a newspaper or a magazine, discuss with your child whether it is one of the polygons mentioned in the unit, and suggest that it might be cut out and saved for the shapes project.

- Have your child share his or her mathematics notebook with you, showing you what has been recorded about the different shapes being studied. Ask your child to explain why these ideas are important, and try to share ways that shapes help you with work or hobbies.

- Look over your child's homework and make sure all questions are answered and that explanations are clear.

A few important mathematical ideas that your child will learn in *Shapes and Designs* are given on the back. As always, if you have any questions or concerns about this unit or your child's progress in class, please feel free to call.

Sincerely,

Important Concepts and Examples

Polygon

A shape formed by line segments so that each of the segments meets exactly two other segments, and all of the points where the segments meet are end points of the segments.

Polygons | Not polygons

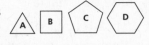  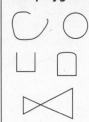

Polygon Names

Triangle 3 sides and 3 angles
Quadrilateral 4 sides and 4 angles
Pentagon 5 sides and 5 angles
Hexagon 6 sides and 6 angles
Heptagon 7 sides and 7 angles
Octagon 8 sides and 8 angles
Nonagon 9 sides and 9 angles
Decagon 10 sides and 10 angles
Dodecagon 12 sides and 12 angles

Regular Polygons

Polygons whose side lengths are equal and interior angle measures are equal.

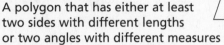

Irregular Polygon

A polygon that has either at least two sides with different lengths or two angles with different measures

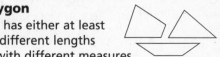

Line (or Mirror) Symmetry

If the polygon is folded over the line of symmetry, the two halves of the shape will match exactly.

Rotational (or Turn) Symmetry

A polygon with turn symmetry can be turned around its center point less than a full turn and still look exactly as it did before it was rotated.

Angles

Angles are figures formed by two rays or line segments that have a common vertex. The **vertex** of an angle is the point where the two rays meet or intersect. Angles are measured in degrees.

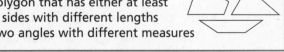

Angle Measures

To develop estimation skills, students relate angles to right angles. Combinations and partitions of 90° are used as benchmarks to estimate angle size.

A **goniometer** (goh nee AHM uh tur), or **angle ruler**, is an instrument for making more precise measurements of angles. This tool is used in the medical field for measuring angle of motion or flexibility in body joints, such as knees.

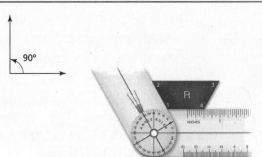

Angles and Parallel Lines

Parallel lines cut by a **transversal** make pairs of equal corresponding angles and pairs of equal alternate interior angles. Angles 1 and 5, angles 2 and 6, angles 3 and 7, and angles 4 and 8 are pairs of **corresponding angles**. Angles 4 and 5 and angles 3 and 6 are pairs of **alternate interior angles**.

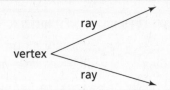

Polygons That Tile a Plane

For regular polygons to tile a plane (or cover a flat surface without gaps or overlaps), the angle measure of an interior angle must be a factor of 360°. The only regular polygons that can tile a plane are an equilateral triangle (60° angles), a square (90° angles), and a regular hexagon (120° angles).

Triangle Inequality Theorem

The sum of two side lengths of a triangle must be greater than the 3rd side length.

If the side lengths are a, b, and c, then: $a + b > c$, $b + c > a$, $c + a > b$

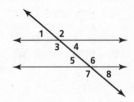

On the **CMP Parent Web Site**, you can learn more about the mathematical goals of each unit, see an illustrated vocabulary list, and examine solutions of selected ACE problems. http://PHSchool.com/cmp2parents

Dear Family,

The next unit in your child's course of study in mathematics class this year is ***Bits and Pieces II: Using Fraction Operations***. This is the second of three number units that focus on developing concepts and procedures for computing with fractions, decimals, and percents.

UNIT GOALS

In this unit, the focus is on understanding and developing systematic ways to add, subtract, multiply, and divide fractions. While working on this unit, students investigate interesting problem situations to help them develop algorithms for fraction computation. In addition, students will use benchmarks and number and operation sense to estimate solutions for computations to help them decide if their answers are reasonable.

HELPING WITH HOMEWORK

You can help with homework and encourage sound mathematical habits as your child studies this unit by asking questions such as:

- What models or diagrams might be helpful in understanding the situation?
- What models or diagrams might help decide which operation is useful in solving a problem?
- What is a reasonable estimate for the answer?
- What strategies or algorithms would help you solve this problem?

In your child's notebook, you can find worked-out examples from problems done in class, notes on the mathematics of the unit, and descriptions of the vocabulary words.

HAVING CONVERSATIONS ABOUT THE MATHEMATICS IN *BITS AND PIECES II*

You can help your child with his or her work for this unit in several ways:

- There are various logical procedures for computing with fractions. At times, students may be working with ideas and algorithms that are different from the ones you learned. Be open to these approaches. Encourage your child to share these methods with you as a way to help them make sense of what they are studying.
- Ask your child to tell you about a problem that he or she has enjoyed solving. Ask for an explanation of the ideas in the problem.
- Look over your child's homework and make sure all questions are answered and explanations are clear.

A few important mathematical ideas that your child will learn in *Bits and Pieces II* are given on the back. As always, if you have any questions or concerns about this unit or your child's progress in class, please feel free to call.

Sincerely,

Important Concepts	Examples
Addition and Subtraction of Fractions Students model problems to develop meaning and skill in addition and subtraction. Students learn to find common denominators so that the numerators can be added or subtracted.	To find the sum of A + B on the rectangle, or $\frac{1}{2} + \frac{1}{8}$, students need to use equivalent fractions to rename $\frac{1}{2}$ as $\frac{4}{8}$. The area model helps students visualize A, $\frac{1}{2}$, as $\frac{4}{8}$ and they write the number sentence, $$\frac{4}{8} + \frac{1}{8} = \frac{5}{8}.$$ 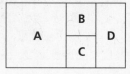 The *number-line model* helps connect fractions to quantities. This illustrates $1\frac{1}{3} - \frac{2}{3} = \frac{2}{3}$. 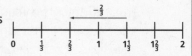
Developing a Multiplication Algorithm Students use models to see that they can just multiply the numerators and multiply the denominators of proper fractions.	An area model can show $\frac{2}{3} \times \frac{3}{4}$. Shade a square to show $\frac{3}{4}$. To represent taking $\frac{2}{3}$ of $\frac{3}{4}$, cut the square into thirds the opposite way and use hash marks on two of the three sections. The overlap sections represent the product, $\frac{6}{12}$. The **denominators** partition and repartition the whole. Breaking the fourths into three parts each makes 12 pieces. In the algorithm, you multiply the denominators (3 × 4) to resize the whole to have the correct number of parts. denominator → $\frac{2}{3} \times \frac{3}{4} = \frac{2 \times 3}{3 \times 4} = \frac{6}{12}$ numerator → $\frac{2}{3} \times \frac{3}{4} = \frac{2 \times 3}{3 \times 4} = \frac{6}{12}$ The **numerator** is keeping track of how many of the parts are being referenced. You need to take 2 out of 3 sections from each part. This can be represented by the product of the numerators 2 × 3.
Developing a Division Algorithm Students may have various ways to think about division of fractions. Our goal in the development of algorithms is to help students develop an efficient algorithm.	**Common Denominator Approach** Students rewrite $\frac{7}{9} \div \frac{1}{3}$ as $\frac{7}{9} \div \frac{3}{9}$. The common denominator allows the reasoning that if you have 7 one-ninth-sized pieces and want to find out how many groups of 3 one-ninth-sized pieces you can make, then $\frac{7}{9} \div \frac{3}{9}$ has the same answer as $7 \div 3 = 2\frac{1}{3}$. **Multiplying by the Denominator and Dividing by the Numerator** With $9 \div \frac{1}{3}$, you can reason: I have to find the total number of $\frac{1}{3}$s in 9. There are three $\frac{1}{3}$s in 1, so there are 9 × 3, or 27, $\frac{1}{3}$s in 9. $9 \div \frac{1}{3} = 9 \times 3 = 27$. With $\frac{2}{3} \div \frac{1}{5}$, we can reason that $1 \div \frac{1}{5}$ is 5, as $\frac{2}{3} \div \frac{1}{5}$ should be $\frac{2}{3}$ of this, or $\frac{2}{3}$ of 5, or $\frac{10}{3}$. We could also rename $\frac{2}{3} \div \frac{1}{5}$ as $\frac{10}{15} \div \frac{3}{15}$ and see this as 10 fifteenths divided by 3 fifteenths, which is the same as $10 \div 3$, or $\frac{10}{3}$. Notice that this requires us to multiply the number of $\frac{2}{3}$s by 5. With $\frac{2}{3} \div \frac{4}{5}$, we can reason that this should be $\frac{1}{4}$ of $\left(\frac{2}{3} \div \frac{1}{5}\right)$, or $\frac{1}{4}\left(\frac{10}{3}\right) = \frac{10}{12}$. Notice that this reasoning requires us to multiply the denominator of $\frac{2}{3}$ by 4. In short, to compare $\frac{2}{3} \div \frac{4}{5}$ we compute $\frac{2}{3} \times \frac{5}{1} \times \frac{1}{4} = \frac{10}{12}$. That is, we multiply the numerator of $\frac{2}{3}$ by 5 and the denominator by 4. **Multiplying by the Reciprocal** We see that $\frac{2}{3} \div \frac{4}{5}$ (see above) gives the same result as $\frac{2}{3} \times \frac{5}{4}$.

On the **CMP Parent Web Site,** you can learn more about the mathematical goals of each unit, see an illustrated vocabulary list, and examine solutions of selected ACE problems. **http://PHSchool.com/cmp2parents**

Dear Family,

The next unit in your child's mathematics class this year is ***Covering and Surrounding: Two-Dimensional Measurement***. The focus is area (covering) and perimeter (surrounding). The unit helps students develop an understanding of perimeters and areas of rectangles, triangles, parallelograms, and circles. Students use estimating and counting to find areas and perimeters of irregular figures.

UNIT GOALS

The overarching goal of this unit is to help students understand what it means to measure. Students study two kinds of measurements: perimeter and area. Since students often do not know how each of these measures affects the other, students study them together to probe the relationships.

Students develop strategies for measuring perimeter and area. Their strategies are discussed and used to formulate rules for finding area and perimeter of different figures. Many ideas from previous units will be revisited and extended in this unit. For example, from the *Prime Time* unit, the connection between factors and dimensions of rectangles will be used.

HELPING WITH HOMEWORK

You can help with homework and encourage sound mathematical habits as your child studies this unit by asking questions such as:

- How do you know which measurements of a figure are involved—area or perimeter?
- How can you find the area and perimeter of an irregular shape?
- How can you find the area and perimeter of a regular shape?
- Is an exact answer required?
- Is there a relationship between area and perimeter that will help solve the problem?

In your child's notebook, you can find worked-out examples from problems done in class, notes on the mathematics of the unit, and descriptions of the vocabulary words.

HAVING CONVERSATIONS ABOUT THE MATHEMATICS IN *COVERING AND SURROUNDING*

You can help your child with his or her work for this unit in several ways:

- Encourage him or her to use the measuring tools you have at home, such as measuring tapes and rulers, to practice making measurements.
- Help your child develop personal referents for estimating lengths and distances. For example, the distance from home to school might be one mile, or the span of your child's hand might be six inches. Use these referents to estimate other distances and lengths.
- Help your child develop personal referents for estimating area. Use the area of his or her bedroom to estimate areas of other rooms.
- Look over your child's homework and make sure all questions are answered and that explanations are clear.

A few important mathematical ideas that your child will learn in *Covering and Surrounding* are given on the back. As always, if you have any questions or concerns about this unit or your child's progress in class, please feel free to call.

Sincerely,

Important Concepts	Examples
The Measurement Process • Identify an object and the attribute to be measured. • Select an appropriate unit. • Repeatedly "match" the unit to the attribute of the object (or phenomenon, such as time). • Determine the number of units.	**Measuring Perimeter** Measuring perimeter requires counting how many linear units are needed to surround an object. **Measuring Area** Measuring area requires counting how many square units are needed to cover an object.
Area of Rectangles Students begin finding the area by counting the number of squares enclosed. To count more efficiently, they find the number of squares in one row and multiply by the number of rows. In other words, find the area by multiplying the length (how many in a row) by the width (the number of rows).	There are 5 squares in the first row and 7 rows in all. The area of the rectangle is $5 \times 7 = 35$ square units or, in general, $\ell \times w$.
Perimeter of Rectangles Students count the number of linear units surrounding the rectangle. To count more efficiently, they can take the measure of the length plus the width and double that amount. They can also calculate two lengths plus two widths to get the perimeter of a rectangle.	The perimeter of the figure above is $2(7 + 5)$ or $2 \times 7 + 2 \times 5$ or, in general, $2(\ell + w)$ or $2\ell + 2w$.
Area of Triangles Students use their knowledge of rectangles to find the area of triangles. If we surround a triangle with a rectangle, we can see that the area of the triangle is half of the area of the rectangle. The triangle may be turned to a convenient side as the base, if needed.	Sections 1 and 2 are congruent. 3 and 4 are congruent. The area of the triangle is $\frac{1}{2} b \times h$ where b is the base of the triangle (length of the rectangle) and h is the height of the triangle (width of the rectangle).
Perimeter of Triangles Students find the perimeter of a triangle by measuring the lengths of the three sides and adding them together.	The perimeter of the triangle is $7 + 10 + 12.2$, or 19.2 ft.
Area of Parallelograms Students draw a diagonal creating two congruent triangles. The parallelogram and triangle have the same length of the base and height. Students find the area of the parallelogram by multiplying the base and height, without dividing by two, as they did when finding the area of a triangle.	The area of a parallelogram is the area of two triangles $2 \times (\frac{1}{2} b \times h)$, or just $b \times h$.
Perimeter of Parallelograms The perimeter of parallelograms is found by measuring the lengths of the four sides and adding them together.	The perimeter of the parallelogram is $2(5 + 6)$ or $2 \times 5 + 2 \times 6 = 22$ cm.
Area of Circles Students find the number of "radius squares," whose side lengths are equal to the radius, that cover the circle. They find they need a little more than three, or pi.	The area of a circle is pi $\times$ a "radius square" or pi $\times$ radius $\times$ radius $= \pi \times r \times r = \pi r^2$ radius square (r^2) 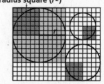
Perimeter of Circles (Circumference) Students count the number of diameter lengths needed to surround the circle. It is a little more than three, or pi.	The circumference of a circle is pi $\times$ diameter $= \pi d$.

On the **CMP Parent Web Site**, you can learn more about the mathematical goals of each unit, see an illustrated vocabulary list, and examine solutions of selected ACE problems. **http://PHSchool.com/cmp2parents**

Dear Family,

The next unit in your child's mathematics class is ***Bits and Pieces III: Computing with Decimals and Percents***. It is the third and final unit in the development of understanding fractions, decimals, and percents.

UNIT GOALS

Like the work done to develop fraction operations, students will engage in many problem situations as they develop algorithms for adding, subtracting, multiplying, and dividing decimals. They will explore percents in the context of tip, tax, discount, and total cost.

Students have two ways of making sense of what decimals mean—extending the place-value system on which our number system is built or interpreting decimals as fractions. In order to have the most complete understanding of and skill with computation, students need to understand each of these meanings. Then they use them to examine why decimal algorithms for addition, subtraction, multiplication, and division make sense. Depending on the operation, the fraction interpretation or the place value interpretation may help in finding short-cut algorithms. Students will draw upon and use the ideas developed in *Bits and Pieces I* and *Bits and Pieces II*. For example, students will use the algorithm they developed for multiplying fractions in *Bits and Pieces II* to help them develop and understand an algorithm for multiplying decimals.

HELPING WITH HOMEWORK

You can help with homework and encourage sound mathematical habits as your child studies this unit by asking questions such as:

- What is a reasonable estimate for the answer? Or, About how large will the sum (difference, product, or quotient) be?
- How do these decimals compare to fractions?
- What strategies or algorithms would help you solve this problem?
- Why are percents useful in this problem?

In your child's notebook, you can find worked-out examples from problems done in class, notes on the mathematics of the unit, and descriptions of the vocabulary words.

HAVING CONVERSATIONS ABOUT THE MATHEMATICS IN *BITS AND PIECES III*

You can help your child with his or her work for this unit in several ways:

- Ask your child for an explanation of the ideas in a problem. For example, why do you line up the decimals when adding and subtracting decimal numbers?
- At times, students may be working with ideas and algorithms that are different from the ones you learned. Encourage your child to share these methods with you as a way to help them make sense of what they are studying.
- When shopping or eating in a restaurant with your child, ask him or her to estimate what the tax will be on a purchase or what the tip should be for a meal.

A few important mathematical ideas that your child will learn in *Bits and Pieces III* are given on the back. As always, if you have any questions or concerns about this unit or your child's progress in class, please feel free to call.

Sincerely,

Important Concepts	Examples
Addition and Subtraction of Decimals **DECIMALS AS FRACTIONS** Write decimals as fractions, find common denominators, add or subtract the fractions, and express the answers as decimals. This confirms that when adding or subtracting, one must compute with digits of the same place value. **PLACE-VALUE INTERPRETATION** Students consider the place value of digits and what that means when adding or subtracting numbers.	Zeke buys cider for $1.97 and donuts for $0.89. The clerk said the bill was $10.87. What did the clerk do wrong? The cider is $1.97 = $\frac{197}{100}$ and the donuts are $0.89 = $\frac{89}{100}$. So the cost is $\frac{197}{100} + \frac{89}{100} = \frac{286}{100} = 2.86$. In $1.97 + 0.89$, we add hundredths to hundredths ($1.9\underline{7} + 0.8\underline{9}$), tenths to tenths ($1.\underline{9}7 + 0.\underline{8}9$), and ones to ones ($\underline{1}.97 + \underline{0}.89$). The clerk incorrectly added dollars and pennies (ones and tenths, tenths and hundredths).
Multiplication of Decimals **DECIMALS AS FRACTIONS** Write decimals as fractions, multiply, write the answer as a decimal, and relate the number of decimal places in the factors to the answer. **PLACE-VALUE INTERPRETATION** Students see why counting decimal points make sense and use the short-cut algorithm: multiply the decimals as whole numbers and adjust the place of the decimal in the product.	We can look at a problem using equivalent fractions. $$0.3 \times 2.3 = \frac{3}{10} \times 2\frac{3}{10} = \frac{3}{10} \times \frac{23}{10}$$ The product as a fraction is $\frac{69}{100}$, as a decimal 0.69. The 100 in the denominator shows that there should be two decimal places (hundredths) in the answer. The denominator of the fraction tells us the place value needed in the decimal. Using the fact that $25 \times 31 = 775$ students reason about a related product: 2.5×0.31 (2.5 is a tenth of 25, 0.31 is a hundredth of 31, so the product is a thousandth of 775) = 0.775.
Division of Decimals **DECIMALS AS FRACTIONS** Write decimals as fractions with common denominators and divide the numerators. **PLACE-VALUE INTERPRETATION** Write an equivalent problem by multiplying both the dividend and the divisor by the same power of ten until both are whole numbers.	$3.25 \div 0.5 = \frac{325}{100} \div \frac{5}{10} = \frac{325}{100} \div \frac{50}{100} = 325 \div 50 = 6.5$ $37.5 \div 0.015 = \frac{375}{10} \div \frac{15}{1,000} = \frac{37,500}{1,000} \div \frac{15}{1,000} = 37,500 \div 15 = 2,500$ This makes a whole number problem with the same quotient as the original decimal problem. The fraction approach explains why moving decimal places works. $$0.015\overline{)37.5} = 0.015 \times 1,000\overline{)37.5 \times 1,000} = 15\overline{)37500}$$
Decimal Forms of Rational Numbers **FINITE (OR TERMINATING) DECIMALS** are decimals that "end." The simplified fraction has prime factors of only 2s or 5s in the denominator. **FNFINITE REPEATING DECIMALS** are decimals that "go on forever" but show a repeating pattern. These fractions have prime factors other than 2 or 5 in the simplest denominator form.	$\frac{1}{2} = 0.5$, $\frac{1}{8} = 0.125$, $\frac{12}{75} = 0.16$. $\frac{4}{25} = \frac{16}{100} = 0.16$ In simplified fraction form $\frac{12}{75} = \frac{4}{25}$ has only factors of five $\left(\frac{4}{5 \times 5}\right)$ in the denominator. $\frac{1}{3} = 0.333...$, $\frac{2}{3} = 0.666...$, $\frac{8}{15} = 0.533...$, $\frac{3}{7} = 0.42857142...$ In simplified fraction form $\frac{26}{150} = \frac{13}{75} = \frac{13}{3 \times 5 \times 5} = 0.1733333....$
Using Percents **PERCENT OF A PRICE** "A CD costs $7.50. The sales tax is 6%. How much is the tax?" **ON WHAT AMOUNT THE PERCENT WAS FIGURED** "Customers left Jill $2.50 as a tip. The tip was 20% of the total. How much was the bill?" **WHAT PERCENT ONE NUMBER IS OF ANOTHER NUMBER** "Sam got a $12 discount off a $48 purchase. What percent discount did he get?"	6% of $7.50 = *cost of tax* 1% of $7.50 = $\frac{1}{100}$ of $7.50 = $7.50 \div 100 = 0.075$ 6 of the 1%'s will give me 6%. So, 6% of $7.50 = $0.45. 20% of *some number* equals $2.50 Find how many 20%s it takes to make 100%. In this case we need five. So, $5 \times 2.50 gives us $12.50. Find *what* % 12 is of 48. Students can solve this by computing how many 12s in 48. It takes four, so the percent is $\frac{1}{4}$ of 100% or 25%.

On the **CMP Parent Web Site**, you can learn more about the mathematical goals of each unit, see the glossary, and examine worked-out examples of ACE problems. http://PHSchool.com/cmp2parents

Dear Family,

The next unit in your child's mathematics class this year is ***How Likely Is It?:
Understanding Probability***. This unit helps students understand and reason
about experimental and theoretical probability and the relationship between
them. Students make important connections between probability and rational
numbers, geometry, statistics, science, and business.

UNIT GOALS

Students will learn to find probabilities in two ways: by conducting trials and
collecting experimental data, and also by analyzing situations to determine
theoretical probabilities. Students use fractions, decimals, and percents to
describe how likely events are.

Students experiment with coins, number cubes, spinners, and paper cups. They
will examine simple games of chance to determine whether the games are fair.
Students will examine how probability is useful in predicting the likelihood of
genetic traits, such as eye color and tongue-curling ability.

HELPING WITH HOMEWORK

You can help with homework and encourage sound mathematical habits as your
child studies this unit by asking questions such as:

- What are the possible outcomes that can occur for the events in this
  situation?
- How could you determine the experimental probability of each of the
  outcomes?
- Is it possible to determine the theoretical probability of each of the
  outcomes?
- If so, what are these probabilities?
- How can you use the probabilities to make decisions about this
  situation?

In your child's notebook, you can find worked-out examples from problems done in
class, notes on the mathematics of the unit, and descriptions of the vocabulary words.

HAVING CONVERSATIONS
ABOUT THE MATHEMATICS IN *HOW LIKELY IS IT?*

You can help your child with his or her work for this unit in several ways:

- Discuss examples of statements or situations in everyday experiences
  that relate to the likelihood of certain events.
- Look at sports statistics with your child and ask questions such as
  how a batting average or a free-throw average can be used to predict
  the likelihood that the player will get a hit the next time at bat or
  make a basket the next time at the free-throw line.
- Look over your child's homework and make sure all questions are
  answered and that explanations are clear.

A few important mathematical ideas that your child will learn in *How Likely
Is It?* are given on the back. As always, if you have any questions or concerns
about this unit or your child's progress in class, please feel free to call.

Sincerely,

Important Concepts	Examples
Probability A number between 0 and 1 that describes the likelihood that an event will occur.	If a bag contains a red marble, a white marble, and a blue marble, then the probability of drawing a red marble is 1 out of 3 or $\frac{1}{3}$. We would write: $P(red) = \frac{1}{3}$.
Once we have a probability—theoretical or experimental—we can use it to make predictions and decisions.	If a number cube is rolled 1000 times, we would predict that a 3 will occur about $\frac{1}{6}$ of the time or about $\frac{1}{6} \times 1000$, or 167 times.
Theoretical Probability A probability obtained by analyzing a situation. If all the **outcomes** (possible results) are equally likely, you can find a theoretical probability of an event by first listing all the possible outcomes, then finding the ratio of the number of outcomes you are interested in to the total number of outcomes.	If a number cube has six sides with the possible outcomes of rolling: 1, 2, 3, 4, 5, or 6, then the probability of rolling a "3" is 1 out of 6. $P(\text{Rolling a 3}) = \dfrac{\text{number of favorable outcomes}}{\text{number of possible outcomes}}$ $= \dfrac{1 \text{ (there is 1 number 3 on the cube)}}{6 \text{ (there are 6 possible outcomes)}}$
Experimental Probability A probability found as a result of an experiment. This probability is the relative frequency of the **event** (a set of outcomes) that is the ratio of the number of times the event occurred compared to the total number of **trials** (one round of an experiment).	If you tossed a coin 50 times and heads occurred 23 times, the relative frequency of heads would be $\frac{23}{50}$. $P(\text{heads}) = \dfrac{\text{number of times the event occurred}}{\text{number of trials}}$ $= \dfrac{\text{number of heads}}{\text{total number of tosses}} = \dfrac{23}{50}$
Random Events In mathematics, random means that any particular outcome is unpredictable, but the long-term behavior exhibits a pattern.	Flipping a coin is a random event because we never know whether the next flip will be heads or tails, but we do know that in the long run we will have close to 50% heads.

Strategies for Finding Outcomes

When situations involve more than one action, we need to generate the outcomes in a systematic way. Organized lists or tree diagrams are particularly useful.

Organized List

First Coin	Second Coin	Outcome
heads	heads	heads-heads
heads	tails	heads-tails
tails	heads	tails-heads
tails	tails	tails-tails

Tree Diagram

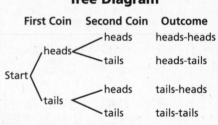

Law of Large Numbers

Experimental data gathered over many trials should produce probabilities that are close to the theoretical probabilities. This idea is sometimes called the Law of Large Numbers.

It is important for students to realize that a small amount of data may produce wide variation. It takes many trials to make good estimates for what will happen in the long run.

The Law of Large Numbers does not say that when flipping a coin, we should expect exactly 50% heads in any given large number of trials. Instead, it says that as the number of trials gets larger, we expect the percentage of heads to be in a smaller range of around 50%.

On the **CMP Parent Web Site,** you can learn more about the mathematical goals of each unit, see an illustrated vocabulary list, and examine solutions of selected ACE problems. **http://PHSchool.com/cmp2parents**

Dear Family,

The next unit in your child's mathematics class this year is *Data About Us: Statistics*. Its focus is data investigation, and it teaches students to organize, display, analyze, and interpret data. Your child will learn to make and interpret many different types of data displays and to compute statistics to help describe data.

UNIT GOALS

The unit provides opportunities for students to ask questions about themselves, and then to collect data to help answer these questions. Students explore the lengths of their names, the distances they live from school, the numbers of times they can jump rope, the numbers of pets they have, their heights, and the lengths of their left feet.

Your child will learn to make line plots, bar graphs, coordinate graphs, and stem-and-leaf plots and to interpret patterns shown in these displays. Your child will also learn to compute the mode, median, mean, and range of a data set and to use these statistics to describe data and to make predictions.

HELPING WITH HOMEWORK

You can help with homework and encourage sound mathematical habits as your child studies this unit by asking questions such as:

- What is the question being asked?
- How do you want to organize the data?
- Which representation is best to use to analyze the distribution of the data?
- How can you use graphs and statistics to describe a data distribution or to compare two data distributions in order to answer the original question?
- How do you think the data were collected?
- Why are these data represented using this kind of graph?

In your child's notebook, you can find worked-out examples from problems done in class, notes on the mathematics of the unit, and descriptions of the vocabulary words.

HAVING CONVERSATIONS
ABOUT THE MATHEMATICS IN *DATA ABOUT US*

You can help your child with his or her work for this unit in several ways:

- Look with your child for uses of data in magazines, newspapers, and on TV.
- Point out examples of graphical displays and ask your child questions about the information shown.
- Ask your child about the data studied in class. What were the typical values (mode, median, or mean) for these data?
- Look over your child's homework and make sure all questions are answered and that explanations are clear.

A few important mathematical ideas that your child will learn in *Data About Us* are given on the back. As always, if you have any questions or concerns about this unit or your child's progress in class, please feel free to call.

Sincerely,

Representing Data Distributions and Reading Data Representations

Statisticians use data representations such as line plots, bar graphs, stem-and-leaf plots, and coordinate graphs to describe and analyze their data.

READING STANDARD DATA REPRESENTATIONS

- *Reading the data* involves "lifting" information from a graph to answer explicit questions.
- *Reading between the data* includes the interpretation and integration of information presented in a graph.
- *Reading beyond the data* involves extending, predicting, or inferring from data to answer implicit questions.

LINE PLOT Each case is represented as an "X" positioned over a labeled number line.

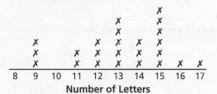

Name Lengths of Ms. Jee's Students

STEM-AND-LEAF PLOT
A plot that permits students to group data in intervals (usually by 10s).

Movies Watched

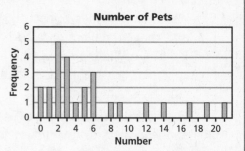

Key: 1 | 5 means 15 movies

FREQUENCY BAR GRAPH
A bar's height is not the value of an individual case but rather the number (frequency) of cases that all have that value.

Number of Pets

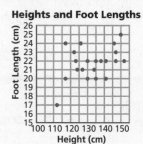

SCATTERPLOT
The relationship between two variables is explored by plotting data values on a Cartesian coordinate system.

Heights and Foot Lengths

Using Measures of Center (Mode, Median, Mean)

MODE The mode is the value that occurs with greatest frequency in a set of data.

MEDIAN The median value marks the location that separates an ordered set of data in half.

MEAN We emphasize the fair share (or evening out) interpretation of mean (average).

14 students said that they had the following number of siblings: 0, 0, 0, 1, 1, 1, 2, 2, 2, 2, 2, 3, 5, 6. The mode is 2.

The median for the data set 3, 4, 4, 7, 8, 9 is 5 , the number halfway between 4 and 7. For 4, 5, 5, and 7, the median is 5.

The mean (average) number of people in these households is 4. There are 24 people shared among 6 households.

	BEFORE		AFTER
Ossie	2 people	Ossie	4
Leon	3 people	Leon	4
Gary	3 people	Gary	4
Ruth	4 people	Ruth	4
Paul	6 people	Paul	4
Arlene	6 people	Arlene	4
Total	24 people		24 people

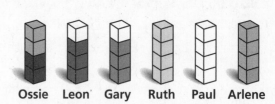

Ossie   Leon   Gary   Ruth   Paul   Arlene

Using Measures of Variability

Measures of variability are used to describe how widely spread or closely clustered the individual data values are.

RANGE The range depends on only two values, the greatest and the smallest.

Distinguishing Different Types of Data

NUMERICAL DATA are values that are counts or measures (pulse, height). We can use mean, median, mode, and range as summary statistics.

CATEGORICAL DATA are data sets that are responses representing categories (favorite color, month of birth, etc.). We can use only the mode as the summary statistic.

On the **CMP Parent Web Site,** you can learn more about the mathematical goals of each unit, see an illustrated vocabulary list, and examine solutions of selected ACE problems. http://PHSchool.com/cmp2parents

Dear Family,

The first unit in your child's mathematics class this year is ***Variables and Patterns: Introducing Algebra***. This is the first formal unit of the *Connected Mathematics™* algebra strand.

UNIT GOALS

This unit's focus is on ways to describe situations that change. In the first part of the unit, students explore three ways of representing a changing situation: with a description in words, with a data table, and with a graph. These representations are compared to one another to elicit the strengths of each presentation.

Students learn to write symbolic expressions as a shorter, quicker way to give a summary of the relationship between two variables. After writing symbolic rules, students learn how to use graphing calculators to make tables and graphs for a given rule, which allows students to interpret and compare more data sets.

HELPING WITH HOMEWORK

The overall goal of *Connected Mathematics* is to help students develop sound mathematical habits. As your child studies this unit, you can help with homework, and at the same time, encourage sound mathematical habits by asking questions such as:

- What are the variables in the problem?
- Which variables depend on or change in relation to others?
- How can the relationships of the problem be described in words?
- How can the relationships between variables be represented and analyzed?
- What does it mean when we see predictable changes in a table of data or a graph?
- How can we use these predictable changes to find out about other possible data?

In your child's notebook, you can find worked-out examples from problems done in class, notes on the mathematics of the unit, and descriptions of the vocabulary words.

HAVING CONVERSATIONS ABOUT THE MATHEMATICS IN *VARIABLES AND PATTERNS*

You can help your child with his or her work for this unit in several ways:

- Look over your child's homework and make sure all questions are answered and that explanations are clear.
- Have your child share his or her mathematics notebook with you, showing you the tables and graphs he or she has constructed and what has been recorded about patterns and variables. Ask your child to explain why these ideas are important.
- Have your child pick a question that was interesting to him or her and explain it to you.

A few important mathematical ideas that your child will learn in *Variables and Patterns* are given on the back. As always, if you have any questions or concerns about this unit or your child's progress in class, please feel free to call.

Sincerely,

Important Concepts	Examples
Variables A variable is a quantity that can change. Letters are often used as symbols to represent variables in rules that describe patterns.	The *number of students, n,* who go on a trip is related to the *price of the trip, p,* for each student.
Patterns A change that occurs in a predictable way. The problems in this unit require students to investigate the patterns of change in values of one variable in relation to changes in value of the other variable.	As the *number of bikes* increases by one, the *rental fee* increases by $30. 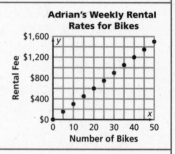

Tables
A list of values for two or more variables that shows the relationship between them.

The table shows how a change in one variable affects the change in the other variable. The table may show a pattern of change.

As the *number of campsites, x,* changes by one unit, the *total campground fee, y,* changes by 12.5 units. The table can be continued by adding 1 to the previous entry in the *x* row and 12.5 to the previous entry in the *y* row.

Campground Fees

Number of Campsites	1	2	3	4	5	6	7	8
Total Campground Fee	$12.50	$25.00	$37.50	$50.00	$62.50	$75.00	$87.50	$100.00

Coordinate Graphs
A representation of pairs of related numerical values that show the relationship between two variables. It relates the independent variable (shown on the *x*-axis) and the dependent variable (shown on the *y*-axis). Graphs are another way to view patterns of change.

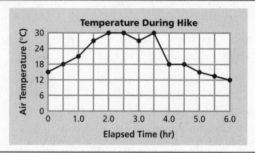

Discrete vs. Continuous Data
There are two basic types of quantitative variables—those with only a countable set of values (discrete data) and those with any real number values (continuous data). Tables can only represent discrete collections of (*x, y*) values. Graphs can represent both but often suggest continuous variables.

The *number of shirts sold* and *revenue* is a discrete relationship. Connecting two points does not make sense. It would imply that part of a shirt could be sold.

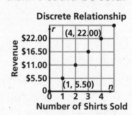 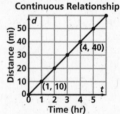

Situations such as the distance/time/rate relation are continuous. If a bicyclist peddles at a rate of 10 miles per hour, it is reasonable to connect the points, because you can go a distance in part of an hour.

Rules and Equations
Rules are a summary of a predictable relationship that tells how to find the values of a variable. A rule may be given in words or as an equation. Equations (or formulas) are rules containing variables that represent a mathematical relationship.

Rule (in words): Total profit equals profit per T-shirt times the number of shirts sold

Rule (written as an Equation): $y = 10x$

A formula or equation for finding the area of a circle: $A = \pi r^2$

On the **CMP Parent Web Site**, you can learn more about the mathematical goals of each unit, see an illustrated vocabulary list, and examine solutions of selected ACE problems. http://PHSchool.com/cmp2parents

Dear Family,

The next unit in your child's mathematics class this year is ***Stretching and Shrinking: Similarity***. Its focus is geometry, and it develops understanding of and skill in the use of concepts of similarity.

UNIT GOALS

In this unit, your child will use properties of similar figures to explore reductions and enlargements such as those made on copy machines. Similarity will also be used to estimate the height of real objects (such as buildings and flagpoles) and the distance across large areas (such as ponds).

The problems are designed to help students begin to reason proportionally by scaling in geometry situations. By the end of this unit, your child will know how to create similar figures, how to determine whether two figures are similar, and how to predict the relationship between lengths and areas for two similar figures. The next unit, *Comparing and Scaling*, continues to develop proportional ideas in numerical, rather than geometric, contexts.

HELPING WITH HOMEWORK

You can help with homework and encourage sound mathematical habits as your child studies this unit by asking questions such as:

- When two figures are similar, what is the same in each figure?
- When two figures are similar, what is different in each figure?
- How might we describe these differences?
- How do ratios relate to similarity?
- When two figures are similar, how can we describe the relationship between their areas?
- When two figures are similar, how can we describe the relationship between their perimeters?

In your child's notebook, you can find worked-out examples from problems done in class, notes on the mathematics of the unit, and descriptions of the vocabulary words.

HAVING CONVERSATIONS ABOUT THE MATHEMATICS IN *STRETCHING AND SHRINKING*

You can help your child with his or her work for this unit in several ways:

- Talk with your child about any situations that are like those in this unit—places in the real world where items are reduced or enlarged, such as models.
- Continue to have your child share his or her mathematics notebook with you, showing you the different ideas about similarity that have been recorded. Ask your child why these ideas are important. Share any ways that reductions or enlargements help you in your work or hobbies.
- Look over your child's homework and make sure all questions are answered and that explanations are clear.

A few important mathematical ideas that your child will learn in *Stretching and Shrinking* are given on the back. As always, if you have any questions or concerns about this unit or your child's progress in class, please feel free to call.

Sincerely,

Important Concepts	**Examples**
Similarity Two figures are similar if: (1) the measures of their **corresponding** angles are equal and (2) the lengths of their **corresponding** sides are related by the same factor, called the **scale factor**.	The Figures A and B below are similar. 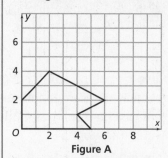 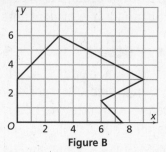 The corresponding angle measures are equal. The side lengths from Figure A to Figure B grow by a factor of 1.5—each side length from A to B is 1.5 times as long. So, the scale factor from Figure A to Figure B is 1.5. (The Figure A stretches or is enlarged to figure B.) We could also say the scale factor from Figure B to Figure A is $\frac{1}{1.5}$ or $\frac{2}{3}$. (The figure B shrinks to figure A.)
Corresponding Corresponding sides or angles have the same relative position in similar figures.	 **Corresponding Sides** AC and DF AB and DE BC and EF **Corresponding angles** A and D B and E C and F
Scale Factor The number used to multiply the lengths of a figure to stretch or shrink it to a similar image. A scale factor larger than 1 will enlarge a figure. A scale factor between 0 and 1 will shrink a figure. The scale factor of two similar figures can be found by a ratio that compares the corresponding sides: $\dfrac{\text{length of a side on the image}}{\text{length of the corresponding side on the original}}$	If we use a scale factor of $\frac{1}{2}$, all lengths in the image are $\frac{1}{2}$ as long as the corresponding lengths in the original. 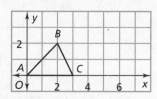 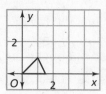 The base of the original triangle is 3 units. The base of the image is 1.5 units. The scale factor is $\frac{1.5}{3} = \frac{3}{6}$ or $\frac{1}{2}$.
Area and Scale Factor Lengths of similar figures will stretch (or shrink) by a scale factor. Areas of the figures will not change by the same factor.	If we apply a scale factor of 2 to a figure, the area becomes 4 times as large. 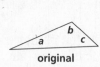 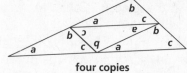 If we apply a scale factor of 3 to a figure, the area becomes 9 times as large. The original area is 6 cm². The area of the image is 9 times as large or 54 cm². 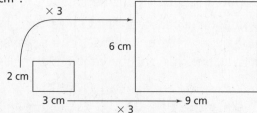

On the **CMP Parent Web Site,** you can learn more about the mathematical goals of each unit, see an illustrated vocabulary list, and examine solutions of selected ACE problems.
http://PHSchool.com/cmp2parents

Dear Family,

The next unit in your child's mathematics class this year is ***Comparing and Scaling: Ratio, Proportion, and Percent***. Students look at problems involving many situations and learn to make comparisons using ratios, fractions, percents, and rates.

UNIT GOALS

One goal of this unit is to develop students' abilities to make useful comparisons of quantitative information using ratios, fractions, decimals, rates, unit rates, and percents. A second goal is to have students learn to use quantitative comparison information to make larger or smaller scale models.

Students should also learn different ways to reason in proportional situations and to recognize when such reasoning is appropriate.

HELPING WITH HOMEWORK

As your child studies this unit you can help with homework, and at the same time, encourage sound mathematical habits by asking questions such as:

- When quantities have different measurements, how can they be compared?
- When can a comparison be made by subtraction? When can division be used?
- Why is a ratio a good means of comparison? How can it be scaled up or down?
- Where can ratios be used in daily life to find unknown quantities or inaccessible measurements?
- How can we use proportions for solving problems?

In your child's notebook, you can find worked-out examples from problems done in class, notes on the mathematics of the unit, and descriptions of the vocabulary words.

HAVING CONVERSATIONS ABOUT THE MATHEMATICS IN *COMPARING AND SCALING*

You can help your child in several ways:

- Ratios, proportions, and percents are found all around us. When you notice such a use in a newspaper or magazine, point it out to your child and discuss with your child what the numbers are telling them about the situation.

- Have your child share his or her mathematics notebook with you, showing you what has been recorded about ratios. Ask your child to explain why these ideas are important.

- Have your child pick a question that was interesting to him or her and explain it to you.

A few important mathematical ideas that your child will learn in *Comparing and Scaling* are given on the back. As always, if you have any questions or concerns about this unit or your child's progress in the class, please feel free to call.

Sincerely,

Important Concepts	Examples
Ratio A comparison of two quantities.	*For every 2 cups of mix, you use 3 cups of water.* Ratios are written in several forms: 2 to 3, or 2:3, or $\frac{2 \text{ cups mix}}{3 \text{ cups water}}$.
Ratios in Fraction Form Ratios are often written in fraction form but do not represent fractions. Fractions have part-to-whole comparisons. Some ratios are part-to-part comparisons.	The statement "the ratio of boys to girls in a class is 15 girls to 9 boys" can be written as a fraction, $\frac{15}{9}$, but it does not mean that the fraction of students in the class that are girls is $\frac{15}{9}$. The total number of students in the class is needed. The sum of the numbers of boys and girls is 24. The part-to-whole comparison is $\frac{15}{24}$. So the fraction of the class that is girls is $\frac{15}{24}$.
Ratios as Percents When the ratio can be thought of as part of a whole you can write a percent comparison statement.	*The ratio of concentrate to water in a mix is 3 cups concentrate to 16 cups water. First, find the total cups the recipe makes, 19 cups.* Then, write the fraction of the mix that is concentrate, $\frac{3}{19}$. To find the percent, we divide the concentrate by the total mix, $3 \div 19 = 0.15789\ldots$ or about 15.8% concentrate.
Rate A statement that compares two different variables.	miles to gallons, sandwiches to people, dollars to hours
Unit Rate You have two options when you divide two numbers. The units help you think through the situations so that you can use either set of unit rates to compare the quantities	*Sascha goes 6 miles in 20 minutes on leg 1 of his bike ride. On leg 2 he goes 8 miles in 24 minutes. On which leg is he faster?* $\frac{6 \text{ miles}}{20 \text{ minutes}} = 0.3$ miles per minute and $\frac{8 \text{ miles}}{24 \text{ minutes}} = 0.333$ miles per minute Now the comparison is clear. The times are the same, 1 minute, and the distances can be directly compared. 8 miles in 24 minutes is faster. But, we could divide the other way: $\frac{20 \text{ minutes}}{6 \text{ miles}} = 3.333$ minutes per mile and $\frac{24 \text{ minutes}}{8 \text{ miles}} = 3$ minutes per mile We see that the smaller number tells the correct answer, 8 miles in 24 minutes.
Scaling Ratios (and Rates) Write the ratios as fractions to help the thinking needed for scaling the ratios up (or down). However, we must recognize the difference between dealing with a fraction and dealing with a ratio written as a fraction.	*Which is less expensive, 3 roses for $5 or 7 roses for $9?* If we want to scale the costs to be the same, we can use the same thinking as that for finding a common denominator. We would look for a common multiple of 5 and 9. $\frac{3}{5} = \frac{3 \times 9}{5 \times 9} = \frac{27 \text{ roses}}{\$45}$ and $\frac{7}{9} = \frac{7 \times 5}{9 \times 5} = \frac{35 \text{ roses}}{\$45}$. The second option gives more for the same amount of money.
Proportions A proportion is a statement of equality between two ratios. If one part is unknown, we can use scaling or equivalent fractions to find the missing part of a proportion.	*It takes Glenda 70 steps on the elliptical machine to go 0.1 of a mile. When her workout is done, she has gone 3 miles. How many steps has she made on the machine?* $\frac{70 \text{ steps}}{0.1 \text{ miles}} = \frac{x \text{ steps}}{3 \text{ miles}} = \frac{70 \times 30 \text{ steps}}{0.1 \times 30 \text{ miles}} = \frac{2{,}100 \text{ steps}}{3 \text{ miles}}$ Glenda took 2,100 steps to go 3 miles.

On the **CMP Parent Web Site**, you can learn more about the mathematical goals of each unit, see an illustrated vocabulary list, and examine solutions of selected ACE problems. http://PHSchool.com/cmp2parents

Dear Family,

The next unit in your child's course of study in mathematics class this year is ***Accentuate the Negative: Positive and Negative Numbers***. Although students have intuitively used operations on integers to make sense of some situations in their everyday world, this unit looks at formal ways to compute with these numbers.

UNIT GOALS

In this unit, the focus is on understanding and developing systematic ways to add, subtract, multiply, and divide positive and negative numbers. Students will develop algorithms for computations and will use the order of operations, the Commutative Property, and the Distributive Property to solve problems.

HELPING WITH HOMEWORK

You can help with homework and encourage sound mathematical habits as your child studies this unit by asking questions such as:

• How do negative and positive numbers help in describing the situation?

• What will addition, subtraction, multiplication, or division of positive and negative numbers tell about the problem?

• What model(s) for positive and negative numbers would help in displaying the relationships in the problem situation?

In your child's notebook, you can find worked-out examples from problems done in class, notes on the mathematics of the unit, and descriptions of the vocabulary words.

HAVING CONVERSATIONS ABOUT THE MATHEMATICS IN *ACCENTUATE THE NEGATIVE*

You can help your child with his or her work for this unit in several ways:

• Ask your child to describe some real-world situations in which integers are used. If your child talks to you about being "in the red" or "in the black," you may relate this idea to earnings or savings he or she has.

• Look at your child's mathematics notebook. You may want to read some of the explanations that have been written and, if they are unclear, talk with your child about why you think they may need more explanation.

• Look over your child's homework and make sure all questions are answered and explanations are clear.

A few important mathematical ideas that your child will learn in *Accentuate the Negative* are given on the back. As always, if you have any questions or concerns about this unit or your child's progress in class, please feel free to call.

Sincerely,

Important Concepts	Examples
Negative Numbers Negative Numbers are the opposites of positive numbers. **INTEGERS** are the set of the whole numbers and their opposites. **RATIONAL NUMBERS** are the positive and negative integers and fractions.	Negative numbers: $-\frac{2}{3}$, -24, -1 Integers: -14, -29, 0 Rational numbers: -2, $-1\frac{2}{3}$, 0, $\frac{3}{4}$, 14

Addition and Subtraction

Students model and symbolize problems to develop meaning and skill in addition and subtraction before developing algorithms.

The **colored chip model** requires an understanding of opposites. For example, 4 black chips represent +4 and 4 red chips represent −4.

$4 + (−4) = 0$ because +4 and −4 are opposites.

The **number line model** helps make the connection to rational numbers as quantities.

Sometimes it is helpful to restate an addition problem as a subtraction or a subtraction problem as an addition.

Chip Board

Johnson owed his sister $6.00. He earned $4.00 delivering papers. What is his net worth?

One color chip (black) represents positive numbers and another chip (red) represents negative numbers.

Collections of black and red chips on a board represent the combination of expense and income. The result, or net worth, is that he is "in the red" 2, or $^-2$ dollars. This problem may be represented with the number sentence $^-6 + {}^+4 = {}^-2$.

To calculate $^+12 + {}^-8$, the result is the same as if you subtract $^+8$ in the problem, $^+12 − {}^+8$. To calculate $^+5 − {}^-7$, the result is the same as if you add $^+7$ in the problem $^+5 + {}^+7$.

Multiplication

Multiplication can be modeled using a number line model and "counting" occurrences of fixed-size movement along the number line.

$$8 \times (−6)$$

This can be represented as 8 jumps of $^-6$ on the number line.

$^-6 + {}^-6 + {}^-6 + {}^-6 + {}^-6 + {}^-6 + {}^-6 + {}^-6 = {}^-48$ or $8 \times {}^-6 = {}^-48$

Division

A multiplication fact can be used to write two related division facts.

We know that $5 \times {}^-2 = {}^-10$. Write the related division sentences: $^-10 \div {}^-2 = 5$ and $^-10 \div 5 = {}^-2$. From this relationship students can determine the answer to a division problem.

Order of Operations

Mathematicians have established rules for the order in which operations ($+$, $−$, $\times$, $\div$) should be carried out.

1. Do any computations in parentheses.

2. Compute exponents.

3. Do all $\div$ or $\times$ operations in order from left to right.

4. Do all $+$ or $−$ operations in order, from left to right.

$3 + 4 \times \underline{(6 \div 2)} \times 5 − 7^2 + 6 \div 3 =$
$3 + 4 \times 3 \times 5 − \underline{7^2} + 6 \div 3 =$
$3 + \underline{4 \times 3} \times 5 − 49 + 6 \div 3 =$
$3 + \underline{12 \times 5} − 49 + \underline{6 \div 3} =$
$\underline{3 + 60} − 49 + 2 =$
$\underline{63 − 49} + 2 =$
$\underline{14 + 2} = 16$

Commutative Property

The order of addends does not matter. The order of factors does not matter. Subtraction and division do not have this property.

$5 + 4 = 4 + 5$	$−2 + 3 = 3 + {}−2$
$5 \times 4 = 4 \times 5$	$−2 \times 3 = 3 \times {}−2$
$5 − 4 \neq 4 − 5$	$−2 − 3 \neq 3 − {}−2$
$5 \div 4 \neq 4 \div 5$	$−2 \div 3 \neq 3 \div {}−2$

Distributive Property

The distributive property shows that multiplication *distributes* over addition. This property is introduced and modeled through finding areas of rectangles.

$$5 \times (17 + 4) = (5 \times 17) + (5 \times 4)$$

On the **CMP Parent Web Site**, you can learn more about the mathematical goals of each unit, see an illustrated vocabulary list, and examine solutions of selected ACE problems.
http://PHSchool.com/cmp2parents

Dear Family,

The next unit in your child's mathematics class this year is ***Moving Straight Ahead: Linear Relationships***. In this unit, students are developing skills in areas that are traditionally known as algebra. This unit introduces them to situations that can be modeled with linear functions and graphed with straight lines.

UNIT GOALS

The primary goal of this unit is to develop understanding of linear relationships or linear functions. Students learn to recognize linear functions by the constant rate of change between two variables in a verbal context, table, graph, and equation.

Students identify, represent, and interpret linear relationships. They solve linear equations and write equations for lines. These last two ideas will be revisited with more complexities in later units—in particular, the *Thinking with Mathematical Models* and *Say It with Symbols* units.

HELPING WITH HOMEWORK

You can help with homework and encourage sound mathematical habits as your child studies this unit by asking questions such as:

- What are the variables in the problem?
- How are the variables related? Is the relationship linear?
- How can I recognize a linear relationship if it is represented in a problem, a table, a graph, or with an equation?
- How can tables, graphs, and equations of linear relationships be used to express and answer given questions?

In your child's notebook, you can find worked-out examples from problems done in class, notes on the mathematics of the unit, and descriptions of the vocabulary words.

HAVING CONVERSATIONS ABOUT THE MATHEMATICS IN *MOVING STRAIGHT AHEAD*

You can help your child with his or her work for this unit in several ways:

- Ask your child to describe some real-world situations in which linear functions are used to explain how the situations can be described using a table, a graph, and an equation. An example is phone charges that increase at a constant rate based on the length of the call
- Look at your child's mathematics notebook. You may want to read some of the explanations that have been written and, if they are unclear, talk with your child about why you think they may need more explanations.
- Look over your child's homework and make sure all questions are answered and that explanations are clear.

A few important mathematical ideas that your child will learn in *Moving Straight Ahead* are given on the back. As always, if you have any questions or concerns about this unit or your child's progress in class, please feel free to call.

Sincerely,

Linear Relationships

A relationship is linear if there is a constant rate of change between the two variables. That is, for each unit change in x there is a constant change in y.

TABLES In the table the **constant rate of change** can be observed as a pattern of consistent change in the variables.

Gilberto's Walking Rate

Time (seconds)	Distance (meters)
0	0
1	2
2	4
3	6
4	8
5	10
6	12
7	14
8	16
9	18

+2 (from 0 to 1), +4 (from 0 to 2); +3 (from 4 to 5), +6 (from 8 to 10)

As time increases by 1 second, the distance increases by 2 meters. The constant rate of change is 2 meters per second.

GRAPHS If we graph the data, the constant rate of change between the two variables shows up as a straight line.

This constant rate of change is called the **slope of the line**. It is the ratio of change between the two variables.

$$\text{Slope} = \frac{\text{vertical change}}{\text{horizontal change}},$$

for any two points on the line.

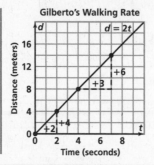

Gilberto's Walking Rate graph, $d = 2t$

Here, the slope is

$\frac{4}{2}$ or $\frac{6}{3}$ or $\frac{2}{1}$.

EQUATIONS In this symbolic representation the constant rate of change shows up as the **coefficient** of t.

$d = 2t$ (Gilberto)

Here, the coefficient is 2.

y-INTERCEPT The point where the graph of a line crosses the y-axis (vertical axis).

Suppose the cost to rent bikes is represented by $C = \$150 + \$10n$, where C is the cost in dollars and n is the number of bikes.

Cost of Bike Rental

The y-intercept is $\$150$.

The y-intercept is the constant term in the equation, $C = 150 + 10n$.

The slope (or the constant rate of change) of the line is 10.

Solving Equations

Write a series of equivalent equations until it is easy to read the value of the variable. Equality or equivalence is maintained when you add, subtract, multiply, and divide the same quantity to each side of the equation. These procedures are called the *properties of equality*.

EQUATION	REASONS
$750 = 150 + 10n$	Original equation
$750 - 150 = 150 - 150 + 10n$	Undo "adding 150" by subtracting 150 from each side.
$600 = 10n$	
$\frac{600}{10} = \frac{600n}{10}$	Undo "multiplying by 10" by dividing by 10.
$60 = n$	The value of n must be 60.

Note that if n is replaced by 60 in each step, we have a true equation. The original equation would give $750 = 750$.

On the **CMP Parent Web Site**, you can learn more about the mathematical goals of each unit, see an illustrated vocabulary list, and examine solutions of selected ACE problems. http://PHSchool.com/cmp2parents

Dear Family,

The next unit in your child's mathematics class this year is ***Filling and Wrapping: Three-Dimensional Measurement***. Its focus is volume (filling) and surface area (wrapping) of objects, especially rectangular prisms, cylinders, cones, and spheres. In addition, students extend their understanding of similarity and scale factors to three-dimensional figures.

UNIT GOALS

Students develop strategies for measuring the surface area and volume. Their strategies are discussed and used to formulate rules for finding the surface area and volume of rectangular prisms and cylinders. They also investigate other solids—including cones and spheres—to develop volume relationships.

Ideas from previous units will be revisited and extended in this unit. For example, from the *Stretching and Shrinking* unit, the connection of how changing the scale of a box affects its surface area and volume will be studied.

HELPING WITH HOMEWORK

You can help with homework and encourage sound mathematical habits as your child studies this unit by asking questions such as:

- Which measures of an object are involved—volume or surface area?
- What method should I use to determine these measures?
- What strategies or formulas might help?

In your child's notebook, you can find worked-out examples from problems done in class, notes on the mathematics of the unit, and descriptions of the vocabulary words.

HAVING CONVERSATIONS ABOUT THE MATHEMATICS IN *FILLING AND WRAPPING*

You can help your child with his or her work for this unit in several ways:

- Ask your child about the different ways the class has explored to find the surface area and volume of various shapes.
- Look at your child's mathematics notebook. You may want to review the section where your child is recording definitions for new words that he or she is encountering in the unit.
- Have your child pick a question that was interesting to him or her and explain it to you.

A few important mathematical ideas that your child will learn in *Filling and Wrapping* are given on the back. As always, if you have any questions or concerns about this unit or your child's progress in class, please feel free to call.

Sincerely,

Important Concepts	**Examples**

Surface Area of Rectangular Prisms
 	
To find the surface area of a box (prism), determine the total area needed to wrap the container. Nets can represent boxes. The area of the net is the surface area of the box.
 	
Surface area is the sum of the areas of the faces.
 	
Surface Area = (area of the front × 2) + (area of the side × 2) + (area of the top × 2) or
 	
Surface Area = (area of the front + area of the side + area of the top) × 2 = $(w \times h + w \times \ell + \ell \times h) \times 2$.
	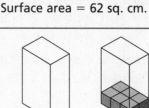
	
	There are two of each of these faces of the prism:
	  2 cm by 3 cm (area is 6 sq. cm.);
	  2 cm by 5 cm (area is 10 sq. cm.);
	  3 cm by 5 cm (area is 15 sq. cm.).
	Surface area = 62 sq. cm.

Volume of Rectangular Prisms To find the volume of a rectangular box, count the number of layers of unit cubes it takes to fill the container. The number of unit cubes in one layer is equal to the area of the base. The volume (the total number of unit cubes) of a rectangular prism is the area of its base (the number of unit cubes in the first layer) multiplied by its height (the total number of layers). Volume = Area of the base × height = $Bh = \ell wh$.	 one layer five layers fill the box $2 \times 3 = 6$ cubes on the area of the base 5 stacks of cubes in the height Volume = $6 \times 5 = 30$ cubic units
Volume of Prisms The volume of any prism is the area of its base multiplied by its height. Volume = Area of the base × height = Bh.	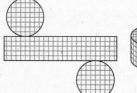 Rectangular Prism Triangular Prism Pentagonal Prism
Surface Area of Cylinders The surface area of the cylinder is the area of the rectangle that forms the lateral surface ($2\pi rh$) plus the areas of the two circular ends ($2\pi r^2$) where r = radius and h = height. Surface Area = $2\pi r^2 + 2\pi rh$.	 Use 3.14 for π. $r = 4$ $h = 5$ $2(\pi 4^2) + 2\pi 4(5) \approx$ $100.48 + 125.6 =$ 226.08 square units
Volume of Cylinders The volume of a cylinder is the number of unit cubes in one layer (the area of the circular base) multiplied by the number of layers (the height) needed to fill the cylinder. The area of the base (πr^2) is multiplied by the height to find the volume. Volume = $Bh = \pi r^2 h$	$r = 1.5$ $h = 7$ Area of the base $\approx 3.14 \times 2.25 = 7.065$ Volume $\approx 7.065 \times 7 = 49.455$ cubic units
Volume of Cones and Spheres When all three have the same radius and the same height, 1 cone fills $\frac{1}{3}$ of a cylinder, and 1 sphere fills $\frac{2}{3}$ of a cylinder. Cone Volume = $\frac{1}{3}$ volume of the cylinder = $\frac{1}{3}\pi r^2 h$ Sphere Volume = $\frac{2}{3}$ volume of the cylinder = $\frac{2}{3}\pi r^2 h$	Volume of the cylinder = 628 cm^3. Volume of the cone is approximately 209 cm^3. Volume of the sphere is approximately 419 cm^3.

On the **CMP Parent Web Site**, you can learn more about the mathematical goals of each unit, see an illustrated vocabulary list, and examine solutions of selected ACE problems.
http://PHSchool.com/cmp2parents

Dear Family,

The next unit in your child's mathematics class this year is ***What Do You Expect?: Probability and Expected Value***. This unit is about the concepts of probability and will help students understand common ideas that they read or hear about every day. They will explore long-range expectations in probability situations and learn how to make better predictions.

UNIT GOALS

Students will learn to find probabilities in two ways: by conducting trials and collecting experimental data, also by analyzing situations to determine theoretical probabilities. As they work, students will be using fractions, decimals, and percents to describe how likely events are.

HELPING WITH HOMEWORK

You can help with your child's homework and encourage sound mathematical habits as your child studies this unit by asking questions such as:

- What are the possible outcomes that can occur for the events in this situation?
- How could I determine the experimental probability of each of the outcomes?
- Is it possible to determine the theoretical probability of each of the outcomes?
- If so, what are these probabilities?
- How can I use the probabilities I have found to make decisions about this situation?

In your child's notebook, you can find worked-out examples from problems done in class, notes on the mathematics of the unit, and descriptions of the vocabulary words.

HAVING CONVERSATIONS ABOUT THE MATHEMATICS IN *WHAT DO YOU EXPECT?*

You can help your child with his or her work for this unit in several ways:

- Discuss examples of statements or situations in everyday experiences that relate to the likelihood of certain events. For example: What would a 50% chance of rain mean, and how might forecasters decide on this figure?
- Look at sports statistics with your child and ask questions such as how a batting average or a free-throw average can be used to predict the likelihood that the player will get a hit the next time at bat or make a basket the next time at the free-throw line.
- Look over your child's homework and make sure all questions are answered and that explanations are clear.

A few important mathematical ideas that your child will learn in *What Do You Expect?* are given on the back. As always, if you have any questions or concerns about this unit or your child's progress in class, please feel free to call.

Sincerely,

Important Concepts	Examples
Probability A number between 0 and 1 that describes the likelihood that an event will occur.	If a bag contains a red marble, a white marble, and a blue marble, then the probability of drawing a red marble is 1 out of 3 or $\frac{1}{3}$. We would write: P(red) = $\frac{1}{3}$.
Theoretical Probability If all the **outcomes** are equally likely, you can find the theoretical probability of the event by first listing all the possible outcomes, then find the ratio of the number of outcomes of interest to the total number of outcomes.	If a number cube has six sides with the possible outcomes of rolling: 1, 2, 3, 4, 5, or 6, the probability of rolling a "3" is 1 out of 6. P(Rolling a 3) = $\frac{\text{number of equally likely favorable outcomes}}{\text{total number of equally likely outcomes}}$ = $\frac{1 \text{ (there is 1 number 3 on the cube)}}{6 \text{ (there are 6 possible outcomes)}}$
Experimental Probability This probability is the relative frequency of the **event**. It is the ratio of the number of times the event occurred compared to the total number of **trials**.	If you tossed a coin 50 times and heads occurred 23 times, the relative frequency of heads would be $\frac{23}{50}$. P(heads) = $\frac{\text{number of times the event occured}}{\text{number of trials}}$ = $\frac{\text{number of heads}}{\text{total number of tosses}}$ = $\frac{23}{50}$
Random Events Outcomes that are uncertain when viewed individually, but which exhibit a predictable pattern over many trials are random.	Rolling a fair number cube is random because although you have no way of knowing what the next roll will be, you do know that, over the long run, you will roll each number on the cube about the same number of times.
Tree Diagram This is a diagram used to determine the number of possible outcomes. The number of final branches is equal to the number of possible outcomes.	**First Coin** **Second Coin** **Outcome** Start — heads — heads → heads-heads heads — tails → heads-tails tails — heads → tails-heads tails — tails → tails-tails
Area Model This is a diagram in which fractions of the area correspond to probabilities in a situation. Area models are particularly helpful when there are 2 events to track and the outcomes of each event are not equally likely.	The area model here shows the probability of getting two red blocks if there are 2 red blocks and 2 blue blocks and one is drawn at a time without replacing it. The probability is $\frac{2}{12}$ or $\frac{1}{6}$. **Second Choice (with red removed)** |	B	B	R
B	BB	BB	BB
B	BR	BR	BB
R	RB	RB	RR
R	RB	RB	RR	 (First Choice)
Expected Value or Long-term Average The average result over many trials is the expected value. A player's average score per shot in a 1-and-1 free throw situation is an expected value. A player's average winning per lottery ticket is also an expected value.	A game is played with two number cubes. You score 2 points when a sum of 6 is rolled, 1 point for a sum of 3, and 0 points for anything else. If you roll the cubes 36 times, you could expect to get a sum of 6 about five times and a sum of 3 twice. You could expect to score (5 × 2) + (2 × 1) = 12 points for 36 rolls, an average of $\frac{12}{36} = \frac{1}{3}$ point per roll. This is the expected value of one roll.
Law of Large Numbers Experimental data gathered over many trials should produce probabilities that are close to the theoretical probabilities.	For 1 million flips, exactly 50% heads is improbable, but it would be extremely unlikely for the percent heads to be very different from 50%.

On the **CMP Parent Web Site**, you can learn more about the mathematical goals of each unit, see an illustrated vocabulary list, and examine solutions of selected ACE problems. http://PHSchool.com/cmp2parents

Dear Family,

The next unit in your child's mathematics class this year is *Data Distributions: Describing Variability and Comparing Groups*. Students will learn to choose among a variety of representations to display distributions and will analyze, describe, and compare sets of data.

UNIT GOALS

Exploring statistics as a process of data investigation involves a set of four interrelated components (Graham, 1987).

- Posing the question: formulating the key question(s) to explore and deciding what data to collect to address the question(s);
- Collecting the data: deciding how to collect the data as well as actually collecting it;
- Analyzing the data: organizing, representing, summarizing, and describing the data and looking for patterns in the data; and
- Interpreting the results: predicting, comparing, and identifying relationships and using the results from the analyses to make decisions about the original question(s).

This dynamic process often involves moving back and forth among the four components.

HELPING WITH HOMEWORK

You can help with homework and encourage sound mathematical habits as your child studies this unit by asking questions such as:

- Is there anything that surprises you about the data and their distribution?
- Where do the data cluster in the distribution?
- How can I use the mean or median and range to help me understand and describe a data distribution?
- What strategies can I use to compare two different data sets?

In your child's notebook, you can find worked-out examples from problems done in class, notes on the mathematics of the unit, and descriptions of the vocabulary words.

HAVING CONVERSATIONS ABOUT THE MATHEMATICS IN *DATA DISTRIBUTIONS*

You can help your child with his or her work for this unit in several ways:

- Look with your child for uses of data in magazines, newspapers, and on TV.
- Point out examples of graphical displays and ask your child questions about the information shown.
- Ask your child about the data studied in class. What were the typical (mode, median, or mean) values for these data?
- Look over your child's homework and make sure all questions are answered and that explanations are clear.

A few important mathematical ideas that your child will learn in *Data Distributions* are given on the back. As always, if you have any questions or concerns about this unit or your child's progress in class, please feel free to call.

Sincerely,

Representing Data Distributions

Statisticians use representations or summary statistics during the analysis part of the process of statistical investigation to describe the data distribution.

READING STANDARD DATA REPRESENTATIONS

- Reading the data involves "lifting" information from a graph to answer explicit questions.
- Reading between the data includes the interpretation and integration of information presented in a graph.
- Reading beyond the data involves extending, predicting, or inferring from data to answer implicit questions.

FREQUENCY BAR GRAPH A bar's height is the number (frequency) of cases that all have that value.

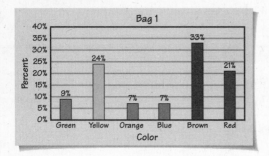

VALUE BAR GRAPH
Each case is represented by a separate bar whose relative length corresponds to the magnitude or value of that case.

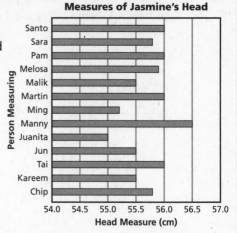

DOT PLOT (OR LINE PLOT)
Each case is represented as a dot (or an "x") positioned over a labeled number line.

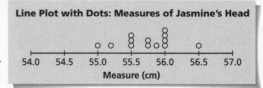

SCATTERPLOT
The relationship between two different attributes is explored by plotting values of two numeric attributes on a Cartesian coordinate system.

Measures of Central Tendency or Location (Mode, Median, Mean)

MODE The data value or category that occurs with greatest frequency. It is not usually used for summarizing numerical data.

Number of siblings: 0, 0, 0, 1, 1, 1, 2, 2, 2, 2, 2, 3, 5, 6.

The mode is 2.

MEDIAN The numerical value that marks the middle of an ordered distribution. It is not influenced by extreme data values. Graphically, the median marks the location that divides a distribution into two equal parts.

The median for the data set 3, 4, 4, 7, 8, 9 is $5\frac{1}{2}$, the number halfway between 4 and 7.

For 4, 5, 5, and 7, the median is 5.

MEAN The numerical value that marks the balance point of a distribution; it is influenced by all values of the distribution including extremes and outliers. It is a good measure to use when working with distributions that are roughly symmetric.

Number of people in household: 2, 3, 3, 4, 6, 6.

The mean (average) number of people in these households is 4. There are 24 people "shared" among 6 households.

Using Measures of Variability

Measures of variability are used to describe how widely spread or closely clustered the individual data values are.

Range depends on two values, the greatest and the smallest. Range is the difference between the greatest value and the least value in the data.

On the **CMP Parent Web Site**, you can learn more about the mathematical goals of each unit, see an illustrated vocabulary list, and examine solutions of selected ACE problems. http://PHSchool.com/cmp2parents

Dear Family,

The first unit in your child's mathematics class this year is ***Thinking With Mathematical Models: Linear and Inverse Variation***. In previous mathematics work, your child has studied some of the basic concepts of algebra. In this unit, we will be exploring a variety of situations that can be represented with different mathematical models.

UNIT GOALS

This first unit in eighth grade has been designed to review and extend student understanding and skill in work with linear functions and to introduce concepts associated with non-linear functions.

When algebraic expressions are used to represent patterns in data, the resulting functions are called *mathematical models* of the relationships. The functions can then be used to write and solve equations that provide estimates of answers to questions about the relationships. One of the central goals of this unit is to develop student understanding and skill in this aspect of the modeling process.

HELPING WITH HOMEWORK

The overall goal of *Connected Mathematics* is to help students develop sound mathematical habits. As your child studies this unit, you can help with homework, and at the same time encourage sound mathematical habits by asking questions such as:

- What are the key variables in this selection?
- What is the pattern relating the variables that are involved? Is it linear?
- What kind of equation will express the relationship among variables?
- How can the equation relating variables be used to answer questions about the relationship?

In your child's notebook, you can find worked-out examples from problems done in class, notes on the mathematics of the unit, and descriptions of the vocabulary words.

HAVING CONVERSATIONS ABOUT THE MATHEMATICS IN *THINKING WITH MATHEMATICAL MODELS*

You can help your child in several ways:

- Have your child share his or her mathematics notebook with you, showing you what has been recorded. Ask your child to explain why these ideas are important.
- Talk about situations in which data might be collected to help represent the situations with mathematical models such as tables and graphs.
- Look over your child's homework and make sure that all questions are answered and that explanations are clear.

A few important mathematical ideas that your child will learn in *Thinking with Mathematical Models* are given on the back. As always, if you have any questions or concerns about this unit or your child's progress in the class, please feel free to call.

Sincerely,

Important Concepts	Examples
Mathematical Models An equation or a graph that describes, at least approximately, the relationship between two variables is a mathematical model. A mathematical model may allow you to make reasonable guesses for values between and beyond the known data points.	**Modeling Bridge Thickness and Strength** 1. Collect data by simulating how much weight a bridge can hold with various layers of thickness. 2. Plot the data and draw a line to model the pattern of the data. 3. Find an equation to model the data. For example, $y = 8x$ (since 0 thickness should suggest 0 strength). 4. Use the equation $y = 8x$ to predict the breaking weights for other bridges: 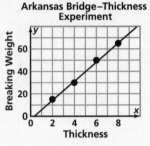 Arkansas Bridge–Thickness Experiment

<table>
<tr><td>thickness in layers</td><td>3.5</td><td>7</td><td>10</td></tr>
<tr><td>strength in penny load</td><td>28</td><td>56</td><td>80</td></tr>
</table>

Linear Relationships In previous units, students learned how to recognize, represent symbolically, and analyze linear relationships. Many questions about linear relationships can be answered by solving equations of the form $c = mx + b$. The problems in this unit are designed to promote review and extension of these skills.	The **rate of change** of y in the equation $y = mx + b$ is the **slope** of its graph. In particular, m, the **coefficient** of x, indicates that constant ratio: $\frac{change\ in\ y}{change\ in\ x}$. The constant term b indicates the **y-intercept** $(0, b)$ of the graph. $5x - 3 = 7x - 2$ may be solved • by graphing (or making tables for) $y = 5x - 3$ and $y = 7x - 2$ and looking for a common solution. • by using Properties of Equality. $\quad 5x - 3 = 7x - 2$ $\quad\ \ -3 = 2x - 2$ (subtract 5x from each side) $\quad\ \ -1 = 2x$ (add 2 to each side) $\quad -\frac{1}{2} = x$ (divide each side by 2)
Direct Variation Direct variation models are those that can be expressed with equations in the form $y = kx$. In a table of data, students may notice $\frac{y}{x} = k$. This is the same relationship as $y = kx$.	This is a special case of linear relationship in which the y-intercept is equal to zero.
Inverse Variation Inverse variation models are those that can be expressed with equations in the form $y = \frac{k}{x}$. It is important to realize that inverse variation gives a non-linear pattern of change. In a table of data, students may notice the pattern $xy = k$, where k is a constant. This is the same relationship as $y = \frac{k}{x}$.	Dividing by an increasing variable has a different effect than does subtracting an increasing variable. This fact is revealed by contrasting graphs of $y = 10 - x$ (the line) and $y = \frac{10}{x}$ (the curve). 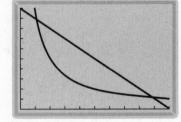 Notice that there is no solution for y when $x = 0$ in $y = \frac{10}{x}$.

On the **CMP Parent Web Site**, you can learn more about the mathematical goals of each unit, see an illustrated vocabulary list, and examine solutions of selected ACE problems. **http://PHSchool.com/cmp2parents**

Dear Family,

The next unit in your child's mathematics class this year is ***Looking for Pythagoras: The Pythagorean Theorem***. Students' work in this unit develops a fundamentally important relationship connecting geometry and algebra: the Pythagorean Theorem.

UNIT GOALS

In this unit, students explore the Pythagorean Theorem, square roots, and strategies for estimating square roots. In addition, irrational numbers are introduced.

The presentation of ideas in the unit reflects the historical development of the concept of irrational numbers. Early Greek mathematicians recognized the need for such numbers as they searched for a ratio of integers to represent the length of the sides of a square with certain areas, such as 2 square units.

HELPING WITH HOMEWORK

You can help with your child's homework and encourage sound mathematical habits as your child studies this unit by asking questions such as:

- Is this a situation where it is appropriate to use the Pythagorean Theorem?
- Do I need to find the distance between two points?
- How are square roots and areas of squares related?
- How can I estimate the square root of a number?
- How can I know the length of something without directly measuring it?

In your child's notebook, you can find worked-out examples from problems done in class, notes on the mathematics of the unit, and descriptions of the vocabulary words.

HAVING CONVERSATIONS ABOUT THE MATHEMATICS IN *LOOKING FOR PYTHAGORAS*

You can help your child with his or her work for this unit in several ways:

- Ask your child to explain the ideas presented in the text about finding distances.
- Discuss with your child how the Pythagorean Theorem is applied by people in some careers, such as carpenters, architects, and pilots.
- Look over your child's homework and make sure that all the questions are answered and that explanations are clear.
- Have your child pick a question that was interesting to him or her and explain it to you.

A few important mathematical ideas that your child will learn in *Looking for Pythagoras* are given on the back. As always, if you have any questions or concerns about this unit or your child's progress in class, please feel free to call.

Sincerely,

Important Concepts	Examples
Finding Area Students find areas of squares drawn on grids. One method is to subdivide the square and add the areas of the component shapes. Another method is to enclose the square in a rectangle and subtract the area outside the figure from the area of the rectangle.	Area of tilted square = Area of 4 triangles + 1 small square = $4\left[\frac{1}{2}(3 \times 4)\right] + 1$ = 25 square units 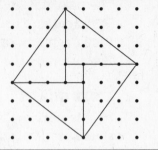
Square Roots If the area of a square is known, its side length is the number whose square is the area. Some of these lengths are not whole numbers, so we use the $\sqrt{}$ symbol.	The area of the tilted square is 10 square units, so the side of the tilted square is $\sqrt{10}$ units.
Estimating Square Roots Students develop benchmarks for estimating square roots.	$\sqrt{5}$ is between 2 and 3 because $2^2 < 5 < 3^2$. It is closer to 2. Try 2.25 ÷ 2.25^2 = 5.06. So $\sqrt{5}$ is between 2 and 2.25, but closer to 2.25. Try 2.24 (2.24^2 = 5.0176), even closer. Continue until the desired accuracy is obtained.
Finding Distances To find various lengths of line segments, students begin by drawing a square that is associated with the length.	The line segment shown is the side of a square with an area of 25 square units, so the segment has length $\sqrt{25}$, or 5. 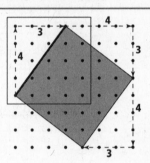
Pythagorean Theorem In a right triangle, the sum of the squares of the lengths of the two legs is equal to the square of the length of the longest side, called the hypotenuse. Symbolically, this is $a^2 + b^2 = c^2$, where a and b are the lengths of the legs and c is the length of the hypotenuse.	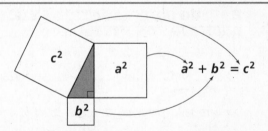
Length of Line Segment On a grid, the length of a horizontal or vertical line segment can be found by counting the distance. If a segment is not vertical or horizontal, it is possible to treat it as the hypotenuse of a right triangle. The Pythagorean Theorem is used to find the length of the hypotenuse.	The length of line segment AB can be the hypotenuse of a right triangle, c. $2^2 + 2^2 = c^2$, so $4 + 4 = 8 = c^2$. $\sqrt{8} = c$ 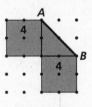
Irrational Numbers A number that cannot be written as a fraction with an integer numerator or denominator is irrational. Decimal representations of irrational numbers never end and never show a repeating pattern for a fixed number of digits.	The numbers $\sqrt{2}$, $\sqrt{3}$, $\sqrt{5}$, and π are examples of irrational numbers. $\sqrt{2}$ is 1.41421356237…. The decimal part goes forever without any pattern of fixed length that repeats.

On the **CMP Parent Web Site,** you can learn more about the mathematical goals of each unit, see an illustrated vocabulary list, and examine solutions of selected ACE problems. **http://PHSchool.com/cmp2parents**

Dear Family,

The next unit in your child's mathematics class this year is ***Growing, Growing, Growing: Exponential Relationships***. This unit focuses on exponential relationships, in which a quantity grows larger or smaller at an increasing rate rather than at a constant rate.

UNIT GOALS

Your child has previously studied linear growth, in which a fixed amount is repeatedly added to a beginning quantity to produce a sequence of values. Exponential growth involves patterns that are based on multiplication rather than addition. For example, in the sequence 3, 9, 27, 81, 243, ..., each term is 3 times the previous term.

The basic goal in *Growing, Growing, Growing* is for students to learn to recognize situations, data patterns, and graphs that are modeled by exponential expressions, and to use tables, graphs, and equations to answer questions about exponential patterns.

HELPING WITH HOMEWORK

You can help with your child's homework and encourage sound mathematical habits as your child studies this unit by asking questions such as:

- Is the relationship between variables an example of exponential growth or decay? Why?
- How can this relationship be detected in a table, graph, or equation? What is the growth factor?
- What table, graph, or equation would model the data or the pattern in a graph relating the variables?
- How could I answer questions about an exponential situation by studying a table, a graph, or an equation of the exponential relationship?
- How does this exponential relationship compare to other relationships between variables I have studied?

In your child's notebook, you can find worked-out examples from problems done in class, notes on the mathematics of the unit, and descriptions of the vocabulary words.

HAVING CONVERSATIONS ABOUT THE MATHEMATICS IN *GROWING, GROWING, GROWING*

You can help your child with his or her work for this unit in several ways:

- Talk with your child about the applications that are presented in the unit and similar applications that you encounter in your daily activities.
- Have your child pick a question that was interesting to him or her and explain it to you.
- Look over your child's homework and make sure that all questions are answered and that explanations are clear.

A few important mathematical ideas that your child will learn in *Growing, Growing, Growing* are given on the back. As always, if you have any questions or concerns about this unit or your child's progress in class, please feel free to call.

Sincerely,

Important Concepts	Examples

Exponential Growth

An exponential pattern of change involves patterns that are based on multiplication and can often be recognized in a verbal description of a situation or in the pattern of change in a table of (x, y) values.

The increasing rate of growth is reflected in the upward curve of the plotted points.

Suppose a reward is offered. At the start, 1¢ is put in a fund. On the first day, 2¢ is added; on the second day, 4¢ is added; and on each succeeding day, the reward is doubled. How much money is added on the eighth day?

Class Party Fund

Good-Work Day	Reward (cents)
0 (start)	1
1	2
2	4
3	8
4	16
5	32
6	64
7	128
8	?

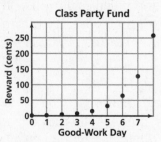

Class Party Fund

Growth Factor

A constant factor can be obtained by dividing each successive y-value by the previous y-value. This ratio is called the *growth factor* of the pattern.

In the example above, you multiply the previous award by 2 to get the new reward. This constant factor can also be obtained by dividing successive y-values: $\frac{2}{1} = 2$, $\frac{4}{2} = 2$, etc.

Exponential Equations

EXPONENTIAL GROWTH An exponential growth pattern, $y = a(b)^x$, increases slowly at first but grows at an increasing rate because its growth is multiplicative. The growth factor is b.

Day	Calculation	Reward (cents)
0	1	1
1	1×2, or 2^1	2
2	$1 \times 2 \times 2$, or 2^2	4
3	$1 \times 2 \times 2 \times 2$, or 2^3	8
⋮	⋮	⋮
6	$1 \times 2 \times 2 \times 2 \times 2 \times 2 \times 2$, or 2^6	256
⋮	⋮	⋮
n	$1 \times 2 \times 2 \times \cdots \times 2$, or 2^n	2^n

On the nth day, the reward, R, will be $R = 1 \times 2^n$. Because the independent variable in this pattern appears as an exponent, the growth pattern is called exponential. The growth factor is the *base*, 2. The *exponent*, n, tells the number of times the 2 is a factor.

EXPONENTIAL DECAY Exponential models describe patterns in which the value decreases. Decay factors result in decreasing relationships because they are less than 1.

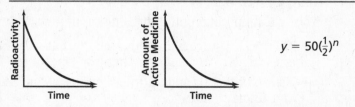

$$y = 50(\tfrac{1}{2})^n$$

Rules of Exponents

The multiplicative structure of bases leads to:

$(b^m)^n = b^{mn}$

$(b^m)(b^n) = b^{m+n}$

$(a^m b^m) = (ab)^m$

$a^m/a^n = a^{m-n}$

$(2^3)^2 = (2 \times 2 \times 2)^2 = (2 \times 2 \times 2) \times (2 \times 2 \times 2) = 2^6$

$3^2 \times 3^3 = (3 \times 3) \times (3 \times 3 \times 3) = 3^5 = 243$

$(2 \times 5)^2 = (2 \times 5) \times (2 \times 5) = (2 \times 2) \times (5 \times 5) = 2^2 \times 5^2$

$5^3/5^2 = (5 \times 5 \times 5)/(5 \times 5) = 5^{3-2} = 5^1 = 5$

On the **CMP Parent Web Site**, you can learn more about the mathematical goals of each unit, see an illustrated vocabulary list, and examine solutions of selected ACE problems. **http://PHSchool.com/cmp2parents**

Dear Family,

The next unit in your child's mathematics class this year is ***Frogs, Fleas, and Painted Cubes: Quadratic Relationships***. In an earlier unit, *Thinking With Mathematical Models*, students studied the use of linear models and investigated examples of inverse variation. In the *Growing, Growing, Growing* unit, students explored exponential models. In *Frogs, Fleas, and Painted Cubes*, the focus switches to a nonlinear polynomial relationship: the second-degree polynomial or the *quadratic* function.

UNIT GOALS

Students will learn to recognize quadratic patterns of change in tables and graphs, and they will learn to write equations to represent those patterns. They will compare and contrast quadratic patterns of change with those of linear and exponential patterns of change, which they have already studied in depth.

Quadratic relationships are encountered in such fields as business, sports, engineering, and economics. We are dealing with quadratic relationships, for example, when we study how the height of a ball—or jumping flea—changes over time. A quadratic graph, called a *parabola*, is shaped like either a U or an upside-down U.

HELPING WITH HOMEWORK

You can help with your child's homework and encourage sound mathematical habits as your child studies this unit by asking questions such as:

- How can I recognize if the relationship among variables in a situation is a quadratic function?
- What equation would represent a quadratic relationship in the table, graph, or problem context relating the variables?
- How could I answer the questions of the situations by studying a table, graph, or equation of the quadratic relationship?

In your child's notebook, you can find worked-out examples from problems done in class, notes on the mathematics of the unit, and descriptions of the vocabulary words.

HAVING CONVERSATIONS ABOUT THE MATHEMATICS IN *FROGS, FLEAS, AND PAINTED CUBES*

You can help your child with his or her work for this unit in several ways:

- Talk with your child about the situations that are presented in the unit.
- Look over your child's homework and make sure that all questions are answered and that explanations are clear.
- Have your child pick a question that was interesting to him or her and explain it to you.

A few important mathematical ideas that your child will learn in *Frogs, Fleas, and Painted Cubes* are given on the back. As always, if you have any questions or concerns about this unit or your child's progress in class, please feel free to call.

Sincerely,

Important Concepts	Examples

Representing Quadratic Patterns of Change With Tables

In linear relationships, the *first differences* of successive values are constant, indicating a constant rate of change. In quadratic relationships, first differences are not constant, but *second differences* are. The first difference is the rate at which y is changing with respect to x. The second difference indicates the rate at which *that rate* is changing. If the second differences are all the same, then the relationship is quadratic.

$y = 6(x - 2)^2$

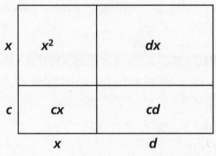

x	y	First Differences	Second Differences
0	24	$6 - 24 = ^-18$	$^-6 - (^-18) = 12$
1	6	$0 - 6 = ^-6$	$0 - (^-6) = 12$
2	0	$6 - 0 = 6$	$18 - 6 = 12$
3	6	$24 - 6 = 18$	$30 - 18 = 12$
4	24	$54 - 24 = 30$	
5	54		

The second differences are all 12, which indicates that the table represents a quadratic relationship.

Representing Quadratic Functions With Equations

Traditionally, quadratic relationships are defined as relationships that have equations fitting the form $y = ax^2 + bx + c$, in which a, b, and c are constants, and $a \neq 0$. This form of the equation is called the *expanded form*. The emphasis is on observing that the equations contain an independent variable raised to the second power. It is also important to understand the *factored form* of such equations.

Many quadratic equations can also be defined as functions whose y-value is equal to the product of two linear factors—the form $y = (ax + c)(bx + d)$, where $a \neq 0$ and $b \neq 0$. The power of this form is that it relates quadratic polynomials as products of linear factors.

The area of the rectangle below can be thought of as the product of two linear expressions, as the result of multiplying the width by the length, or as the sum of the area of the subparts of the rectangle.

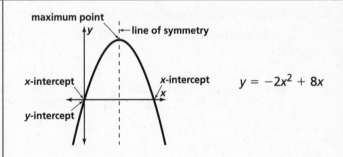

$A = (x + c)(x + d)$ factored form
$A = x^2 + cx + dx + d$ expanded form

Representing Quadratic Patterns of Change With Graphs

The values in the equation affect the shape, orientation, and location of the quadratic graph, a parabolic curve.

If the coefficient of the x^2 term is positive, the curve opens upward and has a minimum point. If negative, the curve opens downward and has a maximum point.

The maximum or minimum point of a quadratic graph **(parabola)** is called the **vertex**. The vertex lies on the vertical *line of symmetry* that separates the parabola into halves that are mirror images. The vertex is located halfway between the **x-intercepts**, if the x-intercepts exist. The x-intercepts are mirror images of each other. The **y-intercept** is where the parabola crosses the y-axis.

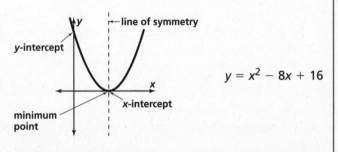

$y = -2x^2 + 8x$

$y = x^2 - 8x + 16$

On the **CMP Parent Web Site**, you can learn more about the mathematical goals of each unit, see an illustrated vocabulary list, and examine solutions of selected ACE problems. **http://PHSchool.com/cmp2parents**

Dear Family,

The next unit your child will be studying in mathematics class this year is *Kaleidoscopes, Hubcaps, and Mirrors: Symmetry and Transformations*. This unit is an introduction to the topic in mathematics called transformational geometry.

UNIT GOALS

Students often have an intuitive understanding of symmetry. Though students begin recognizing symmetric figures at an early age, the analytic understanding needed to confirm symmetry and to construct figures with given symmetries requires greater mathematical sophistication. *Kaleidoscopes, Hubcaps, and Mirrors*, the last geometry and measurement unit in the *Connected Mathematics* curriculum, helps students to refine their knowledge of symmetry and to use it to make mathematical arguments.

Symmetry is commonly described in terms of transformations. Symmetry transformations include reflections, rotations, and translations. These transformations preserve both angle measures and side lengths, resulting in an image that is congruent to the original figure. This unit will stimulate and sharpen students' awareness of symmetry, congruence, and their connections.

HELPING WITH HOMEWORK

You can help with your child's homework and encourage sound mathematical habits as your child studies this unit by asking questions such as:

- How can a systematic design be described so that someone could re-create it?
- Exactly what specific information about distances can we use when we make an image under reflection? Under rotation? Under transformation?
- If figures are the same shape and size, how are measures of the sides and angles related?
- What measures of sides and angles in two shapes are known, and can I conclude from these measures that the two shapes are congruent?
- What connections between geometry and algebra help create certain kinds of designs?

In your child's notebook, you can find worked-out examples from problems done in class, notes on the mathematics of the unit, and descriptions of the vocabulary words.

HAVING CONVERSATIONS ABOUT THE MATHEMATICS IN KALEIDOSCOPES, HUBCAPS, AND MIRRORS

You can help your child with his or her work for this unit in several ways:

- Talk with your child about the ideas presented in the text about symmetry. Look with your child for examples of each type of symmetry.
- Look over your child's homework and make sure that all questions are answered and that explanations are clear.

A few important mathematical ideas that your child will learn in *Kaleidoscopes, Hubcaps, and Mirrors* are given on the back. As always, if you have any questions or concerns about this unit or your child's progress in class, please feel free to call.

Sincerely,

Types of Symmetry

REFLECTION SYMMETRY A design has reflection symmetry if a reflection in a line makes an image that fits exactly onto the original figure or design.

This letter A has reflection symmetry because a reflection in the vertical line will match each point on the left half with a point on the right half. The vertical line is the line of symmetry.

ROTATION SYMMETRY A design has rotation symmetry if a rotation other than a full turn about a point makes an image that fits exactly onto the original figure or design.

This design has rotation symmetry because a rotation of 120° or 240° about point *P* will match each flag with another flag. Point *P* is the center of rotation. The angle of rotation is 120°, the smallest angle through which the design can be rotated to match with the original position.

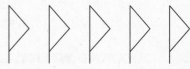

TRANSLATION SYMMETRY A design has translation symmetry if a translation, or slide, maps the figure onto itself.

This figure is part of a translation-symmetric design. If this design continued in both directions, a slide to the right or left would match each flag with another.

Symmetry Transformations

Symmetry transformations—reflections, rotations, and translations—move points to image points so that the distance between any two original points is equal to the distance between their images. Students examine figures and their images under reflections, rotations, and translations, measuring key distances and angles. They use their findings to determine how they can specify a particular transformation so that another person could perform it exactly. They can also use this information about preserved distances to reason about shapes which have symmetry.

REFLECTIONS A reflection can be specified by giving the line of reflection.

The point *A* and its reflection image point *A'* lie on a line that is perpendicular to the line of symmetry and are equidistant from that line.

ROTATIONS A rotation can be specified by giving the center of rotation and the angle of the turn.

Point *B* and its image point *B'* are equidistant from the center of the rotation *P*. A point under a rotation "travels" on the arc of a circle, and the set of circles on which the points of the figure "travel" are concentric circles with *P* as their center. The angles formed by the vertex points of the figure and their rotation images all have measures equal to the angle of turn.

TRANSLATIONS A translation can be specified by giving the length and direction of the slide. Usually, an arrow with the appropriate length and direction is drawn.

If you draw the segments connecting a number of points to their images, the segments will be parallel and all the same length. The length is equal to the magnitude of the translation.

Congruent Figures

Figures of the same size and shape are congruent.

You can make an image of one figure which will fit exactly on top of the other by a combination of symmetry transformations.

On the **CMP Parent Web Site**, you can learn more about the mathematical goals of each unit, see an illustrated vocabulary list, and examine solutions of selected ACE problems. **http://PHSchool.com/cmp2parents**

Dear Family,

The next unit in mathematics class, ***Say It With Symbols: Making Sense of Symbols***, explores the topic that beginning algebra used to focus on almost exclusively: the use of symbols. When you first began studying algebra, you probably spent most of your time learning to manipulate symbols. Chances are you didn't get a chance to think about what the symbols actually meant. This mathematics curriculum emphasizes the *meaning* behind the symbols. This helps students build their own understanding of the basics of algebra and its usefulness for solving problems.

UNIT GOALS

In *Say It With Symbols*, students learn to use symbolic expressions to represent and reason about relationships. Students also manipulate symbolic expressions into equivalent forms to access new information. The emphasis is on using the properties of numbers and properties of equality to look at equivalent expressions and the information each expression represents. In addition, students interpret underlying patterns that a symbolic equation or statement represents. Students look critically at each part of an expression and how each part relates to the original expression, its graph, its table, and the context that is modeled.

HELPING WITH HOMEWORK

You can help with your child's homework and encourage sound mathematical habits as your child studies this unit by asking questions such as:

- What expression or equation captures the underlying pattern or relationship in a context?
- How can one tell if two or more expressions are equivalent?
- What operations would transform an equation or expression into an equivalent form so the solution can be more easily determined?
- What patterns of change does the equation or expression represent?
- In what ways can symbolic reasoning help confirm a conjecture?

In your child's notebook, you can find worked-out examples from problems done in class, notes on the mathematics of the unit, and descriptions of the vocabulary words.

HAVING CONVERSATIONS ABOUT THE MATHEMATICS IN *SAY IT WITH SYMBOLS*

You can help your child with his or her work for this unit in several ways:

- Talk with your child about the situations that are presented and why we can rearrange symbols.
- Talk with your child about the importance of being skillful in algebra.
- Look over your child's homework and make sure that all the questions are answered and that explanations are clear.

A few important mathematical ideas that your child will learn in *Say It With Symbols* are given on the back. As always, if you have any questions or concerns about this unit or your child's progress in class, please feel free to call.

Sincerely,

Important Concepts	Examples
Equivalent Expressions Students are deliberately presented with situations in which contextual clues can be interpreted in several ways to produce different, yet equivalent, equations.	*Find the number of 1-foot-square tiles, N, needed to make a border around a square pool with sides of length s feet.* Different conceptualizations of the situation can lead to different, yet equivalent, expressions for the number of tiles: $N = 4s + 4$ $N = 4(s + 1)$ $N = s + s + s + s + 4$ $N = 8 + 4(s - 1)$ $N = 2s + 2(s + 2)$ $N = (s + 2)^2 - s^2$. 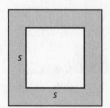

Revisiting the Distributive Property
If an expression is written as a factor multiplied by a sum of two or more terms, the Distributive Property can be applied to *multiply* the factor by each term in the sum. If an expression is written as a sum of terms and the terms have a common factor, the Distributive Property can be applied to rewrite the expression as the common factor multiplied by a sum of two or more terms. This process is called *factoring*.

multiply

$r(s + t) = rs + rt$

factor

The Distributive Property allows students to group symbols (shown on the left side of the equation) or to expand an expression as needed (shown on the right side of the equation).

Checking for Equivalence
Students may use contextual reasoning to decide if expressions are equivalent. Students may check whether equations have the same graphs and tables. Students should also be able to use the Distributive and Commutative Properties to show that expressions are equivalent.

By applying the Distributive Property $4(s + 1) = 4s + 4$.
$8 + 4(s - 1)$ can be shown to be equivalent to $4s + 4$.

$8 + 4(s - 1) = 8 + 4s - 4$	(Distributive Property)
$= 8 - 4 + 4s$	(Commutative Property)
$= 4 + 4s$	(Subtraction)
$= 4s + 4$	(Commutative Property)

Solving Linear Equations
Students have used tables or graphs to find solutions. They can solve simple linear equations using Properties of Equality. In this unit, students solve more complicated equations using Properties of Real Numbers.

$200 = 5x - (100 + 2x)$	
$200 = 5x - (2x + 100)$	(Commutative Property)
$200 = 5x - 2x - 100$	(Distributive Property)
$200 = 3x - 100$	[Distributive Property, $5x - 2x = (5 - 2)x$]
$300 = 3x$	(adding same to each side of an equation)
$100 = x$	(dividing by the same on each side of an equation)

Solving Quadratic Equations
Solving quadratic equations for x when $y = 0$ is equivalent to finding the x-intercepts on the graph. Students are also introduced to solving quadratic equations by factoring.

The connection is made between the linear factors of a quadratic expression and the x-intercepts of the graph of a quadratic equation.

If $y = 2x^2 + 8x$, then the values of x when $y = 0$ can be obtained by rewriting the equation in the equivalent form of $2x(x + 4) = 0$.

This product can be zero only if one of the factors is equal to 0. Solve $2x = 0$ and $x + 4 = 0$. Thus, $x = 0$ or $x = -4$. The x-intercepts are $(0, 0)$ and $(-4, 0)$.

If $0 = x^2 + 5x + 6$, we write $x^2 + 5x + 6$ in factored form $(x + 2)(x + 3)$ and then solve $0 = (x + 2)(x + 3)$. Thus $x + 2 = 0$ or $x = -2$, and $x + 3 = 0$ or $x = -3$. The solutions of $x^2 + 5x + 6 = 0$ are $x = -3$ and $x = -2$.

On the **CMP Parent Web Site,** you can learn more about the mathematical goals of each unit, see an illustrated vocabulary list, and examine solutions of selected ACE problems. **http://PHSchool.com/cmp2parents**

Dear Family,

The next unit in your child's mathematics class this year is ***The Shapes of Algebra: Linear Systems and Inequalities***. This unit was designed to help students capitalize on the strong connections between algebra and geometry in order to extend students' understanding and skill in several aspects of those two key strands in the middle grades curriculum.

UNIT GOALS

In *The Shapes of Algebra*, students will explore the relationship between algebra and geometry. Through this exploration, students will work with equations for lines and curves, and will develop an understanding of how systems of equations and inequalities can help solve problems. Students extend their earlier work in algebra and geometry by making connections between them. For example, students connect the idea of the Pythagorean Theorem to the coordinate equation for a circle, and connect properties of polygons to slopes of lines.

HELPING WITH HOMEWORK

You can help with your child's homework and encourage sound mathematical habits as your child studies this unit by asking questions such as:

- What patterns relate coordinates of points on lines and curves that have been drawn?
- What patterns relate the points whose coordinates satisfy equations that are to be solved?
- Does the problem involve an equation or an inequality?
- Does the problem call for writing and/or solving a system of equations?
- If so, what method would be useful in solving the system?
- Are there some systematic methods that can be used to solve all systems of linear equations?

In your child's notebook, you can find worked-out examples from problems done in class, notes on the mathematics of the unit, and descriptions of the vocabulary words.

HAVING CONVERSATIONS ABOUT THE MATHEMATICS IN *THE SHAPES OF ALGEBRA*

You can help your child with his or her work for this unit in several ways:

- Talk with your child about the importance of being skillful in algebra.
- Look over your child's homework and make sure that all the questions are answered and that explanations are clear.
- Have your child pick a question that was interesting to him or her and explain it to you.

A few important mathematical ideas that your child will learn in *The Shapes of Algebra* are given on the back. As always, if you have any questions or concerns about this unit or your child's progress in class, please feel free to call.

Sincerely,

Important Concepts	**Examples**
Linear Inequalities A relation of inequality between two quantities, in which each quantity is a linear expressions, is called a linear inequality.	$3x + 22 < 8x + 7$ or $3x + 4y < 12$
Solving Linear Inequalities Solving an inequality is much like solving linear equations. The rules for operations with inequalities are identical to those for equations, with one exception. When multiplying (or dividing) an inequality by a negative number, the direction of the inequality is reversed.	$5x + 7 \leq 42$ $5x \leq 35$ $x \leq 7$ Solving this inequality is similar to solving $5x + 7 = 42$. The operations $(+, -, \times, \div)$ are applied to both sides. We usually show this solution on a number line. $-5x + 7 \leq 42$ $-5x \leq 35$ $x \geq -7$ Reverse in the direction of the inequality sign.

Solving Systems of Linear Equations

Solving a system means finding all solutions that satisfy all equations in the system. There are a variety of techniques available for solving systems of two linear equations in two unknowns.

GRAPHIC SOLUTION OF SYSTEMS This method involves producing straight-line graphs for each equation and then reading coordinates of intersection points as the solution(s).

EQUIVALENT FORM The equations in a system can each be changed to $y = ax + b$ form. For $\begin{cases} y = -2x + 5 \\ y = 3x - 5 \end{cases}$

set the two expressions for y equal to each other. This eliminates a variable and gives $(-2x + 5) = (3x - 5)$.

So $5x = 10$, or $x = 2$. Find the corresponding y-value by substituting. $y = -2(2) + 5 = 1$
The solution is $(2, 1)$.

SOLVING SYSTEMS BY SUBSTITUTION In the system $\begin{cases} 3x + 5y = 8 \\ 6x + y = 7 \end{cases}$, the second equation can be

rewritten as $y = 7 - 6x$. Use this information about y and the first equation, $3x + 5(7 - 6x) = 8$. Now solve this equation with one unknown with methods from earlier work to reveal $x = 1$ and then $y = 7 - 6(1)$ or $y = 1$.

SOLVING SYSTEMS BY LINEAR COMBINATION Another method relies on two basic principles:

1. Multiplying a linear equation by the same (non-zero) number does not change the set of solutions.

2. The solution is unchanged if one of the equations is replaced by a new equation formed by adding the two original equations.

For example:
$\begin{cases} 3x + 5y = 8 \\ 6x + y = 7 \end{cases}$ is equivalent to $\begin{cases} -6x - 10y = -16 \\ 6x + y = 7 \end{cases}$

$-9y = -9$, by adding the two equations.
You can see that $y = 1$ and that $x = 1$.

| **Solving Systems of Linear Inequalities**
Systems of inequalities tend to have infinite solution sets as well. The solution to a system of distinct, non-disjoint linear *inequalities* is the intersection of two half-planes, which contain infinitely many points. | In general, there are four regions suggested by a system of linear inequalities such as $\begin{cases} y < y \\ y > x - 5 \end{cases}$.

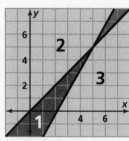 Region 1 contains the solutions to the system. Points in Regions 2 and 3 satisfy one, but not both, of the inequalities. Region 4 satisfies neither inequality. |

On the **CMP Parent Web Site,** you can learn more about the mathematical goals of each unit, see an illustrated vocabulary list, and examine solutions of selected ACE problems. **http://PHSchool.com/cmp2parents**

Dear Family,

The next unit in your child's mathematics class this year is ***Samples and Populations: Data and Statistics***. The unit will involve the process of statistical investigation. As part of this process, we will pay special attention to the ways that data are collected.

UNIT GOALS

Probability is a tool for understanding sampling issues in statistics; statistics is a tool for representing and analyzing data that may then be used to draw conclusions about a population. The problems in *Samples and Populations* help students make connections between probability and statistics.

This unit begins with tools for grouping data and comparing distributions. Then students explore what samples are and how they are related to populations, ways to select samples, and the use of random samples. Finally, students look at relationships between two attributes and what it means to say that information about values from one attribute can be used to understand, explain, or predict values of another attribute.

HELPING WITH HOMEWORK

You can help with homework and encourage sound mathematical habits as your child studies this unit by asking questions such as:

- What is the population? What is the sample? What sampling method was used?
- What kinds of comparisons among the data from the sample can I explore?
- Can I use my results to make predictions or generalizations about the populations?
- Were the ways in which the data were collected or analyzed likely to give results that represent the population?

In your child's notebook, you can find worked-out examples from problems done in class, notes on the mathematics of the unit, and descriptions of the vocabulary words.

HAVING CONVERSATIONS ABOUT THE MATHEMATICS IN *SAMPLES AND POPULATIONS*

You can help your child with his or her work for this unit in several ways:

- Using newspapers, magazines, television, or radio, help your child identify situations in which statistics are being used, paying particular attention to who or what was sampled.
- Talk about whether data from a particular study can be used to make accurate predictions about a larger population.
- Look over your child's homework and make sure that all questions are answered and that explanations are clear.

A few important mathematical ideas that your child will learn in *Samples and Populations* are given on the back. As always, if you have any questions or concerns about this unit or your child's progress in class, please feel free to call.

Sincerely,

Important Concepts	Examples
The Process of Statistical Investigation This process involves four parts: posing a question, collecting the data, analyzing the distribution, and interpreting the analysis in light of the question. When completed, students need to communicate the results.	Students need to think about the process of statistical investigation whether they are collecting their own data or using data provided for them.
Distinguishing Different Types of Data An *attribute* is a name for a particular characteristic of a person, place, or thing about which data are being collected. There are two general kinds of data values: categorical and numerical.	We can have the attribute of *kind of peanut butter* to characterize whether a peanut butter is natural or regular, or the attribute of *quality rating* to characterize the quality (using a number) of a given type of peanut butter. Categorical values are "regular" or "natural" for the kind of peanut butter. Numerical values are the numbers used in the quality ratings for peanut butter.

Making Sense of a Data Set Using Different Representations

DOT PLOT (OR LINE PLOT) Each case is represented as a dot (or an "x") positioned over a labeled number line.

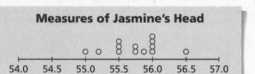

Measures of Jasmine's Head

HISTOGRAM The size of the bar over that interval shows the frequency data values in each interval along the range of data values; frequencies may be displayed as counts or percentages.

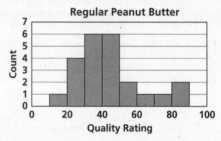

SCATTERPLOT The relationship between two different attributes is explored by plotting values of two numeric attributes on a Cartesian coordinate system.

BOX-AND-WHISKER PLOT The box plot is divided into quartiles and displays the properties of distribution, such as symmetry or skewness. This plot was developed largely because comparing data using frequency bar graphs can often be confusing, especially if one is comparing more than two bar graphs.

Exploring the Concept of Sampling The essential idea behind sampling is to gain information about the whole by analyzing only a part of it. A primary issue in sampling is choosing a sample likely to be unbiased and predictive of the population.	To ensure fair samples, we try to choose random samples. Students consider other types of sampling strategies: convenience sampling, voluntary-response sampling, and systematic sampling. We want students to develop a sound, general sense about what makes a good sample size and how sample size affects the predictive quality of the sample.

On the **CMP Parent Web Site,** you can learn more about the mathematical goals of each unit, see an illustrated vocabulary list, and examine solutions of selected ACE problems. **http://PHSchool.com/cmp2parents**

Connected Mathematics 2

Sugerencias para contribuir al éxito de su hijo

Los objetivos de Connected Mathematics 2 (CMP2) son ayudar a los estudiantes a:

- Desarollar conocimientos, comprensión y destrezas matemáticos.

- Desarrolla la capacidad de definir y resolver problemas con razonamiento, comprensión, inventiva y eficacia técnica.

- Sentar una base y hacer conexiones entre las ideas y los conceptos matemáticos.

- Ver las conexiones entre las matemáticas y otras disciplinas

En CMP2, las prácticas instruccionales del maestro y las maneras en las que los estudiantes interactúan con las matemáticas apoyan estos objetivos. Enseñar, aprender y evaluar están alineados unos con otros como partes integrales de Connected Mathematics 2.

Para más información, por favor visite la página web de CMP, disponible en inglés: **http://www.math.msu.edu/cmp/parents**
O la página Web de CMP2 Prentice Hall: **http://www.PHSchool.com/cmp2**

PEARSON
Prentice Hall

Autores

Glenda T. Lappan, Universidad Estatal de Michigan
James T. Fey, Universidad de Maryland
William M. Fitzgerald, Universidad Estatal de Michigan (Fallecido)
Susan N. Friel, Universidad de Carolina de Norte
Elizabeth Difanis Phillips, Universidad Estatal de Michigan

Premios

La *American Association for the Advancement of Science* (AAAS) clasificó a CMP como el mejor de doce programas de escuela intermedia, declarando que "contiene tanto contenido matemático profundo como excelente apoyo instructivo".
— 22 de enero, 1999

El panel de expertos del Departamento de Educación de Estados Unidos designó *Connected Mathematics* como un plan de estudios de matemáticas ejemplar. Sólo cinco planes de estudio de matemáticas de K a 12 recibieron esta designación. CMP fue el único plan ejemplar de estudios de matemáticas de la escuela intermedia.
— Departamento de Educación de EE.UU., 1999

Derechos

Los autores no reciben derechos de las ventas de los libros de *Connected Mathematics*. Los autores y la administración de la Universidad Estatal de Michigan han decidido que todos los derechos MSU que salgan de la publicación de libros de CMP se pondrán en un fondo de educación matemática para el apoyo de proyectos relacionados con CMP y la educación matemática.

Fondos

La *National Science Foundation*, la Oficina del director de la Universidad Estatal de Michigan, Computación y Tecnología, y el Colegio de Ciencias Naturales proporcionaron fondos para el desarrollo de CMP.

Resumen de investigación y evaluación

La editorial, Prentice Hall, tiene disponible en inglés un Resumen de investigación y evaluación de CMP.
http://www.phschool.com/math/cmp/research_evaluation

¿Cuáles son los puntos fuertes de Connected Mathematics 2?

Como plan de estudios para los grados 6 a 8, *Connected Mathematics 2*:

- Está organizado alrededor de importantes ideas y procesos matemáticos

- Es un plan de estudios centrado en el problema, que usa una base inquisitiva como modelo instruccional.

- Desarrolla una comprensión profunda de ideas, razonamiento y destrezas matemáticas clave.

- Eleva sustancialmente el nivel de pensamiento y razonamiento matemático de los estudiantes.

- Promueve la retención a largo plazo de conceptos, procesos y destrezas matemáticos.

- Conecta ideas matemáticas dentro de la unidad, con otras unidades y con otros grados.

- Promueve tarea para la casa que pone énfasis en la práctica de destrezas y resolución de problemas.

- Incorpora la tecnología a través de todo el plan de estudios.

- Ofrece tareas de evaluación multidimensionales.

- Se basa en tres décadas de experiencia e investigación.

Cuando ayude a su hijo(a) a aprender, un objetivo es que entiendan tanto como puedan por sí mismos. Buenas preguntas y escuchar bien ayudarán a comprender las matemáticas, tener confianza en sí mismos y estimular la comunicación y el pensamiento matemático. Aquí hay algunas preguntas que puede usar para guiar el pensamiento de su hijo(a):

Listos para empezar ....

* ¿Qué necesitas averiguar?
* ¿Qué necesitas saber?
* ¿Qué términos comprendes o no comprendes?
* ¿Has resuelto problemas similares que te ayudarían? Miremos tu cuaderno.

Trabajar en el problema ....

* ¿Cómo puedes organizar la información?
* ¿Ves algún patrón o relación que te ayudará a resolver esto?
* ¿Puedes describir una estrategia que puedas usar para resolver esto?
* ¿Puedes hacer un dibujo para explicar lo que piensas?
* ¿Qué pasaría si...?

Reflexionar sobre la solución ....

* ¿Se ha contestado la pregunta?
* ¿Cómo sabes que la solución es razonable?
* ¿Cómo puedes convencerme de que tu respuesta tiene sentido?
* ¿Qué destrezas e ideas matemáticas usaste para resolver el problema?

Clarificar y ampliar el pensamiento ....

* Ayúdame a comprender esta parte....
* ¿Puedes explicarlo de una manera distinta?
* ¿Hay otra posibilidad o estrategia que funcionaría?
* ¿Cómo se conecta esto con otras ideas que has aprendido?

Busque un lugar de estudio Si es posible, prepare un área tranquila. Tenga disponible material como papel cuadriculado, papel de cuaderno, una regla con unidades métricas y estándares, una calculadora (graficadora para los grados 7 a 12) y un diccionario.

Desarrolle un sistema Ayude a su hijo(a) a desarrollar un sistema para escribir tareas y controlar el progreso. Asegúrese que su hijo(a) lo haga regularmente.

Desarrolle destrezas para tomar notas Ayude a su hijo(a) a desarrollar un sistema para tomar notas con sentido. Frecuentemente, durante la clase se enseña a tomar notas, de modo que puede que sólo deba comprobar si su hijo(a) lo está haciendo bien.

Organice su cuaderno Muchos niños necesitan ayuda para organizar y mantener un cuaderno. Compruebe rutinariamente si su hijo(a) está siguiendo correctamente las guías del programa para mantener un cuaderno.

Fomente destrezas de control de tiempo Anime y espere que su hijo(a) haga el trabajo a tiempo, para que esté al día, para buscar ayuda a tiempo y para corregir errores en su trabajo. Si quiere, puede ayudar a su hijo(a) a repasar trabajo incorrecto o incompleto y hablar sobre cómo se podría mejorar el trabajo.

Domine las destrezas necesarias Se espera en general que los estudiantes de escuela intermedia conozcan la suma, resta, multiplicación y división de números enteros. Si su hijo(a) no domina estas destrezas básicas, ayúdele a dominar las destrezas necesarias.

Busque compañeros de estudio Anime a su hijo a identificar compañeros de estudio u otros estudiantes con los que pueda hablar de las tareas, aclarar cosas o averiguar sobre trabajos pendientes.

Dos objetivos importantes para todos los estudiantes son aprender a valorar las matemáticas y tener confianza en su habilidad para hacer matemáticas. Los padres pueden ayudarles a desarrollar una disposición de "sí puedo" de cara a las matemáticas, nutriendo su curiosidad y proporcionando apoyo y ánimo.

Señale matemáticas del mundo real Las matemáticas están por todas partes, pero muchos niños no lo ven. Señale y refuerce las destrezas matemáticas en casa. Por ejemplo:

* Hable de cómo usa matemáticas en casa o el trabajo.
* Involucre a su hijo(a) en tareas que requieran calcular, medir, estimar, construir, resolver problemas y razonar.
* Busque actividades que requieran usar destrezas matemáticas como construir modelos a escala, cocinar, planear viajes y jugar a juegos de lógica.

Pida a su hijo(a) que le explique lo que ha aprendido Invite a su hijo(a) a explicarle lo que se ha aprendido en clase. Esto le da una oportunidad de clarificar su pensamiento, practicar nuevas destrezas y comunicarse matemáticamente.

Busque juegos Usar juegos y actividades es otra manera de enseñar y/o reforzar las destrezas y pensamiento matemáticos.

Busque artículos Muchos artículos tienen datos interesantes para su hijo(a) (ej., estadísticas deportivas, datos sobre fumadores adolescentes, información sobre desastres naturales). Compártanlos y hablen sobre lo que significan los números.

Comparta estrategias Pida a su hijo(a) que comparta sus estrategias para resolver problemas, calcular mentalmente y estimar. Comparta sus estrategias con ellos.

Busque programas de computadora Si su hijo(a) tiene acceso a una computadora, busque programas que refuercen y enseñen conceptos matemáticos.

Querida familia:

La primera unidad en la clase de matemáticas de su hijo(a) es ***La hora de los primos: Factores y múltiplos***. Ésta es la primera unidad sobre el tema de números de *Connected Mathematics*.

OBJETIVOS DE LA UNIDAD

La hora de los primos se centra en las propiedades de los números enteros, especialmente las relacionadas con la multiplicación y división. Los estudiantes aprenderán sobre factores, múltiplos, divisores, productos, números primos, números compuestos, factores y múltiplos comunes, y muchos otros conceptos sobre números. Los estudiantes participarán en actividades que reflejan muchas de las propiedades clave de los números y aprenderán a usarlas para resolver problemas.

AYUDAR CON LA TAREA

El objetivo de *Connected Mathematics* es ayudar a los estudiantes a desarrollar hábitos matemáticos con sentido. Usted puede ayudar con la tarea y al mismo tiempo propiciar buenos hábitos matemáticos haciendo preguntas como:

- ¿Me ayudará hallar los factores o los múltiplos a resolver el problema?
- ¿Qué relaciones me ayudan a ver los factores o los múltiplos?
- ¿Qué me dicen los factores y múltiplos de los números sobre la situación?
- ¿Cómo puedo hallar los factores de un número?
- ¿Cómo puedo hallar los múltiplos de un número?
- ¿Qué factores comunes y múltiplos comunes tienen los números?

En el cuaderno de su hijo(a), puede encontrar ejemplos de problemas resueltos en clase, notas sobre las matemáticas de la unidad y definiciones de las palabras del vocabulario.

En esta unidad se le pedirá a su hijo(a) que haga un proyecto llamado "Mi número especial". Se introduce al principio de la unidad, cuando se le pide a cada estudiante que escoja un número y escriba varias cosas sobre él. A medida que los estudiantes trabajan en la unidad, aplican lo que han aprendido para escribir nueva información sobre sus números. Al final de la unidad, los estudiantes crean proyectos que incluyen todo lo que han aprendido sobre sus números.

CONVERSAR SOBRE LAS MATEMÁTICAS DE *LA HORA DE LOS PRIMOS*

Puede ayudar a su hijo(a) de varias maneras:

- Pida a su hijo(a) que le muestre su cuaderno de matemáticas y lo que ha anotado sobre los factores y los múltiplos. Pida a su hijo(a) que le explique por qué estos conceptos son importantes.
- Pida a su hijo(a) que le muestre los tableros para jugar al *Juego de los factores* y al *Juego de los productos*. Pídale que le explique las reglas y, si tienen tiempo, ofrezca jugar al juego.
- Pida a su hijo(a) que le explique algo que aprendió con el juego.
- Revise la tarea de su hijo(a) y asegúrese que haya contestado todas las preguntas y que las explicaciones sean claras.

En la parte de atrás se dan unos cuantos conceptos matemáticos importantes que su hijo(a) aprenderá en *La hora de los primos*. Como siempre, si tiene preguntas sobre esta unidad o el progreso en clase de su hijo(a), no dude en llamar.

Atentamente,

Conceptos importantes	Ejemplos
Factor Cada uno de dos o más números que se multiplican para obtener un producto.	Todos los factores de 12 son 1, 2, 3, 4, 6, 12 porque $1 \times 12 = 12$, $2 \times 6 = 12$, $3 \times 4 = 12$.
Múltiplo El producto de un número entero dado y otro número entero.	Algunos múltiplos de 12 incluyen 12, 24, 36, 48, 60 porque $12 \times 1 = 12$, $12 \times 2 = 24$, $12 \times 3 = 36$, $12 \times 4 = 48$ y $12 \times 5 = 60$. Fíjese en que se puede seguir hallando múltiplos infinitamente. Si un número es un múltiplo de 12, entonces 12 es un factor de ese número. Por ejemplo, 36 es un múltiplo de 12 y 12 es un factor de 36.
Primo Un número que tiene exactamente dos factores, 1 y el propio número.	Ejemplos de números primos son 11, 17, 53 y 101. El número 1 no es un número primo, ya que sólo tiene un factor. Todos los factores de 11 son 1 y 11. Todos los factores de 17 son 1 y 17.
Compuesto Un número entero con otros factores además de 1 y él mismo, o un número entero que no es primo.	Algunos números compuestos son 6, 12, 20 y 1,001. Cada uno de estos números tiene más de dos factores. Todos los factores de 6 son 1, 2, 3, 6. Todos los factores de 1,001 son 1, 7, 11, 13, 77, 91, 143, 1001.
Múltiplo común Un múltiplo que comparten dos o más números.	Algunos múltiplos de 5 son 5, 10, 15, 20, 25, 30, <u>35</u>, 40, 45, 50, 55, 60, 65 y <u>70</u>. Algunos múltiplos de 7 son 7, 14, 21, 28, <u>35</u>, 42, 49, 56, 63, <u>70</u> y 77. De estas listas podemos ver que dos múltiplos comunes de 5 y 7 son 35 y 70. Se pueden hallar más múltiplos comunes.
Factor común Un factor que comparten dos o más números.	7 es un factor común de 14 y 35 porque 7 es un factor de 14 $(14 = 7 \times 2)$ y 7 es un factor de 35 $(35 = 7 \times 5)$.
Descomposición en factores primos Un producto de números primos, que acaba en el número deseado. La descomposición en factores primos de un número es exclusiva, excepto por el orden de los factores. Éste es el **Teorema fundamental de la aritmética**.	La descomposición en factores primos de 360 es $2 \times 2 \times 2 \times 3 \times 3 \times 5$. A pesar de que se puede cambiar el orden de los factores, cada tira de productos primos para 360 tendrá tres 2, dos 3 y un 5.

En la **Página Web de CMP para los padres**, disponible en inglés, puede aprender más sobre los objetivos matemáticos de cada unidad. Vea la lista de vocabulario ilustrado y examine las soluciones de algunos de los problemas de ACE. **http://PHSchool.com/cmp2parents**

Querida familia:

La siguiente unidad en la clase de matemáticas de su hijo(a) este año es ***Trozos y piezas I: Comprender fracciones, decimales y porcentajes***. Ésta es la primera de tres unidades dedicadas a desarrollar la comprensión de fracciones, decimales y porcentajes. *Trozos y piezas II* y *III* se centrarán en el cálculo con fracciones, decimales y porcentajes.

OBJETIVOS DE LA UNIDAD

Trozos y piezas I se centra en desarrollar una comprensión profunda de los números racionales. En esta unidad, su hijo(a) aprenderá el significado de las fracciones, los decimales y los porcentajes, y se sentirá cómodo(a) moviéndose entre estas tres maneras de expresar los números racionales. Su hijo(a) trabajará en problemas que reflejan diferentes contextos y que están relacionados con escribir, comparar y ordenar fracciones y decimales.

En esta unidad se usan modelos, como tiras de fracciones, rectas numéricas y cuadrículas. Se desarrolla la destreza para estimar y comparar a través de un conjunto de fracciones de referencia y sus equivalentes decimales. Las fracciones de referencia son aquellas que se encuentran a menudo en situaciones reales. Algunos ejemplos son $\frac{1}{4}$, $\frac{1}{3}$, $\frac{1}{2}$, $\frac{2}{3}$, $\frac{3}{4}$ y $1\frac{1}{2}$.

AYUDAR CON LA TAREA

Usted puede ayudar con la tarea y al mismo tiempo propiciar buenos hábitos matemáticos a medida que su hijo(a) estudia esta unidad, haciendo preguntas como:

- ¿Por qué necesito considerar cantidades que no representen números enteros?
- ¿Por qué puede haber distintos nombres de fracciones para la misma cantidad?
- ¿Cómo puedes saber cuándo dos fracciones son equivalentes?
- ¿Cómo puedo saber qué fracción es mayor?
- ¿En qué situaciones es útil el nombre decimal para una cantidad fraccional?
- ¿Cómo puedo cambiar un nombre fraccional a su equivalente en nombre decimal o en porcentaje?
- ¿Por qué son útiles las fracciones con un denominador de 100?

En el cuaderno de su hijo(a), puede encontrar ejemplos de problemas resueltos en clase, notas sobre las matemáticas de la unidad y definiciones de las palabras del vocabulario.

CONVERSAR SOBRE LAS MATEMÁTICAS DE *TROZOS Y PIEZAS I*

Puede ayudar a su hijo(a) con su trabajo para esta unidad de varias maneras:

- Pida a su hijo(a) que halle ejemplos de cómo se usan fracciones, decimales y porcentajes en periódicos, revistas, radio y televisión.
- Revise la tarea de su hijo(a) y asegúrese que haya contestado todas las preguntas y que las explicaciones sean claras.
- Pida a su hijo(a) que escoja una pregunta que le haya parecido interesante y se la explique.

En la parte de atrás se dan unos cuantos conceptos matemáticos importantes que su hijo(a) aprenderá en *Trozos y piezas I*. Como siempre, si tiene preguntas o preocupaciones sobre esta unidad o el progreso en clase de su hijo(a), no dude en llamar.

Conceptos importantes	Ejemplos
Fracciones como partes de un todo En la interpretación parte-todo de las fracciones, los estudiantes deben: • determinar lo que es el todo; • subdividir el todo en partes de igual tamaño (no necesariamente de igual forma, sino igual tamaño); • reconocer cuántas partes se necesitan para representar la situación; y • formar la fracción poniendo las partes necesarias sobre el número de partes en que se ha dividido el todo	Si hay 24 estudiantes en la clase y 16 son niñas, la parte del todo que es niñas se puede representar como $\frac{16}{24}$.  La porción sombreada de arriba también se puede representar como $\frac{2}{3}$. El **denominador** de 3 dice en cuántas partes de igual tamaño se ha dividido el todo, y el **numerador** de 2 dice cuántas partes de igual tamaño han sido sombreadas.
Fracciones como medidas o cantidades En esta interpretación, se piensa en una fracción como número.	Una fracción puede ser una medida que "está entre" dos medidas enteras. Los estudiantes encuentran esto cada día en referencias como $2\frac{1}{2}$ *brownies*, 11.5 millones de personas ó $7\frac{1}{2}$ pulgadas.
Fracciones como divisiones indicadas Para moverse con flexibilidad entre representaciones en fracciones y representaciones decimales de números racionales, los estudiantes necesitan comprender que se puede pensar en las fracciones como divisiones indicadas.	Compartir 36 manzanas entre 6 personas requiere una división ($36 \div 6 = 6$ manzanas cada una), de modo que compartir 3 manzanas entre 8 personas requiere dividir 3 por 8 para averiguar cuánto le tocará a cada persona ($\frac{3}{8}$ de manzana).
Fracciones como decimales Los estudiantes deben comprender los decimales de dos maneras: como fracciones especiales con denominadores de 10 y potencias de 10 y como extensiones naturales del sistema de valor posicional para representar cantidades menores que 1.	Para la fracción $\frac{2}{5}$, por ejemplo, podemos hallar la representación decimal reescribiéndola como fracción equivalente $\frac{4}{10}$ o dividiendo 2 por 5. En esto se aplica el interpretar las fracciones como divisiones para hallar la representación decimal de la misma cantidad. $$\frac{2}{5} = 2 \div 5 = 0.4$$
Fracciones como porcentajes Esto sirve para desarrollar una conexión entre los conceptos de fracciones, decimales y porcentajes. Los porcentajes se introducen como nombres especiales para centésimas, $\frac{1}{100}$.	Diez por ciento, 10%, es simplemente otra manera de representar 0.10 ó 0.1, que es otra manera de representar $\frac{10}{100}$ ó $\frac{1}{10}$. 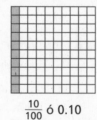 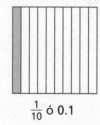 $\frac{10}{100}$ ó 0.10 $\frac{1}{10}$ ó 0.1
Fracciones equivalentes Partir y luego volver a partir es una destreza importante que contribuye a la comprensión de la equivalencia. Las fracciones equivalentes tienen el mismo valor.	Si una barra se marca en cuartos (la primera partición) y luego cada cuarto se divide en tercios (la segunda partición), cada cuarto original tiene tres partes (o tres doceavos) en ella. Así pues un cuarto es equivalente a tres doceavos. $\frac{1}{4} = \frac{1 \times 3}{4 \times 3} = \frac{3}{12}$ 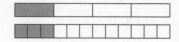

En la **Página Web de CMP para los padres**, disponible en inglés, puede aprender más sobre los objetivos matemáticos de cada unidad. Vea una lista ilustrada de vocabulario y examine las soluciones de algunos problemas de ACE. **http://PHSchool.com/cmp2parents**

Querida familia:

La siguiente unidad en la clase de matemáticas de su hijo(a) es *Figuras y diseños: Geometría bidimensional*. Ésta es la primera unidad sobre el tema de geometría de *Connected Mathematics*. Los estudiantes reconocerán, analizarán, medirán y razonarán sobre figuras y patrones visuales importantes en nuestro mundo. La unidad amplía los conocimientos previos de los estudiantes sobre figuras simples, analizando las propiedades que hacen a ciertas figuras especiales y útiles.

OBJETIVOS DE LA UNIDAD

El objetivo de *Figuras y diseños* es que los estudiantes descubran y analicen muchas de las propiedades clave de las figuras poligonales que las hacen útiles y atractivas. La unidad se centra en polígonos y desarrolla estos dos temas:

- ¿Cómo las medidas de los ángulos de un polígono determinan su forma y sus usos?
- ¿Cómo las longitudes de los lados de un polígono determinan su forma y sus usos?

Cada investigación se centra en algunas propiedades clave de las figuras y en la importancia de esas propiedades en aplicaciones. Se pide periódicamente a los estudiantes que identifiquen las diferencias entre determinados tipos de polígonos. También se les pide que busquen y describan lugares donde vean diferentes polígonos y piensen en cómo se usan esas figuras.

AYUDAR CON LA TAREA

Usted puede ayudar con la tarea y al mismo tiempo propiciar buenos hábitos matemáticos a medida que su hijo(a) estudia haciendo preguntas como:

- ¿Qué tipos de figuras/polígonos cubren una superficie plana?
- ¿Qué tienen en común estas figuras?
- ¿Cómo se pueden estimar las medidas de los ángulos?
- ¿Cómo se pueden medir los ángulos con mayor precisión?

En el cuaderno de su hijo(a), verá ejemplos de problemas resueltos en clase, notas sobre la unidad y definiciones de las palabras del vocabulario.

CONVERSAR SOBRE LAS MATEMÁTICAS DE *FIGURAS Y DISEÑOS*

Puede ayudar a su hijo(a) a ver cómo la geometría es importante en la vida diaria:

- Cuando vea una figura interesante en un periódico o revista, comente con su hijo(a) si es uno de los polígonos mencionados en la unidad, y sugiera que podrían recortarlo y guardarlo para el proyecto de las figuras.
- Pida a su hijo(a) que le muestre su cuaderno de matemáticas y lo que ha anotado sobre las figuras que se están estudiando. Pregúntele por qué estas ideas son importantes y comenten de qué maneras las figuras pueden ayudar en su trabajo o sus aficiones.
- Revise la tarea de su hijo(a) y asegúrese que haya contestado todas las preguntas y que las explicaciones sean claras.

En la parte de atrás se dan unos cuantos conceptos matemáticos importantes que su hijo(a) aprenderá en *Figuras y diseños*. Como siempre, si tiene preguntas sobre esta unidad o el progreso en clase de su hijo(a), no dude en llamar.

Atentamente,

Conceptos importantes y ejemplos

Polígono

Una figura formada por segmentos de recta de modo que cada segmento se une exactamente a otros dos segmentos, y todos los puntos donde los segmentos se unen son los extremos de los segmentos.

Polígonos   No polígonos

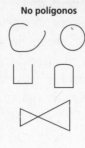

Nombres de los polígonos

Triángulo 3 lados y 3 ángulos
Cuadrilátero 4 lados y 4 ángulos
Pentágono 5 lados y 5 ángulos
Hexágono 6 lados y 6 ángulos
Heptágono 7 lados y 7 ángulos
Octágono 8 lados y 8 ángulos
Nonágono 9 lados y 9 ángulos
Decágono 10 lados y 10 ángulos
Dodecágono 12 lados y 12 ángulos

Polígonos regulares

Polígonos cuyas longitudes de lado son iguales y cuyas medidas de los ángulos interiores son iguales.

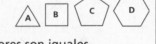

Polígonos irregulares

Un polígono que tiene o dos caras con diferentes longitudes o dos ángulos con diferentes medidas.

Simetría reflexiva (o de espejo)

Si el polígono se dobla por el eje de simetría, las dos mitades de la figura encajarán exactamente.

Simetría rotacional (o de giro)

Un polígono con simetría de giro se puede girar alrededor de su punto central menos de una vuelta entera y seguirá viéndose igual que antes de girar.

Ángulos

Los ángulos son la porción del plano delimitada por dos rayos o segmentos de recta que tienen un vértice en común. El **vértice** de un ángulo es el punto donde se unen o intersecan dos rayos. Los ángulos se miden en grados.

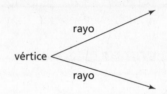

rayo

vértice

rayo

Medidas de ángulos

Para desarrollar destrezas de estimación, los estudiantes relacionan ángulos a ángulos rectos. Las combinaciones y particiones de ángulos de 90° se usan como puntos de referencia para estimar el tamaño de un ángulo.

Los estudiantes usan un **goniómetro** o **regla de ángulos** para hacer mediciones más precisas de los ángulos. Ésta es una herramienta que se usa en el campo médico para medir el ángulo de movimiento o flexibilidad en articulaciones del cuerpo, como las rodillas.

90°

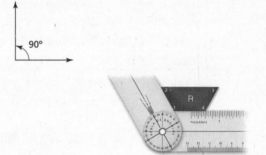

Ángulos y rectas paralelos

Las rectas paralelas cortadas por una **transversal** crean ángulos correspondientes iguales y ángulos interiores alternos iguales. Los ángulos 1 y 5, los ángulos 2 y 6, los ángulos 3 y 7, y los ángulos 4 y 8, son pares de **ángulos correspondientes**. Los ángulos 4 y 5 y los ángulos 3 y 6 son pares de **ángulos alternos internos**.

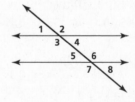

Polígonos que embaldosan un plano

Para que un polígono regular pueda embaldosar un plano (o cubrir una superficie sin espacios ni superposiciones), la medida de los ángulos interiores debe ser un factor de 360°. Los únicos polígonos regulares que pueden embaldosar un plano son un triángulo equilátero (60°), un cuadrado (90°) y un hexágono regular (120°).

Teorema de la desigualdad del triángulo

La suma de las longitudes de dos lados cualesquiera de un triángulo debe ser mayor que la longitud del 3er lado.

Si las longitudes de lado son a, b y c, entonces: $a + b > c$, $b + c > a$, $c + a > b$

Querida familia:

La siguiente unidad en la clase de matemáticas de su hijo(a) este año es ***Trozos y piezas II: Comprender operaciones con fracciones***. Ésta es la segunda de tres unidades que se centran en desarrollar conceptos y procedimientos para hacer cálculos con fracciones, decimales y porcentajes.

OBJETIVOS DE LA UNIDAD

Esta unidad está centrada en la comprensión y el desarrollo de maneras sistemáticas de sumar, restar, multiplicar y dividir fracciones. A medida que trabajan en esta unidad, los estudiantes investigan situaciones de problemas interesantes que los ayudarán a desarrollar algoritmos para hacer cálculos con fracciones. Además, los estudiantes usarán puntos de referencia y sentido numérico y operacional para estimar soluciones a sus cálculos, lo cual los ayudará a determinar si sus respuestas son razonables.

AYUDAR CON LA TAREA

Usted puede ayudar con la tarea y al mismo tiempo propiciar buenos hábitos matemáticos a medida que su hijo(a) estudia esta unidad, haciendo preguntas como:

- ¿Qué modelos o diagramas pueden ser útiles para comprender la situación?
- ¿Qué modelos o diagramas pueden ayudarte a decidir qué operación es útil para resolver el problema?
- ¿Cuál es una estimación razonable para esta respuesta?
- ¿Qué estrategias o algoritmos me ayudarían a resolver este problema?

En el cuaderno de su hijo(a), puede encontrar ejemplos de problemas resueltos en clase, notas sobre las matemáticas de la unidad y definiciones de las palabras del vocabulario.

CONVERSAR SOBRE LAS MATEMÁTICAS DE *TROZOS Y PIEZAS II*

Puede ayudar a su hijo(a) con su trabajo para esta unidad de varias maneras:

- Hay varios procedimientos lógicos para hacer cálculos con fracciones. A veces, los estudiantes pueden trabajar con ideas y algoritmos distintos de los que usted aprendió. Mantenga una mente abierta sobre ellos. Anime a su hijo(a) a compartir estos métodos con usted como ayuda para comprender lo que están estudiando.
- Pida a su hijo(a) que le explique un problema que le haya gustado resolver. Pídale una explicación de las ideas del problema.
- Revise la tarea de su hijo(a) y asegúrese que haya contestado todas las preguntas y que las explicaciones sean claras.

En la parte de atrás se dan unos cuantos conceptos matemáticos importantes que su hijo(a) aprenderá en *Trozos y piezas II*. Como siempre, si tiene preguntas o preocupaciones sobre esta unidad o el progreso en clase de su hijo(a), no dude en llamar.

Atentamente,

Conceptos importantes	Ejemplos
Suma y resta de fracciones Los estudiantes representan problemas para desarrollar la comprensión y destreza en la suma y la resta. Los estudiantes aprenden a hallar denominadores comunes para que los numeradores se puedan sumar o restar.	Para hallar la suma de A + B en el rectángulo, ó $\frac{1}{2} + \frac{1}{8}$, los estudiantes tienen que usar fracciones equivalentes para expresar $\frac{1}{2}$ como $\frac{4}{8}$. El modelo de área ayuda a los estudiantes a visualizar A, $\frac{1}{2}$, como $\frac{4}{8}$ y a que escriban la oración numérica, $\frac{4}{8} + \frac{1}{8} = \frac{5}{8}$. El modelo de *recta numérica* ayuda a relacionar las fracciones con las cantidades. Esto ilustra $1\frac{1}{3} - \frac{2}{3} = \frac{2}{3}$. 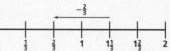

El modelo de área ayuda...

(Above the recta numérica image) $-\frac{2}{3}$

Desarrollar el algoritmo de multiplicación Los estudiantes usan modelos para ver que ellos pueden simplemente multiplicar los numeradores y multiplicar los denominadores de fracciones propias.	Un modelo de área puede mostrar $\frac{2}{3} \times \frac{3}{4}$. Se sombrea un cuadrado para expresar $\frac{3}{4}$. Para representar quitar $\frac{2}{3}$ de $\frac{3}{4}$, se corta el cuadrado en cuartos de la forma opuesta y se sombrean con líneas diagonales dos de las tres secciones. Las secciones que se sobreponen representan el producto, $\frac{6}{12}$. Los **denominadores** parten y vuelven a partir el entero. Romper los cuartos en tres partes forma 12 piezas. En el algoritmo se multiplican los denominadores (3×4) para recalcular el todo y así obtener el número correcto de partes.

$$\text{denominadores} \rightarrow \frac{2}{3} \times \frac{3}{4} = \frac{2 \times 3}{3 \times 4} = \frac{6}{12} \qquad \text{nominadores} \rightarrow \frac{2}{3} \times \frac{3}{4} = \frac{2 \times 3}{3 \times 4} = \frac{6}{12}$$

El **numerador** lleva la cuenta de a cuántas de las partes se hace referencia. Se necesita quitar 2 de las 3 secciones de cada parte. Esto se puede representar con el producto de los numeradores 2×3.

Desarrollar un algoritmo de división Los estudiantes pueden tener varias maneras de pensar en la división de fracciones. Nuestro objetivo en el desarrollo de algoritmos es ayudar a los estudiantes a desarrollar un algoritmo eficiente.	**Modo del denominador común** Los estudiantes reescriben $\frac{7}{9} \div \frac{1}{3}$ como $\frac{7}{9} \div \frac{3}{9}$. El denominador común permite razonar que si tienes 7 piezas de un noveno y quieres hallar cuántos grupos de 3 piezas de un noveno puedes hacer, entonces $\frac{7}{9} \div \frac{3}{9} = 7 \div 3 = 2\frac{1}{3}$. **Multiplicar por el denominador y dividir por el numerador** Con $9 \div \frac{1}{3}$, se puede razonar: Tengo que hallar el número total de $\frac{1}{3}$s que hay en 9. Hay tres $\frac{1}{3}$s en 1, de modo que hay 9×3, ó 27 $\frac{1}{3}$s, en 9. $9 \div \frac{1}{3} = 9 \times 3 = 27$. Con $\frac{2}{3} \div \frac{1}{5}$, podemos razonar que $1 \div \frac{1}{5}$ es 5, como $\frac{2}{3} \div \frac{1}{5}$ debería ser $\frac{2}{3}$ de esto, ó $\frac{2}{3}$ de 5, ó $\frac{10}{3}$. También podríamos renombrar $\frac{2}{3} \div \frac{1}{5}$ como $\frac{10}{15} \div \frac{3}{15}$ y ver esto como 10 quinceavos dividido por 3 quinceavos, que es lo mismo que $10 \div 3$, ó $\frac{10}{3}$. Fíjate que esto requiere que se multiplique el número de $\frac{2}{3}$ por 5. Con $\frac{2}{3} \div \frac{4}{5}$, podemos razonar que debería ser $\frac{1}{4}$ de $\left(\frac{2}{3} \div \frac{1}{5}\right)$ ó $\frac{1}{4}\left(\frac{10}{3}\right) = \frac{10}{12}$. Fíjate que esto requiere que se multiplique el denominador de $\frac{2}{3}$ por 4. Resumiendo, para comparar $\frac{2}{3} \div \frac{4}{5}$ calculamos $\frac{2}{3} \times \frac{5}{1} \times \frac{1}{4} = \frac{10}{12}$. Es decir, multiplicamos el numerador de $\frac{2}{3}$ por 5 y el denominador por 4. **Multiplicar por el recíproco** Vemos que $\frac{2}{3} \div \frac{4}{5}$ (ver arriba) da el mismo resultado que $\frac{2}{3} \times \frac{5}{4}$.

En la **Página Web de CMP para los padres**, disponible en inglés, puede aprender más sobre los objetivos matemáticos de cada unidad. Vea una lista ilustrada de vocabulario y examine las soluciones de algunos problemas de ACE. **http://PHSchool.com/cmp2parents**

Querida familia:

La siguiente unidad en la clase de matemáticas de su hijo(a) este año es ***Cubrir y rodear: Mediciones bidimensionales***. El centro de atención es el área (cubrir) y el perímetro (rodear). La unidad ayuda a los estudiantes a desarrollar una comprensión de los perímetros y las áreas de rectángulos, triángulos, paralelogramos y círculos. Los estudiantes usan la estimación y el conteo para hallar áreas y perímetros de figuras irregulares.

OBJETIVOS DE LA UNIDAD

El objetivo general de esta unidad es ayudar a los estudiantes a comprender lo que significa medir. Los estudiantes estudian dos tipos de mediciones: perímetro y área. Como los estudiantes a menudo no saben cómo cada una de estas medidas afecta a la otra, los estudiantes las estudian juntas para probar las relaciones.

Los estudiantes desarrollan estrategias para medir perímetro y área. Sus estrategias se comentan y se usan para formular reglas para hallar áreas y perímetros de distintas figuras. Muchas ideas de unidades previas se repasarán y ampliarán en esta unidad. Por ejemplo, de la unidad *La hora de los primos* se usará la conexión entre factores y dimensiones de rectángulos.

AYUDAR CON LA TAREA

Usted puede ayudar con la tarea y al mismo tiempo propiciar buenos hábitos matemáticos a medida que su hijo(a) estudia, haciendo preguntas como:

- ¿Cómo sé qué medición está involucrada: área o perímetro?
- ¿Cómo puedo hallar el área y el perímetro de una figura irregular?
- ¿Cómo puedo hallar el área y el perímetro de una figura regular?
- ¿Es necesaria una respuesta exacta?
- ¿Hay una relación entre el área y el perímetro que me ayude a resolver este problema?

En el cuaderno de su hijo(a), verá problemas resueltos en clase, notas sobre las matemáticas de la unidad y definiciones de las palabras del vocabulario.

CONVERSAR SOBRE LAS MATEMÁTICAS DE *CUBRIR Y RODEAR*

Puede ayudar a su hijo(a) con su trabajo para esta unidad de varias maneras:

- Anímelo(a) a usar las herramientas de medición que tengan en casa, como cintas métricas y reglas, para practicar mediciones.
- Ayude a su hijo(a) a desarrollar sus propias referencias para estimar longitudes y distancias. Por ejemplo, la distancia de casa a la escuela puede ser una milla, o el palmo de la mano de su hijo(a) pueden ser seis pulgadas. Úsenlas para estimar otras distancias y longitudes.
- Ayude a su hijo(a) a desarrollar sus propias referencias personales para estimar el área. Usen el área de su dormitorio para estimar áreas de otras habitaciones.
- Revise la tarea de su hijo(a) y asegúrese que haya contestado todas las preguntas y varios conceptos matemáticos que las explicaciones sean claras.

En la parte de atrás se dan varios conceptos matemáticos importantes que su hijo(a) aprenderá en *Cubrir y rodear*. Como siempre, si tiene preguntas sobre esta unidad o el progreso en clase de su hijo(a), no dude en llamar.

Atentamente,

Conceptos importantes	Ejemplos
El proceso de medición • Identificar un objeto y el atributo a medir. • Seleccionar una unidad apropiada. • "Emparejar" repetidamente la unidad al atributo del objeto (o fenómeno como el tiempo). • Determinar el número de unidades.	**Medir el perímetro** Medir el perímetro requiere contar cuántas unidades lineales se necesitan para rodear un objeto. **Medir el área** Medir el área requiere contar cuántas unidades cuadradas se necesitan para cubrir un objeto.
Área de rectángulos Los estudiantes pueden hallar el área contando el número de cuadrados encerrados. Para contar con más eficiencia, hallan el número de cuadrados en una hilera y lo multiplican por el número de hileras. En otras palabras, hallan el área multiplicando la longitud (cuántos por hilera) por el ancho (el número de hileras).	Hay 5 cuadrados en la primera hilera y 7 hileras en total. El área del rectángulo es $5 \times 7 = 35$ unidades cuadradas o, en general, $\ell \times a$. 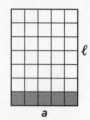
Perímetro de rectángulos Los estudiantes cuentan el número de unidades lineales que rodean el rectángulo. Para contar mejor, pueden tomar la medida de la longitud más el ancho y duplicar esa cantidad. También pueden calcular dos longitudes más dos anchos para obtener el perímetro.	El perímetro de la figura de arriba es $2(7 + 5)$ ó $2 \times 7 + 2 \times 5$ o, en general, $2(\ell + a)$ ó $2\ell + 2a$.
Área de triángulos Los estudiantes pueden usar su conocimiento de rectángulos para hallar el área de los triángulos. Si rodeamos un triángulo con un rectángulo, podemos ver que el área del triángulo es la mitad del área del rectángulo. El triángulo puede rotarse a un lado más conveniente como su base de ser necesario.	 Las secciones 1 y 2 son congruentes. 3 y 4 son congruentes. El área de un triángulo es $\frac{1}{2} b \times h$, donde b es la base del triángulo (la longitud del rectángulo) y h es la altura del triángulo (el ancho del rectángulo).
Perímetro de triángulos Los estudiantes pueden hallar el perímetro de un triángulo midiendo las longitudes de los tres lados y sumándolas.	El perímetro de un triángulo es $7 + 10 + 12.2$, ó 19.2 pies. 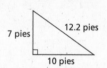
Área de paralelogramos Si se traza una diagonal se producen dos triángulos iguales que tienen la misma longitud de la base y altura que el paralelogramo. Se puede hallar el área del paralelogramo multiplicando la base y la altura, sin dividir por dos, como se haría para el área de un triángulo.	El área de un paralelogramo es el área de dos triángulos $2 \times (\frac{1}{2} b \times h)$, o simplemente $b \times h$. 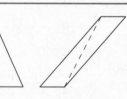
Perímetro de paralelogramos El perímetro de los paralelogramos se halla midiendo las longitudes de los cuatro lados y sumándolas.	El perímetro del paralelogramo es $2(5 + 6)$ ó $2 \times 5 + 2 \times 6 = 22$ cm. 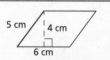
Área de círculos Los estudiantes pueden hallar el número de "cuadrados del radio", cuyos lados son iguales al radio, que cubre el círculo. Ven que necesitan un poco más que tres o pi.	cuadrado del radio (r^2) El área de un círculo es pi × un "cuadrado del radio" o pi × radio × radio = $\pi \times r \times r = \pi r^2$ 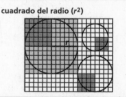
Perímetro de círculos (circunferencia) Pueden contar cuántos diámetros se necesitan para rodear el círculo. Es un poco más que tres o *pi*.	La circunferencia de un círculo es pi × diámetro = πd.

Querida familia:

La siguiente unidad en la clase de matemáticas de su hijo(a) este año es ***Trozos y piezas III: Calcular con decimales y porcentajes***. Ésta es la tercera y última unidad en el desarrollo de la comprensión de fracciones, decimales y porcentajes.

OBJETIVOS DE LA UNIDAD

Como en el trabajo realizado para desarrollar operaciones de fracciones, los estudiantes se sumergirán en muchas situaciones de problemas a medida que desarrollan algoritmos para suma, resta, multiplicación y división de decimales. Explorarán porcentajes calculando propinas, impuestos, descuentos y costo total.

Los estudiantes tienen dos maneras de comprender lo que significan los decimales: extender el sistema de valor posicional en el cual se basa nuestro sistema numérico o interpretar decimales como fracciones. Para poder tener la comprensión más completa del cálculo y destreza con el mismo, los estudiantes necesitan comprender cada uno de estos significados. Luego los usan para examinar por qué los algoritmos decimales de suma, resta, multiplicación y división tienen sentido. Dependiendo de la operación, la interpretación de la fracción o la interpretación del valor de posición puede ayudar a hallar algoritmos de atajos. Los estudiantes se basarán en y usarán los conceptos desarrollados en *Trozos y piezas I* y *Trozos y piezas II*. Por ejemplo, usarán los algoritmos para multiplicar fracciones en *Trozos y piezas II* para desarrollar y comprender un algoritmo para multiplicar decimales.

AYUDAR CON LA TAREA

Usted puede ayudar con la tarea y al mismo tiempo propiciar buenos hábitos matemáticos a medida que su hijo(a) estudia esta unidad, haciendo preguntas como:

- ¿Cuál es una estimación razonable para la respuesta? O, aproximadamente, ¿cuál será la suma (diferencia, producto o cociente)?
- ¿En qué se parecen o diferencian estos decimales y las fracciones?
- ¿Qué estrategias o algoritmos te ayudarían a resolver este problema?
- ¿Por qué los porcentajes son útiles en este problema?

En el cuaderno de su hijo(a), puede encontrar ejemplos de problemas resueltos en clase, notas sobre la unidad y definiciones de las palabras del vocabulario.

CONVERSAR SOBRE LAS MATEMÁTICAS DE *TROZOS Y PIEZAS III*

Puede ayudar a su hijo(a) con su trabajo para esta unidad de varias maneras:

- Pídale a su hijo(a) una explicación de las ideas de un problema. Por ejemplo, ¿por qué alineas los decimales al sumar y restar números decimales?
- A veces, los estudiantes pueden trabajar con conceptos y algoritmos distintos de los que usted aprendió. Anime a su hijo(a) a que comente estos métodos con usted para ayudarle a comprender lo que está estudiando.
- Cuando estén de compras o en un restaurante con su hijo(a), pídale que estime el impuesto de una compra o qué propina deberían dejar por una comida.

En la parte de atrás se dan varios conceptos matemáticos importantes que su hijo(a) aprenderá en *Trozos y piezas III*. Como siempre, si tiene preguntas o preocupaciones sobre esta unidad o el progreso en clase de su hijo(a), no dude en llamar.

Atentamente,

Conceptos importantes	Ejemplos
Suma y resta de decimales **DECIMALES COMO FRACCIONES** Escribir decimales como fracciones, hallar denominadores comunes, sumar o restar las fracciones y expresar las respuestas como decimales. Esto confirma que al sumar o restar, uno debe calcular con dígitos del mismo valor de posición. **INTERPRETACIÓN DEL VALOR DE POSICIÓN** Se considera el valor de posición de los dígitos y lo que significa al sumar o restar números.	Zeke compra jugo por $1.97 y donas por $0.89. El vendedor le dice que la factura era $10.87. ¿Qué hizo mal el vendedor? El jugo cuesta $1.97 = $\frac{197}{100}$ y las donas cuestan $0.89 = $\frac{89}{100}$. De modo que el costo es $\frac{197}{100} + \frac{89}{100} = \frac{286}{100} = 2.86$. En $1.97 + 0.89$, sumamos centésimos a centésimos ($1.9\underline{7} + 0.8\underline{9}$), décimos a décimos ($1.\underline{9}7 + 0.\underline{8}9$) y unidades a unidades ($\underline{1}.97 + \underline{0}.89$). El vendedor sumó dólares y centavos incorrectamente (unidades y décimos, décimos y centésimos).
Multiplicación de decimales **DECIMALES COMO FRACCIONES** Escribir decimales como fracciones, multiplicar, escribir la respuesta como decimal y relacionar el número de las posiciones decimales de los factores con la respuesta. **INTERPRETACIÓN DE LOS VALORES DE POSICIÓN** Vemos por qué contar puntos decimales tiene sentido y usamos el algoritmo de atajo: multiplicar decimales como números enteros y ajustar la posición del decimal en el producto.	Podemos observar un problema usando fracciones equivalentes. $$0.3 \times 2.3 = \frac{3}{10} \times 2\frac{3}{10} = \frac{3}{10} \times \frac{23}{10}$$ El producto como fracción es $\frac{69}{100}$, como decimal, 0.69. El 100 en el denominador muestra que debería haber dos posiciones decimales (centésimas) en la respuesta. El denominador de la fracción nos dice el valor de posición necesario del decimal. Como $25 \times 31 = 775$ pensamos en un producto relacionado: 2.5×0.31 (2.5 es un décimo de 25, 0.3 es un centésimo de 31, y su producto es un milésimo de 775) = 0.775.
División de decimales **DECIMALES COMO FRACCIONES** Escribir decimales como fracciones con denominadores comunes y dividir los numeradores. **INTERPRETACIÓN DEL VALOR DE POSICIÓN** Escribir un problema equivalente multiplicando ambos dividendos y el divisor por la misma potencia de diez hasta que sean números enteros.	$3.25 \div 0.5 = \frac{325}{100} \div \frac{5}{10} = \frac{325}{100} \div \frac{50}{100} = 325 \div 50 = 6.5$ $37.5 \div 0.015 = \frac{375}{10} \div \frac{15}{1,000} = \frac{37,500}{1,000} \div \frac{15}{1,000} = 37,500 \div 15 = 2,500$ Esto lo convierte en un problema de números enteros con el mismo cociente que el problema decimal original. El enfoque fraccional explica por qué mover posiciones decimales funciona. $$0.015\overline{)37.5} = 0.015 \times 1,000\overline{)37.5 \times 1,000} = 15\overline{)37500}$$
Formas decimales de números racionales **DECIMALES FINITOS** son los decimales que "terminan". La fracción simplificada tiene factores primos sólo de 2 ó 5 en el denominador. **DECIMALES PERIÓDICOS (INFINITOS)** son los decimales que "siguen para siempre" pero que muestran un patrón. En su mínima expresión, estas fracciones tienen factores primos distintos de 2 ó 5 en su denominador.	$\frac{1}{2} = 0.5$, $\frac{1}{8} = 0.125$, $\frac{12}{75} = 0.16$. $\frac{4}{25} = \frac{16}{100} = 0.16$ En forma fraccional simplificada $\frac{12}{75} = \frac{4}{25}$ tiene sólo factores de cinco $\left(\frac{4}{5 \times 5}\right)$ en el denominador. $\frac{1}{3} = 0.333...$, $\frac{2}{3} = 0.666...$, $\frac{8}{15} = 0.533...$, $\frac{3}{7} = 0.42857142...$ En forma fraccional simplificada $\frac{26}{150} = \frac{13}{75} = \frac{13}{3 \times 5 \times 5} = 0.1733333....$
Usar porcentajes **PORCENTAJES DE UN PRECIO** "Un CD cuesta $7.50 más 6% de impuesto. ¿Cuánto es el impuesto?" **DE QUÉ CANTIDAD SE CALCULÓ EL PORCENTAJE** "Los clientes le dejaron a Jill una propina de $2.50. La propina era el 20% del total. "¿Cuánto era la factura?" **QUÉ PORCENTAJE DE UN NÚMERO ES OTRO NÚMERO** "Sam obtuvo un descuento de $12 de una compra de $48. ¿Qué porcentaje de descuento le dieron?"	6% of $7.50 = *costo del impuesto* 1% de $7.50 = $\frac{1}{100}$ de $7.50 = $7.50 $\div$ 100 = 0.075 6 del 1% me dará 6%. De modo que, 6% de $7.50 = $0.45 20% de *algún número* es igual a $2.50 Halla cuántos 20% se necesitan para hacer 100%. En este caso necesitamos cinco. De modo que 5 × $2.50 nos da $12.50. Hallar *qué* % es 12 de 48. Los estudiantes pueden resolver esto calculando cuántos 12 hay en 48. Hay cuatro, de modo que el porcentaje es $\frac{1}{4}$ de 100% ó 25%.

En la **Página Web de CMP para los padres**, disponible en inglés, puede aprender más sobre los objetivos matemáticos de cada unidad. Vea el glosario y examine los ejemplos trabajados de los problemas de ACE. **http://PHSchool.com/cmp2parents**

Querida familia:

La siguiente unidad en la clase de matemáticas de su hijo(a) este año es *¿Qué probabilidad hay?: Probabilidad*. Esta unidad ayuda a los estudiantes a comprender y razonar sobre probabilidad experimental y teórica, y las relaciones entre ambas. Los estudiantes hacen conexiones importantes entre probabilidad y números racionales, geometría, estadística, ciencia y negocios.

OBJETIVOS DE LA UNIDAD

Los estudiantes aprenderán a hallar probabilidades de dos maneras: haciendo intentos y recopilando datos experimentales, y también analizando situaciones para determinar probabilidades teóricas. Usarán fracciones, decimales y porcentajes para describir qué probabilidad hay de que ciertos sucesos ocurran.

Los estudiantes experimentan con monedas, cubos numéricos, flechas giratorias y vasos de papel. Examinarán juegos sencillos de azar para determinar si son justos. También analizarán cómo se usa la probabilidad para predecir rasgos genéticos como el color de ojos o la capacidad de curvar la lengua.

AYUDAR CON LA TAREA

Usted puede ayudar con la tarea y al mismo tiempo propiciar buenos hábitos matemáticos a medida que su hijo(a) estudia esta unidad, haciendo preguntas como:

- ¿Cuáles son los resultados posibles que pueden ocurrir para los sucesos de esta situación?
- ¿Cómo puedo determinar la probabilidad experimental de cada uno de los resultados?
- ¿Es posible determinar la probabilidad teórica de cada uno de los resultados?
- Si es así, ¿cuáles son estas probabilidades?
- ¿Cómo puedo usar estas probabilidades para tomar decisiones sobre esta situación?

En el cuaderno de su hijo(a), puede encontrar ejemplos de problemas resueltos en clase, notas sobre las matemáticas de la unidad y definiciones de las palabras del vocabulario.

CONVERSAR SOBRE LAS MATEMÁTICAS DE *¿QUÉ PROBABILIDAD HAY?*

Puede ayudar a su hijo(a) con su trabajo para esta unidad de varias maneras:

- Comenten ejemplos de enunciados o situaciones de la vida cotidiana que se relacionen con la probabilidad de ciertos sucesos.
- Mire estadísticas deportivas con su hijo(a) y haga preguntas como cómo se puede usar un promedio de bateo, o un promedio de tiros libres, para predecir la probabilidad de que el jugador obtenga un golpe en el siguiente turno al bate o enceste la próxima vez que haga tiros libres.
- Revise la tarea de su hijo(a) y asegúrese que haya contestado todas las preguntas y que las explicaciones sean claras.

En la parte de atrás se dan varios conceptos matemáticos importantes que su hijo(a) aprenderá en *¿Qué probabilidad hay?*. Como siempre, si tiene preguntas o preocupaciones sobre esta unidad o el progreso en clase de su hijo(a), no dude en llamar.

Atentamente,

Conceptos importantes	Ejemplos
Probabilidad Un número entre 0 y 1 que describe la probabilidad de que un suceso ocurra.	Si una bolsa contiene una canica roja, una canica blanca y una canica azul, la probabilidad de sacar una canica roja es 1 de 3, ó $\frac{1}{3}$. Escribiríamos: $P(roja) = \frac{1}{3}$.
Una vez que tengamos una probabilidad —teórica o experimental— la podemos usar para hacer predicciones y tomar decisiones.	Si se lanza un cubo numérico 1000 veces, podríamos predecir que un 3 saldría cada $\frac{1}{6}$ de las veces, o aproximadamente $\frac{1}{6} \times 1000$ ó 167 veces.
Probabilidad teórica Probabilidad obtenida analizando una situación. Si todos los **resultados** (resultados posibles) son igualmente probables, puedes hallar la probabilidad teórica de un suceso anotando primero todos los resultados posibles y luego hallando la razón del número de resultados en el que estás interesado al número total de resultados posibles.	Si un cubo numérico tiene seis lados con los resultados posibles de sacar: 1, 2, 3, 4, 5 ó 6, la probabilidad de sacar un "3" es 1 de 6. $P(sacar\ un\ 3) = \dfrac{resultados\ favorables}{resultados\ posibles}$ $= \dfrac{1\ (hay\ 1\ número\ 3\ en\ el\ cubo)}{6\ (hay\ 6\ resultados\ posibles)}$
Probabilidad experimental Probabilidad hallada como resultado de un experimento. Esta probabilidad es la frecuencia relativa del **suceso** (un conjunto de resultados), que es la razón del número de veces que ocurre el suceso comparada con el número total de **intentos** (una ronda de un experimento).	Si lanzas una moneda 50 veces y sale cara 23 veces, la frecuencia relativa de caras sería $\frac{23}{50}$. $P(caras) = \dfrac{veces\ que\ ocurrió\ el\ suceso}{cantidad\ de\ intentos}$ $= \dfrac{número\ de\ caras}{total\ de\ veces\ que\ se\ lanzó} = \dfrac{23}{50}$
Sucesos al azar En matemáticas, al azar significa que un resultado en particular es impredecible, pero que a largo plazo hay un cierto patrón.	Lanzar una moneda es un suceso al azar porque nunca sabemos si el siguiente lanzamiento será cara o cruz, pero sabemos que a largo plazo se aproximará al 50% de caras.

Estrategias para hallar resultados

Cuando una situación tiene más de una acción, necesitamos generar resultados de una manera sistemática. Una lista organizada o los diagramas de árbol son especialmente útiles.

Lista organizada

Primera moneda	Segunda moneda	Resultado
caras	caras	caras-caras
caras	cruz	caras-cruz
cruz	caras	cruz-caras
cruz	cruz	cruz-cruz

Diagrama de árbol

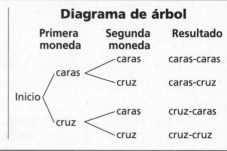

Ley de números extensos

Los datos experimentales recopilados a lo largo de muchos intentos deberían producir probabilidades que se acercaran a las probabilidades teóricas. Esta idea a veces se llama *Ley de números extensos*.

Es importante que los estudiantes se den cuenta de que una cantidad pequeña de datos puede producir una variación amplia. Son necesarios muchos intentos para hacer buenas estimaciones de lo que pasará a largo plazo.

La ley de números extensos no dice que cuando lanzas una moneda deberías esperar exactamente 50% de caras en cualquier número extenso de intentos. Sino que dice que a medida que el número de intentos crece, esperamos que el porcentaje de caras se acerque más al 50%.

En la **Página Web de CMP para los padres**, disponible en inglés, puede aprender más sobre los objetivos matemáticos de cada unidad. Vea una lista ilustrada de vocabulario y examine las soluciones de algunos problemas de ACE. http://PHSchool.com/cmp2parents

Querida familia:

La siguiente unidad en la clase de matemáticas de su hijo(a) este año es *Datos sobre nosotros: Estadística*. Se centra en la investigación de datos y enseña a los estudiantes a organizar, mostrar, analizar e interpretar datos. Su hijo(a) aprenderá a hacer e interpretar muchos tipos de representaciones de datos y a calcular estadísticas como ayuda para describir datos.

OBJETIVOS DE LA UNIDAD

La unidad proporciona oportunidades para que los estudiantes se hagan preguntas sobre ellos mismos, y luego recopilen los datos como ayuda para contestar estas preguntas. Los estudiantes exploran la longitud de sus nombres, las distancias a las que viven de la escuela, los números de veces que pueden saltar a la cuerda, los números de mascotas que tienen, sus alturas y las longitudes de sus pies.

Su hijo(a) aprenderá a hacer diagramas de puntos, gráficas de barras, gráficas de coordenadas y diagramas de tallo y hojas, y a interpretar patrones que se muestren en estas representaciones. Su hijo(a) también aprenderá a calcular la moda, la mediana, la media y el rango de un conjunto de datos y a usar estas estadísticas para describir datos y hacer predicciones.

AYUDAR CON LA TAREA

Usted puede ayudar con la tarea y al mismo tiempo propiciar buenos hábitos matemáticos a medida que su hijo(a) estudia esta unidad, haciendo preguntas como:

- ¿Qué se pregunta?
- ¿Cómo quiero organizar los datos?
- ¿Qué representación es mejor usar para analizar la distribución de los datos?
- ¿Cómo puedo usar las gráficas y estadísticas para describir una distribución de datos o para comparar dos distribuciones de datos a fin de contestar mi pregunta original?
- ¿Cómo crees que se recopilaron los datos?
- ¿Por qué estos datos se representan usando este tipo de gráfica?

En el cuaderno de su hijo(a), puede encontrar ejemplos de problemas resueltos en clase, notas sobre las matemáticas de la unidad y definiciones de las palabras del vocabulario.

CONVERSAR SOBRE LAS MATEMÁTICAS DE *DATOS SOBRE NOSOTROS*

Puede ayudar a su hijo(a) con su trabajo para esta unidad de varias maneras:

- Observe con su hijo(a) los usos de datos en revistas, periódicos y en la televisión. Señale ejemplos de representaciones gráficas y pregúntele a su hijo qué información muestran.
- Pregúntele a su hijo(a) sobre los datos que ha estudiado en clase. ¿Cuáles eran los valores típicos (moda, mediana o media) de estos datos?
- Revise la tarea de su hijo(a) y asegúrese que haya contestado todas las preguntas y que las explicaciones sean claras.

En la parte de atrás se dan varios conceptos matemáticos importantes que su hijo(a) aprenderá en *Datos sobre nosotros*. Como siempre, si tiene preguntas o preocupaciones sobre esta unidad o el progreso en clase de su hijo(a), no dude en llamar.

Atentamente ,

Conceptos importantes y ejemplos

Representar distribuciones de datos y leer representaciones de datos

Los estadistas usan representaciones de datos como diagramas de puntos, gráficas de barras, diagramas de tallo y hojas, y gráficas de coordenadas para describir y analizar sus datos.

LEER REPRESENTACIONES DE DATOS ESTÁNDAR

- *Leer los datos* requiere "extraer" información de una gráfica para contestar preguntas explícitas.
- *Leer entre los datos* incluye la interpretación e integración de información presentada en una gráfica.
- *Leer más allá de los datos* requiere ampliar, predecir o inferir a partir de los datos para contestar preguntas implícitas.

DIAGRAMA DE PUNTOS
Cada caso se representa como una "X" puesta sobre una recta numérica rotulada.

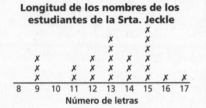

Longitud de los nombres de los estudiantes de la Srta. Jeckle

DIAGRAMA DE TALLO Y HOJAS
Un diagrama que permite que los estudiantes agrupen los datos a intervalos (generalmente de 10 en 10).

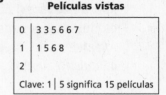

Películas vistas

0	3 3 5 6 6 7
1	1 5 6 8
2	

Clave: 1 | 5 significa 15 películas

GRÁFICA DE BARRAS DE FRECUENCIA
La altura de una barra no es el valor de un caso individual sino el número (frecuencia) de casos que tienen el mismo valor.

Número de mascotas

DIAGRAMA DE DISPERSIÓN
La relación entre dos variables se explora colocando valores de datos en un sistema de coordenadas cartesiano.

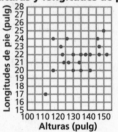

Alturas y longitudes de pie

Usar medidas de tendencia central (moda, mediana, media)

MODA La moda es el valor que ocurre con mayor frecuencia en un conjunto de datos.

MEDIANA El valor de la mediana marca la ubicación que separa al conjunto ordenado de datos por la mitad.

MEDIA Ponemos énfasis en la interpretación de la repartición justa (o igualación) de media (promedio).

14 estudiantes dijeron que tenían el siguiente número de hermanos(as): 0, 0, 0, 1, 1, 1, 2, 2, 2, 2, 2, 3, 5, 6. La moda es 2.

La mediana del conjunto de datos 3, 4, 4, 7, 8, 9 es $5\frac{1}{2}$, el número que está en la mitad entre 4 y 7. Para 4, 5, 5, y 7, la mediana es 5.

La media (promedio) del número de gente de estos hogares es 4. Hay 24 personas repartidas entre 6 hogares.

ANTES		DESPUÉS	
Sara	2 personas	Sara	4
León	3 personas	León	4
Gary	3 personas	Gary	4
Ruth	4 personas	Ruth	4
Paul	6 personas	Paul	4
Arlene	6 personas	Arlene	4
Total	24 personas		24 personas

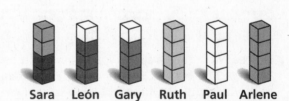

Sara   León   Gary   Ruth   Paul   Arlene

Usar medidas de variabilidad
Las medidas de variabilidad se usan para describir con qué dispersión o acumulación se distribuyen los datos.
RANGO El rango depende sólo de dos valores, el mayor y el menor.

Diferenciar los distintos tipos de datos
DATOS NUMÉRICOS Valores que se pueden contar (pulso, altura). Podemos usar la media, la mediana, la moda y el rango como resumen estadístico.
DATOS CATEGÓRICOS Conjuntos de datos que son respuestas que representan categorías (color favorito, mes de nacimiento, etc.) Podemos usar sólo la moda como resumen estadístico.

En la **Página Web de CMP para los padres**, disponible en inglés, puede aprender más sobre los objetivos matemáticos de cada unidad. Vea una lista ilustrada de vocabulario y examine las soluciones de algunos problemas de ACE. **http://PHSchool.com/cmp2parents**

Querida familia:

La primera unidad en la clase de matemáticas de su hijo(a) es ***Variables y patrones: Introducción al álgebra***. Ésta es la primera unidad formal de la línea de álgebra de *Connected Mathematics*™.

OBJETIVOS DE LA UNIDAD

La unidad se centra en las maneras de describir situaciones que cambian. En la primera parte de la unidad, los estudiantes exploran tres maneras de representar una situación cambiante: con una descripción en palabras, con una tabla de datos y con una gráfica. Estas representaciones se comparan para extraer los puntos fuertes de cada presentación.

Los estudiantes aprenden a escribir expresiones simbólicas de una manera más corta y rápida para hacer un resumen de la relación entre dos variables. Después de escribir las reglas simbólicas, los estudiantes aprenden a usar calculadoras gráficas para hacer tablas y gráficas para una regla dada, que permita a los estudiantes interpretar y comparar más conjuntos de datos.

AYUDAR CON LA TAREA

El objetivo general de *Connected Mathematics* es ayudar a los estudiantes a desarrollar hábitos matemáticos con sentido. Usted puede ayudar con la tarea y al mismo tiempo propiciar buenos hábitos matemáticos haciendo preguntas como:

- ¿Cuáles son las variables del problema?
- ¿Qué variables dependen de, o cambian, en relación a otras?
- ¿Cómo se pueden describir en palabras las relaciones del problema?
- ¿Cómo se pueden representar y analizar las relaciones entre las variables?
- ¿Qué significa cuando vemos cambios predecibles en una tabla de datos o gráfica?
- ¿Cómo podemos usar estos cambios predecibles para averiguar otros datos posibles?

En el cuaderno de su hijo(a), puede encontrar ejemplos trabajados de problemas hechos en clase, notas sobre las matemáticas de la unidad y descripciones de las palabras del vocabulario.

CONVERSAR SOBRE LAS MATEMÁTICAS DE *VARIABLES Y PATRONES*

Puede ayudar a su hijo(a) con su trabajo de varias maneras:

- Repase la tarea de su hijo(a) y asegúrese de que se han contestado todas las preguntas y de que las explicaciones son claras.
- Pida a su hijo(a) que comparta su cuaderno de matemáticas con usted, mostrándole las tablas y gráficas que ha construido y lo que se ha anotado sobre variables y patrones. Pida a su hijo(a) que le explique por qué estas ideas son importantes.
- Pida a su hijo(a) que escoja una pregunta que le pareciera interesante y se la explique.

En la parte de atrás se dan varias ideas matemáticas importantes que su hijo(a) aprenderá en *Variables y patrones*. Como siempre, si tiene preguntas o preocupaciones sobre esta unidad o el progreso en clase de su hijo(a), no dude en llamar.

Atentamente,

Conceptos importantes	Ejemplos
Variables Una variable es una cantidad que cambia. A menudo se usan letras como símbolos para representar variables en reglas que describen patrones.	El *número de estudiantes, n*, que fue de viaje está relacionado al *precio del viaje, p*, por cada estudiante.
Patrones Un cambio que ocurre de forma predecible. Los problemas de esta unidad requieren que los estudiantes investiguen los patrones de cambio en valores de una variable en relación a los cambios en el valor de la otra variable.	A medida que se incrementa el *número de bicicletas* la *tarifa de alquiler* se incrementa en $30. 
Tablas Una lista de valores para dos o más variables que muestra la relación entre ellos. La tabla muestra cómo un cambio en una variable afecta al cambio en la otra variable. La tabla puede mostrar un patrón de cambio.	A medida que el *número de zonas de acampada, x*, cambia por unidad, la *tarifa total del campamento* cambia de 12.5 en 12.5 unidades. La tabla se puede continuar sumando 1 a la entrada previa en la hilera de las x y 12.5 a la entrada previa en la hilera de las *y*.

Tarifas del campamento

Número de campamentos	1	2	3	4	5	6	7	8
Tarifa total de zonas de acampada	$12.50	$25.00	$37.50	$50.00	$62.50	$75.00	$87.50	$100.00

Conceptos importantes	Ejemplos
Gráfica de coordenadas Una representación de pares de valores numéricos relacionados que muestra la relación entre dos variables. Relaciona la variable independiente (mostrada en el *eje de x*) y la variable dependiente (mostrada en el *eje de y*). Las gráficas son otra manera de ver los patrones de cambio.	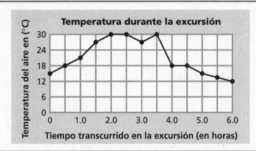
Datos discretos contra Datos continuos Hay dos tipos básicos de variables cuantitativas: los que sólo tienen un conjunto de valores contables (datos discretos) y los que tienen valores cualesquiera de números reales (datos continuos). Las tablas sólo pueden representar colecciones discretas de valores (*x, y*). Las gráficas pueden representar ambas pero a menudo sugieren variables continuas.	El *número de camisetas vendidas* y las *ganancias* es una relación discreta. Conectar los dos puntos no tiene sentido. Implicaría que se podría vender sólo parte de una camiseta.  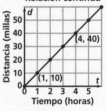 Las situaciones como la relación distancia/tiempo/tasa son continuas. Si un ciclista pedalea a una tasa de 10 millas por hora, es razonable conectar los puntos, porque puedes avanzar cierta distancia en parte de una hora.
Reglas y ecuaciones Las reglas son un resumen de una relación predecible que te dice cómo hallar los valores de una variable. Una regla se puede dar en palabras o como ecuación. Las ecuaciones (o fórmulas) son reglas que contienen variables que representan relaciones matemáticas.	Regla (en palabras): El beneficio total es igual al beneficio por camiseta multiplicado por el número de camisetas vendidas Regla (escrita como una Ecuación): $y = 10x$ Una fórmula o ecuación para hallar el área de un círculo: $A = \pi r^2$

En la **Página Web de CMP para los padres**, disponible en inglés, puede aprender más sobre los objetivos matemáticos de cada unidad. Vea una lista ilustrada de vocabulario y examine las soluciones de algunos problemas de ACE. **http://PHSchool.com/cmp2parents**

Querida familia:

La siguiente unidad en la clase de matemáticas de este año de su hijo(a) es *Estirar y encoger: Comprender la semejanza*. Se centra en geometría y desarrolla la comprensión y la destreza en el uso de los conceptos de semejanza.

OBJETIVOS DE LA UNIDAD

En esta unidad, su hijo(a) usará las propiedades de las figuras semejantes para explorar reducciones y ampliaciones como las que se hacen en fotocopiadoras. La semejanza también se usará para estimar la altura de objetos reales (como edificios y astas de banderas) y la distancia a través de áreas grandes (como estanques).

Los problemas están diseñados para ayudar a los estudiantes a comenzar a razonar proporcionalmente usando escalas en situaciones geométricas. Al final de esta unidad, su hijo(a) sabrá cómo crear figuras semejantes, cómo determinar la semejanza y cómo predecir la relación entre las longitudes y las áreas de dos figuras semejantes. La siguiente unidad, *Comparaciones y escalas*, sigue desarrollando ideas de proporción en un contexto numérico, más que geométrico.

AYUDAR CON LA TAREA

Usted puede ayudar con la tarea y al mismo tiempo propiciar buenos hábitos matemáticos a medida que su hijo(a) estudia esta unidad, haciendo preguntas como:

- Cuando dos figuras son semejantes, ¿qué es igual en cada figura?
- Cuando dos figuras son semejantes, ¿qué es diferente en cada figura?
- ¿Cómo podríamos describir estas diferencias?
- ¿Qué relación hay entre las razones y la semejanza?
- Cuando dos figuras son semejantes, ¿cómo podemos describir la relación entre sus áreas?
- Cuando dos figuras son semejantes, ¿cómo podemos describir la relación entre sus perímetros?

En el cuaderno de su hijo(a), puede encontrar ejemplos trabajados de problemas hechos en clase, notas sobre las matemáticas de la unidad y descripciones de las palabras del vocabulario.

CONVERSAR SOBRE LAS MATEMÁTICAS DE *ESTIRAR Y ENCOGER*

Puede ayudar a su hijo(a) con su trabajo para esta unidad de varias maneras:

- Hable con su hijo(a) sobre situaciones como las que aparecen en esta unidad—lugares del mundo real donde los objetos se reducen o amplían.
- Continúe pidiendo a su hijo(a) que comparta su cuaderno de matemáticas con usted, mostrándole las distintas ideas sobre semejanza que se hayan anotado. Pregúntele a su hijo(a) que por qué son importantes estas ideas. Compartan maneras en las que las reducciones o ampliaciones les ayudan en su trabajo o aficiones.
- Repase la tarea de su hijo(a) y asegúrese de que se han contestado todas las preguntas y de que las explicaciones son claras.

En la parte de atrás se dan unas cuantas ideas matemáticas importantes que su hijo(a) aprenderá en *Estirar y encoger*. Como siempre, si tiene preguntas o preocupaciones sobre esta unidad o el progreso en clase de su hijo(a), no dude en llamar.

Atentamente,

Conceptos importantes	Ejemplos
Semejanza Dos figuras son semejantes si: (1) las medidas de sus ángulos **correspondientes** son iguales y (2) la longitud de sus lados **correspondientes** se relacionan por el mismo factor, llamado **factor de escala**.	Las figuras A y B de abajo son semejantes. 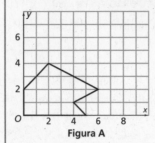 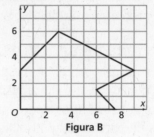 Figura A Figura B Los ángulos correspondientes miden lo mismo. Las longitudes de los lados de la Figura A a la Figura B crecen por un factor de 1.5—cada longitud de lado de A a B es 1.5 veces más largo. De modo que el factor de escala de la Figura A a la Figura B es 1.5. (La Figura A se estira o es ampliada a la figura B.) También podríamos decir que el factor de escala de la Figura B a la Figura A es $\frac{1}{1.5}$ o $\frac{2}{3}$. (La figura B se encoge a la figura A.)
Correspondientes Los lados o ángulos correspondientes tienen la misma posición relativa en figuras semejantes.	**Lados correspondientes** AC y DF AB y DE BC y EF **Ángulos correspondientes** A y D B y E C y F
Factor de escala El número que se usa para multiplicar las longitudes de una figura para estirarla o encogerla a una figura semejante. Un factor de escalar mayor que 1 ampliará una figura. Un factor de escala entre 0 y 1 encogerá la figura. El factor de escala de dos figuras semejantes puede hallarse por una razón que compare los lados correspondientes: $$\frac{\text{long. de un lado en la imagen}}{\text{long. del lado correspondiente en el original}}$$	Si usamos un factor de escala de $\frac{1}{2}$, todas las longitudes de la imagen son $\frac{1}{2}$ más cortas que las longitudes correspondientes en el original. 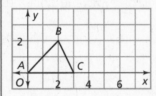 La base del triángulo original es 3 unidades. La base de la imagen es 1.5 unidades. El factor de escala es $\frac{1.5}{3} = \frac{3}{6}$ ó $\frac{1}{2}$.
Área y factor de escala Las longitudes de figuras semejantes se estirarán (o encogerán) por un factor de escala. Las áreas de las figuras no cambiarán por el mismo factor.	Si aplicamos un factor de escala de 2 a una figura, el área se convierte en 4 veces mayor. 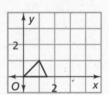 original cuatro copias Si aplicamos un factor de escala de 3 a una figura, el área se convierte en 9 veces mayor. El área original es 6 cm². El área de la imagen es 9 veces mayor, o 54 cm². 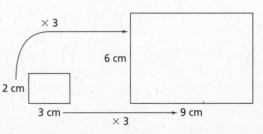

En la **Página Web de CMP para los padres**, disponible en inglés, puede aprender más sobre los objetivos matemáticos de cada unidad. Vea una lista ilustrada de vocabulario y examine las soluciones de algunos problemas de ACE. http://PHSchool.com/cmp2parents

Querida familia:

Lá siguiente unidad en la clase de matemáticas de su hijo(a) este año es *Comparaciones y escalas: Razón, proporción y porcentaje*. Los estudiantes verán problemas relacionados con muchas situaciones y aprenderán a hacer comparaciones usando razones, fracciones, porcentajes y tasas.

OBJETIVOS DE LA UNIDAD

Un objetivo de esta unidad es desarrollar la habilidad de los estudiantes de hacer comparaciones útiles de información cuantitativa usando razones, fracciones, decimales, tasas, tasas unitarias y porcentajes. Un segundo objetivo es que los estudiantes aprendan a usar información cuantitativa comparativa para hacer modelos a escala mayor o menor.

Los estudiantes también deberían aprender distintas maneras de razonar en situaciones de proporción y a reconocer cuándo dicho razonamiento es apropiado.

AYUDAR CON LA TAREA

Usted puede ayudar con la tarea y al mismo tiempo propiciar buenos hábitos matemáticos a medida que su hijo(a) estudia haciendo preguntas como:

- Cuando las cantidades tienen distintas medidas, ¿cómo se pueden comparar?
- ¿Cuándo se puede hacer una comparación por resta? ¿Cuándo se puede usar la división?
- ¿Por qué una razón es una buen medio de comparación? ¿Cómo se puede ampliar o reducir?
- ¿Cuándo se pueden usar las razones en la vida cotidiana para hallar cantidades desconocidas o medidas inaccesibles?

En el cuaderno de su hijo(a), puede encontrar ejemplos trabajados de problemas hechos en clase, notas sobre las matemáticas de la unidad y descripciones de las palabras del vocabulario.

CONVERSAR SOBRE LAS MATEMÁTICAS DE *COMPARACIONES Y ESCALAS*

Puede ayudar a su hijo(a) de varias maneras:

- A nuestro alrededor hay razones, proporciones y porcentajes. Cuando vea alguno que se use en un periódico o revista, señáleselo a su hijo(a) y comenten qué dicen los números sobre la situación.
- Pida a su hijo(a) que comparta su cuaderno de matemáticas con usted, y le muestre lo que se ha anotado sobre razones. Pida a su hijo que le explique por qué estas ideas son importantes.
- Pida a su hijo(a) que escoja una pregunta que le pareciera interesante y que se la explique.

En la parte de atrás se dan unas cuantas ideas matemáticas importantes que su hijo(a) aprenderá en *Comparaciones y escalas*. Como siempre, si tiene preguntas o preocupaciones sobre esta unidad o el progreso en clase de su hijo(a), no dude en llamar.

Atentamente,

Conceptos importantes	Ejemplos
Razón Una comparación de dos cantidades.	*Por cada 2 tazas de mezcla usa 3 tazas de agua.* Las razones se escriben de varias maneras: 2 a 3, o 2:3, o $\frac{2 \text{ tazas de mezcla}}{3 \text{ tazas de agua}}$.
Razones en forma fraccionaria Las razones a menudo se escriben en forma fraccionaria pero no representan fracciones. Las fracciones tienen comparaciones de parte a todo. Algunas razones son comparaciones de parte a parte.	El enunciado "la razón de niños a niñas en la clase es 15 niñas a 9 niños" se puede escribir como fracción $\frac{15}{9}$, pero no significa que la fracción de estudiantes de la clase que son niñas es $\frac{15}{9}$. Se necesita el número total de estudiantes de la clase. La suma de los números de niños y niñas es 24. La comparación parte a todo es $\frac{15}{24}$. De modo que la fracción de la clase que son niñas es $\frac{15}{24}$.
Razones como porcentajes Cuando se puede pensar en una razón como parte de un todo se puede escribir un enunciado comparativo de porcentaje.	*La razón de concentrado a agua en una mezcla es 3 tazas de concentrado por 16 tazas de agua. Primero, halla el total de tazas que lleva la receta, 19 tazas.* Luego, escribe la fracción de la mezcla que es concentrado, $\frac{3}{19}$. Para hallar el porcentaje, dividimos el concentrado por la mezcla total, $3 \div 19 = 0.15789\ldots$ o aproximadamente 15.8% de concentrado.
Tasa Un enunciado que compara dos variables diferentes.	millas por galones, sándwiches por personas, dólares por horas
Tasa unitaria Tienes dos opciones cuando divides dos números. Las unidades te ayudan a pensar en la situación de modo que puedas usar cualquier conjunto de tasas unitarias para comparar las cantidades.	*Sasha va a 6 millas por 20 minutos en la manga 1 de su paseo en bicicleta. En la manga 2, va a 8 millas en 24 minutos. ¿En qué manga va más deprisa?* $\frac{6 \text{ millas}}{20 \text{ minutos}} = 0.3$ millas por minuto y $\frac{8 \text{ millas}}{24 \text{ minutos}} = 0.333$ millas por minuto Ahora la comparación es clara. Los tiempos son los mismos, 1 minuto, y las distancias se pueden comparar directamente. 8 millas en 24 minutos es más rápido. Pero podemos dividir de otra manera: $\frac{20 \text{ minutos}}{6 \text{ millas}} = 3.333$ minutos por millas y $\frac{24 \text{ minutos}}{8 \text{ millas}} = 3$ minutos por millas Podemos ver que el número menor nos da la respuesta correcta, 8 millas en 24 minutos.
Escala de razones (y tasas) Escribe razones como fracciones como ayuda para pensar en la escala de razones (hacia arriba o hacia abajo). Sin embargo, debemos reconocer la diferencia entre trabajar con una fracción y trabajar con una razón escrita como fracción.	*¿Qué es menos caro: 3 rosas por $5 ó 7 rosas por $9?* Si queremos equilibrar los costos para que sean lo mismo, podemos usar el mismo razonamiento que para hallar el denominador común. Buscaríamos un múltiplo común de 5 y 9, $\frac{3}{5} = \frac{3 \times 9}{5 \times 9} = \frac{27 \text{ rosas}}{\$45}$ y $\frac{7}{9} = \frac{7 \times 5}{9 \times 5} = \frac{35 \text{ rosas}}{\$45}$. La segunda opción da más por la misma cantidad de dinero.
Proporciones Una proporción es un enunciado de igualdad entre dos razones. Si se desconoce una parte, podemos usar una escala o fracciones equivalentes para hallar la parte que falta en una proporción.	*Glenda tiene que dar 70 pasos en la máquina elíptica para recorrer 0.1 de milla. Cuando acaba de hacer ejercicio, ha recorrido 3 millas. ¿Cuántos pasos ha dado en la máquina?* $\frac{70 \text{ pasos}}{0.1 \text{ millas}} = \frac{x \text{ pasos}}{3 \text{ millas}} = \frac{70 \times 30 \text{ pasos}}{0.1 \times 30 \text{ millas}} = \frac{2,100 \text{ pasos}}{3 \text{ millas}}$ Glenda dio 2100 pasos para recorrer 3 millas.

En la **Página Web de CMP para los padres**, disponible en inglés, puede aprender más sobre los objetivos matemáticos de cada unidad. Vea una lista ilustrada de vocabulario y examine las soluciones de algunos problemas de ACE. http://PHSchool.com/cmp2parents

Querida familia:

La siguiente unidad en la clase de matemáticas de su hijo(a) este año es ***Resaltar lo negativo: Los números enteros y los números racionales***. A pesar de que los estudiantes han usado intuitivamente operaciones con enteros para comprender algunas situaciones de su vida cotidiana, esta unidad ve maneras formales de calcular con estos números.

OBJETIVOS DE LA UNIDAD

En esta unidad, el centro está en la comprensión y el desarrollo de maneras sistemáticas de sumar, restar, multiplicar y dividir números positivos y negativos. Los estudiantes desarrollarán algoritmos para cálculos y usarán el orden de las operaciones, la propiedad conmutativa y la propiedad distributiva para resolver problemas.

AYUDAR CON LA TAREA

Usted puede ayudar con la tarea y al mismo tiempo propiciar buenos hábitos matemáticos a medida que su hijo(a) estudia esta unidad, haciendo preguntas como:

- ¿Cómo ayudan a describir esta situación los números positivos y negativos?
- ¿Qué dicen sobre el problema la suma, resta, multiplicación o división de números positivos y negativos?
- ¿Qué modelo(s) para números positivos y negativos me ayudaría(n) a representar las relaciones en esta situación de problema?

En el cuaderno de su hijo(a), puede encontrar ejemplos trabajados de problemas hechos en clase, notas sobre las matemáticas de la unidad y descripciones de las palabras del vocabulario.

CONVERSAR SOBRE LAS MATEMÁTICAS DE *RESALTAR LO NEGATIVO*

Puede ayudar a su hijo(a) con su trabajo para esta unidad de varias maneras:

- Pídale a su hijo(a) que describa algunas situaciones del mundo real en que se usen números enteros. Si su hijo(a) le habla sobre estar "en rojo" o "en negro", puede relacionar esta idea con las ganancias o ahorros que tenga.
- Mire el cuaderno de matemáticas de su hijo(a). Si quiere, lea algunas explicaciones que se hayan escrito y, si no son claras, hable con su hijo(a) sobre por qué cree que se deberían explicar más.
- Repase la tarea de su hijo(a) y asegúrese de que se han contestado todas las preguntas y de que las explicaciones son claras.

En la parte de atrás se dan unas cuantas ideas matemáticas importantes que su hijo(a) aprenderá en *Resaltar lo negativo*. Como siempre, si tiene preguntas o preocupaciones sobre esta unidad o el progreso en clase de su hijo(a), no dude en llamar.

Atentamente,

Conceptos importantes	Ejemplos
Números negativos Los números negativos son los números opuestos a los números positivos. El conjunto de números positivos y sus opuestos se llama **ENTEROS**. Los números enteros positivos y negativos y las fracciones son los **NÚMEROS RACIONALES**.	Números negativos: $-\frac{2}{3}$, -24, -1 Enteros: -14, -29, 0 Números racionales: -2, $-1\frac{2}{3}$, 0, $\frac{3}{4}$, 14

Suma y resta

Los estudiantes representan y simbolizan problemas para desarrollar la comprensión y destreza en la suma y la resta antes de desarrollar algoritmos.

El **modelo de fichas de color** requiere que se entiendan los opuestos. Por ejemplo, 4 fichas negras representan $^+4$ y 4 fichas rojas representan -4.

$4 + (-4) = 0$ porque $^+4$ y $^-4$ son opuestos.

El número de **modelo lineal** ayuda a conectar con los números racionales como cantidades.

A veces es útil reescribir un problema de suma como una resta o un problema de resta como una suma.

Tablero de fichas

Johnson le debía a su hermana $6.00. Ganó $4 repartiendo periódicos. ¿Cuál es su valor neto?

Una ficha de color (negra) representa números positivos y otra ficha (roja) representa números negativos.

Las colecciones de fichas de colores negras y rojas en el tablero representan la combinación de gastos e ingresos. El resultado o valor neto es que él está "en rojo" 2, o $^-2$ dólares. Este problema se puede representar con la oración numérica $^-6 + {}^+4 = {}^-2$.

Para calcular $^+12 + {}^-8$, el resultado es el mismo si restas $^+8$ del problema, $^+12 - {}^+8$. Para calcular $^+5 - {}^-7$, el resultado es el mismo que si sumaras $^+7$ en el problema $^+5 + {}^+7$.

Multiplicación

La multiplicación se puede representar usando un modelo de recta numérica y "contando" cuántas veces sucede un movimiento de tamaño fijo a lo largo de la recta numérica.

$$8 \times (-6)$$

Esto se puede representar como 8 saltos de $^-6$ en una recta numérica.

$^-6 + {}^-6 + {}^-6 + {}^-6 + {}^-6 + {}^-6 + {}^-6 + {}^-6 = {}^-48$ ó $8 \times {}^-6 = {}^-48$

División

Una multiplicación se puede usar para escribir dos divisiones relacionadas.

Sabemos que $5 \times {}^-2 = {}^-10$. Escribe las oraciones de división relacionadas: $^-10 \div {}^-2 = 5$ y $^-10 \div 5 = {}^-2$. A partir de esta relación los estudiantes pueden determinar la respuesta a un problema de división.

Orden de las operaciones

Los matemáticos han establecido reglas para el orden en el que las operaciones $(+, -, \times, \div)$ se deben realizar.

1. Haz cualquier operación en paréntesis.
2. Calcular los exponentes.
3. Hacer todas las operaciones de $\div$ o $\times$ en orden de izquierda a derecha.
4. Hacer todas las operaciones de $+$ o $-$ en orden de izquierda a derecha.

$3 + 4 \times \underline{(6 \div 2)} \times 5 - 7^2 + 6 \div 3 =$
$3 + 4 \times 3 \times 5 - 7^2 + 6 \div 3 =$
$3 + \underline{4 \times 3} \times 5 - 49 + 6 \div 3 =$
$3 + \underline{12 \times 5} - 49 + \underline{6 \div 3} =$
$\underline{3 + 60} - 49 + 2 =$
$\underline{63 - 49} + 2 =$
$\underline{14 + 2} = 16$

Propiedad conmutativa

El orden de los adendos no importa. El orden de los factores no importa. Esto no ocurre en la resta o división.

$5 + 4 = 4 + 5$ $-2 + 3 = 3 + -2$
$5 \times 4 = 4 \times 5$ $-2 \times 3 = 3 \times -2$
$5 - 4 \neq 4 - 5$ $-2 - 3 \neq 3 - -2$
$5 \div 4 \neq 4 \div 5$ $-2 \div 3 \neq 3 \div -2$

Propiedad distributiva

La propiedad distributiva *muestra* que la multiplicación *se distribuye* sobre la suma. Esta propiedad se introduce y representa hallando áreas de triángulos.

$5 \times (17 + 4) = (5 \times 17) + (5 \times 4)$

En la **Página Web de CMP para los padres**, disponible en inglés, puede aprender más sobre los objetivos matemáticos de cada unidad. Vea una lista ilustrada de vocabulario y examine las soluciones de algunos problemas de ACE. **http://PHSchool.com/cmp2parents**

Querida familia:

La siguiente unidad en la clase de matemáticas de su hijo(a) este año es *Seguir Adelante: Relaciones lineales*. En esta unidad, los estudiantes están desarrollando destrezas en áreas que tradicionalmente se conocen como álgebra. Esta unidad les presenta situaciones que se pueden representar con funciones lineales y de las que se pueden hacer gráficas con líneas rectas.

OBJETIVOS DE LA UNIDAD

El objetivo principal de esta unidad es desarrollar la comprensión de relaciones lineales o funciones lineales. Los estudiantes aprenden a reconocer funciones lineales por la tasa de cambio constante entre dos variables en un contexto verbal, en una tabla, gráfica o ecuación.

Los estudiantes identifican, representan e interpretan relaciones lineales. Resuelven relaciones lineales y escriben ecuaciones para rectas. Estas dos últimas ideas se volverán a ver de forma más compleja en unidades posteriores, en particular en las unidades *Pensar con modelos matemáticos* y *Dilo con símbolos*.

AYUDAR CON LA TAREA

Usted puede ayudar con la tarea y al mismo tiempo propiciar buenos hábitos matemáticos a medida que su hijo(a) estudia esta unidad, haciendo preguntas como:

- ¿Cuáles son las variables de este problema?
- ¿Qué relación tienen las variables? ¿Es lineal la relación?
- ¿Cómo puedo reconocer una relación lineal si está representada en un problema, una tabla, una gráfica o con una ecuación?
- ¿Cómo se pueden usar tablas, gráficas y ecuaciones de relaciones lineales para expresar y contestar ciertas preguntas?

En el cuaderno de su hijo(a), puede encontrar ejemplos trabajados de problemas hechos en clase, notas sobre las matemáticas de la unidad y descripciones de las palabras del vocabulario.

CONVERSAR SOBRE LAS MATEMÁTICAS DE *SEGUIR ADELANTE*

Puede ayudar a su hijo(a) con su trabajo para esta unidad de varias maneras:

- Pida a su hijo(a) que describa algunas situaciones del mundo real en las que se usen funciones lineales para explicar cómo se pueden describir las situaciones usando una tabla, una gráfica y una ecuación. Un ejemplo son los costos telefónicos que aumentan a una tasa constante según la duración de la llamada.
- Mire el cuaderno de matemáticas de su hijo(a). Si quiere, lea algunas de las explicaciones que se han escrito y, si no son claras, hable con su hijo(a) sobre por qué cree que sean necesarias más explicaciones.
- Repase la tarea de su hijo(a) y asegúrese de que se han contestado todas las preguntas y de que las explicaciones son claras.

En la parte de atrás se dan unas cuantas ideas matemáticas importantes que su hijo(a) aprenderá en *Seguir adelante*. Como siempre, si tiene preguntas o preocupaciones sobre esta unidad o el progreso en clase de su hijo(a), no dude en llamar.

Atentamente,

Conceptos importantes y ejemplos

Relaciones lineales

Una relación es lineal si hay una tasas de cambio constante entre dos variables. Es decir, para cada unidad de cambio en *x* hay un cambio constante en *y*.

TABLAS En la tabla la **tasa de cambio constante** se puede observar como un patrón de cambio regular en las variables.

Distancia de Gilberto

Tiempo (segundos)	Distancia de Gilberto (metros)
0	0
1	2
2	4
3	6
4	8
5	10
6	12
7	14
8	16
9	18

A medida que el tiempo aumenta en 1 segundo la distancia aumenta en una tasa constante de 2 metros por segundo.

GRÁFICAS Si hacemos una gráfica de los datos, la tasa de cambio constante entre las dos variables aparece como una línea recta.

Esta tasa de cambio constante se llama **pendiente de la recta**. Es la razón de cambio entre las dos variables.

$$\text{Pendiente} = \frac{\text{cambio vertical}}{\text{cambio horizontal}},$$

para dos puntos cualesquiera de la recta.

A medida que el tiempo aumenta en 1 segundo la distancia aumenta en una tasa constante de 2 metros por segundo.

Aquí, la pendiente es $\frac{4}{2}$ ó $\frac{6}{3}$ ó $\frac{2}{1}$.

ECUACIONES En esta representación simbólica la tasa de cambio constante aparece como el **coeficiente** de *t*.

$d = 2t$ (Gilberto)

Aquí, el coeficiente es 2.

INTERCEPTO *y* El punto donde la gráfica de una recta cruza el eje de *y* (eje vertical).

Supón que el costo del alquiler de bicicletas se representa por $C = \$150 + \$10n$, donde C es el costo en dólares y *n* es el número de bicicletas.

El intercepto *y* es $150.

El intercepto *y* es el término constante en la ecuación, $C = 150 + 10n$.

La pendiente (o la tasa de cambio constante) de la recta es 10.

Resolver ecuaciones

Escribe una serie de ecuaciones equivalentes hasta que sea fácil leer el valor de la variable. La igualdad o equivalencia se mantiene si sumas, restas, multiplicas y divides la misma cantidad a cada lado de la ecuación. Estos procedimientos se llaman *propiedades de la igualdad*.

ECUACIÓN	RAZONES
$750 = 150 + 10n$	Ecuación original
$750 - 150 = 150 - 150 + 10n$	Deshacer "sumar 150" restando 150 de ambos lados.
$600 = 10n$	
$\frac{600}{10} = \frac{600n}{10}$	Deshacer "multiplicar por 10" dividiendo por 10.
$60 = n$	El valor de *n* debe ser 60.

Fíjate que si *n* se reemplaza por 60 en cada paso, tenemos una ecuación cierta. La ecuación original sería $750 = 750$.

Querida familia:

La siguiente unidad en la clase de matemáticas de su hijo(a) este año es **Llenar y envolver: Mediciones tridimensionales**. Su centro es el volumen (llenar) y el área total (envolver) de objetos, especialmente prismas rectangulares, cilindros, conos y esferas. Además, los estudiantes amplían su comprensión de semejanza y factores de escala de figuras tridimensionales.

OBJETIVOS DE LA UNIDAD

Los estudiantes desarrollan estrategias para medir el área total y el volumen. Sus estrategias se comentan y se usan para formular reglas para hallar el área total y el volumen de prismas rectangulares y cilindros. También investigan otros sólidos, incluidos conos y esferas, para desarrollar relaciones de volumen.

Las ideas de unidades anteriores se volverán a ver y se ampliarán en esta unidad. Por ejemplo, de la unidad *Estirar y encoger*, se estudiará la conexión de cómo el cambio de la escala de una caja afecta su área total y volumen.

AYUDAR CON LA TAREA

Usted puede ayudar con la tarea y al mismo tiempo propiciar buenos hábitos matemáticos a medida que su hijo(a) estudia esta unidad, haciendo preguntas como:

- ¿Qué medidas de un objeto están relacionadas, el volumen o el área total?
- ¿Qué método debo usar para determinar estas medidas?
- ¿Qué estrategias o fórmulas ayudarían?

En el cuaderno de su hijo(a), puede encontrar ejemplos trabajados de problemas hechos en clase, notas sobre las matemáticas de la unidad y descripciones de las palabras del vocabulario.

CONVERSAR SOBRE LAS MATEMÁTICAS DE *LLENAR Y ENVOLVER*

Puede ayudar a su hijo(a) con su trabajo para esta unidad de varias maneras:

- Pregúntele a su hijo(a) sobre las diferentes maneras en que la clase ha explorado para hallar el área total y el volumen de varias figuras.
- Mire el cuaderno matemático de su hijo(a). Si quiere, puede repasar la sección donde su hijo(a) está anotando definiciones para nuevas palabras que va encontrando en la unidad.
- Pídale a su hijo(a) que escoja una pregunta que le pareciera interesante y que se la explique.

En la parte de atrás se dan unas cuantas ideas matemáticas importantes que su hijo(a) aprenderá en *Llenar y envolver*. Como siempre, si tiene preguntas o preocupaciones sobre esta unidad o el progreso en clase de su hijo(a), no dude en llamar.

Atentamente,

Conceptos importantes	Ejemplos

Área total de prismas rectangulares

Para hallar el área total de una caja (prisma) determina el área total necesaria para envolver el recipiente. Las plantillas planas pueden representar cajas. El área de la plantilla es el área total de la caja.

El área total es la suma de las áreas de las caras.

Área total = (área del frente × 2) + (área del lado) × 2 + (área de la parte superior × 2) ó

Área total = (área del frente + área del lado + área de la parte superior)× 2 = ($w × h + w × \ell + \ell × h$) × 2.

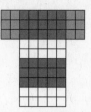

Hay dos de cada una de estas caras del prisma:
2 cm por 3 cm (el área es 6 cm. cuadrados)
2 cm por 5 cm (el área es 10 cm. cuadrados)
3 cm por 5 cm (el área es 15 cm. cuadrados)
Área total = 62 cm. cuadrados

Volumen de prismas rectangulares

Para hallar el volumen de una caja rectangular cuenta el número de capas de cubos unitarios necesarias para llenar el recipiente. El número de cubos unitarios de una capa es igual al área de la base. El volumen (el número total de cubos unitarios) de un prisma rectangular es el área de su base (el número de cubos unitarios de la primera capa) multiplicada por su altura (el número total de capas).

Volumen = Área de base × altura = $Bh = \ell wh$.

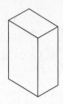

una capa   cinco capas
llenan la caja

2 × 3 = 6 cubos en el área de la base pilas de 5 cubos en la altura
Volumen = 6 × 5 = 30 unidades cúbicas

Volumen de prismas

El volumen de cualquier prisma es el área de su base multiplicada por su altura.

Volumen = Área de la base × altura = Bh.

Prisma rectangular   Prisma triangular   Prisma pentagonal

Área total de cilindros

El área total de un cilindro es el área del rectángulo que forma la superficie lateral ($2\pi rh$) más las áreas de los extremos circulares ($2\pi r^2$) donde r = radio y h = altura.

Área total = $2\pi r^2 + 2\pi rh$.

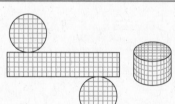

Usa 3.14 para π.
$h = 5$ $r = 4$
$2(\pi 4^2) + 2\pi 4(5) \approx$
$100.48 + 125.6 =$
226.08 unidades cuadradas

Volumen de cilindros

El volumen de un cilindro es el número de cubos unitarios en una capa (el área de la base circular) multiplicado por el número de capas (la altura) necesarios para llenar el cilindro. El área de la base (πr^2) se multiplica por la altura para hallar el volumen.

Volumen = $Bh = \pi r^2 h$

$r = 1.5$ $h = 7$

Área de la base = $3.14 × 2.25 = 7.065$

Volumen ≈ $7.065 × 7 = 49.455$ unidades cúbicas

Volumen de conos y esferas

Cuando los tres tienen el mismo radio y la misma altura llena $\frac{1}{3}$ de un cilindro, y una esfera llena $\frac{2}{3}$ de un cilindro.

Volumen del cono = $\frac{1}{3}$ volumen del cilindro = $\frac{1}{3}\pi r2h$

Volumen de la esfera = $\frac{2}{3}$ volumen del cilindro = $\frac{2}{3}\pi r2h$

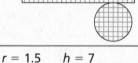

Volumen del cilindro = 628 cm³

El volumen del cono es aproximadamente 209 cm³

El volumen de la esfera es aproximadamente 419 cm³.

Querida familia:

La siguiente unidad en la clase de matemáticas de su hijo(a) este año es ***¿Qué esperas?: Probabilidad y valor esperado***. Esta unidad trata sobre los conceptos de probabilidad y ayudará a los estudiantes a comprender ideas comunes que lean o escuchen cada día. Ellos explorarán las expectativas a largo plazo en situaciones de probabilidad y aprenderán cómo hacer mejores predicciones.

OBJETIVOS DE LA UNIDAD

Los estudiantes aprenderán a hallar probabilidades de dos maneras: haciendo intentos y recopilando datos experimentales, y también analizando situaciones para determinar probabilidades teóricas. A medida que trabajan, los estudiantes usarán fracciones, decimales y porcentajes para describir la probabilidad de sucesos.

AYUDAR CON LA TAREA

Usted puede ayudar con la tarea y al mismo tiempo propiciar buenos hábitos matemáticos a medida que su hijo(a) estudia esta unidad, haciendo preguntas como:

- ¿Cuáles son los resultados posibles que pueden ocurrir para los sucesos de esta situación?
- ¿Cómo puedo determinar la probabilidad experimental de cada uno de los resultados?
- ¿Es posible determinar la probabilidad teórica de cada uno de los resultados?
- Si es así, ¿cuáles son estas probabilidades?
- ¿Cómo puedo usar las probabilidades que he hallado para tomar decisiones sobre esta situación?

En el cuaderno de su hijo(a), puede encontrar ejemplos trabajados de problemas hechos en clase, notas sobre las matemáticas de la unidad y descripciones de las palabras del vocabulario.

CONVERSAR SOBRE LAS MATEMÁTICAS DE *¿QUÉ ESPERAS?*

Puede ayudar a su hijo(a) con su trabajo para esta unidad de varias maneras:

- Comenten ejemplos de enunciados o situaciones de experiencias de la vida cotidiana que se relacionen con la probabilidad de ciertos sucesos. Por ejemplo, ¿qué significa un 50% de probabilidad de lluvia y cómo podrían estimar esta cifra los meteorólogos?
- Mire estadísticas deportivas con su hijo(a) y haga preguntas como cómo se puede usar un promedio de bateo o un promedio de tiros libres para predecir la probabilidad de que el jugador obtenga un golpe en el siguiente turno al bate, o meta una canasta la próxima vez desde la línea de tiros libres.
- Repase la tarea de su hijo(a) y asegúrese de que se han contestado todas las preguntas y de que las explicaciones son claras.

En la parte de atrás se dan unas cuantas ideas matemáticas importantes que su hijo(a) aprenderá en *¿Qué esperas?*. Como siempre, si tiene preguntas o preocupaciones sobre esta unidad o el progreso en clase de su hijo(a), no dude en llamar.

Atentamente,

Conceptos importantes	Ejemplos
Probabilidad Un número entre 0 y 1 que describe la probabilidad de que un suceso ocurra.	Si una bolsa contiene una canica roja, una canica blanca y una canica azul, la probabilidad de sacar una canica roja es 1 de 3, o $\frac{1}{3}$. Escribiríamos: P(roja) $= \frac{1}{3}$.
Probabilidad teórica Si todos los **resultados** son igualmente probables, puedes hallar la probabilidad teórica de un suceso primero haciendo una lista de todos los resultados posibles y luego hallando la razón del número de resultados en el que estás interesado al número total de resultados posibles.	Si un cubo numérico tiene seis lados con los resultados posibles de sacar: 1, 2, 3, 4, 5 ó 6. La probabilidad de sacar un "3" es 1 de 6. $P(\text{sacar un 3}) = \dfrac{\text{número de resultados favorables igualmente posibles}}{\text{número de resultados igualmente posibles}} =$ $\dfrac{1 \,(\text{hay un número 3 en el cubo})}{6 \,(\text{hay 6 resultados posibles})}$
Probabilidad experimental Esta probabilidad es la frecuencia relativa del **suceso**. Es la razón del número de veces que el suceso ocurrió comparado al número total de **intentos**.	Si lanzas una moneda 50 veces y sale cara 23 veces, la frecuencia relativa de caras sería $\frac{23}{50}$ $P(\text{cara}) = \dfrac{\text{número de veces que ocurrió el suceso}}{\text{número de intentos}} =$ $\dfrac{\text{número de caras}}{\text{número total de lanzamientos}} = \dfrac{23}{50}$
Sucesos al azar Sucesos inciertos si se observan individualmente, pero que muestran un patrón predecible a lo largo de varios intentos al azar.	Lanzar un cubo numérico es al azar porque aunque no hay manera de saber qué número saldrá a continuación, sabes que con el tiempo saldrá cada número aproximadamente las mismas veces.
Árbol de conteo Éste es un diagrama que se usa para determinar el número de resultados posibles. El número final de ramas es igual al número de resultados posibles.	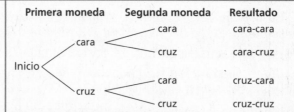
Modelo de área Éste es un diagrama en el cual fracciones del área corresponden a probabilidades de la situación. Los modelos de área son especialmente útiles cuando hay 2 sucesos que seguir y los resultados de cada suceso no son igualmente probables.	El modelo de área de la derecha muestra la probabilidad de sacar dos bloques rojos si hay 2 bloques rojos y 2 bloques azules y se saca uno cada vez, sin volverlo a meter. La probabilidad es $\frac{2}{12}$ ó $\frac{1}{6}$. 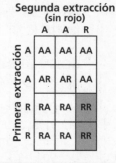
Valor esperado o promedio a largo plazo El promedio a lo largo de muchos intentos es el valor esperado. La puntuación promedio de un jugador por lanzamiento en una situación de tiros libres de 1 más 1 es un valor esperado. El promedio de ganancias por boleto de lotería de un jugador también es un valor esperado.	Se juega un juego con dos cubos numéricos. Anotas 2 puntos cuando sale una suma de 6, 1 punto por una suma de 3, y 0 puntos por cualquier otra suma. Si lanzas los cubos 36 veces, podrías esperar sacar una suma de 6 aproximadamente 5 veces y una suma de 3 dos veces. Podrías esperar anotar $(5 \times 2) + (2 \times 1) = 12$ puntos de 36 lanzamientos, un promedio de $\frac{12}{36} = \frac{1}{3}$ punto por lanzamiento. Éste es el valor esperado de un lanzamiento.
Ley de números grandes Los datos experimentales recopilados a lo largo de muchos intentos deberían producir probabilidades que se acercaran a las probabilidades teóricas.	Para un millón de lanzamientos sería improbable que salieran exactamente 50% de caras, pero sería extremadamente poco probable que el porcentaje de caras fuera muy diferente al 50%.

Querida familia:

La siguiente unidad en la clase de matemáticas de su hijo(a) este año es *Distribución de datos: Describir variabilidad y comparar grupos*. Los estudiantes aprenderán a escoger entre una variedad de representaciones para mostrar distribuciones y analizarán, describirán y compararán grupos de datos.

OBJETIVOS DE LA UNIDAD

Explorar estadísticas como un proceso de investigación de datos que requiere un conjunto de cuatro componentes interrelacionados (Graham, 1987).

- Plantear la pregunta: formular la(s) pregunta(s) clave para explorar y decidir qué datos recopilar para contestar la(s) pregunta(s);
- Recopilar los datos: decidir cómo recopilar los datos además de recopilarlos;
- Analizar los datos: organizar, representar, resumir y describir los datos y buscar patrones en los datos; e
- Interpretar los resultados: predecir, comparar e identificar relaciones y usar los resultados de los análisis para tomar decisiones sobre la(s) pregunta(s) original(es).

Este proceso dinámico a menudo requiere ir de uno a otro de los cuatro componentes.

AYUDAR CON LA TAREA

Usted puede ayudar con la tarea y al mismo tiempo propiciar buenos hábitos matemáticos a medida que su hijo(a) estudia esta unidad, haciendo preguntas como:

- ¿Hay algo que te sorprenda sobre los datos y su distribución?
- ¿Dónde se acumulan los datos en la distribución?
- ¿Cómo puedo usar la media o la mediana y el rango como ayuda para comprender y describir una distribución de datos?
- ¿Qué estrategias puedo usar para comparar dos conjuntos de datos distintos?

En el cuaderno de su hijo(a), puede encontrar ejemplos trabajados de problemas hechos en clase, notas sobre las matemáticas de la unidad y descripciones de las palabras del vocabulario.

CONVERSAR SOBRE LAS MATEMÁTICAS DE *DISTRIBUCIONES DE DATOS*

Puede ayudar a su hijo(a) con su trabajo para esta unidad de varias maneras:

- Observe con su hijo(a) los usos de datos en revistas, periódicos y en la televisión.
- Señale ejemplos de representaciones gráficas y pregúntele a su hijo qué información muestran.
- Pregúntele a su hijo(a) sobre los datos estudiados en clase. ¿Cuáles eran los valores típicos (moda, mediana o media) de estos datos?
- Repase la tarea de su hijo(a) y asegúrese de que se han contestado todas las preguntas y de que las explicaciones son claras.

En la parte de atrás se dan unas cuantas ideas matemáticas importantes que su hijo(a) aprenderá en *Distribuciones de datos*. Como siempre, si tiene preguntas o preocupaciones sobre esta unidad o el progreso en clase de su hijo(a), no dude en llamar.

Atentamente,

Representar distribuciones de datos

Los estadísticos usan representaciones o resúmenes estadísticos durante la parte de análisis del proceso de investigación estadística para describir la distribución de datos.

LEER REPRESENTACIONES DE DATOS ESTÁNDAR

- Leer los datos requiere "extraer" información de una gráfica para contestar preguntas explícitas.
- Leer entre los datos incluye la interpretación e integración de información presentada en una gráfica.
- Leer más allá de los datos requiere ampliar, predecir o inferir a partir de los datos para contestar preguntas implícitas.

GRÁFICA DE BARRAS DE FRECUENCIA La altura de una barra es el número (la frecuencia) de casos que tienen el mismo valor

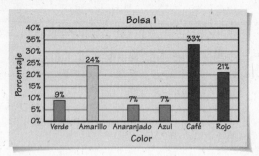

GRÁFICA DE BARRAS DE VALOR Cada caso se representa por una barra separada cuya longitud relativa corresponde a la magnitud o valor del caso.

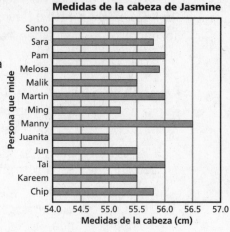

Medidas de la cabeza de Jasmine

DIAGRAMA DE PUNTOS
Cada caso se representa como(o) una "X" un punto puesto sobre una recta numérica rotulada.

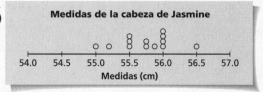

DIAGRAMA DE DISPERSIÓN
La relación entre dos atributos diferentes se explora colocando valores de dos atributos numéricos en un sistema de coordenadas cartesiano.

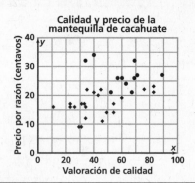

Medidas de tendencia o localización central (moda, mediana, media)

MODA El valor o categoría que ocurre con mayor frecuencia. Generalmente no se usa para resumir datos numéricos.

MEDIANA El valor numérico que marca el medio de una distribución ordenada. No está influida por los valores extremos. Gráficamente, la mediana marca la localización que divide una distribución en dos partes iguales.

MEDIA El valor numérico que marca el punto de equilibrio de una distribución; está influido por todos los valores de la distribución, incluidos los valores extremos. Es una buena medida para usar cuando se trabaja con distribuciones que son poco simétricas.

Número de hermanos: 0, 0, 0, 1, 1, 1, 2, 2, 2, 2, 2, 3, 5, 6.

La moda es 2.

La mediana del conjunto de datos 3, 4, 4, 7, 8, 9 es $5\frac{1}{2}$, el número a medio camino entre 4 y 7.

Para 4, 5, 5 y 7, la mediana es 5.

Número de personas en un hogar: 2, 3, 3, 4, 6, 6.

La media (promedio) del número de gente de estos hogares es 4. Hay 24 personas repartidas entre 6 hogares.

Usar medidas de variabilidad

Las medidas de variabilidad se usan para describir cómo se dispersan o se agrupan los valores individuales de los datos.

El **rango** depende sólo de dos valores, el mayor y el menor. El rango es la diferencia entre el valor mayor y el valor menor en un conjunto de datos.

Querida familia:

La primera unidad en la clase de matemáticas de su hijo(a) este año es ***Pensar con modelos matemáticos: Variación lineal e inversa***. En el trabajo matemático anterior, su hijo(a) ha estudiado algunos de los conceptos básicos de álgebra. En esta unidad, vamos a explorar una variedad de situaciones que se pueden representar con diferentes modelos matemáticos.

OBJETIVOS DE LA UNIDAD

Esta primera unidad del grado octavo se ha diseñado para repasar y ampliar la comprensión y destreza de los estudiantes con las funciones lineales y para presentar conceptos asociados con funciones no lineales.

Cuando se usan expresiones algebraicas para representar patrones en los datos, las funciones resultantes se llaman *modelos matemáticos* de las relaciones. Las funciones entonces se pueden usar para escribir y resolver ecuaciones que proporcionan estimaciones de respuestas a preguntas sobre las relaciones. Uno de los objetivos centrales de esta unidad es desarrollar la comprensión y destreza de los estudiantes en este aspecto del proceso de representación.

AYUDAR CON LA TAREA

El objetivo general de *Connected Mathematics* es ayudar a los estudiantes a desarrollar hábitos matemáticos con sentido. Usted puede ayudar con la tarea y al mismo tiempo propiciar buenos hábitos matemáticos haciendo preguntas como:

- ¿Cuáles son las variables clave en esta selección?
- ¿Cuál es el patrón que relaciona las variables que están involucradas? ¿Es lineal?
- ¿Qué tipo de ecuación expresará la relación entre las variables?
- ¿Cómo se puede usar la ecuación que relaciona las variables para contestar preguntas sobre la relación?

En el cuaderno de su hijo(a), puede encontrar ejemplos trabajados de problemas hechos en clase, notas sobre las matemáticas de la unidad y descripciones de las palabras del vocabulario.

CONVERSAR SOBRE LAS MATEMÁTICAS DE *PENSAR CON MODELOS MATEMÁTICOS*

Puede ayudar a su hijo(a) con su trabajo de varias maneras:

- Pida a su hijo(a) que comparta su cuaderno de matemáticas con usted, mostrándole lo que se ha anotado. Pida a su hijo(a) que le explique por qué estas ideas son importantes.
- Hablen sobre situaciones en los que se recopilarían datos como ayuda para representar la situación con modelos matemáticos como tablas y gráficas.
- Repase la tarea de su hijo(a) y asegúrese de que se han contestado todas las preguntas y de que las explicaciones son claras.

En la parte de atrás se dan unas cuantas ideas matemáticas importantes que su hijo(a) aprenderá en *Pensar con modelos matemáticos*. Como siempre, si tiene preguntas o preocupaciones sobre esta unidad o el progreso en clase de su hijo(a), no dude en llamar.

Atentamente,

Conceptos importantes	Ejemplos
Modelos matemáticos Una ecuación o una gráfica que describe, al menos aproximadamente, la relación entre dos variables es un modelo matemático. Un modelo matemático te puede permitir hacer estimaciones razonables para valores entre, y más allá de, los puntos de datos conocidos.	**Representar el grosor y resistencia de puentes** 1. Recopilar datos que simulen cuánto peso puede aguantar un puente de varias capas de grosor. 2. Colocar los datos en una gráfica y dibujar una recta para representar el patrón de los datos. 3. Hallar una ecuación para representar los datos. Por ejemplo, $y = 8x$ (ya que grosor 0 sugiere resistencia 0). 4. Usar la ecuación $y = 8x$ para predecir los pesos de rotura para otros puentes:  Experimento del grosor del puente de Arkansas

grosor en capas	3.5	7	10
resistencia en carga de centavos	28	56	80

Relaciones lineales En unidades anteriores, los estudiantes aprendieron cómo reconocer, representar simbólicamente y analizar relaciones lineales. Muchas preguntas sobre relaciones lineales se pueden contestar resolviendo ecuaciones de la forma $c = mx + b$. Los problemas de esta unidad están diseñados para promover el repaso y la ampliación de estas destrezas.	La **tasa de cambio** de y en la ecuación $y = mx + b$ es la **pendiente** de su gráfica. En concreto, m, el coeficiente de x, indica la razón constante: $\frac{cambio\ de\ y}{cambio\ de\ x}$. El término constante b indica el **intercepto y** $(0,b)$ de la gráfica. $5x - 3 = 7x - 2$ se puede resolver: • haciendo uno gráfica (o haciendo tablas para) $y = 5x - 3$ y $y = 7x - 2$ y buscando una solución común • usando las propiedades de la igualdad $5x - 3 = 7x - 2$ $-3 = 2x - 2$ (restar $5x$ de cada lado) $-1 = 2x$ (sumar 2 a cada lado) $-\frac{1}{2} = x - 2$ (dividir cada lado por 2)

Variación directa Los modelos de variación directa son aquellos que se pueden expresar con ecuaciones de la forma $y = kx$. En una tabla de datos, los estudiantes pueden notar que $\frac{y}{x} = k$. Ésta es la misma relación que $y = kx$.	Éste es un caso especial de relación lineal, que es uno con el intercepto y igual a cero.

Variación inversa Los modelos de variación inversa son aquellos que se pueden expresar con ecuaciones de la forma $y = \frac{k}{x}$. Es importante darse cuenta de que una variación inversa da un patrón de cambio no lineal. En una tabla de datos los estudiantes pueden notar del patrón $xy = k$, donde k es una constante. Ésta es la misma relación que $y = \frac{k}{x}$.	El hecho de que dividir por una variable en aumento tiene un efecto diferente del que tiene restar por una variable en disminución se revela contrastando las gráficas de $y = 10 - x$ (la recta) e $y = \frac{10}{x}$ (la curva). 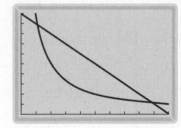 Fíjate que no hay solución para y cuando $x = 0$ en $y = \frac{10}{x}$

En la **Página Web de CMP para los padres**, disponible en inglés, puede aprender más sobre los objetivos matemáticos de cada unidad. Vea una lista ilustrada de vocabulario y examine las soluciones de algunos problemas de ACE. **http://PHSchool.com/cmp2parents**

Querida familia:

La siguiente unidad en la clase de matemáticas de su hijo(a) este año es *En busca de Pitágoras: El teorema de Pitágoras*. El trabajo de los estudiantes en esta unidad desarrolla una relación fundamentalmente importante que conecta la geometría y el álgebra: El teorema de Pitágoras.

OBJETIVOS DE LA UNIDAD

En esta unidad, los estudiantes exploran el teorema de Pitágoras, raíces cuadradas y estrategias para estimar raíces cuadradas. Además, se presentan los números irracionales.

La presentación de las ideas de esta unidad refleja el desarrollo histórico del concepto de los números irracionales. Los antiguos matemáticos griegos reconocían la necesidad de dichos números mientras buscaban una razón de enteros para representar la longitud de los lados de un cuadrado con ciertas áreas, como 2 unidades cuadradas.

AYUDAR CON LA TAREA

Usted puede ayudar con la tarea y al mismo tiempo propiciar buenos hábitos matemáticos a medida que su hijo(a) estudia haciendo preguntas como:

- ¿Es ésta una situación donde es apropiado usar el teorema de Pitágoras?
- ¿Necesito hallar la distancia entre dos puntos?
- ¿Qué relación tienen los números irracionales con las áreas de cuadrados?
- ¿Cómo puedo estimar la raíz cuadrada de un número?
- ¿Cómo puedo saber la longitud de algo sin medirlo directamente?

En el cuaderno de su hijo(a), puede encontrar ejemplos trabajados de problemas hechos en clase, notas sobre las matemáticas de la unidad y descripciones de las palabras del vocabulario.

CONVERSAR SOBRE LAS MATEMÁTICAS DE *EN BUSCA DE PITÁGORAS*

Puede ayudar a su hijo(a) con su trabajo para esta unidad de varias maneras:

- Pida a su hijo(a) que le explique las ideas presentadas en el texto sobre hallar distancias.
- Comente con su hijo(a) cómo la gente en algunas carreras y profesiones, como carpinteros, arquitectos y pilotos, aplica teorema de Pitágoras
- Repase la tarea de su hijo(a) y asegúrese de que se han contestado todas las preguntas y de que las explicaciones son claras.
- Pida a su hijo(a) que escoja una pregunta que le pareciera interesante y que se la explique.

En la parte de atrás se dan unas cuantas ideas matemáticas importantes que su hijo(a) aprenderá en *En busca de Pitágoras*. Como siempre, si tiene preguntas o preocupaciones sobre esta unidad o el progreso en clase de su hijo(a), no dude en llamar.

Atentamente,

Conceptos importantes	Ejemplos
Hallar el área Los estudiantes hallan áreas de cuadrados dibujadas en cuadrículas. Un método es subdividir el cuadrado y sumar las áreas de las figuras que la componen. Otro método es meter el cuadrado en un rectángulo y restar el área de la figura exterior del área del rectángulo.	Área de un cuadrado inclinado = Áreas de los 4 triángulos + 1 cuadrado pequeño = $4\left[\frac{1}{2}(3 \times 4)\right] + 1$ = 25 unidades cuadradas 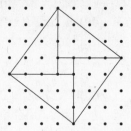
Raíces cuadradas Si se conoce el área de un cuadrado, su longitud de lado es el número cuyo cuadrado es el área. Algunas de estas longitudes no son números enteros, por lo que usamos el símbolo $\sqrt{\ }$.	El área del cuadrado inclinado es 10 unidades cuadradas, o sea que el lado del cuadrado inclinado es $\sqrt{10}$ unidades.
Estimar raíces cuadradas Los estudiantes desarrollan puntos de referencia para estimar raíces cuadradas.	$\sqrt{5}$ está entre 2 y 3, porque $2^2 < 5 < 3^2$. Está más cerca de 2. Prueba $2.25 \div 2.25^2 = 5.06$. De modo que $\sqrt{5}$ está entre 2 y 2.25, pero más cerca de 2.25. Prueba 2.24 ($2.24^2 = 5.0176$), aún más cerca. Sigue hasta que llegues a la precisión deseada.
Hallar distancias Para hallar varias longitudes de segmentos de rectas, los estudiantes empiezan dibujando un cuadrado que esté asociado con la longitud.	El segmento de recta que se muestra es el lado de un cuadrado con un área de 25 unidades cuadradas, de modo que el segmento tiene una longitud de $\sqrt{25}$ ó 5. 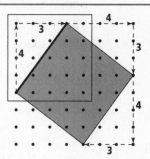
Teorema de Pitágoras En un triángulo recto, la suma de los cuadrados de las longitudes de dos lados es igual al cuadrado de la longitud del lado más largo, llamado hipotenusa. Simbólicamente, esto es $a^2 + b^2 = c^2$, donde a y b son las longitudes de los lados y c es la longitud de la hipotenusa.	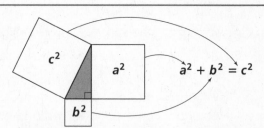 $a^2 + b^2 = c^2$
Longitud del segmento de recta En una cuadrícula, la longitud de un segmento de recta horizontal o vertical se puede hallar contando la distancia. Si un segmento no es vertical u horizontal, es posible tratarlo como la hipotenusa de un triángulo recto. El teorema de Pitágoras se usa para hallar la hipotenusa.	La longitud del segmento AB puede ser la hipotenusa de un triángulo recto, c. $2^2 + 2^2 = c^2$, entonces $4 + 4 = 8 = c^2$. $\sqrt{8} = c$
Números irracionales Un número que no se puede escribir como fracción con un numerador o denominador entero es irracional. Las representaciones decimales de los números irracionales nunca terminan y nunca muestran un patrón para un número fijo de dígitos.	Los números $\sqrt{2}$, $\sqrt{3}$, $\sqrt{5}$ y π son ejemplos de números irracionales. $\sqrt{2}$ es $1.41421356237\ldots$ La parte decimal sigue infinitamente sin ningún patrón de longitud fija que se repita.

Querida familia:

La siguiente unidad en la clase de matemáticas de su hijo(a) este año es *Crecer, crecer, crecer: Relaciones exponenciales*. La unidad se centra en las relaciones exponenciales, en las que una cantidad se hace más grande o más pequeña a una tasa que aumenta, en lugar de a una tasa constante.

OBJETIVOS DE LA UNIDAD

Su hijo(a) ha estudiado anteriormente el crecimiento lineal, en el que una cantidad fija se añade repetidamente a una cantidad inicial para producir una secuencia de valores. El crecimiento exponencial está relacionado con patrones que se basan en la multiplicación en lugar de en la suma. Por ejemplo, en la secuencia 3, 9, 27, 81, 243,... cada término es el triple del término anterior.

El objetivo principal en *Crecer, crecer, crecer* es que los estudiantes aprendan a reconocer situaciones, patrones de datos y gráficas que se representen con expresiones exponenciales y a usar tablas, gráficas y ecuaciones para contestar preguntas sobre patrones exponenciales.

AYUDAR CON LA TAREA

Usted puede ayudar con la tarea y al mismo tiempo propiciar buenos hábitos matemáticos a medida que su hijo(a) estudia esta unidad, haciendo preguntas como:

- ¿Es la relación entre las variables un ejemplo de crecimiento o reducción exponencial? ¿Por qué?
- ¿Cómo se puede detectar esta situación en una tabla, gráfica o ecuación? ¿Cuál es el factor de crecimiento?
- ¿Qué tabla, gráfica o ecuación representaría los datos o los patrones de una gráfica que relacionara las variables?
- ¿Cómo podría contestar preguntas sobre una situación exponencial estudiando una tabla, una gráfica o una ecuación de la relación exponencial?
- ¿En qué se parece o diferencia esta relación exponencial de otras relaciones entre variables que he estudiado?

En el cuaderno de su hijo(a), puede encontrar ejemplos trabajados de problemas hechos en clase, notas sobre las matemáticas de la unidad y descripciones de las palabras del vocabulario.

CONVERSAR SOBRE LAS MATEMÁTICAS DE *CRECER, CRECER, CRECER*

Puede ayudar a su hijo(a) con su trabajo para esta unidad de varias maneras:

- Hable con su hijo(a) sobre las aplicaciones que se presentan en la unidad y sobre aplicaciones parecidas que encuentren en sus actividades cotidianas.
- Pida a su hijo(a) que escoja una pregunta que le pareciera interesante y se la explique.
- Repase la tarea de su hijo(a) y asegúrese de que se han contestado todas las preguntas y de que las explicaciones son claras.

En la parte de atrás se dan unas cuantas ideas matemáticas importantes que su hijo(a) aprenderá en *Crecer, crecer, crecer*. Como siempre, si tiene preguntas sobre esta unidad o el progreso en clase de su hijo(a), no dude en llamar.

Atentamente,

Conceptos importantes	Ejemplos

Crecimiento exponencial

Un patrón exponencial incluye patrones que se basan en la multiplicación y que a menudo se pueden reconocer en una descripción verbal de una situación, o en el patrón de cambio en una tabla de valores (x, y).

La tasa en aumento del crecimiento se refleja en la curva hacia arriba de los puntos de la gráfica.

Supón que se ofrece una recompensa. Al principio, se pone 1¢ en un fondo. El primer día, se añaden 2¢; el segundo día se añaden 4¢; y en cada día sucesivo, la recompensa se dobla. ¿Cuánto dinero se añade al octavo día?

Fondo para la fiesta de la clase

Día de buen trabajo	Recompensa (centavos)
0 (inicio)	1
1	2
2	4
3	8
4	16
5	32
6	64
7	128
8	?

Fondo para la fiesta de la clase

Factor de crecimiento

Un factor constante se puede obtener dividiendo cada valor sucesivo de y por el valor de y anterior. Esta razón se llama *factor de crecimiento* del patrón.

En el ejemplo de arriba, multiplicas el premio anterior por 2 para obtener la nueva recompensa. Este factor constante también se puede obtener dividiendo valores de y sucesivos: $\frac{2}{1} = 2$, $\frac{4}{2} = 2$, etc.

Ecuaciones exponenciales

CRECIMIENTO EXPONENCIAL Un patrón de crecimiento exponencial, $y = a(b)^x$, aumenta lentamente al principio pero crece a una tasa en aumento porque su crecimiento es multiplicativo. El factor de crecimiento es b.

Día	Cálculos	Recompensa (centavos)
0	1	1
1	1×2, ó 2^1	2
2	$1 \times 2 \times 2$, ó 2^2	4
3	$1 \times 2 \times 2 \times 2$, ó 2^3	8
⋮	⋮	⋮
6	$1 \times 2 \times 2 \times 2 \times 2 \times 2 \times 2$, ó 2^6	256
⋮	⋮	⋮
n	$1 \times 2 \times 2 \times \cdots \times 2$, ó 2^n	2^n

En el día n, la recompensa, R, será $R = 1 \times 2^n$. Como la variable independiente de este patrón aparece como exponente, el patrón de crecimiento se llama exponencial. El factor de crecimiento es la *base*, 2. El *exponente, n*, nos dice el número de veces que 2 es un factor.

Reducción exponencial

Los modelos exponenciales describen patrones en los que el valor disminuye. Los factores de reducción producen relaciones en disminución porque son menores que 1.

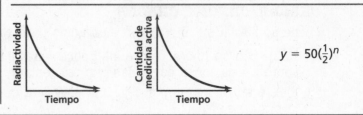

$$y = 50(\tfrac{1}{2})^n$$

Reglas de exponentes

La estructura multiplicativa de las bases lleva a:

$(b^m)^n = b^{mn}$

$(b^m)(b^n) = b^{m+n}$

$(a^m b^m) = (ab)^m$

$a^m/a^n = a^{m-n}$

$(2^3)^2 = (2 \times 2 \times 2)^2 = 2^6$

$3^2 \times 3^3 = (3 \times 3) \times (3 \times 3 \times 3) = 3^5 = 243$

$(2 \times 5)^2 = 10^2 = 100 = 2^2 \times 5^2$

$5^3/5^2 = (5 \times 5 \times 5)/(5 \times 5) = 5^{3-2} = 5^1 = 5$

En la **Página Web de CMP para los padres**, disponible en inglés, puede aprender más sobre los objetivos matemáticos de cada unidad. Vea una lista ilustrada de vocabulario y examine las soluciones de algunos problemas de ACE. **http://PHSchool.com/cmp2parents**

Querida familia:

La siguiente unidad en la clase de matemáticas de su hijo(a) este año es *Ranas, pulgas y cubos pintados: Relaciones cuadráticas*. En la unidad anterior, *Pensar con modelos matemáticos*, los estudiantes estudiaron el uso de los modelos lineales e investigaron ejemplos de variación inversa. En la unidad *Crecer, crecer, crecer*, los estudiantes exploraron modelos exponenciales. En *Ranas, pulgas y cubos pintados*, el centro de atención pasa a las relaciones no lineales polinomiales: la función polinomial de segundo grado o *cuadrática*.

OBJETIVOS DE LA UNIDAD

Los estudiantes aprenderán a reconocer patrones de cambio cuadráticos en tablas y gráficas, y aprenderán a escribir ecuaciones para representar esos patrones. Compararán y contrastarán los patrones de cambio cuadráticos con los patrones de cambio lineales y exponenciales, que ya se han estudiado en profundidad.

Se pueden encontrar relaciones cuadráticas en campos como los negocios, los deportes, la ingeniería y la economía. Estamos tratando con relaciones cuadráticas, por ejemplo, cuando estudiamos cómo una pelota (o una pulga saltando) cambia con el tiempo. Una gráfica cuadrática, llamada *parábola*, tiene forma de U o de U inversa.

AYUDAR CON LA TAREA

Usted puede ayudar con la tarea y al mismo tiempo propiciar buenos hábitos matemáticos a medida que su hijo(a) estudia esta unidad, haciendo preguntas como:

- ¿Cómo puedo reconocer si la relación entre las variables de una situación es una función cuadrática?
- ¿Qué ecuación representaría una relación cuadrática en la tabla, gráfica o contexto del problema que relaciona las variables?
- ¿Cómo puedo contestar las preguntas de las situaciones estudiando una tabla, gráfica o ecuación de la relación cuadrática?

En el cuaderno de su hijo(a), puede encontrar ejemplos trabajados de problemas hechos en clase, notas sobre las matemáticas de la unidad y descripciones de las palabras del vocabulario.

CONVERSAR SOBRE LAS MATEMÁTICAS DE *RANAS, PULGAS Y CUBOS PINTADOS*

Puede ayudar a su hijo(a) con su trabajo para esta unidad de varias maneras:

- Hable con su hijo(a) sobre las situaciones que se presentan en la unidad.
- Repase la tarea de su hijo(a) y asegúrese de que se han contestado todas las preguntas y de que las explicaciones son claras.
- Pida a su hijo(a) que escoja una pregunta que le pareciera interesante y que se la explique.

En la parte de atrás se dan unas cuantas ideas matemáticas importantes que su hijo(a) aprenderá en *Ranas, pulgas y cubos pintados*. Como siempre, si tiene preguntas o preocupaciones sobre esta unidad o el progreso en clase de su hijo(a), no dude en llamar.

Atentamente,

Conceptos importantes	Ejemplos

Representar patrones de cambio cuadrático con tablas

En las relaciones lineales, las *primeras diferencias* de valores sucesivos son constantes, indicando una tasa de cambio constante. En las relaciones cuadráticas, las primeras diferencias no son constantes, pero las *segundas diferencias* sí lo son. La primera diferencia es la tasa a la que *y* está cambiando con respecto a *x*. La segunda diferencia indica la tasa a la que *esa tasa* está cambiando. Si las segundas diferencias son siempre las mismas, entonces la relación es cuadrática.

$y = 6(x - 2)^2$

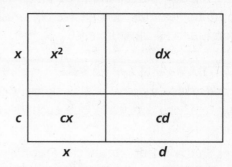

x	y
0	24
1	6
2	0
3	6
4	24
5	54

Primeras diferencias

$6 - 24 = -18$
$0 - 6 = -6$
$6 - 0 = 6$
$24 - 6 = 18$
$54 - 24 = 30$

Segundas diferencias

$-6 - (-18) = 12$
$0 - (-6) = 12$
$18 - 6 = 12$
$30 - 18 = 12$

Las segundas diferencias son todas 12, lo que indica que la tabla representa una relación cuadrática.

Representar funciones cuadráticas con ecuaciones

Tradicionalmente, las relaciones cuadráticas se definen como las relaciones que tienen ecuaciones que encajan en la forma $y = ax^2 + bx + c$, en la que *a*, *b*, y *c* son constantes, $a \neq 0$. Esta forma de la ecuación se llama *forma desarrollada*. El énfasis está en observar que las ecuaciones contienen una variable independiente elevada a la segunda potencia. También es importante comprender la *forma factorial* de estas ecuaciones.

Muchas ecuaciones cuadráticas también se pueden definir como funciones cuyo valor de *y* es igual al producto de dos factores lineales —la forma $y = (ax + c)(bx + d)$, donde $a \neq 0$ y $b \neq 0$. La potencia de esta forma es la que relaciona cuadráticamente a los polinomios como productos de factores lineales.

El área del rectángulo de abajo se puede ver como el producto de dos expresiones lineales, como el resultado de multiplicar el ancho por la longitud, o como la suma del área de las subpartes del rectángulo.

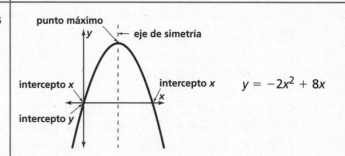

$A = (x + c)(x + d)$ forma factorial
$A = x^2 + cx + dx + d$ forma desarrollada

Representar patrones de cambio cuadráticos con gráficas

Los valores de las ecuaciones afectan la forma, orientación y ubicación de la gráfica cuadrática, una curva parabólica.

Si el coeficiente del término x^2 es positivo, la curva se abre hacia arriba y tiene un punto mínimo. Si es negativo, la curva se abre hacia abajo y tiene un punto máximo.

El punto máximo o mínimo de una gráfica cuadrática (**parábola**) se llama **vértice**. El vértice está en el *eje de simetría* vertical que separa la parábola en mitades que son imágenes de espejo. El vértice se ubica a medio camino entre los **interceptos x**, si el intercepto x existe. Los **interceptos x** son imágenes de espejo uno del otro. El **intercepto y** es donde la parábola cruza el eje de *y*.

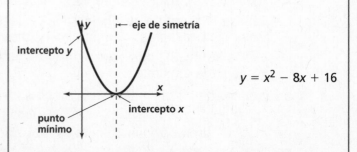

$y = -2x^2 + 8x$

$y = x^2 - 8x + 16$

En la **Página Web de CMP para los padres**, disponible en inglés, puede aprender más sobre los objetivos matemáticos de cada unidad. Vea una lista ilustrada de vocabulario y examine las soluciones de algunos problemas de ACE. **http://PHSchool.com/cmp2parents**

Querida familia:

La siguiente unidad en la clase de matemáticas de su hijo(a) este año es *Caleidoscopios, tapacubos y espejos: Simetría y transformaciones*. Esta unidad es una introducción al tema que en matemáticas se llama geometría transformacional.

OBJETIVOS DE LA UNIDAD

Los estudiantes tienen una comprensión intuitiva de la simetría. A pesar de que han empezado a reconocer figuras simétricas a una edad temprana, se necesita la comprensión analítica para confirmar la simetría, y construir figuras con simetrías dadas requiere mayor sofisticación matemática. *Caleidoscopios, tapacubos y espejo*, la última unidad de geometría y medición en el currículum de *Connected Mathematics*, ayuda a los estudiantes a refinar su conocimiento sobre simetría y a usarlo en afirmaciones matemáticas.

La simetría se describe en términos de transformaciones. Las transformaciones de simetría incluyen reflejos, rotaciones y traslaciones. Estas transformaciones conservan tanto las medidas de los ángulos como las de las longitudes de lado, dando como resultado una imagen que es congruente con la figura original. Esta unidad estimulará y agudizará el reconocimiento de los estudiantes sobre simetría, congruencia y sus conexiones.

AYUDAR CON LA TAREA

Usted puede ayudar con la tarea y al mismo tiempo propiciar buenos hábitos matemáticos a medida que su hijo(a) estudia esta unidad, haciendo preguntas como:

- ¿Cómo se describe un diseño sistemático para que alguien pueda recrearlo?
- Exactamente, ¿qué información sobre las distancias podemos usar cuando hacemos una imagen bajo reflexión? ¿Y bajo rotación? ¿Y bajo transformación?
- Si las figuras tienen la misma forma y tamaño, ¿qué relación tienen las medidas de los lados y los ángulos?
- ¿Qué medidas de lados y ángulos de 2 figuras se conocen y puedo sacar la conclusión, a partir de estas medidas, de que las 2 figuras son congruentes?
- ¿Qué conexiones entre la geometría y el álgebra me pueden ayudar a crear ciertos tipos de diseños?

En el cuaderno de su hijo(a), puede encontrar ejemplos trabajados de problemas hechos en clase, notas sobre las matemáticas de la unidad y descripciones de las palabras del vocabulario.

CONVERSAR SOBRE LAS MATEMÁTICAS DE *CALEIDOSCOPIOS, TAPACUBOS Y ESPEJOS*

Puede ayudar a su hijo(a) con su trabajo para esta unidad de varias maneras:

- Hable con su hijo(a) sobre las ideas presentadas en el texto sobre simetría. Busquen ejemplos de cada tipo de simetría.
- Repase la tarea de su hijo(a) y asegúrese de que se han contestado todas las preguntas y de que las explicaciones son claras.

En la parte de atrás se dan unas ideas matemáticas importantes que su hijo(a) aprenderá en *Caleidoscopios, tapacubos y espejos*. Como siempre, si tiene preguntas sobre esta unidad o el progreso en clase de su hijo(a), no dude en llamar.

Atentamente,

Conceptos importantes y ejemplos

Tipos de simetría

SIMETRÍA DE REFLEXIÓN Un diseño tiene simetría de reflexión si el reflejo en un eje encaja exactamente sobre la figura o diseño original.

Esta letra A tiene simetría de reflexión porque un reflejo en la línea vertical encajará cada punto de la mitad izquierda con un punto en la mitad derecha. La línea vertical es el eje de simetría.

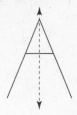

SIMETRÍA DE ROTACIÓN Un diseño tiene simetría de rotación si una rotación, distinta a un giro completo sobre un punto, encaja exactamente sobre la figura o diseño original.

Este diseño tiene simetría de rotación porque una rotación de 120° o 240° sobre un punto *P* encajará cada bandera con otra bandera. El punto *P* es el centro de rotación. El ángulo de rotación es 120°, el menor ángulo por el cual el diseño se puede rotar para encajar con la posición original.

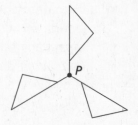

SIMETRÍA DE TRASLACIÓN Un diseño tiene simetría de traslación si una traslación, o deslizamiento, hace encajar la figura sobre sí misma.

Esta figura es parte de un diseño de traslación simétrico. Si este diseño continuara en ambas direcciones, un deslizamiento a la derecha o a la izquierda haría encajar una bandera sobre otra.

Transformaciones de simetría

Las transformaciones de simetría (reflexiones, rotaciones y traslaciones) mueven puntos a puntos de imagen de modo que la distancia entre dos puntos originales cualesquiera, es igual a la distancia entre sus imágenes. Los estudiantes examinan las figuras y sus imágenes bajo reflexiones, rotaciones y traslaciones, midiendo las distancias y los ángulos clave. Usan sus hallazgos para determinar cómo pueden especificar una trasformación particular de modo que otra persona pudiera llevarla a cabo exactamente. También pueden usar esta información sobre distancias conservadas para razonar sobre figuras que tienen simetría.

REFLEXIÓN Una reflexión se puede especificar dando el eje de reflexión.

El punto *A* y su punto reflejo *A*' están en una recta que es perpendicular al eje de simetría y son equidistantes a ese eje.

ROTACIÓN Una rotación se puede especificar dando el centro de rotación y el ángulo de giro.

El punto *B* y su punto imagen *B*' son equidistantes del centro de rotación *P*. Un punto bajo una rotación "viaja" en un arco de círculo y todos los círculos en los cuales los puntos de las figuras "viajan" son círculos concéntricos con *P* como centro. Los ángulos formados por los puntos vértice de la figura y su imagen de rotación tienen la misma medida que el ángulo de giro.

TRASLACIÓN Una traslación se puede especificar dando la longitud y dirección del deslizamiento. Generalmente, se dibuja una flecha con la longitud y dirección apropiada.

Si dibujas segmentos conectando un número de puntos a sus imágenes, los segmentos serán paralelos y todos de la misma longitud. La longitud es igual a la magnitud de la traslación.

Figuras congruentes

Figuras del mismo tamaño y la misma forma son congruentes.

Puedes formar la imagen de una figura que encajará exactamente sobre la otra por una combinación de transformaciones simétricas.

En la **Página Web de CMP para los padres**, disponible en inglés, puede aprender más sobre los objetivos matemáticos de cada unidad. Vea una lista ilustrada de vocabulario y examine las soluciones de algunos problemas de ACE. **http://PHSchool.com/cmp2parents**

Querida familia:

La siguiente unidad en la clase de matemáticas, ***Dilo con símbolos: Comprender los símbolos***, explora el tema en el que se centra el álgebra inicial casi exclusivamente: el uso de símbolos. Cuando usted empezó a estudiar álgebra, probablemente pasó la mayor parte del tiempo aprendiendo a manipular símbolos. Es probable que no tuviera oportunidad de pensar en lo que significaban esos símbolos en realidad. Este currículum de matemáticas pone énfasis en el *significado* detrás de los símbolos. Esto ayuda a que los estudiantes construyan su propia comprensión de las bases del álgebra y su utilidad para resolver problemas.

OBJETIVOS DE LA UNIDAD

En *Dilo con símbolos* los estudiantes aprenden a usar expresiones simbólicas para representar y razonar sobre relaciones. Los estudiantes también manipulan expresiones simbólicas a formas equivalentes para acceder a nueva información. El énfasis se pone en usar las propiedades de los números y las propiedades de la igualdad para observar expresiones equivalentes y la información que representa cada una de estas expresiones. Además, los estudiantes interpretan patrones escondidos que una ecuación o enunciado simbólico representa. Los estudiantes observan críticamente cada parte de una expresión y cómo se relaciona cada parte con la expresión original, su gráfica, su tabla y el contexto que representa.

AYUDAR CON LA TAREA

Usted puede ayudar con la tarea y al mismo tiempo propiciar buenos hábitos matemáticos a medida que su hijo(a) estudia esta unidad, haciendo preguntas como:

- ¿Qué expresión o ecuación recoge el patrón escondido o relación en un contexto?
- ¿Cómo puedo saber si dos o más expresiones son equivalentes?
- ¿Qué operaciones transformarían una ecuación o expresión a una forma equivalente para que se pudiera determinar más fácilmente la solución?
- ¿Qué patrones de cambio representa la ecuación o la expresión?
- ¿Cómo puede ayudar a confirmar una conjetura el razonamiento simbólico?

En el cuaderno de su hijo(a), puede encontrar ejemplos trabajados de problemas hechos en clase, notas sobre las matemáticas de la unidad y descripciones de las palabras del vocabulario.

CONVERSAR SOBRE LAS MATEMÁTICAS DE *DILO CON SÍMBOLOS*

Puede ayudar a su hijo(a) con su trabajo para esta unidad de varias maneras:

- Hable con su hijo(a) sobre las situaciones que se presentan y por qué podemos reorganizar los símbolos.
- Hable con su hijo(a) sobre la importancia de conocer bien en álgebra.
- Repase la tarea de su hijo(a) y asegúrese de que se han contestado todas las preguntas y de que las explicaciones son claras.

En la parte de atrás se dan unas cuantas ideas matemáticas importantes que su hijo(a) aprenderá en *Dilo con símbolos*. Como siempre, si tiene preguntas sobre esta unidad o el progreso en clase de su hijo(a), no dude en llamar.

Atentamente,

Conceptos importantes	Ejemplos

Expresiones equivalentes

A los estudiantes se les presentan deliberadamente situaciones en las cuales pistas de contexto se pueden interpretar de varias maneras para producir ecuaciones diferentes, pero equivalentes.

Halla el número de baldosas cuadradas de 1 pie, N, necesarias para hacer un borde alrededor de una piscina cuadrada con lados de longitud de l pies.

Distintas conceptualizaciones de la situación pueden llevar a expresiones diferentes, pero equivalentes, del número de baldosas:

$N = 4l + 4$
$N = 4(l + 1)$
$N = l + l + l + l + 4$
$N = 8 + 4(l - 1)$
$N = 2l + 2(l + 2)$
$N = (l + 2)^2 - l^2$.

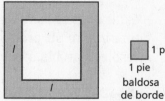

Repasar la propiedad distributiva

Si una expresión se escribe como un factor multiplicado por una suma de dos o más términos, se puede aplicar la propiedad distributiva para *multiplicar* el factor por cada término de la suma. Si una expresión está escrita como una suma de términos y los términos tienen un factor común, se puede aplicar la propiedad distributiva para reescribir la expresión como factor multiplicado por una suma de dos o más términos. Este proceso se llama *factorización*.

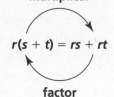

multiplicar

$r(s + t) = rs + rt$

factor

La propiedad distributiva permite a los estudiantes agrupar símbolos (mostrados a la izquierda de la ecuación) o expandir una expresión cuanto sea necesario (mostrado a la derecha de la ecuación).

Comprobar la equivalencia

Los estudiantes pueden usar razonamientos contextuales para decidir si las expresiones son equivalentes. Los estudiantes pueden comprobar si las ecuaciones tienen las mismas gráficas y tablas. Los estudiantes deben poder usar las propiedades distributiva y conmutativa para mostrar expresiones equivalentes.

Aplicando la propiedad distributiva $4(s + 1) = 4s + 4$.

$8 + 4(s - 1)$ se puede mostrar que es equivalente a $4s + 4$.

$$
\begin{aligned}
8 + 4(s - 1) &= 8 + 4s - 4 &&\text{(propiedad distributiva)}\\
&= 8 - 4 + 4s &&\text{(propiedad conmutativa)}\\
&= 4 + 4s &&\text{(resta)}\\
&= 4s + 4 &&\text{(propiedad conmutativa)}
\end{aligned}
$$

Resolver ecuaciones lineales

Los estudiantes han usado tablas o gráficas para hallar soluciones. Pueden resolver ecuaciones lineales simples usando las propiedades de la igualdad. En esta unidad, los estudiantes pueden resolver ecuaciones más complicadas usando las propiedades de los números reales.

$200 = 5x - (100 + 2x)$

$200 = 5x - (2x + 100)$ (propiedad conmutativa)

$200 = 5x - 2x - 100$ (propiedad distributiva)

$200 = 3x - 100$ [propiedad distributiva, $5x - 2x = (5 - 2)x$]

$300 = 3x$ (suma lo mismo a cada lado de la ecuación)

$100 = x$ (dividir por lo mismo a cada lado de la ecuación)

Resolver ecuaciones cuadráticas

Resolver ecuaciones cuadráticas para x cuando $y = 0$ es equivalente a hallar los interceptos x en la gráfica. También se presenta a los estudiantes cómo remover ecuaciones cuadráticas mediante la factorización.

Se hace la conexión entre los factores lineales de una expresión cuadrática y los interceptos x de la gráfica de una ecuación cuadrática.

Si $y = 2x^2 + 8x$, entonces los valores de x cuando $y = 0$, se pueden obtener reescribiendo la ecuación en forma equivalente de $2x(x + 4) = 0$.

Este producto puede ser cero sólo si uno de los factores es igual a 0. Resuelve $2x = 0$ y $x + 4 = 0$. De este modo, $x = 0$ ó $x = -4$. Los interceptos x son $(0, 0)$ y $(-4, 0)$.

Si $0 = x^2 + 5x + 6$, escribimos $x^2 + 5x + 6$ en forma factorial $(x + 2)(x + 3)$ y luego resolvemos $0 = (x + 2)(x + 3)$. De este modo $x + 2 = 0$ ó $x = -2$, y $x + 3 = 0$ ó $x = -3$. Las soluciones de $x^2 + 5x + 6 = 0$ son $x = -3$, y $x = -2$

En la **Página Web de CMP para los padres**, disponible en inglés, puede aprender más sobre los objetivos matemáticos de cada unidad. Vea una lista ilustrada de vocabulario y examine las soluciones de algunos problemas de ACE. **http://PHSchool.com/cmp2parents**

Querida familia:

La siguiente unidad en la clase de matemáticas de su hijo(a) este año es *Figuras de álgebra: Sistemas y desigualdades lineales*. Esta unidad se diseñó para ayudar a los estudiantes a sacar partido de las fuertes conexiones entre álgebra y geometría, con el fin de ampliar la comprensión y destreza de los estudiantes en varios aspectos de esas dos ramas clave del currículum de los grados intermedios.

OBJETIVOS DE LA UNIDAD

En *Figuras de álgebra* los estudiantes explorarán la relación entre álgebra y geometría. A través de esta exploración, los estudiantes trabajarán con ecuaciones para rectas y curvas, y desarrollarán una comprensión de cómo los sistemas de ecuaciones y desigualdades pueden ayudar a resolver problemas. Los estudiantes ampliarán su trabajo previo en álgebra y geometría haciendo conexiones entre ellos. Por ejemplo, los estudiantes conectarán la idea del teorema de Pitágoras a la ecuación coordenada de un círculo y conectarán las propiedades de los polígonos a las pendientes de las rectas.

AYUDAR CON LA TAREA

Usted puede ayudar con la tarea y al mismo tiempo propiciar buenos hábitos matemáticos a medida que su hijo(a) estudia esta unidad, haciendo preguntas como:

- ¿Qué patrones relacionan las coordenadas de puntos en las rectas y curvas que se han dibujado?
- ¿Qué patrones relacionan los puntos cuyas coordenadas satisfacen ecuaciones que se tienen que resolver?
- ¿Incluye el problema una ecuación o una desigualdad?
- ¿Requiere el problema que se escriba y/o resuelva un sistema de ecuaciones?
- Si es así, ¿qué método sería útil para resolver el sistema?
- ¿Hay algunos métodos sistemáticos que se puedan usar para resolver todos los sistemas de ecuaciones lineales?

En el cuaderno de su hijo(a), puede encontrar ejemplos trabajados de problemas hechos en clase, notas sobre las matemáticas de la unidad y descripciones de las palabras del vocabulario.

CONVERSAR SOBRE LAS MATEMÁTICAS DE *FIGURAS DE ÁLGEBRA*

Puede ayudar a su hijo(a) con su trabajo para esta unidad de varias maneras:

- Hable con su hijo(a) sobre la importancia de tener destreza en álgebra.
- Repase la tarea de su hijo(a) y asegúrese de que se han contestado todas las preguntas y de que las explicaciones son claras.
- Pídale a su hijo(a) que escoja una pregunta que le pareciera interesante y que se la explique.

En la parte de atrás se dan unas cuantas ideas matemáticas importantes que su hijo(a) aprenderá en *Figuras de álgebra*. Como siempre, si tiene preguntas o preocupaciones sobre esta unidad o el progreso en clase de su hijo(a), no dude en llamar.

Atentamente,

Conceptos importantes	Ejemplos
Desigualdades lineales Una relación de desigualdad entre dos cantidades, en la que cada cantidad es una expresión lineal, se llama desigualdad lineal.	$3x + 22 < 8x + 7$ ó $3x + 4y < 12$

Resolver desigualdades lineales

Resolver una desigualdad es como resolver ecuaciones lineales. Las reglas para las operaciones con desigualdades son idénticas a las de las ecuaciones, con una excepción. Cuando multiplicas (o divides) una desigualdad por un número negativo, la dirección de la desigualdad cambia.

$$5x + 7 \leq 42$$
$$5x \leq 35$$
$$x \leq 7$$

Resolver esta desigualdad es parecido a resolver $5x + 7 = 42$. Las operaciones $(+, -, \times, \div)$ se aplican a ambos lados. Generalmente mostramos esta solución en una recta numerica.

$$-5x + 7 \leq 42$$
$$-5x \leq 35$$
$$x \geq -7$$

Cambio en la dirección del signo de desigualdad.

Resolver sistemas de ecuaciones lineales

Resolver un sistema significa hallar todas las soluciones que satisfagan todas las ecuaciones del sistema. Hay varias técnicas disponibles para resolver sistemas de dos ecuaciones lineales en dos incógnitas.

SOLUCIÓN GRÁFICA DE SISTEMAS Este método requiere producir gráficas de rectas para cada ecuación y luego leer las coordenadas de los puntos de intersección como soluciones.

FORMA EQUIVALENTE Cada ecuación en un sistema puede cambiar a la forma $y = ax + b$. Para el conjunto

$$\begin{cases} y = -2x + 5 \\ y = 3x - 5 \end{cases}$$

las dos expresiones para y son iguales. Esto elimina la variable y da $(-2x + 5) = (3x - 5)$.

De modo que $5x = 10$, ó $x = 2$. Halla el valor correspondiente de y por sustitución. $y = -2(2) + 5 = 1$. La solución es $(2, 1)$.

RESOLVER SISTEMAS POR SUSTITUCIÓN En el sistema

$$\begin{cases} 3x + 5y = 8 \\ 6x + y = 7 \end{cases}$$

la segunda ecuación se puede reescribir como $y = 7 - 6x$. Usa esta información sobre y y la primera ecuación, $3x + 5(7 - 6x) = 8$. Ahora resuelve esta ecuación con una incógnita con los métodos de trabajo anteriores para revelar $x = 1$ y luego $y = 7 - 6(1)$ ó $y = 1$.

RESOLVER SISTEMAS POR COMBINACIÓN LINEAL Otro método se basa en dos principios básicos:

1. Multiplicar una ecuación lineal por el mismo número (distinto de cero) no cambia el conjunto de soluciones.
2. La solución no cambia si una de las ecuaciones es sustituida por una nueva ecuación formada sumando las dos ecuaciones originales.

Por ejemplo:

$$\begin{cases} 3x + 5y = 8 \\ 6x + y = 7 \end{cases}$$ es equivalente a $$\begin{cases} -6x - 10y = -16 \\ 6x + y = 7 \end{cases}$$

$-9y = -9$, sumando las dos ecuaciones.
Puedes ver que $y = 1$ y que $x = 1$.

Resolver sistemas de desigualdades lineales

Los sistemas de desigualdades también tienden a tener conjuntos soluciones infinitos. La solución para un sistema de *desigualdades* lineales concreto, no disjunto, es la intersección de dos medios-planos que contienen muchos puntos infinitos.

En general, hay cuatro regiones sugeridas por un sistema de desigualdades lineales como $$\begin{cases} y < y \\ y > x - 5 \end{cases}$$

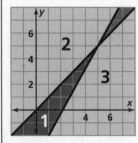

La región 1 contiene las soluciones al sistema. Los puntos de las Regiones 2 y 3 satisfacen una, pero no ambas desigualdades. La Región 4 no satisface ninguna desigualdad.

Querida familia:

La siguiente unidad en la clase de matemáticas de su hijo(a) este año es
Muestras y poblaciones: Datos y estadísticas. La unidad incluirá el proceso de
investigación estadística. Como parte de este proceso, prestaremos especial
atención a la forma en la que se recopilan los datos.

OBJETIVOS DE LA UNIDAD

La probabilidad es una de las herramientas para comprender los problemas de
muestreo en estadística; la estadística es una herramienta para representar y
analizar datos que se pueden usar para sacar conclusiones sobre una población.
Los problemas de *Muestras y poblaciones* ayudan a los estudiantes a hacer
conexiones entre probabilidad y estadística.

Esta unidad empieza con herramientas para agrupar datos y comparar
distribuciones. Luego, los estudiantes exploran qué son las muestras y qué relación
tienen con las poblaciones, las maneras de seleccionar muestras y el uso de
muestras aleatorias. Finalmente, los estudiantes observan las relaciones entre dos
atributos y lo que significa decir que la información sobre los valores de un atributo
se puede usar para comprender, explicar o predecir valores de otro atributo.

AYUDAR CON LA TAREA

Usted puede ayudar con la tarea y al mismo tiempo propiciar buenos hábitos
matemáticos a medida que su hijo(a) estudia esta unidad, haciendo preguntas como:

- ¿Qué es una población? ¿Qué es una muestra? ¿Qué método de muestreo se usó?
- ¿Qué tipos de comparaciones entre los datos de la muestra puedo explorar?
- ¿Puedo usar mis resultados para hacer predicciones o generalizaciones
  sobre las poblaciones?
- ¿Es probable que las maneras en las que se recopilaron o analizaron
  los datos den resultados que representen la población?

En el cuaderno de su hijo(a), puede encontrar ejemplos trabajados de problemas
hechos en clase, notas sobre las matemáticas de la unidad y descripciones de las
palabras del vocabulario.

CONVERSAR SOBRE LAS MATEMÁTICAS DE
MUESTRAS Y POBLACIONES

Puede ayudar a su hijo(a) con su trabajo para esta unidad de varias maneras:

- Usando periódicos, revistas, televisión o radio, ayude a su hijo(a) a
  identificar situaciones en las que se use estadística, prestando especial
  atención a quién o qué se usaba como muestra.
- Hablen de si los datos de un estudio concreto se pueden usar para
  hacer predicciones precisas sobre una población grande.
- Repase la tarea de su hijo(a) y asegúrese de que se han contestado
  todas las preguntas y de que las explicaciones son claras.

En la parte de atrás se dan unas cuantas ideas matemáticas importantes que su
hijo(a) aprenderá en *Muestras y poblaciones*. Como siempre, si tiene preguntas o
preocupaciones sobre esta unidad o el progreso en clase de su hijo(a), no dude en
llamar.

Atentamente,

Conceptos importantes	**Ejemplos**
El proceso de investigación estadística Este proceso tiene cuatro partes: presentar una cuestión, recopilar los datos, analizar la distribución e interpretar el análisis según la cuestión. Cuando esté completo, los estudiantes deben comunicar los resultados.	Los estudiantes necesitan pensar en el proceso de investigación estadística, tanto si están recopilando sus propios datos como si están usando datos que les han sido proporcionados.
Diferenciar distintos tipos de datos Un *atributo* es un nombre para una característica particular de una persona, lugar o cosa sobre la cual se están recopilando los datos. Hay dos tipos generales de valores de datos: categóricos y numéricos.	Podemos tener el atributo de *tipo de mantequilla de cacahuate* para caracterizar si una mantequilla de cacahuate es natural o normal, o el atributo de *valoración de calidad* para caracterizar la calidad (usando un número) de un tipo dado de mantequilla de cacahuate. Los valores categóricos son "normales" o "naturales" para el tipo de mantequilla de cacahuate. Los valores numéricos son los números usados en la valoración de calidad para la mantequilla de cacahuate.

Comprender un conjunto de datos usando distintas representaciones

DIAGRAMA DE PUNTOS Cada caso se representa con un punto (o "x") puesto sobre una recta numérica rotulada.

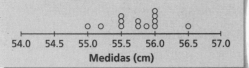

Medidas de la cabeza de Jasmine

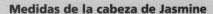

HISTOGRAMA El tamaño de la barra sobre ese intervalo muestra la frecuencia de los valores de datos en cada intervalo a lo largo del rango de los valores de datos; las frecuencias se pueden representar como cuentas o porcentajes.

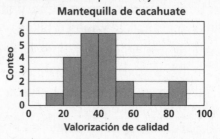

DIAGRAMA DE DISPERSIÓN La relación entre dos atributos diferentes se explora colocando los valores de dos atributos numéricos en un sistema de coordenadas cartesiano.

GRÁFICA DE CAJA Y BRAZOS La gráfica de caja se divide en cuartiles y muestra las propiedades de distribuciones, como la simetría o inclinación. Esta gráfica se desarrolló principalmente porque comparar datos usando gráficas de frecuencia a menudo puede resultar confuso, especialmente si uno está comparando más de dos gráficas de barras.

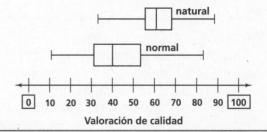

Explorar el concepto de muestreo La idea esencial detrás del muestreo es conseguir información sobre el todo analizando sólo parte de él. Un tema principal del muestreo es escoger una muestra que no sea engañosa y predictiva de la población.	Para asegurar muestras justas, tratamos de escoger muestras al azar. Los estudiantes consideran otros tipos de estrategias de muestreo: muestreo conveniente, muestreo de respuesta voluntaria y muestreo sistemático. Queremos que los estudiantes desarrollen una comprensión general y con sentido sobre lo que es un buen tamaño de muestra y cómo el tamaño de la muestra afecta a la calidad de la muestra.

En la **Página Web de CMP para los padres**, disponible en inglés, puede aprender más sobre los objetivos matemáticos de cada unidad. Vea una lista ilustrada de vocabulario y examine las soluciones de algunos problemas de ACE. **http://PHSchool.com/cmp2parents**

COMPACT
ATLAS
OF THE WORLD

LONDON, NEW YORK, MELBOURNE, MUNICH, DELHI

LONDON, NEW YORK, MELBOURNE, MUNICH, DELHI

PUBLISHER
Jonathan Metcalf

ART DIRECTOR
Bryn Walls

MANAGING CARTOGRAPHER
David Roberts

SENIOR CARTOGRAPHIC EDITOR
Simon Mumford

PROJECT CARTOGRAPHER
Paul Eames

PROJECT DESIGN
Nimbus Design, Langworth, UK

SYSTEMS CO-ORDINATOR
Philip Rowles

PRODUCTION
Sophie Argyris

First American edition 2001
Published in the United States by Dorling Kindersley Publishing, Inc.,
375 Hudson Street
New York, New York 10014

A CIP catalog record for this book is available from the Library of Congress

ISBN 9-7807-5664-2730

Reprographics by MDP Ltd., Wiltshire, UK
Printed and bound by Star Standard, Singapore

see our complete catalog at www.dk.com

Key to map symbols

Physical features

Elevation

	6000m/19,686ft
	4000m/13,124ft
	3000m/9843ft
	2000m/6562ft
	1,000m/3281ft
	500m/1640ft
	250m/820ft
	0
	Below sea level

- △   Mountain
- ▽   Depression
- ⌔   Volcano
-)(Pass/tunnel
- ▦   Sandy desert

Drainage features

- ——— Major perennial river
- ——— Minor perennial river
- – – – Seasonal river
- ——— Canal
- ı   Waterfall
- ⬭   Perennial lake
- ⬭   Seasonal lake
- ▨   Wetland

Ice features

- Permanent ice cap/ice shelf
- Winter limit of pack ice
- Summer limit of pack ice

Borders

- ▬▬▬ Full international border
- – – – – Disputed de facto border
- · · · · · Territorial claim border
- x—x—x Cease-fire line
- – – – Undefined boundary
- ——— Internal administrative boundary

Communications

- ——— Major road
- ——— Minor road
- ——— Rail
- ✈ International airport

Settlements

- ⊡   Above 500,000
- ⊙   100,000 to 500,000
- ○   50,000 to 100,000
- ○   Below 50,000
- ●   National capital
- ◉   Internal administrative capital

Miscellaneous features

- +   Site of interest
- ⊓⊔⊓⊔ Ancient wall

Graticule features

- ——— Line of latitude/longitude/Equator
- – – – Tropic/Polar circle
- 25°   Degrees of latitude/longitude

Names

Physical features

Andes *Sahara* *Ardennes*	Landscape features
Land's End	Headland
Mont Blanc *4,807m*	Elevation/volcano/pass
Blue Nile	River/canal/waterfall
Ross Ice Shelf	Ice feature
PACIFIC *OCEAN* *Sulu Sea* *Palk Strait*	Sea features
Chile Rise	Undersea feature

Regions

FRANCE	Country
JERSEY (to UK)	Dependent territory
KANSAS	Administrative region
Dordogne	Cultural region

Settlements

PARIS	Capital city
SAN JUAN	Dependent territory capital city
Chicago Kettering Burke	Other settlements

Inset map symbols

- Urban area
- City
- Park
- ▪   Place of interest
- ▫   Suburb/district

C O M P A C T
ATLAS
O F   T H E   W O R L D

Contents

The World Atlas

North &
Central America

South America

Africa

Europe

The Political World

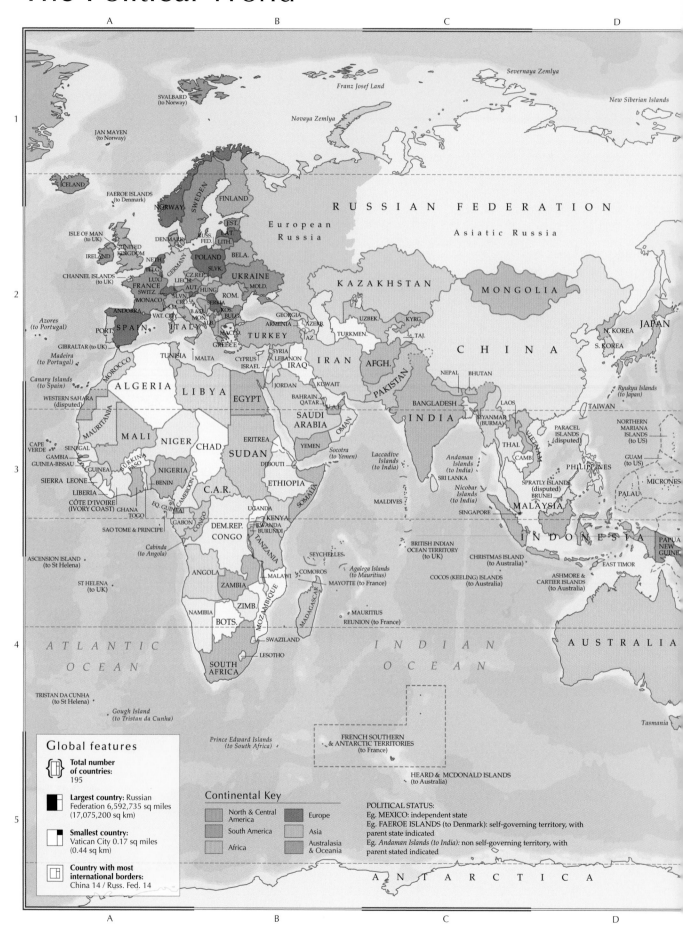

A1 B1 C1 D1
A2 B2 C2 D2
A3 B3 C3 D3
A4 B4 C4 D4
A5 B5 C5 D5

SVALBARD (to Norway)

Franz Josef Land

Severnaya Zemlya

Novaya Zemlya

New Siberian Islands

JAN MAYEN (to Norway)

ICELAND

FAEROE ISLANDS (to Denmark)

NORWAY

SWEDEN

FINLAND

R U S S I A N   F E D E R A T I O N

European Russia

Asiatic Russia

ISLE OF MAN (to UK)

DENMARK

EST.

LAT.

RUSS. FED.

LITH.

UNITED KINGDOM

IRELAND

NETH.

BELG.

GERMANY

POLAND

BELA.

CHANNEL ISLANDS (to UK)

LUX.

CZ.REP.

SLVK.

UKRAINE

LIECH.

FRANCE

SWITZ.

AUT.

HUNG.

MOLD.

K A Z A K H S T A N

M O N G O L I A

J A P A N

SLVN.

MONACO

CRO.

SERBIA

ROM.

Azores (to Portugal)

ANDORRA

B.&H.

MON.

KOS.

BULG.

GEORGIA

N. KOREA

S. KOREA

VAT. CITY

ALB.

MACED.

ARMENIA

AZERB.

UZBEK.

KYRG.

S.M.

PORT.

SPAIN

ITALY

GREECE

TURKEY

AZ.

TURKMEN.

TAJ.

C H I N A

GIBRALTAR (to UK)

Madeira (to Portugal)

TUNISIA

MALTA

CYPRUS

ISRAEL

LEBANON

SYRIA

IRAQ

I R A N

AFGH.

NEPAL

BHUTAN

Ryukyu Islands (to Japan)

Canary Islands (to Spain)

MOROCCO

WESTERN SAHARA (disputed)

A L G E R I A

L I B Y A

E G Y P T

JORDAN

KUWAIT

BAHRAIN

QATAR

U.A.E.

PAKISTAN

BANGLADESH

LAOS

TAIWAN

NORTHERN MARIANA ISLANDS (to US)

MAURITANIA

M A L I

NIGER

CHAD

ERITREA

SAUDI ARABIA

OMAN

YEMEN

Socotra (to Yemen)

I N D I A

MYANMAR (BURMA)

THAI.

Laccadive Islands (to India)

Andaman Islands (to India)

PARACEL ISLANDS (disputed)

GUAM (to US)

CAPE VERDE

SENEGAL

GAMBIA

GUINEA-BISSAU

GUINEA

BURKINA FASO

NIGERIA

BENIN

S U D A N

DJIBOUTI

ETHIOPIA

SRI LANKA

CAMB.

PHILIPPINES

MICRONES

SIERRA LEONE

LIBERIA

CÔTE D'IVOIRE (IVORY COAST)

GHANA

TOGO

CAMEROON

C.A.R.

EQ. GUINEA

GABON

CONGO

UGANDA

KENYA

RWANDA

BURUNDI

SOMALIA

MALDIVES

Nicobar Islands (to India)

SINGAPORE

SPRATLY ISLANDS (disputed)

BRUNEI

M A L A Y S I A

PALAU

SAO TOME & PRINCIPE

DEM.REP. CONGO

TANZANIA

I N D O N E S I A

PAPUA NEW GUINE

Cabinda (to Angola)

ASCENSION ISLAND (to St Helena)

ANGOLA

ZAMBIA

MALAWI

COMOROS

SEYCHELLES

Agalega Islands (to Mauritius)

MAYOTTE (to France)

BRITISH INDIAN OCEAN TERRITORY (to UK)

CHRISTMAS ISLAND (to Australia)

COCOS (KEELING) ISLANDS (to Australia)

EAST TIMOR

ASHMORE & CARTIER ISLANDS (to Australia)

ST HELENA (to UK)

MADAGASCAR

NAMIBIA

ZIMB.

BOTS.

MOZAMBIQUE

MAURITIUS

REUNION (to France)

A U S T R A L I A

SWAZILAND

A T L A N T I C   O C E A N

SOUTH AFRICA

LESOTHO

I N D I A N   O C E A N

TRISTAN DA CUNHA (to St Helena)

Gough Island (to Tristan da Cunha)

Prince Edward Islands (to South Africa)

FRENCH SOUTHERN & ANTARCTIC TERRITORIES (to France)

Tasmania

HEARD & MCDONALD ISLANDS (to Australia)

Global features

Total number of countries: 195

Largest country: Russian Federation 6,592,735 sq miles (17,075,200 sq km)

Smallest country: Vatican City 0.17 sq miles (0.44 sq km)

Country with most international borders: China 14 / Russ. Fed. 14

Continental Key

- North & Central America
- South America
- Africa
- Europe
- Asia
- Australasia & Oceania

POLITICAL STATUS:
Eg. MEXICO: independent state
Eg. FAEROE ISLANDS (to Denmark): self-governing territory, with parent state indicated
Eg. *Andaman Islands (to India)*: non self-governing territory, with parent stated indicated

A N T A R C T I C A

6

E F G H

A R C T I C

O C E A N

Queen Elizabeth Islands

GREENLAND
(to Denmark)

1

Baffin Island

Arctic Circle

Alaska
(to US)

Kurile Islands
(to Russ. Fed.)

Aleutian Islands (to US)

C A N A D A

2

P A C I F I C

O C E A N

ST PIERRE
& MIQUELON
(to France)

A T L A N T I C

UNITED STATES
OF AMERICA

O C E A N

BERMUDA
(to UK)

PUERTO RICO (to US)

MIDWAY ISLANDS
(to US)

Guadelupe
(to Mexico)

DOM. REP.

BRITISH VIRGIN ISLANDS (to UK)

VIRGIN ISLANDS (to US)

TURKS & CAICOS ISLANDS (to UK)

ANGUILLA (to UK)

Tropic of Cancer

CAYMAN ISLANDS
(to UK)

ST KITTS & NEVIS

WAKE ISLAND
(to US)

Hawai'i
(to US)

Revillagigedo
Islands
(to Mexico)

HONDURAS

BAHAMAS

BELIZE

CUBA

ANTIGUA & BARBUDA

MONTSERRAT (to UK)

GUADELOUPE (to France)

MARSHALL
ISLANDS

• JOHNSTON ATOLL (to US)

JAMAICA

NAVASSA I.
(to US)

HAITI

DOMINICA

MARTINIQUE (to France)

GUATEMALA

NETH. ANT.
(to Neth.)

ST LUCIA

WALLIS & FUTUNA
(to France)

CLIPPERTON ISLAND
(to French Polynesia)

EL SALVADOR

ARUBA
(to Neth.)

BARBADOS

3

KINGMAN REEF (to US)

NICARAGUA

ST VINCENT & THE GRENADINES

BAKER &
HOWLAND
ISLANDS
(to US)

PALMYRA ATOLL (to US)

COSTA RICA

VENEZUELA

GRENADA

TRINIDAD & TOBAGO

PANAMA

FRENCH GUIANA
(to France)

JARVIS ISLAND
(to US)

Galapagos Islands
(to Ecuador)

COLOMBIA

NAURU

GUYANA

SURINAME

Equator

ECUADOR

K I R I B A T I

SOLOMON
ISLANDS

TUVALU

TOKELAU
(to NZ)

B R A Z I L

PERU

COOK
ISLANDS
(to NZ)

VANUATU

BOLIVIA

FIJI

FRENCH POLYNESIA
(to France)

PARAGUAY

Tropic of Capricorn

NEW
CALEDONIA
(to France)

TONGA
SAMOA

NIUE (to NZ)

San Felix Island
(to Chile)

...RAL SEA ISLANDS
(Australia)

AMERICAN
SAMOA
(to US)

Easter Island
(to Chile)

Sala y Gomez
(to Chile)

San Ambrosia
Island
(to Chile)

CHILE

4

NORFOLK ISLAND
(to Australia)

PITCAIRN
ISLANDS
(to UK)

A R G E N T I N A

URUGUAY

Lord Howe Island
(to Australia)

Kermadec Island
(to NZ)

Juan Fernandez Island
(to Chile)

NEW
ZEALAND

Chatham Island
(to NZ)

P A C I F I C

Campbell Island
(to NZ)

Bounty Island
(to NZ)

O C E A N

FALKLAND ISLANDS
(to UK)

Macquarie Island (to Australia)

CHILE

ABBREVIATIONS: AFGH. Afghanistan, ALB. Albania, AUT. Austria, AZ. or AZERB. Azerbaijan, BELG. Belgium, BELA. Belarus, B.&H. Bosnia & Herzegovina, BOTS. Botswana, BULG. Bulgaria, CAMB. Cambodia, C.A.R. Central African Republic, CRO. Croatia, CZ. REP. Czech Republic, DOM. REP. Dominican Republic, EST. Estonia, HUNG. Hungary, KOS. Kosovo, KYRG. Kyrgyzstan, LAT. Latvia, LIECH. Liechtenstein, LITH. Lithuania, LUX. Luxembourg,

MACED. Macedonia, MOLD. Moldova, MON. Montenegro, NETH. Netherlands, NETH. ANT. Netherlands Antilles, PORT. Portugal, ROM. Romania, RUSS. FED. Russian Federation, S.M. San Marino, SLVK. Slovakia, SLVN. Slovenia, SWITZ. Switzerland, TAJ. Tajikistan, THAI. Thailand, TURKMEN. Turkmenistan, U.A.E. United Arab Emirates, UZBEK. Uzbekistan, VAT. CITY Vatican City, ZIMB. Zimbabwe.

SOUTH GEORGIA &
SOUTH SANDWICH ISLANDS
(to UK)

5

Antarctic Circle

ANTARCTICA

E F G H

The Physical World

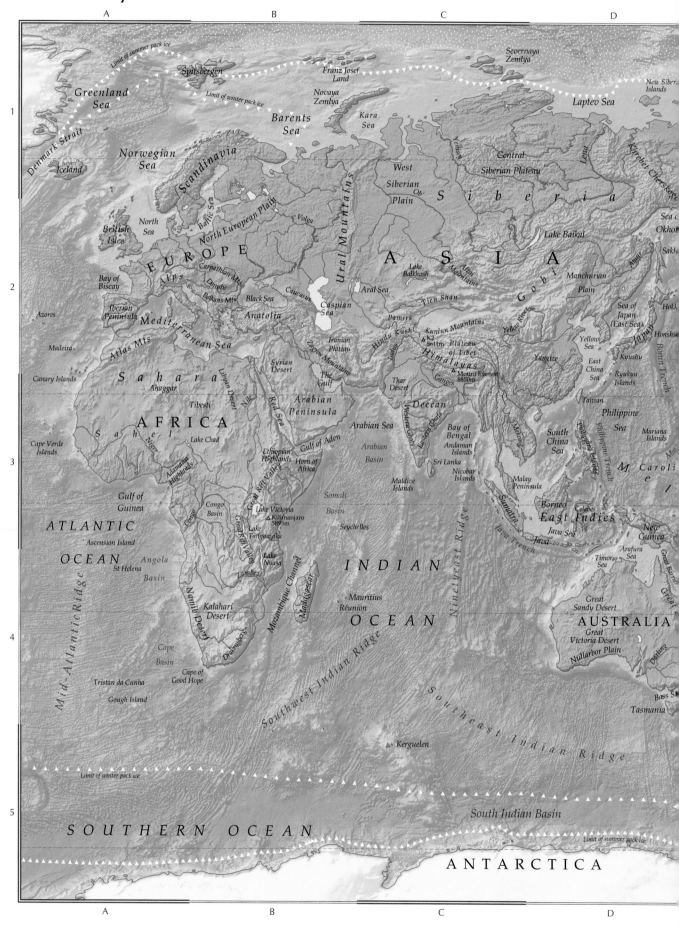

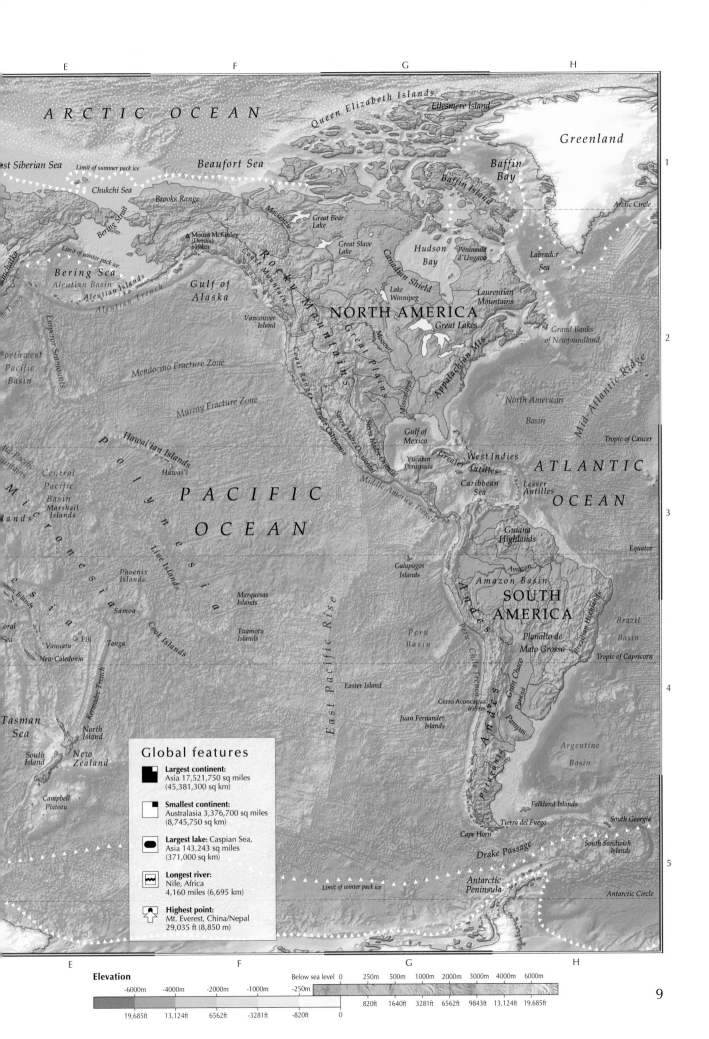

ARCTIC OCEAN

Queen Elizabeth Islands
Ellesmere Island
Greenland

East Siberian Sea
Limit of summer pack ice
Beaufort Sea
Baffin Bay
Arctic Circle
1

Chukchi Sea
Brooks Range
Baffin Island
Bering Strait
Mackenzie
Great Bear Lake
Limit of winter pack ice
△ Mount McKinley (Denali) 6194m
Coast Mountains
Great Slave Lake
Hudson Bay
Péninsule d'Ungava
Labrador Sea

Bering Sea
Aleutian Basin
Aleutian Islands
Aleutian Trench
Gulf of Alaska
Rocky Mountains
Canadian Shield
Laurentian Mountains

Northwest Pacific Basin
Emperor Seamounts
Vancouver Island
Coast Ranges
Great Plains
Lake Winnipeg
NORTH AMERICA
Great Lakes
Appalachian Mts
Grand Banks of Newfoundland
2

Mendocino Fracture Zone
Missouri
Mid-Atlantic Ridge

Murray Fracture Zone
Sierra Madre Occidental
Sierra Madre Oriental
Mississippi
North American Basin

Hawai'ian Islands
Lower California
Gulf of Mexico
Tropic of Cancer

Mid-Pacific Mountains
Central Pacific Basin
Marshall Islands
Hawai'i
Polynesia
Yucatan Peninsula
Greater Antilles
West Indies
ATLANTIC

Micronesia
Islands
PACIFIC OCEAN
Caribbean Sea
Lesser Antilles
OCEAN
3

Line Islands
Middle America Trench
Guiana Highlands

Phoenix Islands
Galapagos Islands
Amazon
Equator

Solomon Islands
Marquesas Islands
Amazon Basin
SOUTH AMERICA
Brazilian Highlands
Brazil Basin

Coral Sea
Samoa
Tuamotu Islands
Peru Basin
Andes
Planalto de Mato Grosso

Vanuatu Fiji Tonga
Cook Islands
Peru-Chile Trench
Gran Chaco
Paraná
Tropic of Capricorn

New Caledonia
East Pacific Rise
Gran Chaco
Pampas
Argentine Basin
4

Tasman Sea
Kermadec Trench
North Island
Easter Island
Cerro Aconcagua 6959m
Patagonia

South Island
New Zealand
Juan Fernandez Islands

Campbell Plateau
Falkland Islands

Global features

■ **Largest continent:**
Asia 17,521,750 sq miles
(45,381,300 sq km)

□ **Smallest continent:**
Australasia 3,376,700 sq miles
(8,745,750 sq km)

● **Largest lake:** Caspian Sea,
Asia 143,243 sq miles
(371,000 sq km)

〰 **Longest river:**
Nile, Africa
4,160 miles (6,695 km)

⛰ **Highest point:**
Mt. Everest, China/Nepal
29,035 ft (8,850 m)

South Georgia
Tierra del Fuego
Cape Horn
South Sandwich Islands

Drake Passage
Limit of winter pack ice
Antarctic Peninsula
Antarctic Circle
5

Elevation

| | | | | | Below sea level 0 | 250m | 500m | 1000m | 2000m | 3000m | 4000m | 6000m |

-6000m   -4000m   -2000m   -1000m   -250m

19,685ft   13,124ft   6562ft   -3281ft   -820ft   0

820ft   1640ft   3281ft   6562ft   9843ft   13,124ft   19,685ft

Time zones

The numbers at the top of the map indicate how many hours each time zone is ahead or behind Coordinated Universal Time (UTC). The row of clocks indicate the time in each zone when it is 12:00 noon UTC.

TIME ZONES

Because Earth is a rotating sphere, the Sun shines on only half of its surface at any one time. Thus, it is simultaneously morning, evening, and night time in different parts of the world. Because of these disparities, each country or part of a country adheres to a local time. A region of the Earth's surface within which a single local time is used is called a time zone.

COORDINATED UNIVERSAL TIME (UTC)

Coordinated Universal Time (UTC) is a reference by which the local time in each time zone is set. UTC is a successor to, and closely approximates, Greenwich Mean Time (GMT). However, UTC is based on an atomic clock, whereas GMT is determined by the Sun's position in the sky relative to the 0° longitudinal meridian, which runs through Greenwich, UK.

THE INTERNATIONAL DATELINE

The International Dateline is an imaginary line from pole to pole that roughly corresponds to the 180° longitudinal meridian. It is an arbitrary marker between calendar days. The dateline is needed because of the use of local times around the world rather than a single universal time.

The
WORLD
ATLAS

North & Central America

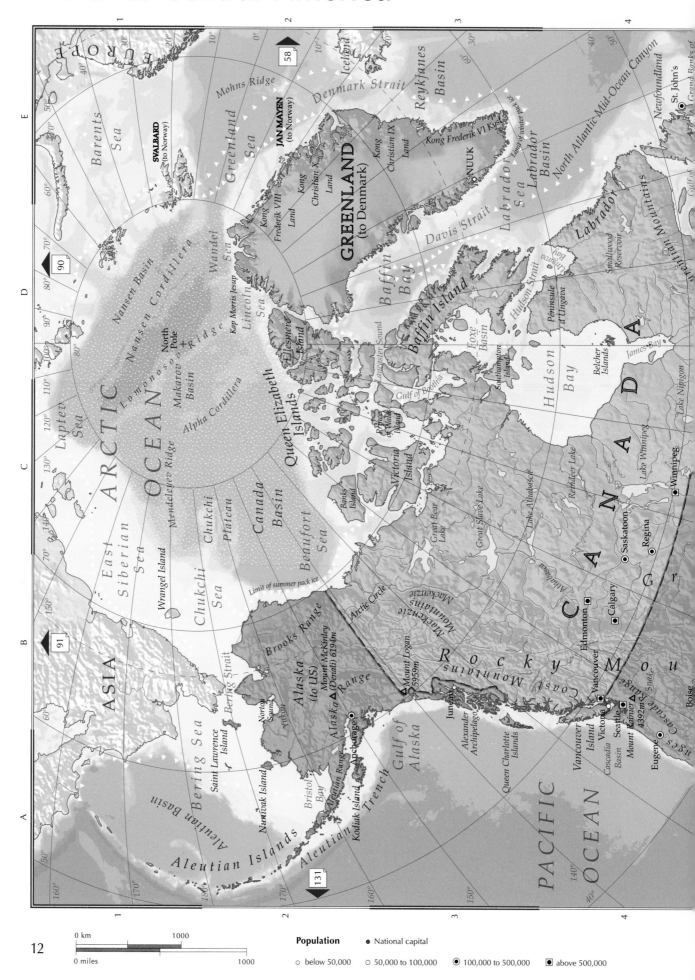

EUROPE

Barents Sea

SVALBARD
(to Norway)

Mohns Ridge

Greenland Sea

JAN MAYEN
(to Norway)

58

Denmark Strait

Iceland

Reykjanes Basin

30°

60°

50°

North Atlantic Mid-Ocean Canyon

Newfoundland

St. John's

Grand Banks of...

Kong Christian IX Land

Kong Frederik VI Kyst

NUUK

North Atlantic...

Labrador Basin

Labrador Sea

90

Nansen Basin

Wandel Sea

Kong Frederik VIII Land

Kong Christian X Land

GREENLAND
(to Denmark)

Davis Strait

Labrador

Labrador Mountains

Nansen Cordillera

Kap Morris Jesup

Lincoln Sea

Baffin Bay

Smallwood Reservoir

North Pole +

Lomonosov Ridge

Makarov Basin

Ellesmere Island

Queen Elizabeth Islands

Péninsule d'Ungava

James Bay

Mendeleyev Ridge

Alpha Cordillera

ARCTIC OCEAN

Lancaster Sound

Foxe Basin

Hudson Strait

Belcher Islands

Lake Nipigon

Laptev Sea

Canada Basin

Banks Island

Victoria Island

Prince of Wales Island

Gulf of Boothia

Southampton Island

Hudson Bay

Reindeer Lake

Lake Winnipeg

Winnipeg

Chukchi Plateau

Beaufort Sea

Great Bear Lake

Lake Athabasca

Saskatoon

Regina

East Siberian Sea

Chukchi Sea

Limit of summer pack ice

Great Slave Lake

C A N A D A

Athabasca

Gr

Wrangel Island

Arctic Circle

Mackenzie Mountains

Mackenzie

Rocky Mountains

Calgary

Edmonton

91

Bering Strait

Brooks Range

Mount McKinley (Denali) 6194m

Mount Logan 5959m

ASIA

Norton Sound

Yukon

Alaska (to US)

Alaska Range

Coast Mountains

Vancouver

R o c k y   M o u

Seattle

Boise

Saint Lawrence Island

Nunivak Island

Anchorage

Juneau

Alexander Archipelago

Victoria

Mount Rainier 4392m

Cascade Range

Bering Sea

Bristol Bay

Kodiak Island

Aleutian Range

Gulf of Alaska

Queen Charlotte Islands

Vancouver Island

Cascadia Basin

Snake

Eugene

Aleutian Basin

Aleutian Islands

Aleutian Trench

131

PACIFIC OCEAN

40°

12

0 km   1000

0 miles   1000

Population   ● National capital

○ below 50,000   ◎ 50,000 to 100,000   ◉ 100,000 to 500,000   ■ above 500,000

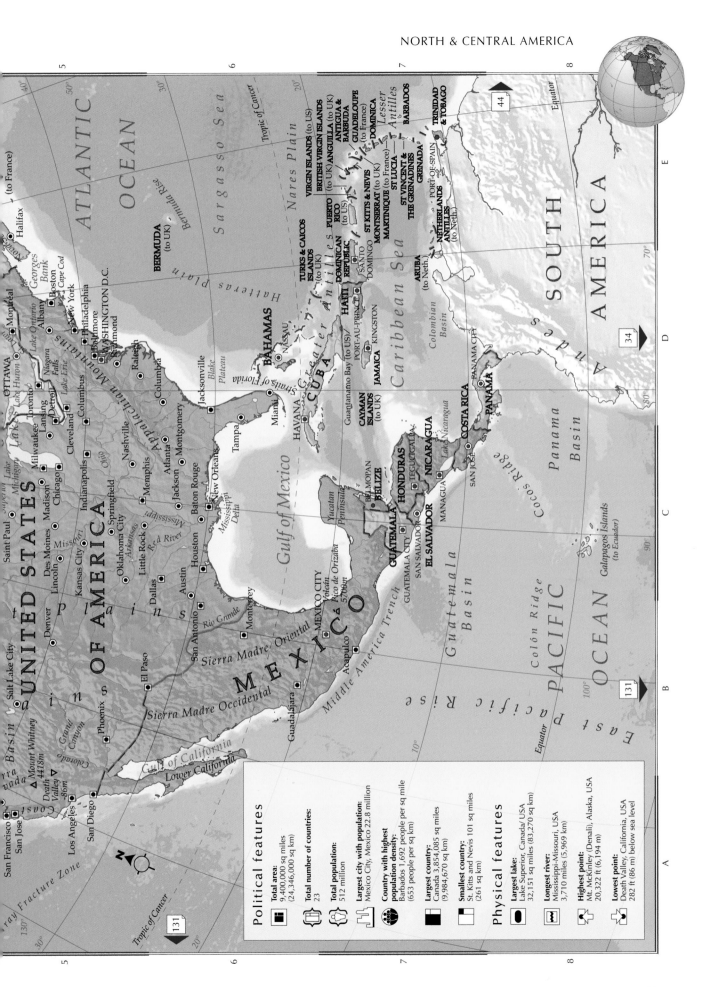

Political features

Total area:
9,400,000 sq miles
(24,346,000 sq km)

Total number of countries:
23

Total population:
512 million

Largest city with population:
Mexico City, Mexico 22.8 million

**Country with highest
population density:**
Barbados 1,692 people per sq mile
(653 people per sq km)

Largest country:
Canada 3,854,085 sq miles
(9,984,670 sq km)

Smallest country:
St. Kitts and Nevis 101 sq miles
(261 sq km)

Physical features

Largest lake:
Lake Superior, Canada / USA
32,151 sq miles (83,270 sq km)

Longest river:
Mississippi-Missouri, USA
3,710 miles (5,969 km)

Highest point:
Mt. McKinley (Denali), Alaska, USA
20,322 ft (6,194 m)

Lowest point:
Death Valley, California, USA
282 ft (86 m) below sea level

Western Canada & Alaska

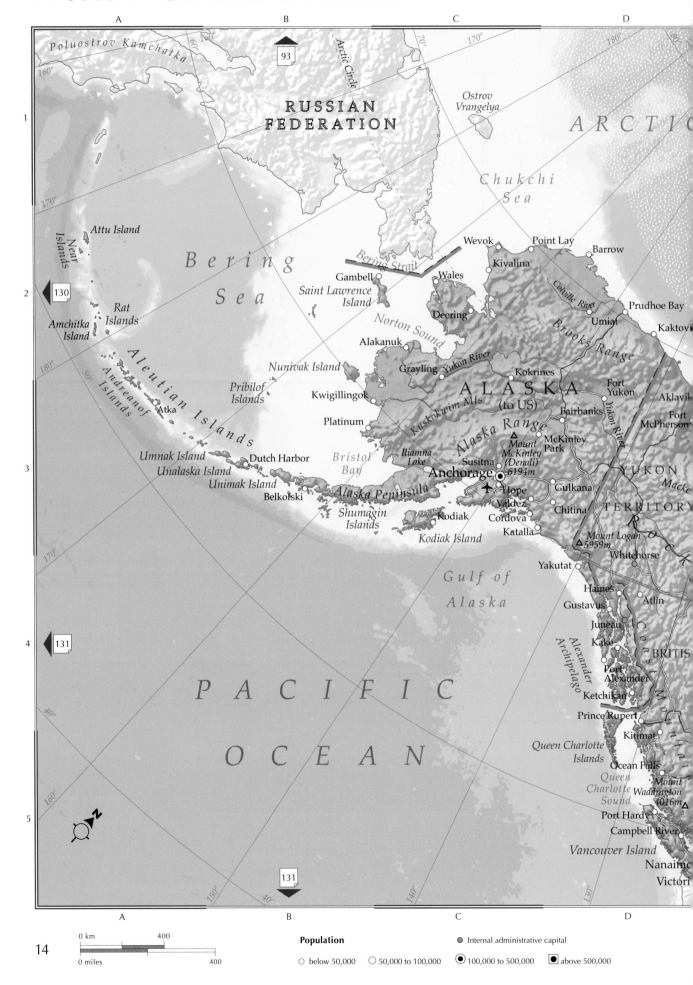

Poluostrov Kamchatka

93

Arctic Circle

RUSSIAN FEDERATION

Ostrov Vrangelya

A R C T I C

Chukchi Sea

Near Islands

Attu Island

130

Rat Islands

Amchitka Island

B e r i n g

S e a

Saint Lawrence Island

Gambell

Wales

Bering Strait

Wevok

Point Lay

Barrow

Kivalina

Deering

Colville River

Prudhoe Bay

Umiat

Kaktovi

Brooks Range

Alakanuk

Norton Sound

Grayling

Yukon River

Kokrines

A L A S K A
(to US)

Fort Yukon

Aklavik

Fort McPherson

Nunivak Island

Pribilof Islands

Kwigillingok

Kuskokwim Mts

Fairbanks

Yukon River

A l e u t i a n   I s l a n d s

Andreanof Islands

Atka

Platinum

Alaska Range

McKinley Park

Mount McKinley (Denali) 6194m

Umnak Island

Unalaska Island

Dutch Harbor

Unimak Island

Belkofski

Bristol Bay

Iliamna Lake

Susitna

Anchorage

Hope

Gulkana

Chitina

Y U K O N

Mackenzie

Alaska Peninsula

Shumagin Islands

Kodiak

Valdez

Cordova

Katalla

T E R R I T O R Y

Kodiak Island

Mount Logan 5959m

Whitehorse

Yakutat

Mount Waddington 4016m

G u l f   o f

A l a s k a

Haines

Gustavus

Atlin

131

Juneau

Kake

BRITIS

Alexander Archipelago

Port Alexander

Ketchikan

P A C I F I C

Prince Rupert

Kitimat

Queen Charlotte Islands

Ocean Falls

Queen Charlotte Sound

O C E A N

Port Hardy

Campbell River

Vancouver Island

Nanaim

Victori

131

0 km   400

0 miles   400

Population

○ below 50,000   ◯ 50,000 to 100,000   ◉ 100,000 to 500,000   ◼ above 500,000

● Internal administrative capital

E   F   G   H

133

GREENLAND
(to Denmark)

Knud Rasmussen Land

Alert

Ellesmere Island

Narces Strait

Axel Heiberg Island

Ellef Ringnes Island

Isachsen

Amund Ringnes Island

Baffin Bay

Arctic Circle

60

Prince Patrick Island

Mould Bay

Devon Island

Bathurst Island

Cornwallis Island

Lancaster Sound

Melville Island

Resolute
(Qausuittuq)

Banks Island

Viscount Melville Sound

Somerset Island

Brodeur Peninsula

Baffin Island

Davis Strait

chs Harbour
(Ikaahuk)

ktoyaktuk

Amundsen Gulf

Holman

McClintock Channel

Prince of Wales Island

Boothia Peninsula

Gulf of Boothia

Igloolik

Cumberland Sound

rik

Paulatuk

Victoria Island

King William Island

Kugaaruk
(Pelly Bay)

Melville Peninsula

Foxe Basin

Nettilling Lake

Fort
Good Hope

Kugluktuk
(Coppermine)

Cambridge Bay
(Ikaluktutiak)

Gjoa Haven
(Uqsuqtuuq)

Amadjuak Lake

Iqaluit
(Frobisher Bay)

Great Bear Lake

Echo Bay

Burnside

Repulse Bay

Southampton Island

Hudson Strait

Mackenzie

Back

N U N A V U T

Garry Lake

Coral Harbour

Péninsule d'Ungava

N O R T H W E S T

Baker Lake

Coats Island

Mansel Island

gsten

T E R R I T O R I E S

Edzo   Yellowknife   Reliance

Dubawnt

Rankin Inlet

Whale Cove

Q U É B E C

Fort Simpson

Great Slave Lake

Lutselk'e
(Snowdrift)

Arviat

H u d s o n

Fort Providence

Fort Liard

Hay River

Fort Smith

Lake Athabasca

B a y

Fort Nelson

LUMBIA

re

16

C A N A D A

Fort Vermilion

Reindeer Lake

Southern Indian Lake

Nelson

Churchill

James Bay

Fort St. John

Wollaston Lake

Belcher Islands

A L B E R T A

Grande Prairie

Fort McMurray

Buffalo Narrows

Lynn Lake

Thompson

rince George

Athabasca

S A S K A T C H E W A N

Flin Flon

O N T A R I O

Athabasca

Edmonton

North Saskatchewan

The Pas

Lake Winnipeg

Mount Robson 3954m

Leduc

Saskatchewan

M A N I T O B A

Red Deer

Prince Albert

Saskatoon

Kamloops

Calgary

Kindersley

Yorkton

Lake Manitoba

Winnipeg

Lake Superior

Kelowna

Regina

Qu'Appelle

Brandon

Lake of the Woods

Lake Huron

ncouver

Cranbrook

Medicine Hat

Lethbridge

Weyburn

Melita

Estevan

Lake Michigan

23

Milk River

U N I T E D   S T A T E S   O F   A M E R I C A

E   F   G   H

1

2

3

4

5

Elevation

-8000m -6000m -4000m -2000m -1000m -500m -250m	Below sea level 0 250m 500m 1000m 2000m 3000m 4000m 6000m	

26,246ft 19,685ft 13,124ft 6562ft -3281ft -1640ft -820ft -100m/-328ft

820ft 1640ft 3281ft 6562ft 9843ft 13,124ft 19,685ft

15

Eastern Canada

NORTHWEST TERRITORIES

NUNAVUT

SASKATCHEWAN

Churchill

Southern Indian Lake

Nelson

Hayes

MANITOBA

Cedar Lake

Lake Winnipeg

Lake Winnipegosis

Lake Manitoba

Coats Island

Mansel Island

Ivujivik

Charles Island

Hudson

HUDSON BAY

Ottawa Islands

Inukjuak (Port Harrison)

Péninsule d'Ungava

Rivière a Feuill

Lac Minto

Fort Severn

Belcher Islands

Bien

Peawanuk

Severn

Winisk

Sandy Lake

C A N

James Bay

Akimiski Island

Attawapiskat

O N T A R I O

Attawapiskat

Albany

Fort Albany

Moosonee

Moose

Harricana

QU

Eastmain

Rivière de Rupert

Lac Mistassini

Lac Seul

Armstrong

Chibougamau

Kenora

Dryden

Lake of the Woods

Lake Nipigon

Longlac

Hearst

Kapuskasing

Réservoir Gouin

Red River

Fort Frances

Atikokan

Nipigon

Marathon

Tip Top Mountain △ 640m

Cochrane

Timmins

Amos

Rouyn-Noranda

NORTH DAKOTA

Rainy Lake

Thunder Bay

Lake Superior

Foleyet

Wawa

Kirkland Lake

Val-d'Or

MINNESOTA

MICHIGAN

Sault Ste.Marie

Sudbury

North Bay

SOUTH DAKOTA

Manitoulin Island

Georgian Bay

Pembroke

Gatineau

Hull

OTTAWA

La

UNITED STATES

WISCONSIN

Lake Michigan

Lake Huron

Midland

Peterborough

Kingston

OF AMERICA

NEBRASKA

IOWA

Brampton

Kitchener

Sarnia

Hamilton

London

Oshawa

Toronto

St.Catharines

Niagara Falls

Lake Ontari

NEW YORK

Windsor

Mississippi River

ILLINOIS

Leamington

Lake Erie

INDIANA

OHIO

PENNSYLVANIA

0 km   300
0 miles   300

Population   ● National capital   ● Internal administrative capital

○ below 50,000   ○ 50,000 to 100,000   ◉ 100,000 to 500,000   ▣ above 500,000

E F G H

65° 60° 55° 60° 50° 45° 40°

60

1

Baffin Island 65°

Resolution Island

Strait

Button Islands

Akpatok Island

Ungava Bay

Kuujjuaq

Rivière à la Baleine

Caniapiscau

Nain

Hopedale

Makkovik

Cape Harrison

L a b r a d o r   S e a

55° 40°

44 2

50°

Schefferville

Cartwright

N E W F O U N D L A N D

Smallwood Reservoir

Lake Melville

Churchill

St.Anthony

&   L A B R A D O R

Réservoir de Caniapiscau

E C D

Gagnon

Réservoir Manicouagan

Laurentian Mountains

Havre-St-Pierre

A

Strait of Belle Isle

Gander

Grand Falls

Newfoundland

St.John's

3

Corner Brook

Île d'Anticosti

Sept-Îles

Baie-Comeau

St. Lawrence

Péninsule de Gaspé

Gaspé

Gulf of St. Lawrence

Channel-Port aux Basques

Cape Race

45°

Lac St-Jean

quière

Chicoutimi

Matane

Rimouski

Îles de la Madeleine

Cabot Strait

ST PIERRE & MIQUELON (to France)

50°

la Tuque

Rivière-du-Loup

Edmundston

Bathurst

PRINCE EDWARD ISLAND

Glace Bay

Sydney

44 4

Charlesbourg

NEW BRUNSWICK

Charlottetown

Cape Breton Island

Québec

Moncton

Amherst

New Glasgow

Trois-Rivières

St-Georges

Oromocto

Truro

Drummondville

Fredericton

NOVA SCOTIA

ontréal

Saint John

MAINE

Dartmouth

Sable Island

Sherbrooke

Bay of Fundy

Halifax

Liverpool

Yarmouth

A T L A N T I C

40°

VERMONT

NEW HAMPSHIRE

5

Cape Cod

O C E A N

N

44

CONNECTICUT RHODE ISLAND 70°

65° 40° 60° 55°

E F G H

Elevation

| Below sea level | 0 | 250m | 500m | 1000m | 2000m | 3000m | 4000m | 6000m |

-8000m -6000m -4000m -2000m -1000m -500m -250m

820ft 1640ft 3281ft 6562ft 9843ft 13,124ft 19,685ft

26,246ft 19,685ft 13,124ft 6562ft -3281ft -1640ft -820ft -100m/-328ft

17

USA: The Northeast

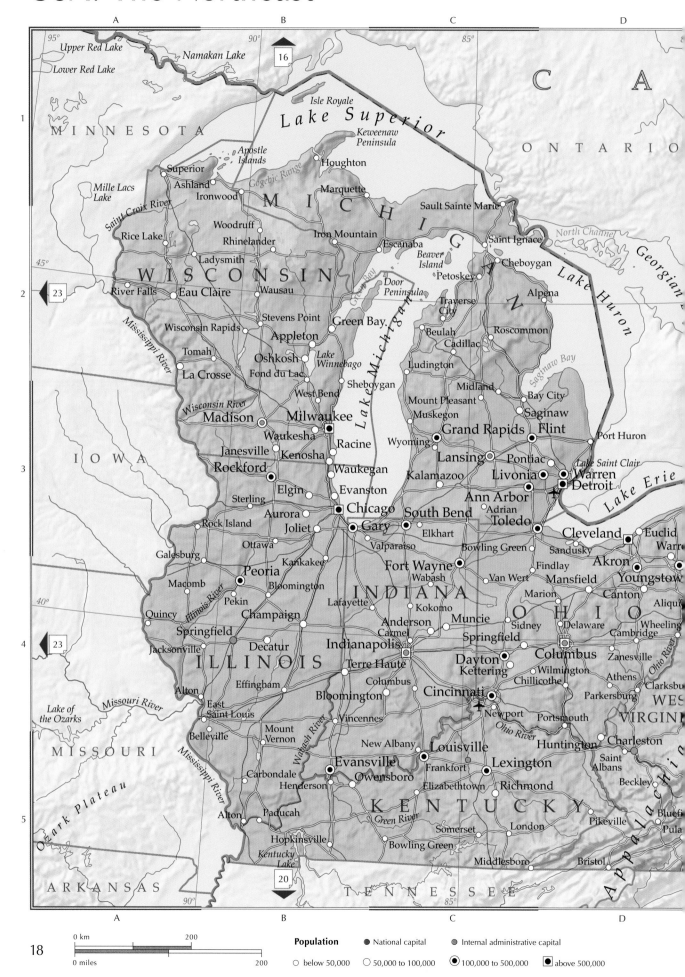

Population ● National capital ● Internal administrative capital
○ below 50,000 ○ 50,000 to 100,000 ◉ 100,000 to 500,000 ■ above 500,000

0 km   200
0 miles   200

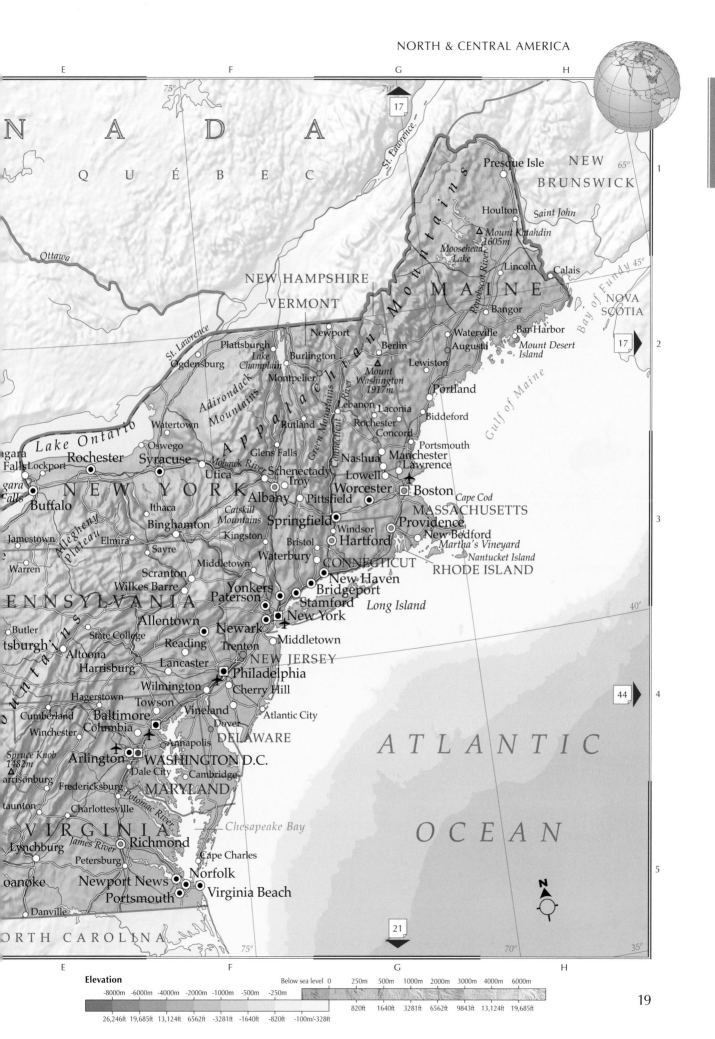

USA: The Southeast

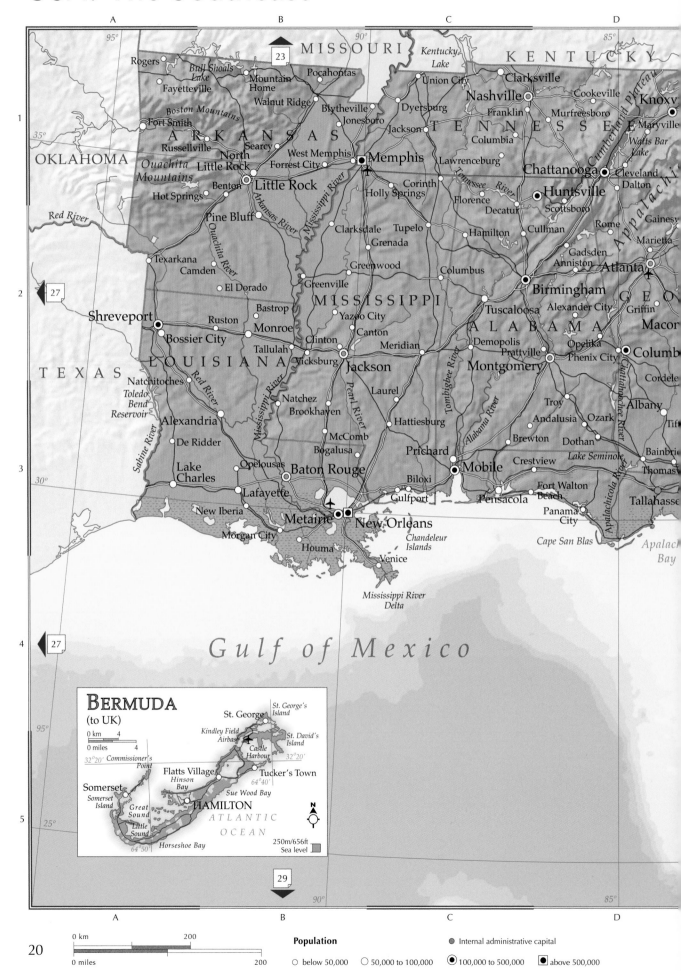

Population

○ below 50,000   ○ 50,000 to 100,000   ◉ 100,000 to 500,000   ■ above 500,000

● Internal administrative capital

MISSOURI

KENTUCKY

Rogers
Fayetteville
Bull Shoals Lake
Mountain Home
Pocahontas
Walnut Ridge
Blytheville
Kentucky Lake
Union City
Clarksville
Nashville
Cookeville
Cumberland Plateau
Knoxv
Fort Smith
Boston Mountains
Searcy
Jonesboro
Dyersburg
Franklin
Murfreesboro
Maryville
ARKANSAS
Russellville
Jackson
Columbia
Watts Bar Lake
TENNESSEE
North Little Rock
West Memphis
Memphis
Lawrenceburg
Chattanooga
Cleveland
OKLAHOMA
Ouachita Mountains
Little Rock
Forrest City
Corinth
Florence
Huntsville
Dalton
Benton
Holly Springs
Decatur
Scottsboro
Appalachi
Hot Springs
Red River
Tennessee River
Hamilton
Cullman
Gainesy
Pine Bluff
Clarksdale
Tupelo
Rome
Ouachita River
Greenwood
Grenada
Gadsden
Marietta
Texarkana
Columbus
Anniston
Atlanta
Camden
Greenville
MISSISSIPPI
Birmingham
GEO
El Dorado
Yazoo City
Tuscaloosa
Alexander City
Griffin
SHREVEPORT
Bastrop
Macor
Ruston
Monroe
Canton
ALABAMA
Bossier City
Clinton
Demopolis
Opelika
Columb
LOUISIANA
Tallulah
Vicksburg
Meridian
Prattville
Phenix City
Cordele
TEXAS
Jackson
Montgomery
Natchitoches
Red River
Natchez
Laurel
Troy
Albany
Toledo Bend Reservoir
Brookhaven
Andalusia
Ozark
Tift
Alexandria
Hattiesburg
Brewton
Dothan
Sabine River
De Ridder
McComb
Prichard
Crestview
Lake Seminole
Bainbri
Lake Charles
Opelousas
Bogalusa
Mobile
Fort Walton Beach
Thomasv
Baton Rouge
Biloxi
Pensacola
Tombigbee River
Lafayette
Gulfport
Panama City
Alabama River
Apalachicola River
Tallahasse
New Iberia
Metairie
New Orleans
Cape San Blas
Apalach Bay
Morgan City
Houma
Chandeleur Islands
Venice
Mississippi River
Pearl River
Apalachicola River
Mississippi River Delta

Gulf of Mexico

BERMUDA
(to UK)

0 km 4
0 miles 4

Commissioner's Point
St. George
St. George's Island
Kindley Field Airbase
St. David's Island
Castle Harbour
Flatts Village
Hinson Bay
Tucker's Town
Somerset
Somerset Island
Sue Wood Bay
Great Sound
HAMILTON
ATLANTIC OCEAN
Little Sound
Horseshoe Bay

250m/656ft
Sea level

N

0 km   200
0 miles   200

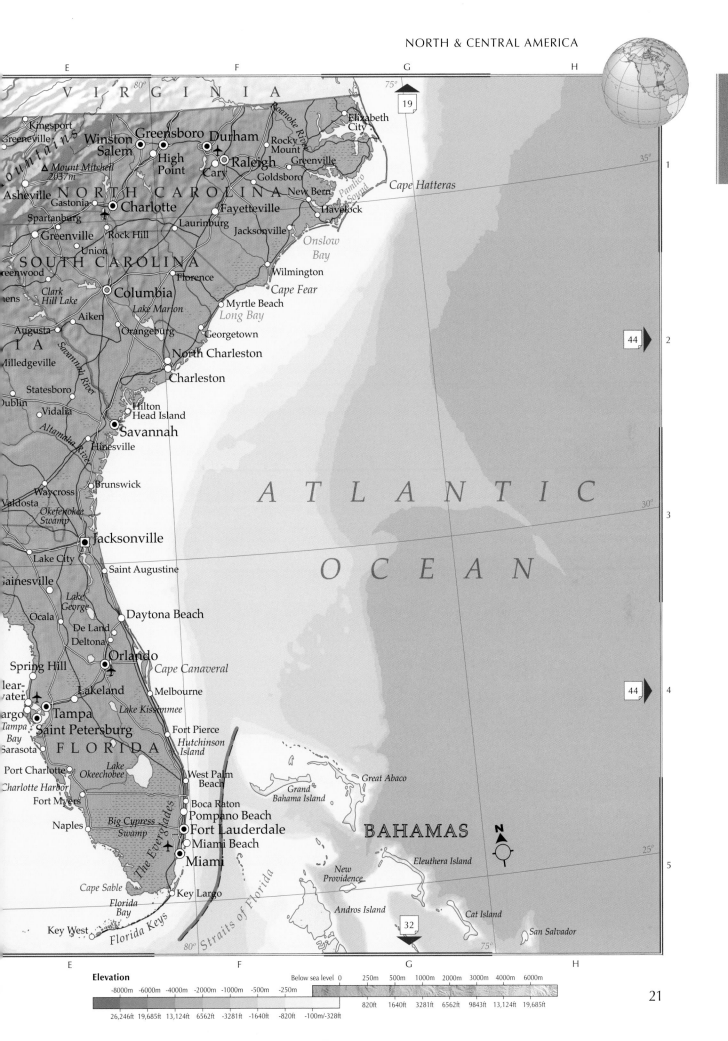

VIRGINIA

Kingsport
Greeneville
Winston Salem
Greensboro
Durham
High Point
Cary
Raleigh
Goldsboro
Rocky Mount
Greenville
Elizabeth City
Mount Mitchell 2037m
Asheville
NORTH CAROLINA
New Bern
Havelock
Cape Hatteras
Gastonia
Charlotte
Fayetteville
Spartanburg
Laurinburg
Jacksonville
Onslow Bay
Greenville
Rock Hill
SOUTH CAROLINA
Union
Pamlico Sound
Greenwood
Florence
Wilmington
Cape Fear
Milledgeville
Columbia
Clark Hill Lake
Lake Marion
Myrtle Beach
Long Bay
Aiken
Augusta
Orangeburg
Georgetown
IA
Savannah River
North Charleston
Statesboro
Charleston
Dublin
Vidalia
Hilton Head Island
Altamaha River
Savannah
Hinesville
Brunswick
ATLANTIC
Waycross
Valdosta
Okefenokee Swamp
Jacksonville
OCEAN
Lake City
Saint Augustine
Gainesville
Lake George
Daytona Beach
Ocala
De Land
Deltona
Orlando
Spring Hill
Cape Canaveral
Clear-water
Lakeland
Melbourne
argo
Tampa
Lake Kissimmee
Saint Petersburg
Fort Pierce
Tampa Bay
Hutchinson Island
Sarasota
FLORIDA
Port Charlotte
Lake Okeechobee
West Palm Beach
Charlotte Harbor
Fort Myers
Boca Raton
Great Abaco
Naples
Big Cypress Swamp
Pompano Beach
Fort Lauderdale
Grand Bahama Island
Miami Beach
BAHAMAS
The Everglades
Miami
Cape Sable
Eleuthera Island
Key Largo
New Providence
Florida Bay
Andros Island
Cat Island
Key West
Florida Keys
San Salvador
Straits of Florida

Roanoke River

75°
80°
35°
30°
25°

19
44
44
32

E   F   G   H

N

Elevation

| Below sea level | 0 | 250m | 500m | 1000m | 2000m | 3000m | 4000m | 6000m |

-8000m -6000m -4000m -2000m -1000m -500m -250m

820ft 1640ft 3281ft 6562ft 9843ft 13,124ft 19,685ft

26,246ft 19,685ft 13,124ft 6562ft -3281ft -1640ft -820ft -100m/-328ft

21

USA: Central States

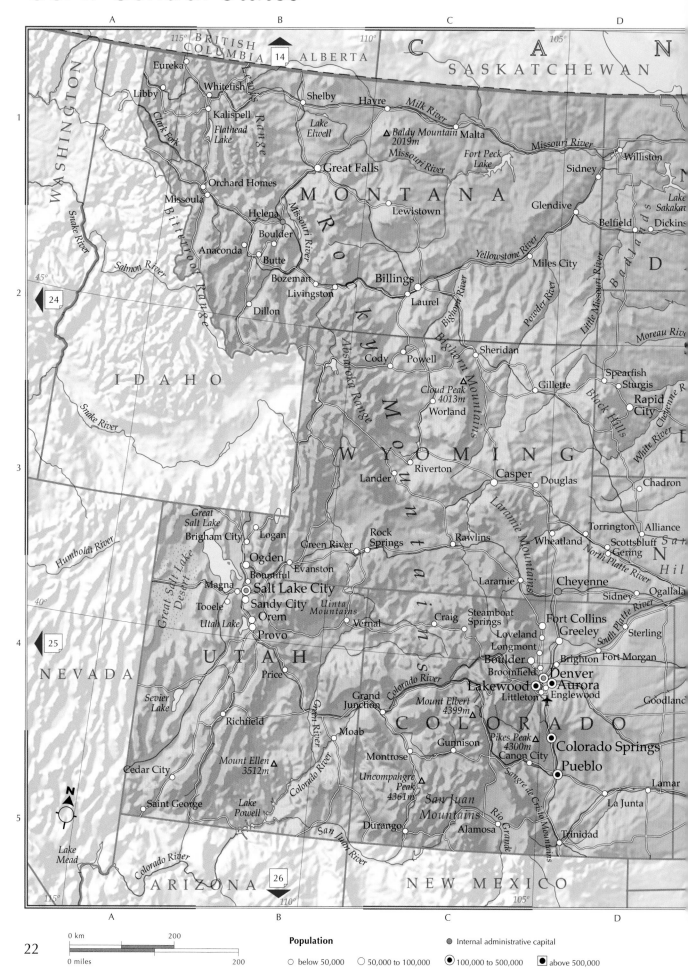

A   B   C   D

BRITISH COLUMBIA   **ALBERTA**   C   A   N

14

SASKATCHEWAN

115°   110°   105°

Eureka

Libby   Whitefish   Shelby   Havre   Milk River

Kalispell   Lake Elwell   △ Baldy Mountain 2019m   Malta   Missouri River   Williston

Flathead Lake   Missouri River   Fort Peck Lake   Sidney

1

Great Falls   M O N T A N A   Glendive   Belfield   Dickins

Orchard Homes   Lewistown   Lake Sakakar

Missoula   Helena   Yellowstone River   Miles City

Boulder   Anaconda   Butte   Billings   Laurel   Powder River   Little Missouri River

45°   Bozeman   Livingston

24   Dillon   Cody   Powell   Sheridan   Moreau River

2

Cloud Peak 4013m   Spearfish   Sturgis

I D A H O   Worland   Gillette   Rapid City

Snake River   W Y O M I N G

Riverton   Casper   Douglas   Chadron

Lander

3

Great Salt Lake   Torrington   Alliance

Brigham City   Logan   Green River   Rock Springs   Rawlins   Wheatland   Scottsbluff   Gering

Ogden   Evanston   Laramie   Cheyenne

Bountiful   Magna   **Salt Lake City**   Sidney   Ogallala

40°   Tooele   Sandy City   Orem   Uinta Mountains   Craig   Steamboat Springs   Fort Collins

25   Utah Lake   Provo   Vernal   Loveland   Greeley   Sterling

4

N E V A D A   U T A H   Price   Longmont   Brighton   Fort Morgan

Boulder   Broomfield   **Denver**

Lakewood   Aurora

Grand Junction   Littleton   Englewood   Goodland

Sevier Lake   Mount Elbert 4399m   C O L O R A D O

Richfield   Moab   Gunnison   Pikes Peak 4300m △   **Colorado Springs**

Cedar City   Mount Ellen 3512m △   Montrose   Canon City   Pueblo

Uncompahgre Peak 4361m △   San Juan Mountains   Lamar

Saint George   Lake Powell   Durango   Alamosa   Trinidad   La Junta

5

Lake Mead   Colorado River   San Juan River

115°   A R I Z O N A   26   N E W   M E X I C O   105°

110°

A   B   C   D

0 km   200   **Population**   ● Internal administrative capital

0 miles   200

○ below 50,000   ○ 50,000 to 100,000   ◉ 100,000 to 500,000   ◼ above 500,000

22

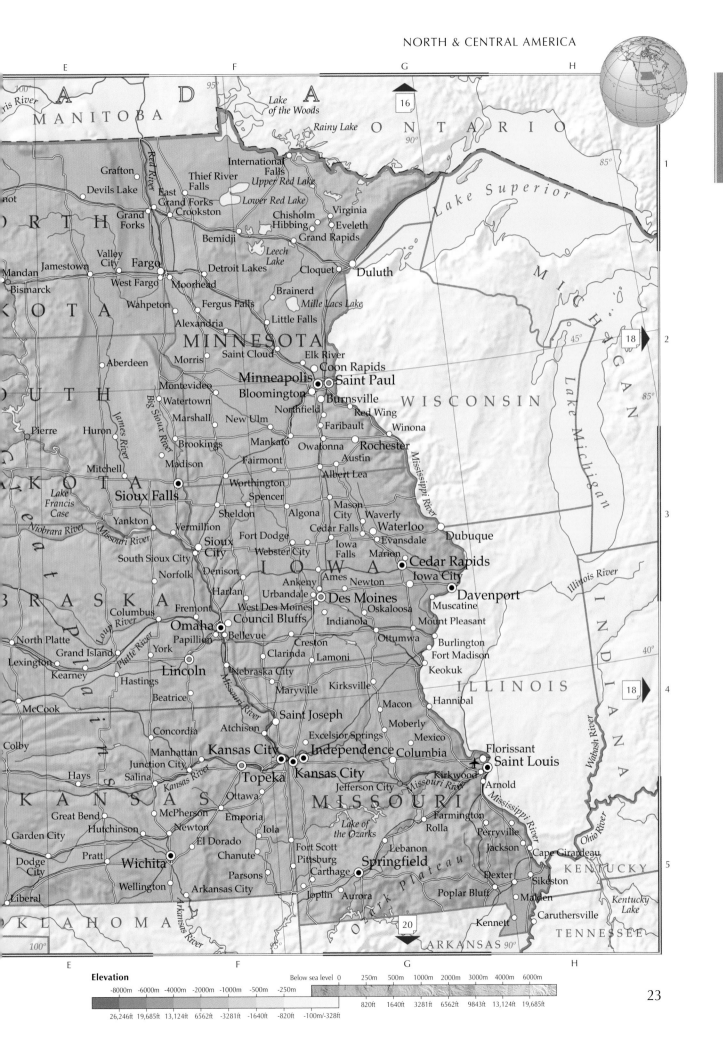

MANITOBA

CANADA

Red River
Lake
of the Woods

Grafton

Devils Lake

Thief River
Falls

International
Falls

Upper Red Lake

ONTARIO

Rainy Lake

Lake Superior

East
Grand Forks

Grand
Forks

Crookston

Bemidji

Lower Red Lake

Chisholm
Hibbing

Virginia
Eveleth

Grand Rapids

M I C H I G A N

Valley
City

Fargo

West Fargo

Moorhead

Detroit Lakes

Leech
Lake

Cloquet

Duluth

Lake Michigan

Mandan

Jamestown

NORTH

Bismarck

Wahpeton

Fergus Falls

Brainerd

Mille Lacs Lake

Little Falls

Aberdeen

DAKOTA

SOUTH

Morris

Alexandria

MINNESOTA

Saint Cloud

Elk River

Coon Rapids

Minneapolis

Saint Paul

WISCONSIN

Pierre

Huron

James River

Montevideo

Watertown

Marshall

Bloomington

Northfield

Burnsville

Red Wing

Winona

Big Sioux River

New Ulm

Brookings

Madison

Mankato

Fairmont

Owatonna

Faribault

Rochester

Austin

Mississippi River

Mitchell

Sioux Falls

Worthington

Spencer

Albert Lea

Lake
Francis
Case

Niobrara River

Missouri River

Yankton

Vermillion

Sheldon

Algona

Mason
City

Waverly

Cedar Falls

Waterloo

Evansdale

Dubuque

Sioux
City

Fort Dodge

Webster City

I O W A

Iowa
Falls

Marion

Cedar Rapids

Iowa City

South Sioux City

Denison

Ames

Newton

Illinois River

Norfolk

Harlan

Ankeny

Urbandale

Des Moines

Oskaloosa

Davenport

Muscatine

N E B R A S K A

Columbus

Loup River

Fremont

West Des Moines

Indianola

Mount Pleasant

North Platte

Platte River

Omaha

Papillion

Bellevue

Creston

Ottumwa

Burlington

Fort Madison

Grand Island

York

Clarinda

Lamoni

Keokuk

Lexington

Lincoln

Nebraska City

Kearney

Hastings

Maryville

Kirksville

Hannibal

I L L I N O I S

McCook

Beatrice

Saint Joseph

Macon

Moberly

Colby

Concordia

Atchison

Excelsior Springs

Mexico

Columbia

Florissant

Missouri River

Manhattan

Kansas City

Independence

Saint Louis

Kirkwood

Hays

Junction City

Salina

Kansas River

Kansas City

Jefferson City

Arnold

Topeka

M I S S O U R I

Missouri River

Mississippi River

K A N S A S

Ottawa

Farmington

Rolla

Perryville

Jackson

Great Bend

McPherson

Emporia

Lake of
the Ozarks

Lebanon

Ohio River

Garden City

Hutchinson

Newton

El Dorado

Iola

Fort Scott

Pittsburg

Springfield

Ozark Plateau

Dexter

Sikeston

Cape Girardeau

KENTUCKY

Dodge
City

Pratt

Wichita

Chanute

Carthage

Poplar Bluff

Malden

Caruthersville

Kentucky
Lake

Liberal

Wellington

Parsons

Arkansas City

Joplin

Aurora

Kennett

O K L A H O M A

Arkansas River

ARKANSAS

TENNESSEE

Wabash River

INDIANA

Elevation

| Below sea level | 0 | 250m | 500m | 1000m | 2000m | 3000m | 4000m | 6000m |

-8000m -6000m -4000m -2000m -1000m -500m -250m

-100m/-328ft

26,246ft 19,685ft 13,124ft 6562ft -3281ft -1640ft -820ft

820ft 1640ft 3281ft 6562ft 9843ft 13,124ft 19,685ft

USA: The West

LOS ANGELES

- Valencia
- Santa Clarita
- San Fernando
- Burbank
- Universal Studios
- Beverly Hills
- Getty Museum
- Santa Monica
- Venice
- Torrance
- San Gabriel Mountains
- Glendale
- Pasadena
- Hollywood
- Inglewood
- Downey
- Buena Park
- Anaheim
- Disneyland
- Santa Ana
- Santa Ana Mountains
- Costa Mesa
- Long Beach
- Riverside

■ Places of interest
□ Regions/suburbs

20 km / 20 miles

CANADA
- ALBERTA
- BRITISH COLUMBIA
- Vancouver Island
- Strait of Georgia
- Strait of Juan de Fuca

WASHINGTON
- Bellingham
- Anacortes
- Oak Harbor
- Mount Vernon
- Skagit River
- Everett
- Edmonds
- Seattle
- Bellevue
- Auburn
- Tacoma
- Bremerton
- Port Angeles
- Olympic Mountains
- Puget Sound
- Olympia
- Aberdeen
- Centralia
- Kelso
- Longview
- Wenatchee
- Banks Lake
- Ellensburg
- Yakima
- Yakima River
- Richland
- Kennewick
- Pasco
- Walla Walla
- Spokane
- Sandpoint
- Lake Pend Oreille
- Coeur d'Alene
- Franklin D. Roosevelt Lake
- Columbia River
- Clark Fork
- Saint Joe River

OREGON
- Vancouver
- Portland
- Gresham
- Oregon City
- Woodburn
- Newberg
- McMinnville
- Salem
- Albany
- Lebanon
- Corvallis
- Springfield
- Eugene
- Roseburg
- Coos Bay
- Cape Blanco
- Grants Pass
- Medford
- Ashland
- Klamath Falls
- Upper Klamath Lake
- Bend
- Burns
- Harney Basin
- Summer Lake
- Goose Lake
- Crescent City
- Yreka
- Klamath Mountains
- Coast
- Cascade
- The Dalles
- Pendleton
- Hermiston
- John Day River
- Deschutes River
- Columbia River
- La Grande
- Baker
- Blue Mountains
- Wallowa Mountains

IDAHO
- Moscow
- Pullman
- Lewiston
- Clearwater Mountains
- Selway River
- Salmon River
- Salmon River Mountains
- Bitterroot Range
- Lemhi Range
- Pioneer Mountains
- Boise
- Nampa
- Caldwell
- Payette River
- Owyhee River
- Malheur Lake
- Snake River
- Snake River Plain
- Twin Falls
- Burley
- American Falls Reservoir
- Pocatello
- Blackfoot
- Idaho Falls
- Rexburg
- Columbia Plateau

MONTANA
- Missouri River
- Pioneer Mountains

WYOMING
- Bear Lake
- Great Salt Lake
- Independence Mountains

PACIFIC

Population

- ○ below 50,000
- ○ 50,000 to 100,000
- ◉ 100,000 to 500,000
- ■ above 500,000
- ● Internal administrative capital

0 km — 200
0 miles — 200

UTAH

Desert

UTAH

a i n s

Schell Creek Range

Lake Powell

Grand Canyon

Colorado River

Lake Mead

Lake Mohave

ARIZONA

Colorado River

Gila River

MEXICO

Ruby Mount

Ely

Alamo

NEVADA

G r e a t

B a s i n

Reese River

Tonopah

Death Valley

-86m ▽

Mojave Desert

Henderson

Las Vegas

Barstow

Victorville

Chocolate Mountains

Blythe

Brawley

El Centro

Lakeside

Hawthorne

Mount Whitney
△ 4418m

Ridgecrest

Salton Sea

Escondido

El Cajon

San Diego

Chula Vista

Humboldt R

Pyramid
Lake

Sparks

Carson
City

Walker
Lake

Mono
Lake

S i e r r a

N e v a d a

Tulare Lake Bed

Porterville

Delano

Bakersfield

Lancaster

San Bernardino

Riverside

Santa Ana

Palm
Springs

Fallbrook

Oceanside

Encinitas

Black R

Honey
Lake

Carson
Sink

Lake
Tahoe

South Lake
Tahoe

C e n t r a l

Visalia

Pasadena

Los Angeles

Long Beach

Huntington Beach

Santa Catalina
Island

San Clemente
Island

Susanville

Reno

Cirrus Heights

V a l l e y

San Joaquin Valley

Selma

Hanford

Oxnard

San Rafael Mountains

Santa
Barbara

Santa Rosa
Island

Santa
Cruz
Island

Channel Islands

Chico

Yuba
City

Sacramento River

Sacramento

Fresno

Madera

Atascadero

Santa Lucia Range

San Luis Obispo

Santa Maria

Lompoc

Redding

Woodland

Napa

Fairfield

Stockton

Manteca

Modesto

Turlock

Gilroy

Salinas

Sacramento Valley

Vallejo

Berkeley

Oakland

San Jose

Santa Cruz

Monterey Bay

Monterey

Ukiah

Santa Rosa

Palo Alto

Sunnyvale

San Francisco

R a n g e s

CALIFORNIA

OCEAN

PACIFIC OCEAN

HAWAI'I

Kaua'i

Ni'ihau

Lihu'e

Wahiawa

Kane'ohe

O'ahu

Honolulu

Moloka'i

Waiiluku

Maui

Mauna Kea
4205m

Hilo

Hawai'i

160°

158°

156°

22°

21°

20°

z

0 km   100
0 miles   100

2000m/6562ft
1000m/3281ft
500m/1640ft
200m/656ft
Sea level

Elevation

Below sea level 0   250m   500m   1000m   2000m   3000m   4000m   6000m

-8000m -6000m -4000m -2000m -1000m -500m -250m

820ft   1640ft 3281ft 6562ft 9843ft 13,124ft 19,685ft

26,246ft 19,685ft 13,124ft 6562ft -3281ft -1640ft -820ft -100m/-328ft

USA: The Southwest

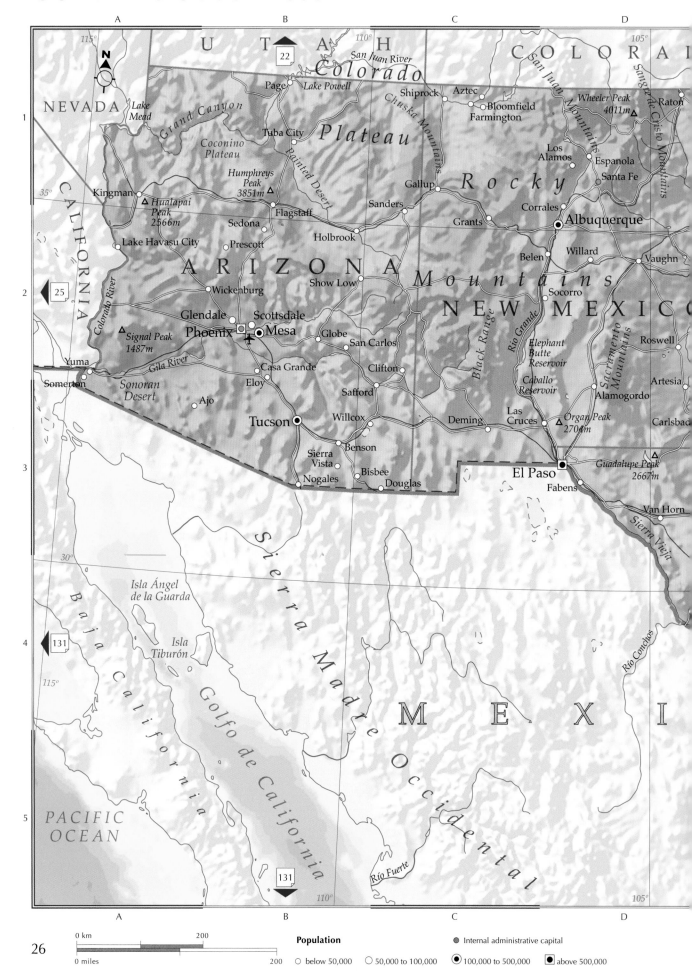

Population

○ below 50,000   ○ 50,000 to 100,000   ◉ 100,000 to 500,000   ■ above 500,000

● Internal administrative capital

0 km   200
0 miles   200

MISSOURI

KANSAS

23

Miami

Table Rock Lake

Beaver River

Boise City
Guymon
Woodward
Alva
Ponca City
Enid
Bartlesville
Vinita
Claremore
Beaver Lake

yton
Dalhart
Perryton
Stillwater
Sand Springs
Tulsa
Broken Arrow
Tahlequah

Dumas
Borger
Pampa
Clinton
El Reno
The Village
Oklahoma City
Sapulpa
Okmulgee
Muskogee
Warner

Lake Meredith
Moore
Norman
Shawnee
Eufaula Lake

nadian River
Amarillo
Canyon
Elk City
Chickasha
Ada
McAlester

cumcari
OKLAHOMA
Altus
Lawton
Duncan
Lake Texoma
Durant
Hugo
Idabel

Hereford
Tulia
Red River
Ardmore

Clovis
Childress
Vernon
Burkburnett
Denison
Paris
Texarkana

Muleshoe
Wichita River
Wichita Falls
Gainesville
Sherman
Atlanta

Plainview
Denton
Greenville
Sulphur Springs
LOUISIANA

Lubbock
Llano Estacado
Levelland
Brownfield
Mineral Wells
Plano
Garland
Lake Tawakoni
Marshall

Snyder
Fort Worth
Dallas
Tyler
Longview
Red River

lobbs
Lamesa
Sweetwater
Abilene
Cleburne
Arlington
Athens
Henderson

Seminole
Colorado City
Stephenville
Ennis
Corsicana
Jacksonville

Andrews
Big Spring
Ballinger
Coleman
Brazos River
Nacogdoches
Toledo Bend Reservoir

Midland
Brownwood
Waco
Trinity River
Lufkin
Pineland

Odessa
San Angelo
TEXAS
Killeen
Neches River
Sabine River

Monahans
McCamey
Brady
Copperas Cove
Temple
Huntsville
Livingston

Pecos
Edwards Plateau
Lake Buchanan
Belton
Taylor
Bryan
College Station
Conroe
Beaumont

Fort Stockton
Pecos River
Lake Travis
Round Rock
Brenham
Port Arthur

t Davis
Stockton Plateau
Kerrville
Austin
Colorado River
Houston
Baytown

lpine
New Braunfels
San Marcos
Brenham
Pasadena

Amistad Reservoir
Schertz
Seguin
Rosenberg
Alvin
Texas City

Emory Peak
△2385m
Del Rio
San Antonio
Hondo
Guadalupe River
El Campo
Angleton
Galveston
Lake Jackson

Uvalde
San Antonio River
Edna
Bay City
Freeport

Eagle Pass
Pearsall
Kenedy
Victoria
Port Lavaca

Rio Grande
Beeville
Port O'Connor

MEXICO

Portland
Robstown
Alice
Corpus Christi

Laredo
Kingsville

Laguna Madre
Padre Island

Gulf of Mexico

Norias

Edinburg
Mission
Harlingen
San Benito

McAllen
Brownsville

1

35°

20

2

3

30°

32

4

5

29

Mexico

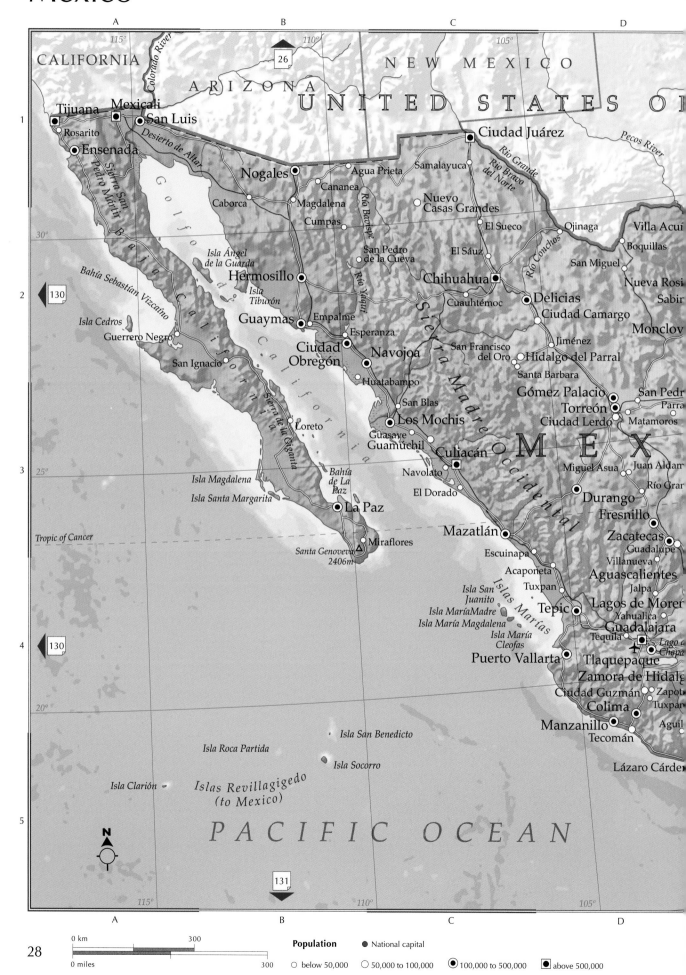

CALIFORNIA

Tijuana Mexicali
Rosarito San Luis
Ensenada

ARIZONA

UNITED STATES OF

NEW MEXICO

26

Colorado River

Desierto de Altar

Sierra San Pedro Mártir

Bahía Sebastián Vizcaíno

130

Isla Cedros

Guerrero Negro

San Ignacio

Golfo de California

Isla Ángel de la Guarda

Isla Tiburón

Nogales
Cananea
Caborca
Magdalena
Cumpas

Agua Prieta Samalayuca
Nuevo
Casas Grandes

Ciudad Juárez

Pecos River

Rio Grande
Rio Bravo del Norte

El Sueco
Ojinaga
Villa Acui
Boquillas

San Pedro de la Cueva
El Sáuz
San Miguel
Nueva Rosi

Hermosillo

Guaymas Empalme
Esperanza
Ciudad Obregón
Huatabampo
Navojoa
San Blas

Chihuahua
Cuauhtémoc Delicias
Ciudad Camargo

Río Yaqui
Río Bavispe

Río Conchos

San Francisco del Oro
Jiménez
Hidalgo del Parral
Santa Barbara

Sabir
Monclov

Gómez Palacio
Torreón
Ciudad Lerdo

San Pedr
Parra
Matamoros

Sierra de la Giganta

Loreto

Isla Magdalena
Isla Santa Margarita

Bahía de La Paz

La Paz

Santa Genoveva
2406m Miraflores

Los Mochis
Guasave
Guamúchil
Culiacán
Navolato
El Dorado

Mazatlán

Escuinapa
Acaponeta
Tuxpan

Isla San Juanito
Isla MaríaMadre
Isla María Magdalena
Isla María Cleofas

Islas Marías

MEX

Miguel Asua Juan Aldam
Río Gran
Durango
Fresnillo

Zacatecas
Guadalupe
Villanueva
Aguascalientes
Jalpa
Lagos de Morer
Yahualica

Sierra Madre Occidental

Tropic of Cancer

Tepic

Guadalajara
Tequila Lago Chapa
Puerto Vallarta
Tlaquepaque
Zamora de Hidalg
Ciudad Guzmán Zapot
Colima Tuxpan
Manzanillo Aguil
Tecomán

Lázaro Cárden

Isla San Benedicto
Isla Roca Partida
Isla Socorro

Isla Clarión
Islas Revillagigedo
(to Mexico)

PACIFIC OCEAN

N

130

131

28

0 km   300
0 miles   300

Population   ● National capital

○ below 50,000   ○ 50,000 to 100,000   ◉ 100,000 to 500,000   ■ above 500,000

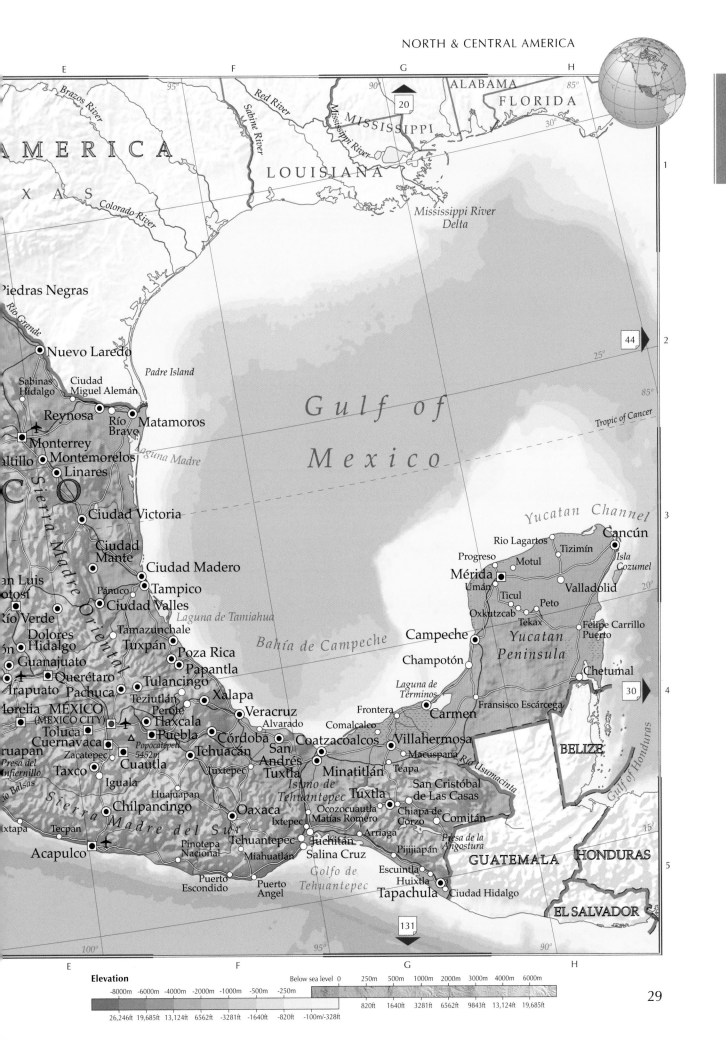

AMERICA

T E X A S

LOUISIANA

ALABAMA

FLORIDA

MISSISSIPPI

Brazos River

Colorado River

Red River

Sabine River

Mississippi River

Mississippi River Delta

20

Piedras Negras

Río Grande

Nuevo Laredo

Padre Island

Sabinas Hidalgo

Ciudad Miguel Alemán

Reynosa

Río Bravo

Matamoros

Monterrey

altillo

Montemorelos

Linares

C O

Laguna Madre

Gulf of

Mexico

44

Tropic of Cancer

Sierra Madre Oriental

Ciudad Victoria

Ciudad Mante

an Luis otosí

Ciudad Madero

Pánuco

Tampico

Río Verde

Ciudad Valles

Laguna de Tamiahua

Yucatan Channel

Rio Lagartos

Cancún

Dolores Hidalgo

ón

Guanajuato

rapuato

Morelia

Tamazunchale

Tuxpán

Poza Rica

Bahía de Campeche

Progreso

Mérida

Motul

Tizimín

Umán

Isla Cozumel

Valladolid

Querétaro

Pachuca

Teziutlán

Papantla

Tulancingo

Ticul

Peto

MÉXICO (MEXICO CITY)

Perote

Xalapa

Tlaxcala

Puebla

Campeche

Oxkutzcab

Tekax

Yucatan Peninsula

Felipe Carrillo Puerto

Champotón

Toluca

Cuernavaca

Popocatépetl 5452m

Córdoba

Veracruz

Alvarado

Frontera

Laguna de Términos

Carmen

Fransisco Escárcega

Chetumal

uapan

Zacatepec

Presa del nfiernillo

Cuautla

Tehuacán

San Andrés Tuxtla

Comalcalco

Coatzacoalcos

Villahermosa

Macuspana

30

BELIZE

Taxco

Iguala

Tuxtepec

Minatitlán

Teapa

Río Usumacinta

Gulf of Honduras

xtapa

Sierra Madre del Sur

Huajuapan

Chilpancingo

Oaxaca

Ixtepec

Istmo de Tehuantepec

Ocozocuautla

Matías Romero

Tuxtla

San Cristóbal de Las Casas

Chiapa de Corzo

Comitán

Tecpan

Pinotepa Nacional

Tehuantepec

Miahuatlán

Juchitán

Salina Cruz

Arriaga

Pijijiapán

Presa de la Angostura

GUATEMALA

HONDURAS

Acapulco

Puerto Escondido

Puerto Angel

Golfo de Tehuantepec

Escuintla

Huixtla

Tapachula

Ciudad Hidalgo

EL SALVADOR

131

Elevation

Below sea level   0   250m   500m   1000m   2000m   3000m   4000m   6000m

-8000m   -6000m   -4000m   -2000m   -1000m   -500m   -250m

820ft   1640ft   3281ft   6562ft   9843ft   13,124ft   19,685ft

26,246ft   19,685ft   13,124ft   6562ft   -3281ft   -1640ft   -820ft   -100m/-328ft

Central America

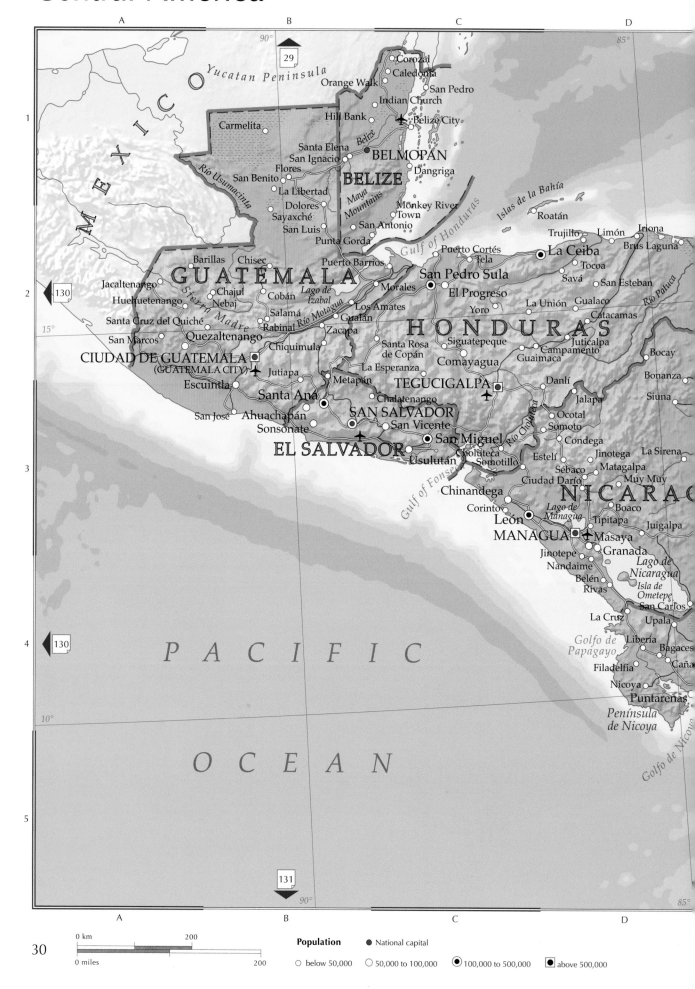

MEXICO

Yucatan Peninsula

Corozal
Caledonia
Orange Walk
San Pedro
Indian Church
Hill Bank
Belize City
Carmelita
Santa Elena
San Ignacio
BELMOPAN
Flores
Dangriga
BELIZE
San Benito
La Libertad
Maya
Dolores
Monkey River
Mountains
Town
Sayaxché
San Antonio
San Luis
Punta Gorda
Gulf of Honduras
Islas de la Bahía
Roatán
Trujillo
Limón
Iriona
Barillas
Chisec
Puerto Barrios
Puerto Cortés
Brus Laguna
Jacaltenango
GUATEMALA
Tela
La Ceiba
Chajul
Lago de
Morales
San Pedro Sula
Tocoa
Huehuetenango
Nebaj
Cobán
Izabal
Savá
San Esteban
Salamá
Los Amates
El Progreso
Santa Cruz del Quiché
Rabinal
Río Motagua
Gualán
Yoro
La Unión
Gualaco
Catacamas
Río Patuca
San Marcos
Quezaltenango
Zacapa
HONDURAS
Chiquimula
Siguatepeque
Juticalpa
CIUDAD DE GUATEMALA
Santa Rosa
Campamento
Bocay
(GUATEMALA CITY)
de Copán
Comayagua
Guaimaca
Jutiapa
La Esperanza
Bonanza
Escuintla
Metapán
TEGUCIGALPA
Danlí
Siuna
Santa Ana
Chalatenango
Jalapa
San José
Ahuachapán
SAN SALVADOR
Ocotal
Sonsonate
San Vicente
Somoto
Condega
EL SALVADOR
San Miguel
Río Choluteca
Estelí
Jinotega
La Sirena
Usulután
Choluteca
Sébaco
Matagalpa
Gulf of Fonseca
Somotillo
Ciudad Darío
Muy Muy
Chinandega
NICARAG
Corinto
Lago de
Boaco
León
Managua
Tipitapa
Juigalpa
MANAGUA
Masaya
Jinotepe
Granada
Nandaime
Lago de
Belén
Nicaragua
Rivas
Isla de
Ometepe
San Carlos
La Cruz
Upala
Golfo de
Liberia
Papagayo
Bagaces
Filadelfia
Caña
Nicoya
Puntarenas
Península
de Nicoya
Golfo de Nicoya

PACIFIC

OCEAN

Sierra Madre

Río Usumacinta

Belize

90°
85°
15°
10°
90°
85°

A
B
C
D

29
130
130
131

0 km   200
0 miles   200

Population   ● National capital

○ below 50,000   ○ 50,000 to 100,000   ◉ 100,000 to 500,000   ■ above 500,000

30

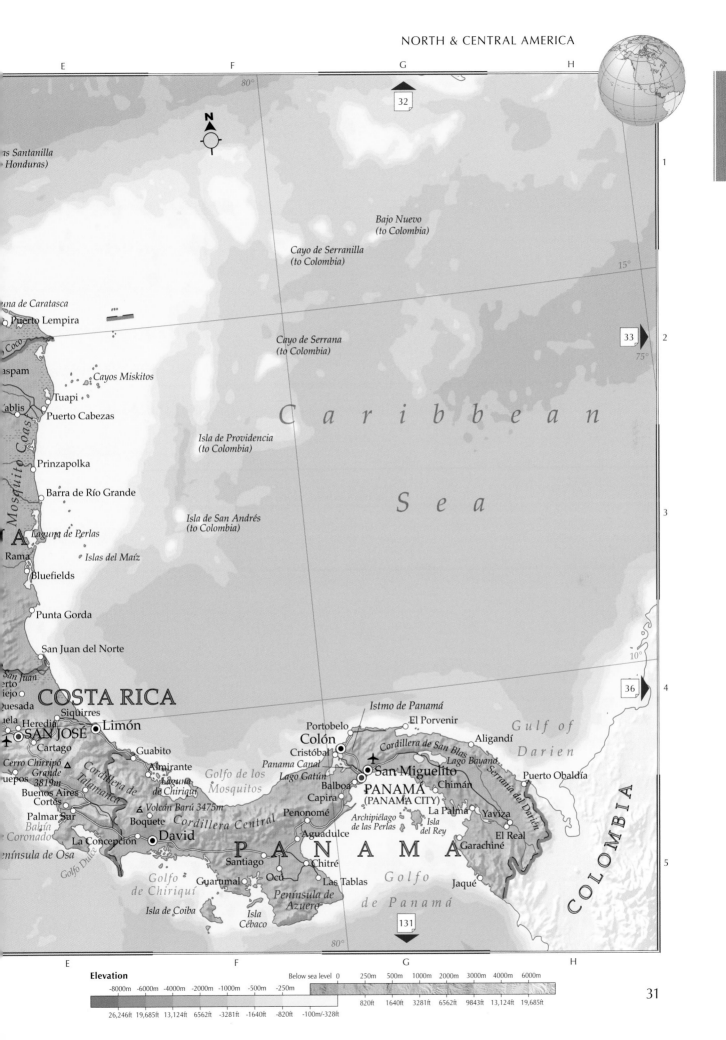

E   F   G   H

80°

N

32

*Bajo Nuevo
(to Colombia)*

*Cayo de Serranilla
(to Colombia)*

15°

*as Santanilla
° Honduras)*

una de Caratasca

Puerto Lempira

*Cayo de Serrana
(to Colombia)*

33

75°

Coco

aspam

Cayos Miskitos

Tuapi

ablis

Puerto Cabezas

*Isla de Providencia
(to Colombia)*

C a r i b b e a n

Mosquito Coast

Prinzapolka

Barra de Río Grande

*Isla de San Andrés
(to Colombia)*

S e a

A

Laguna de Perlas

Rama

Islas del Maíz

Bluefields

Punta Gorda

San Juan del Norte

10°

*San Juan
uerto
iejo*

36

COSTA RICA

uesada

ela

Heredia

Limón

Istmo de Panamá

El Porvenir

Gulf of

Portobelo

Aligandí

SAN JOSÉ

Colón

Darien

Cartago

Guabito

Cristóbal

Cordillera de San Blas

Puerto Obaldía

Cerro Chirripó

Grande

uepos

3819m

Almirante

*Laguna
de Chiriquí*

*Golfo de los
Mosquitos*

Panamá Canal

Lago Gatún

Lago Bayano

San Miguelito

Chimán

Serranía del Darién

*Cordillera de
Talamanca*

Buenos Aires

Cortés

Balboa

PANAMÁ
(PANAMA CITY)

La Palma

Palmar
Sur

Volcán Barú 3475m

Capira

*Archipiélago
de las Perlas*

*Isla
del Rey*

Yaviza

*Bahía
e Coronado*

Boquete

Cordillera Central

Penonomé

P   **A**   **N**   **A**   **M**   **A**

El Real

La Concepción

David

Garachiné

Golfo Dulce

Aguadulce

enínsula de Osa

Santiago

Chitré

Golfo

COLOMBIA

*Golfo
de Chiriquí*

Guarumal

Ocú

Las Tablas

de Panamá

Jaqué

Isla de Coiba

*Península de
Azuero*

*Isla
Cébaco*

131

80°

E   F   G   H

Elevation

Below sea level   0   250m   500m   1000m   2000m   3000m   4000m   6000m

-8000m   -6000m   -4000m   -2000m   -1000m   -500m   -250m

820ft   1640ft   3281ft   6562ft   9843ft   13,124ft   19,685ft

26,246ft   19,685ft   13,124ft   6562ft   -3281ft   -1640ft   -820ft   -100m/-328ft

The Caribbean

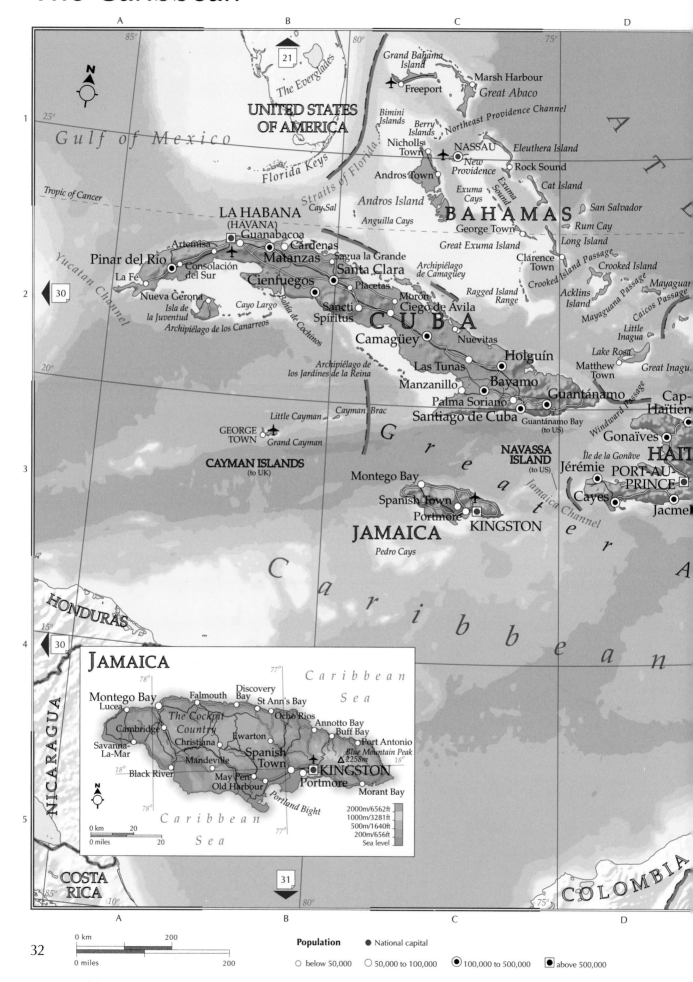

A

B

C

D

21

N

UNITED STATES OF AMERICA

Gulf of Mexico

85°

80°

75°

Grand Bahama Island

Marsh Harbour

Freeport

Great Abaco

Bimini Islands

Berry Islands

Northeast Providence Channel

1

25°

Nicholls Town

NASSAU

Eleuthera Island

New Providence

Rock Sound

Andros Town

Florida Keys

Straits of Florida

Cat Island

Tropic of Cancer

Exuma Cays

Exuma Sound

LA HABANA (HAVANA)

Cay Sal

Andros Island

Anguilla Cays

BAHAMAS

San Salvador

George Town

Rum Cay

Guanabacoa

Artemisa

Cárdenas

Great Exuma Island

Long Island

Pinar del Río

Matanzas

Sagua la Grande

Archipiélago de Camagüey

Clarence Town

Crooked Island

Consolación del Sur

Santa Clara

Crooked Island Passage

La Fé

Cienfuegos

Placetas

Ragged Island Range

Acklins Island

Mayaguana Passage

Mayaguana

2

20°

Nueva Gerona

Cayo Largo

Sancti Spíritus

Morón

Ciego de Ávila

Caicos Passage

Isla de la Juventud

Bahía de Cochinos

CUBA

Little Inagua

Archipiélago de los Canarreos

Camagüey

Nuevitas

Holguín

Lake Rosa

Archipiélago de los Jardines de la Reina

Las Tunas

Great Inagua

Manzanillo

Bayamo

Matthew Town

Palma Soriano

Guantánamo

Cap-Haïtien

Little Cayman

Cayman Brac

Santiago de Cuba

Guantánamo Bay (to US)

Windward Passage

GEORGE TOWN

Grand Cayman

G

NAVASSA ISLAND (to US)

Gonaïves

Île de la Gonâve

HAITI

CAYMAN ISLANDS (to UK)

r

Jérémie

PORT-AU-PRINCE

3

Montego Bay

e

Jamaica Channel

Cayes

Spanish Town

a

Jacmel

Portmore

KINGSTON

t

JAMAICA

Pedro Cays

e

C

r

a

A

HONDURAS

r

i

15°

b

4

30

b

JAMAICA

Caribbean Sea

Montego Bay

Falmouth

Discovery Bay

St Ann's Bay

77°

Lucea

Ocho Rios

Cambridge

The Cockpit Country

Annotto Bay

Buff Bay

Savanna-La-Mar

Christiana

Ewarton

Port Antonio

Blue Mountain Peak

△ 2258m

18°

Mandeville

Spanish Town

Black River

18°

May Pen

KINGSTON

Old Harbour

Portmore

N

Morant Bay

Portland Bight

5

Caribbean Sea

77°

0 km   20

0 miles   20

	2000m/6562ft
	1000m/3281ft
	500m/1640ft
	200m/656ft
	Sea level

COSTA RICA

NICARAGUA

85°

10°

31

80°

75°

COLOMBIA

A

B

C

D

0 km   200

0 miles   200

Population   ● National capital

○ below 50,000   ○ 50,000 to 100,000   ◉ 100,000 to 500,000   ◻ above 500,000

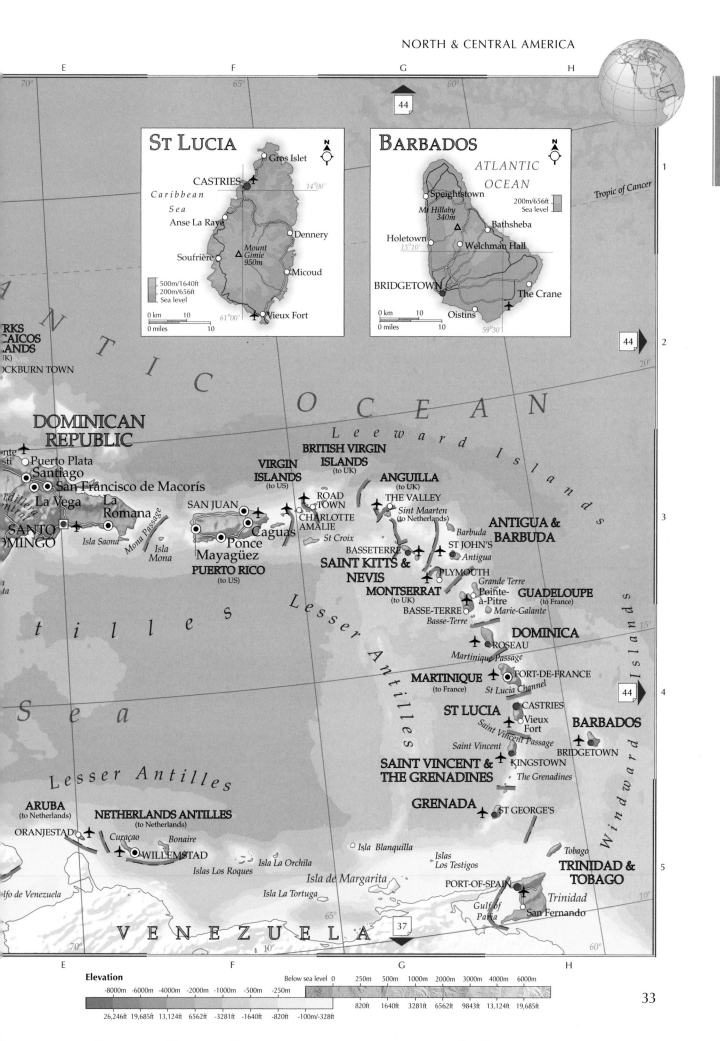

E   F   G   H

44

St Lucia

N

Gros Islet

CASTRIES

Caribbean
Sea

Anse La Raye

Dennery

Soufrière

△ Mount
Gimie
950m

Micoud

14°00'

61°00'

500m/1640ft
200m/656ft
Sea level

0 km   10
0 miles   10

Vieux Fort

Barbados

N

ATLANTIC
OCEAN

Speightstown

Mt Hillaby
340m △

Bathsheba

Holetown

Welchman Hall

13°10'

BRIDGETOWN

The Crane

Oistins

200m/656ft
Sea level

0 km   10
0 miles   10

59°30'

Tropic of Cancer

44

20°

RKS
AICOS
NDS
UK)

CKBURN TOWN

A   N   T   I   C   *O   C   E   A   N*

L e e w a r d   *I s l a n d s*

DOMINICAN
REPUBLIC

sti

Puerto Plata

Santiago

San Francisco de Macorís

La Vega

La Romana

SANTO

MINGO

Isla Saona

Isla
Mona

Mona Passage

SAN JUAN

Caguas

Ponce

Mayagüez

PUERTO RICO
(to US)

BRITISH VIRGIN
ISLANDS
(to UK)

VIRGIN
ISLANDS
(to US)

ROAD
TOWN

CHARLOTTE
AMALIE

St Croix

ANGUILLA
(to UK)

THE VALLEY

Sint Maarten
(to Netherlands)

BASSETERRE

SAINT KITTS &
NEVIS

MONTSERRAT
(to UK)

PLYMOUTH

Barbuda

ANTIGUA &
BARBUDA

ST JOHN'S

Antigua

Pointe-
à-Pitre

BASSE-TERRE

Basse-Terre

Grande Terre

GUADELOUPE
(to France)

Marie-Galante

DOMINICA

ROSEAU

Martinique Passage

MARTINIQUE
(to France)

FORT-DE-FRANCE

St Lucia Channel

ST LUCIA

CASTRIES

Vieux
Fort

Saint Vincent Passage

Saint Vincent

SAINT VINCENT &
THE GRENADINES

KINGSTOWN

The Grenadines

BARBADOS

BRIDGETOWN

W i n d w a r d   I s l a n d s

15°

44

t   i   l   l   e   s

L e s s e r   A n t i l l e s

Sea

GRENADA

ST GEORGE'S

Lesser   Antilles

ARUBA
(to Netherlands)

ORANJESTAD

NETHERLANDS ANTILLES
(to Netherlands)

Curaçao

Bonaire

WILLEMSTAD

Isla La Orchila

Islas Los Roques

Isla Blanquilla

Islas
Los Testigos

Tobago

TRINIDAD &
TOBAGO

lfo de Venezuela

Isla de Margarita

Isla La Tortuga

PORT-OF-SPAIN

Trinidad

Gulf of
Paria

San Fernando

V   E   N   E   Z   U   E   L   A

70°   65°   10°   60°

10°

37

E   F   G   H

Elevation

Below sea level   0   250m   500m   1000m   2000m   3000m   4000m   6000m

-8000m -6000m -4000m -2000m -1000m -500m -250m

820ft   1640ft   3281ft   6562ft   9843ft 13,124ft 19,685ft

26,246ft 19,685ft 13,124ft 6562ft -3281ft -1640ft -820ft -100m/-328ft

South America

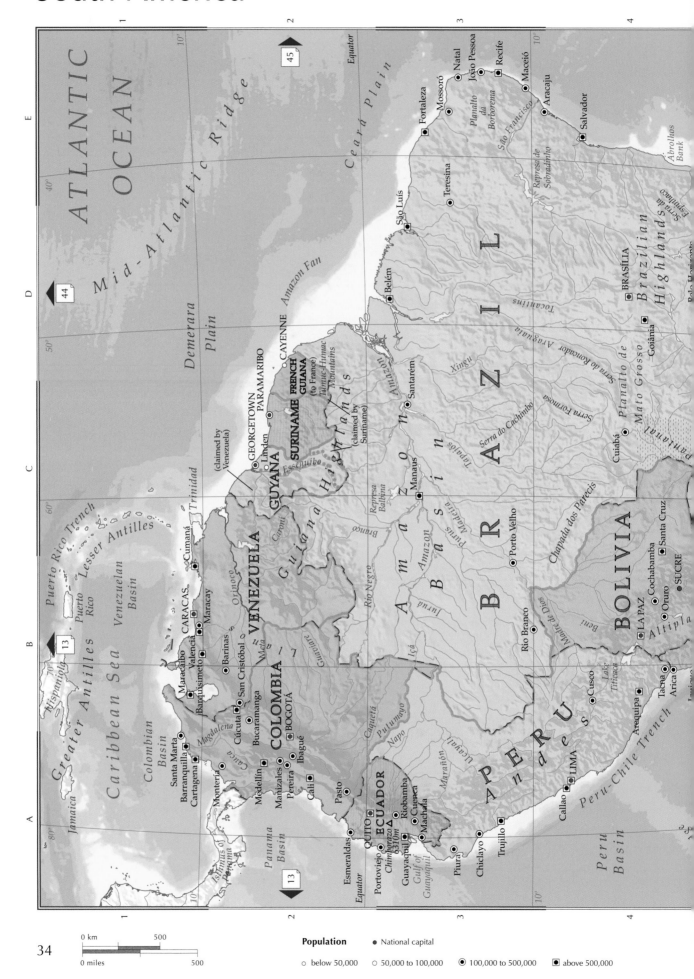

Population   ● National capital

○ below 50,000   ○ 50,000 to 100,000   ◉ 100,000 to 500,000   ▣ above 500,000

0 km   500

0 miles   500

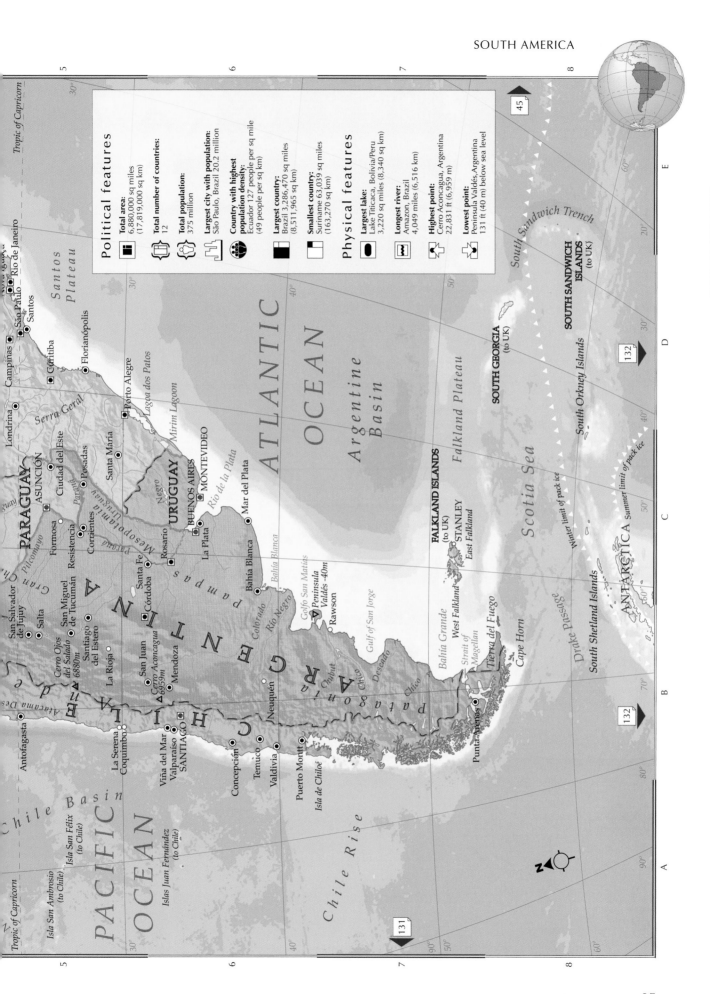

Northern South America

Caribbean Sea

Lesser Ant

NETHERLANDS
ANTILLES
(to Netherlands)

ARUBA
(to Netherlands)

Curaçao   *Bonaire*

Puerto López

Punto Fijo

Golfo de Venezuela

Coro   Puerto Cumarebo

Sabaneta

Islas Los Roques

Isla La Orc

Península de la Guajira

Maicao

Ríohacha

Santa Marta

Barranquilla   Ciénaga

Soledad

Cartagena   Sabanalarga

Pico Cristóbal Colón 5775m

Dabajuro

Maracaibo

La Concepción   Cabimas

San Felipe

Puerto Cabello

CARACA

Valledupar   Machiques   Ciudad Ojeda   Carora   Barquisimeto   Valencia   Maracay

El Carmen de Bolívar

Lago de Maracaibo

San Carlos del Zulia

Valera   Acarigua

San Juan de los Mor

Sincelejo   Magangué

Mérida   Guanare   Calabozo   Valle de la Pascua

Montería   Cereté   Ocaña   El Vigía   *Pico Bolívar 5007m*   Barinas

Planeta Rica

Aguachica   San Fernand

Caucasia   Cúcuta   San Cristóbal   *Río Apure*

Dabeiba   Yarumal   Pamplona   L V E N

Río Cauca   Bucaramanga   Arauca   *Río Arauca*

Bello   Barrancabermeja   *Río Meta*   Puerto Carreño

Medellín   Puerto Berrío   Puerto Ayacuch

Itagüí   Sogamoso

Nuquí   Quibdó   Tunja   Yopal   *Río Orinoco*

Manizales   Zipaquira   *Río Meta*

Pereira   BOGOTÁ

Armenia   Girardot   Villavicencio   *Río Guaviare*   Puerto Inírida

Tuluá   Ibagué

Buenaventura   Buga   Espinal   C O L O M B I A

Palmira

Cali   Neiva

San José del Guaviare

Popayán   Garzón   *Río Vaupés*   Mitú

Tumaco   Pitalito   *Río Apaporis*

Pasto   Mocoa   Florencia

Nevado de Cumbal 4764m

Ipiales   Orito   *O r i n o q u í a - A m a z o n i a*

Equator

Río Putumayo   *Río Caquetá*

E C U A D O R   *Río Napo*   *Río Japurá*

P E R U   *Río Icá*   A

Amazon   *Río Iç*

PANAMA

Panama Canal

Golfo de Panamá

Gulf of Darien

PACIFIC OCEAN

Cordillera Occidental   *Cordillera Central*   *Cordillera Oriental*

Andes

32

31

38

38

36

0 km   200

0 miles   200

Population   ● National capital

○ below 50,000   ◎ 50,000 to 100,000   ◉ 100,000 to 500,000   ▣ above 500,000

E F G H

1

SAINT VINCENT &
THE GRENADINES

GRENADA

Isla Blanquilla

*Isla de
Margarita*

Islas Los Testigos

Tobago

BARBADOS

TRINIDAD &
TOBAGO

Tortuga
La Asunción
Porlamar
maná
Carúpano
Cariaco
Güiria
*Gulf of
Paria*
Trinidad

10°

ATLANTIC

Puerto La Cruz
Barcelona
San Mateo
Anaco
Maturín
The Serpent's Mouth

OCEAN

araza
Cantaura
El Tigre
Tucupita

Río Orinoco
Ciudad Guayana
Upata

45

S

Ciudad
Bolívar

Embalse de Guri
El Callao
Matthews
Ridge
Charity

2

ZUELA

Río Paragua

El Dorado

Cuyuni River

Spring Garden
Aurora
Parika
GEORGETOWN

New
Amsterdam

Peters Mine
Rockstone
Bartica

Totness
PARAMARIBO
Nieuw Amsterdam

Río Caura

*Salto
Angel*
Kamarang

Linden

Nieuw
Nickerie

Kaaimanston

St-Laurent-
du-Maroni
Sinnamary
Kourou

5°

Río Caroní

GUYANA

Orealla
Apoera

Maroni River

CAYENNE

Mount Roraima
2810m

Pakaraima Mountains

Kurupukari

Essequibo River

SURINAME

*W. J. van
Blommesteinmeer*

△ *Juliana Top
1230m*

Grand-
Santi

*Montagnes
de la Trinité*
*Montagne
Tortue*

Ouanary

3

FRENCH

St-Georges

G
u
i
a
n
a

H
i
g
h
l
a
n
d
s

(Venezuela claims all
of Guyana west of
Essequibo River)

Lethem

Río Orinoco

Courantyne River

GUIANA
(to France)

Camopi

Tumuc-Humac Mountains

(claimed by
Suriname)

Acarai Mountains

(claimed by
Suriname)

4

Río Negro

Equator

B R A Z I L

Amazon

Amazon

5

z o n

B a s i n

Amazon

Amazon

Río Purus

Río Tapajós

40

60°

60° 55°

E F G H

Elevation

Below sea level 0 250m 500m 1000m 2000m 3000m 4000m 6000m

-8000m -6000m -4000m -2000m -1000m -500m -250m

820ft 1640ft 3281ft 6562ft 9843ft 13,124ft 19,685ft

26,246ft 19,685ft 13,124ft 6562ft -3281ft -1640ft -820ft -100m/-328ft

Western South America

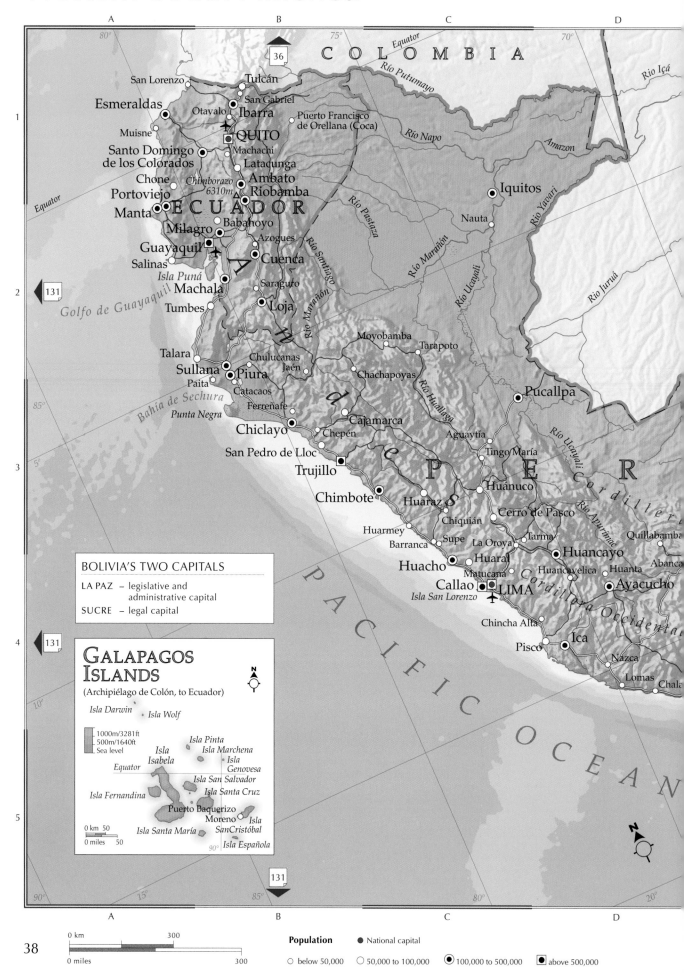

COLOMBIA

Río Putumayo

Río Içá

1

San Lorenzo
Tulcán
Esmeraldas
San Gabriel
Otavalo
Ibarra
Muisne
QUITO
Machachi
Santo Domingo
de los Colorados
Latacunga
Chone
Chimborazo
6310m
Ambato
Riobamba
Portoviejo
ECUADOR
Manta
Babahoyo
Milagro
Azogues
Guayaquil
Cuenca
Salinas
Isla Puná
Saraguro
Machala
Loja
Tumbes

Puerto Francisco
de Orellana (Coca)
Río Napo
Amazon
Iquitos
Nauta
Río Pastaza
Río Santiago
Río Marañón
Río Ucayali
Río Yavarí
Río Juruá

Equator

80°
75°
70°

2

Golfo de Guayaquil

85°

Talara
Chulucanas
Sullana
Piura
Jaén
Paita
Catacaos
Bahía de Sechura
Ferreñafe
Punta Negra
Chiclayo
Chepén
San Pedro de Lloc
Trujillo
Chimbote

Moyobamba
Tarapoto
Chachapoyas
Río Huallaga
Cajamarca
Aguaytía
Pucallpa
Río Ucayali
Tingo María

P E R U

Huánuco
Huaraz
Chiquián
Cerro de Pasco
Tarma
Quillabamba
Abanca
Cordillera

3

5°

Huarmey
Barranca
Supe
La Oroya
Huancayo
Huanta
Huancavelica
Huaral
Matucana
Huacho
Callao
LIMA
Isla San Lorenzo
Ayacucho

P A C I F I C   O C E A N

BOLIVIA'S TWO CAPITALS

LA PAZ – legislative and
administrative capital

SUCRE – legal capital

Chincha Alta

Cordillera Occidental

4

10°

GALAPAGOS ISLANDS

(Archipiélago de Colón, to Ecuador)

Ica
Pisco
Nazca
Lomas
Chala

N

Isla Darwin
Isla Wolf

1000m/3281ft
500m/1640ft
Sea level

Isla Pinta
Isla Marchena
Isla
Isabela
Isla
Genovesa
Equator
Isla San Salvador
Isla Santa Cruz
Isla Fernandina
Puerto Baquerizo
Moreno
Isla
San Cristóbal
Isla Santa María
Isla Española

0 km 50
0 miles 50

90°

5

90°
85°
80°
20°

0 km 300
0 miles 300

Population   ● National capital

○ below 50,000   ○ 50,000 to 100,000   ◉ 100,000 to 500,000   ◼ above 500,000

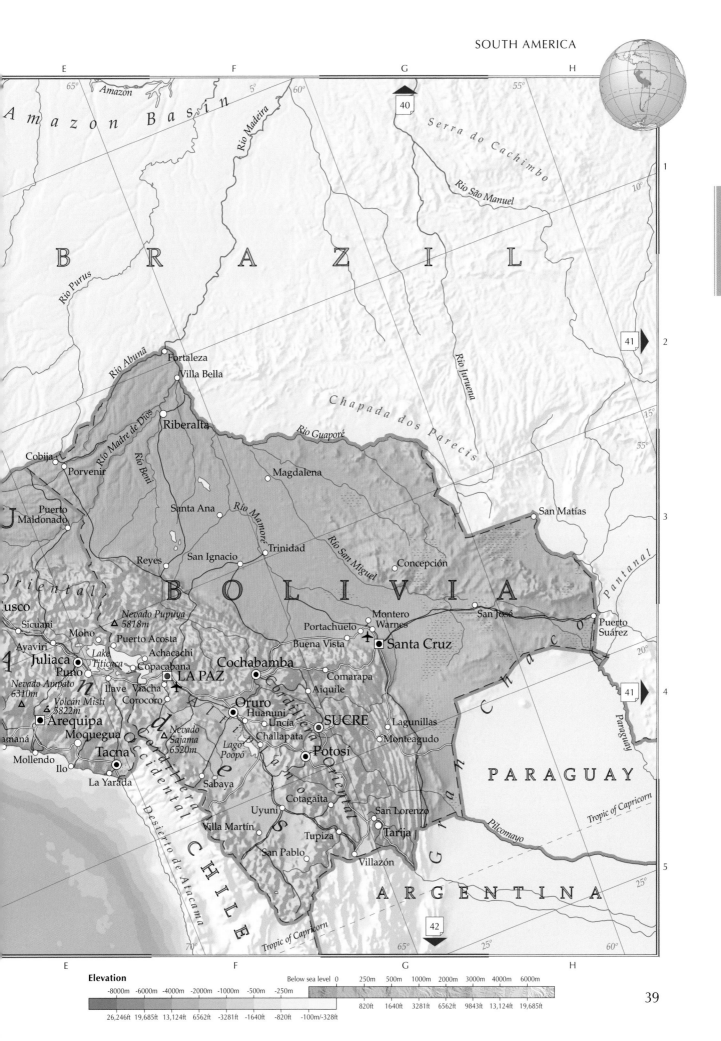

65° Amazon 5° 60° 55° 10°

Amazon Basin

Rio Madeira

Rio Purus

B R A Z I L

Serra do Cachimbo

Rio São Manuel

40

41

15°

55°

Rio Abunã

Fortaleza

Villa Bella

Rio Madre de Dios

Riberalta

Rio Guaporé

Chapada dos Parecis

Rio Juruena

Cobija

Porvenir

Rio Beni

Magdalena

Puerto
Maldonado

Santa Ana

Rio Mamoré

Reyes

San Ignacio

Trinidad

Rio San Miguel

Concepción

San Matías

Pantanal

O r i e n t a l

Cusco

Sicuani

Nevado Pupuya
△ 5818m

Puerto Acosta

B O L I V I A

Montero
Warnes

San José

Puerto
Suárez

20°

Ayaviri

Juliaca

Puno

Achacachi

Lake
Titicaca

Copacabana

Cochabamba

Portachuelo

Buena Vista

Santa Cruz

Comarapa

41

Paraguay

Moho

Nevado Ampato
6310m

Ilave

Viacha

Corocoro

LA PAZ

Aiquile

Volcán Misti
5822m

Arequipa

Moquegua

Oruro

Huanuni

Lincía

Challapata

SUCRE

Lagunillas

Monteagudo

Nevado
Sajama
6520m

Lago
Poopó

Potosí

Tacna

Mollendo

Ilo

La Yarada

Sabaya

Cotagaita

Uyuni

San Lorenzo

Tropic of Capricorn

Villa Martín

Tupiza

Tarija

amaná

San Pablo

Villazón

C o r d i l l e r a   O c c i d e n t a l

A l t i p l a n o

C o r d i l l e r a   O r i e n t a l

D e s i e r t o   d e   A t a c a m a

C H I L E

G r a n   C h a c o

P A R A G U A Y

Pilcomayo

A R G E N T I N A

25°

42

Tropic of Capricorn

70°

65°

60°

25°

Elevation

Below sea level 0   250m 500m 1000m 2000m 3000m 4000m 6000m

-8000m -6000m -4000m -2000m -1000m -500m -250m

820ft 1640ft 3281ft 6562ft 9843ft 13,124ft 19,685ft

26,246ft 19,685ft 13,124ft 6562ft -3281ft -1640ft -820ft -100m/-328ft

Brazil

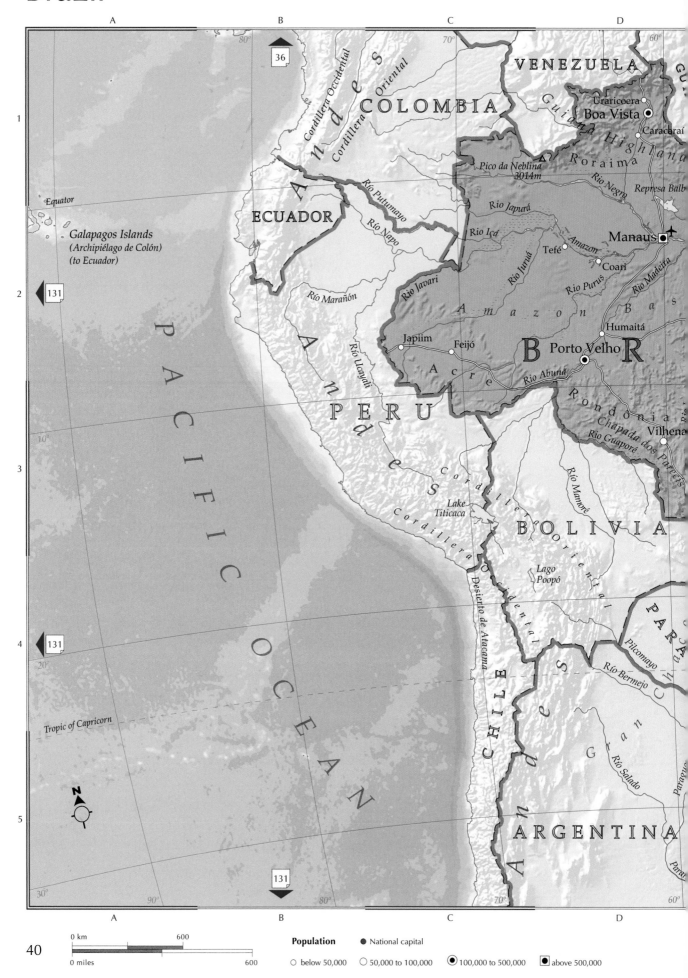

Cordillera Occidental
Cordillera Oriental

COLOMBIA

VENEZUELA

Urarícoera
Boa Vista ◉
Caracaraí

Guiana Highland
Roraima

△ Pico da Neblina
3014m

Rio Negro
Represa Balb

ECUADOR

Equator

Galapagos Islands
(Archipiélago de Colón)
(to Ecuador)

Río Putumayo
Río Napo

Rio Japurá

Rio Içá

Rio Juruá

Tefé
Amazon

Coari

Manaus ◉

A n d e s

Río Marañón

Río Javari

A m a z o n

Rio Purus

Rio Madeira

B a s

Humaitá

PERU

Río Ucayali

Japiim ○
Feijó ○

Acre

B ◉ Porto Velho R

Rio Abunã

Rondônia

R

Chapada dos Parecis

Vilhena ◼

Rio Guaporé

A
n
d
e
s

Cordillera

Lake
Titicaca

Cordillera Oriental

Rio Mamoré

BOLIVIA

Lago
Poopó

P A C I F I C

Cordillera Occidental

Desierto de Atacama

PARA

Pilcomayo

Río Bermejo

Tropic of Capricorn

CHILE

A n d e s

G
G

Río Salado

Parag

O C E A N

N

ARGENTINA

40

0 km _____ 600

0 miles _____ 600

36

131

131

131

Population   ● National capital

○ below 50,000   ○ 50,000 to 100,000   ◉ 100,000 to 500,000   ◼ above 500,000

E   F   G   H

44

45

45

45

ATLANTIC OCEAN

SURINAME

FRENCH
GUIANA
(to France)

*Tumuc-Humac
Mountains*

Amapá

Macapá

Mouths of the Amazon

Ilha Caviana de Fora

Baía de Marajó

Baía de São Marcos

*Ilha
de Marajó*

Belém

São Luís

Parnaíba

Camocim

Alenquer

Amazon

Santarém

Altamira

Itaituba

*Represa de
Tucuruí*

Bacabal

Piripiri

Teresina

Fortaleza

Mossoró

Açu

Rio Grande do Norte

Natal

Cabo de São Roque

Atol das Rocas

*San Fernando de Noronha
(to Brazil)*

Equator

1

Ilpajós

Rio Xingu

Marabá

Imperatriz

Maranhão

Ceará

Juazeiro do Norte

Paraíba

João Pessoa

Campina Grande

Serra do Cachimbo

P a r á

Carolina

Floriano

Balsas

Picos

Piauí

Pernambuco

Alagoas

Recife

Maceió

2

Serra Formosa

São Manuel

Serra dos Graúaus

Rio Tocantins

Palmas do
Tocantins

Juazeiro

Rio São Francisco

*Chapada
Diamantina*

Aracaju

Estância

10°

Mato

Tocantins

Taguatinga

Rio Araguaia

B a h i a

Feira de Santana

Salvador

Baía de Todos os Santos

3

Cuiabá

Grosso

Goiás

Planalto

BRASÍLIA

Central

Janaúba

Itabuna

Vitória da Conquista

Canavieiras

ondonópolis

Anápolis

Goiânia

Jataí

Araguari

Montes Claros

Araçuaí

Minas

Gerais

Governador Valadares

*Espírito
Santo*

Pantanal

*Mato Grosso
do Sul*

Uberlândia

Uberaba

Belo Horizonte

Vitória

Aquidauana

Campo Grande

Ribeirão Preto

Marília

Divinópolis

Juiz de Fora

Campos

20°

4

esidente Prudente

Londrina

Maringá

Campinas

Nova

Iguaçu

Rio de Janeiro

São Paulo

São Paulo

Santos

Paraná

Tropic of Capricorn

UAY

*Represa
de Itaipu*

Saltos do Rio Iguaçu

Iguaçu

Ponta Grossa

Curitiba

Joinville

Santa Catarina

Blumenau

Florianópolis

Paraná

Passo Fundo

Rio Negro

anta Maria

Rio Grande

Canoas

do Sul

Porto Alegre

5

Bagé

Lagoa dos Patos

Rio Grande

Mirim Lagoon

URUGUAY

E   F   G   H

41

Southern South America

Population ● National capital

○ below 50,000   ○ 50,000 to 100,000   ◉ 100,000 to 500,000   ◼ above 500,000

0 km   400
0 miles   400

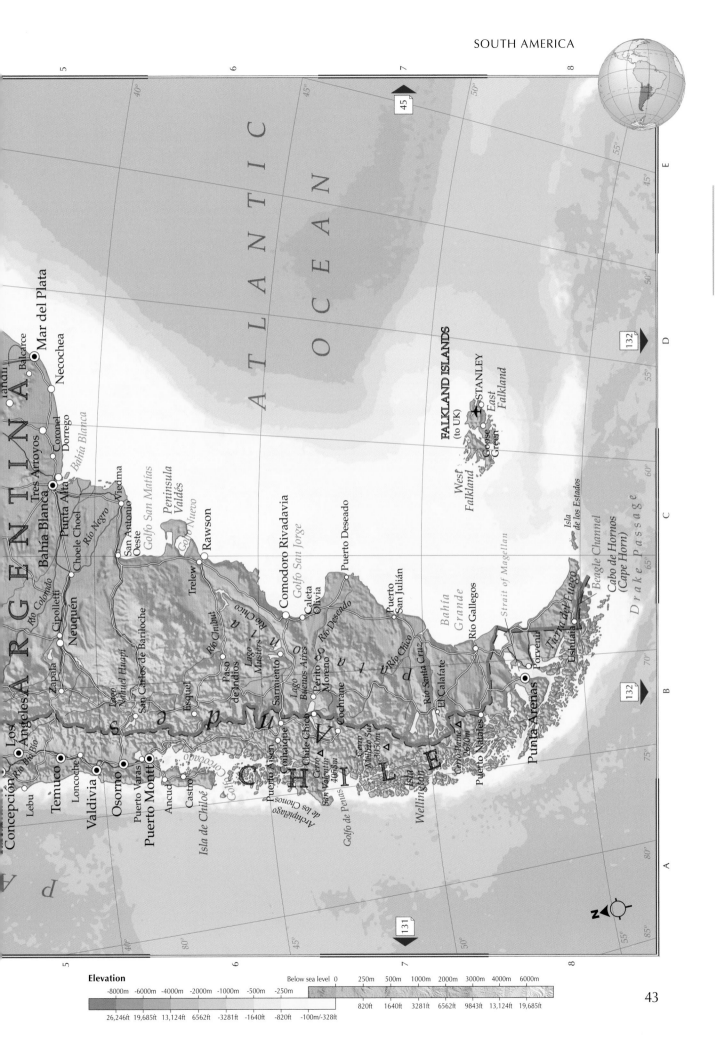

132

132

131

ATLANTIC

OCEAN

A R G E N T I N A

Mar del Plata

Balcarce

Necochea

Coronel
Dorrego

Tres Arroyos

Bahía Blanca

Punta Alta

Bahía Blanca

Viedma

San Antonio
Oeste

Golfo San Matías

Península
Valdés

Golfo Nuevo

Choele Choel

Río Negro

Río Colorado

Cipolletti

Neuquén

Zapala

Rawson

Trelew

Río Chubut

Lago
Musters

Lago
Buenos Aires

Perito
Moreno

Cochrane

Río Chico

Río Deseado

Comodoro Rivadavia

Caleta
Olivia

Puerto Deseado

Golfo San Jorge

Puerto
San Julián

Puerto
Deseado

Río Santa Cruz

Río Chico

Río Gallegos

El Calafate

Bahía
Grande

Puerto Natales

Cerro
Paine
2670m △

Punta Arenas

Porvenir

Tierra del Fuego

Ushuaia

Strait of Magellan

Isla
de los Estados

Beagle Channel

Cabo de Hornos
(Cape Horn)

D r a k e   P a s s a g e

FALKLAND ISLANDS
(to UK)

STANLEY

East
Falkland

Goose
Green

West
Falkland

Los
Ángeles

Concepción

Lebu

Temuco

Loncoche

Valdivia

Osorno

Puerto Varas

Puerto Montt

Ancud

Castro

Isla de Chiloé

Golfo Corcovado

Archipiélago
de los Chonos

Golfo de Penas

Isla
Wellington

Puerto Aisén

Coihaique

Chile Chico

Cerro
San Valentín
4058m △

Cerro
Melimoyu
3050m △

Río Bío Bío

Lago
Nahuel Huapi

San Carlos de Bariloche

Esquel

Paso
de Indios

Sarmiento

San Antonio

C H I L E

R e p ú b l i c a

Río Chico

Ñandu

P

Pd

Z

N

The Atlantic Ocean

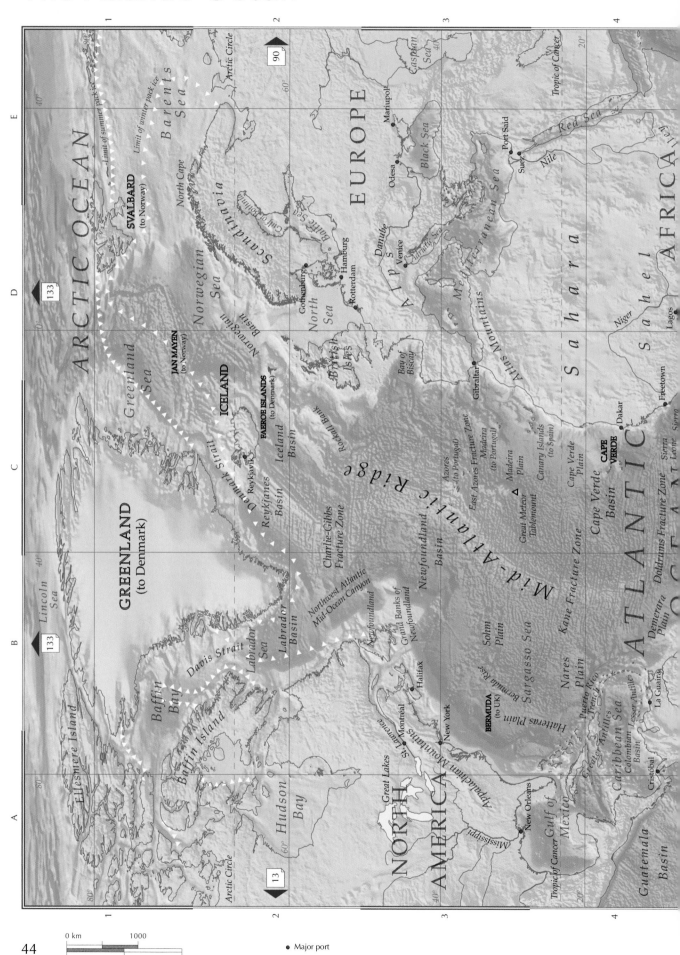

ARCTIC OCEAN

Barents Sea

Limit of summer pack ice

Limit of winter pack ice

Arctic Circle

90

SVALBARD (to Norway)

North Cape

Scandinavia

Gulf of Bothnia

EUROPE

Mariupol

Black Sea

Caspian Sea

Tropic of Cancer

Port Said

Red Sea

Odesa

Suez

Nile

Baltic Sea

Danube

Venice

Alps

Mediterranean Sea

AFRICA

Norwegian Sea

Norwegian Basin

133

Gothenburg

Hamburg

Rotterdam

North Sea

British Isles

Atlas Mountains

Sahara

Sahel

Niger

Lagos

JAN MAYEN (to Norway)

Greenland Sea

ICELAND

FAEROE ISLANDS (to Denmark)

Bay of Biscay

Gibraltar

Denmark Strait

Reykjavik

Reykjanes Basin

Iceland Basin

Rockall Bank

Mid-Atlantic Ridge

Azores (to Portugal)

East Azores Fracture Zone

Madeira (to Portugal)

Madeira Plain

Canary Islands (to Spain)

Cape Verde Plain

Dakar

Freetown

GREENLAND (to Denmark)

Charlie-Gibbs Fracture Zone

Newfoundland Basin

Great Meteor Tablemount

Cape Verde Basin

CAPE VERDE

Sierra Leone

Doldrums Fracture Zone

Lincoln Sea

Labrador Sea

Northwest Atlantic Mid-Ocean Canyon

Newfoundland

Grand Banks of Newfoundland

Sohm Plain

Sargasso Sea

Kane Fracture Zone

Nares Plain

Demerara Plain

Sierra

ATLANTIC OCEAN

133

Baffin Bay

Davis Strait

Labrador Basin

Halifax

Bermuda Rise

Puerto Rico Trench

Ellesmere Island

Baffin Island

Montréal

St. Lawrence

New York

BERMUDA (to UK)

Hatteras Plain

La Guaira

Cristóbal

Lesser Antilles

Greater Antilles

Colombian Basin

Hudson Bay

Great Lakes

Appalachian Mountains

NORTH AMERICA

New Orleans

Gulf of Mexico

Mississippi

Tropic of Cancer

Caribbean Sea

Guatemala Basin

13

Arctic Circle

Major port

44

0 km 1000

0 miles 1000

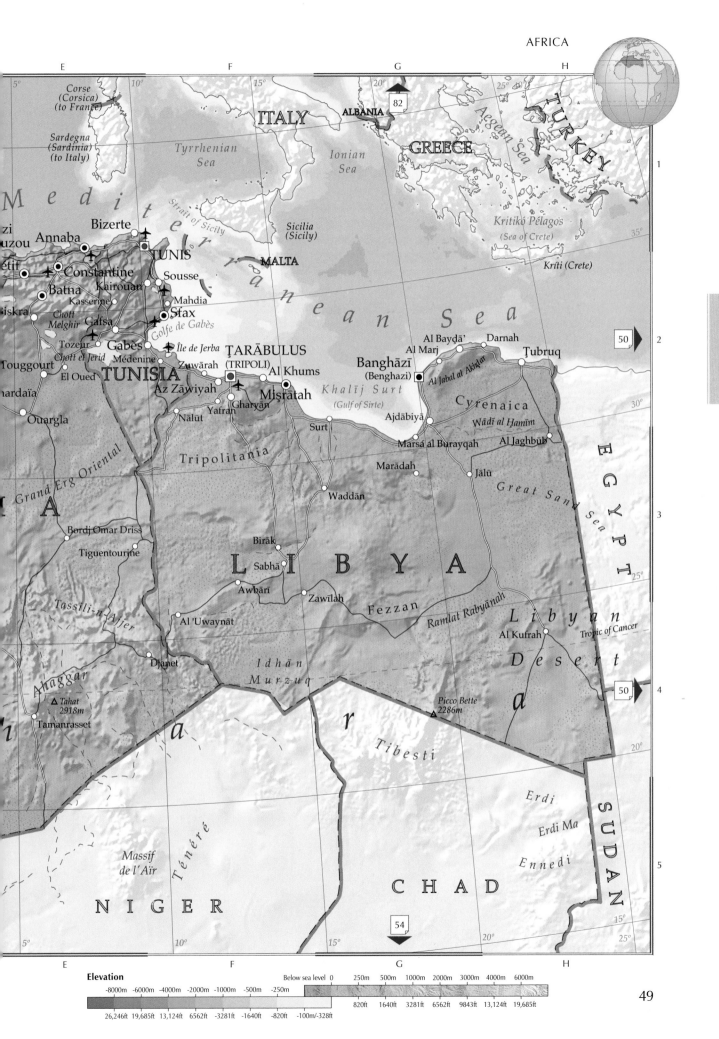

E   10°   F   15°   G   20°   25°   H

5°

Corse
(Corsica)
(to France)

ITALY

82

ALBANIA

Sardegna
(Sardinia)
(to Italy)

Tyrrhenian
Sea

GREECE

TURKEY

Aegean Sea

Ionian
Sea

zi
uzou
Annaba
Bizerte

étif
Constantine
TUNIS
Sousse
Kairouan
Mahdia

Batna
Kasserine
Sfax

Biskra
Chott
Melghir
Gafsa
Golfe de Gabès

Tozeur
Gabes
Île de Jerba
ṬARĀBULUS
(TRIPOLI)

Chott el Jerid
Médenine
Zuwārah
Al Khums

El Oued
TUNISIA
Az Zāwiyah
Miṣrātah

Touggourt
Gharyān
Yafran

hardaïa
Nālūt

Ouargla

MALTA

Mediterranean Sea

Kritikó Pélagos
(Sea of Crete)

35°

Kríti (Crete)

Al Bayḍā'
Darnah

Al Marj
Ṭubruq

Banghāzī
(Benghazi)
Al Jabal al Akhḍar

50

2

Khalīj Surt
(Gulf of Sirte)

Cyrenaica

Ajdābiyā
Wādī al Ḥamīm

Surt
Marsá al Burayqah
Al Jaghbūb

30°

Tripolitania

Marādah
Jālū

EGYPT

Grand Erg Oriental

Waddān

Great Sand Sea

3

A

Bordj Omar Driss

Tiguentourine

Birāk

Sabhā

L I B Y A

25°

Tassili-n-Ajjer

Awbārī

Zawīlah

Fezzan

Libyan

Al 'Uwaynāt

Ramlat Rabyānah

Al Kufrah
Tropic of Cancer

50

4

Djanet

Idhān
Murzuq

Desert

a

Ahaggar

△ Tahat
2918m

Picco Bette
△ 2286m

a

Tamanrasset

r

Tibesti

20°

Erdi

Massif
de l'Air

Ténéré

Erdi Ma

Ennedi

S U D A N

5

N I G E R

C H A D

54

15°

5°
10°
15°
20°
25°

E   F   G   H

Elevation

Below sea level   0   250m   500m   1000m   2000m   3000m   4000m   6000m

-8000m   -6000m   -4000m   -2000m   -1000m   -500m   -250m

820ft   1640ft   3281ft   6562ft   9843ft   13,124ft   19,685ft

26,246ft   19,685ft   13,124ft   6562ft   -3281ft   -1640ft   -820ft   -100m/-328ft

Northeast Africa

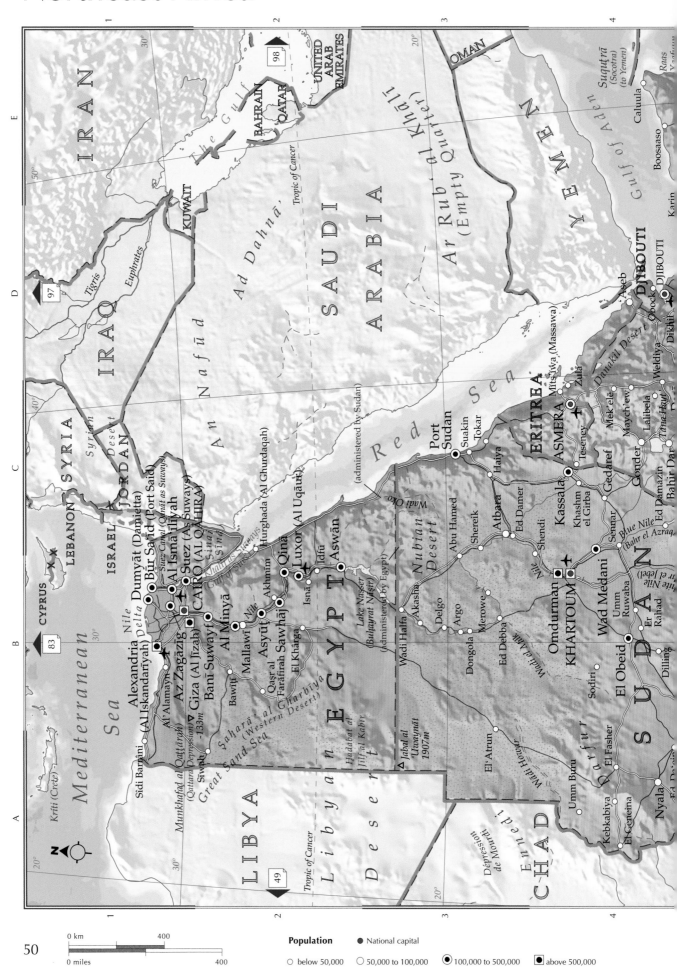

Population ● National capital

○ below 50,000   ◯ 50,000 to 100,000   ◉ 100,000 to 500,000   ■ above 500,000

0 km   400

0 miles   400

Barents Sea

North Cape

Ostrov Kolguyev

133

70°

80°

Murmansk

Kola Peninsula

Irtysh

Ob'

80°

1

Arctic Circle

White Sea

Archangel

Northern Dvina

R U S S I A N

Ural Mountains

FINLAND

Lake Onega

Perm'

90

70°

2

Tampere

F E D E R A T I O N

Ufa

50°

Turku

HELSINKI

Lake Ladoga

Vologda

Kazan'

Gulf of Bothnia

Saint Petersburg

Yaroslavl'

Åland

TALLINN

Nizhniy Novgorod

Ul'yanovsk

Orenburg

STOCKHOLM

Baltic Sea

Uppsala

ESTONIA

MOSCOW

Samara

Ural

LATVIA

Volga Upland

Syr Darya

3

RĪGA

Volga

LITHUANIA

Vitsyebsk

European Plain

Central Russian Upland

Aral Sea

Kaunas

Kaliningrad

VILNIUS

Ural

KALININGRAD (to Russ.Fed).

MINSK

Babruysk

Voronezh

Bydgoszcz

WARSAW

BELARUS

Homyel'

Pripet Marshes

Don

Amu Darya

60°

POLAND

Brest

Bug

Dnieper Lowlands

Kharkiv

Volgograd

40°

Kraków

L'viv

Dniester

Dnieper

Astrakhan'

Volga Delta -28m

SLOVAKIA

UKRAINE

Dnipropetrovs'k

Donets'k

Rostov-na-Donu

Carpathian Mountains

Dniester

BUDAPEST

Chernivtsi

Caspian Sea

HUNGARY

MOLDOVA

Stavropol'

Cluj-Napoca

CHIŞINĂU

90

4

ROMANIA

Odesa

Sea of Azov

Crimea

Caucasus

A S I A

Braşov

BELGRADE

BUCHAREST

Simferopol

El'brus 5642m

SERBIA

Danube

Constanţa

Black Sea

KOSOVO (disputed)

BULGARIA

Varna

Balkan Mountains

MONT.

PRISTINA

Zagros Mountains

PODGORICA

SOFIA

Burgas

MACED.

TURKEY

30°

TIRANA

SKOPJE

ALBANIA

Aegean Sea

Anatolia

5

Pindus Mountains

GREECE

ATHENS

Piraeus

Tigris

Peloponnese

96

Euphrates

50°

Irákleio

Cyprus

Crete

20°

30°

40°

The North Atlantic

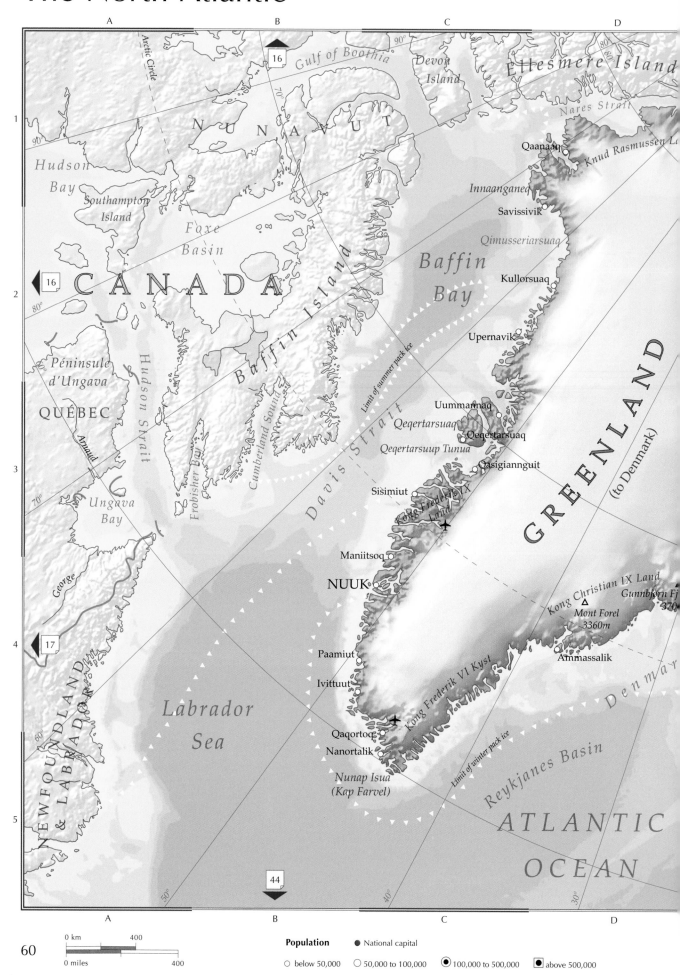

A — B — C — D

Arctic Circle

Gulf of Boothia

Devon Island

Ellesmere Island

Nares Strait

NUNAVUT

Qaanaaq

Knud Rasmussen L

Hudson Bay

Innaanganeq

Southampton Island

Savissivik

Foxe Basin

Qimusseriarsuaq

Baffin Bay

Kullorsuaq

CANADA

Upernavik

Baffin Island

Limit of summer pack ice

Péninsule d'Ungava

Uummannaq

QUÉBEC

Qeqertarsuaq

Qeqertarsuaq

Hudson Strait

Qeqertarsuup Tunua

Qasigianguit

Davis Strait

Sisimiut

Kong Frederik IX Land

GREENLAND

(to Denmark)

Arnaud

Ungava Bay

Maniitsoq

NUUK

Kong Christian IX Land

Gunnbjørn Fj

George

Mont Forel 3360m

370

Kong Frederik VI Kyst

Paamiut

Ammassalik

Ivittuut

Denmar

Labrador Sea

Qaqortoq

Nanortalik

Reykjanes Basin

Nunap Isua (Kap Farvel)

Limit of winter pack ice

ATLANTIC

NEWFOUNDLAND & LABRADOR

OCEAN

16

16

17

44

A — B — C — D

60

0 km 400
0 miles 400

Population ● National capital

○ below 50,000 ○ 50,000 to 100,000 ◉ 100,000 to 500,000 ◼ above 500,000

ARCTIC
OCEAN

Lincoln Sea

Kap Morris Jesup

Wandel Sea

Independence Fjord

Nord

SVALBARD
(to Norway)

133

Zemlya
Frantsa-Iosifa

Kvitøya

Novaya
Zemlya

Nordaustlandet

Kong Karls Land

Spitsbergen

Barentsøya

*Barents
Sea*

LONGYEARBYEN
Barentsburg

Edgeøya

Storfjorden

88

Limit of winter pack ice

*Greenland
Sea*

Kong Frederik VIII Land

Kong Christian X Land

Daneborg

△ Petermann Bjerg
2940m

Limit of summer pack ice

Mohns Ridge

Bjørnøya
(to Norway)

Nordkapp
(North Cape)

FINLAND

Kong Oscar Fjord

Ittoqqortoormiit

Kangertittivaq

Kangikajik

JAN MAYEN
(to Norway)

*Norwegian
Sea*

Vestfjorden

Arctic Circle

62

trait

Norwegian Basin

S
W
E
D
E
N

ICELAND

Bolungarvík
Siglufjördhur
Ísafjördhur
Húsavík
Akureyri
Stykkishólmur
REYKJAVÍK
xaflói
Selfoss
Thorláshöfn
Surtsey
Vestmannaeyjar

Raufarhöfn

Seydhisfjördhur
Neskaupstadhur

Vatnajökull
△ Hvannadalshnúkur
2119m

Djúpivogur

Gulf
of
Bothnia

FAEROE ISLANDS
(to Denmark)

TÓRSHAVN

NORWAY

Shetland
Islands

63

N

Elevation

| | Below sea level 0 | 250m | 500m | 1000m | 2000m | 3000m | 4000m | 6000m |

-8000m -6000m -4000m -2000m -1000m -500m -250m

820ft 1640ft 3281ft 6562ft 9843ft 13,124ft 19,685ft

26,246ft 19,685ft 13,124ft 6562ft -3281ft -1640ft -820ft -100m/-328ft

61

Scandinavia & Finland

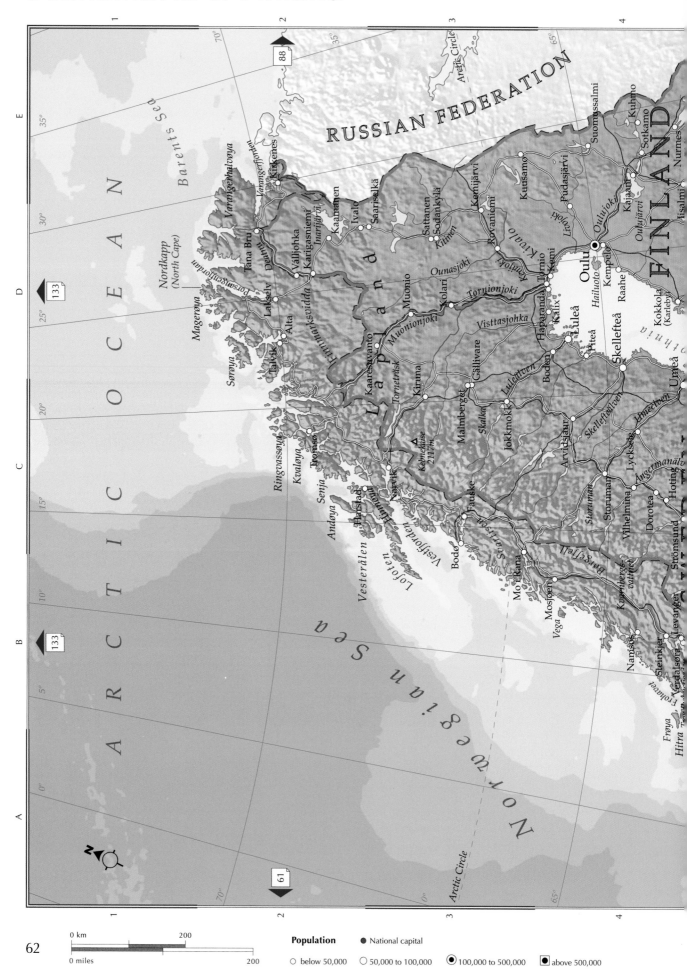

RUSSIAN FEDERATION

FINLAND

Barents Sea

A R C T I C   O C E A N

Norwegian Sea

Arctic Circle

Lapland

Nordkapp
(North Cape)

Kirkenes
Vardø
Vadsø
Tana Bru
Deatnu
Lakselv
Alta
Talvik
Tromsø
Kvaløya
Ringvassøya
Senja
Andøya
Harstad
Narvik
Fauske
Bodø
Mo i Rana
Mosjøen
Vega
Namsos
Steinkjer
Verdalsøra
Levanger
Frohavet
Hitra
Frøya

Magerøya
Sørøya
Vesterålen
Lofoten
Vestfjorden

Vadsøhalvøya
Varangerfjorden
Porsangenfjorden
Finnmarksvidda

Válljohka
Karigasniemi
Inarijärvi
Kaamanen
Ivalo
Saariselkä
Sattanen
Sodankylä
Kitinen
Kemijärvi
Kuusamo
Pudasjärvi
Suomussalmi
Sotkamo
Kuhmo
Nurmes
Iisalmi

Kaaresuvanto
Torneträsk
Kiruna
Malmberget
Gällivare
Jokkmokk
Arvidsjaur
Storuman
Vilhelmina
Dorotea
Hoting
Strömsund

Muonio
Muonionjoki
Kolari
Visttasjohka
Skalka
Luleälven
Boden
Kalix
Haparanda
Tornio
Kemi
Tornionjoki
Rovaniemi
Ounasjoki
Kemijoki
Oulujoki
Oulu
Oulujärvi
Kajaani
Haukipudas
Kempele
Raahe
Kokkola
(Karleby)

Kebnekaise
2117 m

Luleå
Piteå
Skellefteå
Skellefteälven
Lycksele
Ångermanälven
Umeå
Ångermanälven

Kvarberge
vidderne
Børgefjell

Gulf of Bothnia

Population

● National capital

○ below 50,000

○ 50,000 to 100,000

◉ 100,000 to 500,000

◼ above 500,000

0 km   200
0 miles   200

62

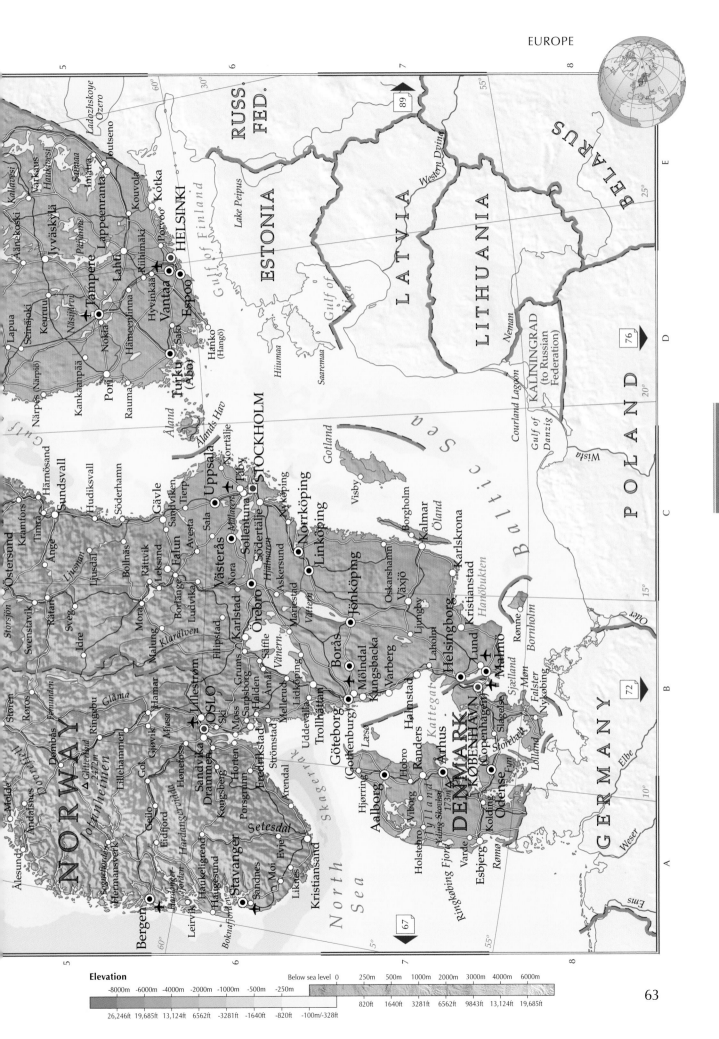

RUSS. FED.

BELARUS

ESTONIA

LATVIA

LITHUANIA

KALININGRAD
(to Russian
Federation)

POLAND

GERMANY

DENMARK

NORWAY

Gulf of Finland

Lake Peipus

Gulf of Riga

Hiiumaa

Saaremaa

Baltic Sea

Gulf of
Danzig

Courland Lagoon

Western Dvina

Neman

Wisła

Oder

Elbe

Weser

Ems

HELSINKI
Espoo
Vantaa
Tampere
Nokia
Pori
Rauma
Turku
(Åbo)
Hanko
(Hangö)
Kotka
Porvoo
Lahti
Kouvola
Lappeenranta
Hyvinkää
Riihimäki
Salo
Hämeenlinna
Jyväskylä
Keuruu
Seinäjoki
Lapua
Närpiö
Kankaanpää
Äänekoski
Varkaus
Iisalmi
Joutseno
Kallavesi
Ladozhskoye
Ozero
Saimaa
Hankavesi
Näsijärvi
Pyhäjärvi

STOCKHOLM
Uppsala
Täby
Sollentuna
Norrtälje
Sigtuna
Västerås
Enköping
Sala
Nora
Örebro
Eskilstuna
Södertälje
Nyköping
Norrköping
Linköping
Motala
Askersund
Mariestad
Jönköping
Borås
Mölndal
Kungsbacka
Göteborg
(Gothenburg)
Trollhättan
Lidköping
Vänern
Vättern
Hjälmaren
Gotland
Visby
Borgholm
Öland
Kalmar
Karlskrona
Kristianstad
Hanöbukten
Helsingborg
Lund
Malmö
Ljungby
Växjö
Oskarshamn
Västervik
Halmstad
Varberg
Falun
Avesta
Ludvika
Borlänge
Leksand
Rättvik
Mora
Malung
Filipstad
Karlstad
Grums
Säffle
Åmål
Mellerud
Uddevalla
Ski
Fredrikstad
Sarpsborg
Halden
Strömstad
Skagerrak
Kattegat
Klarälven
Glåma
Mjøsa
Gävle
Söderhamn
Hudiksvall
Sundsvall
Härnösand
Kramfors
Sollefteå
Timrå
Ånge
Ljusnan
Ljusdal
Bollnäs
Storsjön
Östersund
Svenstavik
Rätan
Sveg
Idre
Vänersborg
Sandviken
Tierp
Hofors

Ålands Hav
Åland
Gulf of Bothnia
North Sea

OSLO
Lillestrøm
Sandvika
Drammen
Kongsberg
Hønefoss
Gjøvik
Hamar
Lillehammer
Gol
Geilo
Eidfjord
Hardangervidda
Haukeligrend
Haugesund
Leirvik
Bergen
Voss
Hermansverk
Sognefjord
Hardanger
Jotunheimen
△ Glittertind
2472m
Dovrefjell
Dombås
Ringebu
Røros
Støren
Åndalsnes
Molde
Ålesund
Stören
Setesdal
Evje
Moi
Liknes
Kristiansand
Mandal
Flekkefjord
Lindesnes
Arendal
Porsgrunn
Horten
Moss
Sandnes
Stavanger
Boknafjorden
Jæren

AALBORG
Hjørring
Holstebro
Viborg
Randers
Hobro
Århus
Jylland
Yding Skovhøj
173m
Ringkøbing Fjord
Varde
Esbjerg
Rømø
Kolding
Odense
Fyn
Svendborg
Storebælt
Slagelse
Sjælland
Nykøbing
Falster
Lolland
Møn
KØBENHAVN
(Copenhagen)
Helsingborg
Rønne
Bornholm

Elevation

| Below sea level | 0 | 250m | 500m | 1000m | 2000m | 3000m | 4000m | 6000m |

-8000m -6000m -4000m -2000m -1000m -500m -250m

26,246ft 19,685ft 13,124ft 6562ft -3281ft -1640ft -820ft -100m/-328ft

820ft 1640ft 3281ft 6562ft 9843ft 13,124ft 19,685ft

The Low Countries

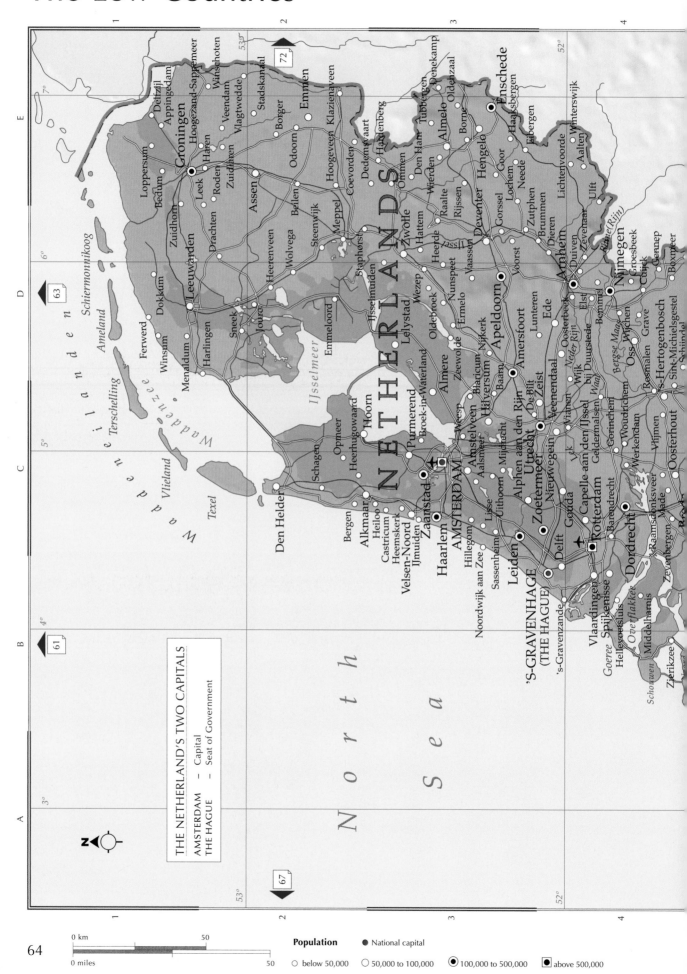

THE NETHERLAND'S TWO CAPITALS

AMSTERDAM – Capital
THE HAGUE – Seat of Government

Population   ● National capital

○ below 50,000   ○ 50,000 to 100,000   ◉ 100,000 to 500,000   ◼ above 500,000

0 km   50

0 miles   50

N

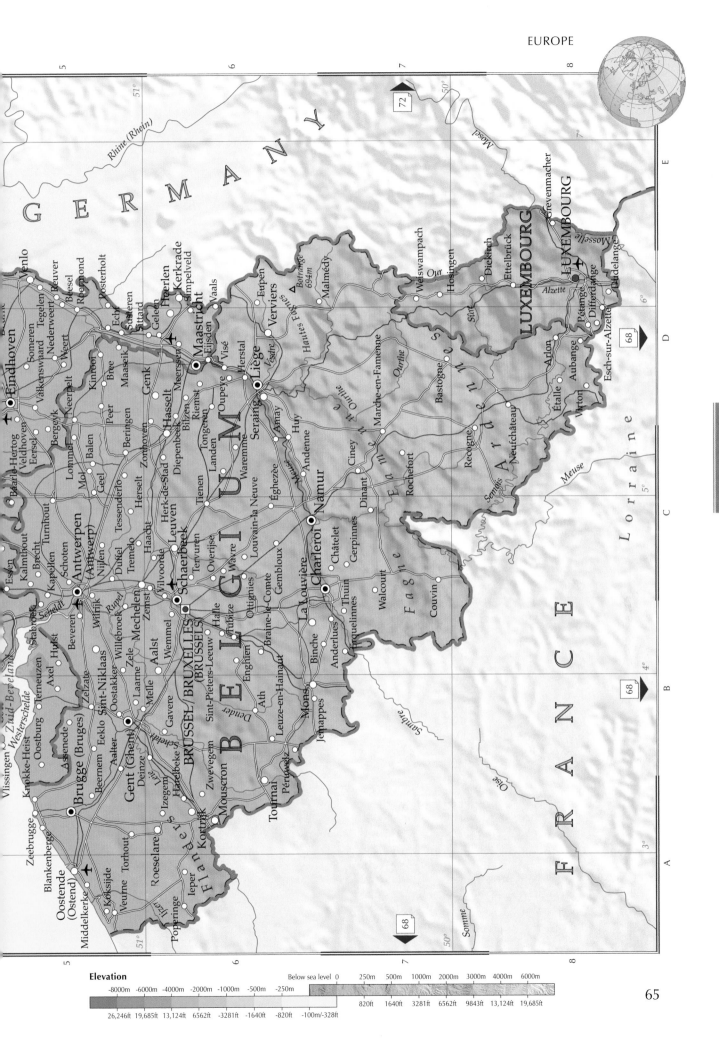

GERMANY

Rhine (Rhein)

Mosel

Venlo
Veldhoven
Reuver
Beesel
Roermond
Posterholt
Eindhoven
Someren
Nederweert
Tegelen
Kerkrade
Kempelveld
Heerlen
Echt
Susteren
Sittard
Geleen
Vaals
Maastricht
Eijsden
Valkenswaard
Bergeyk
Neerpelt
Bree
Maaseik
Genk
Meerssen
Visé
Herstal
Liège
Etten
Verviers
Baarle-Hertog
Eersel
Lommel
Balen
Peer
Beringen
Hasselt
Bilzen
Riemst
Oupeye
Amay
Serang
Huy
Weiswampach
Our
Hosingen
Diekirch
Ettelbrück
Differdange
LUXEMBOURG
LUXEMBOURG
Alzette
Pétange
Dudelange
Esch-sur-Alzette
Botrange
694m
Malmédy
Hautes Fagnes
Grevenmacher
Moselle
Mol
Geel
Zorhoven
Diepenbeek
Herk-de-Stad
Tongeren
Landen
Waremme
Warenne
Andenne
Marche-en-Famenne
Bastogne
Arlon
Aubange
Étalle
Virton
Turnhout
Herselt
Leuven
Tienen
Louvain-la-Neuve
Éghezèe
Ciney
Rochefort
Recogne
Neufchâteau
Ardenne
Lorraine
Antwerpen
(Antwerp)
Nijlen
Duffel
Tremelo
Haacht
Tervuren
Overijse
Wavre
Gembloux
Namur
Dinant
Semois
Meuse
Essen
Kalmthout
Brecht
Kapellen
Schoten
Vilvoorde
Schaerbeek
Ottignies
Braine-le-Comte
Charleroi
Châtelet
Gerpinnes
Walcourt
Couvin
Fagne
Eau d'Heure
BELGIUM
Vlissingen Zuid-Beveland
Westerschelde
Beveren
Mechelen
Zemst
BRUSSEL/BRUXELLES
(BRUSSELS)
Halle
Tubize
La Louvière
Binche
Thuin
Froidchapelle
Sambre
Knokke-Heist
Oostburg
Axel Hulst
Terneuzen
Sint-Niklaas
Laarne
Zele
Willebroek
Sint-Pieters-Leeuw
Enghien
Leuze-en-Hainaut
Mons
Anderlues
Frasnes
Zeebrugge
Blankenberge
Brugge (Bruges)
Eeklo
Gent (Ghent)
Deinze
Gavere
Melle
Aalst
Dender
Ath
Jemappes
Péruwelz
Scheldt
Oostende
(Ostend)
Middelkerke
Koksijde
Veurne
Torhout
Roeselare
Izegem
Zwevegem
Kortrijk
Mouscron
Tournai
Flanders
Ieper
Poperinge
IJzer
FRANCE
Somme
Oise

72

68

68

68

51°
50°
50°
51°

5
6
7
8

E
D
C
B
A

Elevation

Below sea level 0   250m   500m   1000m   2000m   3000m   4000m   6000m

-8000m -6000m -4000m -2000m -1000m -500m -250m

820ft 1640ft 3281ft 6562ft 9843ft 13,124ft 19,685ft

26,246ft 19,685ft 13,124ft 6562ft -3281ft -1640ft -820ft -100m/-328ft

The British Isles

North Sea

ATLANTIC OCEAN

Shetland Islands
Unst
Yell
Fetlar
Mainland
Lerwick
Fair Isle

Orkney Islands
Sanday
Kirkwall
Mainland
Hoy
John o'Groats

Thurso
Ben Hope 927m
Ullapool
North West Highlands
Inverness
Loch Ness
Aviemore
Grampian Mountains
Elgin
Moray Firth
Ness
Dee
SCOTLAND
Fraserburgh
Peterhead
Aberdeen
Montrose
Arbroath
Dundee
St Andrews
Forfar
Tay
Perth
Ben Nevis 1343 m
Fort William
Loch Lomond
Stirling
Dunfermline
Firth of Forth
Edinburgh
Berwick-upon-Tweed
Galashiels
Hawick
Cheviot Hills
Newcastle upon Tyne
South Shields

Stornoway
Isle of Lewis
Harris
North Uist
South Uist
Barra
Outer Hebrides
St Kilda

The Minch
The Little Minch
Isle of Skye
Strontian
Mallaig
Eigg
Rhum
Coll
Tiree
Isle of Mull
Oban
Firth of Lorn
Jura
Islay
Inner Hebrides
Kintyre
Isle of Arran

Greenock
Paisley
Glasgow
Hamilton
East Kilbride
Kilmarnock
Prestwick
Ayr
Clyde
Southern Uplands
Coleraine
NORTHERN

60
62
44

66

Population   ● National capital   ● Internal administrative capital

○ below 50,000   ○ 50,000 to 100,000   ◉ 100,000 to 500,000   ◼ above 500,000

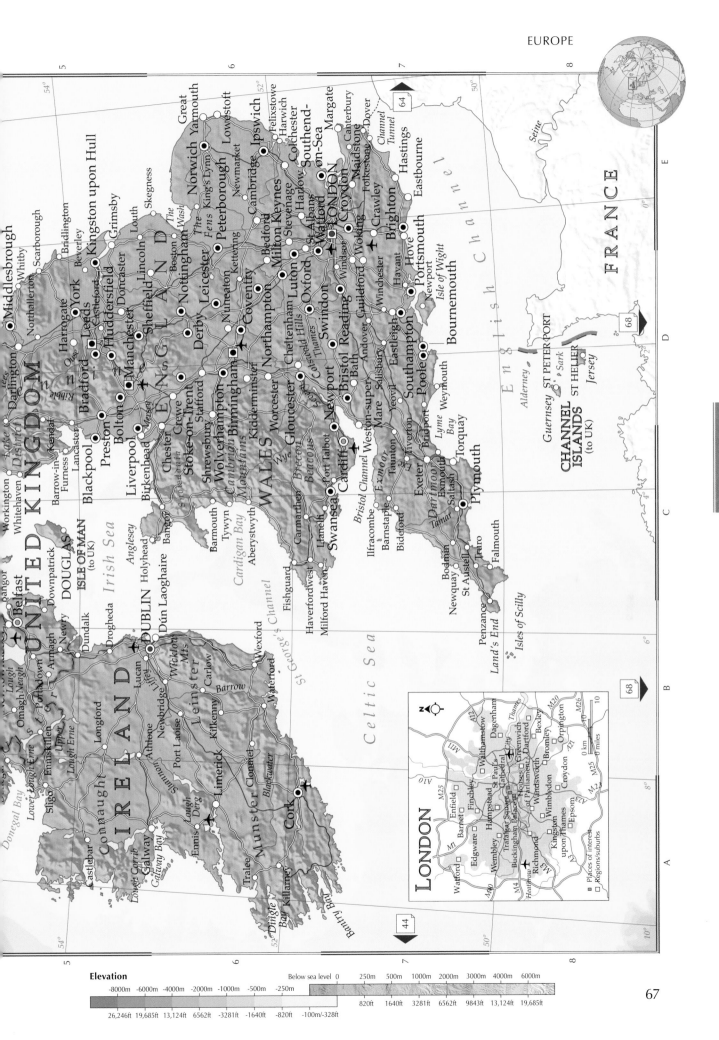

Elevation

| Below sea level | 0 | 250m | 500m | 1000m | 2000m | 3000m | 4000m | 6000m |

-8000m -6000m -4000m -2000m -1000m -500m -250m

-100m/-328ft

26,246ft 19,685ft 13,124ft 6562ft -3281ft -1640ft -820ft

820ft 1640ft 3281ft 6562ft 9843ft 13,124ft 19,685ft

France, Andorra & Monaco

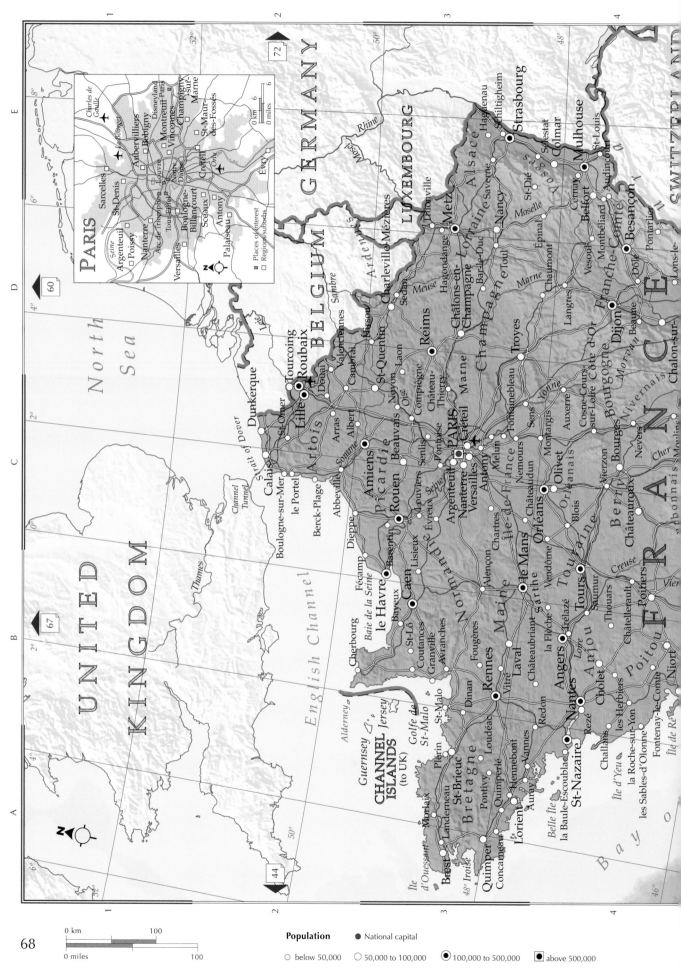

PARIS

Places of interest
Regions/suburbs

SWITZERLAND

GERMANY

LUXEMBOURG

BELGIUM

UNITED KINGDOM

North Sea

Strait of Dover

Channel Tunnel

English Channel

CHANNEL ISLANDS (to UK)

Bay of

FRANCE

Alsace
Lorraine
Champagne
Vosges
Franche-Comté
Île-de-France
Picardie
Artois
Normandie
Bretagne
Maine
Anjou
Touraine
Berry
Bourgogne
Nivernais
Poitou

Strasbourg
Mulhouse
Colmar
Sélestat
St-Louis
Belfort
Montbéliard
Audincourt
Besançon
Dole
Dijon
Metz
Thionville
Hagondange
Nancy
Saverne
Haguenau
Schiltigheim
St-Dié
Épinal
Vesoul
Langres
Chaumont
Bar-le-Duc
Toul
Châlons-en-Champagne
Charleville-Mézières
Sedan
Verdun
Reims
Soissons
Laon
St-Quentin
Compiègne
Château-Thierry
Troyes
Sens
Auxerre
Montargis
Nevers
Cosne-Cours-sur-Loire
Côte d'Or
Beaune
Chalon-sur-Saône
Mâcon
Morvan
Chambéry
Tourcoing
Roubaix
Lille
Douai
Valenciennes
Cambrai
Denain
Dunkerque
St-Omer
Calais
Boulogne-sur-Mer
le Portel
Berck-Plage
Abbeville
Amiens
Arras
Albert
Beauvais
Noyon
Oise
Senlis
Pontoise
Paris
Argenteuil
Nanterre
Créteil
Versailles
Antony
Melun
Nemours
Fontainebleau
Châteaudun
Chartres
Alençon
Orléans
Olivet
Blois
Vendôme
Tours
Amboise
Saumur
Thouars
Châtellerault
Poitiers
Niort
Fontenay-le-Comte
la Roche-sur-Yon
les Sables-d'Olonne
Challans
les Herbiers
Cholet
Angers
Trélazé
Nantes
Rezé
St-Nazaire
la Baule-Escoublac
Redon
Châteaubriant
Vitré
Laval
Rennes
Loudéac
Dinan
St-Malo
Golfe de St-Malo
Guernsey
Alderney
Jersey
St-Brieuc
Plérin
Pontivy
Hennebont
Lorient
Auray
Vannes
Quimperlé
Concarneau
Quimper
Brest
Landerneau
Morlaix
île d'Ouessant
île d'Yeu
Belle île
île de Ré
Cherbourg
Fécamp
Dieppe
le Havre
Bayeux
Caen
Lisieux
Bayeux
Coutances
Granville
Avranches
St-Lô
Fougères
le Mans
la Flèche
Bourges
Issoudun
Vierzon
Cher
Creuse
Châteauroux
Vienne

Seine
Rhine
Moselle
Meuse
Marne
Yonne
Loire
Sarthe
Thames
Baie de la Seine

Rouen
Évreux
Louviers
Bar-le-Duc

0 km 100
0 miles 100

Population   ● National capital

○ below 50,000   ○ 50,000 to 100,000   ◉ 100,000 to 500,000   ▣ above 500,000

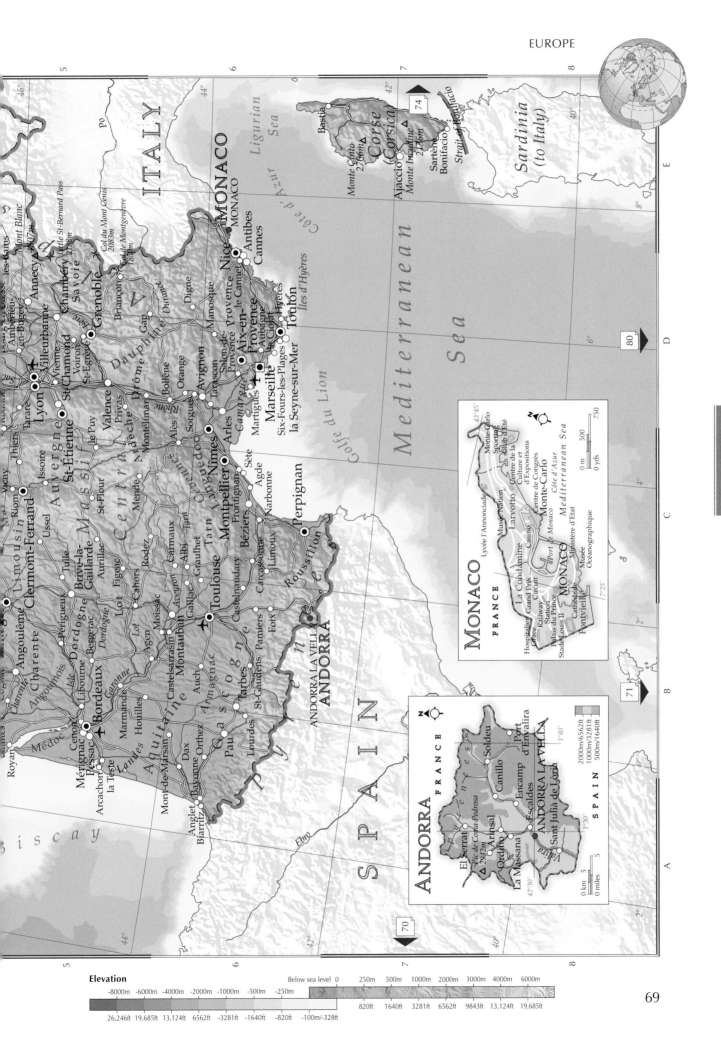

Bastia

Monte Cinto
2706m △

*Corse
(Corsica)*
Monte Incudine
2136m △
Sartène
Ajaccio
Bonifacio
Strait of Bonifacio

*Sardinia
(to Italy)*

*Ligurian
Sea*

Côte d'Azur
MONACO
MONACO
Nice
Antibes
Cannes
le Cannet
Hyères
Toulon
Iles d'Hyères

Mont Blanc
Little St-Bernard Pass
Col du Mont Cenis
Col de Montgenèvre
2083m
Annecy
Albertville
les Bains
Aix-les-Bains
Ambérieu-
en-Bugey
Chambéry
Savoie
Grenoble
Briançon
Voiron
St-Egrève
Gap
Durance
Drôme
Digne
Manosque
Vienne
St-Chamond
Tarare
St-Etienne
le Puy
Privas
Valence
Montélimar
Ardèche
Orange
Avignon
Salon-de-
Provence
Aix-en-
Provence
Aubagne
la Ciotat
Martigues
Six-Fours-les-Plages
la Seyne-sur-Mer
Marseille
Rhône
Bollène
Sorgues
Ales
Gard
Nîmes
Tarascon
Arles
Camargue
Sète
Agde
Montpellier

*Mediterranean
Sea*

Lyon
Villeurbanne
Thiers
Riom
Issoire
Clermont-Ferrand
Ussel
St-Flour
Mende
Aurillac
Auvergne
Limousin
Tulle
Brive-la-
Gaillarde
Figeac
Rodez
Aurillac
Central Massif
Mauriac
Lot
Cahors
Gaillac
Carmaux
Albi
Tarn
Castres
Montauban
Moissac
Garonne
Toulouse
Castelsarrasin
Auch
Pamiers
Foix
Languedoc
Béziers
Narbonne
Limoux
Carcassonne
Castelnaudary
Frontignan
Perpignan
Roussillon
Golfe du Lion

Golfe du Lion

Angoulême
Charente
Périgueux
Bergerac
Libourne
Dordogne
Bordeaux
Cenon
Pessac
Mérignac
Arcachon
la Teste
Médoc
Royan
Marmande
Agen
Houilles
Mont-de-Marsan
Dax
Orthez
Pau
Tarbes
Lourdes
St-Gaudens
Armagnac
Gascogne
Aquitaine
Landes
Isle
Anglet
Biarritz
Bayonne

Biscay

P y r é n é e s

ANDORRA LA VELLA
ANDORRA
Roussillon

SPAIN

ITALY

Ebro

MONACO

FRANCE

Monte-Carlo
Sporting
Club d'Eté
Museé Nation
Larvotto
Centre de la
Culture et
d'Expositions
Lycée l'Annonciade
La Condamine
Hospitalier
Grand Prix
Grace
Circuit
Casino
Centre de Congrès
Monte-Carlo
Côte d'Azur
Mediterranean Sea
Railway
Station
Palais du Prince
StadeLouis II
Cathédrale
Fontvieille
Port de Monaco
Ministère d'Etat
Musée
Océanographique
MONACO

43°45'
7°25'
N
0 m   500
0 yds   750

ANDORRA

FRANCE

N
El Serrat
Soldeu
Ordino
Arinsal
Canillo
La Massana
Encamp
Escaldes
Port
d'Envalira
ANDORRA LA VELLA
Sant Julià de Lòria
Pic de Coma Pedrosa
2942m △
Pyrénées
Valira
SPAIN

1°40'
1°30'
42°30'

2000m/6562ft
1000m/3281ft
500m/1640ft

0 km   5
0 miles   5

74
80
71
70

Elevation

Below sea level   0   250m   500m   1000m   2000m   3000m   4000m   6000m

-8000m   -6000m   -4000m   -2000m   -1000m   -500m   -250m

26,246ft   19,685ft   13,124ft   6562ft   -3281ft   -1640ft   -820ft   -100m/-328ft

820ft   1640ft   3281ft   6562ft   9843ft   13,124ft   19,685ft

Spain & Portugal

Bay of Biscay

Gijon (Xixón) · Costa Verde · Santande
Luarca · Avilés · Villaviciosa · Llanes
Ferrol · Pravia · Oviedo · Torrelavega · Cantab
A Coruña (La Coruña) · Tineo · Mieres del Camino · Reinosa
Betanzos · Asturias · Pola de Lena · Cabañaquinta
Laracha
Santa Comba · Galicia · Cordillera Cantábrica
Cabo Fisterra · Lugo
Oubes · Santiago · Chantada · Ponferrada · León
Muros · Lalín · Monforte de Lemos · Castilla-León
Ribeira · O Carballiño · Astorga · Palencia · Burgo
Pontevedra · Ourense (Orense) · Benavente · Lerm
Marín · Ponteareas · Xinzo de Limia · Zamora · Valladolid · Arand
Vigo · Toro · Duero · de Duer
Miño · Ponte da Barca · Bragança · Embalse de Ricobayo
Viana do Castelo · Chaves · Medina del Campo · Duero
Braga · Vila Real · Salamanca · Segovia · Sierr
Póvoa de Varzim · Guimarães · Embalse de Almendra · S · Guadar
Vila do Conde · P
Matosinhos · Lamego · Central
Porto (Oporto) · Douro · São João da Madeira · Viseu · MADRID
Vila Nova de Gaia · Alto da Torre · Guarda · Ciudad-Rodrigo · Ávila · Getafe
Ovar · 1993m · Serra da Estrela · Béjar · Sistema
Albergaria-a-Velha · Covilhã · Sierra de Gredos
Aveiro · Viseu
Ílhavo · Plasencia · Talavera de la Reina · Aranju
Coimbra · Coria · Toledo
Figueira da Foz · Embalse de Valdecañas
PORTUGAL · Embalse de Alcántara · Cáceres
Leiria · Castelo Branco · Trujillo · Herrera del Duque
Tomar · Tagus · Extremadura · Dam
Entroncamento · Abrantes · Villanueva de la Serena · Ciudad Real
Peniche · Caldas da Rainha · Portalegre · Mérida · Puertollano
Torres Vedras · Santarém · Elvas · Don Benito
Coruche · Estremoz · Badajoz · Castuera
Sintra · LISBOA (LISBON) · Villafranca de los Barros · Pozoblanco
Cascais · Serra d'Osa · Almendralejo · La Caroli
Almada · Barreiro · Évora · Zafra · Azuaga
Setúbal · Jerez de los Caballeros · Morena
Alcácer do Sal · Barragem do Alqueva · Montoro · Bailén
Baía de Setúbal · Córdoba · Linar
Sines · Beja · Cortegana · Guadalquivir · Bujalance · Ja
Nerva · Palma del Río · Martos · Alcaude
Ourique · Valverde del Camino · La Algaba · Andalucí
Algarve · Carmona · Écija · Sistem
Portimão · Lepe · Sevilla (Seville) · Lucena · Granad
Lagos · Isla Cristina · Huelva · Dos Hermanas · Osuna · Archidona · Sierr
Cabo de São Vicente · Faro · Tavira · Antequera · M
Olhão · Las Cabezas de San Juan · Álora
Golfo de Cádiz · Lebrija · Olvera · Ronda · Málaga
Sanlúcar de Barrameda · Ubrique · Can · Fuengirola
El Puerto de Santa María · Jerez de la Frontera · Marbella · Costa del S
Cádiz · Estepona
San Fernando · Vejer de la Frontera
Costa de la Luz · Barbate de France · GIBRALTAR (to UK)
Algeciras · Ceuta (to Spain)
Strait of Gibraltar
MOROCCO

AZORES (to Portugal)

Corvo
Flores · São Jorge · Graciosa
Faial · Pico · Terceira
São Miguel
Ponta Delgada · Santa Maria

0 km 100
0 miles 100
200m/656ft
Sea level

0 km 100
0 miles 100

Population ● National capital
○ below 50,000 ○ 50,000 to 100,000 ◉ 100,000 to 500,000 ▪ above 500,000

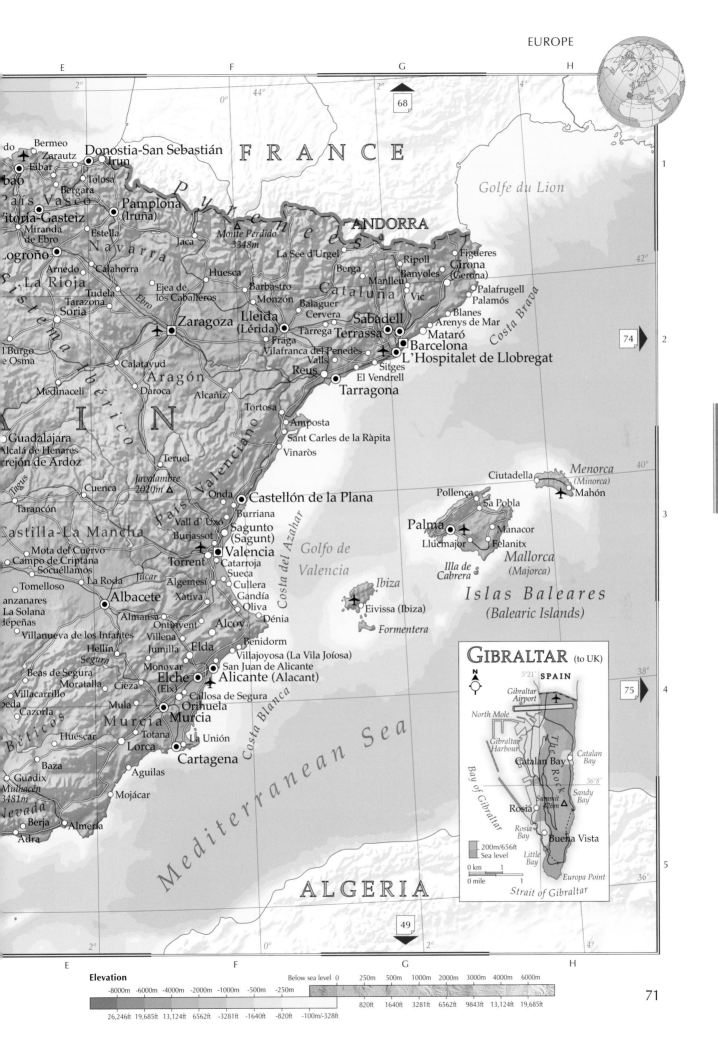

E · F · G · H

FRANCE

Golfe du Lion

ANDORRA

do · Bermeo · Zarautz
Donostia-San Sebastián
Eibar · Irún
bao · Tolosa
Bergara
País Vasco · **Pamplona**
Vitoria-Gasteiz · (Iruña)
Miranda · Estella
de Ebro
ogroño
Navarra · Jaca
Monte Perdido · La See d'Urgel
3348m
S. La Rioja · Huesca · Berga · Manlleu · Vic
Arnedo · Ejea de · Barbastro · Balaguer · Cervera
Tudela · los Caballeros · Monzón
Tarazona
Soria · **Zaragoza** · **Lleida** · Tàrrega · **Terrassa**
l Burgo · (Lérida) · Fraga · Vilafranca del Penedès
e Osma · Calatayud · **Aragón** · Vilafranca del Penedès · Valls
Medinaceli · Daroca · Alcañiz · Reus · Sitges
I · N · Alcañiz · El Vendrell
Guadalajara · Tortosa · **Tarragona**
Alcalá de Henares · Teruel · Amposta
rrejón de Ardoz · Sant Carles de la Ràpita
Tagus · Vinaròs
Javalambre
Tarancón · Cuenca · 2020m · Onda
Castilla-La Mancha · **Castellón de la Plana**
Mota del Cuervo · Burriana
Campo de Criptana · Vall d'Uxó · Sagunto
Socuéllamos · Burjassot · (Sagunt)
Tomelloso · La Roda · **Valencia**
anzanares · Júcar · Torrent · Catarroja
La Solana · Sueca
depeñas · **Albacete** · Xàtiva · Cullera
Villanueva de los Infantes · Almansa · Algemesí · Gandía
Hellín · Ontinyent · Oliva
Segura · Villena · **Alcoy** · Dénia
Beas de Segura · Jumilla · Elda · Benidorm
Moratalla · Monóvar · Villajoyosa (La Vila Joíosa)
Villacarrillo · Cieza · San Juan de Alicante
eda · Mula · **Elche** · **Alicante (Alacant)**
Cazorla · (Elx)
Béticos · **Murcia** · Callosa de Segura
Huéscar · Totana · **Murcia** · Orihuela
Baza · Lorca · La Unión
Guadix · Aguilas · **Cartagena**
Mulhacén
3481m · Mojácar
Jevada · Berja
Adra · Almería

Cataluña
Ripoll · **Girona**
Banyoles · (Gerona) · Figueres
Palafrugell
Palamós
Blanes
Sabadell · Arenys de Mar
Barcelona · Costa Brava
L'Hospitalet de Llobregat
Mataró

*Golfo de
Valencia*

Costa del Azahar

Ibiza
Eivissa (Ibiza)
Formentera

Ciutadella · *Menorca*
(Minorca)
Pollença · Mahón
Sa Pobla
Palma · Manacor
Llucmajor · Felanitx
Illa de · *Mallorca*
Cabrera · (Majorca)

*Islas Baleares
(Balearic Islands)*

Costa Blanca

Mediterranean Sea

ALGERIA

68

49

GIBRALTAR (to UK)

N · 5°21' · **SPAIN**
Gibraltar
Airport
North Mole
Gibraltar · The Rock · Catalan
Harbour · Bay
Catalan Bay
Bay of Gibraltar · 36°8'
Sandy
Summit · Bay
426m
Rosia
Rosia
Bay · Buena Vista
200m/656ft · Little
Sea level · Bay · Europa Point
0 km · 1
0 mile · 1
Strait of Gibraltar

Elevation

Below sea level 0 · 250m · 500m · 1000m · 2000m · 3000m · 4000m · 6000m

-8000m · -6000m · -4000m · -2000m · -1000m · -500m · -250m

820ft · 1640ft · 3281ft · 6562ft · 9843ft · 13,124ft · 19,685ft

26,246ft · 19,685ft · 13,124ft · 6562ft · -3281ft · -1640ft · -820ft · -100m/-328ft

Germany & The Alpine States

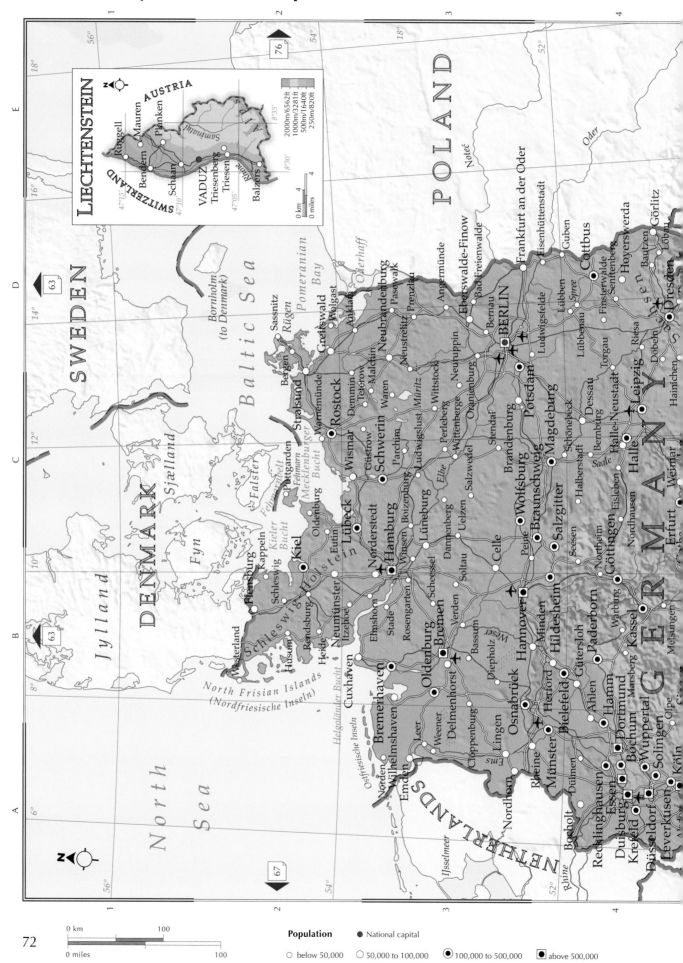

POLAND

SWEDEN

DENMARK

NETHERLANDS

North Sea

Baltic Sea

Jylland

Sjælland

Fyn

Bornholm
(to Denmark)

Pomeranian
Bay

Oder

Noteč

LIECHTENSTEIN

AUSTRIA

SWITZERLAND

Ruggell
Mauren
Planken
Bendern
Schaan
VADUZ
Triesenberg
Triesen
Balzers

Samínatal

Rhine

2000m/6562ft
1000m/3281ft
500m/1640ft
250m/820ft

0 km   4
0 miles   4

GERMANY

Sassnitz
Rügen
Bergen
Stralsund
Warnemünde
Rostock
Wismar
Güstrow
Tetěrow
Schwerin
Parchim
Ludwigslust
Mirštiz
Wittstock
Neuruppin
Oranienburg
Bernau
BERLIN
Potsdam

Greifswald
Wolgast
Anklam
Demmin
Malchin
Waren
Neubrandenburg
Neustrelitz
Pasewalk
Prenzlau
Angermünde
Eberswalde-Finow
Bad Freienwalde
Frankfurt an der Oder
Eisenhüttenstadt
Guben
Cottbus
Senftenberg
Hoyerswerda
Bautzen
Görlitz
Löbau
Dresden
Döbeln
Riesa
Torgau
Leipzig
Halle
Halle-Neustadt
Bernburg
Dessau
Magdeburg
Brandenburg
Wolfsburg
Braunschweig
Salzgitter
Schönebeck
Halberstadt
Stendal
Salzwedel
Uelzen
Lüneburg
Boizenburg
Dannenberg
Perleberg
Wittenberge
Ludwigsfelde
Lübben
Spree
Lübbenau
Finsterwalde
Weimar
Erfurt
Nordhausen
Eisleben
Mansfeld
Göttingen
Northeim
Seesen
Peine
Celle
Soltau
Scheessel
Verden
Bassum
Diepholz
Hannover
Hildesheim
Minden
Herford
Bielefeld
Gütersloh
Paderborn
Warburg
Kassel
Melsungen
Hann.
Hersfeld

Kiel
Flensburg
Kappeln
Schleswig
Rendsburg
Husum
Heide
Neumünster
Itzehoe
Elmshorn
Norderstedt
Hamburg
Lübeck
Eutin
Oldenburg
Fehmarn
Puttgarden
Falster

Cuxhaven
Bremerhaven
Wilhelmshaven
Bremen
Delmenhorst
Oldenburg
Wener
Leer
Emden
Norden
Nordhorn
Rheine
Lingen
Coppenburg
Osnabrück
Münster
Dülmen
Ahlen
Hamm
Dortmund
Bochum
Essen
Recklinghausen
Duisburg
Krefeld
Düsseldorf
Wuppertal
Solingen
Leverkusen
Köln
Bocholt
Olpe

Schleswig-Holstein
Mecklenburger Bucht
Kieler Bucht
Fehmarnbelt
Westerland
North Frisian Islands
(Nordfriesische Inseln)
Ostfriesische Inseln
Helgoländer Bucht
Ijsselmeer
Ems
Weser
Elbe
Saale
Rhine

Oderhaff

63
63
76
67

72

Population   ● National capital

○ below 50,000   ○ 50,000 to 100,000   ◉ 100,000 to 500,000   ▣ above 500,000

0 km   100
0 miles   100

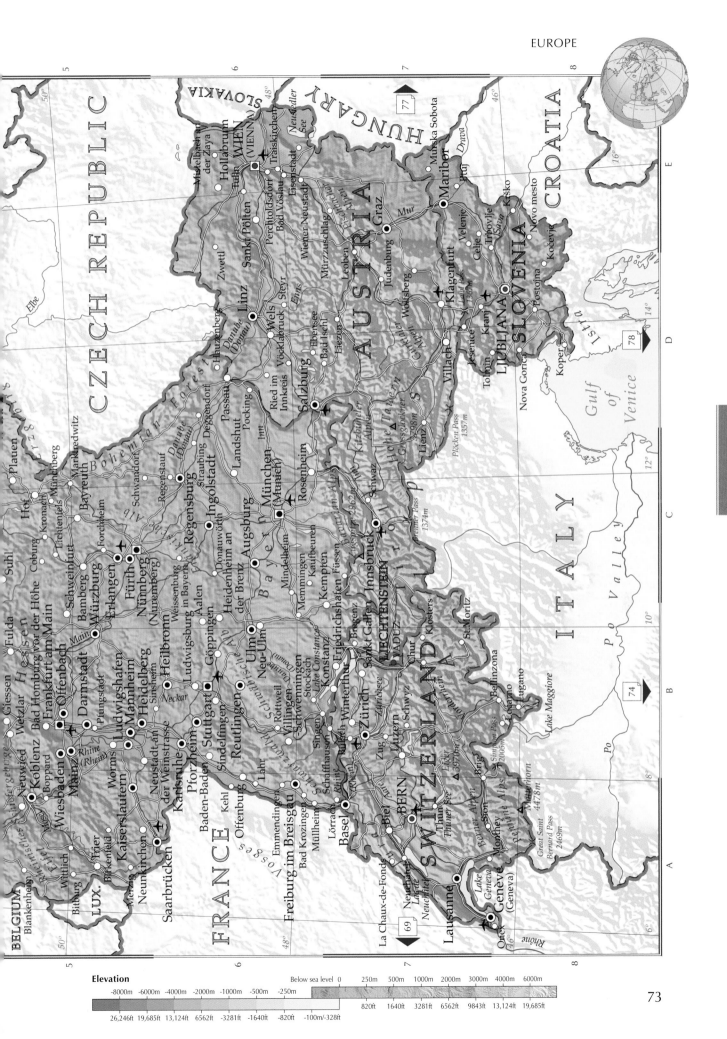

BELGIUM

LUX.

CZECH REPUBLIC

SLOVAKIA

HUNGARY

AUSTRIA

CROATIA

SLOVENIA

ITALY

SWITZERLAND

FRANCE

LIECHTENSTEIN

Hessen

Bayern

Bohemian Forest

Tirol

Hohe Tauern

Gulf of Venice

Po valley

Belgium
Blankenheim

Plauen
Hof
Suhl
Fulda
Giessen
Wetzlar
Netzweil
Koblenz
Boppard
Wiesbaden
Mainz
Rhine (Rhein)
Trier
Wittlich
Bitburg
Birkenfeld
Merzig
Neunkirchen
Saarbrücken
Kaiserslautern
Neustadt an der Weinstrasse
Karlsruhe
Worms
Ludwigshafen
Mannheim
Heidelberg
Sinsheim
Neckar
Pforzheim
Sindelfingen
Stuttgart
Reutlingen
Baden-Baden
Kehl
Offenburg
Lahr
Emmendingen
Freiburg im Breisgau
Bad Krozingen
Müllheim
Lörrach
Basel
La Chaux-de-Fonds
Neuchâtel
Lac de Neuchâtel
Lausanne
Lake Geneva Genève (Geneva)
Rhône
Onex
Bern
Thun
Thuner See
Biel
Brig
Matterhorn 4478m
Great Saint Bernard Pass 2469m
Simplon Pass 2005m
Lugano
Lake Maggiore
Bellinzona
Locarno
Lugano
Chur
VADUZ
Klosters
St Moritz
Zürich
Luzern
Zug
Schwyz
Zürichsee
Winterthur
Sankt Gallen
Bregenz
Friedrichshafen
Lake Constance
Konstanz
Singen
Schaffhausen
Rottweil
Villingen
Schwenningen
Stockach
Ulm
Neu-Ulm
Göppingen
Heilbronn
Heidenheim an der Brenz
Aalen
Weissenburg in Bayern
Ingolstadt
Donauwörth
Augsburg
Mindelheim
Memmingen
Kaufbeuren
Kempten
Füssen
Innsbruck
Schwaz
Kufstein
Rosenheim
München (Munich)
Landshut
Straubing
Deggendorf
Passau
Pocking
Ried im Innkreis
Vöcklabruck
Bad Ischl
Ebensee
Gmunden
Steyr
Enns
Wels
Linz
Danube (Donau)
Schärding
Regensburg
Schwandorf
Nürnberg (Nuremberg)
Fürth
Erlangen
Forchheim
Bamberg
Würzburg
Schweinfurt
Bayreuth
Lichtenfels
Kronach
Coburg
Münchberg
Marktredwitz
Zwettl
Haukenberg
Salzburg
Lienz
Plöcken Pass 1357m
Villach
Wolfsberg
Judenburg
Leoben
Mürzzuschlag
Eisenerz
Graz
Mur
Maribor
Ptuj
Murska Sobota
Drava
Velenje
Trbovlje
Celje
Sava
Krško
Novo mesto
LJUBLJANA
Kranj
Jesenice
Villach
Tolmin
Nova Gorica
Postojna
Kočevje
Koper
Istra
Klagenfurt
Gurktaler Alpen
Grossglockner 3798m
Kitzbüheler Alpen
Karwendel 2962m
Großvenediger 3674m
Brenner Pass 1374m
WIEN (VIENNA)
Mistelbach an der Zaya
Hollabrun
Traiskirchen
Eisenstadt
Neusiedler See
Perchtoldsdorf
Bad Vöslau
Wiener Neustadt
Sankt Pölten
Neustadler

Alb
Schwäbische Alb
Fränkische Alb
Bayerischer Wald
Vosges
Schwarzwald
Erzgebirge
Eifel
Elbe
Inn
Main
Po

Elevation

Below sea level	0	250m	500m	1000m	2000m	3000m	4000m	6000m
		820ft	1640ft	3281ft	6562ft	9843ft	13,124ft	19,685ft

-8000m	-6000m	-4000m	-2000m	-1000m	-500m	-250m
26,246ft	19,685ft	13,124ft	6562ft	-3281ft	-1640ft	-820ft	-100m/-328ft

Italy

SLOVAKIA

HUNGARY

BOSNIA &

HERZEGOVINA

CROATIA

Drava

Sava

D a l m a t i a

Adriatic Sea

SAN MARINO

Dogana
Serravalle
Gualdicciolo
Borgo Maggiore
Fiorina
Cailungo
Faetano
Monte Titano 739m
Murata
Montegiardino
SAN MARINO
ITALY
Chiesanuova

ITALY

500m/1640ft
200m/656ft
100m/328ft

0 km 2
0 miles 2

GERMANY

AUSTRIA

LIECHTENSTEIN

SWITZERLAND

Lake Geneva

Lake Constance

Rhine

Rhône

Inn

FRANCE

Brenner Pass 1374m

Great Saint Bernard Pass 2469m

Little St-Bernard Pass 2188m

Mont Blanc 4807m

Gran Paradiso 4061m

SLOVENIA

Trieste

Tarvisio
Monfalcone
Udine
Cortina d'Ampezzo
Cremona del Friuli
Pordenone
Portogruaro
Mestre
Treviso
Venezia (Venice)
Chioggia
Gulf of Venice
Foci del Po

Bressanone
Alpi
Dolomitiche
Merano
Bolzano
Trento
Edolo
Lago di Garda
Arco
Bassano del Grappa
Vicenza
Padova
Monselice
Ostiglia
Rovigo
Ferrara
Comacchio
Adige
Po

Varese
Lago di Como
Como
Bergamo
Brescia
Verona
Mantova
Carpi
Modena
Bologna
Imola
Faenza
Forlì
Ravenna
Cesena
Rimini
SAN MARINO
Fano
Pesaro
Sansepolcro
Falconara Marittima
Ancona
Civitanova Marche
Fermo
Ascoli Piceno
Giulianova
Teramo
Pescara
Chieti
Ortona
Termoli

Lombardia
Sesto San Giovanni
Monza
Rho
Milano (Milan)
Pavia
Piacenza
Castegio
Parma
Reggio nell'Emilia
Carrara
Massa
Pistoia
Lucca
Prato
Firenze (Florence)
Arezzo
Chianti
Toscana
Siena
Lago Trasimeno
Perugia
Todi
Foligno
Terni
L'Aquila
Avezzano
Tivoli
ROMA
VATICAN CITY

Novara
Vercelli
Asti
Alessandria
Mondovì
Savigliano
Cuneo
Torino (Turin)
Moncalieri
Rivoli
Susa
Aosta
Po
Piemonte
Appennino Ligure
Genova (Genoa)
Savona
Finale Ligure
Imperia
San Remo
Ventimiglia
MONACO

La Spezia
Viareggio
Pisa
Livorno
Cecina
Piombino
Portoferraio
Isola d'Elba
Archipelago Toscano
Grosseto
Orbetello
Civitavecchia
Viterbo

Golfo di Genova
Ligurian Sea

Corse (Corsica) (to France)
Strait of Bonifacio
Isola Asinara
La Maddalena

Marche
Umbro Marchigiana
Appennino
Appennino Pennin

0 km 100
0 miles 100

Population
● National capital
○ below 50,000
◯ 50,000 to 100,000
◉ 100,000 to 500,000
■ above 500,000

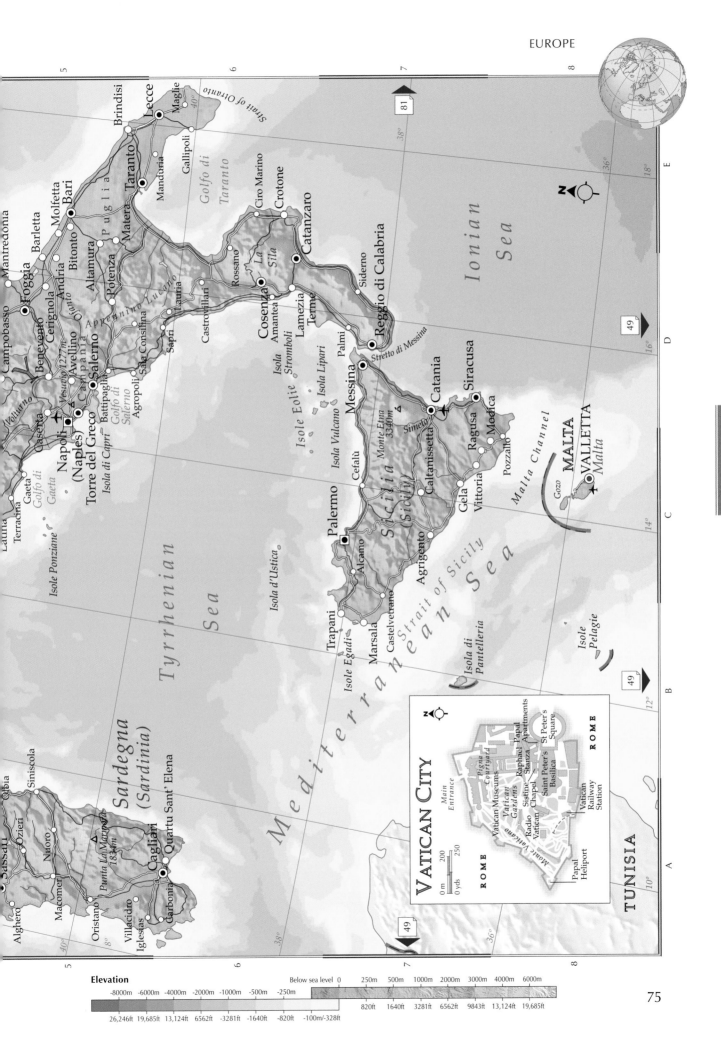

Elevation

| Below sea level | 0 | 250m | 500m | 1000m | 2000m | 3000m | 4000m | 6000m |

| -8000m | -6000m | -4000m | -2000m | -1000m | -500m | -250m |

| 26,246ft | 19,685ft | 13,124ft | 6562ft | -3281ft | -1640ft | -820ft | -100m/-328ft |

| | | | 820ft | 1640ft | 3281ft | 6562ft | 9843ft | 13,124ft | 19,685ft |

VATICAN CITY

Main Entrance
Pigna Courtyard
Papal Apartments
St Peter's Square
ROME
Vatican Museums
Vatican Gardens
Raphael Stanza
Sistine Chapel
Saint Peter's Basilica
Radio Vatican
Monte Vaticano
Vatican Railway Station
Papal Heliport

ROME

0 m   200
0 yds   250

ROME
TUNISIA

Brindisi
Lecce
Maglie
Strait of Otranto
Taranto
Manduria
Gallipoli
Golfo di Taranto
Bari
Molfetta
Barletta
Andria
Bitonto
Puglia
Matera
Altamura
Potenza
Ciro Marino
Crotone
Catanzaro
Rossano
La Sila
Lucania
Cosenza
Amantea
Siderno
Lamezia Terme
Reggio di Calabria
Palmi
Stretto di Messina
Stromboli
Isola Lipari
Isole Eolie
Isola Vulcano
Messina
Catania
Siracusa
Medica
Monte Etna 3340m
Simeto
Ragusa
Caltanissetta
Pozzallo
Sicilia (Sicily)
Cefalù
Palermo
Alcamo
Gela
Vittoria
Agrigento
Malta Channel
Gozo
MALTA
VALLETTA
Malta
Trapani
Marsala
Castelvetrano
Isole Egadi
Strait of Sicily
Isola di Pantelleria
Isole Pelagie
Isola d'Ustica
Tyrrhenian Sea
Mediterranean Sea
Ionian Sea
Manfredonia
Foggia
Cerignola
Campobasso
Benevento
Avellino
Vesuvio 1277m
Salerno
Napoli (Naples)
Torre del Greco
Battipaglia
Golfo di Salerno
Agropoli
Sala Consilina
Sapri
Castrovillari
Caserta
Gaeta
Golfo di Gaeta
Terracina
Latina
Isole Ponziane
Isola di Capri
Volturno
Ofanto
Sele
Appennino
Campania
Sardegna (Sardinia)
Sant'Elena
Quartu Sant'Elena
Cagliari
Punta La Marmora 1834m
Sassari
Ozieri
Nuoro
Macomer
Oristano
Villacidro
Iglesias
Carbonia
Olbia
Siniscola
Alghero
Gallipoli

Central Europe

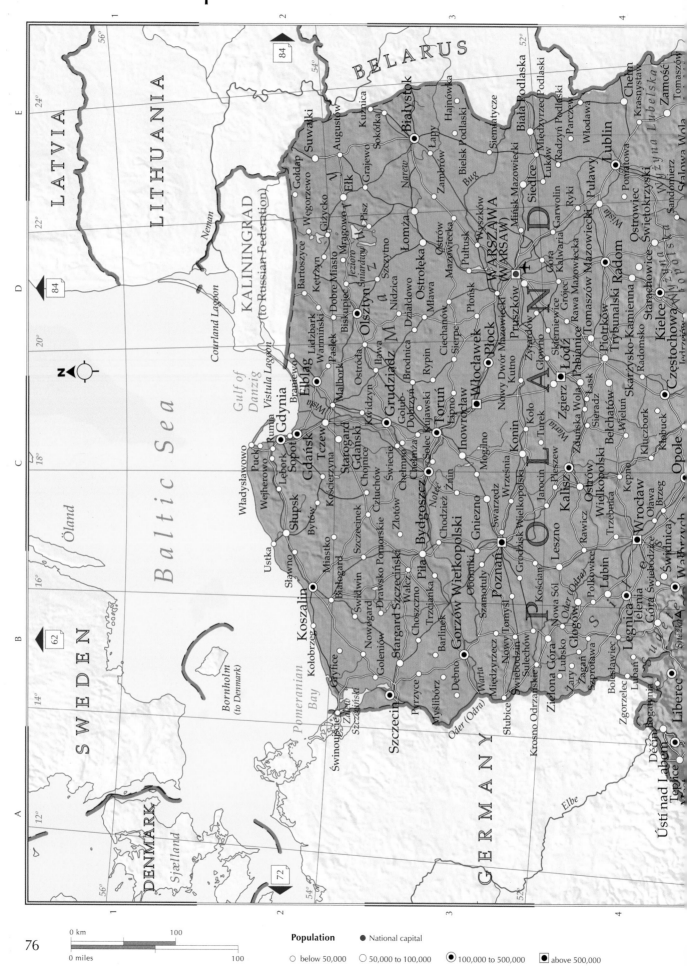

Population

● National capital

○ below 50,000   ○ 50,000 to 100,000   ◉ 100,000 to 500,000   ■ above 500,000

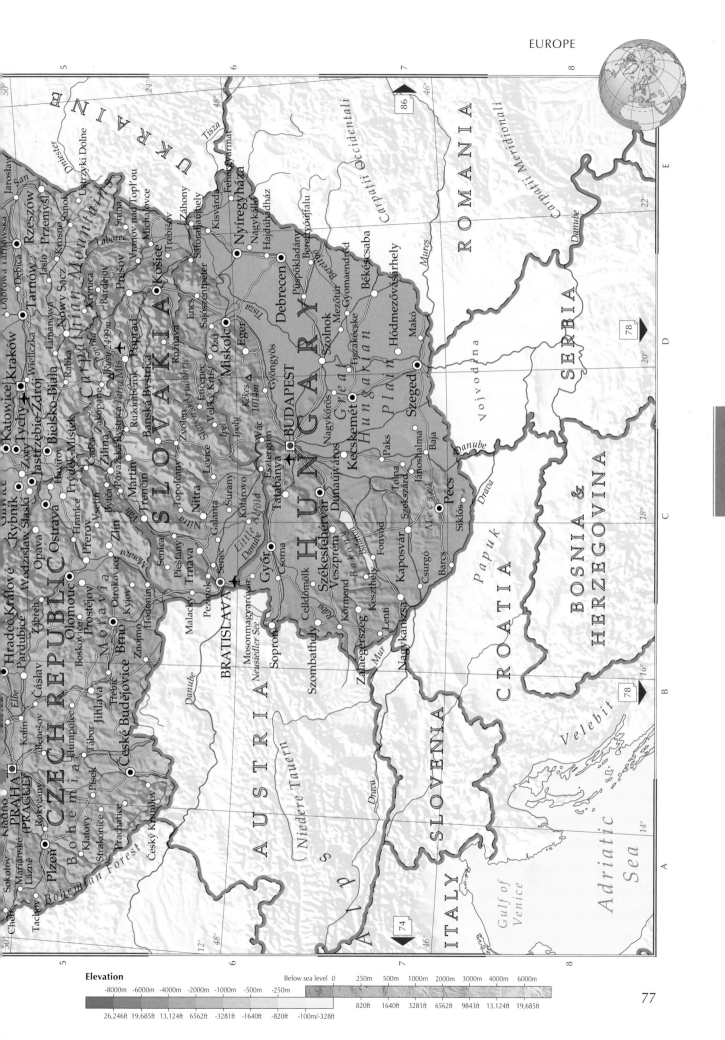

Elevation

| | Below sea level | 0 | 250m | 500m | 1000m | 2000m | 3000m | 4000m | 6000m |

-8000m -6000m -4000m -2000m -1000m -500m -250m

820ft 1640ft 3281ft 6562ft 9843ft 13,124ft 19,685ft

26,246ft 19,685ft 13,124ft 6562ft -3281ft -1640ft -820ft -100m/-328ft

Southeast Europe

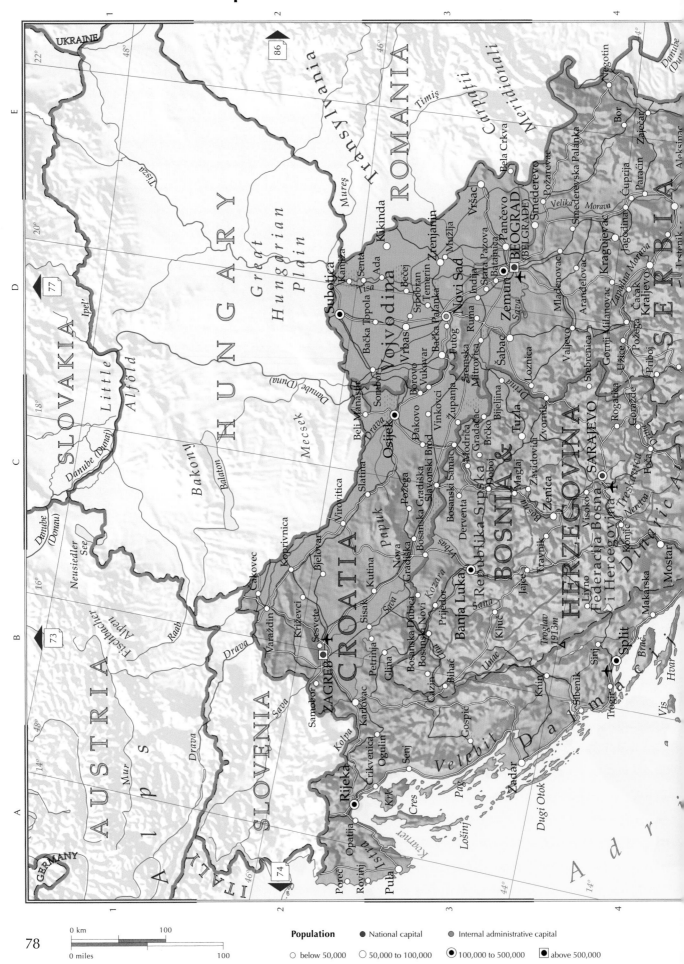

Population
- ● National capital
- ● Internal administrative capital
- ○ below 50,000
- ○ 50,000 to 100,000
- ◉ 100,000 to 500,000
- ◼ above 500,000

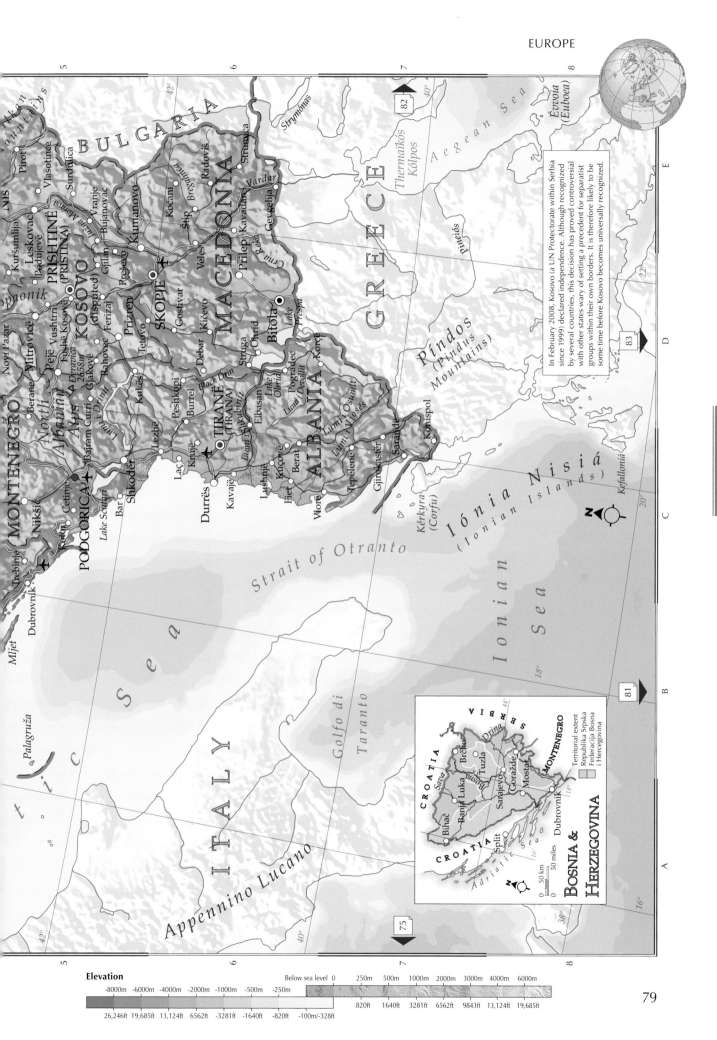

BULGARIA

Pirot
Vlasotince
Surdulica
Kuršumlija
Leskovac
Medveđa
Vranje
Bujanovac
Vlasotince
Vranje
Radoviš
Strumica
Strymónas
Kriva Reka
Bregalnica
Bregalnica
Kočani
Štip
Kumanovo
Gevgelija
Gevgelija
Vardar

NIŠ
Novi Pazar
Berane
Peć
Mitrovicë
Vushtrri
Fushë Kosovë
Gjilan
Preševo
Veles
Prilep
Kavadar
Crna Reka
SKOPJE
Gostivar
Kičevo

Topanik
KOSOVO
PRISHTINË
(PRISTINA)
Gjakovë
Prizren
Ferizaj
Tetovo
(Disputed)
Lake
Prespa
Bitola

Đakovica
Deravica
2656m
Alpet e Shqipërisë
Bajram Curri
Lumi i Drinit
Kukës
Debar
Ohrid
Struga
Lake
Ohrid
Korçë
MACEDONIA

GREECE

Nikšić
Cetinje
MONTENEGRO
PODGORICA
Bar
Shkodër
Lake Scutari
Lezhë
Lumi Shkumbinit
Peshkopi
Burrel
Black Drin
TIRANË
(TIRANA)
Elbasan
Pogradec
Lumi Devollit
Koplik

Trebinje
Dubrovnik
Mljet
Durrës
Kavajë
Krujë
Fier
Berat
Lushnjë
Kuçovë
Vlorë
Tepelenë
Gjirokastër
Sarandë
ALBANIA
Lumi i Osumit
Lumi i Vjosës
Konispol
Kérkyra
(Corfu)

Ríndos
(Pindus
Mountains)

Píneiós
Thermaïkós
Kólpos
Aegean Sea

Évvoia
(Euboea)

Palagruža

A d r i a t i c   S e a

Strait of Otranto

Iónia Nisiá
(Ionian Islands)

Kefallonía

ITALY

Golfo di
Taranto

I o n i a n   S e a

Appennino Lucano

82
83
81
75

In February 2008, Kosovo (a UN Protectorate within Serbia since 1999) declared independence. Although recognized by several countries, this decision has proved controversial with other states wary of setting a precedent for separatist groups within their own borders. It is therefore likely to be some time before Kosovo becomes universally recognized.

BOSNIA & HERZEGOVINA

CROATIA
SERBIA
Sava
Bihać
Banja Luka
Brčko
Tuzla
Bosna
Drina
Sarajevo
Goražde
Mostar
MONTENEGRO
Dubrovnik
Split
CROATIA
Adriatic Sea

Territorial extent
Republika Srpska
Federacija Bosna
i Hercegovina

0   50 km
0   50 miles

Elevation

			Below sea level 0	250m	500m	1000m	2000m	3000m	4000m	6000m

-8000m -6000m -4000m -2000m -1000m -500m -250m

820ft 1640ft 3281ft 6562ft 9843ft 13,124ft 19,685ft

26,246ft 19,685ft 13,124ft 6562ft -3281ft -1640ft -820ft -100m/-328ft

The Mediterranean

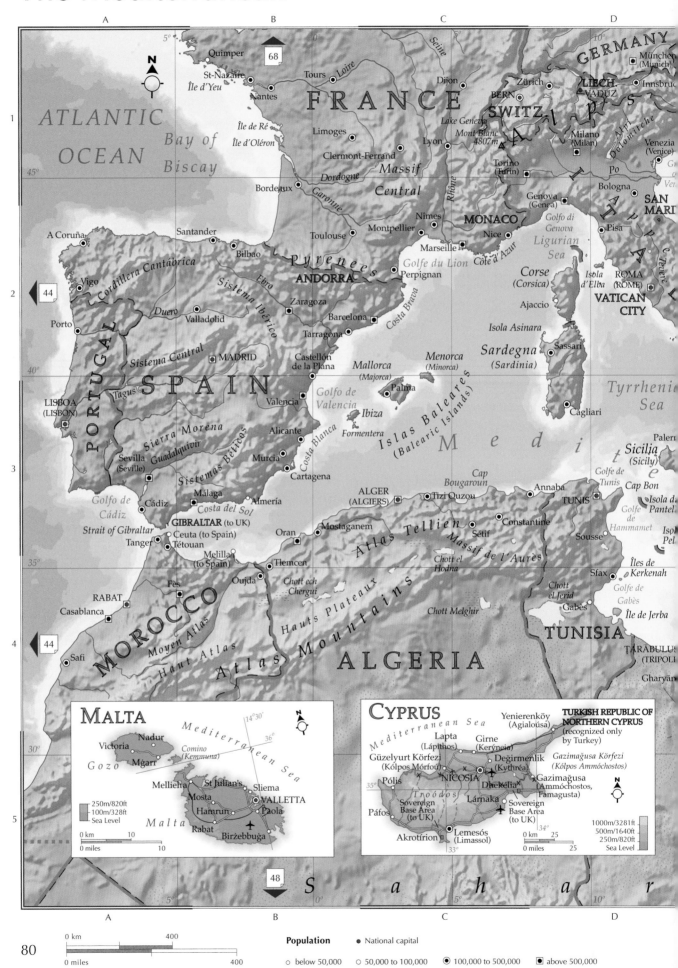

ATLANTIC OCEAN

Bay of Biscay

Quimper
St-Nazaire
Île d'Yeu
Nantes
Île de Ré
Île d'Oléron

FRANCE

Tours
Loire
Seine

Dijon

BERN
SWITZ
Zürich
Lake Geneva
Mont Blanc
4807m
Torino
(Turin)

GERMANY
München
(Munich)
LIECH
VADUZ
Innsbru

Limoges
Clermont-Ferrand
Dordogne
Massif
Central
Garonne
Bordeaux
Toulouse

Nîmes
Montpellier
Rhône
MONACO
Marseille
Nice
Côte d'Azur
Golfe du Lion

Lyon
Milano
(Milan)
Genova
(Genoa)
Po
Bologna
Venezia
(Venice)
Pisa
SAN MARI
ROMA
(ROME)
VATICAN CITY

A Coruña
Santander
Vigo
Cordillera Cantábrica
Bilbao
Porto
Duero
Valladolid
Ebro
Sistema Ibérico
Zaragoza
Pyrenees
ANDORRA
Perpignan
Barcelona
Costa Brava
Tarragona

Corse
(Corsica)
Isola d'Elba
Ligurian Sea
Ajaccio
Isola Asinara
Sardegna
(Sardinia)
Sassari

PORTUGAL
Sistema Central
MADRID
SPAIN
Tagus
LISBOA
(LISBON)
Sierra Morena
Guadalquivir
Sevilla
(Seville)
Castellón de la Plana
Valencia
Golfo de Valencia
Ibiza
Formentera
Mallorca
(Majorca)
Palma
Menorca
(Minorca)
Islas Baleares
(Balearic Islands)
Cagliari
Tyrrhenie
Sea

Alicante
Costa Blanca
Murcia
Cartagena
Sistemas Béticos

Golfo de Cádiz
Cádiz
Málaga
Costa del Sol
Almería
GIBRALTAR (to UK)
Strait of Gibraltar
Ceuta (to Spain)
Tanger
Tétouan
Melilla
(to Spain)
Tlemcen
Oran
Mostaganem
ALGER
(ALGIERS)
Tizi Ouzou
Cap Bougaroun
Annaba
Constantine
Sétif
TUNIS
Sicilia
(Sicily)
Golfe de Tunis
Cap Bon
Isola di Pantel
Golfe de Hammamet
Sousse
Sfax
Paler
Palem

Fes
Oujda
Chott ech Chergui
RABAT
Casablanca
MOROCCO
Moyen Atlas
Safi
Haut Atlas
Atlas Mountains
Hauts Plateaux
ALGERIA
Chott el Hodna
Massif de l'Aurès
Chott Melghir
Chott el Jerid
Gabès
TUNISIA
Îles de Kerkenah
Golfe de Gabès
Île de Jerba
TARABULUS
(TRIPOLI)
Gharyān

S a h a r

MALTA

Mediterranean Sea

Victoria
Nadur
Mġarr
Comino
(Kemmuna)
Gozo
Mellieħa
Mosta
Ħamrun
Rabat
St Julian's
Sliema
VALLETTA
Paola
Birżebbuġa
Malta

250m/820ft
100m/328ft
Sea Level

0 km 10
0 miles 10

CYPRUS

Mediterranean Sea

Yenierenköy
(Agialoúsa)
TURKISH REPUBLIC OF NORTHERN CYPRUS
(recognized only by Turkey)

Lapta
(Lápithos)
Girne
(Kerýneia)
Güzelyurt Körfezi
(Kólpos Mórfou)
Değirmenlik
(Kythréa)
Gazimağusa Körfezi
(Kólpos Ammóchostos)
Pólis
NICOSIA
Dhekélia
Gazimağusa
(Ammóchostos, Famagusta)
Tróödos
Lárnaka
Páfos
Sovereign Base Area (to UK)
Sovereign Base Area (to UK)
Akrotírion
Lemesós
(Limassol)

1000m/3281ft
500m/1640ft
250m/820ft
Sea Level

0 km 25
0 miles 25

Population ● National capital

○ below 50,000 ◎ 50,000 to 100,000 ◉ 100,000 to 500,000 ■ above 500,000

0 km 400
0 miles 400

Elevation

| -8000m | -6000m | -4000m | -2000m | -1000m | -500m | -250m | | Below sea level 0 | 250m | 500m | 1000m | 2000m | 3000m | 4000m | 6000m |

820ft 1640ft 3281ft 6562ft 9843ft 13,124ft 19,685ft

26,246ft 19,685ft 13,124ft 6562ft -3281ft -1640ft -820ft -100m/-328ft

Bulgaria & Greece

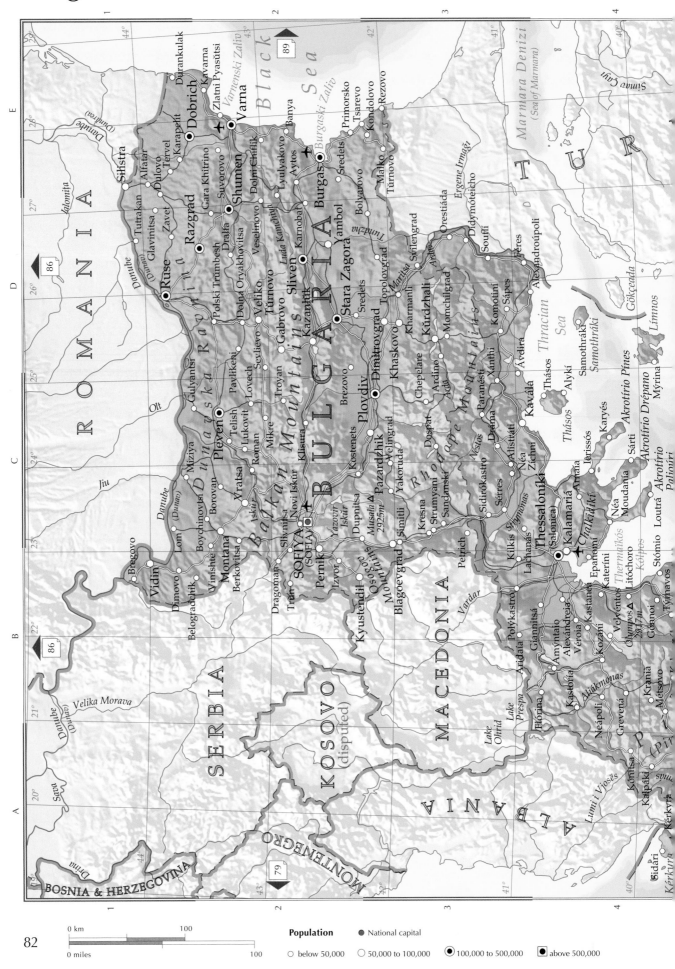

Population ● National capital

○ below 50,000 ○ 50,000 to 100,000 ◉ 100,000 to 500,000 ■ above 500,000

0 km   100
0 miles   100

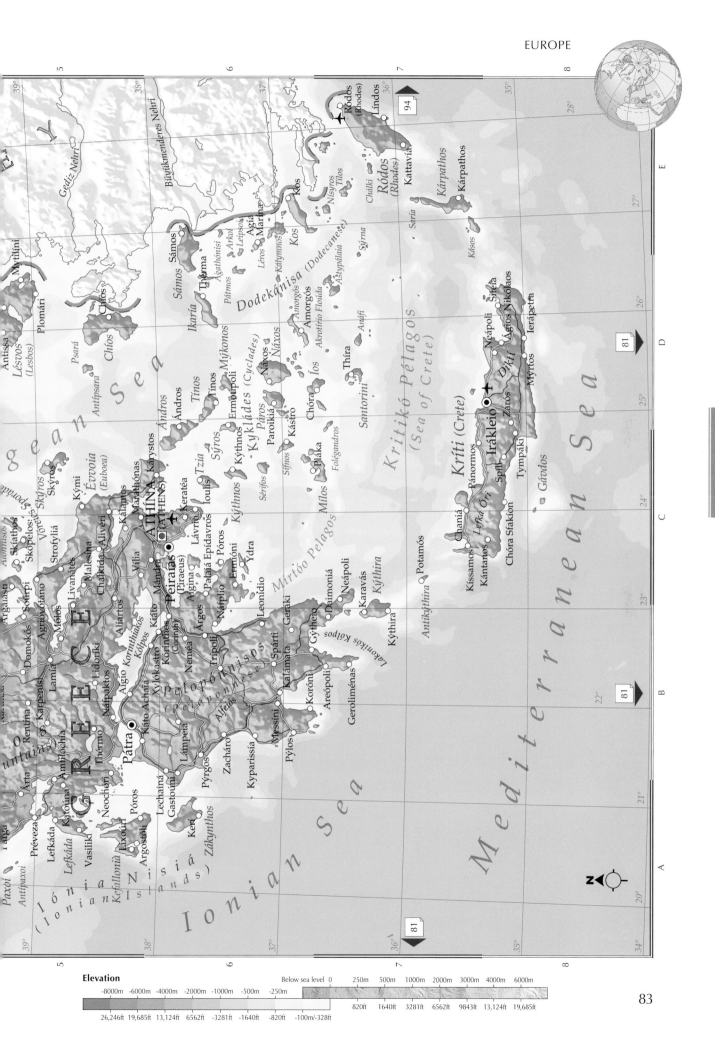

The Baltic States & Belarus

0 km   100

0 miles   100

Population   ● National capital

○ below 50,000   ○ 50,000 to 100,000   ◉ 100,000 to 500,000   ◼ above 500,000

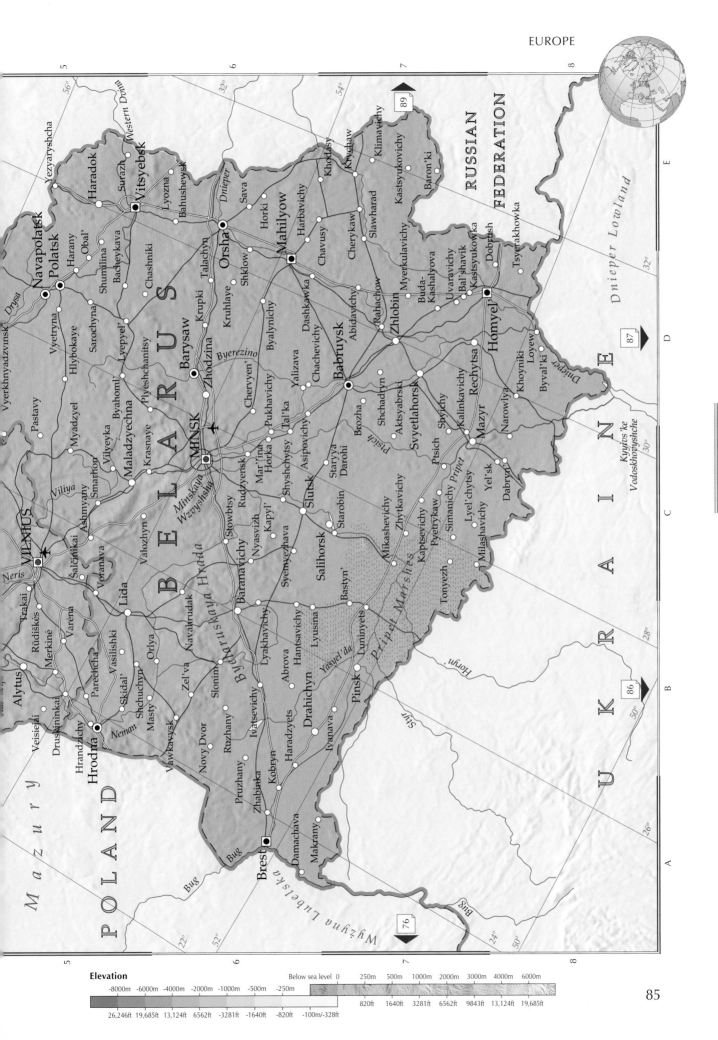

RUSSIAN FEDERATION

POLAND

B E L A R U S

U K R A I N E

Mazury

VILNIUS

Navapolatsk
Polatsk

Vitsyebsk

Yezyaryshcha
Haradok
Surazh

Lyozna
Bahushewsk

Western Dvina

Drysa

Vyerkhnyadzvinsk

Vyetryna
Harany
Obal'
Shumilina
Bacheykava
Chashniki

Dnieper
Sava
Horki
Shklow
Talachyn

Orsha

Mahilyow

Klimavichy
Khodasy
Krychaw

Kastsyukovichy
Baron'ki
Slawharad
Chavusy
Cherykaw
Harbavichy

Myerkulavichy
Uvaravichy
Bal'shavik
Kastsyukowka
Dobrush
Tsyetsyakhowka

Dnieper Lowland

Hlybokaye
Pastavy
Myadzyel
Smarhon'
Vilyeyka
Krasnaye
Plyeshchanitsy
Byahoml'
Byerezino

Barysaw
Zhodzina

Zhlobin
Buda-
Kashalyova
Rabachow
Abidavichy
Babruysk
Dashkawka
Chachevichy
Yalizava
Pukhavichy
Byalynichy

Homyel

Rechytsa
Khoyniki
Loyew
Byval'ki
Narowlya

MINSK

Minskaya
Wzvyshsha

Byelaruskaya Hrada

Minsk
Mar''ina
Horka
Shyshchytsy
Asipovichy
Staryya
Darohi
Brozha
Shchadryn
Aktsyabrski
Svyetlahorsk
Ptsich
Shvichy
Kalinkavichy
Mazyr
Yel'sk
Dabryn'

Lida
Ashmyany
Valozhyn
Stowbtsy
Rudzyensk
Kapyl'
Nyasvizh
Salihorsk
Starobin
Mikashevichy
Zhytkavichy
Kaptsevichy
Pyetrykaw
Simanichy
Lyel'chytsy
Milashavichy

VILNIUS
Trakai
Šalčininkai
Varanava
Neris
Viliya

Rūdiškės
Merkinė
Varėna
Vasilishki
Orlya
Zel'va
Navahrudak
Lyakhavichy
Baranavichy
Syemyezhava
Lyusina
Bastyn'
Luninyets
Tonyezh

Alytus
Veisiejai
Druskininkai
Hrandzichy
Hrodna
Skidal'
Shchuchyn
Masty
Vawkavysk
Novy Dvor
Ruzhany
Ivatsevichy
Abrova
Hantsavichy
Drahichyn
Ivanava
Pinsk
Pripet
Pripet Marshes
Yasyel'da
Stryr

Parechcha
Zhabinka
Pruzhany
Kobryn
Haradzyets
Yasyel'da
Horyn'

Brest
Damachava
Makrany
Bug

Wyżyna Lubelska

Wyżyna
Neman

Kyyiys'ke
Vodoskhovyshche

89
87
86
76

5   6   7   8

56°   54°   52°   50°

32°   30°   28°   26°   24°

A   B   C   D   E

Elevation

Below sea level 0   250m   500m   1000m   2000m   3000m   4000m   6000m

-8000m -6000m -4000m -2000m -1000m -500m -250m

820ft 1640ft 3281ft 6562ft 9843ft 13,124ft 19,685ft

26,246ft 19,685ft 13,124ft 6562ft -3281ft -1640ft -820ft -100m/-328ft

85

Ukraine, Moldova & Romania

0 km 100
0 miles 100

Population ● National capital
○ below 50,000 ○ 50,000 to 100,000 ◉ 100,000 to 500,000 ■ above 500,000

E   30°   32°   F   34°   36°   G   38°   H   40°   52°

88

Dnieper
(Dnyapro)

Desna

Horodnya
Shchors
Shostka
Hlukhiv

Chernihiv
Krolevets'

Konotop

RUSSIAN

Kyyivs'ke
oskhovyshche

Oster

Nizhyn
Bakhmach

Romny
Sumy

FEDERATION

Don

1

YIV
EV)
Brovary
Desna

Pryluky

Lebedyn
Okhtyrka

Zolochiv
Derhachi

Srednerusskaya
Vozvyshennost'

40°

oyarka
Vasyl'kiv
astiv

Yahotyn
Pyryatyn
Hrebinka
Lubny
Myrhorod

Lyubotyn
Kharkiv

50°

Kanius'ke
Vodoskhovyshche

Bila Tserkva
Bohuslav

Kaniv

Merefa

Kup"yans'k

Oskil

88

2

A   N   Horodyshche
Zvenyhorodka

Zolotonosha

Cherkasy
Smila
Shpola
Chyhyryn

Hlobyne
E
Poltava

Donets

Starobil's'k

Izyum
Kreminna
Rubizhne

han
Tal'ne

Kremenchuts'ke
Vodoskhovyshche

Kremenchuk

Slov"yans'k
Kramators'k

Syeverodonets'k
Lysychans'k

Mala Vyska
Oleksandrivka
Svitlovods'k

Dniprodzerzhyns'ke
Vodoskhovyshche

Oleksandriya

Novomoskovs'k

Kostyantynivka

Zolote
Luhans'k

Holovanivs'k
Ulyanivka

Kirovohrad
Zhovti Vody

Dniprodzerzhyns'k

Dnipropetrovs'k

Pavlohrad

Horlivka
Yenakiyeve

Stakhanov

Krasnodon

3

Vil'shanka
Pervomays'k

Dolyns'ka
P"yatykhatky

Synel'nykove

Makiyivka

Krasnyy Luch

48°

Kryve Ozero
Arbuzynka

Bobrynets'
Kryvyy Rih

Pokrovs'ke

Donets'k
Torez

Inhulets'

Zaporizhzhya

Amvrosiyivka

Novyy Buh
Voznesens'k

Ordzhonikidze
Nikopol'
Marhanets'

Orikhiv
Volnovakha

Dokuchayevs'k

Pivdennyy Buh

Kam"yanka-Dniprovs'ka
Dniprorudne

Polohy

Don

B
l
a
c
k

Mykolayiv

Kakhovs'ka
Vodoskhovyshche

Tokmak
Molochans'k

Novoazovs'k

Mariupol'

Dnieper
(Dnipro)

Mykolayiv

Zhovtneve
S   e   a   L   o   w   l   a   n   d

Kakhovka

Melitopol'

Gulf of Taganrog

Yeya

Ochakiv
Kherson

Yakymivka

Prymors'k
Berdyans'k

Odesa

Tsyurupyns'k

Hola Prystan'
Chaplynka

Novotroyits'ke

Heniches'k

Sea of Azov

88

4

Illichivs'k

Kalanchak

Armyans'k

46°

Karkinits'ka Zatoka

Krasnoperekops'k

Rozdol'ne

Dzhankoy

Kerch Strait

RUSSIAN

Chornomors'ke

Krasnohvardiys'ke

Nyzhn'ohirs'kyy

Zatoka
Syvash

Kerch

FEDERATION

Yevpatoriya
Saky

Krym s'kyy
Pivostriv

Lenine
Feodosiya

Kuban'

Simferopol'
Bakhchysaray

Sevastopol'
Alushta

Krymski Hory

Yalta
Alupka

5

44°

B   l   a   c   k   S   e   a

94

E   32°   F   34°   G   36°   38°   H   40°

Elevation

Below sea level   0   250m   500m   1000m   2000m   3000m   4000m   6000m

-8000m   -6000m   -4000m   -2000m   -1000m   -500m   -250m

820ft   1640ft   3281ft   6562ft   9843ft   13,124ft   19,685ft

26,246ft   19,685ft   13,124ft   6562ft   -3281ft   -1640ft   -820ft   -100m/-328ft

European Russia

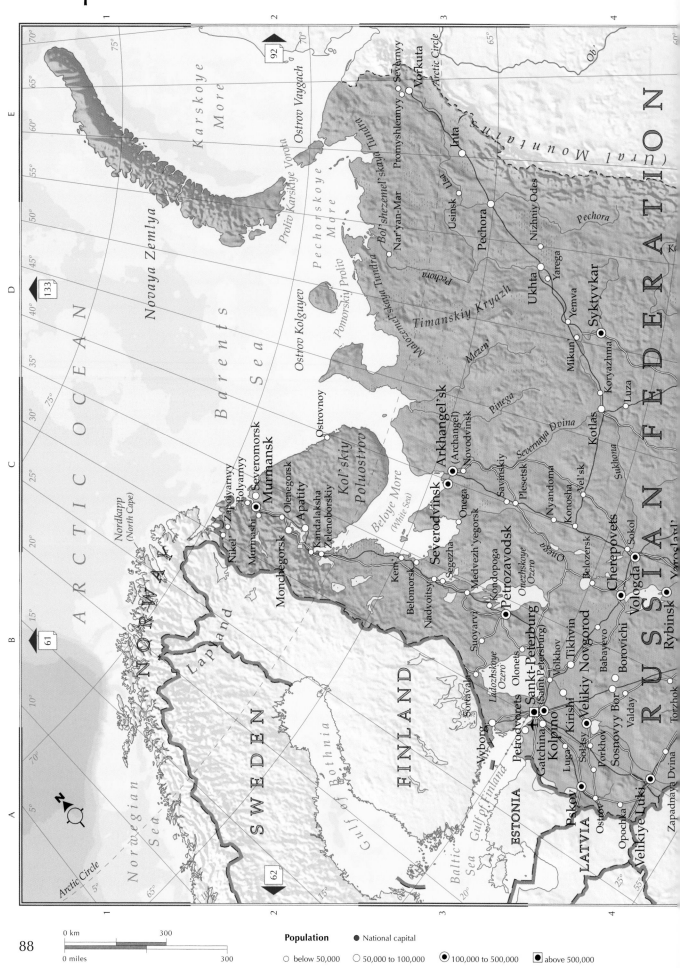

Population   ● National capital

○ below 50,000   ◎ 50,000 to 100,000   ◉ 100,000 to 500,000   ■ above 500,000

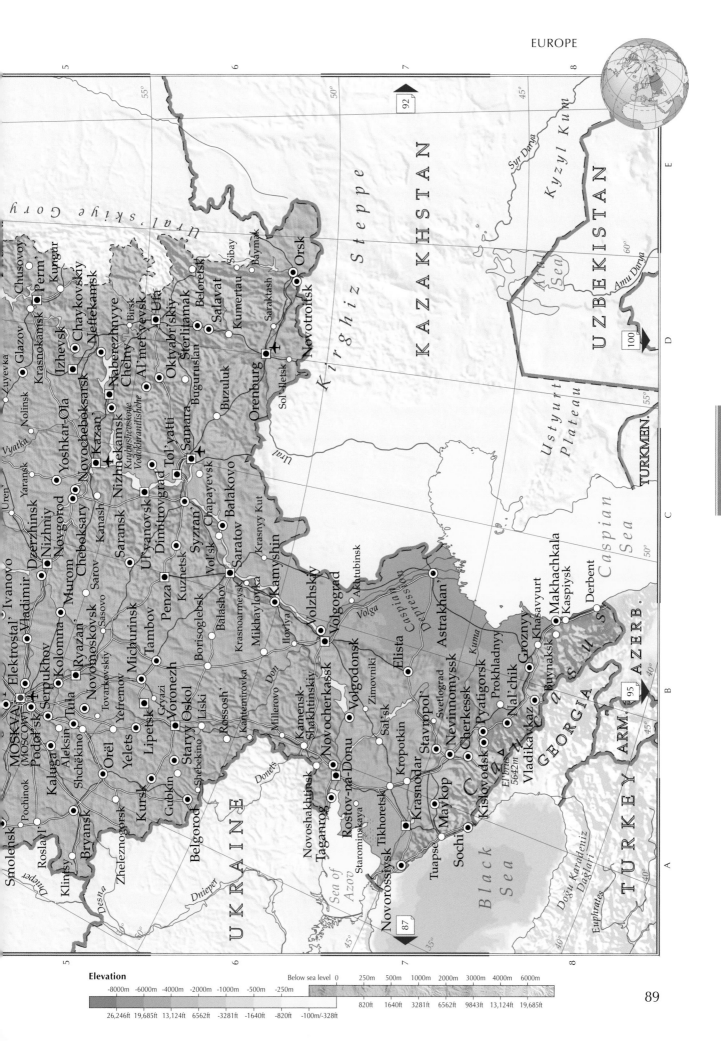

Elevation

| Below sea level | 0 | 250m | 500m | 1000m | 2000m | 3000m | 4000m | 6000m |

-8000m -6000m -4000m -2000m -1000m -500m -250m

26,246ft 19,685ft 13,124ft 6562ft -3281ft -1640ft -820ft -100m/-328ft

820ft 1640ft 3281ft 6562ft 9843ft 13,124ft 19,685ft

89

North & West Asia

A   B   C   D

133

Franz Josef Land   A R C T I C

Severnaya Zem

Ostrov Komsomolets

20°   40°   60°   80°   100°

80°

Ostrov Oktyabr'skoy Revolyutsii
Ostrov Bol'shevik

1

Summer limit of pack ice

Ozer
Tayn

Poluostrov Taymyr

Winter limit of pack ice

Novaya Zemlya

East Novaya Zemlya Trench

Kara Sea

North Siberia

Norwegian Sea   *North Cape*

Barents Sea

Kheta

70°

Ostrov Kolguyev

Poluostrov Yamal

Gulf of Ob'

● Noril'sk

Kureyka

● Murmansk

Kola Peninsula

Central Siberian Plateau

Arctic Circle

59

White Sea

Gulf of Bothnia

R U S S I A N   F E

● Archangel

Lower Tunguska

2

Stony Tunguska

West Siberian Plain

s i

Lake Onega

Northern Dvina

Ob'

60°

Lake Ladoga

● Vologda

● Perm

Angara

● Saint Petersburg

● Yekaterinburg

Irtysh

Chulym

Yaroslavl'

● Nizhniy Novgorod

Ural Mountains

● Chelyabinsk

● Tomsk

● Krasnoyarsk

Volga

MOSCOW ●

● Omsk

● Novosibirsk

Kazan' ●

● Novokuznetsk

● Kaliningrad

Ul'yanovsk ●

● Ufa

Ishim

Central Russian Upland

● Samara

Ob'

KALININGRAD
(to Russ. Fed.)

● Voronezh

● Saratov

● Orenburg

50°

Sayanskiy Khrebet

3

ASTANA ●

A

● Irku

E U R O P E   E

Volgograd ●

Ural'sk ●

Kirghiz Steppe

Karaganda ●

S

● Semipalatinsk

Altai Mountains

● Rostov-na-Donu

Don

Astrakhan' ●

Ural

Kazakh Uplands

Volga

Stavropol' ●

KAZAKHSTAN

Ozero Zaysan

Danube

Black Sea

El'brus 5642m △

Caucasus

Aktau ●

Ustyurt Plateau

Aral'sk ●

Aral Sea

Syr Darya

Lake Balkhash

Ili

40°

Küre Dağları

GEORGIA

TBILISI ●

Caspian Sea

Dasoguz ●

Kyzyl Kum

Kyzylorda ●

Almaty ●

Tien Shan

G

Istanbul ●

ARMENIA

AZERB.

BAKU ●

UZBEKISTAN

Taraz ●

BISHKEK ●

Pik Pobedy 7443m △

ANKARA ●

YEREVAN ●

TASHKENT ●

KYRGYZSTAN

Anatolia

TURKMENISTAN

DUSHANBE ●

Lake Van

TURKEY

Gaziantep ●

● Tabriz

Amu Darya

TAJIKISTAN

ASGABAT ●

Garagum

Mediterranean Sea

Adana ●

Aleppo ●

● Mosul

TEHRAN ●

Hindu Kush

Kunlun Mountains

CYPRUS

SYRIA

IRAQ

Qom ●

IRAN

● KABUL

Jalalabad ●

4

81

DAMASCUS ●

Isfahan ●

Herat ●

Khyber Pass

BEIRUT ●

LEBANON

BAGHDAD ●

Iranian Plateau

AFGHANISTAN

Himalayas

ISRAEL

AMMAN ●

Syrian Desert

Tigris

Zagros Mountains

30°

JERUSALEM ▽

JORDAN

Euphrates

Basra ●

Zahedan ●

Dead Sea
- 392m

An Nafud

KUWAIT ●

Shiraz ●

Thar Desert

Indus Fan

KUWAIT

Bandar-e 'Abbas ●

Ganges

Red Sea

MANAMA ●

Dubai ●

The Gulf

Ganges Fan

BAHRAIN

DOHA ●

Gulf of Oman

Tropic of Cancer

RIYADH ●

QATAR

U.A.E.

MUSCAT ●

Nile

SAUDI ARABIA

ABU DHABI

Sur ●

Murray Ridge

Me

Jedda ●

Arabian Peninsula

20°

At Ta'if ●

OMAN

Ar Rub' al Khali

5

A F R I C A

N

Bay of Bengal

SANA ●

YEMEN

Arabian Sea

Ta'izz ●

Aden ●

Socotra
(to Yemen)

Gulf of Aden

10°

47

20°   40°   60°   80°   100°

A   B   C   D

90

0 km   800

0 miles   800

Population   ● National capital

○ below 50,000   ⊙ 50,000 to 100,000   ◉ 100,000 to 500,000   ■ above 500,000

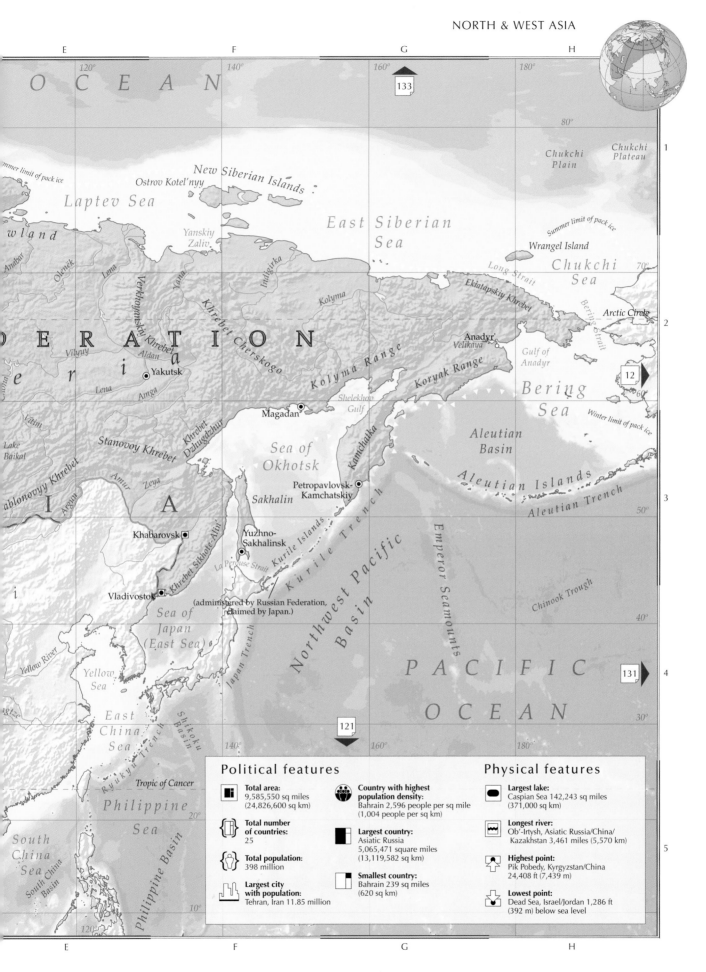

Political features

Total area:
9,585,550 sq miles
(24,826,600 sq km)

Total number of countries:
25

Total population:
398 million

Largest city with population:
Tehran, Iran 11.85 million

Country with highest population density:
Bahrain 2,596 people per sq mile
(1,004 people per sq km)

Largest country:
Asiatic Russia
5,065,471 square miles
(13,119,582 sq km)

Smallest country:
Bahrain 239 sq miles
(620 sq km)

Physical features

Largest lake:
Caspian Sea 142,243 sq miles
(371,000 sq km)

Longest river:
Ob'-Irtysh, Asiatic Russia/China/
Kazakhstan 3,461 miles (5,570 km)

Highest point:
Pik Pobedy, Kyrgyzstan/China
24,408 ft (7,439 m)

Lowest point:
Dead Sea, Israel/Jordan 1,286 ft
(392 m) below sea level

Russia & Kazakhstan

NETH.
DENMARK
GERMANY
NORWAY
SWEDEN
FINLAND
SVALBARD (to Norway)
Zemlya Frantsa Iosifa
61
Arctic Circle
Winter limit of pack ice
Summer limit of pack ice
ARCTI
Barents Sea
Murmansk
Kandalaksha
Nordkapp (North Cape)
Kol'skiy Poluostrov
Beloye More
Ostrov Kolguyev
Novaya Zemlya
Ostrov Belyy
Karskoye More
Dikson
KALININGRAD (to Russ. Fed.)
Kaliningrad
Baltic Sea
Gulf of Bothnia
Gulf of Finland
POLAND
86
LITH.
LAT.
EST.
Sankt-Peterburg
Ladozhskoye Ozero
Onezhskoye Ozero
Severodvinsk
Arkhangel'sk
Nar'yan-Mar
Pechora
Poluostrov Yamal
Obskaya Guba
BELARUS
Pskov
Velikiy Novgorod
Petrozavodsk
Smolensk
Cherepovets
Vel'sk
Severnaya Dvina
Vorkuta
Talna
MOLDOVA
MOSKVA (MOSCOW)
Tver
Vologda
Yaroslavl'
Kineshma
Kotlas
Ukhta
Salekhard
Noril'sk
UKRAINE
Bryansk
Tula
Vladimir
Nizhniy Novgorod
Syktyvkar
Nyagan'
Nadym
Igarka
Belgorod
Ryazan'
Kirov
Ob'
Taz
Yenisey
Voronezh
Tambov
Penza
Kazan'
Glazov
Solikamsk
Perm'
Serov
Khanty-Mansiysk
Zapadno-Sibirskaya
Sea of Azov
Mikhaylovka
Ul'yanovsk
Tol'yatti
Izhevsk
Lesnoy
Yekaterinburg
Surgut
Nizhnevartovsk
Ravnina
Rostov-na-Donu
Saratov
Naberezhnyye Chelny
Ufa
Tyumen'
Tobol'sk
Krasnodar
Balakovo
Samara
Sterlitamak
Chelyabinsk
Ishim
Ishim
Irtysh
Ob'
Chulym
RUSSIAN
Black Sea
Sochi
Stavropol'
Volgograd
Ural'sk
Orenburg
Magnitogorsk
Orsk
Petropavlovsk
Omsk
Seversk
Tomsk
Strel
El'brus 5642m
Nal'chik
Astrakhan'
Alga
Aktobe (Aktyubinsk)
Rudnyy
Kostanay
Ishim
Novosibirsk
Krasnoyar
Vladikavkaz
Groznyy
Makhachkala
Atyrau
Emba
Kokshetau
Atbasar
Shchuchinsk
Barnaul
Kemerovo
Abak
GEORGIA
ARM.
AZERBAIJAN
98
Caspian Sea
Fort-Shevchenko
Aktau
Zhanaozen
Shalkar
KAZAKHSTAN
ASTANA
Pavlodar
Temirtau
Saran'
Karaganda
Novokuznetsk
Semipalatinsk
Leninogorsk
Zyryanovsk
Kyz
Ustyurt Plateau
Aral Sea
Aral'sk
Ayteke Bi
Zhezkazgan
Kazakhskiy Melkosopochnik
Shar
Ust'-Kamenogorsk
Ayagoz
Ozero Zaysan
Altai Mountains
IRAN
UZBEKISTAN
Syr Darya
Dzhusaly
Kyzylorda
Kyzyl Kum
Balkhash
Ozero Balkhash
Gora Belukha 4506m
Kz
Amu Darya
TURKMENISTAN
Turkestan
Kentau
Karatau
Shu
Taldykorgan
Tekeli
Shymkent
Arys'
Taraz
Kirghiz Range
Almaty (Alma-Ata)
Tien Shan
CHINA
TAJIKISTAN
KYRGYZSTAN
AFGHANISTAN
100

0 km   600
0 miles   600

Population ● National capital
○ below 50,000   ○ 50,000 to 100,000   ◉ 100,000 to 500,000   ■ above 500,000

E   F   G   H

80° 100° 120° 140° 160° 180° 80° 170° 70°

ALASKA
(to US)

14

Chukchi
Sea

Bering Strait

Arctic Circle

60°

1

O C E A N

Ostrov
Komsomolets

Ostrov Oktyabr'skoy Revolyutsii

Severnaya
Zemlya

Ostrov
Bol'shevik

Ostrov Kotel'nyy

More
Laptevykh

Poluostrov Taymyr

Ozero
Taymyr

Severo-Sibirskaya Nizmennost'

Kheta

Plato
Putorana

Kotuy

Olenëk

Srednesibirskoye
Ploskogor'ye

Nizhnyaya Tunguska

S I B I R'
(S I B E R I A)

Chunya

F E D E R A T I O N

Angara

Ust'-Ilimsk

Kansk

Bratsk

Tulun

Usol'ye-Sibirskoye

Angarsk

Irkutsk

Eastern Sayans

Ust'-Kut

Ozero
Baykal

Ulan-Ude

Kyakhta

MONGOLIA

G o b i

100° 110°

Ostrov Vrangelya

Proliv Longa

Vostochno-Sibirskoye
More

Novosibirskiye
Ostrova

Ostrov
Novaya Sibir'

Ostrov Bol'shoy
Lyakhovskiy

Pevek

Ambarchik
Cherskiy

Ekvyvatapskiy Khrebet

Anadyr'

Anadyrskiy
Zaliv

Anadyr'

180°

Bering
Sea

170°

Ostrov Karaginskiy

2

Ust'-Olenëk

Tiksi

Kazach'ye

Yana

Indigirka

Alazeya

Kolyma

Khrebet Cherskogo

Adycha

Susuman

Ossora

Zaliv
Shelikhova

Koryakskoye Nagor'ye

Ust'-Kamchatsk

Vulkan
Klyucheyskaya
Sopka 4688m

Atlasovo

Mil'kovo

160°

50°

Verkhoyanskiy Khrebet

Anabar

Olenëk

Lena

Khrebet Aldan

Atka

Magadan

Okhotsk

Poluostrov
Kamchatka

Petropavlovsk-
Kamchatskiy

3

Yakutsk

Nyurba

Mirnyy

Suntar

Olëkminsk

Vilyuy

Lena

Amga

Aldan

Okhotskoye
More

Pervyy Kuril'skiy Proliv

Ostrov
Paramushir

Khrebet Dzhugdzhur

Shantarskiye
Ostrova

Ostrov Sakhalin

Neryungri

Bodaybo

Tynda

Skovorodino

Komsomol'sk-
na-Amure

Ostrov Urup

Ostrov Iturup

Kuril'sk

150°

Olëkma

Vitim

Yablonovyy Khrebet

Shilka

Svobodnyy

Khabarovsk

Birobidzhan

Amur

Amur

Khor

Khrebet Sikhote-Alin'

Yuzhno-Sakhalinsk

Kuril'skiye Ostrova
(Kurile Islands)

130°

4

Chita

Olovyannaya

Blagoveshchensk

Krasnokamensk

Zabaykal'sk

Bikin

La Pérouse
Strait

(administered by
Russian Federation,
claimed by Japan)

40°

C H I N A

Ussuriysk

Vladivostok

Nakhodka

JAPAN

Sea of
Japan
(East Sea)

140°

5

N

NORTH
KOREA

106

120° 40° 130°

E   F   G   H

Elevation

| Below sea level | 0 | 250m | 500m | 1000m | 2000m | 3000m | 4000m | 6000m |

-8000m -6000m -4000m -2000m -1000m -500m -250m

820ft 1640ft 3281ft 6562ft 9843ft 13,124ft 19,685ft

26,246ft 19,685ft 13,124ft 6562ft -3281ft -1640ft -820ft -100m/-328ft

Turkey & The Caucasus

ROMANIA

Danube

Iacul Sinoie

BULGARIA

UKRAINE

Kryms'kyy Pivostriv

Varnenski Zaliv

Burgaski Zaliv

Black Sea

Maritsa

82

Kırklareli

Edirne

Ergéne Çayi

Çorlu

Tekirdağ

İstanbul Boğazı (Bosporus)

Zonguldak

Bartın

Küre Dağları

İnebolu

Cide

Sinop

Gerze

Bafra

Samsun

Ünye

Ordu

İstanbul

İzmit

Adapazarı

Devrek

Karabük

Kastamonu

Kargı

Çerkeş

Merzifon

Marmara Denizi (Sea of Marmara)

Yalova

İznik Gölü

Bolu

Gerede

Çankırı

Kızıl Irmak

Çorum

Tokat

Çanik Dağları

Bandırma

Bursa

Bilecik

ANKARA

Kalecik

Alaca

Za

Çanakkale

Çanakkale Boğazı (Dardanelles)

Balıkesir

Bozüyük

Eskişehir

Kırıkkale

Sorgun

Yıldızeli

Sivas

Simav Çayı

G R E E C E

Edremit

Ayvalık

Kütahya

Polatlı

T U R K

Hirfanlı Barajı

Şarkışla

Boğazlıyan

R

Lésvos

Akhisar

Simav

Gediz

T

Kulu

Tuz Gölü

Bünyan

Hekim

Chíos

Manisa

Gediz Nehri

Uşak

Afyon

Cihanbeyli

Nevşehir

İncesu

Gürün

İzmir

Menemen

Alaşehir

Akşehir

Aksaray

Kayseri

Ödemiş

Aydın

Nazilli

Dinar

Beyşehir Gölü

Göksun

G ü

Sámos

Söke

Büyükmenderes Nehri

Denizli

Burdur

A n a t o l i a

Konya

Niğde

Kahramanmara

Milas

Tavas

İsparta

Burdur Gölü

Ereğli

Sugla Gölü

83

Muğla

Bodrum

T o r o s

Karaman

Ceyhan

Gaziant

Marmaris

Dalaman

Antalya

Manavgat

D a ğ l a r ı

Tarsus

Adana

Osmaniye

Dodekánisa (Dodecánese)

Fethiye

Kaş

Finike

Antalya Körfezi

Alanya

Mut

Mersin (İçel)

İskenderun

Kilis

Ródos (Rhodes)

Silifke

Antakya

Kırıkhan

Kárpathos

Anamur

M e d i t e r r a n e a n

S e a

CYPRUS

TURKISH REPUBLIC OF NORTHERN CYPRUS
(recognized only by Turkey)

Orantes

S

LEBANON

50

0 km   200

0 miles   200

Population   ● National capital

○ below 50,000   ○ 50,000 to 100,000   ◉ 100,000 to 500,000   ■ above 500,000

Elevation

Below sea level	0	250m	500m	1000m	2000m	3000m	4000m	6000m

-8000m -6000m -4000m -2000m -1000m -500m -250m

26,246ft 19,685ft 13,124ft 6562ft -3281ft -1640ft -820ft -100m/-328ft

820ft 1640ft 3281ft 6562ft 9843ft 13,124ft 19,685ft

The Near East

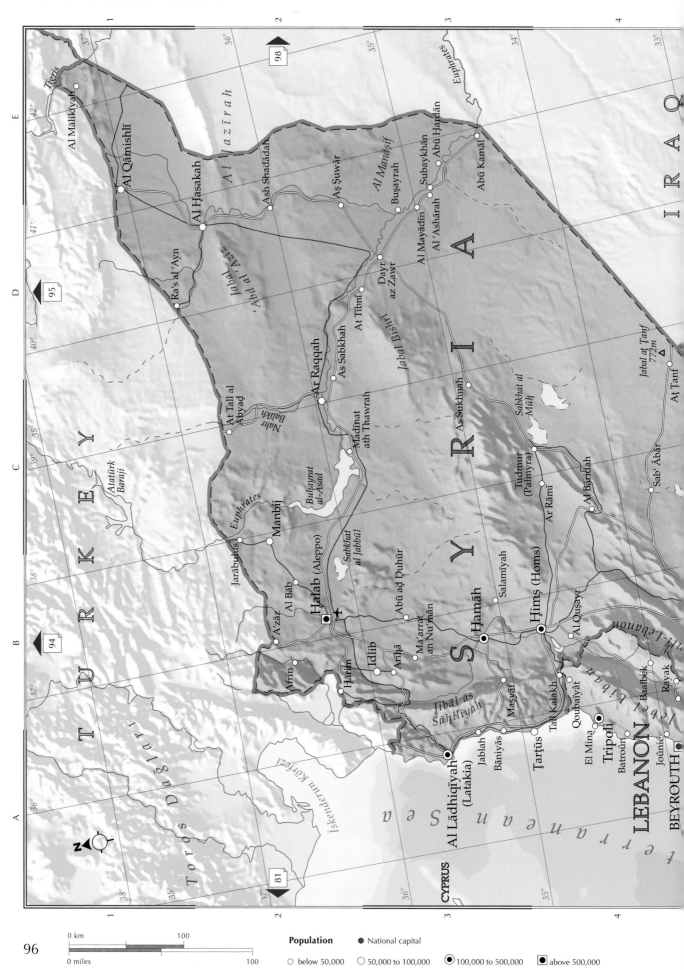

E A S T

Tigris

Al Mālikīyah

Al Qāmishlī

Al Ḥasakah

Ra's al 'Ayn

Ash Shadādah

Al Jazīrah

As Suwār

Al Manāṣif

Buṣayrah

Subaykhān

Abū Ḥardān

Abū Kamāl

Al Mayādīn

Al 'Ashārah

Euphrates

Jabal al 'Abd al 'Azīz

Jabal 'Abd al 'Azīz

At Tall al Abyaḍ

Dayr az Zawr

At Tibnī

Jabal Bishrī

Nahr Balīkh

Ar Raqqah

As Sabkhah

Madīnat ath Thawrah

As Sukhnah

Jabal aṭ Ṭanf 772m

At Tanf

Sab' Ābār

Buḥayrat al-Asad

Tudmur (Palmyra)

Sabkhat al Mūḥ

Ar Rāmī

Al Bāridah

Euphrates

Atatürk Baraji

T U R K E Y

Jarābulus

Manbij

Sabkhat al Jabbūl

Abū aḍ Ḍuhūr

S Y R I A

Salamīyah

Al Bāb

Ḥalab (Aleppo)

A'zāz

Idlib

Arīḥā

Ma'arrat an Nu'mān

Hamāh

Ḥimṣ (Homs)

Al Quṣayr

Afrīn

Ḥārim

Maṣyāf

Anti-Lebanon

Baalbek

Rayak

İskenderun Körfezi

Jibāl as Sāḥilīyah

Tall Kalakh

Qoubaïyāt

Toros Dağları

Jablah

Bāniyās

Ṭarṭūs

El Mîna

Tripoli

Batroûn

Al Lādhiqīyah (Latakia)

Jounié

Jebel Liban

LEBANON

BEYROUTH

CYPRUS

M e d i t e r r a n e a n   S e a

N

| 0 km | | 100 |
| 0 miles | | 100 |

Population ● National capital

○ below 50,000   ◯ 50,000 to 100,000   ◉ 100,000 to 500,000   ■ above 500,000

JAPAN

East China
Sea

Okinawa

(Nansei-shotō)

(Ryukyu Is.)

Tropic of Cancer

Nansei-shotō

(China and Taiwan claim
all of each other's territory)

PACIFIC

OCEAN

PHILIPPINES

Chilung

TAIPEI

Taichung

Chiai

TAIWAN

T'ainan

Kaohsiung

Luzon Strait

Taiwan Strait

Yangzhou

Suzhou
Shanghai

Wuxi
Jiaxing
Ningbo

Nanjing
Hefei
Wuhu
Wenzhou

Huainan
Xinyang

ANHUI

Hangzhou

ZHEJIANG

Maanshan
Anqing

HUBEI

Wuhan
Jingdezhen

Shangrao

Fuzhou

Yichang
Jiujiang
Nanchang

JIANGXI

FUJIAN

Nanping

Yong'an
Quanzhou

Xiamen

SHAANXI

Nanyang
Guangshan

Yueyang

Changsha
Xiangtan
Hengyang

Longyan

Zhangzhou

Shantou

Hong Kong
(Xianggang)

Macao
(Aomen)

Lichuan

HUNAN

Dongting Hu

Loudi

Chenzhou

GUANGDONG

Shaoguan

Guangzhou

Dongguan

Zhangjiang

SPRATLY ISLANDS
(disputed by China,
Malaysia, Philippines,
Taiwan and Vietnam)

Thitu
Island

Flat Island

Nanshan Island

Loaita Island

Namyit Island

Len Dao

Spratly Island

Chengdu

Chongqing

CHONGQING SHI

GUIZHOU

Zunyi

Guiyang

Anshun

GUANGXI
ZHUANGZU
ZIZHIQU

Liuzhou

Yulin

Zhaoqing

Jiangmen

Qinzhou

Beihai

Zhanjiang

Haikou

Hainan Dao

HAINAN

Danzhou

Dongfang

Xuwen

Gulf of Tongking

PARACEL
ISLANDS
(disputed by China,
Taiwan and Vietnam)

Amphitrite Group

Crescent Group

Triton Island

South China

Sea

VIETNAM

SICHUAN

Sichuan
Pendi

Miaoyang

Neijiang

Zigong

Leshan

Ya'an

Xichang

YUNNAN

Kunming

Gejiu

Dali

Baoshan

Wuliang Shan

Jinghong

Mekong

Salween

Jinsha Jiang

Hengduan Shan

Yalong Jiang

Yangtze (Yangtze)

XIZANG
ZIZHIQU

Tibet

INDIA

MYANMAR

(BURMA)

Tropic of Cancer

LAOS

THAILAND

CAMBODIA

Gulf of Thailand

Mekong

Red River

Nanning

Guilin

Quanzhou

Yongzhou

Huaihua

Elevation

Below sea level 0   250m   500m   1000m   2000m   3000m   4000m   6000m

-8000m   -6000m   -4000m   -2000m   -1000m   -500m   -250m

26,246ft   19,685ft   13,124ft   6562ft   -3281ft   -1640ft   -820ft   -100m/-328ft

820ft   1640ft   3281ft   6562ft   9843ft   13,124ft   19,685ft

130

117

114

Japan

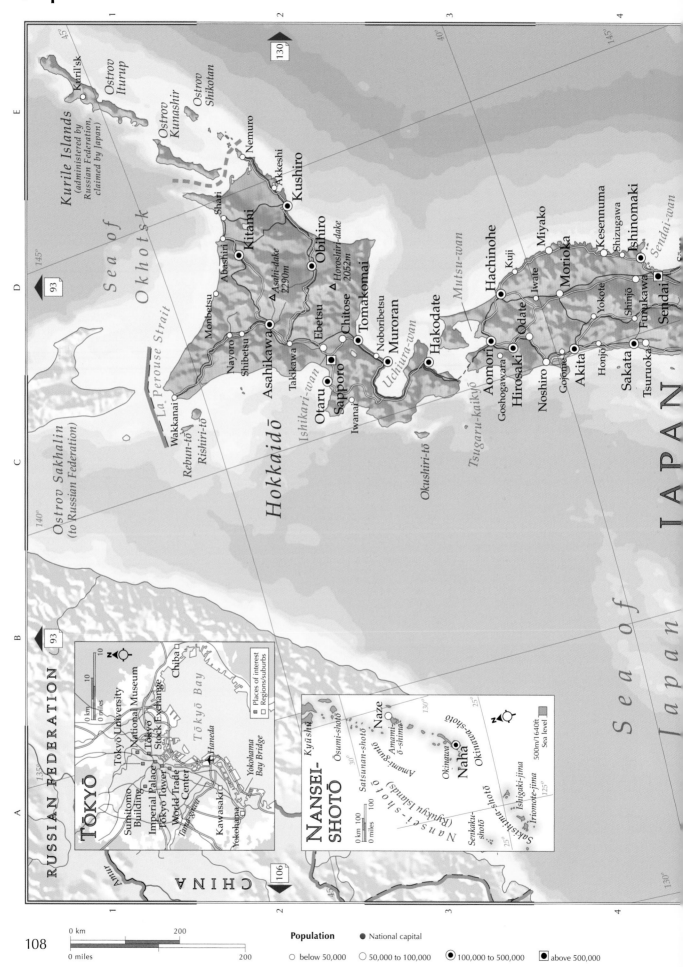

Kurile Islands
(administered by
Russian Federation,
claimed by Japan)

Ostrov Iturup

Kuril'sk

Ostrov Shikotan

Ostrov Kunashir

Nemuro

Sea of Okhotsk

Akkeshi

Kushiro

Shari

Abashiri

Kitami

Monbetsu

Obihiro

△ Asahi-dake 2290m

△ Horoshiri-dake 2052m

Nayoro

Shibetsu

Ebetsu

Chitose

Tomakomai

Noboribetsu

Muroran

Uchiura-wan

Hakodate

Takikawa

Asahikawa

Otaru

Sapporo

Iwanai

Ishikari-wan

Hokkaidō

Wakkanai

Rebun-tō

Rishiri-tō

La Perouse Strait

Okushiri-tō

Tsugaru-kaikyō

Mutsu-wan

Hachinohe

Kuji

Miyako

Morioka

Iwate

Yokote

Kesennuma

Shizugawa

Ishinomaki

Sendai-wan

Sendai

Aomori

Goshogawara

Hirosaki

Odate

Shinjō

Funakawa

Noshiro

Gojome

Akita

Honjō

Sakata

Tsuruoka

Ostrov Sakhalin
(to Russian Federation)

JAPAN

Sea of Japan

TŌKYŌ

□ Places of interest

□ Regions/suburbs

Chiba

Tōkyō University

National Museum

Sumitomo Building

Imperial Palace

Tōkyō Tower

World Trade Center

Tōkyō Stock Exchange

Tōkyō

Hameda

Kawasaki

Yokohama

Tama-gawa

Tōkyō Bay

Yokohama Bay Bridge

NANSEI-SHOTŌ

Kyūshū

Ōsumi-shotō

Satsunan-shotō

Naze

Amami-ō-shima

Amami-guntō

Okinawa

Naha

Okinawa-shotō

Ishigaki-jima

Iriomote-jima

Senkaku-shotō

Sakishima-shotō

Nansei-shotō (Ryūkyū Islands)

500m/1640ft
Sea level

RUSSIAN FEDERATION

Amur

CHINA

0 km   200

0 miles   200

Population   ● National capital

○ below 50,000   ○ 50,000 to 100,000   ◉ 100,000 to 500,000   ■ above 500,000

Honshū

Iwaki
Hitachi
Chōshi
Utsunomiya
Oyama
Mito
Chiba
Kawagoe
Yokohama
TOKYO
Kawasaki
Sukagawa
Maebashi
Kōfu
Fuji
Fujisan △ 3776m
Nagaoka
Matsumoto
Nagano
Shizuoka
Hamamatsu
Jōetsu
Toyama
Toyota
Shinano-gawa
Itoigawa
Nagoya
Okazaki
Ise
Takaoka
Gifu
Ōtsu
Tsu
Owase
Kanazawa
Nakatsugawa
Ogaki
Kyōto
Osaka
Wakayama
Shingū
Komatsu
Tsuruga
Kōbe
Gobō
Tanabe
Fukui

(East Sea)

Toyama-wan

Wakasa-wan

Tottori
Yonago
Matsue
Okayama
Himeji
Kurashiki
Tokushima
Niihama
Kōchi
Nakamura
Sukumo

Oki-shotō
Dōgo
Dōzen

Liancourt Rocks
(claimed by Japan
& South Korea)

Shikoku

Kii-suidō

Tosa-wan

Matsuyama
Kure
Iwakuni
Hiroshima
Hōfu
Ube
Ōita
Nobeoka

Kyūshū

Miyazaki
Miyakonojō

Gōtsu
Hamada
Masuda
Yamaguchi
Nagato
Shimonoseki
Kitakyūshū
Fukuoka
Kurume
Ōmuta
Yatsushiro
Kumamoto
Sasebo
Nagasaki
Sendai
Kagoshima

Bungo-suidō

Shibushi-wan

Tanega-shima
Yaku-shima

Osumi-shotō

Kagoshima-wan

SOUTH
KOREA

Korea Strait

Tsushima
Iki
Kō-saki

Gotō-rettō
Koshikijima-rettō
Amakusa-nada

East
China Sea

PACIFIC OCEAN

Izu-shotō
Ō-shima
Nii-jima
Miyake-jima
Mikura-shima
Hachijō-jima

Sagami-nada
Bōsō-hantō
Izu-hantō
Kōzu-shima

Ise-wan
Suruga-wan

Elevation

Below sea level	0	250m	500m	1000m	2000m	3000m	4000m	6000m

-8000m	-6000m	-4000m	-2000m	-1000m	-500m	-250m	-100m/-328ft

820ft 1640ft 3281ft 6562ft 9843ft 13,124ft 19,685ft

26,246ft 19,685ft 13,124ft 6562ft -3281ft -1640ft -820ft -100m/-328ft

South India & Sri Lanka

A   **B**   **C**   **D**

Arabian Sea

Lakshadweep (Laccadive Islands) (to India)

Amīndīvi Islands

Kavaratti Island

Kalpeni Island

Nine Degree Channel

Minicoy Island

Eight Degree Channel

MALDIVES

Ihavandhippolhu Atoll

Faadhippolhu Atoll

Horsburgh Atoll

Ari Atoll

Male' Atoll

MALE'

Felidhu Atoll

Mulakatholhu

Kolhumadulu

Hadhdhunmathi Atoll

North Huvadhu Atoll

Equator

South Huvadhu Atoll

Addu Atoll   Gan   118

Kalyān
Mumbai (Bombay)
Pune
Ahmadnagar
Bārāmati
Nizāmābād
Nānded
Jagdalpur
Karīmnagar
Vizianagaram
Solāpur
Sāngli
Secunderābād
Visākhapatnam
Kolhāpur
Gulbarga
Hyderābād
Rājahmund
Kākinād
Belgaum
Rāichūr
Krishna
Vijayawāda
Machilīpatnam
Panaji
Gadag
Kurnool
Chīrala
Hubli
Nandyāl
Ongole
Kāvali
Tungabhadra Reservoir
Tādpatri
Dāvangere
Anantapur
Nellore
Shimoga
Cuddapah
Bhadrāvati
Tumkūr
Udupi
Bangalore
Vellore
Chennai (Madras)
Mangalore
Mandya
Kānchīpuram
Kāsaragod
Krishnagiri
Tiruppattūr
Kannur/Cannanore
Mysore
Salem
Pondicherry
Kozhikode/Calicut
Erode
Neyveli
Coimbatore
Thrissur/Trichūr
Tiruchchirāppalli
Ernākulam
Dindigul
Madurai
Kochi/Cochin
Jaffna
Alappuzha/Alleppey
SRI LANKA
Kollam/Quilon
Rājapālaiyam
Mannar
Vavuniya
Thiruvananthapuram/Trivandrum
Tuticorin
Trincomalee
Nāgercoil
Puttalam
Anuradhapura
Batticaloa
Matale
Negombo
Kandy
COLOMBO
Srī Jayewardanapura
Kotte
Kalutara
Ratnapura
Galle
Matara

INDIA   *Deccan*   *Karnātaka*   *Andhra Pradesh*   *Western Ghats*   *Eastern Ghats*   *Godāvari*   *Coromandel Coast*   *Tamil Nādu*   *Palk Strait*   *Gulf of Mannar*

INDIAN

0 km   300

0 miles   300

Population   ● National capital

○ below 50,000   ○ 50,000 to 100,000   ◉ 100,000 to 500,000   ◼ above 500,000

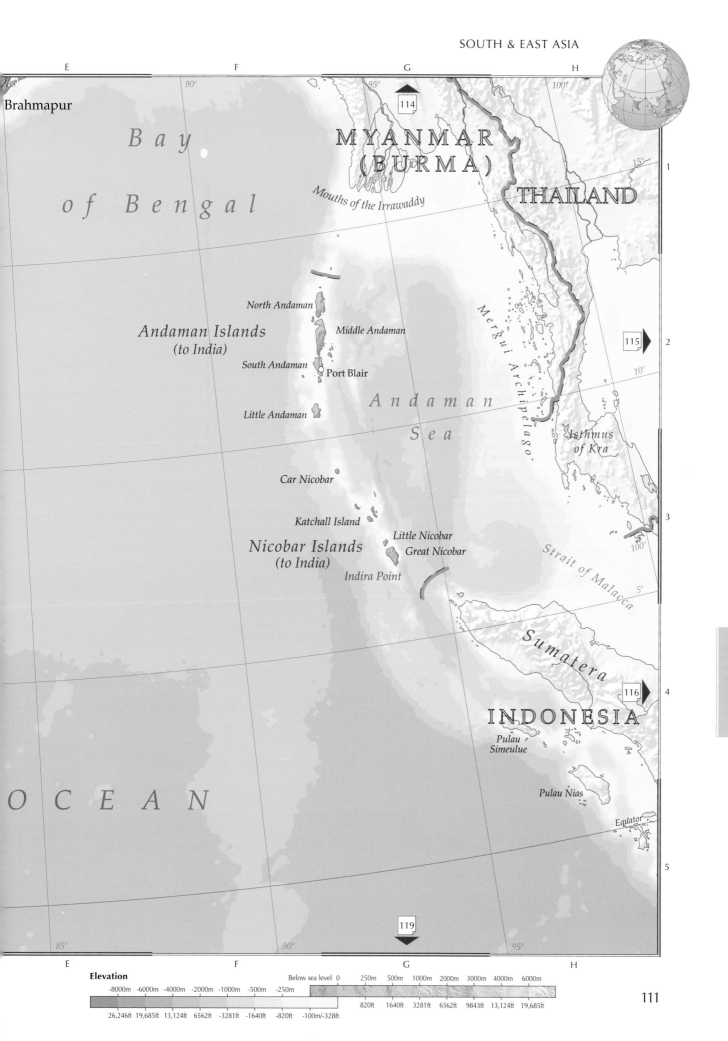

Brahmapur

E

F

G

H

Bay

of Bengal

MYANMAR
(BURMA)

THAILAND

114

Mouths of the Irrawaddy

115

North Andaman

*Andaman Islands
(to India)*

Middle Andaman

South Andaman

○ Port Blair

*Isthmus
of Kra*

A n d a m a n

Little Andaman

S e a

Mergui Archipelago

Car Nicobar

Katchall Island

*Nicobar Islands
(to India)*

Little Nicobar

Great Nicobar

Strait of Malacca

Indira Point

116

Sumatera

INDONESIA

*Pulau
Simeulue*

O C E A N

Pulau Nias

Equator

119

85°

90°

95°

E

F

G

H

Elevation

-8000m -6000m -4000m -2000m -1000m -500m -250m

Below sea level 0   250m   500m 1000m 2000m 3000m 4000m 6000m

26,246ft 19,685ft 13,124ft 6562ft -3281ft -1640ft -820ft -100m/-328ft

820ft   1640ft   3281ft 6562ft 9843ft 13,124ft 19,685ft

111

Northern India, Pakistan & Bangladesh

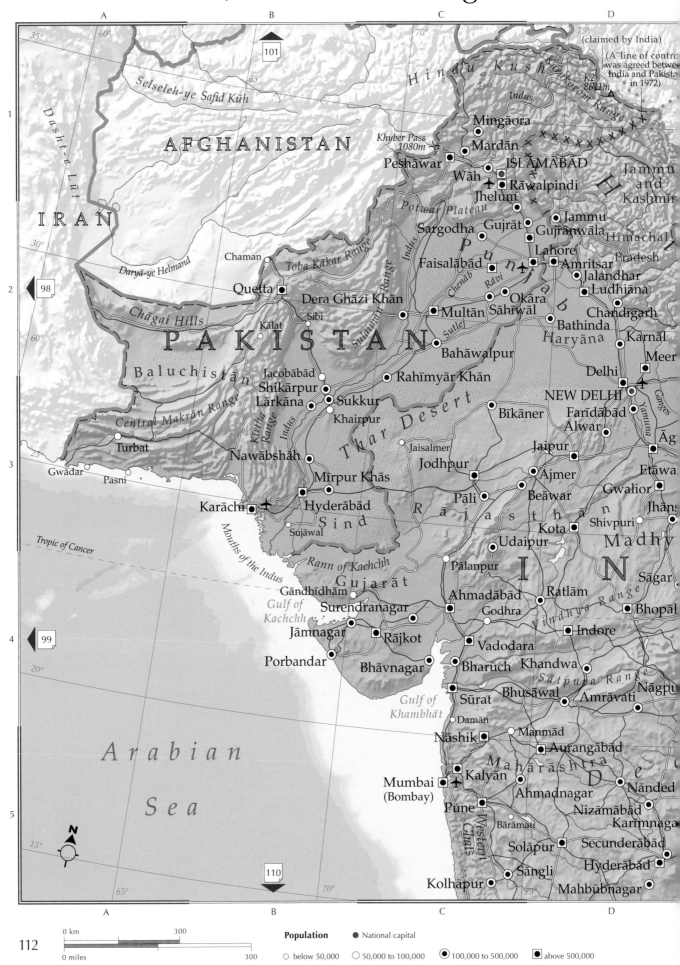

AFGHANISTAN

Selseleh-ye Safid Kūh

Dasht-e Lūt

IRAN

Daryā-ye Helmand

Chaman

98

Quetta

Chāgai Hills

Toba Kākar Range

PAKISTAN

Baluchistān

Kālat

Sibi

Central Makrān Range

Kīrthar Range

Turbat

Gwādar

Pasni

Nawābshāh

Karāchi

Sujāwal

Tropic of Cancer

Mouths of the Indus

Gāndhīdhām

Gulf of Kachchh

Jāmnagar

Porbandar

Arabian

Sea

99

Hindu Kush

Indus

Khyber Pass 1080m

Mingāora

Mardān

Peshāwar

Wāh

ISLĀMĀBĀD

Rāwalpindi

Jhelum

Jammu and Kashmīr

K2 8611m

Karakoram Range

(claimed by India)

(A "line of control was agreed between India and Pakistan in 1972)

Potwar Plateau

Sargodha

Gujrāt

Gujrānwāla

Himachal Pradesh

Lahore

Jammu

Faisalābād

Ravi

Amritsar

Jalandhar

Ludhiāna

Okāra

Sāhīwāl

Chandīgarh

Chenab

Dera Ghāzi Khān

Sulaiman Range

Indus

Sutlej

Multān

Bathinda

Haryāna

Karnāl

Bahāwalpur

Meer

Jacobābād

Shikārpur

Lārkāna

Sukkur

Khairpur

Rahīmyār Khān

Thar Desert

Bīkaner

Delhi

NEW DELHI

Farīdābād

Alwar

Āg

Mīrpur Khās

Jaisalmer

Jodhpur

Jaipur

Etāwa

Hyderābād

Sind

Pāli

Ajmer

Beāwar

Gwalior

Jhān

Rāj

Kota

Shivpuri

Udaipur

Madhy

Rann of Kachchh

Pālanpur

I

N

Sāgar

Gujarāt

Ahmadābād

Ratlām

Surendranagar

Godhra

Bhopāl

Rājkot

Indore

Vindhya Range

Bhāvnagar

Vadodara

Khandwa

Bharūch

Satpura Range

Nāgpu

Sūrat

Bhusāwal

Amrāvati

Damān

Nāshik

Manmād

Aurangābād

Mahārāshtra

De

Mumbai (Bombay)

Kalyān

Ahmadnagar

Nānded

Pune

Nizāmābād

Bārāmati

Karimnaga

Western Ghats

Solāpur

Secunderābād

Sāngli

Hyderābād

Kolhāpur

Mahbūbnagar

110

Population

● National capital

○ below 50,000   ○ 50,000 to 100,000   ◉ 100,000 to 500,000   ■ above 500,000

0 km   300

0 miles   300

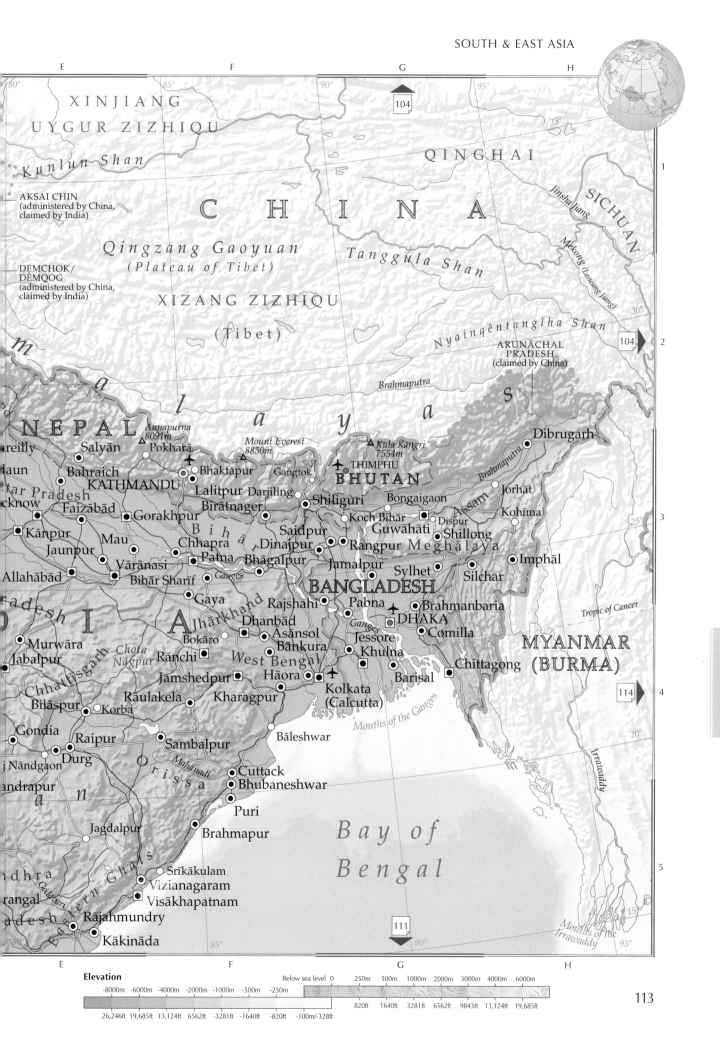

E 80° F 85° G 90° H 95°

104

XINJIANG
UYGUR ZIZHIQU

Kunlun Shan

QINGHAI

SICHUAN

Jinsha Jiang

C H I N A

AKSAI CHIN
(administered by China,
claimed by India)

*Qingzang Gaoyuan
(Plateau of Tibet)*

Tanggula Shan

Mekong (Lancang Jiang)

DEMCHOK/
DÊMQOG
(administered by China,
claimed by India)

XIZANG ZIZHIQU
(Tibet)

Nyainqêntanglha Shan

ARUNĀCHAL
PRADESH
(claimed by China)

104

Brahmaputra

H i m a l a y a s

N E P A L

Annapurna
8091m △
Pokharā

Mount Everest
△ 8850m

△ *Kula Kangri*
7554m

Dibrugarh

Brahmaputra

Bareilly
Salyān

Bahraich

KATHMANDU

Bhaktapur

Gangtok

⊕ THIMPHU
BHUTAN

Jorhāt

Lalitpur Darjiling

Shilīguri

Bongaigaon

Assam

Kohīma

aun

Uttar Pradesh

Faizābād Gorakhpur

Birātnagar

Koch Bihār

Guwāhāti

Dispur
Shillong

cknow

B i h a

Saidpur

Rangpur Meghālaya

Kānpur

Mau

Chhapra

Dinajpur

Imphāl

Jaunpur

Vārānasi

Patna

Bhāgalpur

Jamalpur

Sylhet

Silchar

Allahābād

Bihār Sharif

Ganges

BANGLADESH

Tropic of Cancer

Gaya

Rajshahi

Pabna

DHAKA

Brahmanbaria

Murwāra

Jabalpur

Jharkhand

Dhanbād

Asānsol

Ganges

Comilla

MYANMAR
(BURMA)

Bokāro

Bānkura

Jessore

Khulna

Chittagong

114

*Chota
Nāgpur*

Rānchi

West Bengal

Bilāspur

Jamshedpur

Hāora

Barisal

Chhattisgarh

Korba

Rāulakela

Kharagpur

Kolkata
(Calcutta)

Gondia

Raipur

Durg

Sambalpur

Bāleshwar

Mouths of the Ganges

20°

Irrawaddy

j Nāndgaon

andrapur

O r i s s a

Mahānadi

Cuttack

Bhubaneshwar

B a y   o f
B e n g a l

Jagdalpur

Brahmapur

Puri

ndhra

Srīkākulam

Vizianagaram

Visākhapatnam

Eastern Ghats

Godāvari

rangal

desh

Rājahmundry

Kākināda

15°

*Mouths of the
Irrawaddy*

111

E 85° F G 90° H 95°

Elevation

Below sea level 0   250m 500m 1000m 2000m 3000m 4000m 6000m

-8000m -6000m -4000m -2000m -1000m -500m -250m

820ft 1640ft 3281ft 6562ft 9843ft 13,124ft 19,685ft

26,246ft 19,685ft 13,124ft 6562ft -3281ft -1640ft -820ft -100m/-328ft

113

Mainland Southeast Asia

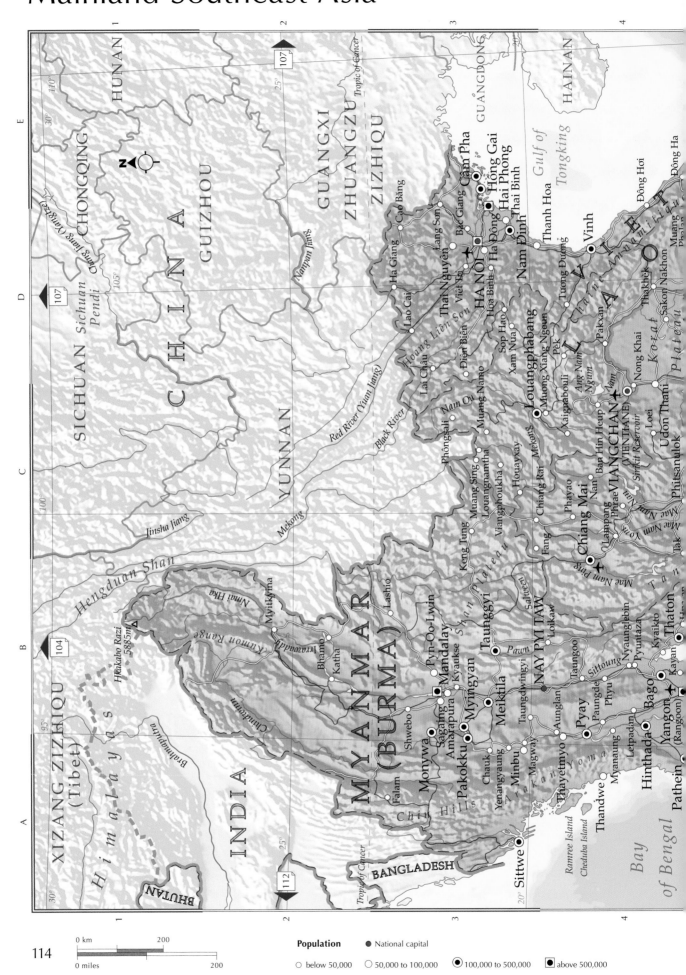

Population ● National capital

○ below 50,000 ○ 50,000 to 100,000 ◉ 100,000 to 500,000 ◼ above 500,000

0 km   200

0 miles   200

117

116

116

111

South China Sea

Kepulauan Natuna (to Indonesia)

Côn Dao

Mouths of the Mekong

MALAYSIA

Malay

Peninsula

Strait of Malacca

INDONESIA

Sumatera

(Sumatra)

Pulau Simeulue

INDIAN OCEAN

Andaman Sea

Nicobar Islands (to India)

Car Nicobar

Katchall Island

Little Nicobar

Great Nicobar

Andaman Islands (to India)

North Andaman

Middle Andaman

South Andaman

Little Andaman

Mergui Archipelago

Gulf of Thailand

Bilauktaung Range

Mouths of the Irrawaddy

VIETNAM

Quang Ngai
Nam Ky
Quy Nhon
Cam Ranh
Plây Cu
Tuy Hoa
Nha Trang
Da Lat
Phan Rang-Tháp Cham
Phan Thiet
Di Linh
Biên Hoa
Hô Chi Minh
Vung Tau
My Tho
Kâmpóng Cham
Svay Riêng
Long Xuyên
Trà Vinh
Soc Trang
Can Tho
Bac Liêu
Ca Mau
Rach Gia
Châu Dôc
Vinh Rach Gia

Muang Khôngxédôn
Pakxé
Champasak
Virôchey
Stung Kông
Samakhixai
Ubon Ratchathani
Surin
Buriram
Phumi Sâmrông
Muang Không
Stoeng Trêng
Krâchéh
Phumi Kâmpóng Trâbék
Trâpeang Vêng
Kâmpóng Chhnang
Suong
Kâmpóng Spoe

CAMBODIA
Tônlé Srêpôk
Tônlé Kông
Tônlé Sap
Mekong

Nakhon Sawan
Nakhon Ratchasima
Lop Buri
Sara Buri
Ayutthaya
KRUNG THEP (BANGKOK)
Samut Prakan
Chon Buri
Pattaya
Rayong
Chanthaburi
Khlong Yai
Trat
Ko Chang
Phumi Kâmpóng Trâbêk
Krâtié
Kâmpóng Roessei
Moung
Pouthisat
Bátdâmbâng
Sisophon
Reang Kesei
Chuor Phnum Krâvanh
PHNUM PENH
Kâmpóng Saôm
Kâmpôt

THAILAND
Srinagarind Reservoir
Nakhon Pathom
Ratchaburi
Phetchaburi
Ban Hua Hin
Ao Krung Thep
Chumphon
Lang Suan
Ranong
Isthmus of Kra
Surat Thani
Sichon
Nakhon Si Thammarat
Ko Phangan
Ko Samui
Pak Phanang
Thung Song
Phang-Nga
Phuket
Ko Phuket
Trang
Ko Lanta
Ko Ta Ru Tao
Phatthalung
Thale Luang
Songkhla
Pattani
Yala
Narathiwat
Hat Yai
Pulau Pinang
Pulau Langkawi

Daweï
Ye
Mali Kyun
Kadan Kyun
Myeik
Daung Kyun
Tenasserim
Letsôk-aw Kyun
Lanbi Kyun
Zadetkyi Kyun
Ko Phra Thong

Elevation

| Below sea level 0 | 250m | 500m | 1000m | 2000m | 3000m | 4000m | 6000m |

-8000m -6000m -4000m -2000m -1000m -500m -250m

820ft 1640ft 3281ft 6562ft 9843ft 13,124ft 19,685ft

26,246ft 19,685ft 13,124ft 6562ft -3281ft -1640ft -820ft -100m/-328ft

Maritime Southeast Asia

MYANMAR (BURMA)

SINGAPORE

0 km   10
0 miles   10

MALAYSIA

Johore Strait

Causeway

Pulau Ubin   *Pulau Tekong*

Lim Chu Kang
Bukit Panjang   Hougang New Town
Choa Chu Kang   Changi
Bukit Timah 176m
Queenstown   Bedok New Town
Jurong Industrial Estate   City
Telok Blangah   Sentosa
Selat Pandan
Pulau Sudong
Pulau Pawai   *Strait of Singapore*

Urban areas
Open areas
Nature reserves

LAOS

THAILAND   VIETNAM

Gulf of Tongking

Hainan Dao (to China)

PARACEL ISLANDS
(disputed by China, Taiwan and Vietnam)

CAMBODIA

South China Sea

SPRATLY ISLANDS
(disputed by China, Malaysia, Philippines, Taiwan and Vietnam)

111

Andaman Sea

Gulf of Thailand

Mouths of the Mekong

Nicobar Islands (to India)

Balabac

Gunung Kinaba   4101

Bandaaceh   Sigli

George Town   Butterworth   Kota Bharu   Kota Kinabalu

Pulau Pinang   Kuala Terengganu   **BANDAR SERI BEGAWAN**

Langsa   Taiping   Dungun   **BRUNEI**
Ipoh   Cukai
Meulaboh   Miri

Medan   Kuantan   Bintulu
Pulau Simeulue   Tebingtinggi   Klang   **KUALA LUMPUR**   M A L A Y S I A
Pematangsiantar   **PUTRAJAYA**   *Kepulauan Natuna*   Sibu   *Batang Rajang*   Sarawak
Danau Toba   Melaka   Keluang   *Selat Serasan*   Kuching   Sri Aman
Kepulauan Banyak   Sibolga   Muar   Johor Bahru   Singkawang   *Sungai Kapuas*   B o r n e o
    Batu Pahat   **SINGAPORE**   Kuching   Sidas   *Pegunungan Müller*   *Sungai Kayan*
Equator   *Pulau Nias*   Pekanbaru   *Kepulauan Lingga*   Pontianak   *Sungai Kapuas*   Samarinda
    Solok   Rengat   Balikpapan
Padang   *Batang Hari*   Kualatungkal   K a l i m a n t a n   *Sungai Mahakam*
Pulau Siberut   Jambi   *Selat Karimata*
Kepulauan Mentawai   *Bangka*   Sampit   Amuntai
    Sungaipenuh   Pangkalpinang   Kandanga
111   **Palembang**   *Sungai Barito*
    Bengkulu   Lahat   I   N   D   *Pulau Belitung*   Banjarmasin
Sumatera (Sumatra)   Kotabumi   *Pulau Laut*
    Java Sea   *Makas*
INDIAN   Bandar Lampung   Cirebon   Tegal
    Serang   **JAKARTA**   Pekalongan   Semarang
OCEAN   Bogor   Kudus   *Pulau Madura*
    Sukabumi   Surabaya
    Bandung   Probolinggo
    Selat Sunda   Tasikmalaya   Jember   Matar
    Cilacap   Malang
Jawa (Java)   Magelang   Kediri   Denpasa
    Yogyakarta   Madiun   *Bali*   *Pulau Lombok*
    Surakarta

MALAYSIA'S TWO CAPITALS

KUALA LUMPUR   – Capital
PUTRAJAYA   – Administrative capital

0 km   400
0 miles   400

Population   ● National capital

○ below 50,000   ○ 50,000 to 100,000   ◉ 100,000 to 500,000   ■ above 500,000

119

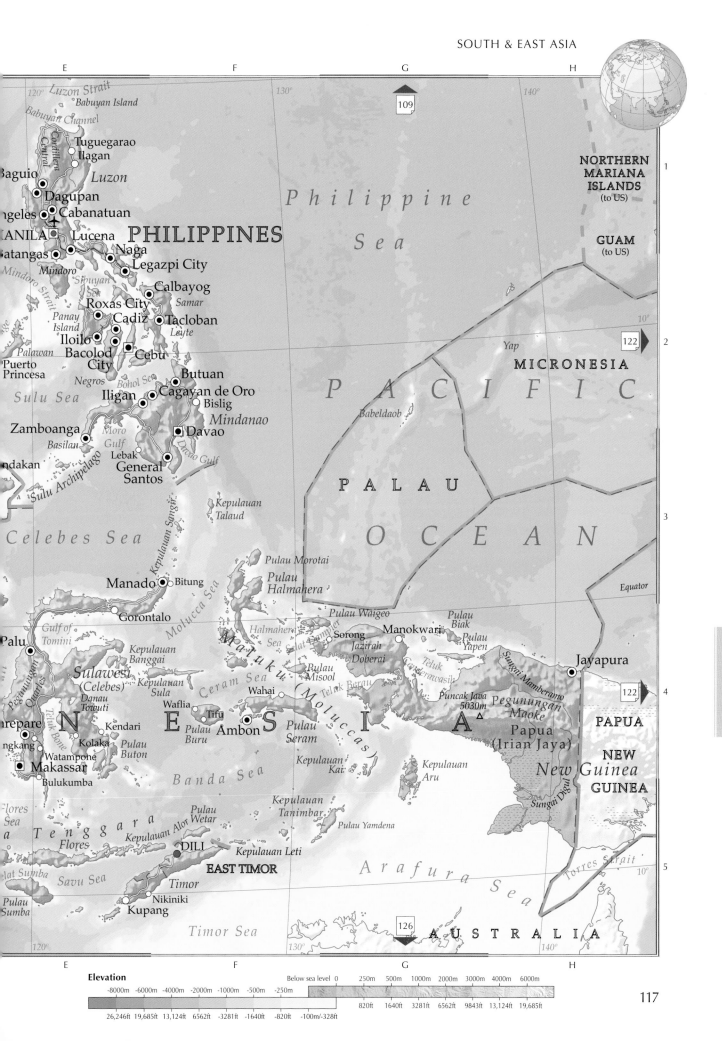

120°
Luzon Strait
Babuyan Island
Babuyan Channel
E

NORTHERN
MARIANA
ISLANDS
(to US)

1

Tuguegarao
Ilagan
Cordillera Central
Baguio
Luzon

GUAM
(to US)

Dagupan
ngeles
Cabanatuan
MANILA
Lucena
Batangas
Naga
PHILIPPINES
Mindoro
Legazpi City
Mindoro Strait
Sibuyan Sea
Calbayog
Samar
Roxas City
Panay Island
Cadiz
Tacloban
Palawan
Iloilo
Bacolod City
Cebu
Leyte

Philippine Sea

130°

140°

10°

Yap

MICRONESIA

109

122

2

Puerto Princesa
Negros
Bohol Sea
Butuan
Cagayan de Oro
Sulu Sea
Iligan
Bislig
Mindanao
Zamboanga
Moro Gulf
Basilan
Davao
ndakan
Lebak
Davao Gulf
Sulu Archipelago
General Santos
Kepulauan Talaud

PACIFIC

Babeldaob

P A L A U

3

Celebes Sea

Kepulauan Sangir

Pulau Morotai
Pulau Halmahera

O C E A N

Equator

Manado
Bitung
Gorontalo
Gulf of Tomini
Palu
Molucca Sea
Kepulauan Banggai
Sulawesi (Celebes)
Pegunungan Quarles
Danau Towuti
Teluk Bone
arepare
N
Kendari
ngkang
Kolaka
Watampone
Pulau Buton
Makassar
Bulukumba

Halmaher Sea
Selat Dampier
Pulau Waigeo
Sorong
Jazirah Doberai
Pulau Misool
Wahai
Ceram Sea
Maluku (Moluccas)
Tifu
Pulau Buru
Ambon
E
S
Pulau Seram
Teluk Berau
Kepulauan Sula
Waflia
Pulau
I
A
Kepulauan Kai

Manokwari
Pulau Biak
Pulau Yapen
Teluk Cenderawasih
Sungai Mamberamo
Jayapura
Puncak Jaya 5030m
Pegunungan Maoke
Papua (Irian Jaya)
New Guinea
Sungai Digul

122

4

PAPUA

NEW

GUINEA

Kepulauan Aru

Banda Sea
Kepulauan Tanimbar
Pulau Yamdena

Flores Sea
a
T e n g g a r a
Flores
Pulau Wetar
Kepulauan Alor
DILI
Kepulauan Leti
EAST TIMOR
Timor
lat Sumba
Savu Sea
Nikiniki
Kupang
Pulau Sumba
Timor Sea

120°

E

130°

Arafura Sea

10°

Torres Strait

5

126

A U S T R A L I A

140°

G

H

Elevation

			Below sea level 0	250m	500m	1000m	2000m	3000m 4000m 6000m

-8000m -6000m -4000m -2000m -1000m -500m -250m

26,246ft 19,685ft 13,124ft 6562ft -3281ft -1640ft -820ft -100m/-328ft

820ft 1640ft 3281ft 6562ft 9843ft 13,124ft 19,685ft

The Indian Ocean

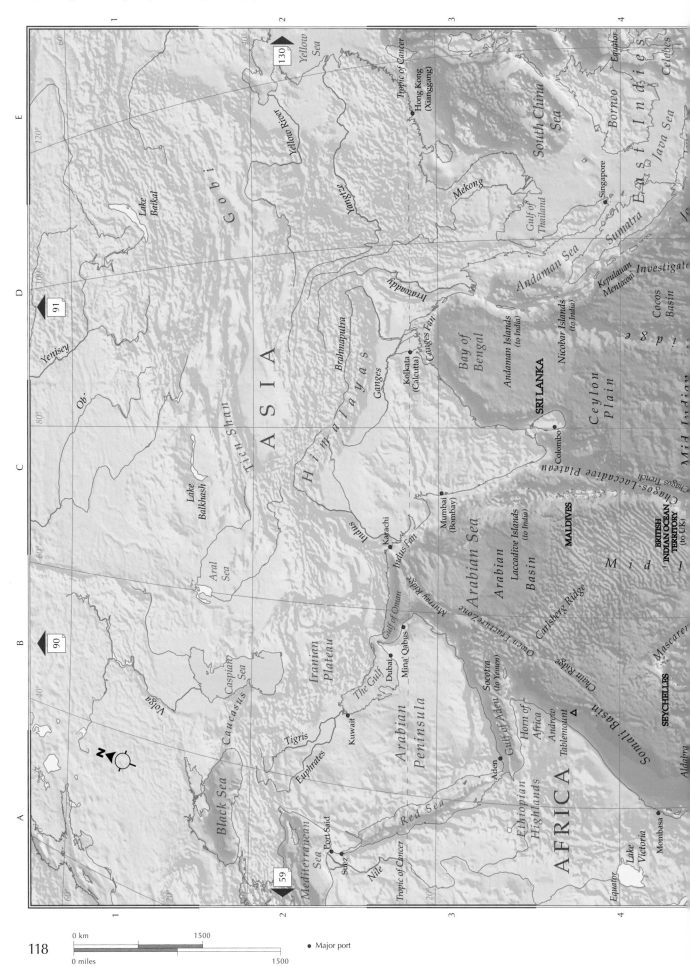

130

91

90

59

Yellow Sea

Tropic of Cancer

Hong Kong (Xianggang)

South China Sea

Borneo

East Indies

Celebes

Java Sea

Equator

Gobi

Yellow River

Yangtze

Mekong

Gulf of Thailand

Singapore

Sumatra

Andaman Sea

Investigate

Lake Baikal

ASIA

Kepulauan Mentawai

Cocos Basin

Irrawaddy

Nicobar Islands (to India)

Ridge

Yenisey

Brahmaputra

Ganges Fan

Bay of Bengal

Andaman Islands (to India)

SRI LANKA

Ceylon Plain

Mid Indian

Ob'

Himalayas

Ganges

Kolkata (Calcutta)

Colombo

Chagos-Laccadive Plateau

Chagos Trench

Tien Shan

Mumbai (Bombay)

MALDIVES

Middle

Lake Balkhash

Indus

Karachi

Indus Fan

Arabian Sea

Laccadive Islands (to India)

Arabian Basin

BRITISH INDIAN OCEAN TERRITORY (to UK)

Aral Sea

Murray Ridge

88g°

Owen Fracture Zone

Carlsberg Ridge

Caspian Sea

Iranian Plateau

Gulf of Oman

Chain Ridge

Mascaren

SEYCHELLES

90

Dubai

Mina' Qabus

Socotra

Volga

The Gulf

Arabian Peninsula

Horn of Africa

Andrew Tablemount

Caucasus

Tigris

Kuwait

Gulf of Aden

Socotra (to Yemen)

Somali Basin

Black Sea

Euphrates

Aden

Aldabra

Mediterranean Sea

Port Said

Red Sea

Ethiopian Highlands

Equator

Lake Victoria

Mombasa

Suez

Nile

Tropic of Cancer

AFRICA

59

N

0 km   1500

0 miles   1500

● Major port

AUSTRALIA

Tropic of Capricorn

Fremantle

North Australian Basin

Exmouth Plateau

Cuvier Plateau

Perth Basin

Naturaliste Plateau

Diamantina Fracture Zone

Wharton Basin

East Indiaman Ridge

Broken Ridge

Southeast Indian Ridge

130

COCOS ISLANDS
(to Australia)

idge

(to Australia)

Osborn Plateau

N i n e t y e a s t

S o u t h e a s t

I n d i a n   R i d g e

South Indian Basin

132

i a n   F r a c t u r e   Z o n e

Argo Fracture

Egeria Fracture Zone

INDIAN

OCEAN

Amsterdam Island

St-Paul Island

SOUTHERN OCEAN

ateau

MAURITIUS
RÉUNION
(to France)

Ridge

I n d i a n   R i d g e

Crozet Basin

FRENCH SOUTHERN &
ANTARCTIC TERRITORIES
(to France)

Kerguelen Plateau

Kerguelen

Banzare Seamounts

ANTARCTICA

Mascarene Basin

Mascarene Plain

Farafangana

MADAGASCAR

Madagascar Basin

S o u t h w e s t

HEARD & McDONALD ISLANDS
(to Australia)

Crozet Plateau

Crozet Islands

△ Lena Tablemount

E n d e r b y   P l a i n

MAYOTTE
(to France)

Davie Ridge

Natal Basin

Madagascar Plateau

Indomed Fracture Zone

△ Ob Tablemount

Atlantic-Indian Basin

Nyasa

Zambezi

Mozambique Channel

Mozambique Plateau

Tropic of Capricorn

Durban

Africana Seamount △

Agulhas Plateau

Agulhas Basin

Prince Edward Islands
(to South Africa)

45

Antarctic Circle

Antarctic Circle

Limit of winter pack ice

Limit of summer pack ice

Antarctic Circle

132

Elevation

-6000m	-4000m	-2000m	-1000m	-250m	0
19,685ft	13,124ft	6562ft	-3281ft	-820ft	0

Australasia & Oceania

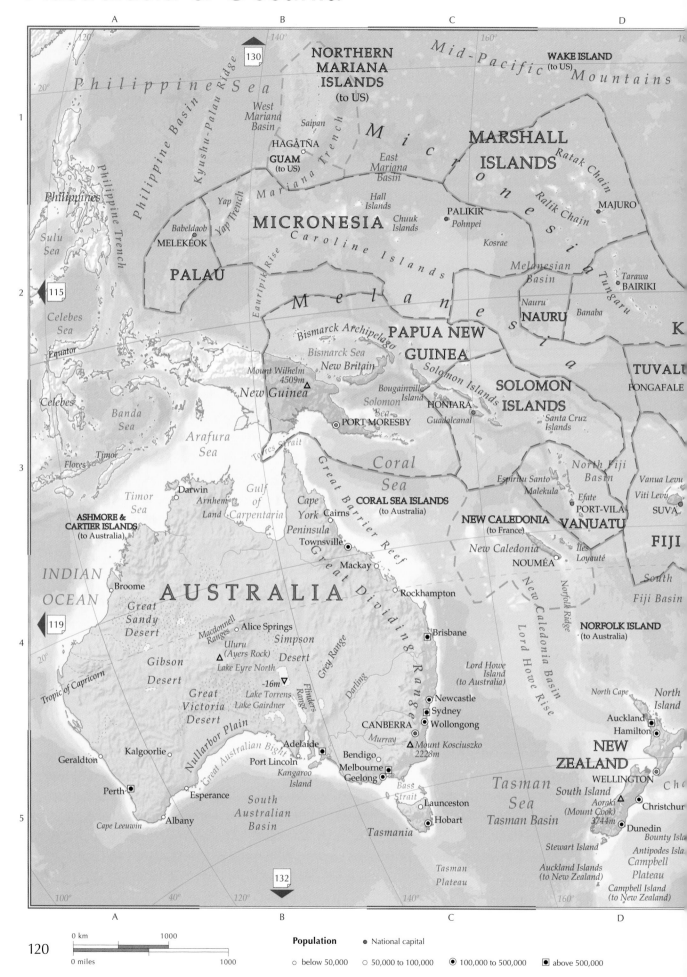

NORTHERN MARIANA ISLANDS (to US)

WAKE ISLAND (to US)

Mid-Pacific *Mountains*

Philippine *Sea*

West Mariana Basin

Saipan

MARSHALL ISLANDS

Ratak Chain

HAGÅTÑA
GUAM (to US)

East Mariana Basin

Ralik Chain

MAJURO

Philippines

Yap

Hall Islands

PALIKIR
Pohnpei

MICRONESIA

Chuuk Islands

Babeldaob
MELEKEOK

Caroline Islands

Kosrae

Melanesian Basin

Tarawa
BAIRIKI

Sulu Sea

PALAU

Eauripik Rise

Nauru
NAURU

Banaba

Celebes Sea

Equator

Melanesia

Tungaru

PAPUA NEW GUINEA

Bismarck Archipelago

Bismarck Sea
New Britain

TUVALU
FONGAFALE

Celebes

Banda Sea

Mount Wilhelm 4509m △
New Guinea

Solomon Islands

SOLOMON ISLANDS

Bougainville Island
Solomon Sea

HONIARA

Santa Cruz Islands

Timor

Flores

Arafura Sea

PORT MORESBY

Guadalcanal

North Fiji Basin

Vanua Levu

Timor Sea

Darwin

Arnhem Land

Gulf of Carpentaria

Cape York

Coral Sea

CORAL SEA ISLANDS (to Australia)

Espiritu Santo
Malekula

Efate
PORT-VILA

Viti Levu
SUVA

ASHMORE & CARTIER ISLANDS (to Australia)

Cairns

Peninsula

Townsville

Great Barrier Reef

NEW CALEDONIA (to France)

New Caledonia
NOUMÉA

VANUATU

Iles Loyauté

FIJI

South Fiji Basin

INDIAN OCEAN

Broome

Great Sandy Desert

AUSTRALIA

Mackay

Rockhampton

Great Dividing Range

New Caledonia Ridge

Norfolk Ridge

NORFOLK ISLAND (to Australia)

Alice Springs

Macdonnell Ranges

Simpson Desert

Brisbane

Lord Howe Island (to Australia)

Lord Howe Rise

Tropic of Capricorn

Gibson Desert

Uluru (Ayers Rock) △

Lake Eyre North ▽

Grey Range

Newcastle

North Cape

North Island

Auckland

Great Victoria Desert

-16m ▽
Lake Torrens
Lake Gairdner

Flinders Range

Darling

Sydney

Wollongong

CANBERRA

Hamilton

Kalgoorlie

Nullarbor Plain

Adelaide

Bendigo

Murray

Mount Kosciuszko 2228m △

NEW ZEALAND

Geraldton

Port Lincoln

Melbourne
Geelong

WELLINGTON

Perth

Great Australian Bight

Kangaroo Island

Bass Strait

Tasman Sea

South Island

Aoraki (Mount Cook) 3744m △

Christchurch

Esperance

South Australian Basin

Launceston

Tasman Basin

Cape Leeuwin

Albany

Hobart

Tasmania

Dunedin

Bounty Isla

Stewart Island

Antipodes Isla

Tasman Plateau

Auckland Islands (to New Zealand)

Campbell Plateau

Campbell Island (to New Zealand)

0 km   1000

0 miles   1000

Population   ● National capital

○ below 50,000   ○ 50,000 to 100,000   ◉ 100,000 to 500,000   ■ above 500,000

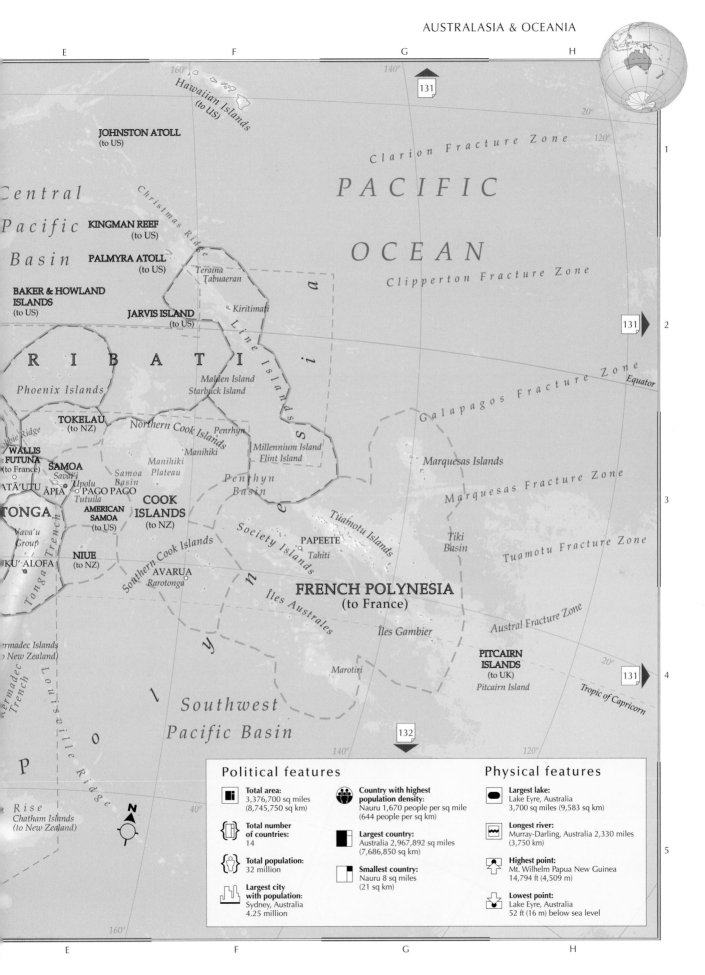

E   F   G   H

160°   140°

131

Hawaiian Islands (to US)

JOHNSTON ATOLL
(to US)

Clarion Fracture Zone   120°   20°

1

Central   **P A C I F I C**

Pacific   **KINGMAN REEF**
(to US)

Basin   **PALMYRA ATOLL**
(to US)

O C E A N

Teraina
Tabuaeran

Clipperton Fracture Zone

**BAKER & HOWLAND
ISLANDS**
(to US)

• *Kiritimati*

JARVIS ISLAND
(to US)

131

2

Equator

K I R I B A T I

Malden Island
Starbuck Island

Galapagos Fracture Zone

Phoenix Islands

Robbie Ridge

TOKELAU
(to NZ)

Northern Cook Islands   *Penrhyn*

Marquesas Islands

**WALLIS &
FUTUNA**
(to France)

Manihiki

Millennium Island
Flint Island

Marquesas Fracture Zone

3

SAMOA
Savai'i

*Manihiki
Plateau*

*Penrhyn
Basin*

ʻATAʻUTU
Upolu
APIA
PAGO PAGO
Tutuila

*Samoa
Basin*

Tuamotu Islands

*Tiki
Basin*

TONGA

**AMERICAN
SAMOA**
(to US)

**COOK
ISLANDS**
(to NZ)

Tuamotu Fracture Zone

*Vava'u
Group*

Southern Cook Islands

Society Islands

PAPEETE
• *Tahiti*

Tonga Trench

NIUE
(to NZ)

AVARUA
Rarotonga

FRENCH POLYNESIA
(to France)

NUKUʻALOFA

Îles Australes

Îles Gambier

Austral Fracture Zone

20°

*Kermadec Islands
(to New Zealand)*

Louisville Ridge

Marotiri

**PITCAIRN
ISLANDS**
(to UK)
Pitcairn Island

131

4

Tropic of Capricorn

**Southwest
Pacific Basin**

132

140°   120°

Rise

*Chatham Islands
(to New Zealand)*

N

40°

Political features

▦	**Total area:**	3,376,700 sq miles (8,745,750 sq km)
▥	**Total number of countries:**	14
⌘	**Total population:**	32 million
⌂	**Largest city with population:**	Sydney, Australia 4.25 million

⚇	**Country with highest population density:**	Nauru 1,670 people per sq mile (644 people per sq km)
◼	**Largest country:**	Australia 2,967,892 sq miles (7,686,850 sq km)
◳	**Smallest country:**	Nauru 8 sq miles (21 sq km)

Physical features

⬬	**Largest lake:**	Lake Eyre, Australia 3,700 sq miles (9,583 sq km)
〰	**Longest river:**	Murray-Darling, Australia 2,330 miles (3,750 km)
⬆	**Highest point:**	Mt. Wilhelm Papua New Guinea 14,794 ft (4,509 m)
⬇	**Lowest point:**	Lake Eyre, Australia 52 ft (16 m) below sea level

160°

E   F   G   H

5

The Southwest Pacific

A

B

C

D

130

Saipan
Tinian
Rota

NORTHERN
MARIANA
ISLANDS
(to US)

GUAM
(to US)

HAGÅTÑA

1

140°

150°

160°

170°

MARSHALL
ISLANDS

Enewetak
Atoll

Bikini Atoll

Rongelap
Atoll

Ailuk Atoll

Wotje Atoll

Ratak Chain

Ralik Chain

Maloelap Ato

Ujelang Atoll

Kwajalein
Atoll

Namu Atoll

Majuro At

Ailinglaplap Atoll

Jaluit Atoll

Mili Atoll

10°

Yap

MICRONESIA

Chuuk
Islands

PALIKIR

Pohnpei

Babeldaob

MELEKEOK

Caroline Islands

Kosrae

Makin

M
i
c
r
o
n
e
s
i
a

Tarawa

PALAU

117

2

Equator

Ebon Atoll

BAIRIKI

Abemar

Nonou

NAURU

Banaba

Admiralty
Islands

St.Matthias Group

New Ireland

Bismarck Archipelago

Bismarck Sea

New Guinea

Madang

INDONESIA

Central Range

Mount Wilhelm
4509m

Lae

Owen Stanley Range

PAPUA NEW GUINEA

New
Britain

Bougainville
Island

Solomon Sea

Choiseul

Santa Isabel

Solomon Islands

New Georgia
Islands

Malaita

SOLOMON
ISLANDS

M
e
l
a
n
e
s
i
a

3

10°

Arafura Sea

Gulf of
Papua

PORT MORESBY

Torres Strait

D'Entrecasteaux
Islands

Louisiade
Archipelago

HONIARA

Guadalcanal

San Cristobal

Rennell

Santa Cruz
Islands

Banks Islands

Maéwo

4

Arnhem
Land

Groote
Eylandt

Gulf of
Carpentaria

Barkly Tableland

Cape
York
Peninsula

Great Barrier Reef

Coral Sea

CORAL SEA ISLANDS
(to Australia)

Espiritu Santo

Malekula

Pentecost

Ambrym

Epi

Efate

Erromango

Tanna

PORT-VILA

VANUATU

124

NEW
CALEDONIA
(to France)

20°

NORTHERN

TERRITORY

Tropic of Capricorn

Macdonnell

Ranges

QUEENSLAND

Great Dividing Range

Ouvéa

New
Caledonia

Îles Loyauté

Lifou

Maré

Aneityum

NOUMÉA

5

AUSTRALIA

127

140°

150°

160°

170°

A

B

C

D

0 km   750
0 miles   750

Population   ● National capital

○ below 50,000   ○ 50,000 to 100,000   ◉ 100,000 to 500,000   ◼ above 500,000

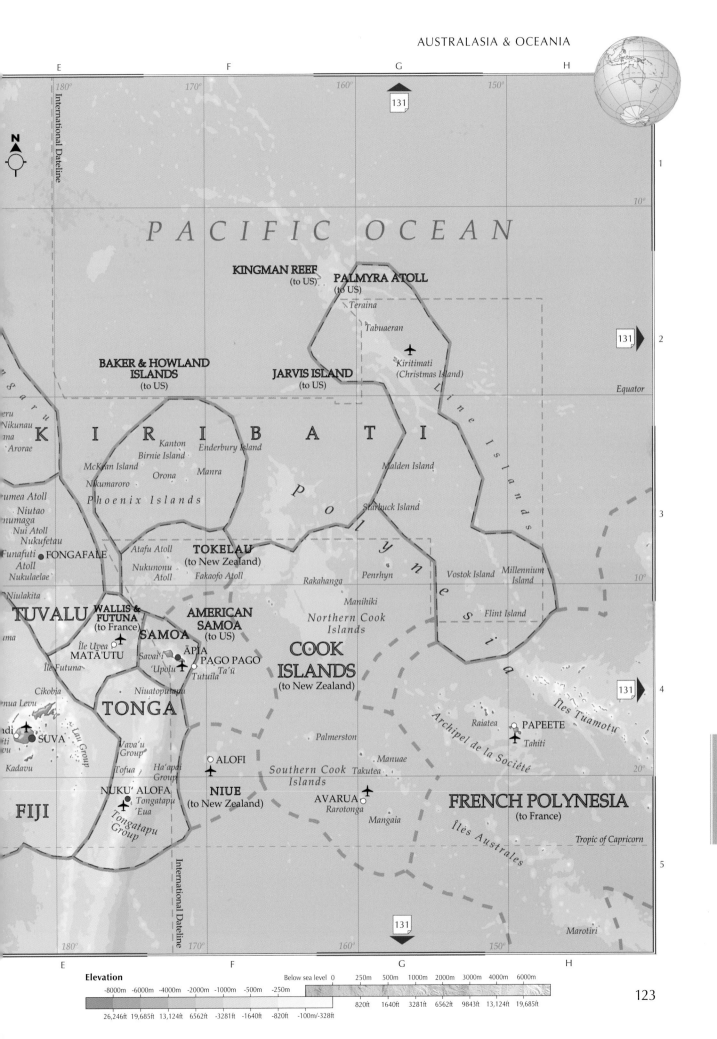

Western Australia

0 km   300

0 miles   300

Population

○ Internal administrative capital

○ below 50,000   ○ 50,000 to 100,000   ◉ 100,000 to 500,000   ■ above 500,000

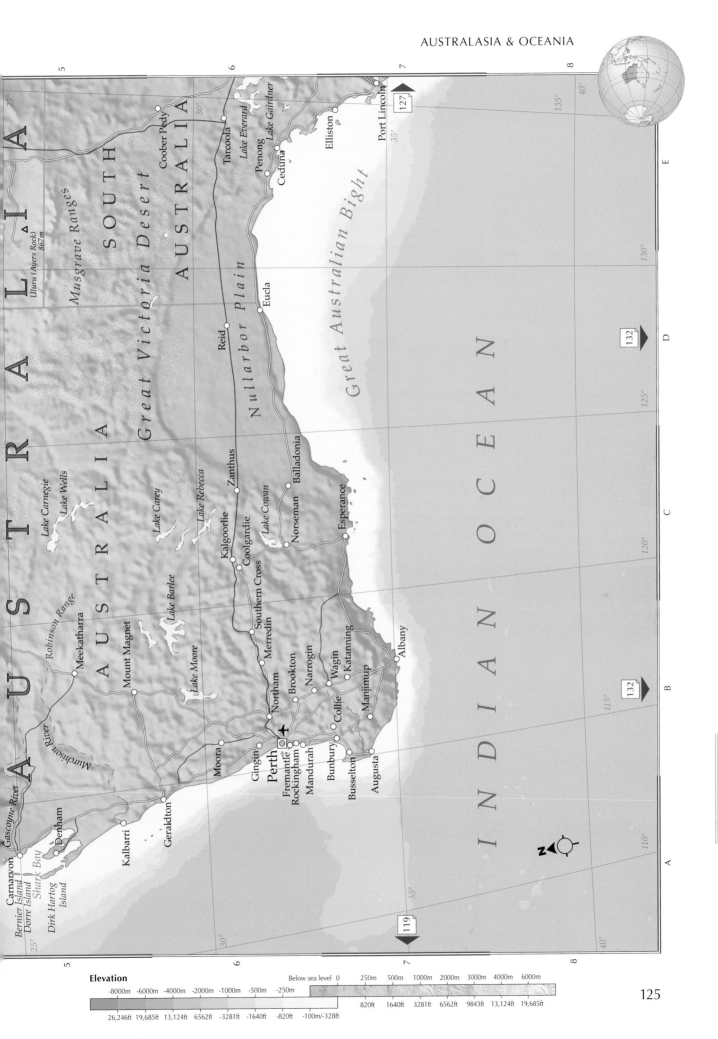

AUSTRALIA

SOUTH AUSTRALIA

Musgrave Ranges

Uluru (Ayers Rock)
867m △

Great Victoria Desert

Coober Pedy

Tarcoola

Lake Everard

Lake Gairdner

Penong

Ceduna

Elliston

Port Lincoln

127

Nullarbor Plain

Reid

Eucla

Great Australian Bight

WESTERN AUSTRALIA

Lake Carnegie

Lake Wells

Lake Carey

Lake Rebecca

Zanthus

Kalgoorlie

Coolgardie

Lake Cowan

Norseman

Balladonia

Esperance

INDIAN OCEAN

132

Robinson Range

Meekatharra

Mount Magnet

Lake Moore

Lake Barlee

Southern Cross

Merredin

Northam

Brookton

Narrogin

Wagin

Katanning

Manjimup

Collie

Albany

Murchison River

Gascoyne River

Carnarvon

Bernier Island

Dorre Island

Dirk Hartog
Island

Denham

Shark Bay

Kalbarri

Geraldton

Moora

Gingin

Perth

Fremantle

Rockingham

Mandurah

Bunbury

Busselton

Augusta

132

N

119

Elevation

Below sea level 0   250m   500m   1000m   2000m   3000m   4000m   6000m

-8000m -6000m -4000m -2000m -1000m -500m -250m

820ft   1640ft   3281ft   6562ft   9843ft   13,124ft   19,685ft

26,246ft 19,685ft 13,124ft 6562ft -3281ft -1640ft -820ft -100m/-328ft

Eastern Australia

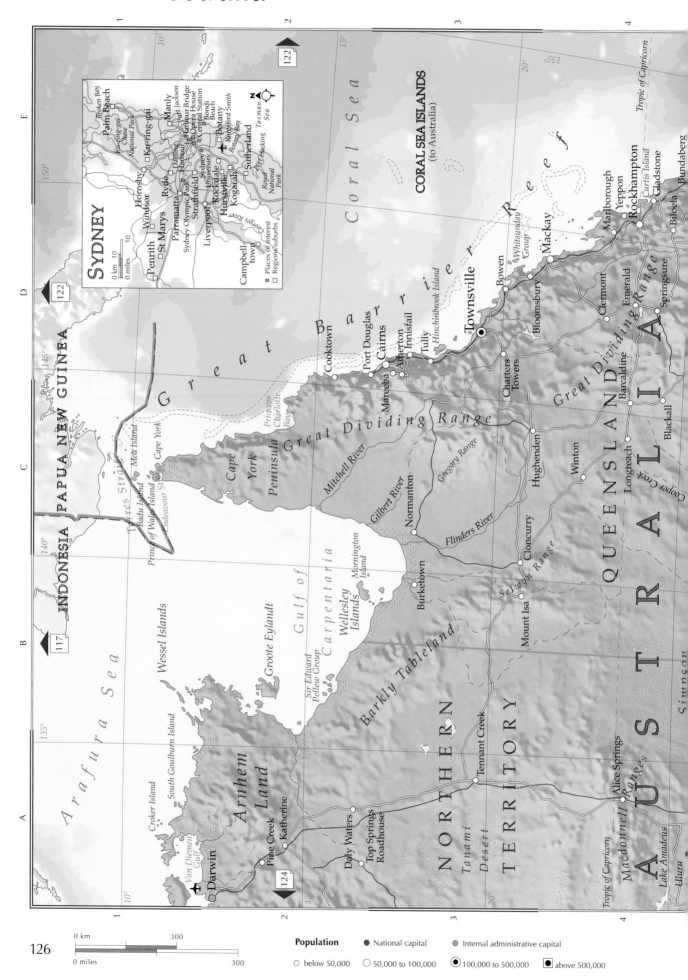

Population
- National capital
- Internal administrative capital
- below 50,000
- 50,000 to 100,000
- 100,000 to 500,000
- above 500,000

SYDNEY

Broken Bay
Palm Beach
Ku-ring-gai
Chase
National Park
Manly
Ryde
Port Jackson
Darling
Harbour Bridge
Opera House
Central Station
Bondi
Beach
Botany
Kingsford Smith
Bondi
Bay
Tasman
Sea
Hornsby
Windsor
Parramatta
Sydney Olympic Park
Strathfield
Sydney
University
Rockdale
Kogarah
Hurstville
Sutherland
Port Hacking
Royal
National
Park
St Marys
Liverpool
Penrith
Campbell-
town
George's River
Places of interest
Regions/suburbs

INDONESIA
PAPUA NEW GUINEA
Arafura Sea
Torres Strait
Badu Island
Moa Island
Prince of Wales Island
Cape York
Endeavour St
Cape York Peninsula

Croker Island
South Goulburn Island
Wessel Islands
Groote Eylandt
Sir Edward Pellew Group
Wellesley Islands
Mornington Island
Gulf of Carpentaria

Van Diemen Gulf
Darwin
Pine Creek
Katherine
Daly Waters
Top Springs Roadhouse
Tennant Creek
Alice Springs
Macdonnell Ranges
Tanami Desert
Lake Amadeus
Uluru
Simpson

NORTHERN TERRITORY
Barkly Tableland
Mount Isa
Burketown
Normanton
Gilbert River
Mitchell River
Princess Charlotte Bay
Cooktown
Port Douglas
Cairns
Mareeba
Atherton
Innisfail
Tully
Hinchinbrook Island
Townsville
Charters Towers
Hughenden
Winton
Cloncurry
Selwyn Range
Gregory Range
Flinders River
Great Dividing Range
Cooper Creek
Longreach
Barcaldine
Blackall
Clermont
Emerald
Springsure
Bowen
Bloomsbury
Whitsunday Group
Mackay
Marlborough
Yeppon
Rockhampton
Curtis Island
Gladstone
Biloela
Bundaberg

QUEENSLAND
AUSTRALIA

Coral Sea
CORAL SEA ISLANDS
(to Australia)
Great Barrier Reef

Tropic of Capricorn

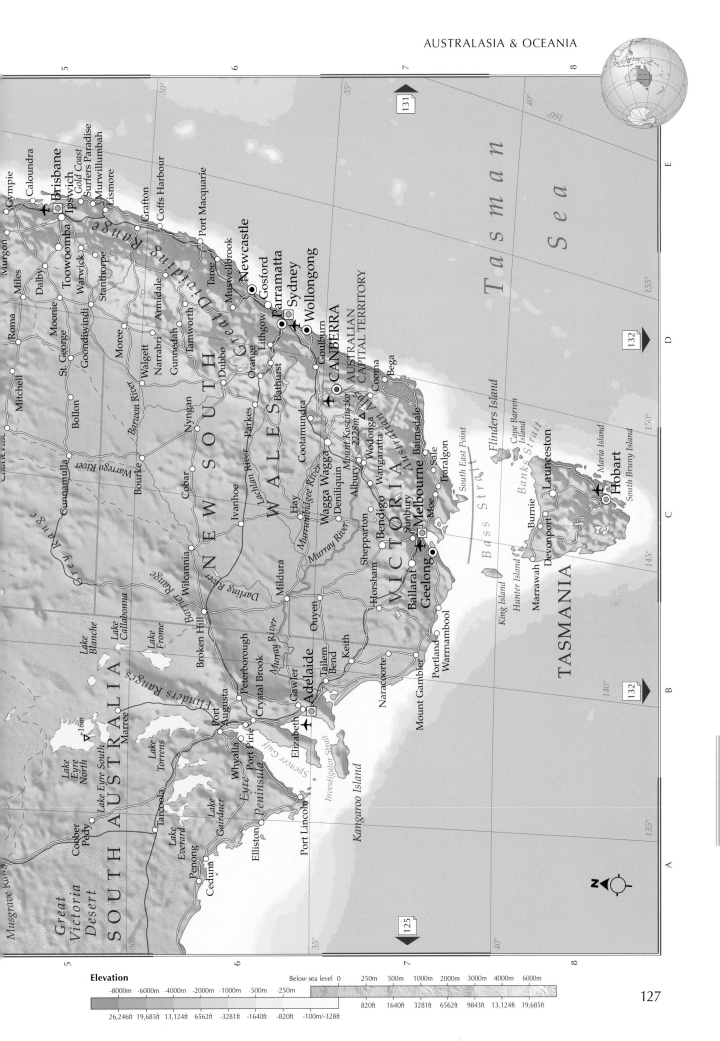

Elevation

| Below sea level | 0 | 250m | 500m | 1000m | 2000m | 3000m | 4000m | 6000m |

| -8000m | -6000m | -4000m | -2000m | -1000m | -500m | -250m |

| 26,246ft | 19,685ft | 13,124ft | 6562ft | -3281ft | -1640ft | -820ft | -100m/-328ft |

| 820ft | 1640ft | 3281ft | 6562ft | 9843ft | 13,124ft | 19,685ft |

New Zealand

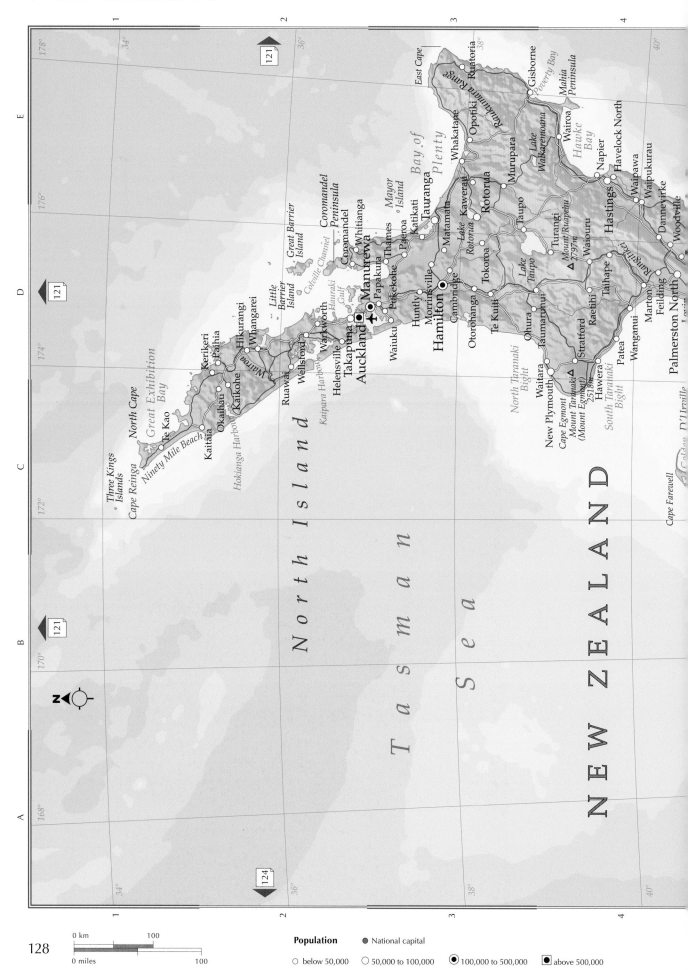

Population

- National capital
- ○ below 50,000
- ○ 50,000 to 100,000
- ◉ 100,000 to 500,000
- ◼ above 500,000

0 km 100
0 miles 100

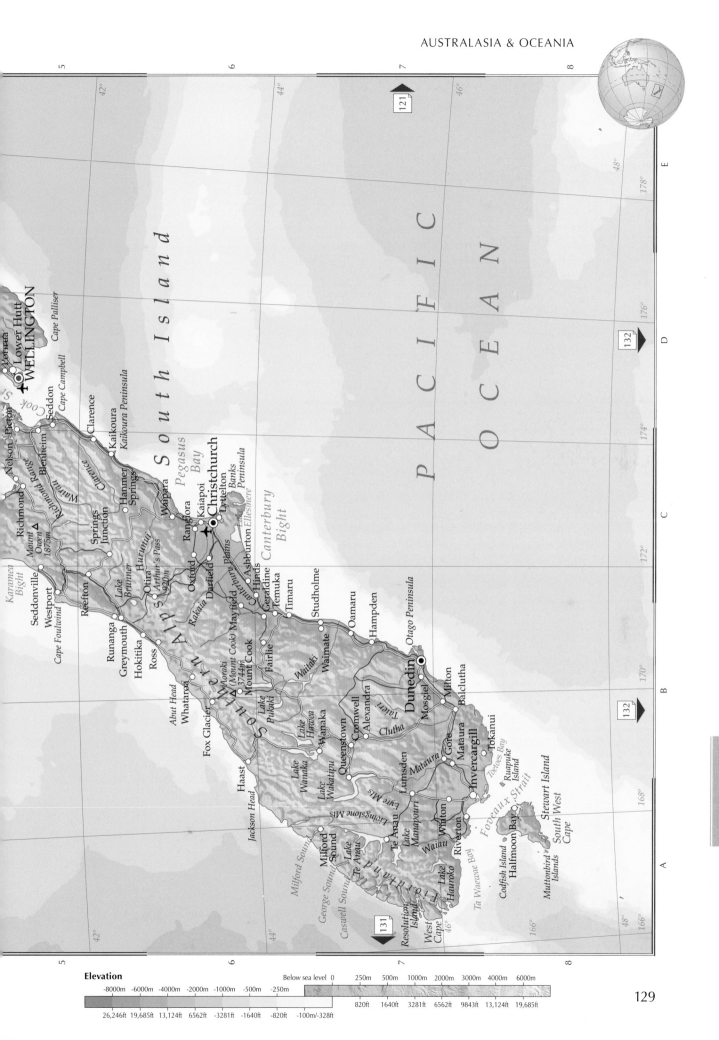

121

132

132

131

South Island

PACIFIC OCEAN

Cook St

Lower Hutt
WELLINGTON
Seddon
Cape Campbell
Cape Palliser

Nelson
Picton
Blenheim
Richmond
Richmond Range
Wairau
Mount Owen 1875m
Seddonville
Westport
Reefton
Springs Junction
Hanner Springs
Clarence
Kaikoura
Kaikoura Peninsula

Karamea Bight
Cape Foulwind
Runanga
Greymouth
Hokitika
Ross
Lake Brunner
Otira
Arthur's Pass 920m
Hurunui
Waipara
Rangiora
Kaiapoi
Christchurch
Lyttelton
Banks Peninsula
Pegasus Bay

Oxford
Darfield
Rakaia
Canterbury Plains
Mayfield
Ashburton
Hinds
Lake Ellesmere
Canterbury Bight

Abut Head
Whataroa
Fox Glacier
Aoraki (Mount Cook) 3744m
Mount Cook
Geraldine
Temuka
Timaru
Studholme
Oamaru
Hampden

Haast
Jackson Head
Lake Pukaki
Fairlie
Waitaki
Waimate

Southern Alps

Lake Hawea
Lake Wanaka
Wanaka
Lake Wakatipu
Queenstown
Cromwell
Alexandra
Clutha
Taieri
Dunedin
Mosgiel
Milton
Balclutha
Otago Peninsula

Eyre Mts
Livingstone Mts
Lumsden
Mataura
Gore
Mataura
Tokanui
Ruapuke Island
Toetoes Bay

Milford Sound
George Sound
Caswell Sound
Lake Te Anau
Te Anau
Lake Manapouri
Waiau
Winton
Invercargill
Riverton
Te Waewae Bay
Codfish Island
Halfmoon Bay
Muttonbird Islands
Stewart Island
South West Cape
South Cape
Foveaux Strait

Fiordland
Puwunu
Lake Hauroko

Resolution Island
West Cape

Elevation

| Below sea level | 0 | 250m | 500m | 1000m | 2000m | 3000m | 4000m | 6000m |

-8000m -6000m -4000m -2000m -1000m -500m -250m

820ft 1640ft 3281ft 6562ft 9843ft 13,124ft 19,685ft

26,246ft 19,685ft 13,124ft 6562ft -3281ft -1640ft -820ft -100m/-328ft

The Pacific Ocean

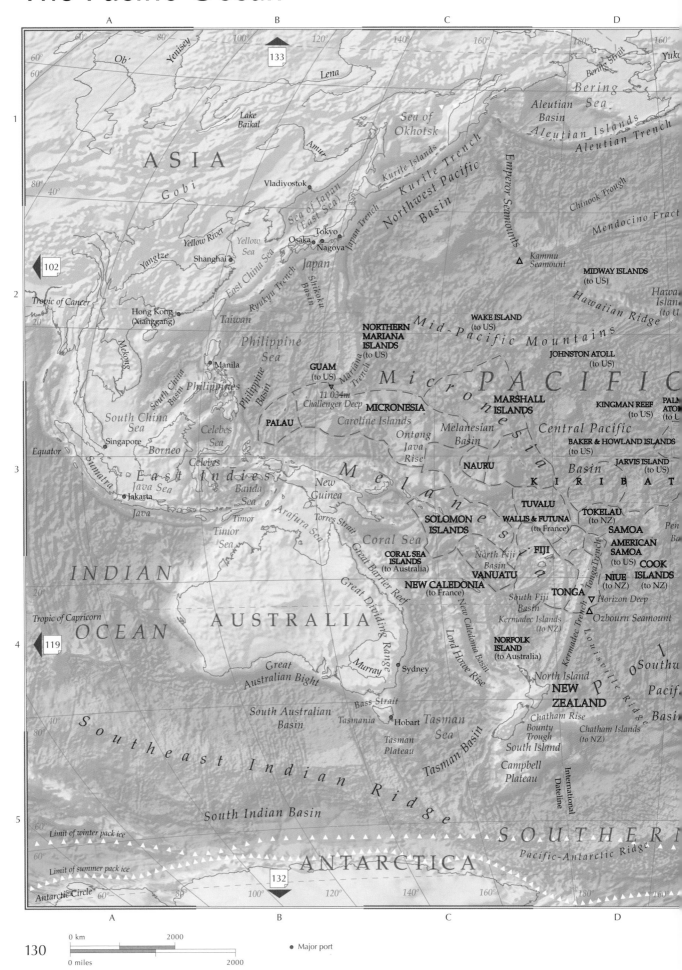

ASIA

Ob'
Yenisey
Lena
Lake Baikal
Amur
Gobi
Vladivostok
Yellow River
Yellow Sea
Shanghai
Yangtze
Osaka Tokyo
Nagoya
Sea of Japan (East Sea)
Sea of Okhotsk
Kurile Islands
Kurile Trench
Japan Trench
Northwest Pacific Basin
Emperor Seamounts
Bering Sea
Aleutian Basin
Aleutian Islands
Aleutian Trench
Bering Strait
Yuko
Chinook Trough
Mendocino Fract

133
102

Tropic of Cancer
Hong Kong (Xianggang)
Taiwan
East China Sea
Ryukyu Trench
Shikoku Basin
Japan
Philippine Sea
Manila
South China Basin
Philippines
Philippine Basin
South China Sea
Celebes Sea
Singapore
Borneo
Celebes Sea
Sumatra
Java Sea
Jakarta
Java
East Indies
Banda Sea
Timor
Timor Sea
Arafura Sea
Torres Strait
New Guinea

GUAM (to US)
11 034m
Challenger Deep
PALAU
Mariana Trench
NORTHERN MARIANA ISLANDS (to US)
WAKE ISLAND (to US)
Mid-Pacific Mountains
MICRONESIA
Caroline Islands
Ontong Java Rise
Melanesian Basin
NAURU
Micronesia
MARSHALL ISLANDS
JOHNSTON ATOLL (to US)
KINGMAN REEF (to US)
PALM ATO (to L
Central Pacific Basin
BAKER & HOWLAND ISLANDS (to US)
JARVIS ISLAND (to US)
KIRIBAT
PACIFIC
Kammu Seamount
MIDWAY ISLANDS (to US)
Hawaiian Ridge
Hawa Islan (to U

Kammu Seamount

Equator

Mekong

Melanesia
SOLOMON ISLANDS
TUVALU
WALLIS & FUTUNA (to France)
TOKELAU (to NZ)
FIJI
SAMOA
AMERICAN SAMOA (to US)
COOK ISLANDS (to NZ)
NIUE (to NZ)
TONGA
Pen Ba
North Fiji Basin
VANUATU
CORAL SEA ISLANDS (to Australia)
NEW CALEDONIA (to France)
Coral Sea
Great Barrier Reef
Great Dividing Range
New Caledonia Basin
Lord Howe Rise
South Fiji Basin
Kermadec Islands (to NZ)
NORFOLK ISLAND (to Australia)
Kermadec Trench
Tonga Trench
Horizon Deep
Ozbourn Seamount
Louisville Ridge

INDIAN
OCEAN

119

Tropic of Capricorn

AUSTRALIA
Great Australian Bight
Murray
Sydney
South Australian Basin
Bass Strait
Tasmania
Hobart
Tasman Plateau
Tasman Sea
Tasman Basin
North Island
NEW ZEALAND
Chatham Rise
Chatham Islands (to NZ)
Bounty Trough
South Island
Campbell Plateau
International Dateline
Southw
Pacific
Basi

Southeast Indian Ridge
South Indian Basin

Limit of winter pack ice
Limit of summer pack ice
Antarctic Circle

SOUTHERN
Pacific-Antarctic Ridge
ANTARCTICA

132

0 km   2000
0 miles   2000

● Major port

130

E   F   G   H

Arctic Circle

Anchorage

Gulf of Alaska

Rocky Mountains

Vancouver

Cascadia Basin

San Francisco

Murray Fracture Zone

Long Beach

Molokai Fracture Zone

NORTH AMERICA

Hudson Bay

Great Lakes

Colorado

Mississippi

Appalachian Mountains

Gulf of California

Gulf of Mexico

Labrador Sea

133

Greater Antilles

Lesser Antilles

Caribbean Sea

ATLANTIC OCEAN

Tropic of Cancer

44

O C E A N

Clarion Fracture Zone

Clipperton Fracture Zone

CLIPPERTON ISLAND
(to France)

Middle America Trench

Guatemala Basin

Cocos Ridge

Panama City

N

Galapagos Fracture Zone

Gallego Rise

Marquesas Islands

Marquesas Fracture Zone

Tiki Basin

Tahiti

FRENCH POLYNESIA
(to France)

Îles Gambier

Austral Fracture Zone

Îles Australes

PITCAIRN ISLANDS
(to UK)

Galapagos Islands
(to Ecuador)

Bauer Basin

Galapagos Rise

Mendaña Fracture Zone

East Pacific Rise

Peru Basin

Peru–Chile Trench

Sala y Gomez
(to Chile)

Sala y Gomez Ridge

Easter Fracture Zone

Easter Island
(to Chile)

Isla San Félix
(to Chile)

Islas Juan Fernández
(to Chile)

Isla San Ambrosio
(to Chile)

Nazca Ridge

Chile Basin

Equator

Amazon

SOUTH AMERICA

Callao

Andes

Paraná

Tropic of Capricorn

45

Challenger Fracture Zone

Chile Rise

Chile Trench

Valparaiso

ATLANTIC OCEAN

Agassiz Fracture Zone

Eltanin Fracture Zone

Mornington Abyssal Plain

Cape Horn

Drake Passage

O C E A N

Southeast Pacific Basin

Bellingshausen Plain

Amundsen Plain

PETER I ØY
(to Norway)

132

Antarctic Circle

E   F   G   H

Elevation

-6000m	-4000m	-2000m	-1000m	-250m	0
19,685ft	13,124ft	6562ft	-3281ft	-820ft	0

131

Antarctica

45

ATLANTIC

OCEAN

SOUTH GEORGIA
(to UK)

SOUTH SANDWICH ISLANDS
(to UK)

Scotia Sea

South Sandwich Trench

America-Antarctica Ridge

Atlantic-Indian Basin

SOUTHERN

OCEAN

Enderby Plain

Antarctic Circle

Lazarev Sea

Limit of winter pack ice

Orcadas
(Argentina)

South Orkney Islands

Signy
(UK)

Weddell Plain

Sanae
(South Africa)

Georg von Neumayer
(Germany)

Novolazarevskaya
(Russian Federation)

Lützow Holmbukta

Syowa
(Japan)

Molodezhnaya
(Russian Federation)

South Shetland Islands

Limit of summer pack ice

Dronning Maud Land

Drake Passage

43

Esperanza
(Argentina)

Capitán Arturo Prat
(Chile)

Halley
(UK)

Weddell Sea

Coats Land

Enderby Land

119

Palmer
(US)

Antarctic Peninsula

Graham Land

Belgrano II
(Argentina)

Berkner Island

Mawson
(Australia)

Rothera
(UK)

San Martin
(Argentina)

Palmer Land

Ronne Ice Shelf

Cape Darnley

Mackenzie Bay

Alexander Island

Princess Elizabeth Land

Prydz Bay

Davis
(Australia)

Bellingshausen Sea

Vinson Massif
4897m △

ANTARCTICA

East

Davis Sea

PETER I ØY
(to Norway)

Ellsworth Land

West Antarctica

Transantarctic Mountains

Amundsen-Scott
+ + (US)
South Pole

Antarctica

Mirny
(Russian Federation)

Limit of winter pack ice

Limit of summer pack ice

South Geomagnetic Pole +

+ Vostok
(Russian Federation)

Shackleton Ice Shelf

Amundsen Sea

Marie Byrd Land

Mount Sidley
4181m △

Mount Kirkpatrick
4528m △

Mount Markham
4351m △

Ross Ice Shelf

Wilkes Land

Casey
(Australia)

Mount Siple
3100m △

Roosevelt Island

Scott Base
(N.Z)

Cape Poinsett

McMurdo Base
(US)

Mount Erebus
3794m △

Victoria Land

131

Ross Sea

Terre Adélie

130

Amundsen Plain

SOUTHERN

Cape Adare

George V Land

Dumont d'Urville
(France)

South Indian Basin

OCEAN

Leningradskaya
(Russian Federation)

Scott Island

Balleny Islands

Eltanin Fracture Zone

Udintsev Fracture Zone

Pacific-Antarctic Ridge

Macquarie Ridge

Limit of winter pack ice

● Antarctic research station

130

132

0 km 500
0 miles 500

Elevation

-6000m -4000m -2000m -1000m

Below sea level 0 250m 500m 1000m 2000m 3000m 4000m 6000m

-250m

19,685ft 13,124ft 6562ft -3281ft

-820ft 0

820ft 1640ft 3281ft 6562ft 9843ft 13,124ft 19,685ft

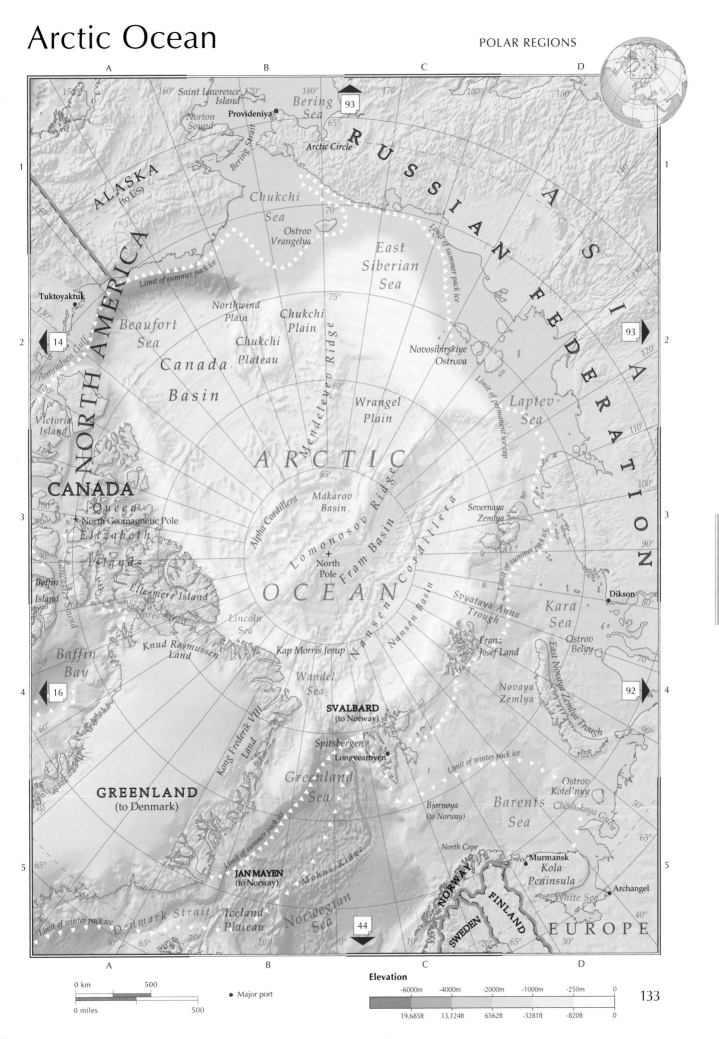

A B C D

Saint Lawrence
Island

Providéniya

Norton
Sound

Bering
Sea

65°

Arctic Circle

R U S S I A N

ALASKA
(to US)

Chukchi
Sea

70°

Ostrov
Vrangelya

East
Siberian
Sea

Limit of summer pack ice

1

140°

160° 170° 180° 170° 160° 150° 140°

130°

93

Tuktoyaktuk

Northwind
Plain

Chukchi
Plain

Limit of summer pack ice

F E D E R A T I O N

2

14

Beaufort
Sea

75°

Chukchi
Plateau

Novosibirskiye
Ostrova

120°

Canada

Basin

Mendeleyev Ridge

80°

Wrangel
Plain

Limit of permanent ice cap

Laptev
Sea

110°

Victoria
Island

NORTH AMERICA

110°

A R C T I C

85°

Severnaya
Zemlya

100°

CANADA

Queen

North Geomagnetic Pole

Elizabeth

90°

Islands

Alpha Cordillera

Makarov
Basin

Lomonosov Ridge

Nansen Cordillera

90°

3

100°

Baffin
Island

Ellesmere Island

Fram Basin

North
Pole

OCEAN

Nansen Basin

Svyataya Anna
Trough

Franz
Josef Land

Kara
Sea

Dikson

Ostrov
Belyy

80°

70°

Nares Strait

Lincoln
Sea

Knud Rasmussen
Land

Kap Morris Jesup

East Novaya Zemlya Trough

Baffin
Bay

70°

Wandel
Sea

Novaya
Zemlya

4

60°

16

SVALBARD
(to Norway)

60°

Kong Frederik VIII Land

Spitsbergen

Longyearbyen

Ostrov
Kotel'nyy

Chëshskaya Guba

50°

GREENLAND
(to Denmark)

Greenland
Sea

Bjørnøya
(to Norway)

Barents
Sea

65°

Limit of winter pack ice

North Cape

Murmansk
Kola
Peninsula

White Sea

Archangel

40°

5

65°

Limit of summer pack ice

JAN MAYEN
(to Norway)

Mohns Ridge

NORWAY

FINLAND

EUROPE

Limit of winter pack ice

Denmark Strait

Iceland
Plateau

Norwegian
Sea

SWEDEN

30°

20° 10° 10° 20° 30°

44

A B C D

0 km 500

0 miles 500

• Major port

Elevation

-6000m -4000m -2000m -1000m -250m 0

19,685ft 13,124ft 6562ft -3281ft -820ft 0

Country Profiles

This Factfile is intended as a guide to a world that is continually changing as political fashions and personalities come and go. Nevertheless, all the material in these factfiles has been researched from the most up-to-date and authoritative sources to give an incisive portrait of the geographical, political, and social characteristics that make each country so unique.

There are currently 195 independent countries in the world - more than at any previous time - and 59 dependencies. Antarctica is the only land area on Earth that is not officially part of, and does not belong to, any single country.

AFGHANISTAN
Central Asia

Page 100 D4

In 2001, following a US-led offensive, the hard-line Muslim taliban militia was replaced by a new interim government under Hamid Karazi

Official name The Islamic Republic of Afghanistan
Formation 1919 / 1919
Capital Kabul
Population 32.3 million / 128 people per sq mile (50 people per sq km) / 24%
Total area 250,000 sq. miles (647,500 sq. km)
Languages Pashtu*, Tajik, Dari*, Farsi, Uzbek, Turkmen
Religions Sunni Muslim 84%, Shi'a Muslim 15%, Other 1%
Ethnic mix Pashtun 38%, Tajik 25%, Hazara 19%, Uzbek and Turkmen 15%, Other 3%
Government Presidential system
Currency Afghani = 100 puls
Literacy rate 28%
Calorie consumption 1539 calories

ALBANIA
Southeast Europe

Page 79 C6

Lying at the southeastern end of the Adriatic Sea, Albania held its first multiparty elections in 1991, after nearly five decades of communism.

Official name Republic of Albania
Formation 1912 / 1921
Capital Tirana
Population 3.2 million / 302 people per sq mile (117 people per sq km) / 44%
Total area 11,100 sq. miles (28,748 sq. km)
Languages Albanian*, Greek
Religions Sunni Muslim 70%, Orthodox Christian 20%, Roman Catholic 10%
Ethnic mix Albanian 93%, Greek 5%, Other 2%
Government Parliamentary system
Currency Lek = 100 qindarka (qintars)
Literacy rate 99%
Calorie consumption 2848 calories

ALGERIA
North Africa

Page 48 C3

Algeria achieved independence from France in 1962. Today, its military-dominated government faces a severe challenge from Islamic extremists.

Official name People's Democratic Republic of Algeria
Formation 1962 / 1962
Capital Algiers
Population 33.9 million / 37 people per sq mile (14 people per sq km) / 59%
Total area 919,590 sq. miles (2,381,740 sq. km)
Languages Arabic*, Tamazight (Kabyle, Shawia, Tamashek), French
Religions Sunni Muslim 99%, Christian and Jewish 1%
Ethnic mix Arab 75%, Berber 24%, European and Jewish 1%
Government Presidential system
Currency Algerian dinar = 100 centimes
Literacy rate 70%
Calorie consumption 3022 calories

ANDORRA
Southwest Europe

Page 69 B6

A tiny landlocked principality, Andorra lies high in the eastern Pyrenees between France and Spain. It held its first full elections in 1993.

Official name Principality of Andorra
Formation 1278 / 1278
Capital Andorra la Vella
Population 71,822 / 399 people per sq mile (154 people per sq km) / 91%
Total area 181 sq. miles (468 sq. km)
Languages Spanish, Catalan*, French, Portuguese
Religions Roman Catholic 94%, Other 6%
Ethnic mix Spanish 46%, Andorran 28%, Other 18%, French 8%
Government Parliamentary system
Currency Euro = 100 cents
Literacy rate 99%
Calorie consumption Not available

ANGOLA
Southern Africa

Page 56 B2

Located in southwest Africa, Angola was in an almost constant state of civil war for nearly 30 years, until a peace deal was agreed in 2002.

Official name Republic of Angola
Formation 1975 / 1975
Capital Luanda
Population 16.9 million / 35 people per sq mile (14 people per sq km) / 36%
Total area 481,351 sq. miles (1,246,700 sq. km)
Languages Portuguese*, Umbundu, Kimbundu, Kikongo
Religions Roman Catholic 50%, Other 30%, Protestant 20%
Ethnic mix Ovimbundu 37%, Other 25%, Kimbundu 25%, Bakongo 13%
Government Presidential system
Currency Readjusted kwanza = 100 lwei
Literacy rate 67%
Calorie consumption 2083 calories

ANTIGUA & BARBUDA
West Indies

Page 33 H3

Lying on the Atlantic edge of the Leeward Islands, Antigua and Barbuda's area includes the uninhabited islet of Redonda.

Official name Antigua and Barbuda
Formation 1981 / 1981
Capital St. John's
Population 69,481 / 409 people per sq mile (158 people per sq km) / 38%
Total area 170 sq. miles (442 sq. km)
Languages English*, English patois
Religions Anglican 45%, Other Protestant 42%, Roman Catholic 10%, Other 2%, Rastafarian 1%
Ethnic mix Black African 95%, Other 5%
Government Parliamentary system
Currency Eastern Caribbean dollar = 100 cents
Literacy rate 86%
Calorie consumption 2349 calories

ARGENTINA
South America

Page 43 B5

Most of the southern half of South America is occupied by Argentina. The country returned to civilian rule in 1983 after a series of military coups.

Official name The Argentine Republic
Formation 1816 / 1816
Capital Buenos Aires
Population 39.5 million / 37 people per sq mile (14 people per sq km) / 90%
Total area 1,068,296 sq. miles (2,766,890 sq. km)
Languages Spanish*, Italian, Amerindian languages
Religions Roman Catholic 90%, Other 6%, Protestant 2%, Jewish 2%
Ethnic mix Indo-European 83%, Mestizo 14%, Jewish 2%, Amerindian 1%
Government Presidential system
Currency new Argentine peso = 100 centavos
Literacy rate 97%
Calorie consumption 2992 calories

ARMENIA
Southwest Asia

Page 95 F3

Smallest of the former USSR's republics, Armenia lies in the Lesser Caucasus mountains. Territorial war with Azerbaijan ended in a 1994 ceasefire.

Official name Republic of Armenia
Formation 1991 / 1991
Capital Yerevan
Population 3 million / 261 people per sq mile (101 people per sq km) / 64%
Total area 11,506 sq. miles (29,800 sq. km)
Languages Armenian*, Azeri, Russian
Religions Armenian Apostolic Church (Orthodox) 88%, Other 6%, Armenian Catholic Church 6%
Ethnic mix Armenian 98%, Other 1%, Yezidi 1%
Government Parliamentary system
Currency Dram = 100 luma
Literacy rate 99%
Calorie consumption 2268 calories

AUSTRALIA
Australasia & Oceania

Page 120 A4

An island continent located between the Indian and Pacific oceans, Australia was settled by Europeans 200 years ago, but now has many Asian immigrants.

Official name Commonwealth of Australia
Formation 1901 / 1901
Capital Canberra
Population 20.9 million / 7 people per sq mile (3 people per sq km) / 92%
Total area 2,967,893 sq. miles (7,686,850 sq. km)
Languages English*, Italian, Cantonese, Greek, Arabic, Vietnamese, Aboriginal languages
Religions Roman Catholic 26%, Protestant 38%, Other 23%, Nonreligious 13%,
   Ethnic mix European 92%, Asian 5%, Aboriginal 2%, Other 1%
Government Parliamentary system
Currency Australian dollar = 100 cents
Literacy rate 99%
Calorie consumption 3054 calories

AUSTRIA
Central Europe

Page 73 D7

Bordering eight countries in the heart of Europe, Austria was created in 1920 after the collapse of the Austro-Hungarian Empire the previous year.

Official name Republic of Austria
Formation 1918 / 1919
Capital Vienna
Population 8.2 million / 257 people per sq mile (99 people per sq km) / 66%
Total area 32,378 sq. miles (83,858 sq. km)
Languages German*, Croatian, Slovenian, Hungarian (Magyar)
Religions Roman Catholic 78%, Other (including Jewish and Muslim) 17%, Protestant 5%
Ethnic mix Austrian 93%, Croat, Slovene, and Hungarian 6%, Other 1%
Government Parliamentary system
Currency Euro = 100 cents
Literacy rate 99%
Calorie consumption 3673 calories

AZERBAIJAN
Southwest Asia

Page 95 G2

Situated on the western coast of the Caspian Sea, Azerbaijan was the first Soviet republic to declare independence from Moscow in 1991.

Official name Republic of Azerbaijan
Formation 1991 / 1991
Capital Baku
Population 8.5 million / 254 people per sq mile (98 people per sq km) / 50%
Total area 33,436 sq. miles (86,600 sq. km)
Languages Azeri*, Russian
Religions Shi'a Muslim 68%, Sunni Muslim 26%, Russian Orthodox 3%, Armenian Apostolic Church (Orthodox) 2%, Other 1%
Ethnic mix Azeri 91%, Other 3%, Lazs 2%, Armenian 2%, Russian 2%
Government Presidential system
Currency New manat = 100 gopik
Literacy rate 99%
Calorie consumption 2575 calories

BAHAMAS
West Indies

Page 32 C1

Located in the western Atlantic, off the Florida coast, the Bahamas comprise some 700 islands and 2,400 cays, only 30 of which are inhabited.

Official name Commonwealth of the Bahamas
Formation 1973 / 1973
Capital Nassau
Population 305,655 / 79 people per sq mile (31 people per sq km) / 90%
Total area 5382 sq. miles (13,940 sq. km)
Languages English*, English Creole, French Creole
Religions Baptist 32%, Anglican 20%, Roman Catholic 19%, Other 17%, Methodist 6%, Church of God 6%
Ethnic mix Black African 85%, Other 15%
Government Parliamentary system
Currency Bahamian dollar = 100 cents
Literacy rate 96%
Calorie consumption 2755 calories

BAHRAIN
Southwest Asia

Page 98 C4

Bahrain is an archipelago of 33 islands between the Qatar peninsula and the Saudi Arabian mainland. Only three of these islands are inhabited.

Official name Kingdom of Bahrain
Formation 1971 / 1971
Capital Manama
Population 708,573 / 2596 people per sq mile (1004 people per sq km) / 90%
Total area 239 sq. miles (620 sq. km)
Languages Arabic
Religions Muslim (mainly Shi'a) 99%, Other 1%
Ethnic mix Bahraini 70%, Iranian, Indian, and Pakistani 24%, Other Arab 4%, European 2%
Government Mixed monarchical–parliamentary system
Currency Bahraini dinar = 1000 fils
Literacy rate 87%
Calorie consumption Not available

BANGLADESH
South Asia

Page 113 G3

Bangladesh lies at the north of the Bay of Bengal. It seceded from Pakistan in 1971 and, after much political instability, returned to democracy in 1991.

Official name People's Republic of Bangladesh
Formation 1971 / 1971
Capital Dhaka
Population 147 million / 2845 people per sq mile (1098 people per sq km) / 25%
Total area 55,598 sq. miles (144,000 sq. km)
Languages Bengali*, Urdu, Chakma, Marma (Magh), Garo, Khasi, Santhali, Tripuri, Mro
Religions Muslim (mainly Sunni) 87%, Hindu 12%, Other 1%
Ethnic mix Bengali 98%, Other 2%
Government Transitional regime
Currency Taka = 100 poisha
Literacy rate 41%
Calorie consumption 2205 calories

BARBADOS
West Indies

Page 33 H4

Barbados is the most easterly of the Caribbean Windward Islands. Under British rule for 339 years, it became fully independent in 1966.

Official name Barbados
Formation 1966 / 1966
Capital Bridgetown
Population 280,946 / 1692 people per sq mile (653 people per sq km) / 52%
Total area 166 sq. miles (430 sq. km)
Languages English*, Bajan (Barbadian English)
Religions Anglican 40%, Other 24%, Nonreligious 17%, Pentecostal 8%, Methodist 7%, Roman Catholic 4%
Ethnic mix Black African 92%, White 3%, Other 3%, Mixed race 2%
Government Parliamentary system
Currency Barbados dollar = 100 cents
Literacy rate 99%
Calorie consumption 3091 calories

BELARUS
Eastern Europe

Page 85 B6

Formerly known as White Russia, Belarus lies landlocked in eastern Europe. The country reluctantly became independent of the USSR in 1991.

Official name Republic of Belarus
Formation 1991 / 1991
Capital Minsk
Population 9.6 million / 120 people per sq mile (46 people per sq km) / 71%
Total area 80,154 sq. miles (207,600 sq. km)
Languages Belorussian*, Russian*
Religions Orthodox Christian 60%, Other 32%, Roman Catholic 8%
Ethnic mix Belorussian 81%, Russian 11%, Polish 4%, Other 2%, Ukrainian 2%
Government Presidential system
Currency Belorussian rouble = 100 kopeks
Literacy rate 99%
Calorie consumption 3000 calories

BELGIUM
Northwest Europe

Page 65 B6

Located in northwestern Europe, Belgium's history has been marked by the division between its Flemish- and French-speaking communities.

Official name Kingdom of Belgium
Formation 1830 / 1919
Capital Brussels
Population 10.5 million / 829 people per sq mile (320 people per sq km) / 97%
Total area 11,780 sq. miles (30,510 sq. km)
Languages Dutch*, French*, German*
Religions Roman Catholic 88%, Other 10%, Muslim 2%
Ethnic mix Fleming 58%, Walloon 33%, Other 6%, Italian 2%, Moroccan 1%
Government Parliamentary system
Currency Euro = 100 cents
Literacy rate 99%
Calorie consumption 3584 calories

BELIZE
Central America

Page 30 B1

The last Central American country to gain independence, this former British colony lies on the eastern shore of the Yucatan Peninsula.

Official name Belize
Formation 1981 / 1981
Capital Belmopan
Population 294,385 / 33 people per sq mile (13 people per sq km) / 48%
Total area 8867 sq. miles (22,966 sq. km)
Languages English*, English Creole, Spanish, Mayan, Garifuna (Carib)
Religions Roman Catholic 62%, Other 16%, Anglican 12%, Methodist 6%, Mennonite 4%,
Ethnic mix Mestizo 49%, Creole 25%, Maya 11%, Other 6%, Garifuna 6%, Asian Indian 3%
Government Parliamentary system
Currency Belizean dollar = 100 cents
Literacy rate 75%
Calorie consumption 2869 calories

BENIN
West Africa

Page 53 F4

Stretching north from the West African coast, Benin became one of the pioneers of African democratization in 1990, ending years of military rule.

Official name Republic of Benin
Formation 1960 / 1960
Capital Porto-Novo
Population 9 million / 211 people per sq mile (81 people per sq km) / 45%
Total area 43,483 sq. miles (112,620 sq. km)
Languages French*, Fon, Bariba, Yoruba, Adja, Houeda, Somba
Religions Voodoo 50%, Muslim 30%, Christian 20%
Ethnic mix Fon 41%, Other 21%, Adja 16%, Yoruba 12%, Bariba 10%
Government Presidential system
Currency CFA franc = 100 centimes
Literacy rate 35%
Calorie consumption 2548 calories

BHUTAN
South Asia

Page 113 G3

The landlocked Buddhist kingdom of Bhutan is perched in the eastern Himalayas between India and China. Gradual reforms protect its cultural identity.

Official name Kingdom of Bhutan
Formation 1656 / 1865
Capital Thimphu
Population 2.3 million / 127 people per sq mile (49 people per sq km) / 9%
Total area 18,147 sq. miles (47,000 sq. km)
Languages Dzongkha*, Nepali, Assamese
Religions Mahayana Buddhist 70%, Hindu 24%, Other 6%
Ethnic mix Bhute 50%, Other 25%, Nepalese 25%
Government Mixed monarchical–parliamentary system
Currency Ngultrum = 100 chetrum
Literacy rate 47%
Calorie consumption Not available

BOLIVIA
South America

Page 39 F3

Bolivia lies landlocked high in central South America. Mineral riches once made it the region's wealthiest state. Today, it is the poorest.

Official name Republic of Bolivia
Formation 1825 / 1938
Capital La Paz (administrative); Sucre (judicial)
Population 9.5 million / 23 people per sq mile (9 people per sq km) / 64%
Total area 424,162 sq. miles (1,098,580 sq. km)
Languages Aymara*, Quechua*, Spanish*
Religions Roman Catholic 93%, Other 7%
Ethnic mix Quechua 37%, Aymara 32%, Mixed race 13%, European 10%, Other 8%
Government Presidential system
Currency Boliviano = 100 centavos
Literacy rate 87%
Calorie consumption 2235 calories

BOSNIA & HERZEGOVINA
Southeast Europe

Page 78 B3

At the heart of the western Balkans, Bosnia and Herzegovina was the focus of the bitter conflict surrounding the breakup of the former Yugoslavia.

Official name Bosnia and Herzegovina
Formation 1992 / 1992
Capital Sarajevo
Population 3.9 million / 198 people per sq mile (76 people per sq km) / 45%
Total area 19,741 sq. miles (51,129 sq. km)
Languages Bosnian*, Croatian*, Serbian*
Religions Muslim (mainly Sunni) 40%, Orthodox Christian 31%, Roman Catholic 15%, Other 10%, Protestant 4%
Ethnic mix Bosniak 44%, Serb 31%, Croat 17%, Other 8%
Government Parliamentary system
Currency Marka = 100 pfeninga
Literacy rate 97%
Calorie consumption 2894 calories

BOTSWANA
Southern Africa

Page 56 C3

Once the British protectorate of Bechuanaland, Botswana lies landlocked in southern Africa. Diamonds provide it with a prosperous economy.

Official name Republic of Botswana
Formation 1966 / 1966
Capital Gaborone
Population 1.8 million / 8 people per sq mile (3 people per sq km) / 52%
Total area 231,803 sq. miles (600,370 sq. km)
Languages English*, Setswana, Shona, San, Khoikhoi, isiNdebele
Religions Traditional beliefs 50%, Christian (mainly Protestant) 30%, Other (including Muslim) 20%
Ethnic mix Tswana 98%, Other 2%
Government Presidential system
Currency Pula = 100 thebe
Literacy rate 81%
Calorie consumption 2151 calories

BRAZIL
South America

Page 40 C2

Brazil covers more than half of South America and is the site of the world's largest rain forest. The country has immense natural resources.

Official name Federative Republic of Brazil
Formation 1822 / 1828
Capital Brasília
Population 191 million / 59 people per sq mile (23 people per sq km) / 84%
Total area 3,286,470 sq. miles (8,511,965 sq. km)
Languages Portuguese*, German, Italian, Spanish, Polish, Japanese, Amerindian languages
Religions Roman Catholic 74%, Protestant 15%, Atheist 7%, Other 4%
Ethnic mix White 54%, Mixed race 38%, Black 6%, Other 2%
Government Presidential system
Currency Real = 100 centavos
Literacy rate 89%
Calorie consumption 3049 calories

BRUNEI
Southeast Asia

Page 116 D3

Lying on the northwestern coast of the island of Borneo, Brunei is surrounded and divided in two by the Malaysian state of Sarawak.

Official name Brunei Darussalam
Formation 1984 / 1984
Capital Bandar Seri Begawan
Population 374,577 / 184 people per sq mile (71 people per sq km) / 77%
Total area 2228 sq. miles (5770 sq. km)
Languages Malay*, English, Chinese
Religions Muslim (mainly Sunni) 66%, Buddhist 14%, Other 10%, Christian 10%
Ethnic mix Malay 67%, Chinese 16%, Other 11%, Indigenous 6%
Government Monarchy
Currency Brunei dollar = 100 cents
Literacy rate 93%
Calorie consumption 2855 calories

BULGARIA
Southeast Europe

Page 82 C2

Located in southeastern Europe, Bulgaria has made slow progress toward democracy since the fall of its communist regime in 1990.

Official name Republic of Bulgaria
Formation 1908 / 1947
Capital Sofia
Population 7.6 million / 178 people per sq mile (69 people per sq km) / 70%
Total area 42,822 sq. miles (110,910 sq. km)
Languages Bulgarian*, Turkish, Romani
Religions Orthodox Christian 83%, Muslim 12%, Other 4%, Roman Catholic 1%
Ethnic mix Bulgarian 84%, Turkish 9%, Roma 5%, Other 2%
Government Parliamentary system
Currency Lev = 100 stotinki
Literacy rate 98%
Calorie consumption 2848 calories

BURKINA FASO
West Africa

Page 53 E4

Known as Upper Volta until 1984, the West African state of Burkina Faso has been under military rule for most of its post-independence history.

Official name Burkina Faso
Formation 1960 / 1960
Capital Ouagadougou
Population 14 million / 132 people per sq mile (51 people per sq km) / 18%
Total area 105,869 sq. miles (274,200 sq. km)
Languages French*, Mossi, Fulani, Tuareg, Dyula, Songhai
Religions Muslim 55%, Traditional beliefs 35%, Roman Catholic 9%, Other Christian 1%
Ethnic mix Mossi 48%, Other 21%, Peul 10%, Lobi 7%, Bobo 7%, Mandé 7%
Government Presidential system
Currency CFA franc = 100 centimes
Literacy rate 22%
Calorie consumption 2462 calories

BURUNDI
Central Africa

Page 51 B7

Small, landlocked Burundi lies just south of the Equator, on the Nile-Congo watershed in Central Africa. Since 1993 it has been marked by violent ethnic conflict.

Official name Republic of Burundi
Formation 1962 / 1962
Capital Bujumbura
Population 8.1 million / 818 people per sq mile (316 people per sq km) / 10%
Total area 10,745 sq. miles (27,830 sq. km)
Languages Kirundi*, French*, Kiswahili
Religions Christian (mainly Roman Catholic) 60%, Traditional beliefs 39%, Muslim 1%
Ethnic mix Hutu 85%, Tutsi 14%, Twa 1%
Government Presidential system
Currency Burundian franc = 100 centimes
Literacy rate 59%
Calorie consumption 1649 calories

CAMBODIA
Southeast Asia

Page 115 D5

Located in mainland Southeast Asia, Cambodia has emerged from two decades of civil war and invasion from Vietnam.

Official name Kingdom of Cambodia
Formation 1953 / 1953
Capital Phnom Penh
Population 14.6 million / 214 people per sq mile (83 people per sq km) / 19%
Total area 69,900 sq. miles (181,040 sq. km)
Languages Khmer*, French, Chinese, Vietnamese, Cham
Religions Buddhist 93%, Muslim 6%, Christian 1%
Ethnic mix Khmer 90%, Other 5%, Vietnamese 4%, Chinese 1%
Government Parliamentary system
Currency Riel = 100 sen
Literacy rate 74%
Calorie consumption 2046 calories

CAMEROON
Central Africa

Page 54 A4

Situated on the central West African coast, Cameroon was effectively a one-party state for 30 years. Multiparty elections were held in 1992.

Official name Republic of Cameroon
Formation 1960 / 1961
Capital Yaoundé
Population 16.3 million / 94 people per sq mile (36 people per sq km) / 52%
Total area 183,567 sq. miles (475,400 sq. km)
Languages English*, French*, Bamileke, Fang, Fulani
Religions Roman Catholic 35%, Traditional beliefs 25%, Muslim 22%, Protestant 18%
Ethnic mix Cameroon highlanders 31%, Other 21%, Equatorial Bantu 19%, Kirdi 11%, Fulani 10%, Northwestern Bantu 8%
Government Presidential system
Currency CFA franc = 100 centimes
Literacy rate 68%
Calorie consumption 2273 calories

CANADA
North America

Page 15 E4

Canada extends from its US border north to the Arctic Ocean. In recent years, French-speaking Quebec has sought independence from the rest of the country.

Official name Canada
Formation 1867 / 1949
Capital Ottawa
Population 32.9 million / 9 people per sq mile (4 people per sq km) / 81%
Total area 3,854,085 sq. miles (9,984,670 sq. km)
Languages English*, French*, Chinese, Italian, German, Ukrainian, Portuguese, Inuktitut, Cree
Religions Roman Catholic 44%, Protestant 29%, Other and nonreligious 27%
Government Parliamentary system
Currency Canadian dollar = 100 cents
Literacy rate 99%
Calorie consumption 3589 calories

CAPE VERDE
Atlantic Ocean

Page 52 A2

Off the west coast of Africa, in the Atlantic Ocean, lies the group of islands that make up Cape Verde, a Portuguese colony until 1975.

Official name Republic of Cape Verde
Formation 1975 / 1975
Capital Praia
Population 423,613 / 272 people per sq mile (105 people per sq km) / 57%
Total area 1557 sq. miles (4033 sq. km)
Languages Portuguese*, Portuguese Creole
Religions Roman Catholic 97%, Other 2%, Protestant (Church of the Nazarene) 1%
Ethnic mix Mestiço 60%, African 30%, Other 10%
Government Mixed presidential–parliamentary system
Currency Cape Verde escudo = 100 centavos
Literacy rate 76%
Calorie consumption 3243 calories

CENTRAL AFRICAN REPUBLIC
Central Africa

Page 54 C4

This landlocked country lies between the basins of the Chad and Congo rivers. Its arid north sustains less than 2% of the population.

Official name Central African Republic
Formation 1960 / 1960
Capital Bangui
Population 4.2 million / 17 people per sq mile (7 people per sq km) / 43%
Total area 240,534 sq. miles (622,984 sq. km)
Languages French*, Sango, Banda, Gbaya
Religions Traditional beliefs 60%, Christian (mainly Roman Catholic) 35%, Muslim 5%
Ethnic mix Baya 34%, Banda 27%, Mandjia 21%, Sara 10%, Other 8%
Government Presidential system
Currency CFA franc = 100 centimes
Literacy rate 49%
Calorie consumption 1980 calories

CHAD
Central Africa

Page 54 C3

Landlocked in north central Africa, Chad has been torn by intermittent periods of civil war since it gained independence from France in 1960.

Official name Republic of Chad
Formation 1960 / 1960
Capital N'Djamena
Population 10.3 million / 21 people per sq mile (8 people per sq km) / 25%
Total area 495,752 sq. miles (1,284,000 sq. km)
Languages Arabic*, French*, Sara, Maba
Religions Muslim 55%, Traditional beliefs 35%, Christian 10%
Ethnic mix Other 30%, Sara 28%, Mayo-Kebbi 12%, Arab 12%, Ouaddai 9%, Kanem-Bornou 9%
Government Presidential system
Currency CFA franc = 100 centimes
Literacy rate 26%
Calorie consumption 2114 calories

CHILE
South America

Page 42 B3

Chile extends in a ribbon down the west coast of South America. It returned to democracy in 1989 after a referendum rejected its military dictator.

Official name Republic of Chile
Formation 1818 / 1883
Capital Santiago
Population 16.6 million / 57 people per sq mile (22 people per sq km) / 87%
Total area 292,258 sq. miles (756,950 sq. km)
Languages Spanish*, Amerindian languages
Religions Roman Catholic 80%, Other and nonreligious 20%
Ethnic mix Mixed race and European 90%, Other Amerindian 9%, Mapuche 1%
Government Presidential system
Currency Chilean peso = 100 centavos
Literacy rate 96%
Calorie consumption 2863 calories

CHINA
East Asia

Page 104 C4

This vast East Asian country was dominated by Mao Zedong for almost 30 years, but since the 1980's it has emerged as one of the world's major political and economic powers.

Official name People's Republic of China
Formation 960 / 1999
Capital Beijing
Population 1.33 billion / 370 people per sq mile (143 people per sq km) / 40%
Total area 3,705,386 sq. miles (9,596,960 sq. km)
Languages Mandarin*, Wu, Cantonese, Hsiang, Min, Hakka, Kan
Religions Nonreligious 59%, Traditional beliefs 20%, Other 13%, Buddhist 6%, Muslim 2%
Ethnic mix Han 92%, Other 4%, Hui 1%, Miao 1%, Manchu 1%, Zhuang 1%
Government One-party state
Currency Renminbi (known as yuan) = 10 jiao = 100 fen
Literacy rate 91%
Calorie consumption 2951 calories

COLOMBIA
South America

Page 36 B3

Lying in northwest South America, Colombia is one of the world's most violent countries, with powerful drugs cartels and guerrilla activity.

Official name Republic of Colombia
Formation 1819 / 1903
Capital Bogotá
Population 47 million / 117 people per sq mile (45 people per sq km) / 77%
Total area 439,733 sq. miles (1,138,910 sq. km)
Languages Spanish*, Wayuu, Páez, and other Amerindian languages
Religions Roman Catholic 95%, Other 5%
Ethnic mix Mestizo 58%, White 20%, European–African 14%, African 4%, African–Amerindian 3%, Amerindian 1%
Government Presidential system
Currency Colombian peso = 100 centavos
Literacy rate 93%
Calorie consumption 2585 calories

COMOROS
Indian Ocean

Page 57 F2

In the Indian Ocean, between Mozambique and Madagascar, lie the Comoros, comprising three main islands, and a number of smaller islets.

Official name Union of the Comoros
Formation 1975 / 1975
Capital Moroni
Population 711,417 / 826 people per sq mile (319 people per sq km) / 36%
Total area 838 sq. miles (2170 sq. km)
Languages Arabic*, Comoran*, French*
Religions Muslim (mainly Sunni) 98%, Other 1%, Roman Catholic 1%
Ethnic mix Comoran 97%, Other 3%
Government Presidential system
Currency Comoros franc = 100 centimes
Literacy rate 56%
Calorie consumption 1754 calories

CONGO
Central Africa

Page 55 B5

Astride the Equator in west central Africa, this former French colony emerged from 26 years of Marxist-Leninist rule in 1990.

Official name Republic of the Congo
Formation 1960 / 1960
Capital Brazzaville
Population 4.2 million / 32 people per sq mile (12 people per sq km) / 54%
Total area 132,046 sq. miles (342,000 sq. km)
Languages French*, Kongo, Teke, Lingala
Religions Traditional beliefs 50%, Roman Catholic 25%, Protestant 23%, Muslim 2%
Ethnic mix Bakongo 51%, Teke 17%, Other 16%, Mbochi 11%, Mbédé 5%
Government Presidential system
Currency CFA franc = 100 centimes
Literacy rate 83%
Calorie consumption 2162 calories

CONGO, DEM. REP.
Central Africa

Page 55 C6

Straddling the Equator in east central Africa, Dem. Rep. Congo is one of Africa's largest countries. It achieved independence from Belgium in 1960.

Official name Democratic Republic of the Congo
Formation 1960 / 1960
Capital Kinshasa
Population 61.2 million / 70 people per sq mile (27 people per sq km) / 33%
Total area 905,563 sq. miles (2,345,410 sq. km)
Languages French*, Kiswahili, Tshiluba, Kikongo, Lingala
Religions Roman Catholic 50%, Protestant 20%, Traditional beliefs and other 20%, Muslim 10%
Ethnic mix Other 55%, Mongo, Luba, Kongo, and Mangbetu-Azande 45%
Government Presidential system
Currency Congolese franc = 100 centimes
Literacy rate 67%
Calorie consumption 1599 calories

COSTA RICA
Central America

Page 31 E4

Costa Rica is the most stable country in Central America. Its neutrality in foreign affairs is long-standing, but it has very strong ties with the US.

Official name Republic of Costa Rica
Formation 1838 / 1838
Capital San José
Population 4.5 million / 228 people per sq mile (88 people per sq km) / 61%
Total area 19,730 sq. miles (51,100 sq. km)
Languages Spanish*, English Creole, Bribri, Cabecar
Religions Roman Catholic 76%, Other (including Protestant) 24%
Ethnic mix Mestizo and European 96%, Black 2%, Chinese 1%, Amerindian 1%
Government Presidential system
Currency Costa Rican colón = 100 céntimos
Literacy rate 95%
Calorie consumption 2876 calories

CÔTE D'IVOIRE
West Africa

Page 52 D4

One of the larger nations along the coast of West Africa, Côte d'Ivoire remains under the influence of its former colonial ruler, France.

Official name Republic of Côte d'Ivoire
Formation 1960 / 1960
Capital Yamoussoukro
Population 18.8 million / 153 people per sq mile (59 people per sq km) / 45%
Total area 124,502 sq. miles (322,460 sq. km)
Languages Akan, French*, Krou, Voltaïque
Religions Muslim 38%, Traditional beliefs 25%, Roman Catholic 25%, Other 6%, Protestant 6%
Ethnic mix Akan 42%, Voltaïque 18%, Mandé du Nord 17%, Krou 11%, Mandé du Sud 10%, Other 2%
Government Presidential system
Currency CFA franc = 100 centimes
Literacy rate 49%
Calorie consumption 2631 calories

CROATIA
Southeast Europe

Page 78 B2

Post-independence fighting in this former Yugoslav republic initially thwarted plans to capitalize on its location along the eastern Adriatic coast. A return to stability has resolved this situation.

Official name Republic of Croatia
Formation 1991 / 1991
Capital Zagreb
Population 4.6 million / 211 people per sq mile (81 people per sq km) / 59%
Total area 21,831 sq. miles (56,542 sq. km)
Languages Croatian*
Religions Roman Catholic 88%, Other 7%, Orthodox Christian 4%, Muslim 1%
Ethnic mix Croat 90%, Other 5%, Serb 5%
Government Parliamentary system
Currency Kuna = 100 lipa
Literacy rate 98%
Calorie consumption 2799 calories

CUBA
West Indies

Page 32 C2

Cuba is the largest island in the Caribbean and the only communist country in the Americas. It was led by Fidel Castro for almost 40 years until he stepped down in 2008.

Official name Republic of Cuba
Formation 1902 / 1902
Capital Havana
Population 11.3 million / 264 people per sq mile (102 people per sq km) / 76%
Total area 42,803 sq. miles (110,860 sq. km)
Languages Spanish
Religions Nonreligious 49%, Roman Catholic 40%, Atheist 6%, Other 4%, Protestant 1%
Ethnic mix White 66%, European–African 22%, Black 12%
Government One-party state
Currency Cuban peso = 100 centavos
Literacy rate 99%
Calorie consumption 3152 calories

CYPRUS
Southeast Europe

Page 80 C5

Cyprus lies in the eastern Mediterranean. Since 1974, it has been partitioned between the Turkish-occupied north and the Greek south (which joined the EU in 2004).

Official name Republic of Cyprus
Formation 1960 / 1960
Capital Nicosia
Population 788,457 / 221 people per sq mile (85 people per sq km) / 69%
Total area 3571 sq. miles (9250 sq. km)
Languages Greek*, Turkish*
Religions Orthodox Christian 78%, Muslim 18%, Other 4%
Ethnic mix Greek 81%, Turkish 11%, Other 8%
Government Presidential system
Currency Euro (Turkish lira in TRNC) = 100 cents (euro); 100 kurus (Turkish lira)
Literacy rate 97%
Calorie consumption 3255 calories

CZECH REPUBLIC
Central Europe

Page 77 A5

Once part of Czechoslovakia in eastern Europe, it became independent in 1993, after peacefully dissolving its federal union with Slovakia.

Official name Czech Republic
Formation 1993 / 1993
Capital Prague
Population 10.2 million / 335 people per sq mile (129 people per sq km) / 74%
Total area 30,450 sq. miles (78,866 sq. km)
Languages Czech*, Slovak, Hungarian (Magyar)
Religions Roman Catholic 39%, Atheist 38%, Other 18%, Protestant 3%, Hussite 2%
Ethnic mix Czech 90%, Other 4%, Moravian 4%, Slovak 2%
Government Parliamentary system
Currency Czech koruna = 100 haleru
Literacy rate 99%
Calorie consumption 3171 calories

DENMARK
Northern Europe

Page 63 A7

The country occupies the Jutland peninsula and over 400 islands in Scandinavia. Greenland and the Faeroe Islands are self-governing associated territories.

Official name Kingdom of Denmark
Formation 950 / 1944
Capital Copenhagen
Population 5.5 million / 336 people per sq mile (130 people per sq km) / 85%
Total area 16,639 sq. miles (43,094 sq. km)
Languages Danish
Religions Evangelical Lutheran 89%, Other 10%, Roman Catholic 1%
Ethnic mix Danish 96%, Other (including Scandinavian and Turkish) 3%, Faeroese and Inuit 1%
Government Parliamentary system
Currency Danish krone = 100 øre
Literacy rate 99%
Calorie consumption 3439 calories

DJIBOUTI
East Africa

Page 50 D4

A city state with a desert hinterland, Djibouti lies in northeast Africa. Once known as French Somaliland, its economy relies on its port.

Official name Republic of Djibouti
Formation 1977 / 1977
Capital Djibouti
Population 496,374 / 55 people per sq mile (21 people per sq km) / 84%
Total area 8494 sq. miles (22,000 sq. km)
Languages Arabic*, French*, Somali, Afar
Religions Muslim (mainly Sunni) 94%, Christian 6%
Ethnic mix Issa 60%, Afar 35%, Other 5%
Government Presidential system
Currency Djibouti franc = 100 centimes
Literacy rate 66%
Calorie consumption 2220 calories

DOMINICA
West Indies

Page 33 H4

The Caribbean island Dominica resisted European colonization until the 18th century, when it first came under the French, and then, the British

Official name Commonwealth of Dominica
Formation 1978 / 1978
Capital Roseau
Population 72,386 / 250 people per sq mile (97 people per sq km) / 72%
Total area 291 sq. miles (754 sq. km)
Languages English*, French Creole
Religions Roman Catholic 77%, Protestant 15%, Other 8%
Ethnic mix Black 87%, Mixed race 9%, Carib 3%, Other 1%
Government Parliamentary system
Currency Eastern Caribbean dollar = 100 cents
Literacy rate 88%
Calorie consumption 2763 calories

DOMINICAN REPUBLIC
West Indies

Page 33 E2

The republic occupies the eastern two-thirds of the island of Hispaniola in the Caribbean. Frequent coups and a strong US influence mark its recent past.

Official name Dominican Republic
Formation 1865 / 1865
Capital Santo Domingo
Population 9.1 million / 487 people per sq mile (188 people per sq km) / 60%
Total area 18,679 sq. miles (48,380 sq. km)
Languages Spanish*, French Creole
Religions Roman Catholic 92%, Other and nonreligious 8%
Ethnic mix Mixed race 75%, White 15%, Black 10%
Government Presidential system
Currency Dominican Republic peso = 100 centavos
Literacy rate 87%
Calorie consumption 2347 calories

EAST TIMOR
Southeast Asia

Page 116 F5

This new nation occupies the eastern half of the island of Timor. Invaded by Indonesia in 1975, it declared independence in 1999.

Official name Democratic Republic of Timor-Leste
Formation 2002 / 2002
Capital Dili
Population 1.1 million / 192 people per sq mile (74 people per sq km) / 8%
Total area 5756 sq. miles (14,874 sq. km)
Languages Tetum (Portuguese/Austronesian)*, Bahasa Indonesia, and Portuguese*
Religions Roman Catholic 95%, Other (including Muslim and Protestant) 5%
Government Parliamentary system
Currency US dollar = 100 cents
Literacy rate 59%
Calorie consumption 2806 calories

ECUADOR
South America

Page 38 A2

Ecuador sits high on South America's western coast. Once part of the Inca heartland, its territory includes the Galapagos Islands, to the west.

Official name Republic of Ecuador
Formation 1830 / 1942
Capital Quito
Population 13.6 million / 127 people per sq mile (49 people per sq km) / 62%
Total area 109,483 sq. miles (283,560 sq. km)
Languages Spanish*, Quechua, other Amerindian languages
Religions Roman Catholic 93%, Protestant, Jewish, and other 7%
Ethnic mix Mestizo 55%, Amerindian 25%, White 10%, Black 10%
Government Presidential system
Currency US dollar = 100 cents
Literacy rate 91%
Calorie consumption 2754 calories

EGYPT
North Africa

Page 50 B2

Egypt occupies the northeast corner of Africa. Its essentially pro-Western, military-backed regime is being challenged by Islamic fundamentalists.

Official name Arab Republic of Egypt
Formation 1936 / 1982
Capital Cairo
Population 76.9 million / 200 people per sq mile (77 people per sq km) / 42%
Total area 386,660 sq. miles (1,001,450 sq. km)
Languages Arabic*, French, English, Berber
Religions Muslim (mainly Sunni) 94%, Coptic Christian and other 6%
Ethnic mix Egyptian 99%, Nubian, Armenian, Greek, and Berber 1%
Government Presidential system
Currency Egyptian pound = 100 piastres
Literacy rate 71%
Calorie consumption 3338 calories

EL SALVADOR
Central America

Page 30 B3

El Salvador is Central America's smallest state. A 12-year war between US-backed government troops and left-wing guerrillas ended in 1992.

Official name Republic of El Salvador
Formation 1841 / 1841
Capital San Salvador
Population 7.1 million / 888 people per sq mile (343 people per sq km) / 60%
Total area 8124 sq. miles (21,040 sq. km)
Languages Spanish
Religions Roman Catholic 80%, Evangelical 18%, Other 2%
Ethnic mix Mestizo 94%, Amerindian 5%, White 1%
Government Presidential system
Currency Salvadorean colón & US dollar = 100 centavos (colón); 100 cents (US dollar)
Literacy rate 80%
Calorie consumption 2584 calories

EQUATORIAL GUINEA
Central Africa

Page 55 A5

The country comprises the Rio Muni mainland and five islands on the west coast of central Africa. Free elections were first held in 1988.

Official name Republic of Equatorial Guinea
Formation 1968 / 1968
Capital Malabo
Population 551,201 / 51 people per sq mile (20 people per sq km) / 49%
Total area 10,830 sq. miles (28,051 sq. km)
Languages French*, Spanish*, Fang, Bubi
Religions Roman Catholic 90%, Other 10%
Ethnic mix Fang 85%, Other 11%, Bubi 4%
Government Presidential system
Currency CFA franc = 100 centimes
Literacy rate 87%
Calorie consumption Not available

ERITREA
East Africa

Page 50 C3

Lying on the shores of the Red Sea, Eritrea effectively seceded from Ethiopia in 1993, following a 30-year war for independence.

Official name State of Eritrea
Formation 1993 / 2002
Capital Asmera
Population 4.7 million / 104 people per sq mile (40 people per sq km) / 20%
Total area 46,842 sq. miles (121,320 sq. km)
Languages Tigrinya*, English*, Tigre, Afar, Arabic*, Bilen, Kunama, Nara, Saho, Hadareb
Religions Christian 45%, Muslim 45%, Other 10%
Ethnic mix Tigray 50%, Tigray and Kunama 40%, Afar 4%, Other 3%, Saho 3%
Government Transitional regime
Currency Nakfa = 100 cents
Literacy rate 57%
Calorie consumption 1513 calories

ESTONIA
Northeast Europe

Page 84 D2

Estonia is the smallest and most developed of the three Baltic states. It has the highest standard of living of any of the former Soviet republics.

Official name Republic of Estonia
Formation 1991 / 1991
Capital Tallinn
Population 1.3 million / 75 people per sq mile (29 people per sq km) / 70%
Total area 17,462 sq. miles (45,226 sq. km)
Languages Estonian*, Russian
Religions Evangelical Lutheran 56%, Orthodox Christian 25%, Other 19%
Ethnic mix Estonian 68%, Russian 26%, Other 4%, Ukrainian 2%
Government Parliamentary system
Currency Kroon = 100 senti
Literacy rate 99%
Calorie consumption 3002 calories

ETHIOPIA
East Africa

Page 51 C5

Located in northeast Africa, Ethiopia was a Marxist regime from 1974–91. It has suffered a series of economic, civil, and natural crises.

Official name Federal Democratic Republic of Ethiopia
Formation 1896 / 2002
Capital Addis Ababa
Population 81.2 million / 189 people per sq mile (73 people per sq km) / 16%
Total area 435,184 sq. miles (1,127,127 sq. km)
Languages Amharic*, Tigrinya, Galla, Sidamo, Somali, English, Arabic
Religions Orthodox Christian 40%, Muslim 40%, Traditional beliefs 15%, Other 5%
Ethnic mix Oromo 32%, Amhara 30%, Other 38%,
Government Parliamentary system
Currency Ethiopian birr = 100 cents
Literacy rate 42%
Calorie consumption 1857 calories

FIJI
Australasia & Oceania

Page 123 E5

A volcanic archipelago, Fiji comprises 882 islands in the southern Pacific Ocean. Ethnic Fijians and Indo-Fijians have been in conflict since 1987.

Official name Republic of the Fiji Islands
Formation 1970 / 1970
Capital Suva
Population 918,675 / 130 people per sq mile (50 people per sq km) / 52%
Total area 7054 sq. miles (18,270 sq. km)
Languages Fijian, English*, Hindi, Urdu, Tamil, Telugu
Religions Hindu 38%, Methodist 37%, Roman Catholic 9%, Other 8%, Muslim 8%
Ethnic mix Melanesian 51%, Indian 44%, Other 5%
Government Transitional regime
Currency Fiji dollar = 100 cents
Literacy rate 93%
Calorie consumption 2894 calories

FINLAND
Northern Europe

Page 62 D4

Finland's distinctive language and national identity have been influenced by both its Scandinavian and its Russian neighbors.

Official name Republic of Finland
Formation 1917 / 1947
Capital Helsinki
Population 5.3 million / 45 people per sq mile (17 people per sq km) / 61%
Total area 130,127 sq. miles (337,030 sq. km)
Languages Finnish*, Swedish*, Sámi
Religions Evangelical Lutheran 89%, Other 9%, Orthodox Christian 1%, Roman Catholic 1%
Ethnic mix Finnish 93%, Other (including Sámi) 7%
Government Parliamentary system
Currency Euro = 100 cents
Literacy rate 99%
Calorie consumption 3100 calories

FRANCE
Western Europe

Page 68 B4

Straddling Western Europe from the English Channel to the Mediterranean Sea, France, is one of the world's leading industrial powers.

Official name French Republic
Formation 987 / 1919
Capital Paris
Population 60.9 million / 287 people per sq mile (111 people per sq km) / 76%
Total area 211,208 sq. miles (547,030 sq. km)
Languages French*, Provençal, German, Breton, Catalan, Basque
Religions Roman Catholic 88%, Muslim 8%, Protestant 2%, Buddhist 1%, Jewish 1%
Ethnic mix French 90%, North African (mainly Algerian) 6%, German (Alsace) 2%, Other 2%
Government Mixed presidential–parliamentary system
Currency Euro = 100 cents
Literacy rate 99%
Calorie consumption 3654 calories

GABON
Central Africa

Page 55 A5

A former French colony straddling the Equator on Africa's west coast, it returned to multiparty politics in 1990, after 22 years of one-party rule.

Official name Gabonese Republic
Formation 1960 / 1960
Capital Libreville
Population 1.4 million / 14 people per sq mile (5 people per sq km) / 84%
Total area 103,346 sq. miles (267,667 sq. km)
Languages Fang, French*, Punu, Sira, Nzebi, Mpongwe
Religions Christian (mainly Roman Catholic) 55%, Traditional beliefs 40%, Other 4%, Muslim 1%
Ethnic mix Fang 26%, Shira-punu 24%, Other 16%, Foreign residents 15%, Nzabi-duma 11%, Mbédé-Teke 8%
Government Presidential system
Currency CFA franc = 100 centimes
Literacy rate 71%
Calorie consumption 2637 calories

GAMBIA
West Africa

Page 52 B3

A narrow state on the west coast of Africa, Gambia was renowned for its stability until its government was overthrown in a coup in 1994.

Official name Republic of the Gambia
Formation 1965 / 1965
Capital Banjul
Population 1.6 million / 414 people per sq mile (160 people per sq km) / 26%
Total area 4363 sq. miles (11,300 sq. km)
Languages English*, Mandinka, Fulani, Wolof, Jola, Soninke
Religions Sunni Muslim 90%, Christian 9%, Traditional beliefs 1%
Ethnic mix Mandinka 40%, Fulani 19%, Wolof 15%, Jola 11%, Serahuli 9%, Other 6%
Government Presidential system
Currency Dalasi = 100 butut
Literacy rate 38%
Calorie consumption 2273 calories

GEORGIA
Southwest Asia

Page 95 F2

Located on the eastern shore of the Black Sea, Georgia's northern provinces have been torn by civil war since independence from the USSR in 1991.

Official name Georgia
Formation 1991 / 1991
Capital Tbilisi
Population 4.4 million / 164 people per sq mile (63 people per sq km) / 52%
Total area 26,911 sq. miles (69,700 sq. km)
Languages Georgian*, Russian, Azeri, Armenian, Mingrelian, Ossetian, Abkhazian* *(in Abkhazia)*
Religions Georgian Orthodox 65%, Muslim 11%, Russian Orthodox 10%, Other 14%
Ethnic mix Georgian 84%, Armenian 6%, Azeri 6%, Russian 2%, Other 1%, Ossetian 1%
Government Presidential system
Currency Lari = 100 tetri
Literacy rate 99%
Calorie consumption 2354 calories

GERMANY
Northern Europe

Page 72 B4

Europe's strongest economic power, Germany's democratic west and Communist east were re-unified in 1990, after the fall of the east's regime.

Official name Federal Republic of Germany
Formation 1871 / 1990
Capital Berlin
Population 82.7 million / 613 people per sq mile (237 people per sq km) / 88%
Total area 137,846 sq. miles (357,021 sq. km)
Languages German*, Turkish
Religions Protestant 34%, Roman Catholic 33%, Other 30%, Muslim 3%
Ethnic mix German 92%, Other European 3%, Other 3%, Turkish 2%
Government Parliamentary system
Currency Euro = 100 cents
Literacy rate 99%
Calorie consumption 3496 calories

GHANA
West Africa

Page 53 E5

Once known as the Gold Coast, Ghana in West Africa has experienced intermittent periods of military rule since independence in 1957.

Official name Republic of Ghana
Formation 1957 / 1957
Capital Accra
Population 23 million / 259 people per sq mile (100 people per sq km) / 46%
Total area 92,100 sq. miles (238,540 sq. km)
Languages English*, Twi, Fanti, Ewe, Ga, Adangbe, Gurma, Dagomba (Dagbani)
Religions Christian 69%, Muslim 16%, Traditional beliefs 9%, Other 6%
Ethnic mix Akan 49%, Mole-Dagbani 17%, Ewe 13%, Other 9%, Ga and Ga-Adangbe 8%, Guan 4%
Government Presidential system
Currency Cedi = 100 pesewas
Literacy rate 58%
Calorie consumption 2667 calories

GREECE
Southeast Europe

Page 83 A5

Greece is the southernmost Balkan nation. Surrounded by the Mediterranean, Aegean, and Ionian Seas, it has a strong seafaring tradition.

Official name Hellenic Republic
Formation 1829 / 1947
Capital Athens
Population 11.2 million / 222 people per sq mile (86 people per sq km) / 61%
Total area 50,942 sq. miles (131,940 sq. km)
Languages Greek*, Turkish, Macedonian, Albanian
Religions Orthodox Christian 98%, Other 1%, Muslim 1%
Ethnic mix Greek 98%, Other 2%
Government Parliamentary system
Currency Euro = 100 cents
Literacy rate 96%
Calorie consumption 3721 calories

GRENADA
West Indies

Page 33 G5

The Windward island of Grenada became a focus of attention in 1983, when the US mounted an invasion to sever its growing links with Cuba.

Official name Grenada
Formation 1974 / 1974
Capital St. George's
Population 89,971 / 687 people per sq mile (265 people per sq km) / 41%
Total area 131 sq. miles (340 sq. km)
Languages English*, English Creole
Religions Roman Catholic 68%, Anglican 17%, Other 15%
Ethnic mix Black African 82%, Mulatto (mixed race) 13%, East Indian 3%, Other 2%
Government Parliamentary system
Currency Eastern Caribbean dollar = 100 cents
Literacy rate 96%
Calorie consumption 2932 calories

GUATEMALA
Central America

Page 30 A2

The largest state on the Central American isthmus, Guatemala returned to civilian rule in 1986, after 32 years of repressive military rule.

Official name Republic of Guatemala
Formation 1838 / 1838
Capital Guatemala City
Population 13.2 million / 315 people per sq mile (122 people per sq km) / 47%
Total area 42,042 sq. miles (108,890 sq. km)
Languages Spanish*, Quiché, Mam, Cakchiquel, Kekchí
Religions Roman Catholic 65%, Protestant 33%, Other and nonreligious 2%
Ethnic mix Amerindian 60%, Mestizo 30%, Other 10%
Government Presidential system
Currency Quetzal = 100 centavos
Literacy rate 69%
Calorie consumption 2219 calories

GUINEA
West Africa

Page 52 C4

Facing the Atlantic Ocean, on the west coast of Africa, Guinea became the first French colony in Africa to gain independence, in 1958.

Official name Republic of Guinea
Formation 1958 / 1958
Capital Conakry
Population 9.8 million / 103 people per sq mile (40 people per sq km) / 36%
Total area 94,925 sq. miles (245,857 sq. km)
Languages French*, Pulaar, Malinke, Soussou
Religions Muslim 65%, Traditional beliefs 33%, Christian 2%
Ethnic mix Peul 39%, Malinké 23%, Other 16%, Soussou 11%, Kissi 6%, Kpellé 5%
Government Presidential system
Currency Guinea franc = 100 centimes
Literacy rate 30%
Calorie consumption 2409 calories

GUINEA-BISSAU
West Africa

Page 52 B4

Known as Portuguese Guinea during its days as a colony, Guinea-Bissau is situated on Africa's west coast, bordered by Senegal and Guinea.

Official name Republic of Guinea-Bissau
Formation 1974 / 1974
Capital Bissau
Population 1.7 million / 157 people per sq mile (60 people per sq km) / 35%
Total area 13,946 sq. miles (36,120 sq. km)
Languages Portuguese*, Portuguese Creole, Balante, Fulani, Malinke
Religions Traditional beliefs 52%, Muslim 40%, Christian 8%
Ethnic mix Balante 30%, Fulani 20%, Other 17%, Mandyako 14%, Mandinka 12%, Papel 7%
Government Presidential system
Currency CFA franc = 100 centimes
Literacy rate 40%
Calorie consumption 2024 calories

GUYANA
South America

Page 37 F3

The only English-speaking country in South America, Guyana gained independence from Britain in 1966, and became a republic in 1970.

Official name The Co-operative Republic of Guyana
Formation 1966 / 1966
Capital Georgetown
Population 769,095 / 10 people per sq mile (4 people per sq km) / 38%
Total area 83,000 sq. miles (214,970 sq. km)
Languages English*, English Creole, Hindi, Tamil, Amerindian languages
Religions Christian 57%, Hindu 33%, Muslim 9%, Other 1%
Ethnic mix East Indian 43%, Black African 30%, Mixed race 17%, Amerindian 9%, Other 1%
Government Presidential system
Currency Guyanese dollar = 100 cents
Literacy rate 97%
Calorie consumption 2692 calories

HAITI
West Indies

Page 32 D3

Haiti shares the Caribbean island of Hispaniola with the Dominican Republic. At independence, in 1804, it became the world's first Black republic.

Official name Republic of Haiti
Formation 1804 / 1844
Capital Port-au-Prince
Population 8.8 million / 827 people per sq mile (319 people per sq km) / 38%
Total area 10,714 sq. miles (27,750 sq. km)
Languages French*, French Creole*
Religions Roman Catholic 80%, Protestant 16%, Other (including Voodoo) 3%, Nonreligious 1%
Ethnic mix Black African 95%, Mulatto (mixed race) and European 5%
Government Presidential system
Currency Gourde = 100 centimes
Literacy rate 52%
Calorie consumption 2086 calories

HONDURAS
Central America

Page 30 C2

Honduras straddles the Central American isthmus. The country returned to full democratic civilian rule in 1984, after a succession of military regimes.

Official name Republic of Honduras
Formation 1838 / 1838
Capital Tegucigalpa
Population 7.5 million / 174 people per sq mile (67 people per sq km) / 46%
Total area 43,278 sq. miles (112,090 sq. km)
Languages Spanish*, Garifuna (Carib), English Creole
Religions Roman Catholic 97%, Protestant 3%
Ethnic mix Mestizo 90%, Black African 5%, Amerindian 4%, White 1%
Government Presidential system
Currency Lempira = 100 centavos
Literacy rate 80%
Calorie consumption 2356 calories

HUNGARY
Central Europe

Page 77 C6

Hungary is bordered by seven states in Central Europe. It has changed its economic and political policies to develop closer ties with the EU.

Official name Republic of Hungary
Formation 1918 / 1947
Capital Budapest
Population 10 million / 280 people per sq mile (108 people per sq km) / 66%
Total area 35,919 sq. miles (93,030 sq. km)
Languages Hungarian (Magyar)*
Religions Roman Catholic 52%, Calvinist 16%, Other 15%, Nonreligious 14%, Lutheran 3%
Ethnic mix Magyar 94%, Other 5%, Roma 1%
Government Parliamentary system
Currency Forint = 100 fillér
Literacy rate 99%
Calorie consumption 3483 calories

ICELAND
Northwest Europe

Page 61 E4

Europe's westernmost country, Iceland lies in the North Atlantic, straddling the mid-Atlantic ridge. Its spectacular, volcanic landscape is largely uninhabited.

Official name Republic of Iceland
Formation 1944 / 1944
Capital Reykjavík
Population 301,931 / 8 people per sq mile (3 people per sq km) / 93%
Total area 39,768 sq. miles (103,000 sq. km)
Languages Icelandic*
Religions Evangelical Lutheran 93%, Nonreligious 6%, Other (mostly Christian) 1%
Ethnic mix Icelandic 94%, Other 5%, Danish 1%
Government Parliamentary system
Currency Icelandic króna = 100 aurar
Literacy rate 99%
Calorie consumption 3249 calories

INDIA
South Asia

Page 112 D4

Separated from the rest of Asia by the Himalayan mountain ranges, India forms a subcontinent. It is the world's second most populous country.

Official name Republic of India
Formation 1947 / 1947
Capital New Delhi
Population 1.14 billion / 989 people per sq mile (382 people per sq km) / 29%
Total area 1,269,338 sq. miles (3,287,590 sq. km)
Languages Hindi*, English*, Urdu, Bengali, Marathi, Telugu, Tamil, Bihari, Gujarati, Kanarese
Religions Hindu 81%, Muslim 13%, Christian 2%, Sikh 2%, Other 1%, Buddhist 1%
Ethnic mix Indo-Aryan 72%, Dravidian 25%, Mongoloid and other 3%
Government Parliamentary system
Currency Indian rupee = 100 paise
Literacy rate 61%
Calorie consumption 2459 calories

INDONESIA
Southeast Asia

Page 116 C4

Formerly the Dutch East Indies, Indonesia, the world's largest archipelago, stretches over 5,000 km (3,100 miles), from the Indian Ocean to the Pacific Ocean.

Official name Republic of Indonesia
Formation 1949 / 1999
Capital Jakarta
Population 228 million / 329 people per sq mile (127 people per sq km) / 47%
Total area 741,096 sq. miles (1,919,440 sq. km)
Languages Bahasa Indonesia*, Javanese, Sundanese, Madurese, Dutch
Religions Sunni Muslim 87%, Protestant 6%, Roman Catholic 3%, Hindu 2%, Other 1%, Buddhist 1%
Ethnic mix Javanese 42%, Sundanese 15%, Coastal Malays 12%, Madurese 3%, Other 28%
Government Presidential system
Currency Rupiah = 100 sen
Literacy rate 90%
Calorie consumption 2904 calories

IRAN
Southwest Asia

Page 98 B3

Since the 1979 revolution led by Ayatollah Khomeini, which sent Iran's Shah into exile, this Middle Eastern country has become the world's largest theocracy.

Official name Islamic Republic of Iran
Formation 1502 / 1990
Capital Tehran
Population 71.2 million / 113 people per sq mile (44 people per sq km) / 67%
Total area 636,293 sq. miles (1,648,000 sq. km)
Languages Farsi*, Azeri, Luri, Gilaki, Kurdish, Mazanderani, Turkmen, Arabic, Baluchi
Religions Shi'a Muslim 93%, Sunni Muslim 6%, Other 1%
Ethnic mix Persian 50%, Azari 24%, Other 10%, Kurdish 8%, Lur and Bakhtiari 8%
Government Islamic theocracy
Currency Iranian rial = 100 dinars
Literacy rate 77%
Calorie consumption 3085 calories

IRAQ
Southwest Asia

Page 98 B3

Oil-rich Iraq is situated in the central Middle East. A US-led invasion in 2003 toppled the regime of Saddam Hussein, prompting an insurgency that led to huge political and social turmoil.

Official name Republic of Iraq
Formation 1932 / 1990
Capital Baghdad
Population 30.3 million / 179 people per sq mile (69 people per sq km) / 67%
Total area 168,753 sq. miles (437,072 sq. km)
Languages Arabic*, Kurdish*, Turkic languages, Armenian, Assyrian
Religions Shi'a Muslim 60%, Sunni Muslim 35%, Other (including Christian) 5%
Ethnic mix Arab 80%, Kurdish 15%, Turkmen 3%, Other 2%
Government Parliamentary system
Currency New Iraqi dinar = 1000 fils
Literacy rate 74%
Calorie consumption 2197 calories

IRELAND
Northwest Europe

Page 67 A6

The Republic of Ireland occupies about 85% of the island of Ireland, with the remainder (Northern Ireland) being part of the United Kingdom.

Official name Ireland
Formation 1922 / 1922
Capital Dublin
Population 4.3 million / 162 people per sq mile (62 people per sq km) / 60%
Total area 27,135 sq. miles (70,280 sq. km)
Languages English*, Irish Gaelic*
Religions Roman Catholic 88%, Other and nonreligious 9%, Anglican 3%
Ethnic mix Irish 99%, Other 1%
Government Parliamentary system
Currency Euro = 100 cents
Literacy rate 99%
Calorie consumption 3656 calories

ISRAEL
Southwest Asia

Page 97 A7

Israel was created as a new state in 1948 on the east coast of the Mediterranean. Following wars with its Arab neighbors, it has extended its boundaries.

Official name State of Israel
Formation 1948 / 1994
Capital Jerusalem (not internationally recognized)
Population 7 million / 892 people per sq mile (344 people per sq km) / 92%
Total area 8019 sq. miles (20,770 sq. km)
Languages Hebrew*, Arabic*, Yiddish, German, Russian, Polish, Romanian, Persian
Religions Jewish 76%, Muslim (mainly Sunni) 16%, Other 4%, Druze 2%, Christian 2%
Ethnic mix Jewish 76%, Other (mostly Arab) 24%
Government Parliamentary system
Currency Shekel = 100 agorot
Literacy rate 97%
Calorie consumption 3666 calories

ITALY
Southern Europe

Page 74 B3

Projecting into the Mediterranean Sea in Southern Europe, Italy is an ancient land, but also one of the continent's newest unified states.

Official name Italian Republic
Formation 1861 / 1947
Capital Rome
Population 58.2 million / 513 people per sq mile (198 people per sq km) / 67%
Total area 116,305 sq. miles (301,230 sq. km)
Languages Italian*, German, French, Rhaeto-Romanic, Sardinian
Religions Roman Catholic 85%, Other and nonreligious 13%, Muslim 2%
Ethnic mix Italian 94%, Other 4%, Sardinian 2%
Government Parliamentary system
Currency Euro = 100 cents
Literacy rate 98%
Calorie consumption 3671 calories

JAMAICA
West Indies

Page 32 C3

First colonized by the Spanish and then, from 1655, by the English, Jamaica was the first of the Caribbean island nations to achieve independence, in 1962.

Official name Jamaica
Formation 1962 / 1962
Capital Kingston
Population 2.7 million / 646 people per sq mile (249 people per sq km) / 52%
Total area 4243 sq. miles (10,990 sq. km)
Languages English*, English Creole
Religions Other and nonreligious 45%, Other Protestant 20%, Church of God 18%, Baptist 10%, Anglican 7%
Ethnic mix Black African 92%, East Indian 1%, Mulatto (mixed race) 6%, Other 1%
Government Parliamentary system
Currency Jamaican dollar = 100 cents
Literacy rate 80%
Calorie consumption 2685 calories

JAPAN
East Asia

Page 108 C4

Japan comprises four principal islands and over 3,000 smaller ones. With the emperor as constitutional head, it is now one of the world's most powerful economies.

Official name Japan
Formation 1590 / 1972
Capital Tokyo
Population 128 million / 883 people per sq mile (341 people per sq km) / 66%
Total area 145,882 sq. miles (377,835 sq. km)
Languages Japanese*, Korean, Chinese
Religions Shinto and Buddhist 76%, Buddhist 16%, Other (including Christian) 8%
Ethnic mix Japanese 99%, Other (mainly Korean) 1%
Government Parliamentary system
Currency Yen = 100 sen
Literacy rate 99%
Calorie consumption 2761 calories

JORDAN
Southwest Asia

Page 97 B6

The kingdom of Jordan lies east of Israel. In 1993, King Hussein responded to calls for greater democracy by agreeing to multiparty elections.

Official name Hashemite Kingdom of Jordan
Formation 1946 / 1967
Capital Amman
Population 6 million / 175 people per sq mile (67 people per sq km) / 79%
Total area 35,637 sq. miles (92,300 sq. km)
Languages Arabic*
Religions Muslim (mainly Sunni) 92%, Other (mostly Christian) 8%
Ethnic mix Arab 98%, Circassian 1%, Armenian 1%
Government Monarchy
Currency Jordanian dinar = 1000 fils
Literacy rate 90%
Calorie consumption 2673 calories

KAZAKHSTAN
Central Asia

Page 92 B4

Second largest of the former Soviet republics, mineral-rich Kazakhstan has the potential to become the major Central Asian economic power.

Official name Republic of Kazakhstan
Formation 1991 / 1991
Capital Astana
Population 14.8 million / 14 people per sq mile (5 people per sq km) / 56%
Total area 1,049,150 sq. miles (2,717,300 sq. km)
Languages Kazakh*, Russian, Ukrainian, German, Uzbek, Tatar, Uighur
Religions Muslim (mainly Sunni) 47%, Orthodox Christian 44%, Other 9%
Ethnic mix Kazakh 57%, Russian 27%, Other 8%, Uzbek 3%, Ukrainian 3%, German 2%
Government Presidential system
Currency Tenge = 100 tiyn
Literacy rate 99%
Calorie consumption 2677 calories

KENYA
East Africa

Page 51 C6

Kenya became a multiparty democracy in 1992 and was led by President Daniel Moi from 1978 until 2002 when he was barred from re-election and Mwai Kibaki subsequently became president.

Official name Republic of Kenya
Formation 1963 / 1963
Capital Nairobi
Population 36 million / 164 people per sq mile (63 people per sq km) / 40%
Total area 224,961 sq. miles (582,650 sq. km)
Languages Kiswahili*, English*, Kikuyu, Luo, Kalenjin, Kamba
Religions Christian 60%, Traditional beliefs 25%, Other 9%, Muslim 6%
Ethnic mix Other 31%, Kikuyu 20%, Luhya 14%, Luo 13%, Kalenjin 11%, Kamba 11%
Government Mixed Presidential–Parliamentary system
Currency Kenya shilling = 100 cents
Literacy rate 74%
Calorie consumption 2090 calories

KIRIBATI
Australasia & Oceania

Page 123 F3

Part of the British colony of the Gilbert and Ellice Islands until independence in 1979, Kiribati comprises 33 islands in the mid-Pacific Ocean.

Official name Republic of Kiribati
Formation 1979 / 1979
Capital Bairiki (Tarawa Atoll)
Population 107,817 / 393 people per sq mile (152 people per sq km) / 49%
Total area 277 sq. miles (717 sq. km)
Languages English*, Kiribati
Religions Roman Catholic 53%, Kiribati Protestant Church 39%, Other 8%
Ethnic mix Micronesian 99%, Other 1%
Government Nonparty system
Currency Australian dollar = 100 cents
Literacy rate 99%
Calorie consumption 2859 calories

KOSOVO (not yet fully recognized)
Southeast Europe

Page 79 D5

In February 2008, Kosovo controversially declared independence from Serbia. It faces numerous economic and political challenges as it seeks to gain full international recognition.

Official name Republic of Kosovo
Formation 2008 / 2008
Capital Pristina
Population 2.1 million / 499 people per sq mile (193 people per sq km) / 40%
Total area 4212 sq miles (10,908 sq km)
Languages Albanian*, Serbian*, Bosniak, Gorani, Roma, Turkish
Religions Muslim 92%, Roman Catholic 4%, Orthodox Christian 4%
Ethnic mix Albanian 92%, Serb 4%, Bosniak and Gorani 2%, Turkish 1%, Roma 1%
Government Parliamentary system
Currency Euro = 100 cents
Literacy rate 92%
Calorie consumption Not available

KUWAIT
Southwest Asia

Page 98 C4

Kuwait lies on the northwest extreme of the Persian Gulf. The state was a British protectorate from 1914 until 1961, when full independence was granted.

Official name State of Kuwait
Formation 1961 / 1961
Capital Kuwait City
Population 2.8 million / 407 people per sq mile (157 people per sq km) / 96%
Total area 6880 sq. miles (17,820 sq. km)
Languages Arabic*, English
Religions Sunni Muslim 45%, Shi'a Muslim 40%, Christian, Hindu, and other 15%
Ethnic mix Kuwaiti 45%, Other Arab 35%, South Asian 9%, Other 7%, Iranian 4%
Government Monarchy
Currency Kuwaiti dinar = 1000 fils
Literacy rate 93%
Calorie consumption 3010 calories

KYRGYZSTAN
Central Asia

Page 101 F2

A mountainous, landlocked state in Central Asia. The most rural of the ex-Soviet republics, it only gradually developed its own cultural nationalism.

Official name Kyrgyz Republic
Formation 1991 / 1991
Capital Bishkek
Population 5.4 million / 70 people per sq mile (27 people per sq km) / 34%
Total area 76,641 sq. miles (198,500 sq. km)
Languages Kyrgyz*, Russian*, Uzbek, Tatar, Ukrainian
Religions Muslim (mainly Sunni) 70%, Orthodox Christian 30%
Ethnic mix Kyrgyz 65%, Uzbek 14%, Russian 13%, Other 6%, Dungan 1%, Ukrainian 1%
Government Presidential system
Currency Som = 100 tyiyn
Literacy rate 99%
Calorie consumption 2999 calories

LAOS
Southeast Asia

Page 114 D4

A former French colony, independent in 1953, Laos lies landlocked in Southeast Asia. It has been under communist rule since 1975.

Official name Lao People's Democratic Republic
Formation 1953 / 1953
Capital Vientiane
Population 6.2 million / 70 people per sq mile (27 people per sq km) / 21%
Total area 91,428 sq. miles (236,800 sq. km)
Languages Lao*, Mon-Khmer, Yao, Vietnamese, Chinese, French
Religions Buddhist 85%, Other (including animist) 15%
Ethnic mix Lao Loum 66%, Lao Theung 30%, Other 2%, Lao Soung 2%
Government One-party state
Currency New kip = 100 at
Literacy rate 69%
Calorie consumption 2312 calories

LATVIA
Northeast Europe

Page 84 C3

Situated on the east coast of the Baltic Sea, Latvia, like its Baltic neighbors, became independent in 1991. It retains a large Russian population.

Official name Republic of Latvia
Formation 1991 / 1991
Capital Riga
Population 2.3 million / 92 people per sq mile (36 people per sq km) / 66%
Total area 24,938 sq. miles (64,589 sq. km)
Languages Latvian*, Russian
Religions Lutheran 55%, Roman Catholic 24%, Other 12%, Orthodox Christian 9%
Ethnic mix Latvian 59%, Russian 29%, Belorussian 4%, Polish 3%, Ukrainian 3%, Other 2%
Government Parliamentary system
Currency Lats = 100 santimi
Literacy rate 99%
Calorie consumption 2938 calories

LEBANON
Southwest Asia

Page 96 A4

Lebanon is dwarfed by its two powerful neighbors, Syria and Israel. The state started rebuilding in 1989, after 14 years of intense civil war.

Official name The Lebanese Republic
Formation 1941 / 1941
Capital Beirut
Population 3.7 million / 937 people per sq mile (362 people per sq km) / 88%
Total area 4015 sq. miles (10,400 sq. km)
Languages Arabic*, French, Armenian, Assyrian
Religions Muslim 70%, Christian 30%
Ethnic mix Arab 94%, Armenian 4%, Other 2%
Government Parliamentary system
Currency Lebanese pound = 100 piastres
Literacy rate 86%
Calorie consumption 3196 calories

LESOTHO
Southern Africa

Page 56 D4

The landlocked kingdom of Lesotho is entirely surrounded by South Africa, which provides all its land transportation links with the outside world.

Official name Kingdom of Lesotho
Formation 1966 / 1966
Capital Maseru
Population 1.8 million / 154 people per sq mile (59 people per sq km) / 18%
Total area 11,720 sq. miles (30,355 sq. km)
Languages English*, Sesotho*, isiZulu
Religions Christian 90%, Traditional beliefs 10%
Ethnic mix Sotho 97%, European and Asian 3%
Government Parliamentary system
Currency Loti = 100 lisente
Literacy rate 82%
Calorie consumption 2638 calories

LIBERIA
West Africa

Page 52 C5

Liberia faces the Atlantic Ocean in equatorial West Africa. Africa's oldest republic, it was established in 1847. Today, it is torn by civil war.

Official name Republic of Liberia
Formation 1847 / 1847
Capital Monrovia
Population 3.5 million / 94 people per sq mile (36 people per sq km) / 47%
Total area 43,000 sq. miles (111,370 sq. km)
Languages English*, Kpelle, Vai, Bassa, Kru, Grebo, Kissi, Gola, Loma
Religions Christian 68%, Traditional beliefs 18%, Muslim 14%
Ethnic mix Indigenous tribes (16 main groups) 95%, Americo-Liberians 5%
Government Presidential system
Currency Liberian dollar = 100 cents
Literacy rate 58%
Calorie consumption 1900 calories

LIBYA
North Africa

Page 49 F3

Libya has been under the leadership of Colonel Gaddafi since 1969. In recent years it has tried to shake off its political isolation and return to the international community.

Official name The Great Socialist People's Libyan Arab Jamahiriyah
Formation 1951 / 1951
Capital Tripoli
Population 6.1 million / 9 people per sq mile (3 people per sq km) / 87%
Total area 679,358 sq. miles (1,759,540 sq. km)
Languages Arabic*, Tuareg
Religions Muslim (mainly Sunni) 97%, Other 3%
Ethnic mix Arab and Berber 95%, Other 5%
Government One-party state
Currency Libyan dinar = 1000 dirhams
Literacy rate 82%
Calorie consumption 3320 calories

LIECHTENSTEIN
Central Europe

Page 73 B7

Tucked in the Alps between Switzerland and Austria, Liechtenstein became an independent principality of the Holy Roman Empire in 1719.

Official name Principality of Liechtenstein
Formation 1719 / 1719
Capital Vaduz
Population 34,247 / 552 people per sq mile (214 people per sq km) / 22%
Total area 62 sq. miles (160 sq. km)
Languages German*, Alemannish dialect, Italian
Religions Roman Catholic 81%, Other 12%, Protestant 7%
Ethnic mix Liechtensteiner 66%, Other 12%, Swiss 10%, Austrian 6%, German 3%, Italian 3%
Government Parliamentary system
Currency Swiss franc = 100 rappen/centimes
Literacy rate 99%
Calorie consumption Not available

LITHUANIA
Northeast Europe

Page 84 B4

The largest, most powerful and stable of the Baltic states, Lithuania was the first Baltic country to declare independence from Moscow, in 1991.

Official name Republic of Lithuania
Formation 1991 / 1991
Capital Vilnius
Population 3.4 million / 135 people per sq mile (52 people per sq km) / 67%
Total area 25,174 sq. miles (65,200 sq. km)
Languages Lithuanian*, Russian
Religions Roman Catholic 83%, Other 12%, Protestant 5%
Ethnic mix Lithuanian 83%, Polish 7%, Russian 6%, Other 3%, Belorussian 1%
Government Parliamentary system
Currency Litas = 100 centu
Literacy rate 99%
Calorie consumption 3324 calories

LUXEMBOURG
Northwest Europe

Page 65 D8

Making up part of the plateau of the Ardennes in Western Europe, Luxembourg is Europe's last independent duchy and one of its richest states.

Official name Grand Duchy of Luxembourg
Formation 1867 / 1867
Capital Luxembourg-Ville
Population 480,222 / 481 people per sq mile (186 people per sq km) / 92%
Total area 998 sq. miles (2586 sq. km)
Languages French*, German*, Luxembourgish*
Religions Roman Catholic 97%, Protestant, Orthodox Christian, and Jewish 3%
Ethnic mix Luxembourger 62%, Foreign residents 38%
Government Parliamentary system
Currency Euro = 100 cents
Literacy rate 99%
Calorie consumption 3701 calories

MACEDONIA
Southeast Europe

Page 79 D6

Landlocked in the southern Balkans, Macedonia has been affected by sanctions imposed on its northern trading partners and by Greek antagonism.

Official name Republic of Macedonia
Formation 1991 / 1991
Capital Skopje
Population 2 million / 201 people per sq mile (78 people per sq km) / 60%
Total area 9781 sq. miles (25,333 sq. km)
Languages Macedonian*, Albanian*, Turkish, Romani, Serbian
Religions Orthodox Christian 59%, Muslim 26%, Other 10%, Roman Catholic 4%, Protestant 1%
Ethnic mix Macedonian 64%, Albanian 25%, Turkish 4%, Roma 3%, Other 2%, Serb 2%
Government Mixed presidential–parliamentary system
Currency Macedonian denar = 100 deni
Literacy rate 96%
Calorie consumption 2655 calories

MADAGASCAR
Indian Ocean

Page 57 F4

Lying in the Indian Ocean, Madagascar is the world's fourth largest island. Free elections in 1993 ended 18 years of radical socialist government.

Official name Republic of Madagascar
Formation 1960 / 1960
Capital Antananarivo
Population 19.6 million / 87 people per sq mile (34 people per sq km) / 27%
Total area 226,656 sq. miles (587,040 sq. km)
Languages French*, Malagasy*, English*
Religions Traditional beliefs 52%, Christian (mainly Roman Catholic) 41%, Muslim 7%
Ethnic mix Other Malay 46%, Merina 26%, Betsimisaraka 15%, Betsileo 12%, Other 1%
Government Presidential system
Currency Ariary = 5 iraimbilanja
Literacy rate 71%
Calorie consumption 2005 calories

MALAWI
Southern Africa

Page 57 E1

A former British colony, Malawi lies landlocked in southeast Africa. Its name means "the land where the sun is reflected in the water like fire."

Official name Republic of Malawi
Formation 1964 / 1964
Capital Lilongwe
Population 13.5 million / 372 people per sq mile (143 people per sq km) / 17%
Total area 45,745 sq. miles (118,480 sq. km)
Languages English*, Chewa, Lomwe, Yao, Ngoni
Religions Protestant 55%, Roman Catholic 20%, Muslim 20%, Traditional beliefs 5%
Ethnic mix Bantu 99%, Other 1%
Government Presidential system
Currency Malawi kwacha = 100 tambala
Literacy rate 64%
Calorie consumption 2155 calories

MALAYSIA
Southeast Asia

Page 116 B3

Malaysia's three separate territories include Malaya, Sarawak, and Sabah. A financial crisis in 1997 ended a decade of spectacular financial growth.

Official name Malaysia
Formation 1963 / 1965
Capital Kuala Lumpur; Putrajaya (administrative)
Population 26.2 million / 207 people per sq mile (80 people per sq km) / 64%
Total area 127,316 sq. miles (329,750 sq. km)
Languages Bahasa Malaysia*, Malay, Chinese, Tamil, English
Religions Muslim (mainly Sunni) 53%, Other 9%, Buddhist 19%, Chinese faiths 12%, Christian 7%,
Ethnic mix Malay 50%, Chinese 25%, Indigenous tribes 11%, Other 7%, Indian 7%
Government Parliamentary system
Currency Ringgit = 100 sen
Literacy rate 89%
Calorie consumption 2881 calories

MALDIVES
Indian Ocean

Page 110 A4

Only 200 of the more than 1,000 Maldivian small coral islands in the Indian Ocean, are inhabited. Government rests in the hands of a few influential families.

Official name Republic of Maldives
Formation 1965 / 1965
Capital Male'
Population 369,031 / 3181 people per sq mile (1230 people per sq km) / 29%
Total area 116 sq. miles (300 sq. km)
Languages Dhivehi (Maldivian)*, Sinhala, Tamil, Arabic
Religions Sunni Muslim 100%
Ethnic mix Arab–Sinhalese–Malay 100%
Government Presidential system
Currency Rufiyaa = 100 laari
Literacy rate 96%
Calorie consumption 2548 calories

MALI
West Africa

Page 53 E2

Landlocked in the heart of West Africa, Mali held its first free elections in 1992, more than 30 years after it gained independence from France.

Official name Republic of Mali
Formation 1960 / 1960
Capital Bamako
Population 14.3 million / 30 people per sq mile (12 people per sq km) / 33%
Total area 478,764 sq. miles (1,240,000 sq. km)
Languages French*, Bambara, Fulani, Senufo, Soninke
Religions Muslim (mainly Sunni) 80%, Traditional beliefs 18%, Christian 1%, Other 1%
Ethnic mix Bambara 32%, Other 26%, Fulani 14%, Senufu 12%, Soninka 9%, Tuareg 7%
Government Presidential system
Currency CFA franc = 100 centimes
Literacy rate 19%
Calorie consumption 2174 calories

MALTA
Southern Europe

Page 80 A5

The Maltese archipelago lies off southern Sicily, midway between Europe and North Africa. The only inhabited islands are Malta, Gozo, and Kemmuna.

Official name Republic of Malta
Formation 1964 / 1964
Capital Valletta
Population 401,880 / 3241 people per sq mile (1256 people per sq km) / 92%
Total area 122 sq. miles (316 sq. km)
Languages Maltese*, English*
Religions Roman Catholic 98%, Other and nonreligious 2%
Ethnic mix Maltese 96%, Other 4%
Government Parliamentary system
Currency Euro = 100 cents
Literacy rate 88%
Calorie consumption 3587 calories

MARSHALL ISLANDS
Australasia & Oceania

Page 122 D1

A group of 34 atolls, the Marshall Islands were under US rule as part of the UN Trust Territory of the Pacific Islands until 1986. The economy depends on US aid.

Official name Republic of the Marshall Islands
Formation 1986 / 1986
Capital Majuro
Population 61,815 / 883 people per sq mile (342 people per sq km) / 67%
Total area 70 sq. miles (181 sq. km)
Languages Marshallese*, English*, Japanese, German
Religions Protestant 90%, Roman Catholic 8%, Other 2%
Ethnic mix Micronesian 97%, Other 3%
Government Presidential system
Currency US dollar = 100 cents
Literacy rate 91%
Calorie consumption Not available

MAURITANIA
West Africa

Page 52 C2

Situated in northwest Africa, two-thirds of Mauritania's territory is desert. A former French colony, it achieved independence in 1960.

Official name Islamic Republic of Mauritania
Formation 1960 / 1960
Capital Nouakchott
Population 3.2 million / 8 people per sq mile (3 people per sq km) / 63%
Total area 397,953 sq. miles (1,030,700 sq. km)
Languages Hassaniyah Arabic*, Wolof, French
Religions Sunni Muslim 100%
Ethnic mix Maure 81%, Wolof 7%, Tukolor 5%, Other 4%, Soninka 3%
Government Presidential system
Currency Ouguiya = 5 khoums
Literacy rate 51%
Calorie consumption 2772 calories

MAURITIUS
Indian Ocean

Page 57 H3

Located to the east of Madagascar in the Indian Ocean, Mauritius became a republic 25 years after it gained independence. Tourism is a mainstay of its economy.

Official name Republic of Mauritius
Formation 1968 / 1968
Capital Port Louis
Population 1.3 million / 1811 people per sq mile (699 people per sq km) / 44%
Total area 718 sq. miles (1860 sq. km)
Languages English*, French Creole, Hindi, Urdu, Tamil, Chinese, French
Religions Hindu 52%, Roman Catholic 26%, Muslim 17%, Other 3%, Protestant 2%
Ethnic mix Indo-Mauritian 68%, Creole 27%, Sino-Mauritian 3%, Franco-Mauritian 2%
Government Parliamentary system
Currency Mauritian rupee = 100 cents
Literacy rate 84%
Calorie consumption 2955 calories

MEXICO
North America

Page 28 D3

Located between the United States of America and the Central American states, Mexico was a Spanish colony for 300 years until 1836.

Official name United Mexican States
Formation 1836 / 1848
Capital Mexico City
Population 110 million / 149 people per sq mile (57 people per sq km) / 76%
Total area 761,602 sq. miles (1,972,550 sq. km)
Languages Spanish*, Nahuatl, Mayan, Zapotec, Mixtec, Otomi, Totonac, Tzotzil, Tzeltal
Religions Roman Catholic 88%, Other 7%, Protestant 5%
Ethnic mix Mestizo 60%, Amerindian 30%, European 9%, Other 1%
Government Presidential system
Currency Mexican peso = 100 centavos
Literacy rate 91%
Calorie consumption 3145 calories

MICRONESIA
Australasia & Oceania

Page 122 B1

The Federated States of Micronesia, situated in the western Pacific, comprise 607 islands and atolls grouped into four main island states.

Official name Federated States of Micronesia
Formation 1986 / 1986
Capital Palikir (Pohnpei Island)
Population 107,862 / 398 people per sq mile (154 people per sq km) / 30%
Total area 271 sq. miles (702 sq. km)
Languages English*, Trukese, Pohnpeian, Mortlockese, Kosraean
Religions Roman Catholic 50%, Protestant 48%, Other 2%
Ethnic mix Chuukese 49%, Pohnpeian 24%, Other 14%, Kosraean 6%, Yapese 5%, Asian 2%
Government Nonparty system
Currency US dollar = 100 cents
Literacy rate 81%
Calorie consumption Not available

MOLDOVA
Southeast Europe

Page 86 D3

The smallest and most densely populated of the ex-Soviet republics, Moldova has strong linguistic and cultural links with Romania to the west.

Official name Republic of Moldova
Formation 1991 / 1991
Capital Chisinau
Population 4.2 million / 323 people per sq mile (125 people per sq km) / 46%
Languages Moldovan*, Ukrainian, Russian
Religions Orthodox Christian 98%, Jewish 2%
Ethnic mix Moldovan 64%, Ukrainian 14%, Russian 13%, Gagauz 4%, Other 3%, Bulgarian 2%
Government Parliamentary system
Currency Moldovan leu = 100 bani
Literacy rate 98%
Calorie consumption 2806 calories

MONACO
Southern Europe

Page 69 E6

The smallest and most densely populated of the ex-Soviet republics, Moldova has strong linguistic and cultural links with Romania to the west.

Official name Principality of Monaco
Formation 1861 / 1861
Capital Monaco-Ville
Population 32,671 / 43,561 people per sq mile (16,754 people per sq km) / 100%
Total area 0.75 sq. miles (1.95 sq. km)
Languages French*, Italian, Monégasque, English
Religions Roman Catholic 89%, Protestant 6%, Other 5%
Ethnic mix French 32%, Other 29%, Italian 20%, Monégasque 19%
Government Mixed monarchical–parliamentary system
Currency Euro = 100 cents
Literacy rate 99%
Calorie consumption Not available

MONGOLIA
East Asia

Page 104 D2

Lying between Russia and China, Mongolia is a vast and isolated country with a small population. Over two-thirds of the country is desert.

Official name Mongolia
Formation 1924 / 1924
Capital Ulan Bator
Population 2.7 million / 4 people per sq mile (2 people per sq km) / 57%
Total area 604,247 sq. miles (1,565,000 sq. km)
Languages Khalkha Mongolian*, Kazakh, Chinese, Russian
Religions Tibetan Buddhist 96%, Muslim 4%
Ethnic mix Khalkh 82%, Other 9%, Kazakh 4%, Dorvod 3%, Bayad 2%
Government Mixed presidential–parliamentary system
Currency Tugrik (tögrög) = 100 mongo
Literacy rate 98%
Calorie consumption 2249 calories

MONTENEGRO
Southeast Europe

Page 79 C5

Montenegro voted to split from Serbia in 2006. Since then the country has developed politically and economically with a view towards eventual membership of the EU.

Official name Republic of Montenegro
Formation 2006 / 2006
Capital Podgorica
Population 684,736 / 128 people per sq mile (50 people per sq km) / 62%
Total area 5332 sq. miles (13,812 sq. km)
Languages Montenegrin*, Serbian, Albanian, Bosniak, Croatian
Religions Orthodox Christian 74%, Muslim 18%, Other 4%Roman Catholic 4%
Ethnic mix Montenegrin 43%, Serb 32%, Other 12%, Bosniak 8%, Albanian 5%
Government Parliamentary system
Currency Euro = 100 cents
Literacy rate 98%
Calorie consumption Not available

MOROCCO
North Africa

Page 48 C2

A former French colony in northwest Africa, independent in 1956, Morocco has occupied the disputed territory of Western Sahara since 1975.

Official name Kingdom of Morocco
Formation 1956 / 1969
Capital Rabat
Population 32.4 million / 188 people per sq mile (73 people per sq km) / 58%
Total area 172,316 sq. miles (446,300 sq. km)
Languages Arabic*, Tamazight (Berber), French, Spanish
Religions Muslim (mainly Sunni) 99%, Other (mostly Christian) 1%
Ethnic mix Arab 70%, Berber 29%, European 1%
Government Mixed monarchical–parliamentary system
Currency Moroccan dirham = 100 centimes
Literacy rate 52%
Calorie consumption 3052 calories

MOZAMBIQUE
Southern Africa

Page 57 E3

Mozambique lies on the southeast African coast. It was torn by a civil war between the Marxist government and a rebel group from 1977–1992.

Official name Republic of Mozambique
Formation 1975 / 1975
Capital Maputo
Population 20.5 million / 68 people per sq mile (26 people per sq km) / 37%
Total area 309,494 sq. miles (801,590 sq. km)
Languages Portuguese*, Makua, Xitsonga, Sena, Lomwe
Religions Traditional beliefs 56%, Christian 30%, Muslim 14%
Ethnic mix Makua Lomwe 47%, Tsonga 23%, Malawi 12%, Shona 11%, Yao 4%, Other 3%
Government Presidential system
Currency New metical = 100 centavos
Literacy rate 46%
Calorie consumption 2079 calories

MYANMAR (BURMA)
Southeast Asia

Page 114 A3

Myanmar forms the eastern shores of the Bay of Bengal and the Andaman Sea in Southeast Asia. Since 1988 it has been ruled by a repressive military regime.

Official name Union of Myanmar
Formation 1948 / 1948
Capital Nay Pyi Taw
Population 51.5 million / 203 people per sq mile (78 people per sq km) / 30%
Total area 261,969 sq. miles (678,500 sq. km)
Languages Burmese*, Shan, Karen, Rakhine, Chin, Yangbye, Kachin, Mon
Religions Buddhist 87%, Christian 6%, Muslim 4%, Other 2%, Hindu 1%
Ethnic mix Burman (Bamah) 68%, Other 13%, Shan 9%, Karen 6%, Rakhine 4%
Government Military-based regime
Currency Kyat = 100 pyas
Literacy rate 90%
Calorie consumption 2937 calories

NAMIBIA
Southern Africa

Page 56 B3

Located in southwestern Africa, Namibia became free of South African control in 1990, after years of uncertainty and guerrilla activity.

Official name Republic of Namibia
Formation 1990 / 1994
Capital Windhoek
Population 2.1 million / 7 people per sq mile (3 people per sq km) / 33%
Total area 318,694 sq. miles (825,418 sq. km)
Languages English*, Ovambo, Kavango, Bergdama, German, Afrikaans
Religions Christian 90%, Traditional beliefs 10%
Ethnic mix Ovambo 50%, Other tribes 24%, Kavango 9%, Damara 8%, Herero 8%, Other 1%
Government Presidential system
Currency Namibian dollar = 100 cents
Literacy rate 85%
Calorie consumption 2278 calories

NAURU
Australasia & Oceania

Page 122 D3

Nauru lies in the Pacific, 2,480 miles (4,000 km) northeast of Australia. For many years phosphate deposits provided great wealth but these are now virtually exhausted.

Official name Republic of Nauru
Formation 1968 / 1968
Capital None
Population 13,528 / 1670 people per sq mile (644 people per sq km)
Total area 8.1 sq. miles (21 sq. km)
Languages Nauruan*, Kiribati, Chinese, Tuvaluan, English
Religions Nauruan Congregational Church 60%, Roman Catholic 35%, Other 5%
Ethnic mix Nauruan 62%, Other Pacific islanders 27%, Asian 8%, European 3%
Government Nonparty system
Currency Australian dollar = 100 cents
Literacy rate 95%
Calorie consumption Not available

NEPAL
South Asia

Page 113 E3

Nepal lies between India and China, on the shoulder of the southern Himalayas. In 2008, after many years of unrest, Nepal was declared a republic and the monarchy was dissolved .

Official name Federal Democratic Republic of Nepal
Formation 1769 / 1769
Capital Kathmandu
Population 28.2 million / 534 people per sq mile (206 people per sq km) / 15%
Total area 54,363 sq. miles (140,800 sq. km)
Languages Nepali*, Maithili, Bhojpuri
Religions Hindu 90%, Buddhist 5%, Muslim 3%, Other (including Christian) 2%
Ethnic mix Other 52%, Chhetri 16%, Hill Brahman 13%, Tharu 7%, Magar 7%, Tamang 5%
Government Parliamentary system
Currency Nepalese rupee = 100 paisa
Literacy rate 49%
Calorie consumption 2453 calories

NETHERLANDS
Northwest Europe

Page 64 C3

Astride the delta of five major rivers in northwest Europe, the Netherlands has a long trading tradition. Rotterdam is the world's largest port.

Official name Kingdom of the Netherlands
Formation 1648 / 1839
Capital Amsterdam; The Hague (administrative)
Population 16.4 million / 1252 people per sq mile (483 people per sq km) / 66%
Total area 16,033 sq. miles (41,526 sq. km)
Languages Dutch*, Frisian
Religions Roman Catholic 36%, Other 34%, Protestant 27%, Muslim 3%
Ethnic mix Dutch 82%, Other 12%, Surinamese 2%, Turkish 2%, Moroccan 2%
Government Parliamentary system
Currency Euro = 100 cents
Literacy rate 99%
Calorie consumption 3362 calories

NEW ZEALAND
Australasia & Oceania

Page 128 A4

One of the Pacific Rim countries, New Zealand lies southeast of Australia, and comprises the North and South Islands, separated by the Cook Strait.

Official name New Zealand
Formation 1947 / 1947
Capital Wellington
Population 4.1 million / 40 people per sq mile (15 people per sq km) / 86%
Total area 103,737 sq. miles (268,680 sq. km)
Languages English*, Maori*
Religions Anglican 24%, Other 22%, Presbyterian 18%, Nonreligious 16%, Roman Catholic 15%, Methodist 5%
Ethnic mix European 75%, Maori 15%, Other 7%, Samoan 3%
Government Parliamentary system
Currency New Zealand dollar = 100 cents
Literacy rate 99%
Calorie consumption 3219 calories

NICARAGUA
Central America

Page 30 D3

Nicaragua lies at the heart of Central America. An 11-year war between left-wing Sandinistas and right-wing US-backed Contras ended in 1989.

Official name Republic of Nicaragua
Formation 1838 / 1838
Capital Managua
Population 5.7 million / 124 people per sq mile (48 people per sq km) / 58%
Total area 49,998 sq. miles (129,494 sq. km)
Languages Spanish*, English Creole, Miskito
Religions Roman Catholic 80%, Protestant Evangelical 17%, Other 3%
Ethnic mix Mestizo 69%, White 14%, Black 8%, Amerindian 5%, Zambo 4%
Government Presidential system
Currency Córdoba oro = 100 centavos
Literacy rate 77%
Calorie consumption 2298 calories

NIGER
West Africa

Page 53 F3

Niger lies landlocked in West Africa, but it is linked to the sea by the River Niger. Since 1973 it has suffered civil unrest and two major droughts.

Official name Republic of Niger
Formation 1960 / 1960
Capital Niamey
Population 14.9 million / 30 people per sq mile (12 people per sq km) / 23%
Total area 489,188 sq. miles (1,267,000 sq. km)
Languages French*, Hausa, Djerma, Fulani, Tuareg, Teda
Religions Muslim 85%, Traditional beliefs 14%, Other (including Christian) 1%
Ethnic mix Hausa 55%, Djerma and Songhai 21%, Peul 9%, Tuareg 9%, Other 6%
Government Presidential system
Currency CFA franc = 100 centimes
Literacy rate 29%
Calorie consumption 2130 calories

NIGERIA
West Africa

Page 53 F4

Africa's most populous state Nigeria, in West Africa, is a federation of 30 states. It adopted civilian rule in 1999 after 33 years of military government.

Official name Federal Republic of Nigeria
Formation 1960 / 1961
Capital Abuja
Population 137 million / 390 people per sq mile (151 people per sq km) / 47%
Total area 356,667 sq. miles (923,768 sq. km)
Languages English*, Hausa, Yoruba, Ibo
Religions Muslim 50%, Christian 40%, Traditional beliefs 10%
Ethnic mix Other 29%, Hausa 21%, Yoruba 21%, Ibo 18%, Fulani 11%
Government Presidential system
Currency Naira = 100 kobo
Literacy rate 67%
Calorie consumption 2726 calories

NORTH KOREA
East Asia

Page 106 E3

North Korea comprises the northern half of the Korean peninsula. A communist state since 1948, it is largely isolated from the outside world.

Official name Democratic People's Republic of Korea
Formation 1948 / 1953
Capital Pyongyang
Population 22.7 million / 488 people per sq mile (189 people per sq km) / 61%
Total area 46,540 sq. miles (120,540 sq. km)
Languages Korean*
Religions Atheist 100%
Ethnic mix Korean 100%
Government One-party state
Currency North Korean won = 100 chon
Literacy rate 98%
Calorie consumption 2142 calories

NORWAY
Northern Europe

Page 63 A5

The Kingdom of Norway traces the rugged western coast of Scandinavia. Settlements are largely restricted to southern and coastal areas.

Official name Kingdom of Norway
Formation 1905 / 1905
Capital Oslo
Population 4.7 million / 40 people per sq mile (15 people per sq km) / 80%
Total area 125,181 sq. miles (324,220 sq. km)
Languages Norwegian* (Bokmål "book language" and Nynorsk "new Norsk"), Sámi
Religions Evangelical Lutheran 89%, Other and nonreligious 10%, Roman Catholic 1%
Ethnic mix Norwegian 93%, Other 6%, Sámi 1%
Government Parliamentary system
Currency Norwegian krone = 100 øre
Literacy rate 99%
Calorie consumption 3484 calories

OMAN
Southwest Asia

Page 99 D6

Situated on the eastern coast of the Arabian Peninsula, Oman is the least developed of the Gulf states, despite modest oil exports.

Official name Sultanate of Oman
Formation 1951 / 1951
Capital Muscat
Population 2.7 million / 33 people per sq mile (13 people per sq km) / 78%
Total area 82,031 sq. miles (212,460 sq. km)
Languages Arabic*, Baluchi, Farsi, Hindi, Punjabi
Religions Ibadi Muslim 75%, Other Muslim and Hindu 25%
Ethnic mix Arab 88%, Baluchi 4%, Persian 3%, Indian and Pakistani 3%, African 2%
Government Monarchy
Currency Omani rial = 1000 baisa
Literacy rate 81%
Calorie consumption Not available

PAKISTAN
South Asia

Page 112 B2

Pakistan was created in 1947 as an independent Muslim state. Today, this nuclear armed country is struggling to deal with complex domestic and international tensions.

Official name Islamic Republic of Pakistan
Formation 1947 / 1971
Capital Islamabad
Population 165 million / 553 people per sq mile (214 people per sq km) / 34%
Total area 310,401 sq. miles (803,940 sq. km)
Languages Urdu*, Punjabi, Sindhi, Pashtu, Baluchi, Brahui
Religions Sunni Muslim 77%, Shi'a Muslim 20%, Hindu 2%, Christian 1%
Ethnic mix Punjabi 56%, Pathan (Pashtun) 15%, Sindhi 14%, Mohajir 7%, Other 4%, Baluchi 4%
Government Presidential system
Currency Pakistani rupee = 100 paisa
Literacy rate 50%
Calorie consumption 2419 calories

PALAU
Australasia & Oceania

Page 122 A2

The Palau archipelago, a group of over 200 islands, lies in the western Pacific Ocean. Since independence in 1994 it has prospered on a thriving tourist industry.

Official name Republic of Palau
Formation 1994 / 1994
Capital Melekeok
Population 20,842 / 106 people per sq mile (41 people per sq km) / 68%
Total area 177 sq. miles (458 sq. km)
Languages Palauan*, English*, Japanese, Angaur, Tobi, Sonsorolese
Religions Christian 66%, Modekngei 34%
Ethnic mix Palauan 74%, Filipino 16%, Other 6%, Chinese and other Asian 4%
Government Nonparty system
Currency US dollar = 100 cents
Literacy rate 98%
Calorie consumption Not available

PANAMA
Central America

Page 31 F5

Southernmost of the Central American countries. The Panama Canal (returned to Panama from US control in 2000) links the Pacific and Atlantic oceans.

Official name Republic of Panama
Formation 1903 / 1903
Capital Panama City
Population 3.3 million / 112 people per sq mile (43 people per sq km) / 57%
Total area 30,193 sq. miles (78,200 sq. km)
Languages English Creole, Spanish*, Amerindian languages, Chibchan languages
Religions Roman Catholic 86%, Other 8%, Protestant 6%
Ethnic mix Mestizo 60%, White 14%, Black 12%, Amerindian 8%, Asian 4%, Other 2%
Government Presidential system
Currency Balboa = 100 centésimos
Literacy rate 92%
Calorie consumption 2272 calories

PAPUA NEW GUINEA
Australasia & Oceania

Page 122 B3

Achieving independence from Australia in 1975, PNG occupies the eastern section of the island of New Guinea and several other island groups.

Official name Independent State of Papua New Guinea
Formation 1975 / 1975
Capital Port Moresby
Population 6.1 million / 35 people per sq mile (13 people per sq km) / 13%
Total area 178,703 sq. miles (462,840 sq. km)
Languages English*, Pidgin English, Papuan, Motu, 750 (est.) native languages
Religions Protestant 60%, Roman Catholic 37%, Other 3%
Ethnic mix Melanesian and mixed race 100%
Government Parliamentary system
Currency Kina = 100 toea
Literacy rate 57%
Calorie consumption 2193 calories

PARAGUAY
South America

Page 42 D2

Landlocked in central South America. Its post-independence history has included periods of military rule. Free elections were held in 1993.

Official name Republic of Paraguay
Formation 1811 / 1938
Capital Asunción
Population 6.4 million / 42 people per sq mile (16 people per sq km) / 58%
Total area 157,046 sq. miles (406,750 sq. km)
Languages Spanish*, Guaraní, German
Religions Roman Catholic 96%, Protestant (including Mennonite) 4%
Ethnic mix Mestizo 91%, Other 7%, Amerindian 2%
Government Presidential system
Currency Guaraní = 100 céntimos
Literacy rate 93%
Calorie consumption 2565 calories

PERU
South America

Page 38 C3

Once the heart of the Inca empire, before the Spanish conquest in the 16th century, Peru lies on the Pacific coast of South America.

Official name Republic of Peru
Formation 1824 / 1941
Capital Lima
Population 28.8 million / 58 people per sq mile (22 people per sq km) / 74%
Total area 496,223 sq. miles (1,285,200 sq. km)
Languages Spanish*, Quechua*, Aymara
Religions Roman Catholic 95%, Other 5%
Ethnic mix Amerindian 50%, Mestizo 40%, White 7%, Other 3%
Government Presidential system
Currency New sol = 100 céntimos
Literacy rate 88%
Calorie consumption 2571 calories

PHILIPPINES
Southeast Asia

Page 117 E1

An archipelago of 7,107 islands between the South China Sea and the Pacific. After 21 years of dictatorship, democracy was restored in 1986.

Official name Republic of the Philippines
Formation 1946 / 1946
Capital Manila
Population 85.9 million / 746 people per sq mile (288 people per sq km) / 62%
Total area 115,830 sq. miles (300,000 sq. km)
Languages English*, Filipino*, Tagalog, Cebuano, Ilocano, Hiligaynon, many other local languages
Religions Roman Catholic 83%, Protestant 9%, Muslim 5%, Other (including Buddhist) 3%
Ethnic mix Other 34%, Tagalog 28%, Cebuano 13%, Ilocano 9%, Hiligaynon 8%, Bisaya 8%
Government Presidential system
Currency Philippine peso = 100 centavos
Literacy rate 93%
Calorie consumption 2379 calories

POLAND
Northern Europe

Page 76 B3

With its seven international borders and strategic location in the heart of Europe, Poland has always played an important role in European affairs.

Official name Republic of Poland
Formation 1918 / 1945
Capital Warsaw
Population 38.5 million / 328 people per sq mile (126 people per sq km) / 62%
Total area 120,728 sq. miles (312,685 sq. km)
Languages Polish*
Religions Roman Catholic 93%, Other and nonreligious 5%, Orthodox Christian 2%
Ethnic mix Polish 97%, Other 3%
Government Parliamentary system
Currency Zloty = 100 groszy
Literacy rate 99%
Calorie consumption 3374 calories

PORTUGAL
Southwest Europe

Page 70 B3

Facing the Atlantic on the western side of the Iberian Peninsula, Portugal is the most westerly country on the European mainland.

Official name The Portuguese Republic
Formation 1139 / 1640
Capital Lisbon
Population 10.6 million / 299 people per sq mile (115 people per sq km) / 55%
Total area 35,672 sq. miles (92,391 sq. km)
Languages Portuguese*
Religions Roman Catholic 97%, Other 2%, Protestant 1%
Ethnic mix Portuguese 98%, African and other 2%
Government Parliamentary system
Currency Euro = 100 cents
Literacy rate 92%
Calorie consumption 3741 calories

Arkansas City – Balıkesir

Arkansas City *23 F5* Kansas, C USA
Arkansas River *27 G1 river* C USA
Arkhangel'sk *92 B2 Eng.* Archangel. Arkhangel'skaya Oblast', NW Russian Federation
Arkoí *83 E6 island* Dodekánisa, Greece, Aegean Sea
Arles *69 D6 var.* Arles-sur-Rhône; *anc.* Arelas, Arelate. Bouches-du-Rhône, SE France
Arles-sur-Rhône *see* Arles
Arlington *27 G2* Texas, SW USA
Arlington *19 E4* Virginia, NE USA
Arlon *65 D8 Dut.* Aarlen, *Ger.* Arel, *Lat.* Orolaunum. Luxembourg, SE Belgium
Armagh *67 B5 Ir.* Ard Mhacha. S Northern Ireland, United Kingdom
Armagnac *69 B6 cultural region* S France
Armenia *36 B3* Quindío, W Colombia
Armenia *95 F3 off.* Republic of Armenia, *var.* Ajastan, *Arm.* Hayastani Hanrapetut'yun; *prev.* Armenian Soviet Socialist Republic. *country* SW Asia
Armenian Soviet Socialist Republic *see* Armenia
Armenia, Republic of *see* Armenia
Armidale *127 D6* New South Wales, SE Australia
Armstrong *16 B3* Ontario, S Canada
Armyans'k *87 F4 Rus.* Armyansk. Respublika Krym, S Ukraine
Arnaía *82 C4 Cont.* Arnea. Kentrikí Makedonía, N Greece
Arnaud *60 A3 river* Québec, E Canada
Arnea *see* Arnaía
Arnedo *71 E2* La Rioja, N Spain
Arnhem *64 D4* Gelderland, SE Netherlands
Arnhem Land *126 A2 physical region* Northern Territory, N Australia
Arno *74 B3 river* C Italy
Arnold *23 G4* Missouri, C USA
Arnswalde *see* Choszczno
Aroe Islands *see* Aru, Kepulauan
Arorae *123 E3 atoll* Tungaru, W Kiribati
Arrabona *see* Győr
Ar Rahad *see* Er Rahad
Ar Ramādī *98 B3 var.* Ramadi, Rumadiya. Al Anbār, SW Iraq
Ar Rāmī *96 C4* Ḩimş, C Syria
Ar Ramthā *97 B5 var.* Ramtha. Irbid, N Jordan
Arran, Isle of *66 C4 island* SW Scotland, United Kingdom
Ar Raqqah *96 C2 var.* Rakka; *anc.* Nicephorium. Ar Raqqah, N Syria
Arras *68 C2 anc.* Nemetocenna. Pas-de-Calais, N France
Ar Rawḑatayn *98 C4 var.* Raudhatain. N Kuwait
Arretium *see* Arezzo
Arriaca *see* Guadalajara
Arriaga *29 G5* Chiapas, SE Mexico
Ar Riyāḑ *99 C5 Eng.* Riyadh. *country capital* Ar Riyāḑ, C Saudi Arabia
Ar Rub 'al Khali *99 C6 Eng.* Empty Quarter, Great Sandy Desert. *desert* SW Asia
Ar Rustāq *99 E5 var.* Rostak, Rustaq. N Oman
Ar Ruţbah *98 B3 var.* Rutba. Al Anbār, SW Iraq
Árta *83 A5 anc.* Ambracia. Ípeiros, W Greece
Artashat *95 F3* S Armenia
Artemisa *32 B2* La Habana, W Cuba
Artesia *26 D3* New Mexico, SW USA
Arthur's Pass *129 C6 pass* South Island, New Zealand
Artigas *42 D3 prev.* San Eugenio, San Eugenio del Cuareim. Artigas, N Uruguay
Art'ik *95 F2* W Armenia
Artois *68 C2 cultural region* N France
Artsiz *see* Artsyz
Artsyz *86 D4 Rus.* Artsiz. Odes'ka Oblast', SW Ukraine
Artvin *95 F2* Artvin, NE Turkey
Arua *51 B6* NW Uganda
Aruba *36 C1 var.* Oruba. *Dutch autonomous region* S West Indies
Aru Islands *see* Aru, Kepulauan
Aru, Kepulauan *117 G4 Eng.* Aru Islands; *prev.* Aroe Islands. *island group* E Indonesia
Arunāchal Pradesh *113 G3 prev.* North East Frontier Agency, North East Frontier Agency of Assam. *cultural region* NE India
Arusha *51 C7* Arusha, N Tanzania
Arviat *15 G4 prev.* Eskimo Point. Nunavut, C Canada
Arvidsjaur *62 C4* Norrbotten, N Sweden
Arys' *92 B5 Kaz.* Arys. Yuzhnyy Kazakhstan, S Kazakhstan
Arys *see* Arys'
Asadābād *101 F4 var.* Asaḑābād; *prev.* Chaghasarāy. Konar, E Afghanistan
Asaḑābād *see* Asadābād
Asahi-dake *108 D2 mountain* Hokkaidō, N Japan
Asahikawa *108 D2* Hokkaidō, N Japan
Asamankese *53 E5* SE Ghana
Āsānsol *113 F4* West Bengal, NE India
Asben *see* Aïr, Massif de l'
Ascension Fracture Zone *47 A5 tectonic Feature* C Atlantic Ocean
Ascension Island *45 C5 dependency of St.Helena* C Atlantic Ocean
Ascoli Piceno *74 C4 anc.* Asculum Picenum. Marche, C Italy
Asculum Picenum *see* Ascoli Piceno
'Aseb *50 D4 var.* Assab, *Amh.* Āseb. SE Eritrea
Aşgabat *100 C3 prev.* Ashgabat, Ashkhabad, Poltoratsk. *country capital* Ahal Welaýaty, C Turkmenistan
Ashara *see* Al 'Ashārah
Ashburton *129 C6* Canterbury, South Island, New Zealand
Ashburton River *124 A4 river* Western Australia
Ashdod *97 A6 anc.* Azotos, *Lat.* Azotus. Central, W Israel
Asheville *21 E1* North Carolina, SE USA
Ashgabat *see* Aşgabat
Ashkelon *97 A6 prev.* Ashqelon. Southern, C Israel
Ashkhabad *see* Aşgabat
Ashland *24 B4* Oregon, NW USA
Ashland *18 B1* Wisconsin, N USA
Ashmore and Cartier Islands *120 A3 Australian external territory* E Indian Ocean
Ashmyany *85 C5 Rus.* Oshmyany. Hrodzyenskaya Voblasts', W Belarus
Ashqelon *see* Ashkelon
Ash Shadādah *96 D2 var.* Ash Shaddādah, Jisr ash Shadadi, Shaddādī, Shedadi, Tell Shedadi. Al Ḩasakah, NE Syria
Ash Shaddādah *see* Ash Shadādah
Ash Sharāh *97 B7 var.* Esh Sharā. *mountain range* W Jordan
Ash Shāriqah *98 D4 Eng.* Sharjah. Ash Shāriqah, NE United Arab Emirates
Ash Shawbak *97 B7* Ma'ān, W Jordan
Ash Shiḩr *99 C6* SE Yemen
Asia *90 continent*
Asinara *74 A4 island* W Italy
Asipovichy *85 D6 Rus.* Osipovichi. Mahilyowskaya Voblasts', C Belarus
Aşkale *95 E3* Erzurum, NE Turkey
Askersund *63 C6* Örebro, C Sweden
Asmara *see* Asmera
Asmera *50 C4 var.* Asmara. *country capital* C Eritrea
Aspadana *see* Eşfahān
Asphaltites, Lacus *see* Dead Sea
Aspinwall *see* Colón
Assab *see* 'Aseb
As Sabkhah *96 D2 var.* Sabkha. Ar Raqqah, NE Syria
Assad, Lake *96 C2 Eng.* Lake Assad. *lake* N Syria
Assad, Lake *see* Asad, Buḩayrat al
Aş Şafāwī *97 C6* Al Mafraq, N Jordan
Aş Şaḩrā' ash Sharqīyah *see* Sahara el Sharqîya
As Salamīyah *see* Salamīyah
'Assal, Lac *46 E4 lake* C Djibouti
As Salţ *97 B6 var.* Salt. Al Balqā', NW Jordan
Assamaka *see* Assamakka
Assamakka *53 F2 var.* Assamaka. Agadez, NW Niger
As Samāwah *98 B3 var.* Samawa. Al Muthannā, S Iraq
Assen *64 E2* Drenthe, NE Netherlands
Assenede *65 B5* Oost-Vlaanderen, NW Belgium
Assiout *see* Asyūţ
Assiut *see* Asyūţ
Assling *see* Jesenice
Assouan *see* Aswān
Assu *see* Açu
Assuan *see* Aswān
As Sukhnah *96 C3 var.* Sukhne, *Fr.* Soukhné. Ḩimş, C Syria
As Sulaymānīyah *98 C3 var.* Sulaimaniya, *Kurd.* Slēmānī. As Sulaymānīyah, NE Iraq
As Sulayyil *99 B5* Ar Riyāḑ, S Saudi Arabia
Aş Şuwār *96 D2 var.* Şuwār. Dayr az Zawr, E Syria
As Suwaydā' *97 B5 var.* El Suweida, Es Suweida, Suweida, *Fr.* Soueida. As Suwaydā', SW Syria
As Suways *see* Suez
Asta Colonia *see* Asti
Astacus *see* İzmit
Astana *92 C4 prev.* Akmola, Akmolinsk, Tselinograd, Aqmola. *country capital* Akmola, N Kazakhstan
Asta Pompeia *see* Asti
Astarabad *see* Gorgān
Asterābād *see* Gorgān
Asti *74 A2 anc.* Asta Colonia, Asta Pompeia, Hasta Colonia, Hasta Pompeia. Piemonte, NW Italy
Astigi *see* Ecija
Astipálaia *see* Astypálaia
Astorga *70 C1 anc.* Asturica Augusta. Castilla-León, N Spain
Astrabad *see* Gorgān
Astrakhan' *89 C7* Astrakhanskaya Oblast', SW Russian Federation
Asturias *70 C1 autonomous community* NW Spain
Asturias *see* Oviedo
Asturica Augusta *see* Astorga
Astypálaia *83 D7 var.* Astipálaia, *It.* Stampalia. *island* Kykládes, Greece, Aegean Sea
Asunción *42 D2 country capital* Central, S Paraguay
Aswān *50 B2 var.* Assouan, Assuan, Aswân; *anc.* Syene. SE Egypt
Aswân *see* Aswān
Asyūţ *50 B2 var.* Assiout, Assiut, Asyût, Siut; *anc.* Lycopolis. C Egypt
Asyût *see* Asyūţ
Atacama Desert *42 B2 Eng.* Atacama Desert. *desert* N Chile
Atacama Desert *see* Atacama, Desierto de
Atafu Atoll *123 E3 island* NW Tokelau
Atamyrat *100 D3 prev.* Kerki. Lebap Welaýaty, E Turkmenistan
Atâr *52 C2* Adrar, W Mauritania
Atas Bogd *104 D3 mountain* SW Mongolia
Atascadero *25 B7* California, W USA
Atatürk Barajı *95 E4 reservoir* S Turkey
Atbara *50 C3 var.* 'Aţbārah. River Nile, NE Sudan
'Aţbārah/'Aţbarah, Nahr *see* Atbara
Atbasar *92 C4* Akmola, N Kazakhstan
Atchison *23 F4* Kansas, C USA
Aternum *see* Pescara
Ath *65 B6 var.* Aat. Hainaut, SW Belgium
Athabasca *15 E5* Alberta, SW Canada
Athabasca *15 E5 var.* Athabaska. *river* Alberta, SW Canada
Athabasca, Lake *15 F4 lake* Alberta/Saskatchewan, SW Canada
Athabaska *see* Athabasca
Athenae *see* Athína
Athens *21 E2* Georgia, SE USA
Athens *18 D4* Ohio, N USA
Athens *27 G3* Texas, SW USA
Athens *see* Athína
Atherton *126 D3* Queensland, NE Australia
Athína *83 C6 Eng.* Athens, *prev.* Athínai; *anc.* Athenae. *country capital* Attikí, C Greece
Athínai *see* Athína
Athlone *67 B5 Ir.* Baile Átha Luain. C Ireland
Ath Thawrah *see* Madīnat ath Thawrah
Ati *54 C3* Batha, C Chad
Atikokan *16 B4* Ontario, S Canada
Atka *93 G3* Magadanskaya Oblast', E Russian Federation
Atka *14 A3* Atka Island, Alaska, USA
Atlanta *20 D2 state capital* Georgia, SE USA
Atlanta *27 H2* Texas, SW USA
Atlantic City *19 F4* New Jersey, NE USA
Atlantic-Indian Basin *45 D7 undersea basin* SW Indian Ocean
Atlantic-Indian Ridge *47 B8 undersea ridge* SW Indian Ocean
Atlantic Ocean *44 B4 ocean*
Atlas Mountains *48 C2 mountain range* NW Africa
Atlasovo *93 H3* Kamchatskaya Oblast', E Russian Federation
Atlas, Tell *80 C3 Eng.* Tell Atlas. *mountain range* N Algeria
Atlas, Tell *see* Atlas Tellien
Atlin *14 D4* British Columbia, W Canada
Aţ Ţafīlah *97 B7 var.* Et Tafila, Tafila. Aţ Ţafīlah, W Jordan
Aţ Ţā'if *99 B5* Makkah, W Saudi Arabia
Attaleia/Attalia *see* Antalya
At Tall al Abyaḑ *96 C2 var.* Tall al Abyaḑ, Tell Abyad, *Fr.* Tell Abiad. Ar Raqqah, N Syria
Aţ Ţanf *96 D4* Ḩimş, S Syria
Attapu *see* Samakhixai
Attawapiskat *16 C3* Ontario, C Canada
Attawapiskat *16 C3 river* Ontario, S Canada
At Tibnī *96 D2 var.* Tibnī. Dayr az Zawr, NE Syria
Attopeu *see* Samakhixai
Attu Island *14 A2 island* Aleutian Islands, Alaska, USA
Atyrau *92 B4 prev.* Gur'yev. Atyrau, W Kazakhstan
Aubagne *69 D6 anc.* Albania. Bouches-du-Rhône, SE France
Aubange *65 D8* Luxembourg, SE Belgium
Aubervilliers *68 E1* Seine-St-Denis, Île-de-France, N France Europe
Auburn *24 B2* Washington, NW USA
Auch *69 B6 Lat.* Augusta Auscorum, Elimberrum. Gers, S France
Auckland *128 D2* Auckland, North Island, New Zealand
Auckland Islands *120 C5 island group* S New Zealand
Audern *see* Audru
Audincourt *68 E4* Doubs, E France
Audru *84 D2 Ger.* Audern. Pärnumaa, SW Estonia
Augathella *127 D5* Queensland, E Australia
Augsbourg *see* Augsburg
Augsburg *73 C6 Fr.* Augsbourg; *anc.* Augusta Vindelicorum. Bayern, S Germany
Augusta *125 A7* Western Australia
Augusta *21 E2* Georgia, SE USA
Augusta *19 G2 state capital* Maine, NE USA
Augusta *see* London
Augusta Auscorum *see* Auch
Augusta Emerita *see* Mérida
Augusta Praetoria *see* Aosta
Augusta Trajana *see* Stara Zagora
Augusta Treverorum *see* Trier
Augusta Vangionum *see* Worms
Augusta Vindelicorum *see* Augsburg
Augustobona Tricassium *see* Troyes
Augustodurum *see* Bayeux
Augustoritum Lemovicensium *see* Limoges
Augustów *76 E2 Rus.* Avgustov. Podlaskie, NE Poland
Aulie Ata/Auliye-Ata *see* Taraz
Aunglan *114 B4 var.* Allanmyo, Myaydo. Magway, C Myanmar (Burma)
Auob *56 B4 var.* Oup. *river* Namibia/South Africa
Aurangābād *112 D5* Mahārāshtra, C India
Auray *68 A3* Morbihan, NW France
Aurelia Aquensis *see* Baden-Baden
Aurelianum *see* Orléans
Aurès, Massif de l' *80 C4 mountain range* NE Algeria
Aurillac *69 C5* Cantal, C France
Aurium *see* Ourense
Aurora *37 F2* NW Guyana
Aurora *22 D4* Colorado, C USA
Aurora *18 B3* Illinois, N USA
Aurora *23 G5* Missouri, C USA
Aurora *see* Maéwo, Vanuatu
Aus *56 B4* Karas, SW Namibia
Ausa *see* Vic
Aussig *see* Ústí nad Labem
Austin *23 G3* Minnesota, N USA
Austin *27 G3 state capital* Texas, SW USA
Australes, Archipel des *see* Australes, Îles
Australes et Antarctiques Françaises, Terres *see* French Southern and Antarctic Territories
Australes, Îles *121 F4 var.* Archipel des Australes, Îles Tubuai, Tubuai Islands, *Eng.* Austral Islands. *island group* SW French Polynesia
Austral Fracture Zone *121 H4 tectonic feature* S Pacific Ocean
Australia *120 A4 off.* Commonwealth of Australia. *country*
Australia, Commonwealth of *see* Australia
Australian Alps *127 C7 mountain range* SE Australia
Australian Capital Territory *127 D7 prev.* Federal Capital Territory. *territory* SE Australia
Australie, Bassin Nord de l' *see* North Australian Basin
Austral Islands *see* Australes, Îles
Austrava *see* Ostrov
Austria *73 D7 off.* Republic of Austria, *Ger.* Österreich. *country* C Europe
Austria, Republic of *see* Austria
Autesiodorum *see* Auxerre
Autissiodorum *see* Auxerre
Autricum *see* Chartres
Auvergne *69 C5 cultural region* C France
Auxerre *68 C4 anc.* Autesiodorum, Autissiodorum. Yonne, C France
Avaricum *see* Bourges
Avarua *123 G5 dependent territory capital* Rarotonga, S Cook Islands
Avasfelsőfalu *see* Negreşti-Oaş
Ávdira *82 C3* Anatolikí Makedonía kai Thráki, NE Greece
Aveiro *70 B2 anc.* Talabriga. Aveiro, W Portugal
Avela *see* Ávila
Avellino *75 D5 anc.* Abellinum. Campania, S Italy
Avenio *see* Avignon
Avesta *63 C6* Dalarna, C Sweden
Aveyron *69 C6 river* S France
Avezzano *74 C4* Abruzzo, C Italy
Avgustov *see* Augustów
Aviemore *66 C3* N Scotland, United Kingdom
Avignon *69 D6 anc.* Avenio. Vaucluse, SE France
Ávila *70 D3 var.* Avila; *anc.* Abela, Abula, Abyla, Avela. Castilla-León, C Spain
Avilés *70 C1* Asturias, NW Spain
Avranches *68 B3* Manche, N France
Avveel *see* Ivalo, Finland
Avvil *see* Ivalo
Awaji-shima *109 C6 island* SW Japan
Āwash *51 D5* Āfar, NE Ethiopia
Awbārī *49 F3* SW Libya
Ax *see* Dax
Axel *65 B5* Zeeland, SW Netherlands
Axel Heiberg Island *15 E1 var.* Axel Heiburg. *island* Nunavut, N Canada
Axel Heiburg *see* Axel Heiberg Island
Axiós *see* Vardar
Ayacucho *38 D4* Ayacucho, S Peru
Ayagoz *92 C5 var.* Ayaguz, *Kaz.* Ayakoz. *river* E Kazakhstan
Ayamonte *70 C4* Andalucía, S Spain
Ayaviri *39 E4* Puno, S Peru
Aydarko'l Ko'li *101 E2 Rus.* Ozero Aydarkul'. *lake* C Uzbekistan
Aydarkul', Ozero *see* Aydarko'l Ko'li
Aydın *94 A4 var.* Aïdin; *anc.* Tralles Aydin. Aydın, SW Turkey
Ayers Rock *see* Uluru
Ayeyarwady *see* Irrawaddy
Ayiá *see* Agiá
Áyios Evstrátios *see* Ágios Efstrátios
Áyios Nikólaos *see* Ágios Nikólaos
Ayorou *53 E3* Tillabéri, W Niger
'Ayoûn el 'Atroûs *52 D3 var.* Aïoun el Atrous, Aïoun el Atroûss. Hodh el Gharbi, SE Mauritania
Ayr *66 C4* W Scotland, United Kingdom
Ayteke Bi *92 B4 Kaz.* Zhangaqazaly; *prev.* Novokazalinsk. Kzylorda, SW Kazakhstan
Aytos *82 E2* Burgas, E Bulgaria
Ayutthaya *115 C5 var.* Phra Nakhon Si Ayutthaya. Phra Nakhon Si Ayutthaya, C Thailand
Ayvalık *94 A3* Balıkesir, W Turkey
Azahar, Costa del *71 F3 coastal region* E Spain
Azaouâd *53 E3 desert* C Mali
Azärbaycan/Azärbaycan Respublikası *see* Azerbaijan
A'zāz *96 B2* Ḩalab, NW Syria
Azerbaijan *95 G2 off.* Azerbaijani Republic, *Az.* Azärbaycan, Azärbaycan Respublikası; *prev.* Azerbaijan SSR. *country* SE Asia
Azerbaijani Republic *see* Azerbaijan
Azerbaijan SSR *see* Azerbaijan
Azimabad *see* Patna
Azizie *see* Telish
Azogues *38 B2* Cañar, S Ecuador
Azores *70 A4 var.* Açores, Ilhas dos Açores, *Port.* Arquipélago dos Açores. *island group* Portugal, NE Atlantic Ocean
Azores-Biscay Rise *58 A3 undersea rise* E Atlantic Ocean
Azotos/Azotus *see* Ashdod
Azoum, Bahr *54 C3 seasonal river* SE Chad
Azov, Sea of *81 H1 Rus.* Azovskoye More, *Ukr.* Azovs'ke More. *sea* NE Black Sea
Azovs'ke More/Azovskoye More *see* Azov, Sea of
Azraq, Wāḩat al *97 C6 oasis* N Jordan
Aztec *26 C1* New Mexico, SW USA
Azuaga *70 C4* Extremadura, W Spain
Azuero, Península de *31 F5 peninsula* S Panama
Azul *43 D5* Buenos Aires, E Argentina
Azur, Côte d' *69 E6 coastal region* SE France
'Azza *see* Gaza
Az Zaqāzīq *50 B1 var.* Zagazig *var.* Az Zaqāzīq. N Egypt
Az Zaqāzīq *see* Az Zaqāzīq
Az Zarqā' *97 B6 var.* Zarqa. Az Zarqā', NW Jordan
Az Zāwiyah *49 F2 var.* Zawia. NW Libya
Az Zilfī *98 B4* Ar Riyāḑ, N Saudi Arabia

B

Baalbek *96 B4 var.* Ba'labakk; *anc.* Heliopolis. E Lebanon
Baardheere *51 D6 var.* Bardere, *It.* Bardera. Gedo, SW Somalia
Baarle-Hertog *65 C5* Antwerpen, N Belgium
Baarn *64 C3* Utrecht, C Netherlands
Babadag *86 D5* Tulcea, SE Romania
Babahoyo *38 B2 prev.* Bodegas. Los Ríos, C Ecuador
Bābā, Kūh-e *101 E4 mountain range* C Afghanistan
Babayevo *88 B4* Vologodskaya Oblast', NW Russian Federation
Babeldaob *122 A1 var.* Babeldaop, Babelthuap. *island* N Palau
Babeldaop *see* Babeldaob
Bab el Mandeb *99 B7 strait* Gulf of Aden/Red Sea
Babelthuap *see* Babeldaob
Babian Jiang *see* Black River
Babruysk *85 D7 Rus.* Bobruysk. Mahilyowskaya Voblasts', E Belarus
Babuyan Channel *117 E1 channel* N Philippines
Babuyan Island *117 E1 island* N Philippines
Bacabal *41 F2* Maranhão, E Brazil
Bacău *86 C4 Hung.* Bákó. Bacău, NE Romania
Băc Bô, Vinh *see* Tongking, Gulf of
Bắc Giang *114 D3* Ha Bắc, N Vietnam
Bacheykava *85 D5 Rus.* Bocheykovo. Vitsyebskaya Voblasts', N Belarus
Back *15 F3 river* Nunavut, N Canada
Bačka Palanka *78 D3 prev.* Palanka. Serbia, NW Serbia
Bačka Topola *78 D3 Hung.* Topolya; *prev. Hung.* Bácstopolya. Vojvodina, N Serbia
Bac Liêu *115 D6 var.* Vinh Loi. Minh Hai, S Vietnam
Bacolod *103 E4 off.* Bacolod City. Negros, C Philippines
Bacolod City *see* Bacolod
Bácsszenttamás *see* Srbobran
Bácstopolya *see* Bačka Topola
Bactra *see* Balkh
Badajoz *70 C4 anc.* Pax Augusta. Extremadura, W Spain
Baden-Baden *73 B6 anc.* Aurelia Aquensis. Baden-Württemberg, SW Germany
Bad Freienwalde *72 D3* Brandenburg, NE Germany
Badger State *see* Wisconsin
Bad Hersfeld *72 B4* Hessen, C Germany
Bad Homburg *see* Bad Homburg vor der Höhe
Bad Homburg vor der Höhe *73 B5 var.* Bad Homburg. Hessen, W Germany
Bad Ischl *73 D7* Oberösterreich, N Austria
Bad Krozingen *73 A6* Baden-Württemberg, SW Germany
Badlands *22 D2 physical region* North Dakota/ South Dakota, N USA
Badu Island *126 C1 island* Queensland, NE Australia
Bad Vöslau *73 E6* Niederösterreich, NE Austria
Baeterrae/Baeterrae Septimanorum *see* Béziers
Baetic Cordillera/Baetic Mountains *see* Béticos, Sistemas
Bafatá *52 C4* C Guinea-Bissau
Baffin Bay *15 G2 bay* Canada/Greenland
Baffin Island *15 G2 island* Nunavut, NE Canada
Bafing *52 C3 river* W Africa
Bafoussam *54 A4* Ouest, W Cameroon
Bafra *94 D2* Samsun, N Turkey
Bāft *98 D4* Kermān, S Iran
Bagaces *30 D4* Guanacaste, NW Costa Rica
Bagdad *see* Baghdād
Bagé *41 E5* Rio Grande do Sul, S Brazil
Baghdād *98 B3 var.* Bagdad, *Eng.* Baghdad. *country capital* Baghdād, C Iraq
Baghdad *see* Baghdād
Baghlān *101 E3* Baghlān, NE Afghanistan
Bago *114 B4 var.* Pegu. Bago, SW Myanmar (Burma)
Bagoé *52 D4 river* Ivory Coast/Mali
Bagrationovsk *84 A4 Ger.* Preussisch Eylau. Kaliningradskaya Oblast', W Russian Federation
Bagrax Hu *see* Bosten Hu
Baguio *117 E1 off.* Baguio City. Luzon, N Philippines
Baguio City *see* Baguio
Bagzane, Monts *53 F3 mountain* N Niger
Bahama Islands *see* Bahamas
Bahamas *32 C2 off.* Commonwealth of the Bahamas. *country* N West Indies
Bahamas *13 D6 var.* Bahama Islands. *island group* N West Indies
Bahamas, Commonwealth of the *see* Bahamas
Baharly *100 C3 var.* Bäherden, *Rus.* Bakharden; *prev.* Bakherden. Ahal Welaýaty, C Turkmenistan
Bahāwalpur *112 C2* Punjab, E Pakistan
Bäherden *see* Baharly
Bahia *41 F3 off.* Estado da Bahia. *region* E Brazil
Bahia *41 F3 off.* Estado da Bahia. *state* E Brazil
Bahía Blanca *43 C5* Buenos Aires, E Argentina
Bahia, Estado da *see* Bahia
Bahir Dar *50 C4 var.* Bahr Dar, Bahrdar Giyorgis. Āmara, N Ethiopia
Bahraich *113 E3* Uttar Pradesh, N India
Bahrain *98 C4 off.* State of Bahrain, Dawlat al Bahrayn, *Ar.* Al Baḩrayn, *prev.* Bahrein; *anc.* Tylos, Tyros. *country* SW Asia
Bahrain, State of *see* Bahrain
Bahrayn, Dawlat al *see* Bahrain
Bahr Dar/Bahrdar Giyorgis *see* Bahir Dar
Bahrein *see* Bahrain
Bahr el, Azraq *see* Blue Nile
Bahr Tabariya, Sea of *see* Tiberias, Lake
Bahushewsk *85 E6 Rus.* Bogushëvsk. Vitsyebskaya Voblasts', NE Belarus
Baia Mare *86 B3 Ger.* Frauenbach, *Hung.* Nagybánya; *prev.* Neustadt. Maramureş, NW Romania
Baia Sprie *86 B3 Ger.* Mittelstadt, *Hung.* Felsőbánya. Maramureş, NW Romania
Baïbokoum *54 B4* Logone-Oriental, SW Chad
Baidoa *see* Baydhabo
Baie-Comeau *17 E3* Québec, SE Canada
Baikal, Lake *93 E4 Eng.* Lake Baikal. *lake* S Russian Federation
Baikal, Lake *see* Baykal, Ozero
Baile Átha Cliath *see* Dublin
Baile Átha Luain *see* Athlone
Bailén *70 D4* Andalucía, S Spain
Baile na Mainistreach *see* Newtownabbey
Băileşti *86 B5* Dolj, SW Romania
Ba Illi *54 B3* Chari-Baguirmi, SW Chad
Bainbridge *20 D3* Georgia, SE USA
Bā'ir *see* Bāyir
Baireuth *see* Bayreuth
Bairiki *122 D2 country capital* Tarawa, NW Kiribati
Bairnsdale *127 C7* Victoria, SE Australia
Baishan *107 E3 prev.* Hunjiang. Jilin, NE China
Baiyin *106 B4* Gansu, C China
Baja *77 C7* Bács-Kiskun, S Hungary
Baja California *28 B2 state* NW Mexico
Bajo Boquete *see* Boquete
Bajram Curri *79 D5* Kukës, N Albania
Bakala *54 C4* Ouaka, C Central African Republic
Bakan *see* Shimonoseki
Baker *24 C3* Oregon, NW USA
Baker and Howland Islands *123 E2 US unincorporated territory* W Polynesia
Baker Lake *15 F3* Nunavut, N Canada
Bakersfield *25 C7* California, W USA
Bakharden *see* Baharly
Bakhchisaray *see* Bakhchysaray
Bakhchysaray *87 F5 Rus.* Bakhchisaray. Respublika Krym, S Ukraine
Bakherden *see* Baharly
Bakhmach *87 F1* Chernihivs'ka Oblast', N Ukraine
Bākhtarān *see* Kermānshāh
Bakı *95 H2 Eng.* Baku. *country capital* E Azerbaijan
Bákó *see* Bacău
Bakony *77 C7 Eng.* Bakony Mountains, *Ger.* Bakonywald. *mountain range* W Hungary
Bakony Mountains/Bakonywald *see* Bakony
Baku *see* Bakı
Bakwanga *see* Mbuji-Mayi
Balabac Island *107 C8 island* W Philippines
Balabac, Selat *see* Balabac Strait
Balabac Strait *116 D2 var.* Selat Balabac. *strait* Malaysia/Philippines
Ba'labakk *see* Baalbek
Balaguer *71 F2* Cataluña, NE Spain
Balakovo *89 C6* Saratovskaya Oblast', W Russian Federation
Bālā Morghāb *100 D4* Laghmān, NW Afghanistan
Balashov *89 B6* Saratovskaya Oblast', W Russian Federation
Balasore *see* Bāleshwar
Balaton, Lake *77 C7 var.* Lake Balaton, *Ger.* Plattensee. *lake* W Hungary
Balaton, Lake *see* Balaton
Balbina, Represa *40 D1 reservoir* NW Brazil
Balboa *31 G4* Panamá, C Panama
Balcarce *43 D5* Buenos Aires, E Argentina
Balclutha *129 B7* Otago, South Island, New Zealand
Baldy Mountain *22 C1 mountain* Montana, NW USA
Bâle *see* Basel
Balearic Plain *see* Algerian Basin
Baleares Major *see* Mallorca
Balearic Islands *71 G3 Eng.* Balearic Islands. *island group* Spain, W Mediterranean Sea
Balearic Islands *see* Baleares, Islas
Balearis Minor *see* Menorca
Baleine, Rivière à la *17 E2 river* Québec, E Canada
Balen *65 C5* Antwerpen, N Belgium
Bāleshwar *113 F4 prev.* Balasore. Orissa, E India
Bälgrad *see* Alba Iulia
Bali *116 D5 island* C Indonesia
Balıkesir *94 A3* Balıkesir, W Turkey

Balīkh, Nahr – Bermeo

Balīkh, Nahr 96 C2 river N Syria
Balikpapan 116 D4 Borneo, C Indonesia
Balkanabat 100 B2 Rus. Nebitdag. Balkan Welaýaty, W Turkmenistan
Balkan Mountains 82 C2 Bul./SCr. Stara Planina. mountain range Bulgaria/Serbia
Balkh 101 E3 anc. Bactra. Balkh, N Afghanistan
Balkhash 92 C5 Kaz. Balqash. Karaganda, SE Kazakhstan
Lake Balkhash 92 C5 Eng. Lake Balkhash, Kaz. Balqash. lake SE Kazakhstan
Balkhash, Lake see Balkhash, Ozero
Balladonia 125 C6 Western Australia
Ballarat 127 C7 Victoria, SE Australia
Balleny Islands 132 B5 island group Antarctica
Ballinger 27 F3 Texas, SW USA
Balochistān see Baluchistān
Balqash see Balkhash/Balkhash, Ozero
Balş 86 B5 Olt, S Romania
Balsas 41 F2 Maranhão, E Brazil
Balsas, Río 29 E5 var. Río Mexcala. river S Mexico
Bal'shavik 85 D7 Rus. Bol'shevik. Homyel'skaya Voblasts', SE Belarus
Balta 86 D3 Odes'ka Oblast', SW Ukraine
Bălţi 86 D3 Rus. Bel'tsy. N Moldova
Baltic Port see Paldiski
Baltic Sea 63 C7 Ger. Ostee, Rus. Baltiskoye More. sea N Europe
Baltimore 19 F4 Maryland, NE USA
Baltischport/Baltiski see Paldiski
Baltiskoye More see Baltic Sea
Baltkrievija see Belarus
Baluchistān 112 B3 var. Balochistān, Beluchistan. province SW Pakistan
Balvi 84 D4 Balvi, NE Latvia
Balykchy 101 G2 Kir. Ysyk-Köl; prev. Issyk-Kul', Rybach'ye. Issyk-Kul'skaya Oblast', NE Kyrgyzstan
Balzers 72 E2 S Liechtenstein
Bam 98 E4 Kermān, SE Iran
Bamako 52 D4 country capital Capital District, SW Mali
Bambari 54 C4 Ouaka, C Central African Republic
Bamberg 73 C5 Bayern, SE Germany
Bamenda 54 A4 Nord-Ouest, W Cameroon
Banaba 122 D2 var. Ocean Island. island Tungaru, W Kiribati
Banaras see Vārānasi
Bandaaceh 116 A3 var. Banda Atjeh; prev. Koetaradja, Kutaradja, Kutaraja. Sumatera, W Indonesia
Banda Atjeh see Bandaaceh
Banda, Laut see Banda Sea
Bandama 52 D5 var. Bandama Fleuve. river S Ivory Coast
Bandama Fleuve see Bandama
Bandar 'Abbās see Bandar-e 'Abbās
Bandarbeyla 51 E5 var. Bender Beila, Bender Beyla. Bari, NE Somalia
Bandar-e 'Abbās 98 D4 var. Bandar 'Abbās; prev. Gombroon. Hormozgān, S Iran
Bandar-e Būshehr 98 C4 var. Būshehr, Eng. Bushire. Būshehr, S Iran
Bandar-e Kangān 98 D4 var. Kangān. Būshehr, S Iran
Bandar-e Khamīr 98 D4 Hormozgān, S Iran
Bandar-e Langeh see Bandar-e Lengeh
Bandar-e Lengeh 98 D4 var. Bandar-e Langeh, Lingeh. Hormozgān, S Iran
Bandar Kassim see Boosaaso
Bandar Lampung 116 C4 var. Bandarlampung, Tanjungkarang-Telukbetung; prev. Tandjoengkarang, Tanjungkarang, Teloekbetoeng, Telukbetung. Sumatera, W Indonesia
Bandarlampung see Bandar Lampung
Bandar Maharani see Muar
Bandar Masulipatnam see Machilipatnam
Bandar Penggaram see Batu Pahat
Bandar Seri Begawan 116 D3 prev. Brunei Town. country capital N Brunei
Banda Sea 117 F5 var. Laut Banda. sea E Indonesia
Bandiagara 53 E3 Mopti, C Mali
Bandırma 94 A3 var. Penderma. Balıkesir, NW Turkey
Bandjarmasin see Banjarmasin
Bandoeng see Bandung
Bandundu 55 C6 prev. Banningville. Bandundu, W Dem. Rep. Congo
Bandung 116 C5 prev. Bandoeng. Jawa, C Indonesia
Bangalore 110 C2 var. Bengalooru. state capital Karnātaka, S India
Bangassou 54 D4 Mbomou, SE Central African Republic
Banggai, Kepulauan 117 E4 island group C Indonesia
Banghāzī 49 G2 Eng. Bengazi, Benghazi, It. Bengasi. NE Libya
Bangka, Pulau 116 C4 island W Indonesia
Bangkok see Krung Thep
Bangkok, Bight of see Krung Thep, Ao
Bangladesh 113 G3 off. People's Republic of Bangladesh; prev. East Pakistan. country S Asia
Bangladesh, People's Republic of see Bangladesh
Bangor 67 C6 NW Wales, United Kingdom
Bangor 67 B5 Ir. Beannchar. E Northern Ireland, United Kingdom
Bangor 19 G2 Maine, NE USA
Bang Pla Soi see Chon Buri
Bangui 55 B5 country capital Ombella-Mpoko, SW Central African Republic
Bangweulu, Lake 51 B8 var. Lake Bengweulu. lake N Zambia
Ban Hat Yai see Hat Yai
Ban Hin Heup 114 C4 Viangchan, C Laos
Ban Houayxay/Ban Houei Sai see Houayxay
Ban Hua Hin 115 C6 var. Hua Hin. Prachuap Khiri Khan, SW Thailand
Bani 52 D3 river S Mali
Banias see Bāniyās
Banijska Palanka see Glina
Banī Suwayf 50 B2 var. Beni Suef. N Egypt
Bāniyās 96 B3 var. Banias, Baniyas, Paneas. Tarṭūs, W Syria
Banjak, Kepulauan see Banyak, Kepulauan
Banja Luka 78 B3 Republika Srpska, NW Bosnia and Herzegovina
Banjarmasin 116 D4 prev. Bandjarmasin. Borneo, C Indonesia
Banjul 52 B3 prev. Bathurst. country capital W Gambia
Banks, Îles see Banks Islands
Banks Island 15 E2 island Northwest Territories, NW Canada
Banks Islands 122 D4 Fr. Îles Banks. island group N Vanuatu
Banks Lake 24 B1 reservoir Washington, NW USA
Banks Peninsula 129 C6 peninsula South Island, New Zealand
Banks Strait 127 C8 strait SW Tasman Sea
Bānkura 113 F4 West Bengal, NE India
Ban Mak Khaeng see Udon Thani
Banmo see Bhamo
Banningville see Bandundu
Bañolas see Banyoles
Ban Pak Phanang see Pak Phanang
Ban Sichon see Sichon
Banská Bystrica 77 C6 Ger. Neusohl, Hung. Besztercebánya. Banskobystricky Kraj, C Slovakia
Bantry Bay 67 A7 Ir. Bá Bheanntraí. bay SW Ireland
Banya 82 E2 Burgas, E Bulgaria
Banyak, Kepulauan 116 A3 prev. Kepulauan Banjak. island group NW Indonesia
Banyo 54 B4 Adamaoua, NW Cameroon
Banyoles 71 G2 var. Bañolas. Cataluña, NE Spain
Banzare Seamounts 119 C7 seamount range S Indian Ocean
Banzart see Bizerte
Baoji 106 B4 var. Pao-chi, Paoki. Shaanxi, C China
Baoro 54 B4 Nana-Mambéré, W Central African Republic
Baoshan 106 A6 var. Pao-shan. Yunnan, SW China
Baotou 105 F3 var. Pao-t'ou, Paotow. Nei Mongol Zizhiqu, N China
Ba'qūbah 98 B3 var. Qubba. Diyālá, C Iraq
Baquerizo Moreno see Puerto Baquerizo Moreno
Bar 79 C5 It. Antivari. S Montenegro
Baraawe 51 D6 It. Brava. Shabeellaha Hoose, S Somalia
Bārāmati 112 C5 Mahārāshtra, W India
Baranavichy 85 B6 Pol. Baranowicze, Rus. Baranovichi. Brestskaya Voblasts', SW Belarus
Baranovichi/Baranowicze see Baranavichy
Barbados 33 G1 country SE West Indies
Barbastro 71 F2 Aragón, NE Spain
Barbate de Franco 70 C5 Andalucía, S Spain
Barbuda 33 G3 island N Antigua and Barbuda
Barcaldine 126 C4 Queensland, E Australia
Barcarozsnyó see Râşnov
Barcău see Berettyó
Barce see Al Marj
Barcelona 71 G2 anc. Barcino, Barcinona. Cataluña, E Spain
Barcelona 37 E2 Anzoátegui, NE Venezuela
Barcino/Barcinona see Barcelona
Barcoo see Cooper Creek
Barcs 77 C7 Somogy, SW Hungary
Bardaï 54 C1 Borkou-Ennedi-Tibesti, N Chad
Bardejov 77 D5 Ger. Bartfeld, Hung. Bártfa. Presovský Kraj, E Slovakia
Bardera/Bardere see Baardheere
Barduli see Barletta
Bareilly 113 E3 var. Bareli. Uttar Pradesh, N India
Bareli see Bareilly
Barendrecht 64 C4 Zuid-Holland, SW Netherlands
Barentin 68 C3 Seine-Maritime, N France
Barentsburg 61 G2 Spitsbergen, W Svalbard
Barentsevo More/Barents Havet see Barents Sea
Barentsøya 61 G2 island E Svalbard
Barents Sea 88 C2 Nor. Barents Havet, Rus. Barentsevo More. sea Arctic Ocean
Bar Harbor 19 H2 Mount Desert Island, Maine, NE USA
Bari 75 E5 var. Bari delle Puglie; anc. Barium. Puglia, SE Italy
Bāridah see Al Bāridah
Bari delle Puglie see Bari
Barikot see Barīkowṭ
Barīkowṭ 101 F4 var. Barikot. Konar, NE Afghanistan
Barillas 30 A2 var. Santa Cruz Barillas. Huehuetenango, NW Guatemala
Barinas 36 C2 Barinas, W Venezuela
Barisal 113 G4 Barisal, S Bangladesh
Barisan, Pegunungan 116 B4 mountain range Sumatera, W Indonesia
Barito, Sungai 116 D4 river Borneo, C Indonesia
Barium see Bari
Barka see Al Marj
Barkly Tableland 126 B3 plateau Northern Territory/Queensland, N Australia
Bârlad 86 D4 prev. Bîrlad. Vaslui, E Romania
Barlavento, Ilhas de 52 A2 var. Windward Islands. island group N Cape Verde
Bar-le-Duc 68 D3 var. Bar-sur-Ornain. Meuse, NE France
Barlee, Lake 125 B6 lake Western Australia
Barlee Range 124 A4 mountain range Western Australia
Barletta 75 D5 anc. Barduli. Puglia, SE Italy
Barlinek 76 B3 Ger. Berlinchen. Zachodnio-pomorskie, NW Poland
Barmen-Elberfeld see Wuppertal
Barmouth 67 C6 NW Wales, United Kingdom
Barnaul 92 D4 Altayskiy Kray, C Russian Federation
Barnet 67 A7 United Kingdom
Barnstaple 67 C7 SW England, United Kingdom
Baroda see Vadodara
Baroghil Pass 101 F3 var. Kowtal-e Barowghīl. pass Afghanistan/Pakistan
Baron'ki 85 E7 Rus. Boron'ki. Mahilyowskaya Voblasts', E Belarus
Barowghīl, Kowtal-e see Baroghil Pass
Barquisimeto 36 C2 Lara, NW Venezuela
Barra 66 B3 island NW Scotland, United Kingdom
Barra de Río Grande 31 E3 Región Autónoma Atlántico Sur, E Nicaragua
Barranca 38 C3 Lima, W Peru
Barrancabermeja 36 B2 Santander, N Colombia
Barranquilla 36 B1 Atlántico, N Colombia
Barreiro 70 B4 Setúbal, W Portugal
Barrier Range 127 C6 hill range New South Wales, SE Australia
Barrow 14 D2 Alaska, USA
Barrow 67 B6 Ir. An Bhearú. river SE Ireland
Barrow-in-Furness 67 C5 NW England, United Kingdom
Barrow Island 124 A4 island Western Australia
Barstow 25 C7 California, W USA
Bar-sur-Ornain see Bar-le-Duc
Bartang 101 F3 river SE Tajikistan
Bartenstein see Bartoszyce
Bártfa/Bartfeld see Bardejov
Bartica 37 F3 N Guyana
Bartın 94 C2 Bartın, NW Turkey
Bartlesville 27 G1 Oklahoma, C USA
Bartoszyce 76 D2 Ger. Bartenstein. Warmińsko-mazurskie, NE Poland
Baruun-Urt 105 F2 Sühbaatar, E Mongolia
Barú, Volcán 31 E5 var. Volcán de Chiriquí. volcano W Panama
Barwon River 127 D5 river New South Wales, SE Australia
Barysaw 85 D6 Rus. Borisov. Minskaya Voblasts', NE Belarus
Basarabeasca 86 D4 Rus. Bessarabka. SE Moldova
Basel 73 A7 Eng. Basle, Fr. Bâle. Basel-Stadt, NW Switzerland
Basilan 117 E3 island Mindanao, SW Philippines Asia Celebes Sea/Sulu Sea Pacific Ocean
Basle see Basel
Basra see Al Başrah
Bassano del Grappa 74 C2 Veneto, NE Italy
Bassein see Pathein
Basseterre 33 G4 country capital Saint Kitts, Saint Kitts and Nevis
Basse-Terre 33 G3 dependent territory capital Basse Terre, SW Guadeloupe
Basse Terre 33 G4 island W Guadeloupe
Bassikounou 52 D3 Hodh ech Chargui, SE Mauritania
Bass, Îlots de see Marotiri
Bass Strait 127 C7 strait SE Australia
Bassum 72 B3 Niedersachsen, NW Germany
Bastia 69 E7 Corse, France, C Mediterranean Sea
Bastogne 65 D7 Luxembourg, SE Belgium
Bastrop 20 B2 Louisiana, S USA
Bastyn' 85 B7 Rus. Bostyn'. Brestskaya Voblasts', SW Belarus
Basuo see Dongfang
Basutoland see Lesotho
Bata 55 A5 NW Equatorial Guinea
Batae Coritanorum see Leicester
Batajnica 78 D3 Vojvodina, N Serbia
Batangas 117 E2 off. Batangas City. Luzon, N Philippines
Batangas City see Batangas
Batavia see Jakarta
Bătdâmbâng 115 C5 prev. Battambang. Bătdâmbâng, NW Cambodia
Batéké, Plateaux 55 B6 plateau S Congo
Bath 67 D7 hist. Akermanceaster; anc. Aquae Calidae, Aquae Solis. SW England, United Kingdom
Bathinda 112 D2 Punjab, NW India
Bathsheba 33 G1 E Barbados
Bathurst 127 D6 New South Wales, SE Australia
Bathurst 17 F4 New Brunswick, SE Canada
Bathurst see Banjul
Bathurst Island 124 D2 island Northern Territory, N Australia
Bathurst Island 15 F2 island Parry Islands, Nunavut, N Canada
Wadi al Batin 98 C4 dry watercourse SW Asia
Batman 95 E4 var. Iluh. Batman, SE Turkey
Batna 49 E2 NE Algeria
Baton Rouge 20 B3 state capital Louisiana, S USA
Batroûn 96 A4 var. Al Batrūn. N Lebanon
Battambang see Bătdâmbâng
Batticaloa 110 D3 Eastern Province, E Sri Lanka
Battipaglia 75 D5 Campania, S Italy
Battle Born State see Nevada
Bat'umi 95 F2 W Georgia
Batu Pahat 116 B3 prev. Bandar Penggaram. Johor, Peninsular Malaysia
Bauchi 53 G4 Bauchi, NE Nigeria
Bauer Basin 131 F3 undersea basin E Pacific Ocean
Bauska 84 C3 Ger. Bauske. Bauska, S Latvia
Bauske see Bauska
Bautzen 72 D4 Lus. Budyšin. Sachsen, E Germany
Bauzanum see Bolzano
Bavaria see Bayern
Bavarian Alps 73 C7 Ger. Bayrische Alpen. mountain range Austria/Germany
Bavière see Bayern
Bavispe, Río 28 C2 river NW Mexico
Bawīṭī 50 B2 var. Bawīṭi. N Egypt
Bawīṭi see Bawīṭī
Bawku 53 E4 N Ghana
Bayamo 32 C3 Granma, E Cuba
Bayan Har Shan 104 D4 var. Bayan Khar. mountain range C China
Bayanhongor 104 D2 Bayanhongor, C Mongolia
Bayan Khar see Bayan Har Shan
Bayano, Lago 31 G4 lake E Panama
Bay City 18 C3 Michigan, N USA
Bay City 27 G4 Texas, SW USA
Baydhabo 51 D6 var. Baydhowa, Isha Baydhabo, It. Baidoa. Bay, SW Somalia
Baydhowa see Baydhabo
Bayern 73 C6 Eng. Bavaria, Fr. Bavière. state SE Germany
Bayeux 68 B3 anc. Augustodurum. Calvados, N France
Bāyir 97 C7 var. Bā'ir. Ma'ān, S Jordan
Bay Islands 30 C1 Eng. Bay Islands. island group N Honduras
Bay Islands see Bahía, Islas de la
Baymak 89 D6 Respublika Bashkortostan, W Russian Federation
Bayonne 69 A6 anc. Lapurdum. Pyrénées-Atlantiques, SW France
Bayou State see Mississippi
Bayram-Ali see Baýramaly
Baýramaly 100 D3 var. Bayramaly; prev. Bayram-Ali. Mary Welaýaty, S Turkmenistan
Bayreuth 73 C5 var. Baireuth. Bayern, SE Germany
Bayrische Alpen see Bavarian Alps
Bayrūt see Beyrouth
Bay State see Massachusetts
Baysun see Boysun
Bayt Laḥm see Bethlehem
Baytown 27 H4 Texas, SW USA
Baza 71 E4 Andalucía, S Spain
Bazargic see Dobrich
Bazin see Pezinok
Beagle Channel 43 C8 channel Argentina/Chile
Béal Feirste see Belfast
Beannchar see Bangor, Northern Ireland, UK
Bear Island see Bjørnøya
Bear Lake 24 E4 lake Idaho/Utah, NW USA
Beas de Segura 71 E4 Andalucía, S Spain
Beata, Isla 33 E3 island SW Dominican Republic
Beatrice 23 F4 Nebraska, C USA
Beaufort Sea 14 D2 sea Arctic Ocean
Beaufort-Wes see Beaufort West
Beaufort West 56 C5 Afr. Beaufort-Wes. Western Cape, SW South Africa
Beaumont 27 H3 Texas, SW USA
Beaune 68 D4 Côte d'Or, C France
Beauvais 68 C3 anc. Bellovacum, Caesaromagus. Oise, N France
Beaver Island 18 C2 island Michigan, N USA
Beaver Lake 27 H1 reservoir Arkansas, C USA
Beaver River 27 F1 river Oklahoma, C USA
Beaver State see Oregon
Beāwar 112 C3 Rājasthān, N India
Bečej 78 D3 Ger. Altbetsche, Hung. Óbecse, Rácz-Becse; prev. Magyar-Becse, Stari Bečej. Vojvodina, N Serbia
Béchar 48 D2 prev. Colomb-Béchar. W Algeria
Beckley 18 D5 West Virginia, NE USA
Bécs see Wien
Bedford 67 D6 E England, United Kingdom
Bedum 64 E1 Groningen, NE Netherlands
Beehive State see Utah
Be'er Menuha 97 B7 prev. Be'ér Menuḥa. Southern, S Israel
Be'ér Menuḥa see Be'er Menuha
Beernem 65 A5 West-Vlaanderen, NW Belgium
Beersheba see Be'er Sheva
Be'er Sheva 97 A7 var. Beersheba, Ar. Bir es Saba; prev. Be'ér Sheva'. Southern, S Israel
Be'ér Sheva' see Be'er Sheva
Beesel 65 D5 Limburg, SE Netherlands
Beeville 27 G4 Texas, SW USA
Bega 127 D7 New South Wales, SE Australia
Begoml' see Byahoml'
Begovat see Bekobod
Behagle see Laï
Behar see Bihār
Beibu Wan see Tongking, Gulf of
Beida see Al Bayḍā'
Beihai 106 B6 Guangxi Zhuangzu Zizhiqu, S China
Beijing 106 C3 var. Pei-ching, Eng. Peking; prev. Pei-p'ing. country capital Beijing Shi, E China
Beilen 64 E2 Drenthe, NE Netherlands
Beira 57 E3 Sofala, C Mozambique
Beirut see Beyrouth
Beiuş 86 B3 Hung. Belényes. Bihor, NW Romania
Beja 70 B4 anc. Pax Julia. Beja, SE Portugal
Béjar 70 C3 Castilla-León, N Spain
Bejraburi see Phetchaburi
Bekabad see Bekobod
Békás see Bicaz
Bek-Budi see Qarshi
Békéscsaba 77 D7 Rom. Bichiş-Ciaba. Békés, SE Hungary
Bekobod 101 E2 Rus. Bekabad; prev. Begovat. Toshkent Viloyati, E Uzbekistan
Bela Crkva 78 E3 Ger. Weisskirchen, Hung. Fehértemplom. Vojvodina, W Serbia
Belarus 85 B6 off. Republic of Belarus, var. Belorussia, Latv. Baltkrievija; prev. Belorussian SSR, Rus. Belorusskaya SSR. country E Europe
Belarus, Republic of see Belarus
Belau see Palau
Belaya Tserkov' see Bila Tserkva
Bełchatów 76 C4 var. Belchatow. Łódzski, C Poland
Belchatow see Bełchatów
Belcher, Îles see Belcher Islands
Belcher Islands 16 C2 Fr. Îles Belcher. island group Nunavut, SE Canada
Beledweyne 51 D5 var. Belet Huen, It. Belet Uen. Hiiraan, C Somalia
Belém 41 F1 var. Pará. state capital Pará, N Brazil
Belén 30 D4 Rivas, SW Nicaragua
Belen 26 D2 New Mexico, SW USA
Belényes see Beiuş
Belet Huen/Belet Uen see Beledweyne
Belfast 67 B5 Ir. Béal Feirste. national capital E Northern Ireland, United Kingdom
Belfield 22 D2 North Dakota, N USA
Belfort 68 E4 Territoire-de-Belfort, E France
Belgard see Białogard
Belgaum 110 B1 Karnātaka, W India
Belgian Congo see Congo (Democratic Republic of)
België/Belgique see Belgium
Belgium 65 B6 off. Kingdom of Belgium, Dut. België, Fr. Belgique. country NW Europe
Belgium, Kingdom of see Belgium
Belgorod 89 A6 Belgorodskaya Oblast', W Russian Federation
Belgrano II 132 A2 Argentinian research station Antarctica
Belice see Belize/Belize City
Beligrad see Berat
Beli Manastir 78 C3 Hung. Pélmonostor; prev. Monostor. Osijek-Baranja, NE Croatia
Bélinga 55 B5 Ogooué-Ivindo, NE Gabon
Belitung, Pulau 116 C4 island W Indonesia
Belize 30 B1 Sp. Belice; prev. British Honduras, Colony of Belize. country Central America
Belize 30 B1 river Belize/Guatemala
Belize see Belize City
Belize City 30 C1 var. Belize, Sp. Belice. Belize, NE Belize
Belize, Colony of see Belize
Beljak see Villach
Belkofski 14 B3 Alaska, USA
Belle Île 68 A4 island NW France
Belle Isle, Strait of 17 G3 strait Newfoundland and Labrador, E Canada
Bellenz see Bellinzona
Belleville 18 B4 Illinois, N USA
Bellevue 23 F4 Iowa, C USA
Bellevue 24 B2 Washington, NW USA
Bellingham 24 B1 Washington, NW USA
Belling Hausen Mulde see Southeast Pacific Basin
Bellingshausen Abyssal Plain see Bellingshausen Plain
Bellingshausen Plain 131 F5 var. Bellingshausen Abyssal Plain. abyssal plain SE Pacific Ocean
Bellingshausen Sea 132 A3 sea Antarctica
Bellinzona 73 B8 Ger. Bellenz. Ticino, S Switzerland
Bello 36 B2 Antioquia, W Colombia
Bello Horizonte see Belo Horizonte
Bellovacum see Beauvais
Bellville 56 B5 Western Cape, SW South Africa
Belmopan 30 C1 country capital Cayo, C Belize
Belogradchik 82 B1 Vidin, NW Bulgaria
Belo Horizonte 41 F4 prev. Bello Horizonte. state capital Minas Gerais, SE Brazil
Belomorsk 88 B3 Respublika Kareliya, NW Russian Federation
Beloretsk 89 D6 Respublika Bashkortostan, W Russian Federation
Belorussia/Belorussian SSR see Belarus
Belorusskaya Gryada see Byelaruskaya Hrada
Belorusskaya SSR see Belarus
Beloshchel'ye see Nar'yan-Mar
Belostok see Białystok
Belovár see Bjelovar
Belozërsk 88 B4 Vologodskaya Oblast', NW Russian Federation
Belton 27 G3 Texas, SW USA
Bel'tsy see Bălţi
Beluchistan see Baluchistān
Belukha, Gora 92 D5 mountain Kazakhstan/Russian Federation
Belynichi see Byalynichy
Belyy, Ostrov 92 D2 island N Russian Federation
Bemaraha 57 F3 var. Plateau du Bemaraha. mountain range W Madagascar
Bemaraha, Plateau du see Bemaraha
Bemidji 23 F1 Minnesota, N USA
Bemmel 64 D4 Gelderland, SE Netherlands
Benaco see Garda, Lago di
Benares see Vārānasi
Benavente 70 D2 Castilla-León, N Spain
Bend 24 B3 Oregon, NW USA
Bender see Tighina
Bender Beila/Bender Beyla see Bandarbeyla
Bender Cassim/Bender Qaasim see Boosaaso
Bendern 72 E1 NW Liechtenstein Europe
Bendery see Tighina
Bendigo 127 C7 Victoria, SE Australia
Beneschau see Benešov
Beneški Zaliv see Venice, Gulf of
Benešov 77 B5 Ger. Beneschau. Středočeský Kraj, W Czech Republic
Benevento 75 D5 anc. Beneventum, Malventum. Campania, S Italy
Beneventum see Benevento
Bengal, Bay of 102 C4 bay N Indian Ocean
Bengalooru see Bangalore
Bengasi see Banghāzī
Bengazi see Banghāzī
Bengbu 106 D5 var. Peng-pu. Anhui, E China
Benghazi see Banghāzī
Bengkulu 116 B4 prev. Bengkoeloe, Benkoelen, Benkulen. Sumatera, W Indonesia
Benguela 56 A2 var. Benguella. Benguela, W Angola
Benguella see Benguela
Bengweulu, Lake see Bangweulu, Lake
Ben Hope 66 B2 mountain N Scotland, United Kingdom
Beni 55 E5 Nord-Kivu, NE Dem. Rep. Congo
Benidorm 71 F4 País Valenciano, SE Spain
Beni-Mellal 48 C2 C Morocco
Benin 53 F4 off. Republic of Benin; prev. Dahomey. country W Africa
Benin, Bight of 53 F5 gulf W Africa
Benin City 53 F5 Edo, SW Nigeria
Benin, Republic of see Benin
Beni, Río 39 E3 river N Bolivia
Beni Suef see Banī Suwayf
Ben Nevis 66 C3 mountain N Scotland, United Kingdom
Bénoué see Benue
Benson 26 B3 Arizona, SW USA
Bent Jbaïl 97 A5 var. Bint Jubayl. S Lebanon
Benton 20 B1 Arkansas, C USA
Benue 54 B4 Fr. Bénoué. river Cameroon/Nigeria
Beograd 78 D3 Eng. Belgrade. Serbia, N Serbia
Berane 79 D5 prev. Ivangrad. E Montenegro
Berat 79 C6 var. Berati, SCr. Beligrad. Berat, C Albania
Berătău see Berettyó
Berati see Berat
Berau, Teluk 117 G4 var. MacCluer Gulf. bay Papua, E Indonesia
Berbera 50 D4 Sahil, NW Somalia
Berbérati 55 B5 Mambéré-Kadéï, SW Central African Republic
Berck-Plage 68 C2 Pas-de-Calais, N France
Berdichev see Berdychiv
Berdyans'k 87 G4 Rus. Berdyansk; prev. Osipenko. Zaporiz'ka Oblast', SE Ukraine
Berdychiv 86 D2 Rus. Berdichev. Zhytomyrs'ka Oblast', N Ukraine
Beregovo/Beregszász see Berehove
Berehove 86 B3 Cz. Berehovo, Hung. Beregszász, Rus. Beregovo. Zakarpats'ka Oblast', W Ukraine
Berehovo see Berehove
Bereket 100 B2 prev. Rus. Gazandzhyk, Kazandzhik, Turkm. Gazanjyk. Balkan Welaýaty, W Turkmenistan
Beretău see Berettyó
Berettyó 77 D7 Rom. Barcău; prev. Berătău, Beretău. river Hungary/Romania
Berettyóújfalu 77 D6 Hajdú-Bihar, E Hungary
Berezhany 86 C2 Pol. Brzeżany. Ternopil's'ka Oblast', W Ukraine
Berezina see Byerezino
Berezniki 89 D5 Permskaya Oblast', NW Russian Federation
Berga 71 G2 Cataluña, NE Spain
Bergamo 74 B2 anc. Bergomum. Lombardia, N Italy
Bergara 71 E1 País Vasco, N Spain
Bergen 72 D2 Mecklenburg-Vorpommern, NE Germany
Bergen 64 C2 Noord-Holland, NW Netherlands
Bergen 63 A5 Hordaland, S Norway
Bergen see Mons
Bergerac 69 B5 Dordogne, SW France
Bergeyk 65 C5 Noord-Brabant, S Netherlands
Bergomum see Bergamo
Bergse Maas 64 D4 river S Netherlands
Beringen 65 C5 Limburg, NE Belgium
Beringov Proliv see Bering Strait
Bering Sea 14 A2 sea N Pacific Ocean
Bering Strait 14 C2 Rus. Beringov Proliv. strait Bering Sea/Chukchi Sea
Berja 71 E5 Andalucía, S Spain
Berkeley 25 B6 California, W USA
Berkner Island 132 A2 island Antarctica
Berkovitsa 82 C2 Montana, NW Bulgaria
Berlin 72 D3 country capital Berlin, NE Germany
Berlin 19 G2 New Hampshire, NE USA
Berlinchen see Barlinek
Bermejo, Río 42 C2 river N Argentina
Bermeo 71 E1 País Vasco, N Spain

Bermuda – Bravo, Río

Bermuda 13 D6 var. Bermuda Islands, Bermudas; prev. Somers Islands. UK crown colony NW Atlantic Ocean
Bermuda Islands see Bermuda
Bermuda Rise 13 E6 undersea rise C Sargasso Sea
Bermudas see Bermuda
Bern 73 A7 Fr. Berne. country capital Bern, W Switzerland
Bernau 72 D3 Brandenburg, NE Germany
Bernburg 72 C4 Sachsen-Anhalt, C Germany
Berne see Bern
Berner Alpen 73 A7 var. Berner Oberland, Eng. Bernese Oberland. mountain range SW Switzerland
Berner Oberland/Bernese Oberland see Berner Alpen
Bernier Island 125 A5 island Western Australia
Beroea see Ḩalab
Berry 68 C4 cultural region C France
Berry Islands 32 C1 island group N Bahamas
Bertoua 55 B5 Est, E Cameroon
Beru 123 E2 var. Peru. atoll Tungaru, W Kiribati
Berwick-upon-Tweed 66 D4 N England, United Kingdom
Berytus see Beyrouth
Besançon 68 D4 anc. Besontium, Vesontio. Doubs, E France
Beskra see Biskra
Besontium see Besançon
Bessarabka see Basarabeasca
Beszterce see Bistriţa
Besztercebánya see Banská Bystrica
Betafo 57 G3 Antananarivo, C Madagascar
Betanzos 70 B1 Galicia, NW Spain
Bethlehem 56 D4 Free State, C South Africa
Bethlehem 97 B6 Ar. Bayt Laḩm, Heb. Bet Leḥem. C West Bank
Béticos, Sistemas 70 D4 var. Sistema Penibético, Eng. Baetic Cordillera, Baetic Mountains. mountain range S Spain
Bet Leḥem see Bethlehem
Bétou 55 C5 Likouala, N Congo
Bette, Picco 49 G4 var. Bikkū Bittī, It. Picco Bette. mountain S Libya
Bette, Picco see Bette, Picco
Beulah 18 C2 Michigan, N USA
Beuthen see Bytom
Beveren 65 B5 Oost-Vlaanderen, N Belgium
Beverley 67 D5 E England, United Kingdom
Bexley 67 B8 Bexley, SE England, United Kingdom
Beyla 52 D4 SE Guinea
Beyrouth 96 A4 var. Bayrūt, Eng. Beirut; anc. Berytus. country capital W Lebanon
Beyşehir 94 B4 Konya, SW Turkey
Beyşehir Gölü 94 B4 lake C Turkey
Béziers 69 C6 anc. Baeterrae, Baeterrae Septimanorum, Julia Beterrae. Hérault, S France
Bezmein see Abadan
Bezwada see Vijayawāda
Bhadrāvati 110 C2 Karnātaka, SW India
Bhāgalpur 113 F3 Bihār, NE India
Bhaktapur 113 F3 Central, C Nepal
Bhamo 114 B2 var. Banmo. Kachin State, N Myanmar (Burma)
Bhārat see India
Bharūch 112 C4 Gujarāt, W India
Bhaunagar see Bhāvnagar
Bhāvnagar 112 C4 prev. Bhaunagar. Gujarāt, W India
Bheanntraí, Bá see Bantry Bay
Bhopāl 112 D4 state capital Madhya Pradesh, C India
Bhubaneshwar 113 F5 prev. Bhubaneswar, Bhuvaneshwar. state capital Orissa, E India
Bhubaneswar see Bhubaneshwar
Bhuket see Phuket
Bhusaval see Bhusāwal
Bhusāwal 112 D4 prev. Bhusaval. Mahārāshtra, C India
Bhutan 113 G3 off. Kingdom of Bhutan, var. Druk-yul. country S Asia
Bhutan, Kingdom of see Bhutan
Bhuvaneshwar see Bhubaneshwar
Biak, Pulau 117 G4 island E Indonesia
Biała Podlaska 76 E3 Lubelskie, E Poland
Białogard 76 B2 Ger. Belgard. Zachodnio-pomorskie, NW Poland
Białystok 76 E3 Rus. Belostok, Bielostok. Podlaskie, NE Poland
Bianco, Monte see Blanc, Mont
Biarritz 69 A6 Pyrénées-Atlantiques, SW France
Bicaz 86 C3 Hung. Békás. Neamţ, NE Romania
Bichiş-Ciaba see Békéscsaba
Biddeford 19 G2 Maine, NE USA
Bideford 67 C7 SW England, United Kingdom
Biel 73 A7 Fr. Bienne. Bern, W Switzerland
Bielefeld 72 B4 Nordrhein-Westfalen, NW Germany
Bielitz/Bielitz-Biala see Bielsko-Biała
Bielostok see Białystok
Bielsko-Biała 77 C5 Ger. Bielitz, Bielitz-Biala. Śląskie, S Poland
Bielsk Podlaski 76 E3 Białystok, E Poland
Bien Bien see Điện Biên
Biên Đông see South China Sea
Biên Hoa 115 E6 Đông Nai, S Vietnam
Bienne see Biel
Bienville, Lac 16 D2 lake Québec, C Canada
Bié Plateau 56 B2 var. Bié Plateau. plateau C Angola
Bié Plateau see Bié, Planalto do
Big Cypress Swamp 21 E5 wetland Florida, SE USA
Bigge Island 124 C2 island Western Australia
Bighorn Mountains 22 C2 mountain range Wyoming, C USA
Bighorn River 22 C2 river Montana/Wyoming, NW USA
Bignona 52 B3 SW Senegal
Bigorra see Tarbes
Bigosovo see Bihosava
Big Sioux River 23 E2 river Iowa/South Dakota, N USA
Big Spring 27 E3 Texas, SW USA
Bihać 78 B3 Federacija Bosna I Hercegovina, NW Bosnia and Herzegovina
Bihār 113 F3 prev. Behar. cultural region N India
Bihār see Bihār Sharīf
Biharamulo 51 B7 Kagera, NW Tanzania
Bihār Sharīf 113 F3 var. Bihār. Bihār, N India
Bihosava 85 D5 Rus. Bigosovo. Vitsyebskaya Voblasts', NW Belarus
Bijeljina 78 C3 Republika Srpska, NE Bosnia and Herzegovina
Bijelo Polje 79 D5 E Montenegro
Bikāner 112 C3 Rājasthān, NW India
Bikin 93 G4 Khabarovskiy Kray, SE Russian Federation
Bikini Atoll 122 C1 var. Pikinni. atoll Ralik Chain, NW Marshall Islands
Bikkū Bittī see Bette, Picco
Bilāspur 113 E4 Chhattīsgarh, C India
Biläsuvar 95 H3 Rus. Bilyasuvar; prev. Pushkino. SE Azerbaijan
Bila Tserkva 87 E2 Rus. Belaya Tserkov'. Kyyivs'ka Oblast', N Ukraine
Bilauktaung Range 115 C6 var. Thanintari Taungdan. mountain range Myanmar (Burma)/ Thailand
Bilbao 71 E1 Basq. Bilbo. País Vasco, N Spain
Bilbo see Bilbao
Bilecik 94 B3 Bilecik, NW Turkey
Billings 22 C2 Montana, NW USA
Bilma, Grand Erg de 53 H3 desert NE Niger
Biloela 126 D4 Queensland, E Australia
Biloxi 20 C3 Mississippi, S USA
Biltine 54 C3 Biltine, E Chad
Bilwi see Puerto Cabezas
Bilyasuvar see Biläsuvar
Bilzen 65 D6 Limburg, NE Belgium
Bimini Islands 32 C1 island group W Bahamas
Binche 65 B7 Hainaut, S Belgium
Bindloe Island see Marchena, Isla
Bin Ghalfān, Jazā'ir see Ḩalāniyāt, Juzur al
Binghamton 19 F3 New York, NE USA
Bingöl 95 E3 Bingöl, E Turkey
Bint Jubayl see Bent Jbaïl
Bintulu 116 D3 Sarawak, East Malaysia
Binzhou 106 D4 Shandong, E China
Bío Bío, Río 43 B5 river C Chile
Bioco, Isla de 55 A5 var. Bioko, Eng. Fernando Po, Sp. Fernando Póo; prev. Macías Nguema Biyogo. island NW Equatorial Guinea
Bioko see Bioco, Isla de
Birāk 49 F3 var. Brak. C Libya
Birao 54 D3 Vakaga, NE Central African Republic
Birātnagar 113 F3 Eastern, SE Nepal
Bir es Saba see Be'er Sheva
Bīrjand 98 E3 Khorāsān-e Janūbī, E Iran
Birkenfeld 73 A5 Rheinland-Pfalz, SW Germany
Birkenhead 67 C5 NW England, United Kingdom
Bîrlad see Bârlad
Birmingham 67 C6 C England, United Kingdom
Birmingham 20 C2 Alabama, S USA
Bir Moghrein see Bîr Mogreïn
Bîr Mogreïn 52 C1 var. Bir Moghrein; prev. Fort-Trinquet. Tiris Zemmour, N Mauritania
Birnie Island 123 E3 atoll Phoenix Islands, C Kiribati
Birnin Konni 53 F3 var. Birni-Nkonni. Tahoua, SW Niger
Birni-Nkonni see Birnin Konni
Birobidzhan 93 G4 Yevreyskaya Avtonomnaya Oblast', SE Russian Federation
Birsen see Biržai
Birsk 89 D5 Respublika Bashkortostan, W Russian Federation
Biržai 84 C4 Ger. Birsen. Panevėžys, NE Lithuania
Birżebbuġa 80 B5 SE Malta
Bisanthe see Tekirdağ
Bisbee 26 B3 Arizona, SW USA
Biscaia, Baía de see Biscay, Bay of
Biscay, Bay of 58 B4 Sp. Golfo de Vizcaya, Port. Baía de Biscaia. bay France/Spain
Biscay Plain 58 B3 abyssal plain SE Bay of Biscay
Bischofsburg see Biskupiec
Bishah, Wadi 99 B5 dry watercourse C Saudi Arabia
Bishkek 101 G2 var. Pishpek; prev. Frunze. country capital Chuyskaya Oblast', N Kyrgyzstan
Bishop's Lynn see King's Lynn
Bishri, Jabal 96 D3 mountain range E Syria
Biskara see Biskra
Biskra 49 E2 var. Beskra, Biskara. NE Algeria
Biskupiec 76 D2 Ger. Bischofsburg. Warmińsko-Mazurskie, NE Poland
Bislig 117 F2 Mindanao, S Philippines
Bismarck 23 E2 state capital North Dakota, N USA
Bismarck Archipelago 122 B3 island group NE Papua New Guinea
Bismarck Sea 122 B3 sea W Pacific Ocean
Bisnulok see Phitsanulok
Bissau 52 B4 country capital W Guinea-Bissau
Bistriţa 86 B3 Ger. Bistritz, Hung. Beszterce; prev. Nösen. Bistriţa-Năsăud, N Romania
Bistritz see Bistriţa
Bitam 55 B5 Woleu-Ntem, N Gabon
Bitburg 73 A5 Rheinland-Pfalz, SW Germany
Bitlis 95 F3 Bitlis, SE Turkey
Bitoeng see Bitung
Bitola 79 D6 Turk. Monastir; prev. Bitolj. S FYR Macedonia
Bitolj see Bitola
Bitonto 75 D5 anc. Butuntum. Puglia, SE Italy
Bitterroot Range 24 D2 mountain range Idaho/ Montana, NW USA
Bitung 117 F3 prev. Bitoeng. Sulawesi, C Indonesia
Biu 53 H4 Borno, E Nigeria
Biwa-ko 109 C6 lake Honshū, SW Japan
Bizerta see Bizerte
Bizerte 49 E1 Ar. Banzart, Eng. Bizerta. N Tunisia
Bjelovar 78 B2 Hung. Belovár. Bjelovar-Bilogora, N Croatia
Bjeshkët e Namuna see North Albanian Alps
Björneborg see Pori
Bjørnøya 61 F3 Eng. Bear Island. island N Norway
Blackall 126 C4 Queensland, E Australia
Black Drin 79 D6 Alb. Lumi i Drinit të Zi, SCr. Crni Drim. river Albania/FYR Macedonia
Blackfoot 24 E4 Idaho, NW USA
Black Forest 73 B6 Eng. Black Forest. mountain range SW Germany
Black Forest see Schwarzwald
Black Hills 22 D3 mountain range South Dakota/ Wyoming, N USA
Blackpool 67 C5 NW England, United Kingdom
Black Range 26 C2 mountain range New Mexico, SW USA
Black River 32 A5 W Jamaica
Black River 114 C3 Chin. Babian Jiang, Lixian Jiang, Fr. Rivière Noire, Vtn. Sông Đa. river China/Vietnam
Black Rock Desert 25 C5 desert Nevada, W USA
Black Sand Desert see Garagum
Black Sea 94 B1 var. Euxine Sea, Bul. Cherno More, Rom. Marea Neagră, Rus. Chernoye More, Turk. Karadeniz, Ukr. Chorne More. sea Asia/Europe
Black Sea Lowland 87 E4 Ukr. Prychornomor'ska Nyzovyna. depression SE Europe
Black Volta 53 E4 var. Borongo, Mouhoun, Moun Hou, Fr. Volta Noire. river W Africa
Blackwater 67 A6 Ir. An Abhainn Mhór. river S Ireland
Blackwater State see Nebraska
Blagoevgrad 82 C3 prev. Gorna Dzhumaya. Blagoevgrad, W Bulgaria
Blagoveshchensk 93 G4 Amurskaya Oblast', SE Russian Federation
Blake Plateau 13 D6 var. Blake Terrace. undersea plateau W Atlantic Ocean
Blake Terrace see Blake Plateau
Blanca, Bahía 43 C5 bay E Argentina
Blanca, Costa 71 F4 physical region SE Spain
Blanche, Lake 127 B5 lake South Australia
Blanc, Mont 69 D5 It. Monte Bianco. mountain France/Italy
Blanco, Cape 24 A4 headland Oregon, NW USA
Blanes 71 G2 Cataluña, NE Spain
Blankenberge 65 A5 West-Vlaanderen, NW Belgium
Blankenheim 73 A5 Nordrhein-Westfalen, W Germany
Blanquilla, Isla 37 E1 var. La Blanquilla. island N Venezuela
Blanquilla, La see Blanquilla, Isla
Blantyre 57 E2 var. Blantyre-Limbe. Southern, S Malawi
Blantyre-Limbe see Blantyre
Blaricum 64 C3 Noord-Holland, C Netherlands
Blatnitsa see Durankulak
Blenheim 129 C5 Marlborough, South Island, New Zealand
Blesae see Blois
Blida 48 D2 var. El Boulaida, El Boulaïda. N Algeria
Bloemfontein 56 C4 var. Mangaung. country capital Free State, C South Africa
Blois 68 C4 anc. Blesae. Loir-et-Cher, C France
Bloomfield 26 C1 New Mexico, SW USA
Bloomington 18 B4 Illinois, N USA
Bloomington 18 C4 Indiana, N USA
Bloomington 23 F2 Minnesota, N USA
Bloomsbury 126 D3 Queensland, NE Australia
Bluefield 18 D5 West Virginia, NE USA
Bluefields 31 E3 Región Autónoma Atlántico Sur, SE Nicaragua
Bluegrass State see Kentucky
Blue Hen State see Delaware
Blue Law State see Connecticut
Blue Mountain Peak 32 B5 mountain E Jamaica
Blue Mountains 24 C3 mountain range Oregon/ Washington, NW USA
Blue Nile 50 C4 var. Abai, Bahr el, Azraq, Amh. Ābay Wenz, Ar. An Nīl al Azraq. river Ethiopia/ Sudan
Blumenau 41 E5 Santa Catarina, S Brazil
Blythe 25 D8 California, W USA
Blytheville 20 C1 Arkansas, C USA
Bo 52 C4 S Sierra Leone
Boaco 30 D3 Boaco, S Nicaragua
Boa Vista 40 D1 state capital Roraima, NW Brazil
Boa Vista 52 A3 island Ilhas de Barlavento, E Cape Verde
Bobaomby, Tanjona 57 G2 Fr. Cap d'Ambre. headland N Madagascar
Bobigny 68 E1 Seine-St-Denis, N France
Bobo-Dioulasso 52 D4 SW Burkina
Bobrinets see Bobrynets'
Bobruysk see Babruysk
Bobrynets' 87 E3 Rus. Bobrinets. Kirovohrads'ka Oblast', C Ukraine
Boca Raton 21 F5 Florida, SE USA
Bocay 30 D2 Jinotega, N Nicaragua
Bocheykovo see Bacheykava
Bocholt 72 A4 Nordrhein-Westfalen, W Germany
Bochum 72 A4 Nordrhein-Westfalen, W Germany
Bocşa 86 A4 Ger. Bokschen, Hung. Boksánbánya. Caraş-Severin, SW Romania
Bodaybo 93 F4 Irkutskaya Oblast', E Russian Federation
Bodegas see Babahoyo
Boden 62 D4 Norrbotten, N Sweden
Bodensee see Constance, Lake, C Europe
Bodmin 67 C7 SW England, United Kingdom
Bodø 62 C3 Nordland, C Norway
Bodrum 94 A4 Muğla, SW Turkey
Boeloekoemba see Bulukumba
Boende 55 C5 Equateur, C Dem. Rep. Congo
Boeroe see Buru, Pulau
Boetoeng see Buton, Pulau
Bogale 114 B4 Ayeyarwady, SW Myanmar (Burma)
Bogalusa 20 B3 Louisiana, S USA
Bogatynia 76 B4 Ger. Reichenau. Dolnośląskie, SW Poland
Boğazlıyan 94 D3 Yozgat, C Turkey
Bogendorf see Łuków
Bogor 116 C5 Dut. Buitenzorg. Jawa, C Indonesia
Bogotá 36 B3 prev. Santa Fe, Santa Fe de Bogotá. country capital Cundinamarca, C Colombia
Bogushëvsk see Bahushewsk
Boguslav see Bohuslav
Bo Hai 106 D4 var. Gulf of Chihli. gulf NE China
Bohemia 77 A5 Cz. Čechy, Ger. Böhmen. W Czech Republic
Bohemian Forest 73 C5 Cz. Ceský Les, Šumava, Ger. Böhmerwald. mountain range C Europe
Böhmen see Bohemia
Böhmerwald see Bohemian Forest
Böhmisch-Krumau see Český Krumlov
Bohol Sea 117 E2 var. Mindanao Sea. sea S Philippines
Bohuslav 87 E2 Rus. Boguslav. Kyyivs'ka Oblast', N Ukraine
Boise 24 D3 var. Boise City. state capital Idaho, NW USA
Boise City 27 E1 Oklahoma, C USA
Boise City see Boise
Bois, Lac des see Woods, Lake of the
Bois-le-Duc see 's-Hertogenbosch
Boizenburg 72 C3 Mecklenburg-Vorpommern, N Germany
Bojador see Boujdour
Bojnūrd 98 D2 var. Bujnurd. Khorāsān-e Shemālī, N Iran
Bokāro 113 F4 Jhārkhand, N India
Boké 52 C4 W Guinea
Bokhara see Buxoro
Boknafjorden 63 A6 fjord S Norway
Boksánbánya/Bokschen see Bocşa
Bol 54 B3 Lac, W Chad
Bolgatanga 53 E4 N Ghana
Bolgrad see Bolhrad
Bolhrad 86 D4 Rus. Bolgrad. Odes'ka Oblast', SW Ukraine
Bolívar, Pico 36 C2 mountain W Venezuela
Bolivia 39 F3 off. Republic of Bolivia. country W South America
Bolivia, Republic of see Bolivia
Bollène 69 D6 Vaucluse, SE France
Bollnäs 63 C5 Gävleborg, C Sweden
Bollon 127 D5 Queensland, C Australia
Bologna 74 C3 Emilia-Romagna, N Italy
Bol'shevik see Bal'shavik
Bol'shevik, Ostrov 93 E2 island Severnaya Zemlya, N Russian Federation
Bol'shezemel'skaya Tundra 88 E3 physical region NW Russian Federation
Bol'shoy Lyakhovskiy, Ostrov 93 F2 island NE Russian Federation
Bolton 67 D5 prev. Bolton-le-Moors. NW England, United Kingdom
Bolton-le-Moors see Bolton
Bolu 94 B3 Bolu, NW Turkey
Bolungarvík 61 E4 Vestfirdhir, NW Iceland
Bolyarovo 82 D3 prev. Pashkeni. Yambol, E Bulgaria
Bolzano 74 C1 Ger. Bozen; anc. Bauzanum. Trentino-Alto Adige, N Italy
Boma 55 B6 Bas-Congo, W Dem. Rep. Congo
Bombay see Mumbai
Bomu 54 D4 var. Mbomou, Mbomu, M'Bomu. river Central African Republic/Dem. Rep. Congo
Bonaire 33 F5 island E Netherlands Antilles
Bonanza 30 D2 Región Autónoma Atlántico Norte, NE Nicaragua
Bonaparte Archipelago 124 C2 island group Western Australia
Bon, Cap 80 D3 headland N Tunisia
Bonda 55 B6 Ogooué-Lolo, C Gabon
Bondoukou 53 E4 E Ivory Coast
Bône see Annaba, Algeria
Bone see Watampone, Indonesia
Bone, Teluk 117 E4 bay Sulawesi, C Indonesia
Bongaigaon 113 G3 Assam, NE India
Bongo, Massif des 54 D4 var. Chaîne des Mongos. mountain range NE Central African Republic
Bongor 54 B3 Mayo-Kébbi, SW Chad
Bonifacio 69 E7 Corse, France, C Mediterranean Sea
Bonifacio, Bocche de/Bonifacio, Bouches de see Bonifacio, Strait of
Bonifacio, Strait of 74 A4 Fr. Bouches de Bonifacio, It. Bocche di Bonifacio. strait C Mediterranean Sea
Bonn 73 A5 Nordrhein-Westfalen, W Germany
Bononia see Vidin, Bulgaria
Bononia see Boulogne-sur-Mer, France
Boosaaso 50 E4 var. Bandar Kassim, Bender Qaasim, Bosaso, It. Bender Cassim. Bari, N Somalia
Boothia Felix see Boothia Peninsula
Boothia, Gulf of 15 F2 gulf Nunavut, NE Canada
Boothia Peninsula 15 F2 prev. Boothia Felix. peninsula Nunavut, NE Canada
Boppard 73 A5 Rheinland-Pfalz, W Germany
Boquete 31 E5 var. Bajo Boquete. Chiriquí, W Panama
Boquillas 28 D2 var. Boquillas del Carmen. Coahuila de Zaragoza, NE Mexico
Boquillas del Carmen see Boquillas
Bor 78 E4 Serbia, E Serbia
Bor 51 B5 Jonglei, S Sudan
Borås 63 B7 Västra Götaland, S Sweden
Borbetomagus see Worms
Borborema, Planalto da 34 E3 plateau NE Brazil
Bordeaux 69 B5 anc. Burdigala. Gironde, SW France
Bordj Omar Driss 49 E3 E Algeria
Borgå see Porvoo
Børgefjelt 62 C4 mountain range C Norway
Borger 64 E2 Drenthe, NE Netherlands
Borger 27 E1 Texas, SW USA
Borgholm 63 C7 Kalmar, S Sweden
Borgo Maggiore 74 E1 NW San Marino
Borislav see Boryslav
Borisoglebsk 89 B6 Voronezhskaya Oblast', W Russian Federation
Borisov see Barysaw
Borlänge 63 C6 Dalarna, C Sweden
Borne 64 E3 Overijssel, E Netherlands
Borneo 116 C4 island Brunei/Indonesia/Malaysia
Bornholm 63 B8 island E Denmark
Borohoro Shan 104 B2 mountain range NW China
Borongo see Black Volta
Boron'ki see Baron'ki
Borosjenő see Ineu
Borovan 82 C2 Vratsa, NW Bulgaria
Borovichi 88 B4 Novgorodskaya Oblast', W Russian Federation
Borovo 78 C3 Vukovar-Srijem, NE Croatia
Borşa 86 C3 Hung. Borsa. Maramureş, N Romania
Boryslav 86 B2 Pol. Borysław, Rus. Borislav. L'vivs'ka Oblast', NW Ukraine
Borysław see Boryslav
Bosanska Dubica 78 B3 var. Kozarska Dubica. Republika Srpska, NW Bosnia and Herzegovina
Bosanska Gradiška 78 B3 var. Gradiška. Republika Srpska, N Bosnia and Herzegovina
Bosanski Novi 78 B3 var. Novi Grad. Republika Srpska, NW Bosnia and Herzegovina
Bosanski Šamac 78 C3 var. Šamac. Republika Srpska, N Bosnia and Herzegovina
Bosaso see Boosaaso
Bösing see Pezinok
Boskovice 77 B5 Ger. Boskowitz. Jihomoravský Kraj, SE Czech Republic
Boskowitz see Boskovice
Bosna 78 C4 river N Bosnia and Herzegovina
Bosnia and Herzegovina 78 B3 off. Republic of Bosnia and Herzegovina. country SE Europe
Bosnia and Herzegovina, Republic of see Bosnia and Herzegovina
Bōsō-hantō 109 D6 peninsula Honshū, S Japan
Bosphorus/Bosporus see İstanbul Boğazı
Bosporus 94 B2 var. Bosporus Thracius, Eng. Bosphorus, Bosporus, Turk. Karadeniz Boğazi. strait NW Turkey
Bosporus Cimmerius see Kerch Strait
Bosporus Thracius see İstanbul Boğazı
Bossangoa 54 C4 Ouham, C Central African Republic
Bossembélé 54 C4 Ombella-Mpoko, C Central African Republic
Bossier City 20 A2 Louisiana, S USA
Bosten Hu 104 C3 var. Bagrax Hu. lake NW China
Boston 67 E6 prev. St.Botolph's Town. E England, United Kingdom
Boston 19 G3 state capital Massachusetts, NE USA
Boston Mountains 20 B1 mountain range Arkansas, C USA
Bostyn' see Bastyn'
Botany 126 E2 New South Wales, E Australia
Botany Bay 126 E2 inlet New South Wales, SE Australia
Boteti 56 C3 var. Botletle. river N Botswana
Bothnia, Gulf of 63 D5 Fin. Pohjanlahti, Swe. Bottniska Viken. gulf N Baltic Sea
Botletle see Boteti
Botoşani 86 C3 Hung. Botosány. Botoşani, NE Romania
Botosány see Botoşani
Botou 106 C4 prev. Bozhen. Hebei, E China
Botrange 65 D6 mountain E Belgium
Botswana 56 C3 off. Republic of Botswana. country S Africa
Botswana, Republic of see Botswana
Bottniska Viken see Bothnia, Gulf of
Bouar 54 B4 Nana-Mambéré, W Central African Republic
Bou Craa 48 B3 var. Bu Craa. NW Western Sahara
Bougainville Island 120 B3 island NE Papua New Guinea
Bougaroun, Cap 80 C3 headland NE Algeria
Bougouni 52 D4 Sikasso, SW Mali
Boujdour 48 A3 var. Bojador. W Western Sahara
Boulder 22 C4 Colorado, C USA
Boulder 22 B2 Montana, NW USA
Boulogne see Boulogne-sur-Mer
Boulogne-Billancourt 68 D1 Hauts-de-Seine, Île-de-France, N France Europe
Boulogne-sur-Mer 68 C2 var. Boulogne; anc. Bononia, Gesoriacum, Gessoriacum. Pas-de-Calais, N France
Boûmdeïd 52 C3 var. Boumdeït. Assaba, S Mauritania
Boumdeït see Boûmdeïd
Boundiali 52 D4 N Ivory Coast
Bountiful 22 B4 Utah, W USA
Bounty Basin see Bounty Trough
Bounty Islands 120 D5 island group S New Zealand
Bounty Trough 130 C5 var. Bounty Basin. trough S Pacific Ocean
Bourbonnais 68 C4 cultural region C France
Bourbon Vendée see la Roche-sur-Yon
Bourg see Bourg-en-Bresse
Bourgas see Burgas
Bourge-en-Bresse see Bourg-en-Bresse
Bourg-en-Bresse 69 D5 var. Bourg, Bourge-en-Bresse. Ain, E France
Bourges 68 C4 anc. Avaricum. Cher, C France
Bourgogne 68 C4 Eng. Burgundy. cultural region E France
Bourke 127 C5 New South Wales, SE Australia
Bournemouth 67 D7 S England, United Kingdom
Boutilimit 52 C3 Trarza, SW Mauritania
Bouvet Island 45 D7 Norwegian dependency S Atlantic Ocean
Bowen 126 D3 Queensland, NE Australia
Bowling Green 18 B5 Kentucky, S USA
Bowling Green 18 C3 Ohio, N USA
Boxmeer 64 D4 Noord-Brabant, SE Netherlands
Boyarka 87 E2 Kyyivs'ka Oblast', N Ukraine
Boysun 101 E3 Rus. Baysun. Surkhondaryo Viloyati, S Uzbekistan
Bozeman 22 B2 Montana, NW USA
Bozen see Bolzano
Bozhen see Botou
Bozüyük 94 B3 Bilecik, NW Turkey
Brač 78 B4 var. Brach, It. Brazza; anc. Brattia. island S Croatia
Bracara Augusta see Braga
Brach see Brač
Bradford 67 D5 N England, United Kingdom
Brady 27 F3 Texas, SW USA
Braga 70 B2 anc. Bracara Augusta. Braga, NW Portugal
Bragança 70 C2 Eng. Braganza; anc. Julio Briga. Bragança, NE Portugal
Braganza see Bragança
Brahestad see Raahe
Brahmanbaria 113 G4 Chittagong, E Bangladesh
Brahmapur 113 F5 Orissa, E India
Brahmaputra 113 H3 var. Padma, Tsangpo, Ben. Jamuna, Chin. Yarlung Zangbo Jiang, Ind. Bramaputra, Dihang, Siang. river S Asia
Brăila 86 D4 Brăila, E Romania
Braine-le-Comte 65 B6 Hainaut, SW Belgium
Brainerd 23 F2 Minnesota, N USA
Brak see Birāk
Bramaputra see Brahmaputra
Brampton 16 D5 Ontario, S Canada
Branco, Rio 34 C3 river N Brazil
Brandberg 56 A3 mountain NW Namibia
Brandenburg 72 C3 var. Brandenburg an der Havel. Brandenburg, NE Germany
Brandenburg an der Havel see Brandenburg
Brandon 15 F5 Manitoba, S Canada
Braniewo 76 D2 Ger. Braunsberg. Warmińsko-mazurskie, N Poland
Brasil see Brazil
Brasília 41 F3 country capital Distrito Federal, C Brazil
Brasil, República Federativa do see Brazil
Braşov 86 C4 Ger. Kronstadt, Hung. Brassó; prev. Oraşul Stalin. Braşov, C Romania
Brassó see Braşov
Bratislava 77 C6 Ger. Pressburg, Hung. Pozsony. country capital Bratislavský Kraj, W Slovakia
Bratsk 93 E4 Irkutskaya Oblast', C Russian Federation
Brattia see Brač
Braunsberg see Braniewo
Braunschweig 72 C4 Eng./Fr. Brunswick. Niedersachsen, N Germany
Brava see Baraawe
Brava, Costa 71 H2 coastal region NE Spain
Bravo del Norte, Río/Bravo, Río see Grande, Rio
Bravo, Río 28 C1 river Mexico/USA North America

Brawley – Cardigan Bay

Brawley 25 D8 California, W USA
Brazil 40 C2 off. Federative Republic of Brazil, Port. Repùblica Federativa do Brasil, Sp. Brasil; prev. United States of Brazil. country South America
Brazil Basin 45 C5 var. Brazilian Basin, Brazil'skaya Kotlovina. undersea basin W Atlantic Ocean
Brazil, Federative Republic of see Brazil
Brazilian Basin see Brazil Basin
Brazilian Highlands 41 F3 var. Brazilian Highlands. mountain range E Brazil
Brazilian Highlands see Central, Planalto
Brazil'skaya Kotlovina see Brazil Basin
Brazil, United States of see Brazil
Brazos River 27 G3 river Texas, SW USA
Brazza see Brač
Brazzaville 55 B6 country capital Capital District, S Congo
Brčko 78 C3 Republika Srpska, NE Bosnia and Herzegovina
Brecht 65 C5 Antwerpen, N Belgium
Brecon Beacons 67 C6 mountain range S Wales, United Kingdom
Breda 64 C4 Noord-Brabant, S Netherlands
Bree 65 D5 Limburg, NE Belgium
Bregalnica 79 E6 river E FYR Macedonia
Bregenz 35 B7 anc. Brigantium. Vorarlberg, W Austria
Bregovo 82 B1 Vidin, NW Bulgaria
Bremen 72 B3 Fr. Brême. Bremen, NW Germany
Bremerhaven 72 B3 Bremen, NW Germany
Bremerton 24 B2 Washington, NW USA
Brenham 27 G3 Texas, SW USA
Brenner, Col du/Brennero, Passo del see Brenner Pass
Brenner Pass 74 C1 var. Brenner Sattel, Fr. Col du Brenner, Ger. Brennerpass, It. Passo del Brennero. pass Austria/Italy
Brennerpass see Brenner Pass
Brenner Sattel see Brenner Pass
Brescia 74 B2 anc. Brixia. Lombardia, N Italy
Breslau see Wrocław
Bressanone 74 C1 Ger. Brixen. Trentino-Alto Adige, N Italy
Brest 85 A6 Pol. Brześć nad Bugiem, Rus. Brest-Litovsk; prev. Brześć Litewski. Brestskaya Voblasts', SW Belarus
Brest 68 A3 Finistère, NW France
Brest-Litovsk see Brest
Bretagne 68 A3 Eng. Brittany, Lat. Britannia Minor. cultural region NW France
Brewster, Kap see Kangikajik
Brewton 20 C3 Alabama, S USA
Brezhnev see Naberezhnyye Chelny
Brezovo 82 D2 prev. Abrashlare. Plovdiv, C Bulgaria
Bria 54 D4 Haute-Kotto, C Central African Republic
Briançon 69 D5 anc. Brigantio. Hautes-Alpes, SE France
Bricgstow see Bristol
Bridgeport 19 F3 Connecticut, NE USA
Bridgetown 33 G2 country capital SW Barbados
Bridlington 67 D5 E England, United Kingdom
Bridport 67 D7 S England, United Kingdom
Brieg see Brzeg
Brig 73 A7 Fr. Brigue, It. Briga. Valais, SW Switzerland
Briga see Brig
Brigantio see Briançon
Brigantium see Bregenz
Brigham City 22 B3 Utah, W USA
Brighton 67 E7 SE England, United Kingdom
Brighton 22 D4 Colorado, C USA
Brigue see Brig
Brindisi 75 E5 anc. Brundisium, Brundusium. Puglia, SE Italy
Briovera see St-Lô
Brisbane 127 E5 state capital Queensland, E Australia
Bristol 67 D7 anc. Bricgstow. SW England, United Kingdom
Bristol 19 F3 Connecticut, NE USA
Bristol 18 D5 Tennessee, S USA
Bristol Bay 14 B3 bay Alaska, USA
Bristol Channel 67 C7 inlet England/Wales, United Kingdom
Britain 58 C3 var. Great Britain. island United Kingdom
Britannia Minor see Bretagne
British Columbia 14 D4 Fr. Colombie-Britannique. province SW Canada
British Guiana see Guyana
British Honduras see Belize
British Indian Ocean Territory 119 B5 UK dependent territory C Indian Ocean
British Isles 67 island group NW Europe
British North Borneo see Sabah
British Solomon Islands Protectorate see Solomon Islands
British Virgin Islands 33 F3 var. Virgin Islands. UK dependent territory E West Indies
Brittany see Bretagne
Briva Curretia see Brive-la-Gaillarde
Briva Isarae see Pontoise
Brive see Brive-la-Gaillarde
Brive-la-Gaillarde 69 C5 prev. Brive; anc. Briva Curretia. Corrèze, C France
Brixen see Bressanone
Brixia see Brescia
Brno 77 B5 Ger. Brünn. Jihomoravský Kraj, SE Czech Republic
Broceni 84 B3 Saldus, SW Latvia
Brod/Bród see Slavonski Brod
Brodeur Peninsula 15 F2 peninsula Baffin Island, Nunavut, NE Canada
Brod na Savi see Slavonski Brod
Brodnica 76 C3 Ger. Buddenbrock. Kujawski-pomorskie, C Poland
Broek-in-Waterland 64 C3 Noord-Holland, C Netherlands
Broken Arrow 27 G1 Oklahoma, C USA
Broken Bay 126 E1 bay New South Wales, SE Australia
Broken Hill 127 B6 New South Wales, SE Australia
Broken Ridge 119 D6 undersea plateau S Indian Ocean
Bromberg see Bydgoszcz
Bromley 67 B8 United Kingdom
Brookhaven 20 B3 Mississippi, S USA
Brookings 23 F3 South Dakota, N USA
Brooks Range 14 D2 mountain range Alaska, USA
Brookton 125 B6 Western Australia
Broome 124 B3 Western Australia
Broomfield 22 D4 Colorado, C USA
Broucsella see Brussel/Bruxelles
Brovary 87 E2 Kyyivs'ka Oblast', N Ukraine
Brownfield 27 E2 Texas, SW USA
Brownsville 27 G5 Texas, SW USA
Brownwood 27 F3 Texas, SW USA
Brozha 85 D7 Mahilyowskaya Voblasts', E Belarus
Bruges see Brugge
Brugge 65 A5 Fr. Bruges. West-Vlaanderen, NW Belgium
Brummen 64 D3 Gelderland, E Netherlands
Brundisium/Brundusium see Brindisi
Brunei 116 D3 off. Brunei Darussalam, Mal. Negara Brunei Darussalam. country SE Asia
Brunei Darussalam see Brunei
Brunei Town see Bandar Seri Begawan
Brünn see Brno
Brunner, Lake 129 C5 lake South Island, New Zealand
Brunswick 21 E3 Georgia, SE USA
Brunswick see Braunschweig
Brusa see Bursa
Brus Laguna 30 D2 Gracias a Dios, E Honduras
Brussa see Bursa
Brussel 65 C6 var. Brussels, Fr. Bruxelles, Ger. Brüssel; anc. Broucsella. country capital Brussels, C Belgium
Brüssel/Brussels see Brussel/Bruxelles
Brüx see Most
Bruxelles see Brussel
Bryan 27 G3 Texas, SW USA
Bryansk 89 A5 Bryanskaya Oblast', W Russian Federation
Brzeg 76 C4 Ger. Brieg; anc. Civitas Altae Ripae. Opolskie, S Poland
Brześć Litewski/Brześć nad Bugiem see Brest
Brzeżany see Berezhany
Bucaramanga 36 B2 Santander, N Colombia
Buchanan 52 C5 prev. Grand Bassa. SW Liberia
Buchanan, Lake 27 F3 reservoir Texas, SW USA
Bucharest see București
Buckeye State see Ohio
Bu Craa see Bou Craa
București 86 C5 Eng. Bucharest, Ger. Bukarest, prev. Altenburg; anc. Cetatea Damboviței. country capital București, S Romania
Buda-Kashalyova 85 D7 Rus. Buda-Koshelëvo. Homyel'skaya Voblasts', SE Belarus
Buda-Koshelëvo see Buda-Kashalyova
Budapest 77 C6 off. Budapest Főváros, SCr. Budimpešta. country capital Pest, N Hungary
Budapest Főváros see Budapest
Budaun 112 D3 Uttar Pradesh, N India
Buddenbrock see Brodnica
Budimpešta see Budapest
Budweis see České Budějovice
Budyšin see Bautzen
Buena Park 24 E2 California, W USA North America
Buenaventura 36 A3 Valle del Cauca, W Colombia
Buena Vista 39 G4 Santa Cruz, C Bolivia
Buena Vista 71 H5 S Gibraltar Europe
Buena Vista 71 H5 S Gibraltar Europe
Buenavista 71 H5 Baja California Sur, W Mexico
Buenavista 71 H5 Sonora, NW Mexico
Buena Vista 71 H5 Cerro Largo, Uruguay
Buena Vista 71 H5 Colorado, C USA
Buena Vista 71 H5 Georgia, SE USA
Buena Vista 71 H5 Virginia, NE USA
Buenos Aires 42 D4 hist. Santa Maria del Buen Aire. country capital Buenos Aires, E Argentina
Buenos Aires 31 E5 Puntarenas, SE Costa Rica
Buenos Aires, Lago 43 B6 var. Lago General Carrera. lake Argentina/Chile
Buffalo 19 E3 New York, NE USA
Buffalo Narrows 15 F4 Saskatchewan, C Canada
Buff Bay 32 B5 E Jamaica
Buftea 86 C5 Ilfov, S Romania
Bug 59 E3 Bel. Zakhodni Buh, Eng. Western Bug, Rus. Zapadnyy Bug, Ukr. Zakhidnyy Buh. river E Europe
Buga 36 B3 Valle del Cauca, W Colombia
Bughotu see Santa Isabel
Buguruslan 89 D6 Orenburgskaya Oblast', W Russian Federation
Buitenzorg see Bogor
Bujalance 70 D4 Andalucía, S Spain
Bujanovac 79 E5 Kosovo, SE Serbia
Bujnurd see Bojnūrd
Bujumbura 51 B7 prev. Usumbura. country capital W Burundi
Bukarest see București
Bukavu 55 E6 prev. Costermansville. Sud-Kivu, E Dem. Rep. Congo
Bukhara see Buxoro
Bukoba 51 B6 Kagera, NW Tanzania
Bülach 73 B7 Zürich, NW Switzerland
Bulawayo 56 D3 Matabeleland North, SW Zimbabwe
Bulgan 105 E2 Bulgan, N Mongolia
Bulgaria 82 C2 off. Republic of Bulgaria, Bul. Bŭlgariya; prev. People's Republic of Bulgaria. country SE Europe
Bulgaria, People's Republic of see Bulgaria
Bulgaria, Republic of see Bulgaria
Bŭlgariya see Bulgaria
Bullion State see Missouri
Bull Shoals Lake 20 B1 reservoir Arkansas/Missouri, C USA
Bulukumba 117 E4 prev. Boeloekoemba. Sulawesi, C Indonesia
Bumba 55 D5 Equateur, N Dem. Rep. Congo
Bunbury 125 A7 Western Australia
Bundaberg 126 E4 Queensland, E Australia
Bungo-suidō 109 B7 strait SW Japan
Bunia 55 E5 Orientale, NE Dem. Rep. Congo
Bünyan 94 D3 Kayseri, C Turkey
Buraida see Buraydah
Buraydah 98 B4 var. Buraida. Al Qaşīm, N Saudi Arabia
Burdigala see Bordeaux
Burdur 94 B4 var. Buldur. Burdur, SW Turkey
Burdur Gölü 94 B4 salt lake SW Turkey
Burē 50 C4 Āmara, N Ethiopia
Burgas 82 E2 var. Bourgas. Burgas, E Bulgaria
Burgaski Zaliv 82 E2 gulf E Bulgaria
Burgos 70 D2 Castilla-León, N Spain
Burgundy see Bourgogne
Burhan Budai Shan 104 D4 mountain range C China
Buriram 115 D5 var. Buri Ram, Puriramya. Buri Ram, E Thailand
Buri Ram see Buriram
Burjassot 71 F3 País Valenciano, E Spain
Burkburnett 27 F2 Texas, SW USA
Burketown 126 B3 Queensland, NE Australia
Burkina 53 E4 off. Burkina Faso; prev. Upper Volta. country W Africa
Burkina see Burkina
Burkina Faso see Burkina
Burley 24 D4 Idaho, NW USA
Burlington 23 G4 Iowa, C USA
Burlington 19 F2 Vermont, NE USA
Burma 114 A3 off. Union of Myanmar. country SE Asia
Burnie 127 C8 Tasmania, SE Australia
Burns 24 C3 Oregon, NW USA
Burnside 15 F3 river Nunavut, NW Canada
Burnsville 23 F2 Minnesota, N USA
Burrel 79 D6 var. Burreli. Dibër, C Albania
Burreli see Burrel
Burriana 71 F3 País Valenciano, E Spain
Bursa 94 B3 var. Brussa, prev. Brusa; anc. Prusa. Bursa, NW Turkey
Būr Sa'īd 50 B1 var. Port Said. N Egypt
Burtnieks 84 C3 var. Burtnieks Ezers. lake N Latvia
Burtnieks Ezers see Burtnieks
Burundi 51 B7 off. Republic of Burundi; prev. Kingdom of Burundi, Urundi. country C Africa
Burundi, Kingdom of see Burundi
Burundi, Republic of see Burundi
Buru, Pulau 117 F4 prev. Boeroe. island E Indonesia
Busan see Pusan
Buşayrah 96 D3 Dayr az Zawr, E Syria
Būshehr/Bushire see Bandar-e Būshehr
Busra see Al Başrah, Iraq
Busselton 125 A7 Western Australia
Bussora see Al Başrah
Buta 55 D5 Orientale, N Dem. Rep. Congo
Butembo 55 E5 Nord-Kivu, NE Dem. Rep. Congo
Butler 19 E4 Pennsylvania, NE USA
Buton, Pulau 117 E4 var. Pulau Butung; prev. Boetoeng. island C Indonesia
Bütow see Bytów
Butte 22 B2 Montana, NW USA
Butterworth 116 B3 Pinang, Peninsular Malaysia
Button Islands 17 E1 island group Nunavut, NE Canada
Butuan 117 F2 off. Butuan City. Mindanao, S Philippines
Butuan City see Butuan
Butung, Pulau see Buton, Pulau
Butuntum see Bitonto
Buulobarde 51 D5 var. Buulo Berde. Hiiraan, C Somalia
Buulo Berde see Buulobarde
Buur Gaabo 51 D6 Jubbada Hoose, S Somalia
Buxoro 100 D2 var. Bokhara, Rus. Bukhara. Buxoro Viloyati, C Uzbekistan
Buynaksk 89 B8 Respublika Dagestan, SW Russian Federation
Büyükmenderes Nehri 94 A4 river SW Turkey
Buzău 86 C4 Buzău, SE Romania
Būzmeyin see Abadan
Buzuluk 89 D6 Orenburgskaya Oblast', W Russian Federation
Byahoml' 85 D5 Rus. Begoml'. Vitsyebskaya Voblasts', N Belarus
Byalynichy 85 D6 Rus. Belynichi. Mahilyowskaya Voblasts', E Belarus
Byan Tumen see Choybalsan
Bydgoszcz 76 C3 Ger. Bromberg. Kujawski-pomorskie, C Poland
Byelaruskaya Hrada 85 B6 Rus. Belorusskaya Gryada. ridge N Belarus
Byerezino 85 D6 Rus. Berezina. river C Belarus
Byron Island see Nikunau
Bystrovka see Kemin
Bytča 77 C5 Žilinský Kraj, N Slovakia
Bytom 77 C5 Ger. Beuthen. Śląskie, S Poland
Bytów 76 C2 Ger. Bütow. Pomorskie, N Poland
Byuzmeyin see Abadan
Byval'ki 85 D8 Homyel'skaya Voblasts', SE Belarus
Byzantium see İstanbul

C

Caála 56 B2 var. Kaala, Robert Williams, Port. Vila Robert Williams. Huambo, C Angola
Caazapá 42 D3 Caazapá, S Paraguay
Caballo Reservoir 26 C3 reservoir New Mexico, SW USA
Cabañaquinta 70 D1 Asturias, N Spain
Cabanatuan 117 E1 off. Cabanatuan City. Luzon, N Philippines
Cabanatuan City see Cabanatuan
Cabillonum see Chalon-sur-Saône
Cabimas 36 C1 Zulia, NW Venezuela
Cabinda 56 A1 var. Kabinda. Cabinda, NW Angola
Cabinda 56 A1 var. Kabinda. province NW Angola
Lake Cabora Bassa 56 D2 var. Lake Cabora Bassa. reservoir NW Mozambique
Cabora Bassa, Lake see Cahora Bassa, Albufeira de
Caborca 28 B1 Sonora, NW Mexico
Cabot Strait 17 G4 strait E Canada
Cabo Verde, Ilhas do see Cape Verde
Cabras, Ilha das 54 E2 island S Sao Tome and Principe, Africa, E Atlantic Ocean
Cabrera 71 G3 river NW Spain
Cáceres 70 C3 Ar. Qazris. Extremadura, W Spain
Cachimbo, Serra do 41 E2 mountain range C Brazil
Caconda 56 B2 Huíla, C Angola
Čadca 77 C5 Hung. Csaca. Žilinský Kraj, N Slovakia
Cadillac 18 C2 Michigan, N USA
Cadiz 117 E2 off. Cadiz City. Negros, C Philippines
Cádiz 70 C5 anc. Gades, Gadier, Gadir, Gadire. Andalucía, SW Spain
Cadiz City see Cadiz
Gulf of Cadiz 70 B5 Eng. Gulf of Cadiz. gulf Portugal/Spain
Cadiz, Gulf of see Cádiz, Golfo de
Cadurcum see Cahors
Caen 68 B3 Calvados, N France
Caene/Caenepolis see Qinā
Caerdydd see Cardiff
Caer Glou see Gloucester
Caer Gybi see Holyhead
Caerleon see Chester
Caer Luel see Carlisle
Caesaraugusta see Zaragoza
Caesarea Mazaca see Kayseri
Caesarobriga see Talavera de la Reina
Caesarodunum see Tours
Caesaromagus see Beauvais
Caesena see Cesena
Cafayate 42 C2 Salta, N Argentina
Cagayan de Oro 117 E2 off. Cagayan de Oro City. Mindanao, S Philippines
Cagayan de Oro City see Cagayan de Oro
Cagliari 75 A6 anc. Caralis. Sardegna, Italy, C Mediterranean Sea
Caguas 33 F3 E Puerto Rico
Cahors 69 C5 anc. Cadurcum. Lot, S France
Cahul 86 D4 Rus. Kagul. S Moldova
Caicos Passage 32 D2 strait Bahamas/Turks and Caicos Islands
Caiffa see Hefa
Cailungo 74 E1 N San Marino
Caiphas see Hefa
Cairns 126 D3 Queensland, NE Australia
Cairo 50 B2 var. El Qâhira, Ar. Al Qāhirah. country capital N Egypt
Caisleán an Bharraigh see Castlebar
Cajamarca 38 B3 prev. Caxamarca. Cajamarca, NW Peru
Čakovec 78 B2 Ger. Csakathurn, Hung. Csáktornya; prev. Ger. Tschakathurn. Medimurje, N Croatia
Calabar 53 G5 Cross River, S Nigeria
Calabozo 36 D2 Guárico, C Venezuela
Calafat 86 B5 Dolj, SW Romania
Calafate see El Calafate
Calahorra 71 E2 La Rioja, N Spain
Calais 68 C2 Pas-de-Calais, N France
Calais 19 H2 Maine, NE USA
Calais, Pas de see Dover, Strait of
Calama 42 B2 Antofagasta, N Chile
Călăras see Călărași
Călărași 86 D3 var. Călăras, Rus. Kalarash. C Moldova
Călărași 86 C5 Călărași, SE Romania
Calatayud 71 E2 Aragón, NE Spain
Calbayog 117 E2 off. Calbayog City. Samar, C Philippines
Calbayog City see Calbayog
Calcutta 113 G4 West Bengal, N India
Caldas da Rainha 70 B3 Leiria, W Portugal
Caldera 42 B3 Atacama, N Chile
Caldwell 24 C3 Idaho, NW USA
Caledonia 30 C1 Corozal, N Belize
Caleta Olivia 43 B6 Santa Cruz, SE Argentina
Calgary 15 E5 Alberta, SW Canada
Cali 36 B3 Valle del Cauca, W Colombia
Calicut 110 C2 var. Kozhikode. Kerala, SW India
California 25 B7 off. State of California, also known as El Dorado, The Golden State. state W USA
Gulf of California 28 B2 Eng. Gulf of California; prev. Sea of Cortez. gulf W Mexico
California, Gulf of see California, Golfo de
Călimănești 86 B4 Vâlcea, SW Romania
Calisia see Kalisz
Callabonna, Lake 127 B5 lake South Australia
Callao 38 C4 Callao, W Peru
Callatis see Mangalia
Callosa de Segura 71 F4 País Valenciano, E Spain
Calmar see Kalmar
Caloundra 127 E5 Queensland, E Australia
Caltanissetta 75 C7 Sicilia, Italy, C Mediterranean Sea
Caluula 50 E4 Bari, NE Somalia
Camabatela 56 B1 Cuanza Norte, NW Angola
Camacupa 56 B2 var. General Machado, Port. Vila General Machado. Bié, C Angola
Camagüey 32 C2 prev. Puerto Príncipe. Camagüey, C Cuba
Camagüey, Archipiélago de 32 C2 island group C Cuba
Camana 39 E4 var. Camaná. Arequipa, SW Peru
Camargue 69 D6 physical region SE France
Ca Mau 115 D6 var. Quan Long. Minh Hai, S Vietnam
Cambay, Gulf of see Khambhāt, Gulf of
Camberia see Chambéry
Cambodia 115 D5 off. Kingdom of Cambodia, var. Democratic Kampuchea, Roat Kampuchea, Cam. Kampuchea; prev. People's Democratic Republic of Kampuchea. country SE Asia
Cambodia, Kingdom of see Cambodia
Cambrai 68 C2 Flem. Kambryk, prev. Cambray; anc. Cameracum. Nord, N France
Cambray see Cambrai
Cambrian Mountains 67 C6 mountain range C Wales, United Kingdom
Cambridge 32 A4 W Jamaica
Cambridge 128 D3 Waikato, North Island, New Zealand
Cambridge 67 E6 Lat. Cantabrigia. E England, United Kingdom
Cambridge 19 F4 Maryland, NE USA
Cambridge 18 D4 Ohio, NE USA
Cambridge Bay 15 F3 var. Ikaluktutiak. Victoria Island, Nunavut, NW Canada
Camden 20 B2 Arkansas, C USA
Camellia State see Alabama
Cameracum see Cambrai
Cameroon 54 A4 off. Republic of Cameroon, Fr. Cameroun. country W Africa
Cameroon, Republic of see Cameroon
Cameroun see Cameroon
Camocim 41 F2 Ceará, E Brazil
Camopi 37 H3 E French Guiana
Campamento 30 C2 Olancho, C Honduras
Campania 75 D5 Eng. Champagne. region S Italy
Campbell, Cape 129 D5 headland South Island, New Zealand
Campbell Island 120 D5 island S New Zealand
Campbell Plateau 120 D5 undersea plateau SW Pacific Ocean
Campbell River 14 D5 Vancouver Island, British Columbia, SW Canada
Campeche 29 G4 Campeche, SE Mexico
Bay of Campeche 29 F4 Eng. Bay of Campeche. bay E Mexico
Campeche, Bay of see Campeche, Bahía de
Câm Pha 114 E3 Quang Ninh, N Vietnam
Câmpina 86 C4 prev. Cîmpina. Prahova, SE Romania
Campina Grande 41 G2 Paraíba, E Brazil
Campinas 41 F4 São Paulo, S Brazil
Campobasso 75 D5 Molise, C Italy
Campo Criptana see Campo de Criptana
Campo de Criptana 71 E3 var. Campo Criptana. Castilla-La Mancha, C Spain
Campo dos Goitacazes see Campos
Campo Grande 41 E4 state capital Mato Grosso do Sul, SW Brazil
Campos 41 F4 var. Campo dos Goitacazes. Rio de Janeiro, SE Brazil
Câmpulung 86 B4 prev. Câmpulung-Mușcel, Cîmpulung. Argeș, S Romania
Câmpulung-Mușcel see Câmpulung
Campus Stellae see Santiago
Cam Ranh 115 E6 Khanh Hoa, S Vietnam
Canada 12 B4 country N North America
Canada Basin 12 C2 undersea basin Arctic Ocean
Canadian River 27 E2 river SW USA
Çanakkale 94 A3 var. Dardanelli; prev. Chanak, Kale Sultanie. Çanakkale, W Turkey
Cananea 28 B1 Sonora, NW Mexico
Canarreos, Archipiélago de los 32 B2 island group W Cuba
Canary Islands 48 A2 Eng. Canary Islands. island group Spain, NE Atlantic Ocean
Canary Islands see Canarias, Islas
Cañas 30 D4 Guanacaste, NW Costa Rica
Canaveral, Cape 21 E4 headland Florida, SE USA
Canavieiras 41 G3 Bahia, E Brazil
Canberra 120 C4 country capital Australian Capital Territory, SE Australia
Cancún 29 H3 Quintana Roo, SE Mexico
Candia see Irákleio
Canea see Chaniá
Cangzhou 106 D4 Hebei, E China
Caniapiscau 17 E2 river Québec, E Canada
Caniapiscau, Réservoir de 16 D3 reservoir Québec, C Canada
Canik Dağları 94 D2 mountain range N Turkey
Canillo 69 A7 Canillo, C Andorra Europe
Çankırı 94 C3 var. Chankiri; anc. Gangra, Germanicopolis. Çankın, N Turkey
Cannanore 110 B2 var. Kannur. Kerala, SW India
Cannes 69 D6 Alpes-Maritimes, SE France
Canoas 41 E5 Rio Grande do Sul, S Brazil
Canon City 22 C5 Colorado, C USA
Cantabria 70 D1 autonomous community N Spain
Cantábrica, Cordillera 70 C1 mountain range N Spain
Cantabrigia see Cambridge
Cantaura 37 E2 Anzoátegui, NE Venezuela
Canterbury 67 E7 hist. Cantwaraburh; anc. Durovernum, Lat. Cantuaria. SE England, United Kingdom
Canterbury Bight 129 C6 bight South Island, New Zealand
Canterbury Plains 129 C6 plain South Island, New Zealand
Cần Thơ 115 E6 Cần Thơ, S Vietnam
Canton 20 B2 Mississippi, S USA
Canton 18 D4 Ohio, N USA
Canton see Guangzhou
Canton Island see Kanton
Cantuaria/Cantwaraburh see Canterbury
Canyon 27 E2 Texas, SW USA
Cao Bằng 114 D3 var. Caobang. Cao Bằng, N Vietnam
Caobang see Cao Bằng
Cap-Breton, Île du see Cape Breton Island
Cape Barren Island 127 C8 island Furneaux Group, Tasmania, SE Australia
Cape Basin 47 B7 undersea basin S Atlantic Ocean
Cape Breton Island 17 G4 Fr. Île du Cap-Breton. island Nova Scotia, SE Canada
Cape Charles 19 F5 Virginia, NE USA
Cape Coast 53 E5 prev. Cape Coast Castle. S Ghana
Cape Coast Castle see Cape Coast
Cape Girardeau 23 H5 Missouri, C USA
Capelle aan den IJssel 64 C4 Zuid-Holland, SW Netherlands
Cape Palmas see Harper
Cape Saint Jacques see Vung Tau
Cape Town 56 B5 var. Ekapa, Afr. Kaapstad, Kapstad. country capital Western Cape, SW South Africa
Cape Verde 52 A2 off. Republic of Cape Verde, Port. Cabo Verde, Ilhas do Cabo Verde. country E Atlantic Ocean
Cape Verde Basin 44 C4 undersea basin E Atlantic Ocean
Cape Verde Plain 44 C4 abyssal plain E Atlantic Ocean
Cape Verde, Republic of see Cape Verde
Cape York Peninsula 126 C2 peninsula Queensland, N Australia
Cap-Haïtien 32 D3 var. Le Cap. N Haiti
Capira 31 G5 Panamá, C Panama
Capitán Arturo Prat 132 A2 Chilean research station South Shetland Islands, Antarctica
Capitán Pablo Lagerenza 42 D1 var. Mayor Pablo Lagerenza. Chaco, N Paraguay
Capodistria see Koper
Capri 75 C5 island S Italy
Caprivi Concession see Caprivi Strip
Caprivi Strip 56 C3 Ger. Caprivizipfel; prev. Caprivi Concession. cultural region NE Namibia
Caprivizipfel see Caprivi Strip
Cap Saint-Jacques see Vung Tau
Caquetá, Río 36 C5 var. Rio Japurá, Yapurá. river Brazil/Colombia
Caquetá, Río see Japurá, Rio
CAR see Central African Republic
Caracal 86 B5 Olt, S Romania
Caracaraí 40 D1 Rondônia, W Brazil
Caracas 36 D1 country capital Distrito Federal, N Venezuela
Caralis see Cagliari
Caratasca, Laguna de 31 E2 lagoon NE Honduras
Carballiño see O Carballiño
Carbondale 18 B5 Illinois, N USA
Carbonia 75 A6 var. Carbonia Centro. Sardegna, Italy, C Mediterranean Sea
Carbonia Centro see Carbonia
Carcaso see Carcassonne
Carcassonne 69 C6 anc. Carcaso. Aude, S France
Cardamomes, Chaîne des see Krâvanh, Chuŏr Phnum
Cardamom Mountains see Krâvanh, Chuŏr Phnum
Cárdenas 32 B2 Matanzas, W Cuba
Cardiff 67 C7 Wel. Caerdydd. national capital S Wales, United Kingdom
Cardigan Bay 67 C6 bay W Wales, United Kingdom

Carei – Chisholm

Carei 86 B3 Ger. Gross-Karol, Karol, Hung. Nagykároly; prev. Careii-Mari. Satu Mare, NW Romania
Careii-Mari see Carei
Carey, Lake 125 B6 lake Western Australia
Cariaco 37 E1 Sucre, NE Venezuela
Caribbean Sea 32 C4 sea W Atlantic Ocean
Caribrod see Dimitrovgrad
Carlisle 66 C4 anc. Caer Luel, Luguvallium, Luguvallum. NW England, United Kingdom
Carlow 67 B6 Ir. Ceatharlach. SE Ireland
Carlsbad 26 D3 New Mexico, SW USA
Carlsbad see Karlovy Vary
Carlsberg Ridge 118 B4 undersea ridge S Arabian Sea
Carlsruhe see Karlsruhe
Carmana/Carmania see Kermān
Carmarthen 67 C6 SW Wales, United Kingdom
Carmaux 69 C6 Tarn, S France
Carmel 18 C4 Indiana, N USA
Carmelita 30 B1 Petén, N Guatemala
Carmen 29 G4 var. Ciudad del Carmen. Campeche, SE Mexico
Carmona 70 C4 Andalucía, S Spain
Carmona see Uíge
Carnaro see Kvarner
Carnarvon 125 A5 Western Australia
Carnegie, Lake 125 B5 salt lake Western Australia
Car Nicobar 111 F3 island Nicobar Islands, India, NE Indian Ocean
Caroço, Ilha 54 E1 island N Sao Tome and Principe, Africa, E Atlantic Ocean
Carolina 41 F2 Maranhão, E Brazil
Caroline Island see Millennium Island
Caroline Islands 122 B2 island group C Micronesia
Carolopois see Châlons-en-Champagne
Caroní, Río 37 E3 river E Venezuela
Caronium see A Coruña
Carora 36 C1 Lara, N Venezuela
Carpathian Mountains 59 E4 var. Carpathians, Cz./Pol. Karpaty, Ger. Karpaten. mountain range E Europe
Carpathians see Carpathian Mountains
Carpathos/Carpathus see Kárpathos
Carpaţii Sudici see Carpaţii Meridionali
Carpentaria, Gulf of 126 B2 gulf N Australia
Carpi 74 C2 Emilia-Romagna, N Italy
Carrara 74 B3 Toscana, C Italy
Carson City 25 C5 state capital Nevada, W USA
Carson Sink 25 C5 salt flat Nevada, W USA
Carstensz, Puntjak see Jaya, Puncak
Cartagena 36 B1 var. Cartagena de los Indes. Bolívar, NW Colombia
Cartagena 71 F4 anc. Carthago Nova. Murcia, SE Spain
Cartagena de los Indes see Cartagena
Cartago 31 E4 Cartago, C Costa Rica
Carthage 23 F5 Missouri, C USA
Carthago Nova see Cartagena
Cartwright 17 F2 Newfoundland and Labrador, E Canada
Carúpano 37 E1 Sucre, NE Venezuela
Carusbur see Cherbourg
Caruthersville 23 H5 Missouri, C USA
Cary 21 F1 North Carolina, SE USA
Casablanca 48 C2 Ar. Dar-el-Beida. NW Morocco
Casa Grande 26 B2 Arizona, SW USA
Cascade Range 24 B3 mountain range Oregon/Washington, NW USA
Cascadia Basin 12 A4 undersea basin NE Pacific Ocean
Cascais 70 B4 Lisboa, C Portugal
Caserta 75 D5 Campania, S Italy
Casey 132 D4 Australian research station Antarctica
Čáslav 77 B5 Ger. Tschaslau. Střední Čechy, C Czech Republic
Casper 22 C3 Wyoming, C USA
Caspian Depression 89 B7 Kaz. Kaspīy Mangy Oypaty, Rus. Prikaspiyskaya Nizmennost'. depression Kazakhstan/Russian Federation
Caspian Sea 92 A4 Az. Xäzär Dänizi, Kaz. Kaspiy Tengizi, Per. Baḩr-e Khazar, Daryā-ye Khazar, Rus. Kaspiyskoye More. inland sea Asia/Europe
Cassai see Kasai
Cassel see Kassel
Castamoni see Kastamonu
Casteggio 74 B2 Lombardia, N Italy
Castelló de la Plana see Castellón de la Plana
Castellón see Castellón de la Plana
Castellón de la Plana 71 F3 var. Castellón, Cat. Castelló de la Plana. País Valenciano, E Spain
Castelnaudary 69 C6 Aude, S France
Castelo Branco 70 C3 Castelo Branco, C Portugal
Castelsarrasin 69 B6 Tarn-et-Garonne, S France
Castelvetrano 75 C7 Sicilia, Italy, C Mediterranean Sea
Castilla-La Mancha 71 E3 autonomous community NE Spain
Castilla-León 70 C2 var. Castillia y Leon. autonomous community NW Spain
Castillia y Leon see Castilla-León
Castlebar 67 A5 Ir. Caisleán an Bharraigh. W Ireland
Castleford 67 D5 N England, United Kingdom
Castle Harbour 20 B5 inlet Bermuda, NW Atlantic Ocean
Castra Regina see Regensburg
Castricum 64 C3 Noord-Holland, W Netherlands
Castries 33 F1 country capital N Saint Lucia
Castro 43 B6 Los Lagos, W Chile
Castrovillari 75 D6 Calabria, SW Italy
Castuera 70 D4 Extremadura, W Spain
Caswell Sound 129 A7 sound South Island, New Zealand
Catacamas 30 D2 Olancho, C Honduras
Catacaos 38 B3 Piura, NW Peru
Catalan Bay 71 H4 bay E Gibraltar, Mediterranean Sea
Cataluña 71 G2 N Spain
Catamarca see San Fernando del Valle de Catamarca
Catania 75 D7 Sicilia, Italy, C Mediterranean Sea
Catanzaro 75 D6 Calabria, SW Italy
Catarroja 71 F3 País Valenciano, E Spain
Cat Island 32 C1 island C Bahamas
Catskill Mountains 19 F3 mountain range New York, NE USA
Cattaro see Kotor
Cauca, Río 36 B2 river N Colombia
Caucasia 36 B2 Antioquia, NW Colombia
Caucasus 59 G4 Rus. Kavkaz. mountain range Georgia/Russian Federation
Caura, Río 37 E3 river C Venezuela
Cavaia see Kavajë
Cavalla 52 D5 var. Cavally, Cavally Fleuve. river Ivory Coast/Liberia
Cavally/Cavally Fleuve see Cavalla
Caviana de Fora, Ilha 41 E1 var. Ilha Caviana. island N Brazil
Caviana, Ilha see Caviana de Fora, Ilha
Cawnpore see Kānpur
Caxamarca see Cajamarca
Caxito 56 B1 Bengo, NW Angola
Cayenne 37 H3 dependent territory/arrondissement capital NE French Guiana
Cayes 32 D3 var. Les Cayes. SW Haiti
Cayman Brac 32 B3 island E Cayman Islands
Cayman Islands 32 B3 UK dependent territory W West Indies
Cayo see San Ignacio
Cay Sal 32 B2 islet SW Bahamas
Cazin 78 B3 Federacija Bosna I Hercegovina, NW Bosnia and Herzegovina
Cazorla 71 E4 Andalucía, S Spain
Ceadâr-Lunga see Ciadîr-Lunga
Ceará 41 F2 off. Estado do Ceará. state C Brazil
Ceará 41 F2 off. Estado do Ceará. region C Brazil
Ceará see Fortaleza
Ceara Abyssal Plain see Ceará Plain
Ceará, Estado do see Ceará
Ceará Plain 34 E3 var. Ceara Abyssal Plain. abyssal plain W Atlantic Ocean
Ceatharlach see Carlow
Cébaco, Isla 31 F5 island SW Panama
Cebu 117 E2 off. Cebu City. Cebu, C Philippines
Cebu City see Cebu
Čechy see Bohemia
Cecina 74 B3 Toscana, C Italy
Cedar City 22 A5 Utah, W USA
Cedar Falls 23 G3 Iowa, C USA
Cedar Lake 16 A2 lake Manitoba, C Canada
Cedar Rapids 23 G3 Iowa, C USA
Cedros, Isla 28 A2 island W Mexico
Ceduna 127 A6 South Australia
Cefalù 75 C7 anc. Cephaloedium. Sicilia, Italy, C Mediterranean Sea
Celebes 117 E4 Eng. Celebes. island C Indonesia
Celebes see Sulawesi
Celebes Sea 117 E3 Ind. Laut Sulawesi. sea Indonesia/Philippines
Celje 73 E7 Ger. Cilli. C Slovenia
Celldömölk 77 C6 Vas, W Hungary
Celle 72 B3 var. Zelle. Niedersachsen, N Germany
Celovec see Klagenfurt
Celtic Sea 67 B7 Ir. An Mhuir Cheilteach. sea SW British Isles
Celtic Shelf 58 B3 continental shelf E Atlantic Ocean
Cenderawasih, Teluk 117 G4 var. Teluk Irian, Teluk Sarera. bay W Pacific Ocean
Cenon 69 B5 Gironde, SW France
Centennial State see Colorado
Centrafricaine, République see Central African Republic
Central African Republic 54 C4 var. République Centrafricaine, abbrev. CAR; prev. Ubangi-Shari, Oubangui-Chari, Territoire de l'Oubangui-Chari. country C Africa
Central, Cordillera 36 B3 mountain range W Colombia
Cordillera Central 33 E3 mountain range C Dominican Republic
Cordillera Central 31 F5 mountain range C Panama
Central, Cordillera 117 E1 mountain range Luzon, N Philippines
Central Group see Inner Islands
Centralia 24 B2 Washington, NW USA
Central Indian Ridge see Mid-Indian Ridge
Central Makran Range 112 A3 mountain range W Pakistan
Central Pacific Basin 120 D1 undersea basin C Pacific Ocean
Central Provinces and Berar see Madhya Pradesh
Central Range 122 B3 mountain range NW Papua New Guinea
Central Russian Upland 87 G1 Eng. Central Russian Upland. mountain range W Russian Federation
Central Russian Upland see Srednerusskaya Vozvyshennost'
Central Siberian Plateau 92 D3 var. Central Siberian Uplands, Eng. Central Siberian Plateau. mountain range N Russian Federation
Central Siberian Plateau/Central Siberian Uplands see Srednesibirskoye Ploskogor'ye
Central, Sistema 70 D3 mountain range C Spain
Central Valley 25 B6 valley California, W USA
Centum Cellae see Civitavecchia
Ceos see Tziá
Cephaloedium see Cefalù
Ceram see Seram, Pulau
Ceram Sea 117 F4 Ind. Laut Seram. sea E Indonesia
Cerasus see Giresun
Cereté 36 B2 Córdoba, NW Colombia
Cergy-Pontoise see Pontoise
Cerignola 75 D5 Puglia, SE Italy
Çerkeş 94 C2 Çankırı, N Turkey
Cernăuţi see Chernivtsi
Cernay 68 E4 Haut-Rhin, NE France
Cerro de Pasco 38 C3 Pasco, C Peru
Cervera 71 F2 Cataluña, NE Spain
Cervino, Monte see Matterhorn
Cesena 74 C3 anc. Caesena. Emilia-Romagna, N Italy
Cēsis 84 D3 Ger. Wenden. Cēsis, C Latvia
Česká Republika see Czech Republic
České Budějovice 77 B5 Ger. Budweis. Jihočeský Kraj, S Czech Republic
Český Krumlov 77 A5 var. Böhmisch-Krumau, Ger. Krummau. Jihočeský Kraj, S Czech Republic
Ceský Les see Bohemian Forest
Cetatea Damboviţei see Bucureşti
Cetinje 79 C5 It. Cettigne. S Montenegro
Cette see Sète
Cettigne see Cetinje
Ceuta 48 C2 enclave Spain, N Africa
Cévennes 69 C6 mountain range S France
Ceyhan 94 D4 Adana, S Turkey
Ceylanpınar 95 E4 Şanlıurfa, SE Turkey
Ceylon see Sri Lanka
Ceylon Plain 102 B4 abyssal plain N Indian Ocean
Ceyre to the Caribs see Marie-Galante
Chachapoyas 38 B2 Amazonas, NW Peru
Chachevichy 85 D6 Rus. Chechevichi. Mahilyowskaya Voblasts', E Belarus
Chaco see Gran Chaco
Chad 54 C3 off. Republic of Chad, Fr. Tchad. country C Africa
Chad, Lake 54 B3 Fr. Lac Tchad. lake C Africa
Chad, Republic of see Chad
Chadron 22 D3 Nebraska, C USA
Chadyr-Lunga see Ciadîr-Lunga
Chagai Hills 112 A2 var. Chāh Gay. mountain range Afghanistan/Pakistan
Chaghasarāy see Asadābād
Chagos-Laccadive Plateau 102 B4 undersea plateau N Indian Ocean
Chagos Trench 119 C5 trench N Indian Ocean
Chāh Gay see Chāgai Hills
Chaillu, Massif du 55 B6 mountain range C Gabon
Chain Ridge 118 B4 undersea ridge W Indian Ocean
Chajul 30 B2 Quiché, W Guatemala
Chakhānsūr 100 D5 Nīmrūz, SW Afghanistan
Chala 38 D4 Arequipa, SW Peru
Chalatenango 30 C3 Chalatenango, N El Salvador
Chalcidice see Chalkidikí
Chalcis see Chalkída
Chalki 83 E7 island Dodekánisa, Greece, Aegean Sea
Chalkída 83 C5 var. Halkida, prev. Khalkís; anc. Chalcis. Evvoia, E Greece
Chalkidikí 82 C4 var. Khalkidhikí; anc. Chalcidice. peninsula NE Greece
Challans 68 B4 Vendée, NW France
Challapata 39 F4 Oruro, SW Bolivia
Challenger Deep 130 B3 trench W Pacific Ocean
Challenger Deep see Mariana Trench
Challenger Fracture Zone 131 F4 tectonic feature SE Pacific Ocean
Châlons-en-Champagne 68 D3 prev. Châlons-sur-Marne, hist. Arcae Remorum; anc. Carolopois. Marne, NE France
Châlons-sur-Marne see Châlons-en-Champagne
Chalon-sur-Saône 68 D4 anc. Cabillonum. Saône-et-Loire, C France
Cha Mai see Thung Song
Chaman 112 B2 Baluchistān, SW Pakistan
Chambéry 69 D5 anc. Camberia. Savoie, E France
Champagne 68 D3 cultural region N France
Champagne see Campania
Champaign 18 B4 Illinois, N USA
Champasak 115 D5 Champasak, S Laos
Champlain, Lake 19 F2 lake Canada/USA
Champotón 29 G4 Campeche, SE Mexico
Chanak see Çanakkale
Chañaral 42 B3 Atacama, N Chile
Chan-chiang/Chanchiang see Zhanjiang
Chandeleur Islands 20 C3 island group Louisiana, S USA
Chandīgarh 112 D2 state capital Punjab, N India
Chandrapur 113 E5 Mahārāshtra, C India
Changan see Xi'an, Shaanxi, C China
Changane 57 E3 river S Mozambique
Changchun 106 D3 var. Ch'angch'un, Ch'ang-ch'un; prev. Hsinking. province capital Jilin, NE China
Ch'angch'un/Ch'ang-ch'un see Changchun
Changkiakow see Zhangjiakou
Chang, Ko 115 C6 island S Thailand
Changsha 106 C5 var. Ch'angsha, Ch'ang-sha. province capital Hunan, S China
Ch'angsha/Ch'ang-sha see Changsha
Changzhi 106 C4 Shanxi, C China
Chaniá 83 C7 var. Hania, Khaniá, Eng. Canea; anc. Cydonia. Kríti, Greece, E Mediterranean Sea
Chañi, Nevado de 42 B2 mountain NW Argentina
Chankiri see Çankırı
Channel Islands 67 C8 Fr. Iles Normandes. island group S English Channel
Channel Islands 25 B8 island group California, W USA
Channel-Port aux Basques 17 G4 Newfoundland and Labrador, SE Canada
Channel, The see English Channel
Channel Tunnel 68 C2 tunnel France/United Kingdom
Chantabun/Chantaburi see Chanthaburi
Chantada 70 C1 Galicia, NW Spain
Chanthaburi 115 C6 var. Chantabun, Chantaburi. Chantaburi, S Thailand
Chanute 23 F5 Kansas, C USA
Chaouèn see Chefchaouen
Chaoyang 106 D3 Liaoning, NE China
Chapala, Lago de 28 D4 lake C Mexico
Chapan, Gora 100 B3 mountain C Turkmenistan
Chapayevsk 89 C6 Samarskaya Oblast', W Russian Federation
Chaplynka 87 F4 Khersons'ka Oblast', S Ukraine
Chapra see Chhapra
Charcot Seamounts 58 B3 seamount range E Atlantic Ocean
Chardzhev see Türkmenabat
Chardzhou/Chardzhui see Türkmenabat
Charente 69 B5 cultural region W France
Charente 69 B5 river W France
Chari 54 B3 var. Shari. river Central African Republic/Chad
Chārīkār 101 E4 Parvān, NE Afghanistan
Charity 37 F2 NW Guyana
Chärjew see Türkmenabat
Charkhlik/Charkhliq see Ruoqiang
Charleroi 65 C7 Hainaut, S Belgium
Charlesbourg 17 E4 Québec, SE Canada
Charles de Gaulle 68 E1 international airport Seine-et-Marne, N France
Charles Island 16 D1 island Nunavut, NE Canada
Charles Island see Santa María, Isla
Charleston 21 F2 South Carolina, SE USA
Charleston 18 D5 state capital West Virginia, NE USA
Charleville 127 D5 Queensland, E Australia
Charleville-Mézières 68 D3 Ardennes, N France
Charlie-Gibbs Fracture Zone 44 C2 tectonic feature N Atlantic Ocean
Charlotte 21 E1 North Carolina, SE USA
Charlotte Amalie 33 F3 prev. Saint Thomas. dependent territory capital Saint Thomas, N Virgin Islands (US)
Charlotte Harbor 21 E5 inlet Florida, SE USA
Charlottenhof see Aegviidu
Charlottesville 19 E5 Virginia, NE USA
Charlottetown 17 F4 province capital Prince Edward Island, Prince Edward Island, SE Canada
Charlotte Town see Roseau, Dominica
Charsk see Shar
Charters Towers 126 D3 Queensland, NE Australia
Chartres 68 C3 anc. Autricum, Civitas Carnutum. Eure-et-Loir, C France
Chashniki 85 D5 Vitsyebskaya Voblasts', N Belarus
Châteaubriant 68 B4 Loire-Atlantique, NW France
Châteaudun 68 C3 Eure-et-Loir, C France
Châteauroux 68 C4 prev. Indreville. Indre, C France
Château-Thierry 68 C3 Aisne, N France
Châtelet 65 C7 Hainaut, S Belgium
Châtelherault see Châtellerault
Châtellerault 68 B4 var. Châtelherault. Vienne, W France
Chatham Island see San Cristóbal, Isla
Chatham Island Rise see Chatham Rise
Chatham Islands 121 E5 island group New Zealand, SW Pacific Ocean
Chatham Rise 120 D5 var. Chatham Island Rise. undersea rise S Pacific Ocean
Chatkal Range 101 F2 Rus. Chatkal'skiy Khrebet. mountain range Kyrgyzstan/Uzbekistan
Chatkal'skiy Khrebet see Chatkal Range
Chāttagām see Chittagong
Chattahoochee River 20 D3 river SE USA
Chattanooga 20 D1 Tennessee, S USA
Chatyr-Tash 101 G2 Narynskaya Oblast', C Kyrgyzstan
Châu Đốc 115 D6 var. Chauphu, Chau Phu. An Giang, S Vietnam
Chauk 114 A3 Magway, W Myanmar (Burma)
Chaumont 68 D4 prev. Chaumont-en-Bassigny. Haute-Marne, N France
Chaumont-en-Bassigny see Chaumont
Chau Phu see Châu Đốc
Chausy see Chavusy
Chaves 70 C2 anc. Aquae Flaviae. Vila Real, N Portugal
Chávez, Isla see Santa Cruz, Isla
Chavusy 85 E6 Rus. Chausy. Mahilyowskaya Voblasts', E Belarus
Chaykovskiy 89 D5 Permskaya Oblast', NW Russian Federation
Cheb 77 A5 Ger. Eger. Karlovarský Kraj, W Czech Republic
Cheboksary 89 C5 Chuvashskaya Respublika, W Russian Federation
Cheboygan 18 C2 Michigan, N USA
Chechaouèn see Chefchaouen
Chech, Erg 52 D1 desert Algeria/Mali
Chechevichi see Chachevichy
Che-chiang see Zhejiang
Cheduba Island 114 A4 island W Myanmar (Burma)
Chefchaouen 48 C2 var. Chaouèn, Chechaouèn, Sp. Xauen. N Morocco
Chefoo see Yantai
Cheju-do 107 E4 Jap. Saishū; prev. Quelpart. island S South Korea
Cheju Strait 107 E4 Eng. Cheju Strait. strait S South Korea
Cheju Strait see Cheju-haehyŏp
Chekiang see Zhejiang
Cheleken see Hazar
Chelkar see Shalkar
Chełm 76 E4 Rus. Kholm. Lubelskie, SE Poland
Chełmno 76 C3 Ger. Culm, Kulm. Kujawski-pomorskie, C Poland
Chełmża 76 C3 Ger. Culmsee, Kulmsee. Kujawski-pomorskie, C Poland
Cheltenham 67 D6 C England, United Kingdom
Chelyabinsk 92 C3 Chelyabinskaya Oblast', C Russian Federation
Chemnitz 72 D4 prev. Karl-Marx-Stadt. Sachsen, E Germany
Chemulpo see Inch'ŏn
Chenāb 112 C2 river India/Pakistan
Chengchiatun see Liaoyuan
Ch'eng-chou/Chengchow see Zhengzhou
Chengde 106 D3 var. Jehol. Hebei, E China
Chengdu 106 B5 var. Chengtu, Ch'eng-tu. province capital Sichuan, C China
Chenghsien see Zhengzhou
Chengtu/Ch'eng-tu see Chengdu
Chennai 110 D2 prev. Madras. state capital Tamil Nādu, S India
Chenstokhov see Częstochowa
Chen Xian/Chenxian/Chen Xiang see Chenzhou
Chenzhou 106 C6 var. Chenxian, Chen Xian, Chen Xiang. Hunan, S China
Chepelare 82 C3 Smolyan, S Bulgaria
Chepén 38 B3 La Libertad, C Peru
Cher 68 C4 river C France
Cherbourg 68 B3 anc. Carusbur. Manche, N France
Cherepovets 88 B4 Vologodskaya Oblast', NW Russian Federation
Chergui, Chott ech 48 D2 salt lake NW Algeria
Cherikov see Cherykaw
Cherkassy see Cherkasy
Cherkasy 87 E2 Rus. Cherkassy. Cherkas'ka Oblast', C Ukraine
Cherkessk 89 B7 Karachayevo-Cherkesskaya Respublika, SW Russian Federation
Chernigov see Chernihiv
Chernihiv 87 E1 Rus. Chernigov. Chernihivs'ka Oblast', NE Ukraine
Chernivtsi 86 C3 Ger. Czernowitz, Rom. Cernăuţi, Rus. Chernovtsy. Chernivets'ka Oblast', W Ukraine
Cherno More see Black Sea
Chernomorskoye More see Chornomors'ke
Chernovtsy see Chernivtsi
Chernoye More see Black Sea
Chernyakhovsk 84 A4 Ger. Insterburg. Kaliningradskaya Oblast', W Russian Federation
Cherry Hill 19 F4 New Jersey, NE USA
Cherski Range see Cherskogo, Khrebet
Cherskiy 93 G2 Respublika Sakha (Yakutiya), NE Russian Federation
Cherskogo, Khrebet 93 F2 var. Cherski Range. mountain range NE Russian Federation
Cherso see Cres
Cherven' see Chervyen'
Chervonograd see Chervonohrad
Chervonohrad 86 C2 Rus. Chervonograd. L'vivs'ka Oblast', NW Ukraine
Chervyen' 85 D6 Rus. Cherven'. Minskaya Voblasts', C Belarus
Cherykaw 85 E7 Rus. Cherikov. Mahilyowskaya Voblasts', E Belarus
Chesapeake Bay 19 F5 inlet NE USA
Chesha Bay see Chëshskaya Guba
Chëshskaya Guba 133 D5 var. Archangel Bay, Chesha Bay, Dvina Bay. bay NW Russian Federation
Chester 67 C6 Wel. Caerleon, hist. Legaceaster, Lat. Deva, Devana Castra. C England, United Kingdom
Chetumal 29 H4 var. Payo Obispo. Quintana Roo, SE Mexico
Cheviot Hills 66 D4 hill range England/Scotland, United Kingdom
Cheyenne 22 D4 state capital Wyoming, C USA
Cheyenne River 22 D3 river South Dakota/Wyoming, N USA
Chezdi-Oşorheiu see Târgu Secuiesc
Chhapra 113 F3 prev. Chapra. Bihār, N India
Chhattīsgarh 113 E4 cultural region E India
Chiai 106 D6 var. Chia-i, Chiayi, Kiayi, Jiayi, Jap. Kagi. C Taiwan
Chia-i see Chiai
Chiang-hsi see Jiangxi
Chiang Mai 114 B4 var. Chiangmai, Chiengmai, Kiangmai. Chiang Mai, NW Thailand
Chiangmai see Chiang Mai
Chiang Rai 114 C3 var. Chianpai, Chienrai, Muang Chiang Rai. Chiang Rai, NW Thailand
Chiang-su see Jiangsu
Chianning/Chian-ning see Nanjing
Chianpai see Chiang Rai
Chianti 74 C3 cultural region C Italy
Chiapa see Chiapa de Corzo
Chiapa de Corzo 29 G5 var. Chiapa. Chiapas, SE Mexico
Chiayi see Chiai
Chiba 108 B1 var. Tiba. Chiba, Honshū, S Japan
Chibougamau 16 D3 Québec, SE Canada
Chicago 18 B3 Illinois, N USA
Ch'i-ch'i-ha-erh see Qiqihar
Chickasha 27 G2 Oklahoma, C USA
Chiclayo 38 B3 Lambayeque, NW Peru
Chico 25 B5 California, W USA
Chico, Río 43 B7 river SE Argentina
Chico, Río 43 B6 river S Argentina
Chicoutimi 17 E4 Québec, SE Canada
Chiengmai see Chiang Mai
Chienrai see Chiang Rai
Chiesanuova 74 D2 SW San Marino
Chieti 74 D4 var. Teate. Abruzzo, C Italy
Chifeng 105 G2 var. Ulanhad. Nei Mongol Zizhiqu, N China
Chigirin see Chyhyryn
Chih-fu see Yantai
Chihli see Hebei
Chihli, Gulf of see Bo Hai
Chihuahua 28 C2 Chihuahua, NW Mexico
Childress 27 F2 Texas, SW USA
Chile 42 B3 off. Republic of Chile. country SW South America
Chile Basin 35 A5 undersea basin E Pacific Ocean
Chile Chico 43 B6 Aisén, W Chile
Chile, Republic of see Chile
Chile Rise 35 A7 undersea rise SE Pacific Ocean
Chilia-Nouă see Kiliya
Chililabombwe 56 D2 Copperbelt, C Zambia
Chi-lin see Jilin
Chillán 43 B5 Bío Bío, C Chile
Chillicothe 18 D4 Ohio, N USA
Chill Mhantáin, Sléibhte see Wicklow Mountains
Chiloé, Isla de 43 A6 var. Isla Grande de Chiloé. island W Chile
Chilpancingo 29 E5 var. Chilpancingo de los Bravos. Guerrero, S Mexico
Chilpancingo de los Bravos see Chilpancingo
Chilung 106 D6 var. Keelung, Jap. Kirun, Kirun'; prev. Sp. Santissima Trinidad. N Taiwan
Chimán 31 G5 Panamá, E Panama
Chimbay see Chimboy
Chimborazo 38 A1 volcano C Ecuador
Chimbote 38 C3 Ancash, W Peru
Chimboy 100 D1 Rus. Chimbay. Qoraqalpog'iston Respublikasi, NW Uzbekistan
Chimkent see Shymkent
Chimoio 57 E3 Manica, C Mozambique
China 102 C2 off. People's Republic of China, Chin. Chung-hua Jen-min Kung-ho-kuo, Zhonghua Renmin Gongheguo; prev. Chinese Empire. country E Asia
Chi-nan/Chinan see Jinan
Chinandega 30 C3 Chinandega, NW Nicaragua
China, People's Republic of see China
China, Republic of see Taiwan
Chincha Alta 38 D4 Ica, SW Peru
Chin-chiang see Quanzhou
Chin-chou/Chinchow see Jinzhou
Chindwin see Chindwinn
Chindwinn 114 B2 var. Chindwin. river N Myanmar (Burma)
Chinese Empire see China
Chinghai see Qinghai
Ch'ing Hai see Qinghai Hu, China
Chingola 56 D2 Copperbelt, C Zambia
Ching-Tao/Ch'ing-tao see Qingdao
Chinguețți 52 C2 var. Chinguetti. Adrar, C Mauritania
Chin Hills 114 A3 mountain range W Myanmar (Burma)
Chinhsien see Jinzhou
Chinnereth see Tiberias, Lake
Chinook Trough 91 H4 trough N Pacific Ocean
Chioggia 74 C2 anc. Fossa Claudia. Veneto, NE Italy
Chíos 83 D5 var. Hios, Khíos, It. Scio, Turk. Sakiz-Adasi. Chíos, E Greece
Chíos 83 D5 var. Khíos. island E Greece
Chipata 56 D2 prev. Fort Jameson. Eastern, E Zambia
Chiquián 38 C3 Ancash, W Peru
Chiquimula 30 B2 Chiquimula, SE Guatemala
Chīrāla 110 D1 Andhra Pradesh, E India
Chirchik see Chirchiq
Chirchiq 101 E2 Rus. Chirchik. Toshkent Viloyati, E Uzbekistan
Chiriqui Gulf 31 E5 Eng. Chiriqui Gulf. gulf SW Panama
Chiriqui Gulf see Chiriquí, Golfo de
Chiriquí, Laguna de 31 E5 lagoon NW Panama
Chiriquí, Volcán de see Barú, Volcán
Chirripó, Cerro see Chirripó Grande, Cerro
Chirripó Grande, Cerro 30 D4 var. Cerro Chirripó. mountain SE Costa Rica
Chisec 30 B2 Alta Verapaz, C Guatemala
Chisholm 23 F1 Minnesota, N USA

Chisimaio/Chisimayu – Crooked Island

Chisimaio/Chisimayu see Kismaayo
Chişinău 86 D4 Rus. Kishinev. country capital C Moldova
Chita 93 F4 Chitinskaya Oblast', S Russian Federation
Chitangwiza see Chitungwiza
Chitato 56 C1 Lunda Norte, NE Angola
Chitina 14 D3 Alaska, USA
Chitose 108 D2 var. Titose. Hokkaidō, NE Japan
Chitré 31 F5 Herrera, S Panama
Chittagong 113 G4 Ben. Chāttagām. Chittagong, SE Bangladesh
Chitungwiza 56 D3 prev. Chitangwiza. Mashonaland East, NE Zimbabwe
Chkalov see Orenburg
Chlef 48 D2 var. Ech Cheliff, Ech Chleff; prev. Al-Asnam, El Asnam, Orléansville. NW Algeria
Chocolate Mountains 25 D8 mountain range California, W USA
Chodorów see Khodoriv
Chodzież 76 C3 Wielkopolskie, C Poland
Choele Choel 43 C5 Río Negro, C Argentina
Choiseul 122 C3 var. Lauru. island NW Solomon Islands
Chojnice 76 C2 Ger. Konitz. Pomorskie, N Poland
Ch'ok'ē 50 C4 var. Choke Mountains. mountain range NW Ethiopia
Choke Mountains see Ch'ok'ē
Cholet 68 B4 Maine-et-Loire, NW France
Choluteca 30 C3 Choluteca, S Honduras
Choluteca, Río 30 C3 river SW Honduras
Choma 56 D2 Southern, S Zambia
Chomutov 76 A4 Ger. Komotau. Ústecký Kraj, NW Czech Republic
Chona 91 E2 river C Russian Federation
Chon Buri 115 C5 prev. Bang Pla Soi. Chon Buri, S Thailand
Chone 38 A1 Manabí, W Ecuador
Ch'ŏngjin 107 E3 NE North Korea
Chongqing 106 B5 var. Ch'ung-ching, Ch'ung-ch'ing, Chungking, Pahsien, Tchongking, Yuzhou. Chongqing Shi, C China
Chonnacht see Connaught
Chonos, Archipiélago de los 43 A6 island group S Chile
Chóra Sfakíon 83 C8 var. Sfákia. Kríti, Greece, E Mediterranean Sea
Chorne More see Black Sea
Chornomors'ke 87 E4 Rus. Chernomorskoye. Respublika Krym, S Ukraine
Chorokh/Chorokhi see Çoruh Nehri
Chortkiv 86 C2 Rus. Chortkov. Ternopil's'ka Oblast', W Ukraine
Chortkov see Chortkiv
Chorzów 77 C5 Ger. Königshütte; prev. Królewska Huta. Śląskie, S Poland
Chośebuz see Cottbus
Chōsen-kaikyō see Korea Strait
Chōshi 109 D5 var. Tyôsi. Chiba, Honshū, S Japan
Chosŏn-minjujuŭi-inmin-kanghwaguk see North Korea
Choszczno 76 B3 Ger. Arnswalde. Zachodnio-pomorskie, NW Poland
Chota Nagpur 113 E4 plateau N India
Choûm 52 C2 Adrar, C Mauritania
Choybalsan 105 F2 prev. Byan Tumen. Dornod, E Mongolia
Christchurch 129 C6 Canterbury, South Island, New Zealand
Christiana 32 B5 C Jamaica
Christiania see Oslo
Christiansand see Kristiansand
Christianshåb see Qasigiannguit
Christiansund see Kristiansund
Christmas Island 119 D5 Australian external territory E Indian Ocean
Christmas Island see Kiritimati
Christmas Ridge 121 E1 undersea ridge C Pacific Ocean
Chuan see Sichuan
Ch'uan-chou see Quanzhou
Chubek see Moskva
Chubut, Río 43 B6 river SE Argentina
Ch'u-chiang see Shaoguan
Chudskoye Ozero see Peipus, Lake
Chugoku-sanchi 109 B6 mountain range Honshū, SW Japan
Chuí see Chuy
Chukai see Cukai
Chukchi Plain 133 B2 abyssal plain Arctic Ocean
Chukchi Plateau 12 C2 undersea plateau Arctic Ocean
Chukchi Sea 12 B2 Rus. Chukotskoye More. sea Arctic Ocean
Chukotskoye More see Chukchi Sea
Chula Vista 25 C8 California, W USA
Chulucanas 38 B2 Piura, NW Peru
Chulym 92 D4 river C Russian Federation
Chumphon 115 C6 var. Jumporn. Chumphon, SW Thailand
Ch'unch'ŏn 107 E4 Jap. Shunsen. N South Korea
Ch'ung-ch'ing/Ch'ung-ching see Chongqing
Chung-hua Jen-min Kung-ho-kuo see China
Chungking see Chongqing
Chunya 93 E3 river C Russian Federation
Chuquicamata 42 B2 Antofagasta, N Chile
Chuquisaca see Sucre
Chur 73 B7 Fr. Coire, It. Coira, Rmsch. Cuera, Quera; anc. Curia Rhaetorum. Graubünden, E Switzerland
Churchill 15 G4 Manitoba, C Canada
Churchill 16 B2 river Manitoba/Saskatchewan, C Canada
Churchill 17 F2 river Newfoundland and Labrador, E Canada
Chuska Mountains 26 C1 mountain range Arizona/New Mexico, SW USA
Chusovoy 89 D5 Permskaya Oblast', NW Russian Federation
Chust see Khust
Chuuk Islands 122 B2 var. Hogoley Islands; prev. Truk Islands. island group Caroline Islands, C Micronesia
Chuy 42 E4 var. Chuí. Rocha, E Uruguay
Chyhyryn 87 E2 Rus. Chigirin. Cherkas'ka Oblast', N Ukraine
Ciadîr-Lunga 86 D4 var. Ceadâr-Lunga, Rus. Chadyr-Lunga. S Moldova
Cide 94 C2 Kastamonu, N Turkey
Ciechanów 76 D3 prev. Zichenau. Mazowieckie, C Poland
Ciego de Ávila 32 C2 Ciego de Ávila, C Cuba
Ciénaga 36 B1 Magdalena, N Colombia
Cienfuegos 32 B2 Cienfuegos, C Cuba
Cieza 71 E4 Murcia, SE Spain
Cihanbeyli 94 C3 Konya, C Turkey
Cikobia 123 E4 prev. Thikombia. island N Fiji
Cilacap 116 C5 prev. Tjilatjap. Jawa, C Indonesia
Cill Airne see Killarney
Cill Chainnigh see Kilkenny
Cilli see Celje
Cill Mhantáin see Wicklow
Cimpina see Câmpina
Cimpulung see Câmpulung
Cina Selatan, Laut see South China Sea
Cincinnati 18 C4 Ohio, N USA
Ciney 65 C7 Namur, SE Belgium
Cinto, Monte 69 E7 mountain Corse, France, C Mediterranean Sea
Cintra see Sintra
Cipolletti 43 B5 Río Negro, C Argentina
Cirebon 116 C4 prev. Tjirebon. Jawa, S Indonesia
Cirkvenica see Crikvenica
Ciro Marina 75 E6 Calabria, S Italy
Cirquenizza see Crikvenica
Cisnădie 86 B4 Ger. Heltau, Hung. Nagydisznód. Sibiu, SW Romania
Citharista see la Ciotat
Citlaltépetl see Orizaba, Volcán Pico de
Citrus Heights 25 B5 California, W USA
Ciudad Acuña see Villa Acuña
Ciudad Bolívar 37 E2 prev. Angostura. Bolívar, E Venezuela
Ciudad Camargo 28 D2 Chihuahua, N Mexico
Ciudad Cortés see Cortés
Ciudad Darío 30 D3 var. Dario. Matagalpa, W Nicaragua
Ciudad de Dolores Hidalgo see Dolores Hidalgo
Ciudad de Guatemala 30 B2 Eng. Guatemala City; prev. Santiago de los Caballeros. country capital Guatemala, C Guatemala
Ciudad del Carmen see Carmen
Ciudad del Este 42 E2 prev. Ciudad Presidente Stroessner, Presidente Stroessner, Puerto Presidente Stroessner. Alto Paraná, SE Paraguay
Ciudad Delicias see Delicias
Ciudad de México see México
Ciudad de Panama see Panamá
Ciudad Guayana 37 E2 prev. San Tomé de Guayana, Santo Tomé de Guayana. Bolívar, NE Venezuela
Ciudad Guzmán 28 D4 Jalisco, SW Mexico
Ciudad Hidalgo 29 G5 Chiapas, SE Mexico
Ciudad Juárez 28 C1 Chihuahua, N Mexico
Ciudad Lerdo 28 D3 Durango, C Mexico
Ciudad Madero 29 E3 var. Villa Cecilia. Tamaulipas, C Mexico
Ciudad Mante 29 E3 Tamaulipas, C Mexico
Ciudad Miguel Alemán 29 E2 Tamaulipas, C Mexico
Ciudad Obregón 28 B2 Sonora, NW Mexico
Ciudad Ojeda 36 C1 Zulia, NW Venezuela
Ciudad Porfirio Díaz see Piedras Negras
Ciudad Presidente Stroessner see Ciudad del Este
Ciudad Quesada see Quesada
Ciudad Real 70 D3 Castilla-La Mancha, C Spain
Ciudad-Rodrigo 70 C3 Castilla-León, N Spain
Ciudad Trujillo see Santo Domingo
Ciudad Valles 29 E3 San Luis Potosí, C Mexico
Ciudad Victoria 29 E3 Tamaulipas, C Mexico
Ciutadella 71 H3 var. Ciutadella de Menorca. Menorca, Spain, W Mediterranean Sea
Ciutadella Ciutadella de Menorca see Ciutadella
Civitanova Marche 74 D3 Marche, C Italy
Civitas Altae Ripae see Brzeg
Civitas Carnutum see Chartres
Civitas Eburovicum see Évreux
Civitavecchia 74 C4 anc. Centum Cellae, Trajani Portus. Lazio, C Italy
Claremore 27 G1 Oklahoma, C USA
Clarence 129 C5 Canterbury, South Island, New Zealand
Clarence 129 C5 river South Island, New Zealand
Clarence Town 32 D2 Long Island, C Bahamas
Clarinda 23 F4 Iowa, C USA
Clarion Fracture Zone 131 E2 tectonic feature NE Pacific Ocean
Clarión, Isla 28 A5 island W Mexico
Clark Fork 22 A1 river Idaho/Montana, NW USA
Clark Hill Lake 21 E2 var. J.Storm Thurmond Reservoir. reservoir Georgia/South Carolina, SE USA
Clarksburg 18 D4 West Virginia, NE USA
Clarksdale 20 B2 Mississippi, S USA
Clarksville 20 C1 Tennessee, S USA
Clausentum see Southampton
Clayton 27 E1 New Mexico, SW USA
Clearwater 21 E4 Florida, SE USA
Clearwater Mountains 24 D2 mountain range Idaho, NW USA
Cleburne 27 G3 Texas, SW USA
Clermont 126 D4 Queensland, E Australia
Clermont-Ferrand 69 C5 Puy-de-Dôme, C France
Cleveland 18 D3 Ohio, N USA
Cleveland 20 D1 Tennessee, S USA
Clifton 26 C2 Arizona, SW USA
Clinton 20 B2 Mississippi, S USA
Clinton 27 F1 Oklahoma, C USA
Clipperton Fracture Zone 131 E3 tectonic feature E Pacific Ocean
Clipperton Island 13 A7 French dependency of French Polynesia E Pacific Ocean
Cloncurry 126 B3 Queensland, C Australia
Clonmel 67 B6 Ir. Cluain Meala. S Ireland
Cloppenburg 72 B3 Niedersachsen, NW Germany
Cloquet 23 G2 Minnesota, N USA
Cloud Peak 22 C3 mountain Wyoming, C USA
Clovis 27 E2 New Mexico, SW USA
Cluain Meala see Clonmel
Cluj see Cluj-Napoca
Cluj-Napoca 86 B3 Ger. Klausenburg, Hung. Kolozsvár; prev. Cluj. Cluj, NW Romania
Clutha 129 B7 river South Island, New Zealand
Clyde 66 C4 river W Scotland, United Kingdom
Coari 40 D2 Amazonas, N Brazil
Coast Mountains 14 D4 Fr. Chaîne Côtière. mountain range Canada/USA
Coast Ranges 24 A4 mountain range W USA
Coats Island 15 G3 island Nunavut, NE Canada
Coats Land 132 B2 physical region Antarctica
Coatzacoalcos 29 G4 var. Quetzalcoalco; prev. Puerto México. Veracruz-Llave, E Mexico
Cobán 30 B2 Alta Verapaz, C Guatemala
Cobar 127 C6 New South Wales, SE Australia
Cobija 39 E3 Pando, NW Bolivia
Coblence/Coblenz see Koblenz
Coburg 73 C5 Bayern, SE Germany
Coca see Puerto Francisco de Orellana
Cocanada see Kākināda
Cochabamba 39 F4 hist. Oropeza. Cochabamba, C Bolivia
Cochin 110 C3 var. Kochchi, Kochi. Kerala, SW India
Cochrane 16 C4 Ontario, S Canada
Cochrane 43 B7 Aisén, S Chile
Cocibolca see Nicaragua, Lago de
Cockade State see Maryland
Cockburn Town 33 E2 San Salvador, E Bahamas
Cockpit Country, The 32 A4 physical region W Jamaica
Cocobeach 55 A5 Estuaire, NW Gabon
Coconino Plateau 26 B1 plain Arizona, SW USA
Coco, Río 31 E2 var. Río Wanki, Segoviao Wangkí. river Honduras/Nicaragua
Cocos Basin 102 C5 undersea basin E Indian Ocean
Cocos Island Ridge see Cocos Ridge
Cocos Islands 119 D5 island group E Indian Ocean
Cocos Ridge 13 C8 var. Cocos Island Ridge. undersea ridge E Pacific Ocean
Cod, Cape 19 G3 headland Massachusetts, NE USA
Codfish Island 129 A8 island SW New Zealand
Codlea 86 C4 Ger. Zeiden, Hung. Feketehalom. Braşov, C Romania
Cody 22 C2 Wyoming, C USA
Coeur d'Alene 24 C2 Idaho, NW USA
Coevorden 64 E2 Drenthe, NE Netherlands
Coffs Harbour 127 E6 New South Wales, SE Australia
Cognac 69 B5 anc. Compniacum. Charente, W France
Cohalm see Rupea
Coiba, Isla de 31 E5 island SW Panama
Coihaique 43 B6 var. Coyhaique. Aisén, S Chile
Coimbatore 110 C3 Tamil Nādu, S India
Coimbra 70 B3 anc. Conimbria, Conimbriga. Coimbra, W Portugal
Coín 70 D5 Andalucía, S Spain
Coira/Coire see Chur
Coirib, Loch see Corrib, Lough
Colby 23 E4 Kansas, C USA
Colchester 67 E6 Connecticut, NE USA
Coleman 27 F3 Texas, SW USA
Coleraine 66 B4 Ir. Cúil Raithin. N Northern Ireland, United Kingdom
Colesberg 56 C5 Northern Cape, C South Africa
Colima 28 D4 Colima, S Mexico
Coll 66 B3 island W Scotland, United Kingdom
College Station 27 G3 Texas, SW USA
Collie 125 A7 Western Australia
Collipo see Leiria
Colmar 68 E4 Ger. Kolmar. Haut-Rhin, NE France
Cöln see Köln
Cologne see Köln
Colomb-Béchar see Béchar
Colombia 36 B3 off. Republic of Colombia. country N South America
Colombian Basin 34 A1 undersea basin SW Caribbean Sea
Colombia, Republic of see Colombia
Colombie-Britannique see British Columbia
Colombo 110 C4 country capital Western Province, W Sri Lanka
Colón 31 G4 prev. Aspinwall. Colón, C Panama
Colonia Agrippina see Köln
Colón Ridge 13 B8 undersea ridge E Pacific Ocean
Colorado 22 C4 off. State of Colorado, also known as Centennial State, Silver State. state C USA
Colorado City 27 F3 Texas, SW USA
Colorado Plateau 26 B1 plateau W USA
Colorado, Río 43 C5 river E Argentina
Colorado, Río see Colorado River
Colorado River 13 B5 var. Río Colorado. river Mexico/USA
Colorado River 27 G4 river Texas, SW USA
Colorado Springs 22 D5 Colorado, C USA
Columbia 19 E4 Maryland, NE USA
Columbia 23 G4 Missouri, C USA
Columbia 21 E2 state capital South Carolina, SE USA
Columbia 20 C1 Tennessee, S USA
Columbia River 24 B3 river Canada/USA
Columbia Plateau 24 C3 plateau Idaho/Oregon, NW USA
Columbus 20 D2 Georgia, SE USA
Columbus 18 C4 Indiana, N USA
Columbus 20 C2 Mississippi, S USA
Columbus 23 F4 Nebraska, C USA
Columbus 18 D4 state capital Ohio, N USA
Colville Channel 128 D2 channel North Island, New Zealand
Colville River 14 D2 river Alaska, USA
Comacchio 74 C3 var. Commachio; anc. Comactium. Emilia-Romagna, N Italy
Comactium see Comacchio
Comalcalco 29 G4 Tabasco, SE Mexico
Coma Pedrosa, Pic de 69 A7 mountain NW Andorra
Comarapa 39 F4 Santa Cruz, C Bolivia
Comayagua 30 C2 Comayagua, W Honduras
Comer See see Como, Lago di
Comilla 113 G4 Ben. Kumillā. Chittagong, E Bangladesh
Comino 80 A5 Malt. Kemmuna. island C Malta
Comitán 29 G5 var. Comitán de Domínguez. Chiapas, SE Mexico
Comitán de Domínguez see Comitán
Commachio see Comacchio
Commissioner's Point 20 A5 headland W Bermuda
Communism Peak 101 F3 prev. Qullai Kommunizm. mountain E Tajikistan
Como 74 B2 anc. Comum. Lombardia, N Italy
Comodoro Rivadavia 43 B6 Chubut, SE Argentina
Como, Lake 74 B2 var. Lario, Eng. Lake Como, Ger. Comer See. lake N Italy
Como, Lake see Como, Lago di
Comores, République Fédérale Islamique des see Comoros
Comoros 57 F2 off. Federal Islamic Republic of the Comoros, Fr. République Fédérale Islamique des Comores. country W Indian Ocean
Comoros, Federal Islamic Republic of the see Comoros
Compiègne 68 C3 Oise, N France
Complutum see Alcalá de Henares
Compniacum see Cognac
Compostella see Santiago
Comrat 86 D4 Rus. Komrat. S Moldova
Comum see Como
Conakry 52 C4 country capital SW Guinea
Conca see Cuenca
Concarneau 68 A3 Finistère, NW France
Concepción 39 G3 Santa Cruz, E Bolivia
Concepción 43 B5 Bío Bío, C Chile
Concepción 42 D2 var. Villa Concepción. Concepción, C Paraguay
Concepción see La Concepción
Concepción de la Vega see La Vega
Conchos, Río 26 D4 river NW Mexico
Conchos, Río 28 D2 river C Mexico
Concord 19 G3 state capital New Hampshire, NE USA
Concordia 42 D4 Entre Ríos, E Argentina
Concordia 23 E4 Kansas, C USA
Côn Đao 115 E7 var. Con Son. island S Vietnam
Condate see Rennes, Ille-et-Vilaine, France
Condate see St-Claude, Jura, France
Condega 30 D3 Estelí, NW Nicaragua
Condivincum see Nantes
Confluentes see Koblenz
Công Hoa Xa Hôi Chu Nghia Viêt Nam see Vietnam
Congo 55 D5 off. Republic of the Congo, Fr. Moyen-Congo; prev. Middle Congo. country C Africa
Congo 55 C6 off. Democratic Republic of Congo; prev. Zaire, Belgian Congo, Congo (Kinshasa). country C Africa
Congo 55 C6 var. Kongo, Fr. Zaire. river C Africa
Congo Basin 55 C6 drainage basin W Dem. Rep. Congo
Congo/Congo (Kinshasa) see Congo (Democratic Republic of)
Coni see Cuneo
Conimbria/Conimbriga see Coimbra
Conjeeveram see Kānchīpuram
Connacht see Connaught
Connaught 67 A5 var. Connacht, Ir. Chonnacht, Cúige. province W Ireland
Connecticut 19 F3 off. State of Connecticut, also known as Blue Law State, Constitution State, Land of Steady Habits, Nutmeg State. state NE USA
Connecticut 19 G3 river Canada/USA
Conroe 27 G3 Texas, SW USA
Consentia see Cosenza
Consolación del Sur 32 A2 Pinar del Río, W Cuba
Con Son see Côn Đao
Constance see Konstanz
Constance, Lake 73 B7 Ger. Bodensee. lake C Europe
Constanţa 86 D5 var. Küstendje, Eng. Constanza, Ger. Konstanza, Turk. Küstence. Constanţa, SE Romania
Constantia see Coutances
Constantia see Konstanz
Constantine 49 E2 var. Qacentina, Ar. Qoussantina. NE Algeria
Constantinople see İstanbul
Constantiola see Olteniţa
Constanz see Konstanz
Constanza see Constanţa
Constitution State see Connecticut
Coo see Kos
Coober Pedy 127 A5 South Australia
Cookeville 20 D1 Tennessee, S USA
Cook Islands 123 F4 territory in free association with New Zealand S Pacific Ocean
Cook, Mount see Aoraki
Cook Strait 129 D5 var. Raukawa. strait New Zealand
Cooktown 126 D2 Queensland, NE Australia
Coolgardie 125 B6 Western Australia
Cooma 127 D7 New South Wales, SE Australia
Coomassie see Kumasi
Coon Rapids 23 F2 Minnesota, N USA
Cooper Creek 126 C4 var. Barcoo, Cooper's Creek. seasonal river Queensland/South Australia
Cooper's Creek see Cooper Creek
Coos Bay 24 A3 Oregon, NW USA
Cootamundra 127 D6 New South Wales, SE Australia
Copacabana 39 E4 La Paz, W Bolivia
Copenhagen see København
Copiapó 42 B3 Atacama, N Chile
Copperas Cove 27 G3 Texas, SW USA
Coppermine see Kugluktuk
Copper State see Arizona
Coquilhatville see Mbandaka
Coquimbo 42 B3 Coquimbo, N Chile
Corabia 86 B5 Olt, S Romania
Coral Harbour 15 G3 Southampton Island, Nunavut, NE Canada
Coral Sea 120 B3 sea SW Pacific Ocean
Coral Sea Islands 122 B4 Australian external territory SW Pacific Ocean
Corantijn River see Courantyne River
Corcovado, Golfo 43 B6 gulf S Chile
Corcyra Nigra see Korčula
Cordele 20 D3 Georgia, SE USA
Córdoba 42 C3 Córdoba, C Argentina
Córdoba 29 F4 Veracruz-Llave, E Mexico
Córdoba 70 D4 var. Cordoba, Eng. Cordova; anc. Corduba. Andalucía, SW Spain
Cordova 14 C3 Alaska, USA
Cordova/Cordoba see Córdoba
Corduba see Córdoba
Corentyne River see Courantyne River
Corfu 82 A4 var. Kérkira, Eng. Corfu. island Iónia Nisiá, Greece, C Mediterranean Sea
Corfu see Kérkyra
Coria 70 C3 Extremadura, W Spain
Corinth 20 C1 Mississippi, S USA
Corinth see Kórinthos
Corinth, Gulf of 83 B5 Eng. Gulf of Corinth; anc. Corinthiacus Sinus. gulf C Greece
Corinth, Gulf of/Corinthiacus Sinus see Korinthiakós Kólpos
Corinthus see Kórinthos
Corinto 30 C3 Chinandega, NW Nicaragua
Cork 67 A6 Ir. Corcaigh. S Ireland
Çorlu 94 A2 Tekirdağ, NW Turkey
Corner Brook 17 G3 Newfoundland, Newfoundland and Labrador, E Canada
Cornhusker State see Nebraska
Corn Islands 31 E3 var. Corn Islands. island group SE Nicaragua
Corn Islands see Maíz, Islas del
Cornwallis Island 15 F2 Island Nunavut, N Canada
Coro 36 C1 prev. Santa Ana de Coro. Falcón, NW Venezuela
Corocoro 39 F4 La Paz, W Bolivia
Coromandel 128 D2 Waikato, North Island, New Zealand
Coromandel Coast 110 D2 coast E India
Coromandel Peninsula 128 D2 peninsula North Island, New Zealand
Coronado, Bahía de 30 D5 bay S Costa Rica
Coronel Dorrego 43 C5 Buenos Aires, E Argentina
Coronel Oviedo 42 D2 Caaguazú, SE Paraguay
Corozal 30 C1 Corozal, N Belize
Corpus Christi 27 G4 Texas, SW USA
Corrales 26 D2 New Mexico, SW USA
Corrib, Lough 67 A5 Ir. Loch Coirib. lake W Ireland
Corrientes 42 D3 Corrientes, NE Argentina
Corriza see Korçë
Corsica 69 E7 Eng. Corsica. island France, C Mediterranean Sea
Corsica see Corse
Corsicana 27 G3 Texas, SW USA
Cortegana 70 C4 Andalucía, S Spain
Cortés 31 E5 var. Ciudad Cortés. Puntarenas, SE Costa Rica
Cortez, Sea of see California, Golfo de
Cortina d'Ampezzo 74 C1 Veneto, NE Italy
Coruche 70 B3 Santarém, C Portugal
Çoruh Nehri 95 E3 Geor. Chorokh, Rus. Chorokhi. river Georgia/Turkey
Çorum 94 D3 var. Chorum. Çorum, N Turkey
Corunna see A Coruña
Corvallis 24 B3 Oregon, NW USA
Corvo 70 A5 var. Ilha do Corvo. island Azores, Portugal, NE Atlantic Ocean
Corvo, Ilha do see Corvo
Cos see Kos
Cosenza 75 D6 anc. Consentia. Calabria, SW Italy
Cosne-Cours-sur-Loire 68 C4 Nièvre, Bourgogne, C France Europe
Costa Mesa 24 D2 California, W USA North America
Costa Rica 31 E4 off. Republic of Costa Rica. country Central America
Costa Rica, Republic of see Costa Rica
Costermansville see Bukavu
Cotagaita 39 F5 Potosí, S Bolivia
Côte d'Ivoire see Ivory Coast
Côte d'Ivoire, République de la see Ivory Coast
Côte d'Or 68 D4 cultural region C France
Côte Française des Somalis see Djibouti
Côtière, Chaîne see Coast Mountains
Cotonou 53 F5 var. Kotonu. S Benin
Cotrone see Crotone
Cotswold Hills 67 D6 var. Cotswolds. hill range S England, United Kingdom
Cotswolds see Cotswold Hills
Cottbus 72 D4 Lus. Chośebuz; prev. Kottbus. Brandenburg, E Germany
Cotton State, The see Alabama
Cotyora see Ordu
Couentrey see Coventry
Council Bluffs 23 F4 Iowa, C USA
Courantyne River 37 G4 var. Corantijn Rivier, Corentyne River. river Guyana/Suriname
Courland Lagoon 84 A4 Ger. Kurisches Haff, Rus. Kurskiy Zaliv. lagoon Lithuania/Russian Federation
Courtrai see Kortrijk
Coutances 68 B3 anc. Constantia. Manche, N France
Couvin 65 C7 Namur, S Belgium
Coventry 67 D6 anc. Couentrey. C England, United Kingdom
Covilhã 70 C3 Castelo Branco, E Portugal
Cowan, Lake 125 B6 lake Western Australia
Coxen Hole see Roatán
Coxin Hole see Roatán
Coyhaique see Coihaique
Coyote State, The see South Dakota
Cozhê 104 C5 Xizang Zizhiqu, W China
Cozumel, Isla 29 H3 island SE Mexico
Cracovia/Cracow see Kraków
Cradock 56 C5 Eastern Cape, S South Africa
Craig 22 C4 Colorado, C USA
Craiova 86 B5 Dolj, SW Romania
Cranbrook 15 E5 British Columbia, SW Canada
Crane see The Crane
Cranz see Zelenogradsk
Crawley 67 E7 SE England, United Kingdom
Cremona 74 B2 Lombardia, N Italy
Creole State see Louisiana
Cres 78 A3 It. Cherso; anc. Crexa. island W Croatia
Crescent City 24 A4 California, W USA
Crescent Group 106 C7 island group C Paracel Islands
Creston 23 F4 Iowa, C USA
Crestview 20 D3 Florida, SE USA
Crete 83 C7 Eng. Crete. island Greece, Aegean Sea
Créteil 68 E2 Val-de-Marne, N France
Sea of Crete 83 D7 var. Kretikon Delagos, Eng. Sea of Crete; anc. Mare Creticum. sea Greece, Aegean Sea
Crete, Sea of/Creticum, Mare see Kritikó Pélagos
Creuse 68 B4 river C France
Crewe 67 D6 C England, United Kingdom
Crexa see Cres
Crikvenica 78 A3 It. Cirquenizza; prev. Cirkvenica, Crjkvenica. Primorje-Gorski Kotar, NW Croatia
Crimea 59 F4 peninsula SE Ukraine Europe
Cristóbal 31 G4 Colón, C Panama
Cristóbal Colón, Pico 36 B1 mountain N Colombia
Cristur/Cristuru Săcuiesc see Cristuru Secuiesc
Cristuru Secuiesc 86 C4 prev. Cristur, Cristuru Săcuiesc, Sitaş Cristuru, Ger. Kreutz, Hung. Székelykeresztúr, Szitás-Keresztúr. Harghita, C Romania
Crjkvenica see Crikvenica
Crna Gora see Montenegro
Crna Reka 79 D6 river S FYR Macedonia
Crni Drim see Black Drin
Croatia 78 B3 off. Republic of Croatia, Ger. Kroatien, SCr. Hrvatska. country SE Europe
Croatia, Republic of see Croatia
Crocodile see Limpopo
Croia see Krujë
Croker Island 124 E2 island Northern Territory, N Australia
Cromwell 129 B7 Otago, South Island, New Zealand
Crooked Island 32 D2 island SE Bahamas

Crooked Island Passage – Doberai Peninsula

Crooked Island Passage *32 D2 channel* SE Bahamas
Crookston *23 F1* Minnesota, N USA
Crossen *see* Krosno Odrzańskie
Croton/Crotona *see* Crotone
Crotone *75 E6 var.* Cotrone; *anc.* Croton, Crotona. Calabria, SW Italy
Croydon *67 A8* SE England, United Kingdom
Crozet Basin *119 B6 undersea basin* S Indian Ocean
Crozet Islands *119 B7 island group* French Southern and Antarctic Territories
Crozet Plateau *119 B7 var.* Crozet Plateaus. *undersea plateau* SW Indian Ocean
Crozet Plateaus *see* Crozet Plateau
Crystal Brook *127 B6* South Australia
Csaca *see* Čadca
Csakathurn/Csáktornya *see* Čakovec
Csíkszereda *see* Miercurea-Ciuc
Csorna *77 C6* Győr-Moson-Sopron, NW Hungary
Csurgó *77 C7* Somogy, SW Hungary
Cuando *56 C2 var.* Kwando. *river* S Africa
Cuango *56 B1 var.* Kwango. *river* Angola/Dem. Rep. Congo
Cuango *see* Kwango
Cuanza *56 B1 var.* Kwanza. *river* C Angola
Cuauhtémoc *28 C2* Chihuahua, N Mexico
Cuautla *29 E4* Morelos, S Mexico
Cuba *32 B2 off.* Republic of Cuba. *country* W West Indies
Cubal *56 B2* Benguela, W Angola
Cubango *56 B2 var.* Kuvango, *Port.* Vila Artur de Paiva, Vila da Ponte. Huíla, SW Angola
Cubango *56 B2 var.* Kavango, Kavengo, Kubango, Okavango, Okavanggo. *river* S Africa
Cuba, Republic of *see* Cuba
Cúcuta *36 C2 var.* San José de Cúcuta. Norte de Santander, N Colombia
Cuddapah *110 C2* Andhra Pradesh, S India
Cuenca *38 B2* Azuay, S Ecuador
Cuenca *71 E3 anc.* Conca. Castilla-La Mancha, C Spain
Cuera *see* Chur
Cuernavaca *29 E4* Morelos, S Mexico
Cuiabá *41 E3 prev.* Cuyabá. *state capital* Mato Grosso, SW Brazil
Cúige *see* Connaught
Cúige Laighean *see* Leinster
Cúige Mumhan *see* Munster
Cuijck *64 D4* Noord-Brabant, SE Netherlands
Cúil Raithin *see* Coleraine
Cuito *56 B2 var.* Kwito. *river* SE Angola
Cukai *116 B3 var.* Chukai, Kemaman. Terengganu, Peninsular Malaysia
Cularo *see* Grenoble
Culiacán *28 C3 var.* Culiacán Rosales, Culiacán-Rosales. Sinaloa, C Mexico
Culiacán-Rosales/Culiacán Rosales *see* Culiacán
Cullera *71 F3* País Valenciano, E Spain
Cullman *20 C2* Alabama, S USA
Culm *see* Chełmno
Culmsee *see* Chełmża
Cumaná *37 E1* Sucre, NE Venezuela
Cumbal, Nevado de *36 A4 elevation* S Colombia
Cumberland *19 E4* Maryland, NE USA
Cumberland Plateau *20 D1 plateau* E USA
Cumberland Sound *15 H3 inlet* Baffin Island, Nunavut, NE Canada
Cumpas *28 B2* Sonora, NW Mexico
Cuneo *74 A2 Fr.* Coni. Piemonte, NW Italy
Cunnamulla *127 C5* Queensland, E Australia
Ćuprija *78 E4* Serbia, E Serbia
Curaçao *33 E5 island* Netherlands Antilles
Curia Rhaetorum *see* Chur
Curicó *42 B4* Maule, C Chile
Curieta *see* Krk
Curitiba *41 E4 prev.* Curytiba. *state capital* Paraná, S Brazil
Curtbunar *see* Tervel
Curtea de Argeş *86 C4 var.* Curtea-de-Arges. Argeş, S Romania
Curtea-de-Arges *see* Curtea de Argeş
Curtici *86 A4 Ger.* Kurtitsch, *Hung.* Kürtös. Arad, W Romania
Curtis Island *126 E4 island* Queensland, SE Australia
Curytiba *see* Curitiba
Curzola *see* Korčula
Cusco *39 E4 var.* Cuzco. Cusco, C Peru
Cusset *69 C5* Allier, C France
Cutch, Gulf of *see* Kachchh, Gulf of
Cuttack *113 F4* Orissa, E India
Cuvier Plateau *119 E6 undersea plateau* E Indian Ocean
Cuxhaven *72 B2* Niedersachsen, NW Germany
Cuyabá *see* Cuiabá
Cuyuni, Río *see* Cuyuni River
Cuyuni River *37 F3 var.* Río Cuyuni. *river* Guyana/Venezuela
Cuzco *see* Cusco
Cyclades *83 D6 var.* Kikládhes, *Eng.* Cyclades. *island group* SE Greece
Cyclades *see* Kykládes
Cydonia *see* Chaniá
Cymru *see* Wales
Cyprus *80 C4 off.* Republic of Cyprus, *Gk.* Kypros, *Turk.* Kıbrıs, Kıbrıs Cumhuriyeti. *country* E Mediterranean Sea
Cyprus, Republic of *see* Cyprus
Cythnos *see* Kýthnos
Czech Republic *77 A5 Cz.* Česká Republika. *country* C Europe
Czenstochau *see* Częstochowa
Czernowitz *see* Chernivtsi
Częstochowa *76 C4 Ger.* Czenstochau, Tschenstochau, *Rus.* Chenstokhov. Śląskie, S Poland
Człuchów *76 C3 Ger.* Schlochau. Pomorskie, NW Poland

D

Dabajuro *36 C1* Falcón, NW Venezuela
Dabeiba *36 B2* Antioquia, NW Colombia
Dąbrowa Tarnowska *77 D5* Małopolskie, S Poland
Dabryn' *85 C8 Rus.* Dobryn'. Homyel'skaya Voblasts', SE Belarus
Dacca *see* Dhaka
Daegu *see* Taegu
Dagana *52 B3* N Senegal
Dagda *84 D4* Krāslava, SE Latvia
Dagden *see* Hiiumaa
Dagenham *67 B8* United Kingdom
Dağliq Quarabağ *see* Nagorno-Karabakh
Dagö *see* Hiiumaa
Dagupan *117 E1 off.* Dagupan City. Luzon, N Philippines
Dagupan City *see* Dagupan
Dahm, Ramlat *99 B6 desert* NW Yemen
Dahomey *see* Benin
Daihoku *see* T'aipei
Daimiel *70 D3* Castilla-La Mancha, C Spain
Daimoniá *83 B7* Pelopónnisos, S Greece
Dainan *see* T'ainan
Daingin, Bá an *see* Dingle Bay
Dairen *see* Dalian
Dakar *52 B3 country capital* W Senegal
Dakhla *see* Ad Dakhla
Dakoro *53 G3* Maradi, S Niger
Đakovica *see* Gjakovë
Đakovo *78 C3 var.* Djakovo, *Hung.* Diakovár. Osijek-Baranja, E Croatia
Dakshin *see* Deccan
Dalain Hob *104 D3 var.* Ejin Qi. Nei Mongol Zizhiqu, N China
Dalai Nor *see* Hulun Nur
Dalaman *94 A4* Muğla, SW Turkey
Dalandzadgad *105 E3* Ömnögovĭ, S Mongolia
Đa Lat *115 E6* Lâm Đông, S Vietnam
Dalby *127 D5* Queensland, E Australia
Dale City *19 E4* Virginia, NE USA
Dalhart *27 E1* Texas, SW USA
Dali *106 A6 var.* Xiaguan. Yunnan, SW China
Dalian *106 D4 var.* Dairen, Dalien, Jay Dairen, Lüda, Ta-lien, *Rus.* Dalny. Liaoning, NE China
Dalien *see* Dalian
Dallas *27 G2* Texas, SW USA
Dalmacija *78 B4 Eng.* Dalmatia, *Ger.* Dalmatien, *It.* Dalmazia. *cultural region* S Croatia
Dalmatia/Dalmatien/Dalmazia *see* Dalmacija
Dalny *see* Dalian
Dalton *20 D1* Georgia, SE USA
Dálvvadis *see* Jokkmokk
Daly Waters *126 A2* Northern Territory, N Australia
Damachava *85 A6 var.* Damachova, *Pol.* Domaczewo, *Rus.* Domachëvo. Brestskaya Voblasts', SW Belarus
Damachova *see* Damachava
Damān *112 C4* Damān and Diu, W India
Damara *54 C4* Ombella-Mpoko, S Central African Republic
Damas *see* Dimashq
Damasco *see* Dimashq
Damascus *see* Dimashq
Qolleh-ye Damavand *98 D3 mountain* N Iran
Damietta *see* Dumyāṭ
Dammām *see* Ad Dammān
Damoûr *97 A5 var.* Ad Dāmūr. W Lebanon
Dampier *124 A4* Western Australia
Dampier, Selat *117 F4 strait* Papua, E Indonesia
Damqawt *99 D6 var.* Damqut. E Yemen
Damqut *see* Damqawt
Damxung *104 C5 var.* Gongtang. Xizang Zizhiqu, W China
Danakil Desert *50 D4 var.* Afar Depression, Danakil Plain. *desert* E Africa
Danakil Plain *see* Danakil Desert
Danané *52 D5* W Ivory Coast
Đă Nẵng *115 E5 prev.* Tourane. Quang Nam-Đa Nẵng, C Vietnam
Danborg *see* Daneborg
Dandong *106 D3 var.* Tan-tung; *prev.* An-tung. Liaoning, NE China
Daneborg *61 E3 var.* Danborg. Tunu, N Greenland
Dänew *see* Galkynyş
Dangara *see* Danghara
Dangerous Archipelago *see* Tuamotu, Îles
Danghara *101 E3 Rus.* Dangara. SW Tajikistan
Danghe Nanshan *104 D3 mountain range* W China
Dang Raek, Phanom/Dangrek, Chaîne des *see* Dângrêk, Chuŏr Phnum
Chuor Phnum Dangrek *115 D5 var.* Phanom Dang Raek, Phanom Dong Rak, *Fr.* Chaîne des Dangrek. *mountain range* Cambodia/Thailand
Dangriga *30 C1 prev.* Stann Creek. Stann Creek, E Belize
Danish West Indies *see* Virgin Islands (US)
Danlí *30 D2* El Paraíso, S Honduras
Danmark *see* Denmark
Danmarksstraedet *see* Denmark Strait
Dannenberg *72 C3* Niedersachsen, N Germany
Dannevirke *128 D4* Manawatu-Wanganui, North Island, New Zealand
Dantzig *see* Gdańsk
Danube *59 E4 Bul.* Dunav, *Cz.* Dunaj, *Ger.* Donau, *Hung.* Duna, *Rom.* Dunărea. *river* C Europe
Danubian Plain *82 C2 Eng.* Danubian Plain. *lowlands* N Bulgaria
Danubian Plain *see* Dunavska Ravnina
Danum *see* Doncaster
Danville *19 E5* Virginia, NE USA
Danxian/Dan Xian *see* Danzhou
Danzhou *106 C7 prev.* Danxian, Dan Xian, Nada. Hainan, S China
Danzig *see* Gdańsk
Danziger Bucht *see* Danzig, Gulf of
Danzig, Gulf of *76 C2 var.* Gulf of Gdańsk, *Ger.* Danziger Bucht, *Pol.* Zakota Gdańska, *Rus.* Gdan'skaya Bukhta. *gulf* N Poland
Daqm *see* Duqm
Dar'ā *97 B5 var.* Der'a, *Fr.* Déraa. Dar'ā, SW Syria
Darabani *86 C3* Botoşani, NW Romania
Daraut-Kurgan *see* Daroot-Korgon
Dardanelles *94 A2 Eng.* Dardanelles. *strait* NW Turkey
Dardanelles *see* Çanakkale Boğazı
Dardanelli *see* Çanakkale
Dar-el-Beida *see* Casablanca
Dar es Salaam *51 C7* Dar es Salaam, E Tanzania
Darfield *129 C6* Canterbury, South Island, New Zealand
Darfur *50 A4 var.* Darfur Massif. *cultural region* W Sudan
Darfur Massif *see* Darfur
Darhan *105 E2* Darhan Uul, N Mongolia
Darién, Golfo del *see* Darien, Gulf of
Darien, Gulf of *36 A2 Sp.* Golfo del Darién. *gulf* S Caribbean Sea
Darien, Isthmus of *see* Panama, Istmo de
Darién, Serranía del *31 H5 mountain range* Colombia/Panama
Dario *see* Ciudad Darío
Dariorigum *see* Vannes
Darjeeling *see* Dārjiling
Dārjiling *113 F3 prev.* Darjeeling. West Bengal, NE India
Darling River *127 C6 river* New South Wales, SE Australia
Darlington *67 D5* N England, United Kingdom
Darmstadt *73 B5* Hessen, SW Germany
Darnah *49 G2 var.* Dérna. NE Libya
Darnley, Cape *132 D2 cape* Antarctica
Daroca *71 E2* Aragón, NE Spain
Daroot-Korgon *101 F3 var.* Daraut-Kurgan. Oshskaya Oblast', SW Kyrgyzstan
Dartford *67 B8* SE England, United Kingdom
Dartmoor *67 C7 moorland* SW England, United Kingdom
Dartmouth *17 F4* Nova Scotia, SE Canada
Darvaza *see* Derweze, Turkmenistan
Darwin *124 D2 prev.* Palmerston, Port Darwin. *territory capital* Northern Territory, N Australia
Darwin, Isla *38 A4 island* Galápagos, Galapagos Islands, W Ecuador
Dashhowuz *see* Daşoguz
Dashkawka *85 D6 Rus.* Dashkovka. Mahilyowskaya Voblasts', E Belarus
Dashkovka *see* Dashkawka
Daşoguz *100 C2 Rus.* Dashkhovuz, *Turkm.* Dashhowuz; *prev.* Tashauz. Daşoguz Welaýaty, N Turkmenistan
Đa, Sông *see* Black River
Datong *106 C3 var.* Tatung, Ta-t'ung. Shanxi, C China
Daugava *see* Western Dvina
Daugavpils *84 D4 Ger.* Dünaburg; *prev. Rus.* Dvinsk. Daugvapils, SE Latvia
Daung Kyun *115 B6 island* S Myanmar (Burma)
Dauphiné *69 D5 cultural region* E France
Dāvangere *110 C2* Karnātaka, W India
Davao *117 F3 off.* Davao City. Mindanao, S Philippines
Davao City *see* Davao
Davao Gulf *117 F3 gulf* Mindanao, S Philippines
Davenport *23 G3* Iowa, C USA
David *31 E5* Chiriquí, W Panama
Davie Ridge *119 A5 undersea ridge* W Indian Ocean
Davis *132 D3 Australian research station* Antarctica
Davis Sea *132 D3 sea* Antarctica
Davis Strait *60 B3 strait* Baffin Bay/Labrador Sea
Dawei *115 B5 var.* Tavoy, Htawei. Tanintharyi, S Myanmar (Burma)
Dawlat Qaṭar *see* Qatar
Dax *69 B6 var.* Ax; *anc.* Aquae Augustae, Aquae Tarbelicae. Landes, SW France
Dayr az Zawr *96 D3 var.* Deir ez Zor. Dayr az Zawr, E Syria
Dayton *18 C4* Ohio, N USA
Daytona Beach *21 E4* Florida, SE USA
De Aar *56 C5* Northern Cape, C South Africa
Dead Sea *97 B6 var.* Bahret Lut, Lacus Asphaltites, *Ar.* Al Baḥr al Mayyit, Baḥrat Lūt, *Heb.* Yam HaMelaḥ. *salt lake* Israel/Jordan
Deán Funes *42 C3* Córdoba, C Argentina
Death Valley *25 C7 valley* California, W USA
Deatnu *62 D2 Fin.* Tenojoki, *Nor.* Tana. *river* Finland/Norway
Debar *79 D6 Ger.* Dibra, *Turk.* Debre. W FYR Macedonia
De Behagle *see* Laï
Dębica *77 D5* Podkarpackie, SE Poland
De Bildt *see* De Bilt
De Bilt *64 C3 var.* De Bildt. Utrecht, C Netherlands
Dębno *76 B3* Zachodnio-pomorskie, NW Poland
Debre *see* Debar
Debrecen *77 D6 Ger.* Debreczin, *Rom.* Debreţin; *prev.* Debreczen. Hajdú-Bihar, E Hungary
Debreczen/Debreczin *see* Debrecen
Debreţin *see* Debrecen
Decatur *20 C1* Alabama, S USA
Decatur *18 B4* Illinois, N USA
Deccan *112 D5 Hind.* Dakshin. *plateau* C India
Děčín *76 B4 Ger.* Tetschen. Ústecký Kraj, NW Czech Republic
Dedeagaç/Dedeagach *see* Alexandroúpoli
Dedemsvaart *64 E3* Overijssel, E Netherlands
Dee *66 C3 river* NE Scotland, United Kingdom
Deering *14 C2* Alaska, USA
Deés *see* Dej
Deggendorf *73 D6* Bayern, SE Germany
Değirmenlik *80 C5 Gk.* Kythréa. N Cyprus
Deh Bīd *see* Şafāshahr
Dehli *see* Delhi
Deh Shū *100 D5 var.* Deshu. Helmand, S Afghanistan
Deinze *65 B5* Oost-Vlaanderen, NW Belgium
Deir ez Zor *see* Dayr az Zawr
Deirgeirt, Loch *see* Derg, Lough
Dej *86 B3 Hung.* Dés; *prev.* Deés. Cluj, NW Romania
De Jouwer *see* Joure
Dekéleia *see* Dhekélia
Dékoa *54 C4* Kémo, C Central African Republic
De Land *21 E4* Florida, SE USA
Delano *25 C7* California, W USA
Delārām *100 D5* Nimrūz, SW Afghanistan
Delaware *18 D4* Ohio, N USA
Delaware *19 F4 off.* State of Delaware, *also known as* Blue Hen State, Diamond State, First State. *state* NE USA
Delft *64 B4* Zuid-Holland, W Netherlands
Delfzijl *64 E1* Groningen, NE Netherlands
Delgo *50 B3* Northern, N Sudan
Delhi *112 D3 var.* Dehli, *Hind.* Dilli, *hist.* Shahjahanabad. *union territory capital* Delhi, N India
Delicias *28 D2 var.* Ciudad Delicias. Chihuahua, N Mexico
Déli-Kárpátok *see* Carpaţii Meridionali
Delmenhorst *72 B3* Niedersachsen, NW Germany
Del Rio *27 F4* Texas, SW USA
Deltona *21 E4* Florida, SE USA
Demba *55 D6* Kasai-Occidental, C Dem. Rep. Congo
Dembia *54 D4* Mbomou, SE Central African Republic
Demchok *104 A5 var.* Dêmqog. *disputed region* China/India
Demerara Plain *34 C2 abyssal plain* W Atlantic Ocean
Deming *26 C3* New Mexico, SW USA
Demmin *72 C2* Mecklenburg-Vorpommern, NE Germany
Demopolis *20 C2* Alabama, S USA
Dêmqog *104 A5 var.* Demchok. China/India
Denali *see* McKinley, Mount
Denau *see* Denow
Dender *65 B6 Fr.* Dendre. *river* W Belgium
Dendre *see* Dender
Denekamp *64 E3* Overijssel, E Netherlands
Den Haag *see* 's-Gravenhage
Denham *125 A5* Western Australia
Den Ham *64 E3* Overijssel, E Netherlands
Den Helder *64 C2* Noord-Holland, NW Netherlands
Dénia *71 F4* País Valenciano, E Spain
Deniliquin *127 C7* New South Wales, SE Australia
Denison *23 F3* Iowa, C USA
Denison *27 G2* Texas, SW USA
Denizli *94 B4* Denizli, SW Turkey
Denmark *63 A7 off.* Kingdom of Denmark, *Dan.* Danmark; *anc.* Hafnia. *country* N Europe
Denmark, Kingdom of *see* Denmark
Denmark Strait *60 D4 var.* Danmarksstraedet. *strait* Greenland/Iceland
Dennery *33 F1* E Saint Lucia
Denow *101 E3 Rus.* Denau. Surkhondaryo Viloyati, S Uzbekistan
Denpasar *116 D5 prev.* Paloe. Bali, C Indonesia
Denton *27 G2* Texas, SW USA
D'Entrecasteaux Islands *122 B3 island group* SE Papua New Guinea
Denver *22 D4 state capital* Colorado, C USA
Der'a/Derá/Déraa *see* Dar'ā
Dera Ghāzi Khān *112 C2 var.* Dera Ghāzikhān. Punjab, C Pakistan
Dera Ghāzikhān *see* Dera Ghāzi Khān
Đeravica *79 D5 mountain* S Serbia
Derbent *89 B8* Respublika Dagestan, SW Russian Federation
Derby *67 D6* C England, United Kingdom
Dereli *see* Gónnoi
Dergachi *see* Derhachi
Derg, Lough *67 A6 Ir.* Loch Deirgeirt. *lake* W Ireland
Derhachi *87 G2 Rus.* Dergachi. Kharkivs'ka Oblast', E Ukraine
De Ridder *20 A3* Louisiana, S USA
Dérna *see* Darnah
Derry *see* Londonderry
Dertosa *see* Tortosa
Derventa *78 B3* Republika Srpska, N Bosnia and Herzegovina
Derweze *100 C2 Rus.* Darvaza. Ahal Welaýaty, C Turkmenistan
Dés *see* Dej
Deschutes River *24 B3 river* Oregon, NW USA
Desē *50 C4 var.* Desse, *It.* Dessie. Āmara, N Ethiopia
Deseado, Río *43 B7 river* S Argentina
Desertas, Ilhas *48 A2 island group* Madeira, Portugal, NE Atlantic Ocean
Deshu *see* Deh Shū
Des Moines *23 F3 state capital* Iowa, C USA
Desna *87 E2 river* Russian Federation/Ukraine
Dessau *72 C4* Sachsen-Anhalt, E Germany
Desse *see* Desē
Dessie *see* Desē
Destêrro *see* Florianópolis
Detroit *18 D3* Michigan, N USA
Detroit Lakes *23 F2* Minnesota, N USA
Deurne *65 D5* Noord-Brabant, SE Netherlands
Deutschendorf *see* Poprad
Deutsch-Eylau *see* Iława
Deutsch Krone *see* Wałcz
Deutschland/Deutschland, Bundesrepublik *see* Germany
Deutsch-Südwestafrika *see* Namibia
Deva *86 B4 Ger.* Diemrich, *Hung.* Déva. Hunedoara, W Romania
Déva *see* Deva
Deva *see* Chester
Devana *see* Aberdeen
Devana Castra *see* Chester
Đevđelija *see* Gevgelija
Deventer *64 D3* Overijssel, E Netherlands
Devils Lake *23 E1* North Dakota, N USA
Devoll *see* Devollit, Lumi i
Devollit, Lumi i *79 D6 var.* Devoll. *river* SE Albania
Devon Island *15 F2 prev.* North Devon Island. *island* Parry Islands, Nunavut, NE Canada
Devonport *127 C8* Tasmania, SE Australia
Devrek *94 C2* Zonguldak, N Turkey
Dexter *23 H5* Missouri, C USA
Deynau *see* Galkynyş
Dezfūl *98 C3 var.* Dizful. Khūzestān, SW Iran
Dezhou *106 D4* Shandong, E China
Dhaka *113 G4 prev.* Dacca. *country capital* Dhaka, C Bangladesh
Dhanbād *113 F4* Jhārkhand, NE India
Dhekélia *80 C5 Eng.* Dhekelia, *Gk.* Dekéleia. *UK air base* SE Cyprus
see Dhekélia
Dhidhimótikhon *see* Didymóteicho
Dhíkti Ori *see* Díkti
Dhodhekánisos *see* Dodekánisa
Dhomokós *see* Domokós
Dhráma *see* Dráma
Dhrepanon, Akrotírio *see* Drépano, Akrotírio
Dhún na nGall, Bá *see* Donegal Bay
Dhuusa Marreeb *51 E5 var.* Dusa Marreb, *It.* Dusa Mareb. Galguduud, C Somalia
Diakovár *see* Đakovo
Diamantina, Chapada *41 F3 mountain range* E Brazil
Diamantina Fracture Zone *119 E6 tectonic feature* E Indian Ocean
Diamond State *see* Delaware
Diarbekr *see* Diyarbakır
Dibio *see* Dijon
Dibra *see* Debar
Dibrugarh *113 H3* Assam, NE India
Dickinson *22 D2* North Dakota, N USA
Dicle *see* Tigris
Didimotiho *see* Didymóteicho
Didymóteicho *82 D3 var.* Dhidhimótikhon, Didimotiho. Anatolikí Makedonía kai Thráki, NE Greece
Diedenhofen *see* Thionville
Diekirch *65 D7* Diekirch, C Luxembourg
Diemrich *see* Deva
Điên Biên *114 D3 var.* Bien Bien, Dien Bien Phu. Lai Châu, N Vietnam
Dien Bien Phu *see* Điên Biên
Diepenbeek *65 D6* Limburg, NE Belgium
Diepholz *72 B3* Niedersachsen, NW Germany
Dieppe *68 C2* Seine-Maritime, N France
Dieren *64 D4* Gelderland, E Netherlands
Differdange *65 D8* Luxembourg, SW Luxembourg
Digne *69 D6 var.* Digne-les-Bains. Alpes-de-Haute-Provence, SE France
Digne-les-Bains *see* Digne
Digoel *see* Digul, Sungai
Digoin *68 C4* Saône-et-Loire, C France
Digul, Sungai *117 H5 prev.* Digoel. *river* Papua, E Indonesia
Dihang *see* Brahmaputra
Dijlah *see* Tigris
Dijon *68 D4 anc.* Dibio. Côte d'Or, C France
Dikhil *50 D4* SW Djibouti
Dikson *92 D2* Taymyrskiy (Dolgano-Nenetskiy) Avtonomnyy Okrug, N Russian Federation
Díkti *83 D8 var.* Dhíkti Ori. *mountain range* Kríti, Greece, E Mediterranean Sea
Dili *117 F5 var.* Dilli, Dilly. *country capital* N East Timor
Dilia *53 G3 var.* Dillia. *river* SE Niger
Di Linh *115 E6* Lâm Đông, S Vietnam
Dilli *see* Dili, East Timor
Dilli *see* Delhi, India
Dillia *see* Dilia
Dilling *50 B4 var.* Ad Dalanj. Southern Kordofan, C Sudan
Dillon *22 B2* Montana, NW USA
Dilly *see* Dili
Dilolo *55 D7* Katanga, S Dem. Rep. Congo
Dimashq *97 B5 var.* Ash Shām, Esh Sham, *Eng.* Damascus, *Fr.* Damas, *It.* Damasco. *country capital* Dimashq, SW Syria
Dimitrovgrad *82 D3* Khaskovo, S Bulgaria
Dimitrovgrad *89 C6 prev.* Caribrod. Serbia, SE Serbia
Dimitrovo *see* Pernik
Dimovo *82 B1* Vidin, NW Bulgaria
Dinajpur *113 F3* Rajshahi, NW Bangladesh
Dinan *68 B3* Côtes d'Armor, NW France
Dinant *65 C7* Namur, S Belgium
Dinar *94 B4* Afyon, SW Turkey
Dinara *see* Dinaric Alps
Dinaric Alps *78 C4 var.* Dinara. *mountain range* Bosnia and Herzegovina/Croatia
Dindigul *110 C3* Tamil Nādu, SE India
Dingle Bay *67 A6 Ir.* Bá an Daingin. *bay* SW Ireland
Dinguiraye *52 C4* N Guinea
Diourbel *52 B3* W Senegal
Dirē Dawa *51 D5* Dirē Dawa, E Ethiopia
Dirk Hartog Island *125 A5 island* Western Australia
Dirschau *see* Tczew
Disappointment, Lake *124 C4 salt lake* Western Australia
Discovery Bay *32 B4* Middlesex, Jamaica, Greater Antilles, C Jamaica Caribbean Sea
Disko Bugt *see* Qeqertarsuup Tunua
Dispur *113 G3 state capital* Assam, NE India
Divinópolis *41 F4* Minas Gerais, SE Brazil
Divo *52 D5* S Ivory Coast
Divodurum Mediomatricum *see* Metz
Diyarbakır *95 E4 var.* Diarbekr; *anc.* Amida. Diyarbakır, SE Turkey
Dizful *see* Dezfūl
Djailolo *see* Halmahera, Pulau
Djajapura *see* Jayapura
Djakarta *see* Jakarta
Djakovo *see* Đakovo
Djambala *55 B6* Plateaux, C Congo
Djambi *see* Hari, Batang
Djambi *see* Jambi
Djanet *49 E4 prev.* Fort Charlet. SE Algeria
Djéblé *see* Jablah
Djelfa *48 D2 var.* El Djelfa. N Algeria
Djéma *54 D4* Haut-Mbomou, E Central African Republic
Djember *see* Jember
Djérablous *see* Jarābulus
Djerba *49 F2 var.* Djerba, Jazīrat Jarbah. *island* E Tunisia
Djerba *see* Jerba, Île de
Djérem *54 B4 river* C Cameroon
Djevdjelija *see* Gevgelija
Djibouti *50 D4 var.* Jibuti. *country capital* E Djibouti
Djibouti *50 D4 off.* Republic of Djibouti, *var.* Jibuti; *prev.* French Somaliland, French Territory of the Afars and Issas, *Fr.* Côte Française des Somalis, Territoire Français des Afars et des Issas. *country* E Africa
Djibouti, Republic of *see* Djibouti
Djokjakarta *see* Yogyakarta
Djourab, Erg du *54 C2 desert* N Chad
Djúpivogur *61 E5* Austurland, SE Iceland
Dmitriyevsk *see* Makiyivka
Dnepr *see* Dnieper
Dneprodzerzhinsk *see* Romaniv
Dneprodzerzhinskoye Vodokhranilishche *see* Dniprodzerzhyns'ke Vodoskhovyshche
Dnepropetrovsk *see* Dnipropetrovs'k
Dneprorudnoye *see* Dniprorudne
Dnestr *see* Dniester
Dnieper *59 F4 Bel.* Dnyapro, *Rus.* Dnepr, *Ukr.* Dnipro. *river* E Europe
Dnieper Lowland *87 E2 Bel.* Prydnyaprowskaya Nizina, *Ukr.* Prydniprovs'ka Nyzovyna. *lowlands* Belarus/Ukraine
Dniester *59 E4 Rom.* Nistru, *Rus.* Dnestr, *Ukr.* Dnister; *anc.* Tyras. *river* Moldova/Ukraine
Dnipro *see* Dnieper
Dniprodzerzhyns'k *see* Romaniv
Dniprodzerzhyns'ke Vodoskhovyshche *87 F3 Rus.* Dneprodzerzhinskoye Vodokhranilishche. *reservoir* C Ukraine
Dnipropetrovs'k *87 F3 Rus.* Dnepropetrovsk; *prev.* Yekaterinoslav. Dnipropetrovs'ka Oblast', E Ukraine
Dniprorudne *87 F3 Rus.* Dneprorudnoye. Zaporiz'ka Oblast', SE Ukraine
Dnister *see* Dniester
Dnyapro *see* Dnieper
Doba *54 C4* Logone-Oriental, S Chad
Döbeln *72 D4* Sachsen, E Germany
Doberai Peninsula *117 G4 Dut.* Vogelkop. *peninsula* Papua, E Indonesia

Doboj 78 C3 Republiks Srpska, N Bosnia and Herzegovina

Dobre Miasto 76 D2 *Ger.* Guttstadt. Warmińsko-mazurskie, NE Poland

Dobrich 82 E1 *Rom.* Bazargic; *prev.* Tolbukhin. Dobrich, NE Bulgaria

Dobrush 85 D7 Homyel'skaya Voblasts', SE Belarus

Dobryn' *see* Dabryn'

Dodecanese 83 D6 *var.* Nóties Sporádes, *Eng.* Dodecanese; *prev.* Dhodhekánisos, Dodekanisos. *island group* SE Greece

Dodecanese *see* Dodekánisa

Dodekanisos *see* Dodekánisa

Dodge City 23 E5 Kansas, C USA

Dodoma 47 D5 *country capital* Dodoma, C Tanzania

Dogana 74 E1 NE San Marino Europe

Dogo 109 B6 *island* Oki-shotō, SW Japan

Dogondoutchi 53 F3 Dosso, SW Niger

Dogrular *see* Pravda

Doğubayazıt 95 F3 Ağrı, E Turkey

Doğu Karadeniz Dağları 95 E3 *var.* Anadolu Dağları. *mountain range* NE Turkey

Doha *see* Ad Dawhah

Doire *see* Londonderry

Dokkum 64 D1 Friesland, N Netherlands

Dokuchayevs'k 87 G3 *var.* Dokuchayevsk. Donets'ka Oblast', SE Ukraine

Dokuchayevsk *see* Dokuchayevs'k

Doldrums Fracture Zone 44 C4 *fracture zone* W Atlantic Ocean

Dôle 68 D4 Jura, E France

Dolina *see* Dolyna

Dolinskaya *see* Dolyns'ka

Dolisie 55 B6 *prev.* Loubomo. Niari, S Congo

Dolomites 74 C1 *var.* Dolomiti, *Eng.* Dolomites. *mountain range* NE Italy

Dolomites/Dolomiti *see* Dolomitiche, Alpi

Dolores 42 D4 Buenos Aires, E Argentina

Dolores 30 B1 Petén, N Guatemala

Dolores 42 D4 Soriano, SW Uruguay

Dolores Hidalgo 29 E4 *var.* Ciudad de Dolores Hidalgo. Guanajuato, C Mexico

Dolyna 86 B2 *Rus.* Dolina. Ivano-Frankivs'ka Oblast', W Ukraine

Dolyns'ka 87 F3 *Rus.* Dolinskaya. Kirovohrads'ka Oblast', S Ukraine

Domachèvo/Domaczewo *see* Damachava

Dombås 63 B5 Oppland, S Norway

Domel Island *see* Letsôk-aw Kyun

Domesnes, Cape *see* Kolkasrags

Domeyko 42 B3 Atacama, N Chile

Dominica 33 H4 *off.* Commonwealth of Dominica. *country* E West Indies

Dominica Channel *see* Martinique Passage

Dominica, Commonwealth of *see* Dominica

Dominican Republic 33 E2 *country* C West Indies

Domokós 83 B5 *var.* Dhomokós. Stereá Ellás, C Greece

Don 89 B6 *var.* Duna, Tanais. *river* SW Russian Federation

Donau *see* Danube

Donauwörth 73 C6 Bayern, S Germany

Don Benito 70 C4 Extremadura, W Spain

Doncaster 67 D5 *anc.* Danum. N England, United Kingdom

Dondo 56 B1 Cuanza Norte, NW Angola

Donegal 67 B5 *Ir.* Dún na nGall. Donegal, NW Ireland

Donegal Bay 67 A5 *Ir.* Bá Dhún na nGall. *bay* NW Ireland

Donets 87 G2 *river* Russian Federation/Ukraine

Donets'k 87 G3 *Rus.* Donetsk; *prev.* Stalino. Donets'ka Oblast', E Ukraine

Dongfang 106 B7 *var.* Basuo. Hainan, S China

Dongguan 106 C6 Guangdong, S China

Đông Ha 114 E4 Quang Tri, C Vietnam

Dong Hai *see* East China Sea

Đông Hơi 114 D4 Quang Binh, C Vietnam

Dongliao *see* Liaoyuan

Dongola 50 B3 *var.* Donqola, Dunqulah. Northern, N Sudan

Dongou 55 C5 Likouala, NE Congo

Dong Rak, Phanom *see* Dângrêk, Chuôr Phnum

Dongting Hu 106 C5 *var.* Tung-t'ing Hu. *lake* S China

Donostia-San Sebastián 71 E1 País Vasco, N Spain

Donqola *see* Dongola

Doolow 51 D5 Sumalē, E Ethiopia

Doornik *see* Tournai

Door Peninsula 18 C2 *peninsula* Wisconsin, N USA

Dooxo Nugaaleed 51 E5 *var.* Nogal Valley. *valley* E Somalia

Dordogne 69 B5 *cultural region* SW France

Dordogne 69 B5 *river* W France

Dordrecht 64 C4 *var.* Dordt, Dort. Zuid-Holland, SW Netherlands

Dordt *see* Dordrecht

Dorohoi 86 C3 Botoşani, NE Romania

Dorotea 62 C4 Västerbotten, N Sweden

Dorpat *see* Tartu

Dorre Island 125 A5 *island* Western Australia

Dort *see* Dordrecht

Dortmund 72 A4 Nordrhein-Westfalen, W Germany

Dos Hermanas 70 C4 Andalucía, S Spain

Dospad Dagh *see* Rhodope Mountains

Dospat 82 C3 Smolyan, S Bulgaria

Dothan 20 D3 Alabama, S USA

Dotnuva 84 B4 Kaunas, C Lithuania

Douai 68 C2 *prev.* Douay; *anc.* Duacum. Nord, N France

Douala 55 A5 *var.* Duala. Littoral, W Cameroon

Douay *see* Douai

Douglas 67 C5 *dependent territory capital* E Isle of Man

Douglas 26 C3 Arizona, SW USA

Douglas 22 D3 Wyoming, C USA

Douma *see* Dūmā

Douro *see* Duero

Douvres *see* Dover

Dover 67 E7 *Fr.* Douvres, *Lat.* Dubris Portus. SE England, United Kingdom

Dover 19 F4 *state capital* Delaware, NE USA

Dover, Strait of 68 C2 *var.* Straits of Dover, *Fr.* Pas de Calais. *strait* England, United Kingdom/ France

Dover, Straits of *see* Dover, Strait of

Dovrefjell 63 B5 *plateau* S Norway

Downpatrick 67 B5 *Ir.* Dún Pádraig. SE Northern Ireland, United Kingdom

Dozen 109 B6 *island* Oki-shotō, SW Japan

Drâa, Hammada du *see* Dra, Hamada du

Drač/Draç *see* Durrës

Drachten 64 D2 Friesland, N Netherlands

Drăgăşani 86 B5 Vâlcea, SW Romania

Dra, Hamada du 48 C3 *var.* Hammada du Drâa, Haut Plateau du Dra. *plateau* W Algeria

Dra, Haut Plateau du *see* Dra, Hamada du

Drahichyn 85 B6 *Pol.* Drohiczyn Poleski, *Rus.* Drogichin. Brestskaya Voblasts', SW Belarus

Drakensberg 56 D5 *mountain range* Lesotho/ South Africa

Drake Passage 35 B8 *passage* Atlantic Ocean/ Pacific Ocean

Dralfa 82 D2 Türgovishte, N Bulgaria

Dráma 82 C3 *var.* Dhráma. Anatolikí Makedonía kai Thráki, NE Greece

Dramburg *see* Drawsko Pomorskie

Drammen 63 B6 Buskerud, S Norway

Drau *see* Drava

Drava 78 C3 *var.* Drau, *Eng.* Drave, *Hung.* Dráva. *river* C Europe

Dráva/Drave *see* Drau/Drava

Drawsko Pomorskie 76 B3 *Ger.* Dramburg. Zachodnio-pomorskie, NW Poland

Drépano, Akrotírio 82 C4 *var.* Akrotírio Dhrepanon. *headland* N Greece

Drepanum *see* Trapani

Dresden 72 D4 Sachsen, E Germany

Drin *see* Drinit, Lumi

Drina 78 C3 *river* Bosnia and Herzegovina/Serbia

Drinit, Lumi 79 D5 *var.* Drin. *river* NW Albania

Drinit të Zi, Lumi i *see* Black Drin

Drissa *see* Drysa

Drobeta-Turnu Severin 86 B5 *prev.* Turnu Severin. Mehedinţi, SW Romania

Drogheda 67 B5 *Ir.* Droichead Átha. NE Ireland

Drogichin *see* Drahichyn

Drogobych *see* Drohobych

Drohiczyn Poleski *see* Drahichyn

Drohobych 86 B2 *Pol.* Drohobycz, *Rus.* Drogobych. L'vivs'ka Oblast', NW Ukraine

Drohobycz *see* Drohobych

Droichead Átha *see* Drogheda

Drôme 69 D5 *cultural region* E France

Dronning Maud Land 132 B2 *physical region* Antarctica

Drontheim *see* Trondheim

Drug *see* Durg

Druk-yul *see* Bhutan

Drummondville 17 E4 Québec, SE Canada

Druskienniki *see* Druskininkai

Druskininkai 85 B5 *Pol.* Druskienniki. Alytus, S Lithuania

Dryden 16 B3 Ontario, C Canada

Drysa 85 D5 *Rus.* Drissa. *river* N Belarus

Duacum *see* Douai

Duala *see* Douala

Dubai *see* Dubayy

Dubăsari 86 D3 *Rus.* Dubossary. NE Moldova

Dubawnt 15 F4 *river* Nunavut, NW Canada

Dubayy 98 D4 *Eng.* Dubai. Dubayy, NE United Arab Emirates

Dubbo 127 D6 New South Wales, SE Australia

Dublin 67 B5 *Ir.* Baile Átha Cliath; *anc.* Eblana. *country capital* Dublin, E Ireland

Dublin 21 E2 Georgia, SE USA

Dubno 86 C2 Rivnens'ka Oblast', NW Ukraine

Dubossary *see* Dubăsari

Dubris Portus *see* Dover

Dubrovnik 79 B5 *It.* Ragusa. Dubrovnik-Neretva, SE Croatia

Dubuque 23 G3 Iowa, C USA

Dudelange 65 D8 *var.* Forge du Sud, *Ger.* Dudelingen. Luxembourg, S Luxembourg

Dudelingen *see* Dudelange

Duero 70 D2 Port. Douro. *river* Portugal/Spain

Duero 70 B2 Port. Duero. *river* Portugal/Spain

Duesseldorf *see* Düsseldorf

Duffel 65 C5 Antwerpen, C Belgium

Dugi Otok 78 A4 *var.* Isola Grossa, *It.* Isola Lunga. *island* W Croatia

Duinekerke *see* Dunkerque

Duisburg 72 A4 *prev.* Duisburg-Hamborn. Nordrhein-Westfalen, W Germany

Duisburg-Hamborn *see* Duisburg

Duiven 64 D4 Gelderland, E Netherlands

Duk Faiwil 51 B5 Jonglei, SE Sudan

Dulan 104 D4 *var.* Qagan Us. Qinghai, C China

Dulce, Golfo 31 E5 *gulf* S Costa Rica

Dulce, Golfo *see* Izabal, Lago de

Dülmen 72 A4 Nordrhein-Westfalen, W Germany

Dulovo 82 E1 Silistra, NE Bulgaria

Duluth 23 G2 Minnesota, N USA

Dūmā 97 B5 *Fr.* Douma. Dimashq, SW Syria

Dumas 27 E1 Texas, SW USA

Dumfries 66 C4 S Scotland, United Kingdom

Dumont d'Urville 132 C4 *French research station* Antarctica

Dumyāt 50 B1 *var.* Dumyât, *Eng.* Damietta. N Egypt

Duna *see* Danube, C Europe

Düna *see* Western Dvina

Duna *see* Don, Russian Federation

Dünaburg *see* Daugavpils

Dunaj *see* Wien, Austria

Dunaj *see* Danube, C Europe

Dunărea *see* Danube

Dunaújváros 77 C7 *prev.* Dunapentele, Sztálinváros. Fejér, C Hungary

Dunav *see* Danube

Duncan 27 G2 Oklahoma, C USA

Dundalk 67 B5 *Ir.* Dún Dealgan. Louth, NE Ireland

Dún Dealgan *see* Dundalk

Dundee 56 D4 KwaZulu/Natal, E South Africa

Dundee 66 C4 E Scotland, United Kingdom

Dunedin 129 B7 Otago, South Island, New Zealand

Dunfermline 66 C4 C Scotland, United Kingdom

Dungu 55 E5 Orientale, NE Dem. Rep. Congo

Dungun 116 B3 *var.* Kuala Dungun. Terengganu, Peninsular Malaysia

Dunholme *see* Durham

Dunkerque 68 C2 *Eng.* Dunkirk, *Flem.* Duinekerke; *prev.* Dunquerque. Nord, N France

Dunkirk *see* Dunkerque

Dún Laoghaire 67 B6 *Eng.* Dunleary; *prev.* Kingstown. E Ireland

Dunleary *see* Dún Laoghaire

Dún Pádraig *see* Downpatrick

Dunquerque *see* Dunkerque

Dunqulah *see* Dongola

Dupnitsa 82 C2 *prev.* Marek, Stanke Dimitrov. Kyustendil, W Bulgaria

Duqm 99 E5 *var.* Daqm. E Oman

Durance 69 D6 *river* SE France

Durango 28 D3 *var.* Victoria de Durango. Durango, W Mexico

Durango 22 C5 Colorado, C USA

Durankulak 82 E1 *Rom.* Răcari; *prev.* Blatnitsa, Duranulac. Dobrich, NE Bulgaria

Durant 27 G2 Oklahoma, C USA

Duranulac *see* Durankulak

Durazzo *see* Durrës

Durban 56 D4 *var.* Port Natal. KwaZulu/Natal, E South Africa

Durbe 84 B3 *Ger.* Durben. Liepāja, W Latvia

Durben *see* Durbe

Durg 113 E4 *prev.* Drug. Chhattīsgarh, C India

Durham 67 D5 *hist.* Dunholme. N England, United Kingdom

Durham 21 F1 North Carolina, SE USA

Durocortorum *see* Reims

Durostorum *see* Silistra

Durovernum *see* Canterbury

Durrës 79 C6 *var.* Durrësi, Dursi, *It.* Durazzo, *SCr.* Drač, *Turk.* Draç. Durrës, W Albania

Durrësi *see* Durrës

Dursi *see* Durrës

Durūz, Jabal ad 97 C5 *mountain* SW Syria

D'Urville Island 128 C4 *island* C New Zealand

Dusa Mareb/Dusa Marreb *see* Dhuusa Marreeb

Dushanbe 101 E3 *var.* Dyushambe; *prev.* Stalinabad, *Taj.* Stalinobod. *country capital* W Tajikistan

Düsseldorf 72 A4 *var.* Duesseldorf. Nordrhein-Westfalen, W Germany

Düsti 101 E3 *Rus.* Dusti. SW Tajikistan

Dutch East Indies *see* Indonesia

Dutch Guiana *see* Suriname

Dutch Harbor 14 B3 Unalaska Island, Alaska, USA

Dutch New Guinea *see* Papua

Dutch West Indies *see* Netherlands Antilles

Duzdab *see* Zāhedān

Dvina Bay *see* Chëshskaya Guba

Dvinsk *see* Daugavpils

Dyanev *see* Galkynyş

Dyersburg 20 C1 Tennessee, S USA

Dza Chu *see* Mekong

Dzaudzhikau *see* Vladikavkaz

Dzerzhinsk 89 C5 Nizhegorodskaya Oblast', W Russian Federation

Dzerzhinskiy *see* Nar'yan-Mar

Dzhalal-Abad 101 F2 *Kir.* Jalal-Abad. Dzhalal-Abadskaya Oblast', W Kyrgyzstan

Dzhambul *see* Taraz

Dzhankoy 87 F4 Respublika Krym, S Ukraine

Dzharkurgan *see* Jarqo'rg'on

Dzhelandy 101 F3 SE Tajikistan

Dzhergalan 101 G2 *Kir.* Jyrgalan. Issyk-Kul'skaya Oblast', NE Kyrgyzstan

Dzhezkazgan *see* Zhezkazgan

Dzhizak *see* Jizzax

Dzhugdzhur, Khrebet 93 G3 *mountain range* E Russian Federation

Dzhusaly 92 B4 *Kaz.* Zhosaly. Kzylorda, SW Kazakhstan

Działdowo 76 D3 Warmińsko-Mazurskie, C Poland

Dzuunmod 105 E2 Töv, C Mongolia

Dzüün Soyonï Nuruu *see* Eastern Sayans

Dzvina *see* Western Dvina

E

Eagle Pass 27 F4 Texas, SW USA

East Açores Fracture Zone *see* East Azores Fracture Zone

East Antarctica 132 C3 *var.* Greater Antarctica. *physical region* Antarctica

East Australian Basin *see* Tasman Basin

East Azores Fracture Zone 44 C3 *var.* East Açores Fracture Zone. *tectonic feature* E Atlantic Ocean

Eastbourne 67 E7 SE England, United Kingdom

East Cape 128 E3 *headland* North Island, New Zealand

East China Sea 103 E2 *Chin.* Dong Hai. *sea* W Pacific Ocean

Easter Fracture Zone 131 G4 *tectonic feature* E Pacific Ocean

Easter Island 131 F4 *var.* Rapa Nui, Easter Island. *island* E Pacific Ocean

Easter Island *see* Pascua, Isla de

Eastern Desert 46 D3 *var.* Aş Şahrā' ash Sharqīyah, *Eng.* Arabian Desert, Eastern Desert. *desert* E Egypt

Eastern Desert *see* Sahara el Sharqīya

Eastern Ghats 102 B3 *mountain range* SE India

Eastern Sayans 93 E4 *Mong.* Dzüün Soyonï Nuruu, *Rus.* Vostochnyy Sayan. *mountain range* Mongolia/Russian Federation

Eastern Sierra Madre *see* Madre Oriental, Sierra

East Falkland 43 D8 *var.* Isla Soledad. *island* E Falkland Islands

East Frisian Islands 72 A3 *Eng.* East Frisian Islands. *island group* NW Germany

East Frisian Islands *see* Ostfriesische Inseln

East Grand Forks 23 E1 Minnesota, N USA

East Indiaman Ridge 119 D6 *undersea ridge* E Indian Ocean

East Indies 130 A3 *island group* SE Asia

East Kilbride 66 C4 S Scotland, United Kingdom

East London 56 D5 *Afr.* Oos-Londen; *prev.* Emonti, Port Rex. Eastern Cape, S South Africa

Eastleigh 67 D7 S England, United Kingdom

Eastmain 16 D3 *river* Québec, C Canada

East Mariana Basin 120 B1 *undersea basin* W Pacific Ocean

East Novaya Zemlya Trough 90 C1 *var.* Novaya Zemlya Trough. *trough* W Kara Sea

East Pacific Rise 131 F4 *undersea rise* E Pacific Ocean

East Pakistan *see* Bangladesh

East Saint Louis 18 B4 Illinois, N USA

East Scotia Basin 45 C7 *undersea basin* SE Scotia Sea

East Sea 108 A4 *var.* Sea of Japan, *Rus.* Yaponskoye More. *Sea* NW Pacific Ocean

---

East Siberian Sea 93 F1 *Eng.* East Siberian Sea. *sea* Arctic Ocean

East Siberian Sea *see* Vostochno-Sibirskoye More

East Timor 117 F5 *var.* Loro Sae; *prev.* Portuguese Timor, Timor Timur. *country* S Indonesia

Eau Claire 18 A2 Wisconsin, N USA

Eau Claire, Lac à L' *see* St. Clair, Lake

Eauripik Rise 120 B2 *undersea rise* W Pacific Ocean

Ebensee 73 D6 Oberösterreich, N Austria

Eberswalde-Finow 72 D3 Brandenburg, E Germany

Ebetsu 108 D2 *var.* Ebetu. Hokkaidō, NE Japan

Ebetu *see* Ebetsu

Eblana *see* Dublin

Ebolowa 55 A5 Sud, S Cameroon

Ebon Atoll 122 D2 *var.* Epoon. *atoll* Ralik Chain, S Marshall Islands

Ebora *see* Évora

Eboracum *see* York

Ebro 71 E2 *river* NE Spain

Eburacum *see* York

Ebusus *see* Eivissa

Ebusus *see* Eivissa

Ecbatana *see* Hamadān

Ech Cheliff/Ech Chleff *see* Chlef

Echo Bay 15 E3 Northwest Territories, NW Canada

Écija 70 D4 *anc.* Astigi. Andalucía, SW Spain

Eckengraf *see* Viesīte

Ecuador 38 B1 *off.* Republic of Ecuador. *country* NW South America

Ecuador, Republic of *see* Ecuador

Ed Da'ein 50 A4 Southern Darfur, W Sudan

Ed Damazin 50 C4 *var.* Ad Damazin. Blue Nile, E Sudan

Ed Damer 50 C3 *var.* Ad Dāmir, Ad Damar. River Nile, NE Sudan

Ed Debba 50 B3 Northern, N Sudan

Ede 64 D4 Gelderland, C Netherlands

Ede 53 F5 Osun, SW Nigeria

Edéa 55 A5 Littoral, SW Cameroon

Edessa *see* Şanlıurfa

Edfu *see* Idfū

Edgeoya 61 G2 *island* S Svalbard

Edgware 67 A7 Harrow, SE England, United Kingdom

Edinburg 27 G5 Texas, SW USA

Edinburgh 66 C4 *national capital* S Scotland, United Kingdom

Edingen *see* Enghien

Edirne 94 A2 *Eng.* Adrianople; *anc.* Adrianopolis, Hadrianopolis. Edirne, NW Turkey

Edmonds 24 B2 Washington, NW USA

Edmonton 15 E5 *province capital* Alberta, SW Canada

Edmundston 17 E4 New Brunswick, SE Canada

Edna 27 G4 Texas, SW USA

Edolo 74 B1 Lombardia, N Italy

Edremit 94 A3 Balıkesir, NW Turkey

Edward, Lake 55 E5 *var.* Albert Edward Nyanza, Edward Nyanza, Lac Idi Amin, Lake Rutanzige. *lake* Uganda/Dem. Rep. Congo

Edward Nyanza *see* Edward, Lake

Edwards Plateau 27 F3 *plain* Texas, SW USA

Edzo 31 E4 *prev.* Rae-Edzo. Northwest Territories, NW Canada

Eekloo 65 B5 *var.* Eekloo. Oost-Vlaanderen, NW Belgium

Eekloo *see* Eeklo

Eems *see* Ems

Eersel 65 C5 Noord-Brabant, S Netherlands

Eesti Vabariik *see* Estonia

Efate 122 D4 *var.* Efate, *Fr.* Vaté; *prev.* Sandwich Island. *island* C Vanuatu

Efate *see* Efaté

Effingham 18 B4 Illinois, N USA

Eforie Sud 86 D5 Constanţa, E Romania

Egadi Is. 75 B7 *island group* S Italy

Ege Denizi *see* Aegean Sea

Eger 77 D6 *Ger.* Erlau. Heves, NE Hungary

Eger *see* Cheb, Czech Republic

Egeria Fracture Zone 119 C5 *tectonic feature* W Indian Ocean

Éghezée 65 C6 Namur, C Belgium

Egina *see* Aígina

Egio *see* Aígio

Egmont *see* Taranaki, Mount

Egmont, Cape 128 C4 *headland* North Island, New Zealand

Egoli *see* Johannesburg

Egypt 50 B2 *off.* Arab Republic of Egypt, *Ar.* Jumhūrīyah Misr al 'Arabīyah, *prev.* United Arab Republic; *anc.* Aegyptus. *country* N Africa

Eibar 71 E1 País Vasco, N Spain

Eibergen 64 E3 Gelderland, E Netherlands

Eidfjord 63 A5 Hordaland, S Norway

Eier-Berg *see* Suur Munamägi

Eifel 73 A5 *plateau* W Germany

Eiger 73 B7 *mountain* C Switzerland

Eigg 66 B3 *island* W Scotland, United Kingdom

Eight Degree Channel 110 B3 *channel* India/ Maldives

Eighty Mile Beach 124 B4 *beach* Western Australia

Eijsden 65 D6 Limburg, SE Netherlands

Eilat *see* Elat

Eindhoven 65 D5 Noord-Brabant, S Netherlands

Eipel *see* Ipel'

Éire *see* Ireland

Éireann, Muir *see* Irish Sea

Eisenhüttenstadt 72 D4 Brandenburg, E Germany

Eisenmarkt *see* Hunedoara

Eisenstadt 73 E6 Burgenland, E Austria

Eisleben 72 C4 Sachsen-Anhalt, C Germany

Eivissa 71 G3 *var.* Iviza, *Cast.* Ibiza; *anc.* Ebusus. Ibiza, Spain, W Mediterranean Sea

Eivissa 71 G3 *var.* Iviza, *Cast.* Ibiza; *anc.* Ebusus. Ibiza, Spain, W Mediterranean Sea

Eivissa 71 G3 *var.* Iviza, *Cast.* Ibiza; *anc.* Ebusus. Ibiza, Spain, W Mediterranean Sea

Ejea de los Caballeros 71 E2 Aragón, NE Spain

Ejin Qi *see* Dalain Hob

Ekapa *see* Cape Town

Ekaterinodar *see* Krasnodar

Ekonda/Ekonda 119 D6 Western Australia

Ekvaraatkiy Khrebet 93 G1 *mountain range* NE Russian Federation

El 'Alamein *see* Al 'Alamayn

El Asnam *see* Chlef

Elat 97 B8 *var.* Eilat, Elath. Southern, S Israel

Elath *see* Elat, Israel

Elath *see* Al 'Aqabah, Jordan

El 'Atrun 50 B3 Northern Darfur, NW Sudan

Elâzîğ 95 E3 *var.* Elâziz, Elâziz. Elâzığ, E Turkey

Elba 74 B4 *island* Archipelago Toscano, C Italy

Elbasan 79 D6 *var.* Elbasani. Elbasan, C Albania

Elbasani *see* Elbasan

Elbe 58 C3 *Cz.* Labe. *river* Czech Republic/ Germany

Elbert, Mount 22 C4 *mountain* Colorado, C USA

Elbing *see* Elbląg

Elbląg 76 C2 *var.* Elblag, *Ger.* Elbing. Warmińsko-Mazurskie, NE Poland

El Boulaïda/El Boulaïda *see* Blida

El'brus 89 A8 *var.* Gora El'brus. *mountain* SW Russian Federation

El'brus, Gora *see* El'brus

El Burgo de Osma 71 E2 Castilla-León, C Spain

Elburz Mountains 98 C2 *Eng.* Elburz Mountains. *mountain range* N Iran

Elburz Mountains *see* Alborz, Reshteh-ye Kūhhā-ye

El Cajon 25 C8 California, W USA

El Calafate 43 B7 *var.* Calafate. Santa Cruz, S Argentina

El Callao 37 E2 Bolívar, E Venezuela

El Campo 27 G4 Texas, SW USA

El Carmen de Bolívar 36 B2 Bolívar, NW Colombia

El Cayo *see* San Ignacio

El Centro 25 D8 California, W USA

Elche 71 F4 *Cat.* Elx; *anc.* Ilici, *Lat.* Illicis. País Valenciano, E Spain

Elda 71 F4 País Valenciano, E Spain

El Djazaïr *see* Alger

El Djelfa *see* Djelfa

Eldorado 42 E3 Misiones, NE Argentina

El Dorado 28 C3 Sinaloa, C Mexico

El Dorado 20 B2 Arkansas, C USA

El Dorado 23 F5 Kansas, C USA

El Dorado 37 F2 Bolívar, E Venezuela

El Dorado *see* California

Eldoret 51 C6 Rift Valley, W Kenya

Elektrostal' 89 B5 Moskovskaya Oblast', W Russian Federation

Elemi Triangle 51 B5 *disputed region* Kenya/Sudan

Elephant Butte Reservoir 26 C2 *reservoir* New Mexico, SW USA

Élesd *see* Aleşd

Eleuthera Island 32 C1 *island* N Bahamas

El Fasher 50 A4 *var.* Al Fāshir. Northern Darfur, W Sudan

El Ferrol/El Ferrol del Caudillo *see* Ferrol

El Gedaref *see* Gedaref

El Geneina 50 A4 *var.* Ajjinena, Al-Genain, Al Junaynah. Western Darfur, W Sudan

Elgin 66 C3 NE Scotland, United Kingdom

Elgin 18 B3 Illinois, N USA

El Gîza *see* Giza

El Goléa 48 D3 *var.* Al Golea. C Algeria

El Haseke *see* Al Hasakah

Elimberrum *see* Auch

Eliocroca *see* Lorca

Élisabethville *see* Lubumbashi

Elista 89 B7 Respublika Kalmykiya, SW Russian Federation

Elizabeth 127 B6 South Australia

Elizabeth City 21 G1 North Carolina, SE USA

Elizabethtown 18 C5 Kentucky, S USA

El-Jadida 48 C2 *prev.* Mazagan. W Morocco

Ełk 76 E2 *Ger.* Lyck. Warmińsko-mazurskie, NE Poland

Elk City 27 F1 Oklahoma, C USA

El Khalil *see* Hebron

El Khârga *see* Al Khārijah

Elkhart 18 C3 Indiana, N USA

El Khartum *see* Khartoum

Elk River 23 F2 Minnesota, N USA

El Kuneitra *see* Al Qunaytirah

Ellás *see* Greece

Ellef Ringnes Island 15 E1 *island* Nunavut, N Canada

Ellen, Mount 22 B5 *mountain* Utah, W USA

Ellensburg 24 B2 Washington, NW USA

Ellesmere Island 15 F1 *island* Queen Elizabeth Islands, Nunavut, N Canada

Ellesmere, Lake 129 C6 *lake* South Island, New Zealand

Ellice Islands *see* Tuvalu

Elliston 127 A6 South Australia

Ellsworth Land 132 A3 *physical region* Antarctica

El Mahbas 48 B3 *var.* Mahbés. SW Western Sahara

El Mina 96 B4 *var.* Al Mînâ'. N Lebanon

El Minya *see* Al Minyā

Elmira 19 E3 New York, NE USA

El Mreyyé 52 D2 *desert* E Mauritania

Elmshorn 72 B3 Schleswig-Holstein, N Germany

El Muglad 50 B4 Western Kordofan, C Sudan

El Obeid 50 B4 *var.* Al Obayyid, Al Ubayyid. Northern Kordofan, C Sudan

El Ouâdi *see* El Oued

El Oued 49 E2 *var.* Al Oued, El Ouâdi, El Wad. NE Algeria

Eloy 26 B2 Arizona, SW USA

El Paso 26 D3 Texas, SW USA

El Porvenir 31 G4 Kuna Yala, N Panama

El Progreso 30 C2 Yoro, NW Honduras

El Puerto de Santa María 70 C5 Andalucía, S Spain

El Qâhira *see* Cairo

El Quneitra *see* Al Qunaytirah

El Quseir *see* Al Quşayr

El Quweira *see* Al Quwayrah

El Rama 31 E3 Región Autónoma Atlántico Sur, SE Nicaragua

El Real 31 H5 *var.* El Real de Santa María. Darién, SE Panama

El Real de Santa María *see* El Real

El Reno 27 F1 Oklahoma, C USA

El Salvador 30 B3 *off.* Republica of El Salvador. *country* Central America

El Salvador, Republica de *see* El Salvador

El Sáuz 28 C2 Chihuahua, N Mexico

El Serrat 69 A7 N Andorra Europe

Elst 64 D4 Gelderland, E Netherlands

El Suweida *see* As Suwaydā'

El Suweis *see* Suez

Eltanin Fracture Zone 131 E5 *tectonic feature* SE Pacific Ocean

El Tigre 37 E2 Anzoátegui, NE Venezuela

Elvas 70 C4 Portalegre, C Portugal

El Vendrell 71 G2 Cataluña, NE Spain

El Vigía – Fort Pierce

El Vigía 36 C2 Mérida, NW Venezuela
El Wad see El Oued
Elwell, Lake 22 B1 reservoir Montana, NW USA
Elx see Elche
Ely 25 D5 Nevada, W USA
El Yopal see Yopal
Emajõgi 84 D3 Ger. Embach. river SE Estonia
Emāmrūd see Shāhrūd
Emāmshahr see Shāhrūd
Emba 92 B4 Kaz. Embi. Aktyubinsk, W Kazakhstan
Embach see Emajõgi
Embi see Emba
Emden 72 A3 Niedersachsen, NW Germany
Emerald 126 D4 Queensland, E Australia
Emerald Isle see Montserrat
Emesa see Ḩimş
Emmaste 84 C2 Hiiumaa, W Estonia
Emmeloord 64 D2 Flevoland, N Netherlands
Emmen 64 E2 Drenthe, NE Netherlands
Emmendingen 73 A6 Baden-Württemberg, SW Germany
Emona see Ljubljana
Emonti see East London
Emory Peak 27 E4 mountain Texas, SW USA
Empalme 28 B2 Sonora, NW Mexico
Emperor Seamounts 91 G3 seamount range NW Pacific Ocean
Empire State of the South see Georgia
Emporia 23 F5 Kansas, C USA
Empty Quarter see Ar Rub 'al Khālī
Ems 72 A3 Dut. Eems. river NW Germany
Enareträsk see Inarijärvi
Encamp 69 A8 Encamp, C Andorra Europe
Encarnación 42 D3 Itapúa, S Paraguay
Encinitas 25 C8 California, W USA
Encs 77 D6 Borsod-Abaúj-Zemplén, NE Hungary
Endeavour Strait 126 C1 strait Queensland, NE Australia
Enderbury Island 123 F3 atoll Phoenix Islands, C Kiribati
Enderby Land 132 C2 physical region Antarctica
Enderby Plain 132 D2 abyssal plain S Indian Ocean
Endersdorf see Jędrzejów
Enewetak Atoll 122 C1 var. Ānewetak, Eniwetok. atoll Ralik Chain, W Marshall Islands
Enfield 67 A7 United Kingdom
Engeten see Aiud
Enghien 65 B6 Dut. Edingen. Hainaut, SW Belgium
England 67 D5 Lat. Anglia. cultural region England, United Kingdom
Englewood 22 D4 Colorado, C USA
English Channel 67 D8 var. The Channel, Fr. la Manche. channel NW Europe
Engure 84 C3 Tukums, W Latvia
Engures Ezers 84 B3 lake NW Latvia
Enguri 95 F1 Rus. Inguri. river NW Georgia
Enid 27 F1 Oklahoma, C USA
Enikale Strait see Kerch Strait
Eniwetok see Enewetak Atoll
En Nâqoûra 97 A5 var. An Nāqūrah. SW Lebanon
En Nazira see Natzrat
Ennedi 54 D2 plateau E Chad
Ennis 67 A6 Ir. Inis. Clare, W Ireland
Ennis 27 G3 Texas, SW USA
Enniskillen 67 B5 var. Inniskilling, Ir. Inis Ceithleann. SW Northern Ireland, United Kingdom
Enns 73 D6 river C Austria
Enschede 64 E3 Overijssel, E Netherlands
Ensenada 28 A1 Baja California, NW Mexico
Entebbe 51 B6 S Uganda
Entroncamento 70 B3 Santarém, C Portugal
Enugu 53 G5 Enugu, S Nigeria
Epanomí 82 B4 Kentrikí Makedonía, N Greece
Epéna 55 B5 Likouala, NE Congo
Eperies/Eperjes see Prešov
Epi 122 D4 var. Épi. island C Vanuatu
Épi see Epi
Épinal 68 D4 Vosges, NE France
Epiphania see Ḩamāh
Epitoli see Tshwane
Epoon see Ebon Atoll
Epsom 67 A8 United Kingdom
Equality State see Wyoming
Equatorial Guinea 55 A5 off. Equatorial Guinea, Republic of. country C Africa
Equatorial Guinea, Republic of see Equatorial Guinea
Erautini see Johannesburg
Erbil see Arbīl
Erciş 95 F3 Van, E Turkey
Erdély see Transylvania
Erdélyi-Havasok see Carpaţii Meridionali
Erdenet 105 E2 Orhon, N Mongolia
Erdi 54 C2 plateau NE Chad
Erdi Ma 54 D2 desert NE Chad
Erebus, Mount 132 B4 volcano Ross Island, Antarctica
Ereğli 94 C4 Konya, S Turkey
Erenhot 105 F2 var. Erlian. Nei Mongol Zizhiqu, NE China
Erfurt 72 C4 Thüringen, C Germany
Ergene Çayı 94 A2 var. Ergene Irmağī. river NW Turkey
Ergene Irmağī see Ergene Çayı
Ergun 105 F1 var. Labudalin; prev. Ergun Youqi. Nei Mongol Zizhiqu, N China
Ergun He see Argun
Ergun Youqi see Ergun
Erie 18 D3 Pennsylvania, NE USA
Érié, Lac see Erie, Lake
Erie, Lake 18 D3 Fr. Lac Érié. lake Canada/USA
Eritrea 50 C4 off. State of Eritrea, Ērtra. country E Africa
Eritrea, State of see Eritrea
Erivan see Yerevan
Erlangen 73 C5 Bayern, S Germany
Erlau see Eger
Erlian see Erenhot
Ermelo 64 D3 Gelderland, C Netherlands
Ermióni 83 C6 Pelopónnisos, S Greece
Ermoúpoli 83 D6 var. Hermoupolis; prev. Ermoúpolis. Sýyros, Kykládes, Greece, Aegean Sea
Ermoúpolis see Ermoúpoli
Ernākulam 110 C3 Kerala, SW India
Erode 110 C2 Tamil Nādu, SE India
Erquelinnes 65 B7 Hainaut, S Belgium
Er-Rachidia 48 C2 var. Ksar al Soule. E Morocco
Er Rahad 50 B4 var. Ar Rahad. Northern Kordofan, C Sudan
Erromango 122 D4 island S Vanuatu
Ertis see Irtysh, C Asia
Ērtra see Eritrea
Erzerum see Erzurum
Erzincan 95 E3 var. Erzinjan. Erzincan, E Turkey
Erzinjan see Erzincan
Erzurum 95 E3 prev. Erzerum. Erzurum, NE Turkey
Esbjerg 63 A7 Ribe, W Denmark
Esbo see Espoo
Escaldes 69 A8 Escaldes Engordany, C Andorra Europe
Escanaba 18 C2 Michigan, N USA
Escaut see Scheldt
Esch-sur-Alzette 65 D8 Luxembourg, S Luxembourg
Esclaves, Grand Lac des see Great Slave Lake
Escondido 25 C8 California, W USA
Escuinapa 28 D3 var. Escuinapa de Hidalgo. Sinaloa, C Mexico
Escuinapa de Hidalgo see Escuinapa
Escuintla 30 B2 Escuintla, S Guatemala
Escuintla 29 G5 Chiapas, SE Mexico
Esenguly 100 B3 Rus. Gasan-Kuli. Balkan Welaýaty, W Turkmenistan
Eşfahān 98 C3 Eng. Isfahan; anc. Aspadana. Eşfahān, C Iran
Esh Sharā see Ash Sharāh
Esil see Ishim, Kazakhstan/Russian Federation
Eskimo Point see Arviat
Eskişehir 94 B3 var. Eskishehr. Eskişehir, W Turkey
Eskishehr see Eskişehir
Eslāmābād 98 C3 var. Eslāmābād-e Gharb; prev. Harunabad, Shāhābād. Kermānshāhān, W Iran
Eslāmābād-e Gharb see Eslāmābād
Esmeraldas 38 A1 Esmeraldas, N Ecuador
Esna see Isnā
España see Spain
Espanola 26 D1 New Mexico, SW USA
Esperance 125 B7 Western Australia
Esperanza 28 B2 Sonora, NW Mexico
Esperanza 132 A2 Argentinian research station Antarctica
Espinal 36 B3 Tolima, C Colombia
Espinhaço, Serra do 34 D4 mountain range SE Brazil
Espírito Santo 41 F4 off. Estado do Espírito Santo. state E Brazil
Espírito Santo 41 F4 off. Estado do Espírito Santo. region E Brazil
Espírito Santo, Estado do see Espírito Santo
Espiritu Santo 122 C4 var. Santo. island W Vanuatu
Espoo 63 D6 Swe. Esbo. Etelä-Suomi, S Finland
Esquel 43 B6 Chubut, SW Argentina
Essaouira 48 B2 prev. Mogador. W Morocco
Esseg see Osijek
Es Semara see Smara
Essen 65 C5 Antwerpen, N Belgium
Essen 72 A4 var. Essen an der Ruhr. Nordrhein-Westfalen, W Germany
Essen an der Ruhr see Essen
Essequibo River 37 F3 river C Guyana
Es Suweida see As Suwaydā'
Estacado, Llano 27 E2 plain New Mexico/Texas, SW USA
Estados, Isla de los 43 C8 prev. Eng. Staten Island. island S Argentina
Estância 41 G3 Sergipe, E Brazil
Estelí 30 D3 Estelí, NW Nicaragua
Estella 71 E1 Bas. Lizarra. Navarra, N Spain
Estepona 70 D5 Andalucía, S Spain
Estevan 15 F5 Saskatchewan, S Canada
Estland see Estonia
Estonia 84 D2 off. Republic of Estonia, Est. Eesti Vabariik, Ger. Estland, Latv. Igaunija; prev. Estonian SSR, Rus. Estonskaya SSR. country NE Europe
Estonian SSR see Estonia
Estonia, Republic of see Estonia
Estonskaya SSR see Estonia
Estrela, Serra da 70 C3 mountain range C Portugal
Estremadura see Extremadura
Estremoz 70 C4 Évora, S Portugal
Eszék see Osijek
Esztergom 77 C6 Ger. Gran; anc. Strigonium. Komárom-Esztergom, N Hungary
Étalle 65 D8 Luxembourg, SE Belgium
Etāwah 112 D3 Uttar Pradesh, N India
Ethiopia 51 C5 off. Federal Democratic Republic of Ethiopia; prev. Abyssinia, People's Democratic Republic of Ethiopia. country E Africa
Ethiopia, Federal Democratic Republic of see Ethiopia
Ethiopian Highlands 51 C5 var. Ethiopian Plateau. plateau N Ethiopia
Ethiopian Plateau see Ethiopian Highlands
Ethiopia, People's Democratic Republic of see Ethiopia
Mount Etna 75 C7 Eng. Mount Etna. volcano Sicilia, Italy, C Mediterranean Sea
Etna, Mount see Etna, Monte
Etosha Pan 56 B3 salt lake N Namibia
Etoumbi 55 B5 Cuvette Ouest, NW Congo
Etsch see Adige
Et Tafila see At Ţafilah
Ettelbrück 65 D8 Diekirch, C Luxembourg
'Eua 123 E5 prev. Middleburg Island. island Tongatapu Group, SE Tonga
Euboea 83 C5 Lat. Euboea. island C Greece
Euboea see Évvoia
Eucla 125 D6 Western Australia
Euclid 18 D3 Ohio, N USA
Eufaula Lake 27 G1 var. Eufaula Reservoir. reservoir Oklahoma, C USA
Eufaula Reservoir see Eufaula Lake
Eugene 24 B3 Oregon, NW USA
Eumolpias see Plovdiv
Eupen 65 D6 Liège, E Belgium
Euphrates 90 B4 Ar. Al-Furāt, Turk. Firat Nehri. river SW Asia
Eureka 25 A5 California, W USA
Eureka 22 A1 Montana, NW USA
Europa Point 71 H5 headland S Gibraltar
Europe 58 continent
Eutin 72 C2 Schleswig-Holstein, N Germany
Euxine Sea see Black Sea
Evansdale 23 G3 Iowa, C USA
Evanston 18 B3 Illinois, N USA
Evanston 22 B4 Wyoming, C USA
Evansville 18 B5 Indiana, N USA
Eveleth 23 G1 Minnesota, N USA
Everard, Lake 127 A6 salt lake South Australia
Everest, Mount 104 B5 Chin. Qomolangma Feng, Nep. Sagarmāthā. mountain China/Nepal
Everett 24 B2 Washington, NW USA
Everglades, The 21 F5 wetland Florida, SE USA
Evje 63 A6 Aust-Agder, S Norway
Evmolpia see Plovdiv
Évora 70 B4 anc. Ebora, Lat. Liberalitas Julia. Évora, C Portugal
Évreux 68 C3 anc. Civitas Eburovicum. Eure, N France
Évros see Maritsa
Évry 68 E2 Essonne, N France
Ewarton 32 B5 C Jamaica
Excelsior Springs 23 F4 Missouri, C USA
Exe 67 C7 river SW England, United Kingdom
Exeter 67 C7 anc. Isca Damnoniorum. SW England, United Kingdom
Exmoor 67 C7 moorland SW England, United Kingdom
Exmouth 124 A4 Western Australia
Exmouth 67 C7 SW England, United Kingdom
Exmouth Gulf 124 A4 gulf Western Australia
Exmouth Plateau 119 E5 undersea plateau E Indian Ocean
Extremadura 70 C3 var. Estremadura. autonomous community W Spain
Exuma Cays 32 C1 islets C Bahamas
Exuma Sound 32 C1 sound C Bahamas
Eyre Mountains 129 A7 mountain range South Island, New Zealand
Eyre North, Lake 127 A5 salt lake South Australia
Eyre Peninsula 127 A6 peninsula South Australia
Eyre South, Lake 127 A5 salt lake South Australia
Ezo see Hokkaidō

F

Faadhippolhu Atoll 110 B4 var. Fadiffolu, Lhaviyani Atoll. atoll N Maldives
Fabens 26 D3 Texas, SW USA
Fada 54 C2 Borkou-Ennedi-Tibesti, E Chad
Fada-Ngourma 53 E4 E Burkina
Fadiffolu see Faadhippolhu Atoll
Faenza 74 C3 anc. Faventia. Emilia-Romagna, N Italy
Faeroe-Iceland Ridge 58 C1 undersea ridge NW Norwegian Sea
Faeroe Islands 61 E5 Dan. Færøerne, Faer. Føroyar. Danish external territory N Atlantic Ocean
Færøerne see Faeroe Islands
Faeroe-Shetland Trough 58 C2 trough NE Atlantic Ocean
Faetano 74 E2 E San Marino
Făgăraş 86 C4 Ger. Fogarasch, Hung. Fogaras. Braşov, C Romania
Fagibina, Lake see Faguibine, Lac
Fagne 65 C7 hill range S Belgium
Faguibine, Lac 53 E3 var. Lake Fagibina. lake NW Mali
Fahlun see Falun
Fahraj 98 E4 Kermān, SE Iran
Faial 70 A5 var. Ilha do Faial. island Azores, Portugal, NE Atlantic Ocean
Faial, Ilha do see Faial
Faifo see Hôi An
Fairbanks 14 D3 Alaska, USA
Fairfield 25 B6 California, W USA
Fair Isle 66 D2 island NE Scotland, United Kingdom
Fairlie 129 B6 Canterbury, South Island, New Zealand
Fairmont 23 F3 Minnesota, N USA
Faisalābād 112 C2 prev. Lyallpur. Punjab, NE Pakistan
Faizābād 113 E3 Uttar Pradesh, N India
Faizabad/Faizābād see Feyẓābād
Fakaofo Atoll 123 F3 island SE Tokelau
Falam 114 A3 Chin State, W Myanmar (Burma)
Falconara Marittima 74 C3 Marche, C Italy
Falkenau an der Eger see Sokolov
Falkland Islands 43 D7 var. Falklands, Islas Malvinas. UK dependent territory SW Atlantic Ocean
Falkland Plateau 35 D7 var. Argentine Rise. undersea feature SW Atlantic Ocean
Falklands see Falkland Islands
Falknov nad Ohří see Sokolov
Fallbrook 25 C8 California, W USA
Falmouth 32 A4 W Jamaica
Falmouth 67 C7 SW England, United Kingdom
Falster 63 B8 island SE Denmark
Fălticeni 86 C3 Hung. Falticsén. Suceava, NE Romania
Falticsén see Fălticeni
Falun 63 C6 var. Fahlun. Kopparberg, C Sweden
Famagusta see Gazimağusa
Famagusta Bay 80 C5 var. Famagusta Bay, Gk. Kólpos Ammóchostos. bay E Cyprus
Famagusta Bay see Gazimağusa Körfezi
Famenne 65 C7 physical region SE Belgium
Fang 114 C3 Chiang Mai, NW Thailand
Fanning Island see Tabuaeran
Fanø 74 C3 island W Denmark
Farafangana 57 G4 Fianarantsoa, SE Madagascar
Farāh 100 D4 var. Farah, Fararud. Farāh, W Afghanistan
Farah Rud 100 D4 river W Afghanistan
Faranah 52 C4 Haute-Guinée, S Guinea
Fararud see Farāh
Farasan, Jaza'ir 99 A6 island group SW Saudi Arabia
Farewell, Cape 128 C4 headland South Island, New Zealand
Farewell, Cape see Nunap Isua
Fargo 23 F2 North Dakota, N USA
Farg'ona 101 F2 Rus. Fergana; prev. Novyy Margilan. Farg'ona Viloyati, E Uzbekistan
Faribault 23 F2 Minnesota, N USA
Farīdābād 112 D3 Haryāna, N India
Farkhor 101 E3 Rus. Parkhar. SW Tajikistan
Farmington 23 G5 Missouri, C USA
Farmington 26 C1 New Mexico, SW USA
Faro 70 B5 Faro, S Portugal
Farquhar Group 57 G2 island group S Seychelles
Fars, Khalīj-e see Gulf, The
Farvel, Kap see Nunap Isua
Fastiv 87 E2 Rus. Fastov. Kyyivs'ka Oblast', NW Ukraine
Fastov see Fastiv
Fauske 62 C3 Nordland, C Norway
Faventia see Faenza
Faxa Bay see Faxaflói
Faxaflói 60 D5 Eng. Faxa Bay. bay W Iceland
Faya 54 C2 prev. Faya-Largeau, Largeau. Borkou-Ennedi-Tibesti, N Chad
Faya-Largeau see Faya
Fayetteville 20 A1 Arkansas, C USA
Fayetteville 21 F1 North Carolina, SE USA
Fdérick see Fdérik
Fdérik 52 C2 var. Fdérick, Fr. Fort Gouraud. Tiris Zemmour, NW Mauritania
Fear, Cape 21 F2 headland Bald Head Island, North Carolina, SE USA
Fécamp 68 B3 Seine-Maritime, N France
Fédala see Mohammedia
Federal Capital Territory see Australian Capital Territory
Fehérgyarmat 77 E6 Szabolcs-Szatmár-Bereg, E Hungary
Fehértemplom see Bela Crkva
Fehmarn 72 C2 island N Germany
Fehmarn Belt 72 C2 Dan. Femern Bælt, Ger. Fehmarnbelt. strait Denmark /Germany
Fehmarnbelt Fehmarn Belt/Femer Bælt
Feijó 40 C2 Acre, W Brazil
Feilding 128 D4 Manawatu-Wanganui, North Island, New Zealand
Feira see Feira de Santana
Feira de Santana 41 G3 var. Feira. Bahia, E Brazil
Feketehalom see Codlea
Felanitx 71 G3 Mallorca, Spain, W Mediterranean Sea
Felicitas Julia see Lisboa
Felidhu Atoll 110 B4 atoll C Maldives
Felipe Carrillo Puerto 29 H4 Quintana Roo, SE Mexico
Felixstowe 67 E6 E England, United Kingdom
Fellin see Viljandi
Felsőbánya see Baia Sprie
Felsőmuzslya see Mužlja
Femunden 63 B5 lake S Norway
Fénérive see Fenoarivo Atsinanana
Fengcheng 106 D3 var. Feng-cheng, Fenghwangcheng. Liaoning, NE China
Feng-cheng see Fengcheng
Fenghwangcheng see Fengcheng
Fengtien see Shenyang, China
Fengtien see Liaoning, China
Fenoarivo Atsinanana 57 G3 Fr. Fénérive. Toamasina, E Madagascar
Fens, The 67 E6 wetland E England, United Kingdom
Feodosiya 87 F5 var. Kefe, It. Kaffa; anc. Theodosia. Respublika Krym, S Ukraine
Ferdinand see Montana, Bulgaria
Ferdinandsberg see Oţelu Roşu
Féres 82 D3 Anatolikí Makedonía kai Thráki, NE Greece
Fergana see Farg'ona
Fergus Falls 23 F2 Minnesota, N USA
Ferizaj 79 D5 Serb. Uroševac. C Kosovo
Ferkessédougou 52 D4 N Ivory Coast
Fermo 74 C4 anc. Firmum Picenum. Marche, C Italy
Fernandina, Isla 38 A5 var. Narborough Island. island Galapagos Islands, Ecuador, E Pacific Ocean
Fernando de Noronha 41 H2 island E Brazil
Fernando Po/Fernando Póo see Bioco, Isla de
Ferrara 74 C2 anc. Forum Alieni. Emilia-Romagna, N Italy
Ferreñafe 38 B3 Lambayeque, W Peru
Ferro see Hierro
Ferrol 70 B1 var. El Ferrol; prev. El Ferrol del Caudillo. Galicia, NW Spain
Fertő see Neusiedler See
Ferwerd 64 D1 Fris. Ferwert. Friesland, N Netherlands
Ferwert see Ferwerd
Fès 48 C2 Eng. Fez. N Morocco
Feteşti 86 D5 Ialomiţa, SE Romania
Fethiye 94 B4 Muğla, SW Turkey
Fetlar 66 D1 island NE Scotland, United Kingdom
Feyẓābād 101 F3 var. Faizabad, Faizābād, Feyzābād, Fyzabad. Badakhshān, NE Afghanistan
Feyzābād see Feyẓābād
Fez see Fès
Fianarantsoa 57 F3 Fianarantsoa, C Madagascar
Fianga 54 B4 Mayo-Kébbi, SW Chad
Fier 79 C6 var. Fieri. Fier, SW Albania
Fieri see Fier
Figeac 69 C5 Lot, S France
Figig see Figuig
Figueira da Foz 70 B3 Coimbra, W Portugal
Figueres 71 G2 Cataluña, E Spain
Figuig 48 D2 var. Figig. E Morocco
Fiji 123 E5 off. Sovereign Democratic Republic of Fiji, Fij. Viti. country SW Pacific Ocean
Fiji, Sovereign Democratic Republic of see Fiji
Filadelfia 30 D4 Guanacaste, W Costa Rica
Filiaşi 86 B5 Dolj, SW Romania
Filipstad 63 B6 Värmland, C Sweden
Finale Ligure 74 A3 Liguria, NW Italy
Finchley 67 A7 United Kingdom
Findlay 18 C4 Ohio, N USA
Finike 94 B4 Antalya, SW Turkey
Finland 62 D4 off. Republic of Finland, Fin. Suomen Tasavalta, Suomi. country N Europe
Finland, Gulf of 63 D6 Est. Soome Laht, Fin. Suomenlahti, Ger. Finnischer Meerbusen, Rus. Finskiy Zaliv, Swe. Finska Viken. gulf E Baltic Sea
Finland, Republic of see Finland
Finnischer Meerbusen see Finland, Gulf of
Finnmarksvidda 62 D2 physical region N Norway
Finska Viken/Finskiy Zaliv see Finland, Gulf of
Finsterwalde 72 D4 Brandenburg, E Germany
Fiordland 129 A7 physical region South Island, New Zealand
Fiorina 74 E1 NE San Marino
Firat Nehri see Euphrates
Firenze 74 C3 Eng. Florence; anc. Florentia. Toscana, C Italy
Firmum Picenum see Fermo
First State see Delaware
Fischbacher Alpen 73 E7 mountain range E Austria
Fischhausen see Primorsk
Fish 56 B4 var. Vis. river S Namibia
Fishguard 67 C6 Wel. Abergwaun. SW Wales, United Kingdom
Fisterra, Cabo 70 B1 headland NW Spain
Fitzroy Crossing 124 C3 Western Australia
Fitzroy River 124 C3 river Western Australia
Fiume see Rijeka
Flagstaff 26 B2 Arizona, SW USA
Flanders 65 A6 Dut. Vlaanderen, Fr. Flandre. cultural region Belgium/France
Flandre see Flanders
Flathead Lake 22 B1 lake Montana, NW USA
Flat Island 106 C8 island NE Spratly Islands
Flatts Village 20 B5 var. The Flatts Village. C Bermuda
Flensburg 72 B2 Schleswig-Holstein, N Germany
Flessingue see Vlissingen
Flickertail State see North Dakota
Flinders Island 127 C8 island Furneaux Group, Tasmania, SE Australia
Flinders Ranges 127 B6 mountain range South Australia
Flinders River 126 C3 river Queensland, NE Australia
Flin Flon 15 F5 Manitoba, C Canada
Flint 18 C3 Michigan, N USA
Flint Island 123 G4 island Line Islands, E Kiribati
Floreana, Isla see Santa María, Isla
Florence 20 C1 Alabama, S USA
Florence 21 F2 South Carolina, SE USA
Florence see Firenze
Florencia 36 B4 Caquetá, S Colombia
Florentia see Firenze
Flores 30 B1 Petén, N Guatemala
Flores 117 E5 island Nusa Tenggara, C Indonesia
Flores 70 A5 island Azores, Portugal, NE Atlantic Ocean
Flores, Laut see Flores Sea
Flores Sea 116 D5 Ind. Laut Flores. sea C Indonesia
Floriano 41 F2 Piauí, E Brazil
Florianópolis 41 F5 prev. Destêrro. state capital Santa Catarina, S Brazil
Florida 42 D4 Florida, S Uruguay
Florida 21 E4 off. State of Florida, also known as Peninsular State, Sunshine State. state SE USA
Florida Bay 21 E5 bay Florida, SE USA
Florida Keys 21 E5 island group Florida, SE USA
Florida, Straits of 32 B1 strait Atlantic Ocean/ Gulf of Mexico
Flórina 82 B4 var. Phlórina. Dytikí Makedonía, N Greece
Florissant 23 G4 Missouri, C USA
Floúda, Ákrotírio 83 D7 headland Astypálaia, Kykládes, Greece, Aegean Sea
Flushing see Vlissingen
Flylân see Vlieland
Foča 78 C4 var. Srbinje, Republika Srpska. SE Bosnia and Herzegovina
Focşani 86 C4 Vrancea, E Romania
Fogaras/Fogarasch see Făgăraş
Foggia 75 D5 Puglia, SE Italy
Fogo 52 A3 island Ilhas de Sotavento, SW Cape Verde
Foix 69 B6 Ariège, S France
Folégandros 83 C7 island Kykládes, Greece, Aegean Sea
Foleyet 16 C4 Ontario, S Canada
Foligno 74 C4 Umbria, C Italy
Folkestone 67 E7 SE England, United Kingdom
Fond du Lac 18 B2 Wisconsin, N USA
Fongafale 123 E3 var. Funafuti. country capital Funafuti Atoll, SE Tuvalu
Fonseca, Golfo de see Fonseca, Gulf of
Fonseca, Gulf of 30 C3 Sp. Golfo de Fonseca. gulf C Central America
Fontainebleau 68 C3 Seine-et-Marne, N France
Fontenay-le-Comte 68 B4 Vendée, NW France
Fontvieille 69 B8 SW Monaco Europe
Fonyód 77 C7 Somogy, W Hungary
Foochow see Fuzhou
Foochow see Fuzhou
Forchheim 73 C5 Bayern, SE Germany
Forel, Mont 60 D4 mountain SE Greenland
Forfar 66 C3 E Scotland, United Kingdom
Forge du Sud see Dudelange
Forlì 74 C3 anc. Forum Livii. Emilia-Romagna, N Italy
Formentera 71 G4 anc. Ophiusa, Lat. Frumentum. island Islas Baleares, Spain, W Mediterranean Sea
Formosa 42 D2 Formosa, NE Argentina
Formosa/Formo'sa see Taiwan
Formosa, Serra 41 E3 mountain range C Brazil
Formosa Strait see Taiwan Strait
Føroyar see Faeroe Islands
Forrest City 20 B1 Arkansas, C USA
Fort Albany 16 C3 Ontario, C Canada
Fortaleza 39 F2 Pando, N Bolivia
Fortaleza 41 G2 prev. Ceará. state capital Ceará, NE Brazil
Fort-Archambault see Sarh
Fort-Bayard see Zhanjiang
Fort-Cappolani see Tidjikja
Fort Charlet see Djanet
Fort-Chimo see Kuujjuaq
Fort Collins 22 D4 Colorado, C USA
Fort-Crampel see Kaga Bandoro
Fort Davis 27 E3 Texas, SW USA
Fort-de-France 33 H4 prev. Fort-Royal. dependent territory capital W Martinique
Fort Dodge 23 F3 Iowa, C USA
Fortescue River 124 A4 river Western Australia
Fort-Foureau see Kousséri
Fort Frances 16 B4 Ontario, S Canada
Fort Good Hope 15 E3 var. Rádeyilikóé. Northwest Territories, NW Canada
Fort Gouraud see Fdérik
Forth 66 C4 river C Scotland, United Kingdom
Forth, Firth of 66 C4 estuary E Scotland, United Kingdom
Fortín General Eugenio Garay see General Eugenio A. Garay
Fort Jameson see Chipata
Fort-Lamy see Ndjamena
Fort Lauderdale 21 F5 Florida, SE USA
Fort Liard 15 E4 var. Liard. Northwest Territories, W Canada
Fort Madison 23 G4 Iowa, C USA
Fort McMurray 15 E4 Alberta, C Canada
Fort McPherson 14 D3 var. McPherson. Northwest Territories, NW Canada
Fort Morgan 22 D4 Colorado, C USA
Fort Myers 21 E5 Florida, SE USA
Fort Nelson 15 E4 British Columbia, W Canada
Fort Peck Lake 22 C1 reservoir Montana, NW USA
Fort Pierce 21 F4 Florida, SE USA

James Bay – Káristos

James Bay 16 C3 bay Ontario/Québec, E Canada
James River 23 E2 river North Dakota/South Dakota, N USA
James River 19 E5 river Virginia, NE USA
Jamestown 19 E3 New York, NE USA
Jamestown 23 E2 North Dakota, N USA
Jamestown see Holetown
Jammu 112 D2 prev. Jummoo. state capital Jammu and Kashmir, NW India
Jammu and Kashmir 112 D1 disputed region India/Pakistan
Jāmnagar 112 C4 prev. Navanagar. Gujarāt, W India
Jamshedpur 113 F4 Jhārkhand, NE India
Jamuna see Brahmaputra
Janaúba 41 F3 Minas Gerais, SE Brazil
Janesville 18 B3 Wisconsin, N USA
Janina see Ioánnina
Janischken see Joniškis
Jankovac see Jánoshalma
Jan Mayen 61 F4 Norwegian dependency N Atlantic Ocean
Jánoshalma 77 C7 SCr. Jankovac. Bács-Kiskun, S Hungary
Janów see Ivanava, Belarus
Janow/Janów see Jonava, Lithuania
Janów Poleski see Ivanava
Japan 108 C4 var. Nippon, Jap. Nihon. country E Asia
Japan, Sea of 108 A4 var. East Sea, Rus. Yapanskoye More. sea NW Pacific Ocean
Japan Trench 103 F1 trench NW Pacific Ocean
Japen see Yapen, Pulau
Japiim 40 C2 var. Máncio Lima. Acre, W Brazil
Japurá, Rio 40 C2 var. Río Caquetá, Yapurá. river Brazil/Colombia
Japurá, Rio see Caquetá, Río
Jaqué 31 G5 Darién, SE Panama
Jaquemel see Jacmel
Jarablos see Jarābulus
Jarābulus 96 C2 var. Jarablos, Jerablus, Fr. Djérablous. Ḥalab, N Syria
Jarbah, Jazīrat see Jerba, Île de
Jardines de la Reina, Archipiélago de los 32 B2 island group C Cuba
Jarīd, Shaṭṭ al see Jerid, Chott el
Jarocin 76 C4 Wielkopolskie, C Poland
Jaroslau see Jarosław
Jarosław 77 E5 Ger. Jaroslau, Rus. Yaroslav. Podkarpackie, SE Poland
Jarqo'rg'on 101 E3 Rus. Dzharkurgan. Surkhondaryo Viloyati, S Uzbekistan
Jarvis Island 123 G2 US unincorporated territory C Pacific Ocean
Jasło 77 D5 Podkarpackie, SE Poland
Jastrzębie-Zdrój 77 C5 Śląskie, S Poland
Jataí 41 E3 Goiás, C Brazil
Jativa see Xàtiva
Jauf see Al Jawf
Jaunpiebalga 84 D3 Gulbene, NE Latvia
Jaunpur 113 E3 Uttar Pradesh, N India
Java 130 A3 South Dakota, N USA
Javalambre 71 E3 mountain E Spain
Java Sea 116 D4 Ind. Laut Jawa. sea W Indonesia
Java Trench 102 D5 var. Sunda Trench. trench E Indian Ocean
Jawa, Laut see Java Sea
Jawhar 51 D6 var. Jowhar, It. Giohar. Shabeellaha Dhexe, S Somalia
Jaworów see Yavoriv
Jaya, Puncak 117 G4 prev. Puntjak Carstensz, Puntjak Sukarno. mountain Papua, E Indonesia
Jayapura 117 H4 var. Djajapura, Dut. Hollandia; prev. Kotabaru, Sukarnapura. Papua, E Indonesia
Jay Dairen see Dalian
Jayhawker State see Kansas
Jaz Murian, Hamun-e 98 E4 lake SE Iran
Jebba 53 F4 Kwara, W Nigeria
Jebel, Bahr el see White Nile
Jeble see Jablah
Jedda see Jiddah
Jędrzejów 76 D4 Ger. Endersdorf. Świętokrzyskie, C Poland
Jefferson City 23 G5 state capital Missouri, C USA
Jega 53 F4 Kebbi, NW Nigeria
Jehol see Chengde
Jēkabpils 84 D4 Ger. Jakobstadt. Jēkabpils, S Latvia
Jelalabad see Jalālābād
Jelenia Góra 76 B4 Ger. Hirschberg, Hirschberg im Riesengebirge, Hirschberg in Riesengebirge, Hirschberg in Schlesien. Dolnośląskie, SW Poland
Jelgava 84 C3 Ger. Mitau. Jelgava, C Latvia
Jemappes 65 B6 Hainaut, S Belgium
Jember 116 D5 prev. Djember. Jawa, C Indonesia
Jena 72 C4 Thüringen, C Germany
Jenin 97 A6 N West Bank
Jerablus see Jarābulus
Jerada 48 D2 NE Morocco
Jérémie 32 D3 SW Haiti
Jerez see Jeréz de la Frontera, Spain
Jeréz de la Frontera 70 C5 var. Jerez; prev. Xeres. Andalucía, SW Spain
Jeréz de los Caballeros 70 C4 Extremadura, W Spain
Jericho 97 B6 Ar. Arīḥā, Heb. Yeriḥo. E West Bank
Jerid, Chott el 49 E2 var. Shaṭṭ al Jarīd. salt lake SW Tunisia
Jersey 67 D8 uk crown dependency Channel Islands, NW Europe
Jerusalem 81 H4 Ar. Al Quds, Al Quds ash Sharīf, Heb. Yerushalayim; anc. Hierosolyma. country capital Jerusalem, NE Israel
Jesenice 73 D7 Ger. Assling. NW Slovenia
Jesselton see Kota Kinabalu
Jessore 113 G4 Khulna, W Bangladesh
Jesús María 42 C3 Córdoba, C Argentina
Jeypore see Jaipur, Rājasthān, India
Jhānsi 112 D3 Uttar Pradesh, N India
Jhārkhand 113 F4 cultural region NE India
Jhelum 112 C2 Punjab, NE Pakistan
Ji see Hebei, China
Ji see Jilin, China
Jiangmen 106 C6 Guangdong, S China
Jiangsu 106 D4 var. Chiang-su, Jiangsu Sheng, Kiangsu, Su. province E China
Jiangsu see Nanjing
Jiangsu Sheng see Jiangsu
Jiangxi 106 C6 var. Chiang-hsi, Gan, Jiangxi Sheng, Kiangsi. province S China
Jiangxi Sheng see Jiangxi
Jiaxing 106 D5 Zhejiang, SE China
Jiayi see Chiai
Jibuti see Djibouti
Jiddah 99 A5 Eng. Jedda. (Saudi Arabia) Makkah, W Saudi Arabia
Jih-k'a-tse see Xigazê
Jihlava 77 B5 Ger. Iglau, Pol. Igława. Vysocina, S Czech Republic
Jilib 51 D6 It. Gelib. Jubbada Dhexe, S Somalia
Jilin 106 E3 var. Chi-lin, Girin, Kirin; prev. Yungki, Yunki. Jilin, NE China
Jilin 106 E3 var. Chi-lin, Girin, Ji, Jilin Sheng, Kirin. province NE China
Jilin Sheng see Jilin
Jīma 51 C5 var. Jimma, It. Gimma. Oromīya, C Ethiopia
Jimbolia 86 A4 Ger. Hatzfeld, Hung. Zsombolya. Timiș, W Romania
Jiménez 28 D2 Chihuahua, N Mexico
Jimma see Jīma
Jimsar 104 C3 Xinjiang Uygur Zizhiqu, NW China
Jin see Shanxi
Jin see Tianjin Shi
Jinan 106 C4 var. Chinan, Chi-nan, Tsinan. province capital Shandong, E China
Jingdezhen 106 C5 Jiangxi, S China
Jinghong 106 A6 var. Yunjinghong. Yunnan, SW China
Jinhua 106 D5 Zhejiang, SE China
Jining 105 F3 Shandong, E China
Jinja 51 C6 S Uganda
Jinotega 30 D3 Jinotega, NW Nicaragua
Jinotepe 30 D3 Carazo, SW Nicaragua
Jinsen see Inch'ŏn
Jinsha Jiang 106 A5 Eng. Yangtze. river SW China
Jinzhong 106 C4 var. Yuci. Shanxi, C China
Jinzhou 106 D3 var. Chin-chou, Chinchow; prev. Chinhsien. Liaoning, NE China
Jirgalanta see Hovd
Jisr ash Shadadi see Ash Shadādah
Jiu 86 B5 Ger. Schil, Schyl, Hung. Zsil, Zsily. river S Romania
Jiujiang 106 C5 Jiangxi, S China
Jixi 107 E2 Heilongjiang, NE China
Jīzān 99 B6 var. Qīzān. Jīzān, SW Saudi Arabia
Jizzax 101 E2 Rus. Dzhizak. Jizzax Viloyati, C Uzbekistan
João Belo see Xai-Xai
João Pessoa 41 G2 prev. Paraíba. state capital Paraíba, E Brazil
Joazeiro see Juazeiro
Job'urg see Johannesburg
Jo-ch'iang see Ruoqiang
Jodhpur 112 C3 Rājasthān, NW India
Joensuu 63 E5 Itä-Suomi, SE Finland
Jōetsu 109 C5 var. Zyôetu. Niigata, Honshū, C Japan
Jogjakarta see Yogyakarta
Johannesburg 56 D4 var. Egoli, Erautini, Gauteng, abbrev. Job'urg. Gauteng, NE South Africa
Johannisburg see Pisz
John Day River 24 C3 river Oregon, NW USA
John o'Groats 66 C2 N Scotland, United Kingdom
Johnston Atoll 121 E1 US unincorporated territory C Pacific Ocean
Johor Baharu see Johor Bahru
Johor Bahru 116 B3 var. Johor Baharu, Johore Bahru. Johor, Peninsular Malaysia
Johore Bahru see Johor Bahru
Johore Strait 116 A1 strait Johor, Peninsular Malaysia, Malaysia/Singapore Asia Andaman Sea/South China Sea
Joinvile see Joinville
Joinville 41 E4 var. Joinvile. Santa Catarina, S Brazil
Jokkmokk 62 C3 Lapp. Dálvvadis. Norrbotten, N Sweden
Jokyakarta see Yogyakarta
Joliet 18 B3 Illinois, N USA
Jonava 84 B4 Ger. Janow, Pol. Janów. Kaunas, C Lithuania
Jonesboro 20 B1 Arkansas, C USA
Joniškis 84 C3 Ger. Janischken. Šiaulai, N Lithuania
Jönköping 63 B7 Jönköping, S Sweden
Jonquière 17 E4 Québec, SE Canada
Joplin 23 F5 Missouri, C USA
Jordan 97 B6 off. Hashemite Kingdom of Jordan, Ar. Al Mamlaka al Urduniya al Hashemīyah, Al Urdunn; prev. Transjordan. country SW Asia
Jordan 97 B5 Ar. Urdunn, Heb. HaYarden. river SW Asia
Jorhāt 113 H3 Assam, NE India
Jos 53 G4 Plateau, C Nigeria
Joseph Bonaparte Gulf 124 D2 gulf N Australia
Jos Plateau 53 G4 plateau C Nigeria
Jotunheimen 63 A5 mountain range S Norway
Joûnié 96 A4 var. Juniyah. W Lebanon
Joure 64 D2 Fris. De Jouwer. Friesland, N Netherlands
Joutseno 63 E5 Etelä-Suomi, SE Finland
Jowhar see Jawhar
J.Storm Thurmond Reservoir see Clark Hill Lake
Juan Aldama 28 D3 Zacatecas, C Mexico
Juan de Fuca, Strait of 24 A1 strait Canada/USA
Juan Fernandez Islands 35 A6 Eng. Juan Fernandez Islands. island group W Chile
Juan Fernandez Islands see Juan Fernández, Islas
Juazeiro 41 G2 prev. Joazeiro. Bahia, E Brazil
Juazeiro do Norte 41 G2 Ceará, E Brazil
Juba 51 B5 var. Jūbā. Bahr el Gabel, S Sudan
Juba 51 D6 Amh. Genalē Wenz, It. Guiba, Som. Ganaane, Webi Jubba. river Ethiopia/Somalia
Jubba, Webi see Juba
Jubbulpore see Jabalpur
Júcar 71 E3 var. Jucar. river C Spain
Juchitán 29 F5 var. Juchitán de Zaragosa. Oaxaca, SE Mexico
Juchitán de Zaragosa see Juchitán
Judayyidat Hāmir 98 B3 Al Anbār, S Iraq
Judenburg 73 D7 Steiermark, C Austria
Jugoslavija see Serbia
Juigalpa 30 D3 Chontales, S Nicaragua
Juiz de Fora 41 F4 Minas Gerais, SE Brazil
Jujuy see San Salvador de Jujuy
Jūlā see Jālū, Libya
Julia Beterrae see Béziers
Juliaca 39 E4 Puno, SE Peru
Juliana Top 37 G3 mountain C Suriname
Julianehåb see Qaqortoq
Julio Briga see Bragança
Juliobriga see Logroño
Juliomagus see Angers
Jullundur see Jalandhar
Jumilla 71 E4 Murcia, SE Spain
Jummoo see Jammu
Jumna see Yamuna
Jumporn see Chumphon
Junction City 23 F4 Kansas, C USA
Juneau 14 D4 state capital Alaska, USA
Junín 42 C4 Buenos Aires, E Argentina
Juniyah see Joûnié
Junkseylon see Phuket
Jur 51 B5 river C Sudan
Jura 68 D4 cultural region E France
Jura 73 A7 var. Jura Mountains. mountain range France/Switzerland
Jura 66 B4 island SW Scotland, United Kingdom
Jura Mountains see Jura
Jurbarkas 84 B4 Ger. Georgenburg, Jurburg. Tauragė, W Lithuania
Jurburg see Jurbarkas
Jūrmala 84 C3 Riga, C Latvia
Juruá, Rio 40 C2 var. Río Yuruá. river Brazil/Peru
Juruena, Rio 40 D3 river W Brazil
Jutiapa 30 B2 Jutiapa, S Guatemala
Juticalpa 30 D2 Olancho, C Honduras
Jutland 63 A7 Eng. Jutland. peninsula W Denmark
Jutland see Jylland
Juvavum see Salzburg
Južna Morava 79 E5 Ger. Südliche Morava. river SE Serbia
Jwaneng 56 C4 Southern, S Botswana
Jyrgalan see Dzhergalan
Jyväskylä 63 D5 Länsi-Suomi, C Finland

K

K2 104 A4 Chin. Qogir Feng, Eng. Mount Godwin Austen. mountain China/Pakistan
Kaafu Atoll see Male' Atoll
Kaaimanston 37 G3 Sipaliwini, N Suriname
Kaakhka see Kaka
Kaala see Caála
Kaamanen 62 D2 Lapp. Gámas. Lappi, N Finland
Kaapstad see Cape Town
Kaaresuvanto 62 C3 Lapp. Gárassavon. Lappi, N Finland
Kabale 51 B6 SW Uganda
Kabinda 55 D7 Kasai-Oriental, SE Dem. Rep. Congo
Kabinda see Cabinda
Kābol 101 E4 var. Kabul, Pash. Kābul. country capital Kābul, E Afghanistan
Kabompo 56 C2 river W Zambia
Kabul 101 E4 var. Daryā-ye Kābul. river Afghanistan/Pakistan
Kābul see Kābol
Kābul, Daryā-ye see Kabul
Kabwe 56 D2 Central, C Zambia
Kachchh, Gulf of 112 B4 var. Gulf of Cutch, Gulf of Kutch. gulf W India
Kachchh, Rann of 112 B4 var. Rann of Kachh, Rann of Kutch. salt marsh India/Pakistan
Kachh, Rann of see Kachchh, Rann of
Kadan Kyun 115 B5 prev. King Island. island Mergui Archipelago, S Myanmar (Burma)
Kadavu 123 E4 prev. Kandavu. island S Fiji
Kadoma 56 D3 prev. Gatooma. Mashonaland West, C Zimbabwe
Kadugli 50 B4 Southern Kordofan, S Sudan
Kaduna 53 G4 Kaduna, C Nigeria
Kadzhi-Say 101 G2 Kir. Kajisay. Issyk-Kul'skaya Oblast', NE Kyrgyzstan
Kaédi 52 C3 Gorgol, S Mauritania
Kaffa see Feodosiya
Kafue 56 D2 Lusaka, SE Zambia
Kafue 56 C2 river C Zambia
Kaga Bandoro 54 C4 prev. Fort-Crampel. Nana-Grébizi, C Central African Republic
Kagan see Kogon
Kâghet 52 D1 var. Karet. physical region N Mauritania
Kagi see Chiai
Kagoshima 109 B8 var. Kagosima. Kagoshima, Kyūshū, SW Japan
Kagoshima-wan 109 A8 bay SW Japan
Kagosima see Kagoshima
Kagul see Cahul
Darya-ye Kahmard 101 E4 prev. Darya-i-surkhab. river NE Afghanistan
Kahramanmaraş 94 D4 var. Kahraman Maraş, Maraş, Marash. Kahramanmaraş, S Turkey
Kaiapoi 129 C6 Canterbury, South Island, New Zealand
Kaifeng 106 C4 Henan, C China
Kai, Kepulauan 117 F4 prev. Kei Islands. island group Maluku, SE Indonesia
Kaikohe 128 C2 Northland, North Island, New Zealand
Kaikoura 129 C5 Canterbury, South Island, New Zealand
Kaikoura Peninsula 129 C5 peninsula South Island, New Zealand
Kainji Lake see Kainji Reservoir
Kainji Reservoir 53 F4 var. Kainji Lake. reservoir W Nigeria
Kaipara Harbour 128 C2 harbour North Island, New Zealand
Kairouan 49 E2 var. Al Qayrawān. E Tunisia
Kaisaria see Kayseri
Kaiserslautern 73 A5 Rheinland-Pfalz, SW Germany
Kaišiadorys 85 B5 Kaunas, S Lithuania
Kaitaia 128 C2 Northland, North Island, New Zealand
Kajaani 62 E4 Swe. Kajana. Oulu, C Finland
Kajan see Kayan, Sungai
Kajana see Kajaani
Kajisay see Kadzhi-Say
Kaka 100 C2 Rus. Kaakhka. Ahal Welaýaty, S Turkmenistan
Kake 14 D4 Kupreanof Island, Alaska, USA
Kakhovka 87 F4 Khersons'ka Oblast', S Ukraine
Kakhovs'ke Vodoskhovyshche 87 F4 Rus. Kakhovskoye Vodokhranilishche. reservoir SE Ukraine
Kakhovskoye Vodokhranilishche see Kakhovs'ke Vodoskhovyshche
Kākināda 110 D1 prev. Cocanada. Andhra Pradesh, E India
Kakshaal-Too, Khrebet see Kokshaal-Tau
Kaktovik 14 D2 Alaska, USA
Kalaallit Nunaat see Greenland
Kalahari Desert 56 B4 desert Southern Africa
Kalaikhum see Qal'aikhum
Kalámai see Kalámata
Kalamariá 82 B4 Kentrikí Makedonía, N Greece
Kalamás 82 A4 var. Thiamis; prev. Thýamis. river W Greece
Kalámata 83 B6 prev. Kalámai. Pelopónnisos, S Greece
Kalamazoo 18 C3 Michigan, N USA
Kalambaka see Kalampáka
Kálamos 83 C5 Attikí, C Greece
Kalampáka 82 B4 var. Kalambaka. Thessalía, C Greece
Kalanchak 87 F4 Khersons'ka Oblast', S Ukraine
Kalarash see Călărași
Kalasin 114 D4 var. Muang Kalasin. Kalasin, E Thailand
Kalāt 112 B2 var. Kelat, Khelat. Baluchistān, SW Pakistan
Kalāt see Qalāt
Kalbarri 125 A5 Western Australia
Kalecik 94 C3 Ankara, N Turkey
Kalemie 55 E6 prev. Albertville. Katanga, SE Dem. Rep. Congo
Kale Sultanie see Çanakkale
Kalgan see Zhangjiakou
Kalgoorlie 125 B6 Western Australia
Kalima 55 D6 Maniema, E Dem. Rep. Congo
Kalimantan 116 D4 Eng. Indonesian Borneo. geopolitical region Borneo, C Indonesia
Kalinin see Tver'
Kaliningrad 84 A4 Kaliningradskaya Oblast', W Russian Federation
Kaliningrad see Kaliningradskaya Oblast'
Kaliningradskaya Oblast' 84 B4 var. Kaliningrad. province and enclave W Russian Federation
Kalinkavichy 85 C7 Rus. Kalinkovichi. Homyel'skaya Voblasts', SE Belarus
Kalinkovichi see Kalinkavichy
Kalisch/Kalish see Kalisz
Kalispell 22 B1 Montana, NW USA
Kalisz 76 C4 Ger. Kalisch, Rus. Kalish; anc. Calisia. Wielkopolskie, C Poland
Kalix 62 D4 Norrbotten, N Sweden
Kalixälven 62 D3 river N Sweden
Kallaste 84 E3 Ger. Krasnogor. Tartumaa, SE Estonia
Kallavesi 63 E5 lake SE Finland
Kalloní 83 D5 Lésvos, E Greece
Kalmar 63 C7 var. Calmar. Kalmar, S Sweden
Kalmthout 65 C5 Antwerpen, N Belgium
Kalpáki 82 A4 Ípeiros, W Greece
Kalpeni Island 110 B3 island Lakshadweep, India, N Indian Ocean
Kaltdorf see Pruszków
Kaluga 89 B5 Kaluzhskaya Oblast', W Russian Federation
Kalush 86 C2 Pol. Kałusz. Ivano-Frankivs'ka Oblast', W Ukraine
Kałusz see Kalush
Kalutara 110 D4 Western Province, SW Sri Lanka
Kalvarija 85 B5 Pol. Kalwaria. Marijampolė, S Lithuania
Kalwaria see Kalvarija
Kalyān 112 C5 Mahārāshtra, W India
Kálymnos 83 D6 var. Kálimnos. island Dodekánisa, Greece, Aegean Sea
Kama 88 D4 river NW Russian Federation
Kamarang 37 F3 W Guyana
Kambryk see Cambrai
Kamchatka 93 G3 Eng. Kamchatka. peninsula E Russian Federation
Kamchatka see Kamchatka, Poluostrov
Kamenets-Podol'skiy see Kam"yanets'-Podil's'kyy
Kamenka Dneprovskaya see Kam"yanka-Dniprovs'ka
Kamenskoye see Romaniv
Kamensk-Shakhtinskiy 89 B6 Rostovskaya Oblast', SW Russian Federation
Kamina 55 D7 Katanga, S Dem. Rep. Congo
Kamishli see Al Qāmishlī
Kamloops 15 E5 British Columbia, SW Canada
Kammu Seamount 130 C2 guyot N Pacific Ocean
Kampala 51 B6 country capital S Uganda
Kâmpóng Cham 115 D6 prev. Kompong Cham. Kâmpóng Cham, C Cambodia
Kâmpóng Chhnăng 115 D6 prev. Kompong. Kâmpóng Chhnăng, C Cambodia
Kâmpóng Saôm 115 D6 prev. Kompong Som, Sihanoukville. Kâmpóng Saôm, SW Cambodia
Kâmpóng Spoe 115 D6 prev. Kompong Speu. Kâmpóng Spœ, S Cambodia
Kâmpôt 115 D6 Kâmpôt, SW Cambodia
Kampuchea see Cambodia
Kampuchea, Democratic see Cambodia
Kampuchea, People's Democratic Republic of see Cambodia
Kam"yanets'-Podil's'kyy 86 C3 Rus. Kamenets-Podol'skiy. Khmel'nyts'ka Oblast', W Ukraine
Kam"yanka-Dniprovs'ka 87 F3 Rus. Kamenka Dneprovskaya. Zaporiz'ka Oblast', SE Ukraine
Kamyshin 89 B6 Volgogradskaya Oblast', SW Russian Federation
Kanaky see New Caledonia
Kananga 55 D6 prev. Luluabourg. Kasai-Occidental, S Dem. Rep. Congo
Kanara see Karnātaka
Kanash 89 C5 Chuvashskaya Respublika, W Russian Federation
Kanazawa 109 C5 Ishikawa, Honshū, SW Japan
Kanbe 114 B4 Yangon, SW Myanmar (Burma)
Kānchīpuram 110 C2 prev. Conjeeveram. Tamil Nādu, SE India
Kandahār 101 E5 Per. Qandahār. Kandahār, S Afghanistan
Kandalakša see Kandalaksha
Kandalaksha 88 B2 var. Kandalakša, Fin. Kantalahti. Murmanskaya Oblast', NW Russian Federation
Kandangan 116 D4 Borneo, C Indonesia
Kandau see Kandava
Kandava 84 C3 Ger. Kandau. Tukums, W Latvia
Kandavu see Kadavu
Kandi 53 F4 N Benin
Kandy 110 D3 Central Province, C Sri Lanka
Kane Fracture Zone 44 B4 fracture zone NW Atlantic Ocean
Kāne'ohe 25 A8 var. Kaneohe. O'ahu, Hawaii, USA, C Pacific Ocean
Kanestron, Akrotírio see Palioúri, Akrotírio
Kanëv see Kaniv
Kanevskoye Vodokhranilishche see Kanivs'ke Vodoskhovyshche
Kangān see Bandar-e Kangān
Kangaroo Island 127 A7 island South Australia
Kangertittivaq 61 E4 Dan. Scoresby Sund. fjord E Greenland
Kangikajik 61 E4 var. Kap Brewster. headland E Greenland
Kaniv 87 E2 Rus. Kanëv. Cherkas'ka Oblast', C Ukraine
Kanivs'ke Vodoskhovyshche 87 E2 Rus. Kanevskoye Vodokhranilishche. reservoir C Ukraine
Kanjiža 78 D2 Ger. Altkanischa, Hung. Magyarkanizsa, Ókanizsa; prev. Stara Kanjiža. Vojvodina, N Serbia
Kankaanpää 63 D5 Länsi-Suomi, SW Finland
Kankakee 18 B3 Illinois, N USA
Kankan 52 D4 E Guinea
Kano 53 G4 Kano, N Nigeria
Kānpur 113 E3 Eng. Cawnpore. Uttar Pradesh, N India
Kansas 23 F5 off. State of Kansas, also known as Jayhawker State, Sunflower State. state C USA
Kansas City 23 F4 Kansas, C USA
Kansas City 23 F4 Missouri, C USA
Kansas River 23 F5 river Kansas, C USA
Kansk 93 E4 Krasnoyarskiy Kray, S Russian Federation
Kansu see Gansu
Kantalahti see Kandalaksha
Kántanos 83 C7 Kriti, Greece, E Mediterranean Sea
Kantemirovka 89 B6 Voronezhskaya Oblast', W Russian Federation
Kantipur see Kathmandu
Kanton 123 F3 var. Abariringa, Canton Island; prev. Mary Island. atoll Phoenix Islands, C Kiribati
Kanye 56 C4 Southern, SE Botswana
Kaohsiung 106 D6 var. Gaoxiong, Jap. Takao, Takow. S Taiwan
Kaolack 52 B3 var. Kaolak. W Senegal
Kaolak see Kaolack
Kaolan see Lanzhou
Kaoma 56 C2 Western, W Zambia
Kapelle 65 B5 Zeeland, SW Netherlands
Kapellen 65 C5 Antwerpen, N Belgium
Kapka, Massif du 54 C2 mountain range E Chad
Kaplangky, Plato see Gaplaňgyr Platosy
Kapoeas see Kapuas, Sungai
Kapoeta 51 C5 Eastern Equatoria, SE Sudan
Kaposvár 77 C7 Somogy, SW Hungary
Kappeln 72 B2 Schleswig-Holstein, N Germany
Kapronca see Koprivnica
Kapstad see Cape Town
Kapsukas see Marijampolė
Kaptsevichy 85 C7 Rus. Koptsevichi. Homyel'skaya Voblasts', SE Belarus
Kapuas, Sungai 116 C4 prev. Kapoeas. river Borneo, C Indonesia
Kapuskasing 16 C4 Ontario, S Canada
Kapyl' 85 C6 Rus. Kopyl'. Minskaya Voblasts', C Belarus
Kara-Balta 101 F2 Chuyskaya Oblast', N Kyrgyzstan
Karabil', Vozvyshennost' see Garabil Belentligi
Kara-Bogaz-Gol, Zaliv see Garabogaz Aylagy
Karabük 94 C2 Karabük, NW Turkey
Karāchi 112 B3 Sind, SE Pakistan
Karácsonkő see Piatra-Neamț
Karadeniz see Black Sea
Karadeniz Boğazi see İstanbul Boğazı
Karaferiye see Véroia
Karaganda 92 C4 Kaz. Qaraghandy. Karaganda, C Kazakhstan
Karaginskiy, Ostrov 93 H2 island E Russian Federation
Karagumskiy Kanal see Garagum Kanaly
Karak see Al Karak
Karakax see Moyu
Karakılısse see Ağrı
Karakol 101 G2 prev. Przheval'sk. Issyk-Kul'skaya Oblast', NE Kyrgyzstan
Karakol 101 G2 var. Karakolka. Issyk-Kul'skaya Oblast', NE Kyrgyzstan
Karakolka see Karakol
Karakoram Range 112 D1 mountain range C Asia
Karaköse see Ağrı
Karakul' see Qarokŭl, Tajikistan
Kara Kum see Garagum
Kara Kum Canal/Karakumskiy Kanal see Garagum Kanaly
Karakumy, Peski see Garagum
Karamai see Karamay
Karaman 94 C4 Karaman, S Turkey
Karamay 104 B2 var. Karamai, Kelamayi; prev. Chin. K'o-la-ma-i. Xinjiang Uygur Zizhiqu, NW China
Karamea Bight 129 B5 gulf South Island, New Zealand
Karapelit 82 E1 Rom. Stejarul. Dobrich, NE Bulgaria
Kara-Say 101 G2 Issyk-Kul'skaya Oblast', NE Kyrgyzstan
Karasburg 56 B4 Karas, S Namibia
Kara Sea 92 D2 Eng. Kara Sea. sea Arctic Ocean
Kara Sea see Karskoye More
Kara Strait 88 E2 Eng. Kara Strait. strait N Russian Federation
Kara Strait see Karskiye Vorota, Proliv
Karatau 92 C5 Kaz. Qaratau. Zhambyl, S Kazakhstan
Karavás 83 B7 Kýthira, S Greece
Karbalā' 98 B3 var. Kerbala, Kerbela. Karbalā', S Iraq
Kardeljevo see Ploče
Kardhítsa see Kardítsa
Kardítsa 83 B5 var. Kardhítsa. Thessalía, C Greece
Kärdla 84 C2 Ger. Kertel. Hiiumaa, W Estonia
Karet see Kâghet
Kargı 94 C2 Çorum, N Turkey
Kargilik see Yecheng
Kariba 56 D2 Mashonaland West, N Zimbabwe
Kariba, Lake 56 D3 reservoir Zambia/Zimbabwe
Karibib 56 B3 Erongo, C Namibia
Karies see Karyés
Karigasniemi 62 D2 Lapp. Garegegasnjárga. Lappi, N Finland
Karimata, Selat 116 C4 strait W Indonesia
Karīmnagar 112 D5 Andhra Pradesh, C India
Karin 50 D4 Sahil, N Somalia
Kariot see Ikaría
Káristos see Kárystos

Klisura – Kuzi

Klisura 82 C2 Plovdiv, C Bulgaria
Ključ 78 B3 Federacija Bosna I Hercegovina, NW Bosnia and Herzegovina
Kłobuck 76 C4 Śląskie, S Poland
Klosters 73 B7 Graubünden, SE Switzerland
Kluang see Keluang
Kluczbork 76 C4 Ger. Kreuzburg, Kreuzburg in Oberschlesien. Opolskie, S Poland
Klyuchevskaya Sopka, Vulkan 93 H3 volcano E Russian Federation
Knin 78 B4 Šibenik-Knin, S Croatia
Knjaževac 78 E4 Serbia, E Serbia
Knokke-Heist 65 A5 West-Vlaanderen, NW Belgium
Knoxville 20 D1 Tennessee, S USA
Knud Rasmussen Land 60 D1 physical region N Greenland
Kobdo see Hovd
Kōbe 109 C6 Hyōgo, Honshū, SW Japan
København 63 B7 Eng. Copenhagen; anc. Hafnia. country capital Sjælland, København, E Denmark
Kobenni 52 D3 Hodh el Gharbi, S Mauritania
Koblenz 73 A5 prev. Coblenz, Fr. Coblence; anc. Confluentes. Rheinland-Pfalz, W Germany
Kobrin see Kobryn
Kobryn 85 A6 Rus. Kobrin. Brestskaya Voblasts', SW Belarus
K'obulet'i 95 F2 W Georgia
Kočani 79 E6 NE FYR Macedonia
Kočevje 73 D8 Ger. Gottschee. S Slovenia
Koch Bihār 113 G3 West Bengal, NE India
Kochchi Cochin/Kochi
Kōchi 109 B7 var. Kôti. Kōchi, Shikoku, SW Japan
Kochiu see Gejiu
Kodiak 14 C3 Kodiak Island, Alaska, USA
Kodiak Island 14 C3 island Alaska, USA
Koedoes see Kudus
Koeln see Köln
Koepang see Kupang
Ko-erh-mu see Golmud
Koetai see Mahakam, Sungai
Koetaradja see Bandaaceh
Kōfu 109 D5 var. Kôhu. Yamanashi, Honshū, S Japan
Kogarah 126 E2 New South Wales, E Australia
Kogon 100 D2 Rus. Kagan. Buxoro Viloyati, C Uzbekistan
Kőhalom see Rupea
Kohima 113 H3 state capital Nāgāland, E India
Koh I Noh see Büyükağrı Dağı
Kohtla-Järve 84 E2 Ida-Virumaa, NE Estonia
Kôhu see Kōfu
Kokand see Qo'qon
Kokchetav see Kokshetau
Kokkola 62 D4 Swe. Karleby; prev. Swe. Gamlakarleby. Länsi-Suomi, W Finland
Koko 53 F4 Kebbi, W Nigeria
Kokomo 18 C4 Indiana, N USA
Koko Nor see Qinghai, China
Koko Nor see Qinghai Hu, China
Kokrines 14 C2 Alaska, USA
Kokshaal-Tau 101 G2 Rus. Khrebet Kakshaal-Too. mountain range China/Kyrgyzstan
Kokshetau 92 C4 Kaz. Kökshetaū; prev. Kokchetav. Kokshetau, N Kazakhstan
Kökshetaū see Kokshetau
Koksijde 65 A5 West-Vlaanderen, W Belgium
Koksoak 16 D2 river Québec, E Canada
Kokstad 56 D5 KwaZulu/Natal, E South Africa
Kolaka 117 E4 Sulawesi, C Indonesia
K'o-la-ma-i see Karamay
Kola Peninsula 88 C2 Eng. Kola Peninsula. peninsula NW Russian Federation
Kola Peninsula see Kol'skiy Poluostrov
Kolari 62 D3 Lappi, NW Finland
Kolárovo 77 C6 Ger. Gutta; prev. Guta, Hung. Gúta. Nitriansky Kraj, SW Slovakia
Kolberg see Kołobrzeg
Kolda 52 C3 S Senegal
Kolding 63 A7 Vejle, C Denmark
Kölen 59 E1 Nor. Kjølen. mountain range Norway/Sweden
Kolguyev, Ostrov 88 C2 island NW Russian Federation
Kolhāpur 110 B1 Mahārāshtra, SW India
Kolhumadulu 110 A5 var. Thaa Atoll. atoll S Maldives
Kolín 77 B5 Ger. Kolin. Střední Čechy, C Czech Republic
Kolka 84 C2 Talsi, NW Latvia
Kolkasrags 84 C2 prev. Eng. Cape Domesnes. headland NW Latvia
Kolmar see Colmar
Köln 72 A4 var. Koeln, Eng./Fr. Cologne, prev. Cöln; anc. Colonia Agrippina, Oppidum Ubiorum. Nordrhein-Westfalen, W Germany
Koło 76 C3 Wielkopolskie, C Poland
Kołobrzeg 76 B2 Ger. Kolberg. Zachodnio-pomorskie, NW Poland
Kolokani 52 D3 Koulikoro, W Mali
Kolomea see Kolomyya
Kolomna 89 B5 Moskovskaya Oblast', W Russian Federation
Kolomyya 86 C3 Ger. Kolomea. Ivano-Frankivs'ka Oblast', W Ukraine
Kolosjoki see Nikel'
Kolozsvár see Cluj-Napoca
Kolpa 78 A2 Ger. Kulpa, SCr. Kupa. river Croatia/Slovenia
Kolpino 88 B4 Leningradskaya Oblast', NW Russian Federation
Kólpos Mórfu see Güzelyurt
Kolwezi 55 D7 Katanga, S Dem. Rep. Congo
Kolyma 93 G2 river NE Russian Federation
Komatsu 109 C5 var. Komatu. Ishikawa, Honshū, SW Japan
Komatu see Komatsu
Kommunizm, Qullai see Ismoili Somoní, Qullai
Komoé 53 E4 var. Komoé Fleuve. river E Ivory Coast
Komoé Fleuve see Komoé
Komotau see Chomutov
Komotiní 82 D3 var. Gümüljina, Turk. Gümülcine. Anatolikí Makedonía kai Thráki, NE Greece
Kompong see Kâmpóng Chhnăng
Kompong Cham see Kâmpóng Cham
Kompong Som see Kâmpóng Saôm
Kompong Speu see Kâmpóng Spoe
Komrat see Comrat
Komsomolets, Ostrov 93 E1 island Severnaya Zemlya, N Russian Federation
Komsomol'sk-na-Amure 93 G4 Khabarovskiy Kray, SE Russian Federation
Kondolovo 82 E3 Burgas, E Bulgaria
Kondopoga 88 B3 Respublika Kareliya, NW Russian Federation
Kondoz 101 E3 Pash. Kunduz. province NE Afghanistan
Köneurgench 100 C2 var. Köneürgench, Rus. Këneurgench; prev. Kunya-Urgench. Daşoguz Welaýaty, N Turkmenistan
Kong Christian IX Land 60 D4 Eng. King Christian IX Land. physical region SE Greenland
Kong Frederik IX Land 60 C3 physical region SW Greenland
Kong Frederik VIII Land 61 E2 Eng. King Frederik VIII Land. physical region NE Greenland
Kong Frederik VI Kyst 60 C4 Eng. King Frederik VI Coast. physical region SE Greenland
Kong Karls Land 61 G2 Eng. King Charles Islands. island group SE Svalbard
Kongo see Congo (river)
Kongolo 55 D6 Katanga, E Dem. Rep. Congo
Kongor 51 B5 Jonglei, SE Sudan
Kong Oscar Fjord 61 E3 fjord E Greenland
Kongsberg 63 B6 Buskerud, S Norway
Kông, Tônle 115 E5 var. Xê Kong. river Cambodia/Laos
Kong, Xê see Kông, Tônle
Königgrätz see Hradec Králové
Königshütte see Chorzów
Konin 76 C3 Ger. Kuhnau. Weilkopolskie, C Poland
Koninkrijk der Nederlanden see Netherlands
Konispol 79 C7 var. Konispoli. Vlorë, S Albania
Konispoli see Konispol
Kónitsa 82 A4 Ípeiros, W Greece
Konitz see Chojnice
Konjic 78 C4 Federacija Bosna I Hercegovina, S Bosnia and Herzegovina
Konosha 88 C4 Arkhangel'skaya Oblast', NW Russian Federation
Konotop 87 F1 Sums'ka Oblast', NE Ukraine
Konstantinovka see Kostyantynivka
Konstanz 73 B7 var. Constanz, Eng. Constance, hist. Kostnitz; anc. Constantia. Baden-Württemberg, S Germany
Konstanza see Constanţa
Konya 94 C4 var. Konieh, prev. Konia; anc. Iconium. Konya, C Turkey
Kopaonik 79 D5 mountain range S Serbia
Kopar see Koper
Koper 73 D8 It. Capodistria; prev. Kopar. SW Slovenia
Kōpetdag Gershi 100 C3 mountain range Iran/Turkmenistan
Kōpetdag Gershi/Kopetdag, Khrebet see Koppeh Dāgh
Koppeh Dāgh 98 D2 Rus. Khrebet Kopetdag, Turkm. Köpetdag Gershi. mountain range Iran/Turkmenistan
Kopreinitz see Koprivnica
Koprivnica 78 B2 Ger. Kopreinitz, Hung. Kaproncza. Koprivnica-Kri»evci, N Croatia
Köprülü see Veles
Koptsevichi see Kaptsevichy
Kopyl' see Kapyl'
Korat see Nakhon Ratchasima
Korat Plateau 114 D4 plateau E Thailand
Korba 113 E4 Chhattīsgarh, C India
Korça see Korçë
Korçë 79 D6 var. Korça, Gk. Korytsa, It. Corriza; prev. Koritsa. Korçë, SE Albania
Korčula 78 B4 It. Curzola; anc. Corcyra Nigra. island S Croatia
Korea Bay 105 G3 bay China/North Korea
Korea, Democratic People's Republic of see North Korea
Korea, Republic of see South Korea
Korea Strait 109 A7 Jap. Chōsen-kaikyō, Kor. Taehan-haehyŏp. channel Japan/South Korea
Korhogo 52 D4 N Ivory Coast
Korinthos 83 B6 anc. Corinthus Eng. Corinth. Pelopónnisos, S Greece
Koritsa see Korçë
Kōriyama 109 D5 Fukushima, Honshū, C Japan
Korla 104 C3 Chin. K'u-erh-lo. Xinjiang Uygur Zizhiqu, NW China
Körmend 77 B7 Vas, W Hungary
Koróni 83 B6 Pelopónnisos, S Greece
Koror 122 A2 var. Oreor. Oreor, N Palau
Kőrös see Križevci
Korosten' 86 D1 Zhytomyrs'ka Oblast', NW Ukraine
Koro Toro 54 C2 Borkou-Ennedi-Tibesti, N Chad
Korsovka see Kārsava
Kortrijk 65 A6 Fr. Courtrai. West-Vlaanderen, W Belgium
Koryak Range 93 H2 var. Koryakskiy Khrebet, Eng. Koryak Range. mountain range NE Russian Federation
Koryak Range see Koryakskoye Nagor'ye
Koryakskiy Khrebet see Koryakskoye Nagor'ye
Koryazhma 88 C4 Arkhangel'skaya Oblast', NW Russian Federation
Korytsa see Korçë
Kos 83 E6 Kos, Dodekánisa, Greece, Aegean Sea
Kos 83 E6 It. Coo; anc. Cos. island Dodekánisa, Greece, Aegean Sea
Ko-saki 109 A7 headland Nagasaki, Tsushima, SW Japan
Kościan 76 B4 Ger. Kosten. Wielkopolskie, C Poland
Kościerzyna 76 C2 Pomorskie, NW Poland
Kosciusko, Mount see Kosciuszko, Mount
Kosciuszko, Mount 127 C7 prev. Mount Kosciusko. mountain New South Wales, SE Australia
K'o-shih see Kashi
Koshikijima-retto 109 A8 var. Kosikizima Rettô. island group SW Japan
Kōshū see Kwangju
Košice 77 D6 Ger. Kaschau, Hung. Kassa. Košický Kraj, E Slovakia
Kosikizima Rettô see Koshikijima-retto
Köslin see Koszalin
Koson 101 E3 Rus. Kasan. Qashqadaryo Viloyati, S Uzbekistan
Kosovo 79 D5 prev. Autonomous Province of Kosovo and Metohija. country SE Europe
Kosovo and Metohija, Autonomous Province of see Kosovo
Kosovo Polje see Fushë Kosovë
Kosovska Mitrovica see Mitrovicë
Kosrae 122 C2 prev. Kusaie. island Caroline Islands, E Micronesia
Kossou, Lac de 52 D5 lake C Ivory Coast
Kostanay 92 C4 var. Kustanay, Kaz. Qostanay. Kostanay, N Kazakhstan
Kosten see Kościan
Kostenets 82 C2 prev. Georgi Dimitrov. Sofiya, W Bulgaria
Kostnitz see Konstanz
Kostroma 88 B4 Kostromskaya Oblast', NW Russian Federation
Kostyantynivka 87 G3 Rus. Konstantinovka. Donets'ka Oblast', SE Ukraine
Kostyukovichi see Kastsyukovichy
Kostyukovka see Kastsyukowka
Koszalin 76 B2 Ger. Köslin. Zachodnio-pomorskie, NW Poland
Kota 112 D3 prev. Kotah. Rājasthān, N India
Kota Baharu see Kota Bharu
Kota Bahru see Kota Bharu
Kotabaru see Jayapura
Kota Bharu 116 B3 var. Kota Baharu, Kota Bahru. Kelantan, Peninsular Malaysia
Kotaboemi see Kotabumi
Kotabumi 116 B4 prev. Kotaboemi. Sumatera, W Indonesia
Kotah see Kota
Kota Kinabalu 116 D3 prev. Jesselton. Sabah, East Malaysia
Kotel'nyy, Ostrov 93 E2 island Novosibirskiye Ostrova, N Russian Federation
Kotka 63 E5 Etelä-Suomi, S Finland
Kotlas 88 C4 Arkhangel'skaya Oblast', NW Russian Federation
Kotonu see Cotonou
Kotor 79 C5 It. Cattaro. SW Montenegro
Kotovs'k 86 D3 Rus. Kotovsk. Odes'ka Oblast', SW Ukraine
Kotovsk see Hînceşti
Kottbus see Cottbus
Kotto 54 D4 river Central African Republic/Dem. Rep. Congo
Kotuy 93 E2 river N Russian Federation
Koudougou 53 E4 C Burkina
Koulamoutou 55 B6 Ogooué-Lolo, C Gabon
Koulikoro 52 D3 Koulikoro, SW Mali
Koumra 54 C4 Moyen-Chari, S Chad
Kourou 37 H3 N French Guiana
Kousseir see Al Quşayr
Kousséri 54 B3 prev. Fort-Foureau. Extrême-Nord, NE Cameroon
Koutiala 52 D4 Sikasso, S Mali
Kouvola 63 E5 Etelä-Suomi, S Finland
Kovel' 86 C1 Pol. Kowel. Volyns'ka Oblast', NW Ukraine
Kovno see Kaunas
Koweit see Kuwait
Kowel see Kovel'
Kowloon 106 A2 Hong Kong, S China
Kowno see Kaunas
Kozáni 82 B4 Dytikí Makedonía, N Greece
Kozara 78 B3 mountain range NW Bosnia and Herzegovina
Kozarska Dubica see Bosanska Dubica
Kozu-shima 109 D6 island E Japan
Kozyatyn 86 D2 Rus. Kazatin. Vinnyts'ka Oblast', C Ukraine
Kpalimé 53 E5 var. Palimé. SW Togo
Krâchéh 115 D6 prev. Kratie. Krâchéh, E Cambodia
Kragujevac 78 D4 Serbia, C Serbia
Krainburg see Kranj
Kra, Isthmus of 115 B6 isthmus Malaysia/Thailand
Krakau see Kraków
Kraków 77 D5 Eng. Cracow, Ger. Krakau; anc. Cracovia. Małopolskie, S Poland
Krâlănh 115 D5 Siĕmréab, NW Cambodia
Kraljevo 78 D4 prev. Rankovićevo. Serbia, C Serbia
Kramators'k 87 G3 Rus. Kramatorsk. Donets'ka Oblast', SE Ukraine
Kramatorsk see Kramators'k
Kramfors 63 C5 Västernorrland, C Sweden
Kranéa see Kraniá
Kraniá 82 B4 var. Kranéa. Dytikí Makedonía, N Greece
Kranj 73 D7 Ger. Krainburg. NW Slovenia
Kranz see Zelenogradsk
Krāslava 84 D4 Krāslava, SE Latvia
Krasnaye 85 C5 Rus. Krasnoye. Minskaya Voblasts', C Belarus
Krasnoarmeysk 89 C6 Saratovskaya Oblast', W Russian Federation
Krasnodar 89 A7 prev. Ekaterinodar, Yekaterinodar. Krasnodarskiy Kray, SW Russian Federation
Krasnodon 87 H3 Luhans'ka Oblast', E Ukraine
Krasnogor see Kallaste
Krasnogvardeyskoye see Krasnohvardiys'ke
Krasnohvardiys'ke 87 F4 Rus. Krasnogvardeyskoye. Respublika Krym, S Ukraine
Krasnokamensk 93 F4 Chitinskaya Oblast', S Russian Federation
Krasnokamsk 89 D5 Permskaya Oblast', W Russian Federation
Krasnoperekops'k 87 F4 Rus. Krasnoperekopsk. Respublika Krym, S Ukraine
Krasnoperekopsk see Krasnoperekops'k
Krasnostav see Krasnystaw
Krasnovodsk see Türkmenbaşy
Krasnovodskiy Zaliv see Türkmenbasy Aylagy
Krasnowodsk Aylagy see Türkmenbasy Aylagy
Krasnoyarsk 92 D4 Krasnoyarskiy Kray, S Russian Federation
Krasnoye see Krasnaye
Krasnystaw 76 E4 Rus. Krasnostav. Lubelskie, SE Poland
Krasnyy Kut 89 C6 Saratovskaya Oblast', W Russian Federation
Krasnyy Luch 87 H3 prev. Krindachevka. Luhans'ka Oblast', E Ukraine
Kratie see Krâchéh
Krâvanh, Chuŏr Phnum 115 C6 Eng. Cardamom Mountains, Fr. Chaîne des Cardamomes. mountain range W Cambodia
Krefeld 72 A4 Nordrhein-Westfalen, W Germany
Kreisstadt see Krosno Odrzańskie
Kremenchug see Kremenchuk
Kremenchugskoye Vodokhranilishche/Kremenchuk Reservoir see Kremenchuts'ke Vodoskhovyshche
Kremenchuk 87 F2 Rus. Kremenchug. Poltavs'ka Oblast', NE Ukraine
Kremenchuk Reservoir 87 F2 Eng. Kremenchuk Reservoir, Rus. Kremenchugskoye Vodokhranilishche. reservoir C Ukraine
Kremenets' 86 C2 Pol. Krzemieniec, Rus. Kremenets. Ternopil's'ka Oblast', W Ukraine
Kremennaya see Kreminna
Kreminna 87 G2 Rus. Kremennaya. Luhans'ka Oblast', E Ukraine
Kresena see Kresna
Kresna 82 C3 var. Kresena. Blagoevgrad, SW Bulgaria
Kretikon Delagos see Kritikó Pélagos
Kretinga 84 B3 Ger. Krottingen. Klaipėda, NW Lithuania
Kreutz see Cristuru Secuiesc
Kreuz see Križevci, Croatia
Kreuz see Risti, Estonia
Kreuzburg/Kreuzburg in Oberschlesien see Kluczbork
Krichëv see Krychaw
Krievija see Russian Federation
Krindachevka see Krasnyy Luch
Krishna 110 C1 prev. Kistna. river C India
Krishnagiri 110 C2 Tamil Nādu, SE India
Kristiania see Oslo
Kristiansand 63 A6 var. Christiansand. Vest-Agder, S Norway
Kristianstad 63 B7 Skåne, S Sweden
Kristiansund 62 A4 var. Christiansund. Møre og Romsdal, S Norway
Krivoy Rog see Kryvyy Rih
Križevci 78 B2 Ger. Kreuz, Hung. Kőrös. Varaždin, NE Croatia
Krk 78 A3 It. Veglia; anc. Curieta. island NW Croatia
Kroatien see Croatia
Krolevets' 87 F1 Rus. Krolevets. Sums'ka Oblast', NE Ukraine
Krolevets see Krolevets'
Królewska Huta see Chorzów
Kronach 73 C5 Bayern, E Germany
Kronstadt see Braşov
Kroonstad 56 D4 Free State, C South Africa
Kropotkin 89 A7 Krasnodarskiy Kray, SW Russian Federation
Krosno 77 D5 Ger. Krossen. Podkarpackie, SE Poland
Krosno Odrzańskie 76 B3 Ger. Crossen, Kreisstadt. Lubuskie, W Poland
Krossen see Krosno
Krottingen see Kretinga
Krško 73 E8 Ger. Gurkfeld; prev. Videm-Krško. E Slovenia
Krugloye see Kruhlaye
Kruhlaye 85 D6 Rus. Krugloye. Mahilyowskaya Voblasts', E Belarus
Kruja see Krujë
Krujë 79 C6 var. Kruja, It. Croia. Durrës, C Albania
Krummau see Český Krumlov
Krung Thep 115 C5 var. Krung Thep Mahanakhon, Eng. Bangkok. country capital Bangkok, C Thailand
Krung Thep, Ao 115 C5 var. Bight of Bangkok. bay S Thailand
Krung Thep Mahanakhon see Krung Thep
Krupki 85 D6 Minskaya Voblasts', C Belarus
Krušné Hory see Erzgebirge
Krychaw 85 E7 Rus. Krichëv. Mahilyowskaya Voblasts', E Belarus
Kryms'ki Hory 87 F5 mountain range S Ukraine
Kryms'kyy Pivostriv 87 F5 peninsula S Ukraine
Krynica 77 D5 Ger. Tannenhof. Małopolskie, S Poland
Kryve Ozero 87 E3 Odes'ka Oblast', SW Ukraine
Kryvyy Rih 87 F3 Rus. Krivoy Rog. Dnipropetrovs'ka Oblast', SE Ukraine
Krzemieniec see Kremenets'
Ksar al Kabir see Ksar-el-Kebir
Ksar al Soule see Er-Rachidia
Ksar-el-Kebir 48 C2 var. Alcázar, Ksar al Kabir, Ksar-el-Kébir, Ar. Al-Kasr al-Kebir, Al-Qsar al-Kbir, Sp. Alcazarquivir. NW Morocco
Ksar-el-Kébir see Ksar-el-Kebir
Kuala Dungun see Dungun
Kuala Lumpur 116 B3 country capital Kuala Lumpur, Peninsular Malaysia
Kuala Terengganu 116 B3 var. Kuala Trengganu. Terengganu, Peninsular Malaysia
Kualatungkal 116 B4 Sumatera, W Indonesia
Kuang-chou see Guangzhou
Kuang-hsi see Guangxi Zhuangzu Zizhiqu
Kuang-tung see Guangdong
Kuang-yuan see Guangyuan
Kuantan 116 B3 Pahang, Peninsular Malaysia
Kuba see Quba
Kuban' 87 G5 var. Hypanis. river SW Russian Federation
Kubango see Cubango/Okavango
Kuching 116 C3 prev. Sarawak. Sarawak, East Malaysia
Kūchnay Darweyshān 100 D5 Helmand, S Afghanistan
Kuçova see Kuçovë
Kuçovë 79 C6 var. Kuçova; prev. Qyteti Stalin. Berat, C Albania
Kudara see Ghŭdara
Kudus 116 C5 prev. Koedoes. Jawa, C Indonesia
Kuei-lin see Guilin
Kuei-Yang/Kuei-yang see Guiyang
K'u-erh-lo see Korla
Kueyang see Guiyang
Kugaaruk 15 G3 prev. Pelly Bay. Nunavut, N Canada
Kugluktuk 31 E3 var. Qurlurtuuq; prev. Coppermine. Nunavut, NW Canada
Kuhmo 62 E4 Oulu, E Finland
Kuhnau see Konin
Kühnö see Kihnu
Kuibyshev see Kuybyshevskoye Vodokhranilishche
Kuito 56 B2 Port. Silva Porto. Bié, C Angola
Kuji 108 D3 var. Kuzi. Iwate, Honshū, C Japan
Kukës 79 D5 var. Kukësi. Kukës, NE Albania
Kukësi see Kukës
Kukong see Shaoguan
Kukukhoto see Hohhot
Kula Kangri 113 G3 var. Kulhakangri. mountain Bhutan/China
Kuldīga 84 B3 Ger. Goldingen. Kuldīga, W Latvia
Kuldja see Yining
Kulhakangri see Kula Kangri
Kullorsuaq 60 D2 var. Kuvdlorssuak. Kitaa, C Greenland
Kulm see Chełmno
Kulmsee see Chełmża
Kŭlob 101 F3 Rus. Kulyab. SW Tajikistan
Kulpa see Kolpa
Kulu 94 C3 Konya, W Turkey
Kulunda Steppe 92 C4 Kaz. Qulyndy Zhazyghy, Rus. Kulundinskaya Ravnina. grassland Kazakhstan/Russian Federation
Kulundinskaya Ravnina see Kulunda Steppe
Kulyab see Kŭlob
Kum see Qom
Kuma 89 B7 river SW Russian Federation
Kumamoto 109 A7 Kumamoto, Kyūshū, SW Japan
Kumanova see Kumanovo
Kumanovo 79 E5 Turk. Kumanova. N Macedonia
Kumasi 53 E5 prev. Coomassie. C Ghana
Kumayri see Gyumri
Kumba 55 A5 Sud-Ouest, W Cameroon
Kumertau 89 D6 Respublika Bashkortostan, W Russian Federation
Kumillā see Comilla
Kumo 53 G4 Gombe, E Nigeria
Kumon Range 114 B2 mountain range N Myanmar (Burma)
Kumul see Hami
Kunashiri see Kunashir, Ostrov
Kunashir, Ostrov 108 E1 var. Kunashiri. island Kuril'skiye Ostrova, SE Russian Federation
Kunda 84 E2 Lääne-Virumaa, NE Estonia
Kunduz see Kondoz
Kunene 47 C6 var. Kunene. river Angola/Namibia
Kunene see Cunene
Kungsbacka 63 B7 Halland, S Sweden
Kungur 89 D5 Permskaya Oblast', NW Russian Federation
Kunlun Mountains see Kunlun Shan
Kunlun Shan 104 B4 Eng. Kunlun Mountains. mountain range NW China
Kunming 106 B6 var. K'un-ming; prev. Yunnan. province capital Yunnan, SW China
K'un-ming see Kunming
Kununurra 124 D3 Western Australia
Kunya-Urgench see Köneürgench
Kuopio 63 E5 Itä-Suomi, C Finland
Kupa see Kolpa
Kupang 117 E5 prev. Koepang. Timor, C Indonesia
Kup"yans'k 87 G2 Rus. Kupyansk. Kharkivs'ka Oblast', E Ukraine
Kupyansk see Kup"yans'k
Kür see Kura
Kura 95 H3 Az. Kür, Geor. Mtkvari, Turk. Kura Nehri. river SW Asia
Kura Nehri see Kura
Kurashiki 109 B6 var. Kurasiki. Okayama, Honshū, SW Japan
Kurasiki see Kurashiki
Kurdistan 95 F4 cultural region SW Asia
Kŭrdzhali 82 D3 var. Kirdzhali. Kŭrdzhali, S Bulgaria
Kure 109 B7 Hiroshima, Honshū, SW Japan
Küre Dağları 94 C2 mountain range N Turkey
Kuressaare 84 C2 Ger. Arensburg; prev. Kingissepp. Saaremaa, W Estonia
Kureyka 90 D2 river N Russian Federation
Kurgan-Tyube see Qŭrghonteppa
Kuria Muria Islands see Ḩalāniyāt, Juzur al
Kurile Islands 93 H4 Eng. Kurile Islands. island group SE Russian Federation
Kurile Islands see Kuril'skiye Ostrova
Kurile-Kamchatka Depression see Kurile Trench
Kurile Trench 91 F3 var. Kurile-Kamchatka Depression. trench NW Pacific Ocean
Kuril'sk 108 E1 Jap. Shana. Kuril'skiye Ostrova, Sakhalinskaya Oblats', SE Russian Federation
Ku-ring-gai 126 E1 New South Wales, E Australia
Kurisches Haff see Courland Lagoon
Kurkund see Kilingi-Nõmme
Kurnool 110 C1 var. Karnul. Andhra Pradesh, S India
Kursk 89 A6 Kurskaya Oblast', W Russian Federation
Kurskiy Zaliv see Courland Lagoon
Kuršumlija 79 D5 Serbia, S Serbia
Kurtbunar see Tervel
Kurtitsch/Kürtös see Curtici
Kuruktag 104 C3 mountain range NW China
Kurume 109 A7 Fukuoka, Kyūshū, SW Japan
Kurupukari 37 F3 C Guyana
Kusaie see Kosrae
Kushiro 108 D2 var. Kusiro. Hokkaidō, NE Japan
Kushka see Serhetabat
Kusiro see Kushiro
Kuskokwim Mountains 14 C3 mountain range Alaska, USA
Kustanay see Kostanay
Küstence/Küstendje see Constanţa
Kütahya 94 B3 prev. Kutaia. Kütahya, W Turkey
Kutai see Mahakam, Sungai
K'ut'aisi 95 F2 W Georgia
Kūt al 'Amārah see Al Kūt
Kut al Imara see Al Kūt
Kutaradja/Kutaraja see Bandaaceh
Kutch, Gulf of see Kachchh, Gulf of
Kutch, Rann of see Kachchh, Rann of
Kutina 78 B3 Sisak-Moslavina, NE Croatia
Kutno 76 C3 Łódzkie, C Poland
Kuujjuaq 17 E2 prev. Fort-Chimo. Québec, E Canada
Kuusamo 62 E3 Oulu, E Finland
Kuvango see Cubango
Kuvdlorssuak see Kullorsuaq
Kuwait 98 C4 off. State of Kuwait, var. Dawlat al Kuwait, Koweit, Kuweit. country SW Asia
Kuwait see Al Kuwayt
Kuwait City see Al Kuwayt
Kuwait, Dawlat al see Kuwait
Kuwait, State of see Kuwait
Kuwajleen see Kwajalein Atoll
Kuwayt 98 C3 Maysān, E Iraq
Kuweit see Kuwait
Kuybyshev see Samara
Kuybyshev Reservoir 89 C5 var. Kuibyshev, Eng. Kuybyshev Reservoir. reservoir W Russian Federation
Kuybyshev Reservoir see Kuybyshevskoye Vodokhranilishche
Kuytun 104 B2 Xinjiang Uygur Zizhiqu, NW China
Kuzi see Kuji

Kuznetsk – Lichtenvoorde

Kuznetsk 89 B6 Penzenskaya Oblast', W Russian Federation
Kuźnica 76 E2 Białystok, NE Poland Europe
Kvaløya 62 C2 island N Norway
Kvarnbergsvattnet 62 B4 var. Frostviken. lake N Sweden
Kvarner 78 A3 var. Carnaro, It. Quarnero. gulf W Croatia
Kvitøya 61 G1 island NE Svalbard
Kwajalein Atoll 122 C1 var. Kuwajleen. atoll Ralik Chain, C Marshall Islands
Kwando see Cuando
Kwangchow see Guangzhou
Kwangchu see Kwangju
Kwangju 107 E4 off. Kwangju-gwangyŏksi, var. Guangju, Kwangchu, Jap. Kōshū. SW South Korea
Kwangju-gwangyŏksi see Kwangju
Kwango 55 C7 Port. Cuango. river Angola/Dem. Rep. Congo
Kwango see Cuango
Kwangsi/Kwangsi Chuang Autonomous Region see Guangxi Zhuangzu Zizhiqu
Kwangtung see Guangdong
Kwangyuan see Guangyuan
Kwanza see Cuanza
Kweichu see Guiyang
Kweilin see Guilin
Kweisui see Hohhot
Kweiyang see Guiyang
Kwekwe 56 D3 prev. Que Que. Midlands, C Zimbabwe
Kwesui see Hohhot
Kwidzyń 76 C2 Ger. Marienwerder. Pomorskie, N Poland
Kwigillingok 14 C3 Alaska, USA
Kwilu 55 C6 river W Dem. Rep. Congo
Kwito see Cuito
Kyabé 54 C4 Moyen-Chari, S Chad
Kyaikkami 115 B5 prev. Amherst. Mon State, S Myanmar (Burma)
Kyaiklat 114 B4 Ayeyarwady, SW Myanmar (Burma)
Kyaikto 114 B4 Mon State, S Myanmar (Burma)
Kyakhta 93 E5 Respublika Buryatiya, S Russian Federation
Kyaukse 114 B3 Mandalay, C Myanmar (Burma)
Kyjov 77 C5 Ger. Gaya. Jihomoravský Kraj, SE Czech Republic
Kými 83 C5 prev. Kími. Évvoia, C Greece
Kyŏngsŏng see Sŏul
Kyōto 109 C6 Kyōto, Honshū, SW Japan
Kyparissía 83 B6 var. Kiparissía. Pelopónnisos, S Greece
Kypros see Cyprus
Kyrá Panagía 83 C5 island Vóreies Sporádes, Greece, Aegean Sea
Kyrenia see Girne
Kyrgyz Republic see Kyrgyzstan
Kyrgyzstan 101 F2 off. Kyrgyz Republic, var. Kirghizia; prev. Kirgizskaya SSR, Kirghiz SSR, Republic of Kyrgyzstan. country C Asia
Kyrgyzstan, Republic of see Kyrgyzstan
Kythira 83 C7 var. Kíthira, It. Cerigo, Lat. Cythera. island S Greece
Kýthnos 83 C6 Kńythnos, Kykládes, Greece, Aegean Sea
Kythnos 83 C6 var. Kíthnos, Thermiá, It. Termia; anc. Cythnos. island Kykládes, Greece, Aegean Sea
Kythréa see Değirmenlik
Kyushu 109 B7 var. Kyûsyû. island SW Japan
Kyushu-Palau Ridge 103 F3 var. Kyusyu-Palau Ridge. undersea ridge W Pacific Ocean
Kyustendil 82 B2 anc. Pautalia. Kyustendil, W Bulgaria
Kyûsyû see Kyūshū
Kyusyu-Palau Ridge see Kyushu-Palau Ridge
Kyyiv 87 E2 Eng. Kiev, Rus. Kiyev. country capital Kyyivs'ka Oblast', N Ukraine
Kyzyl 92 D4 Respublika Tyva, C Russian Federation
Kyzyl Kum 100 D2 var. Kizil Kum, Qizil Qum, Uzb. Qizilqum. desert Kazakhstan/Uzbekistan
Kyzylorda 92 B5 var. Kzyl-Orda, Qizil Orda, Qyzylorda; prev. Perovsk. Kyzylorda, S Kazakhstan
Kyzylrabot see Qizilrabot
Kyzyl-Suu 101 G2 prev. Pokrovka. Issyk-Kul'skaya Oblast', NE Kyrgyzstan
Kzyl-Orda see Kyzylorda

L

Laaland see Lolland
La Algaba 70 C4 Andalucía, S Spain
Laarne 65 B5 Oost-Vlaanderen, NW Belgium
La Asunción 37 E1 Nueva Esparta, NE Venezuela
Laatokka see Ladozhskoye, Ozero
Laâyoune 48 B3 var. Aaiún. country capital NW Western Sahara
La Banda Oriental see Uruguay
La Baule-Escoublac 68 A4 Loire-Atlantique, NW France
Labé 52 C4 NW Guinea
Labe see Elbe
Laborca see Laborec
Laborec 77 E5 Hung. Laborca. river E Slovakia
Labrador 17 F2 cultural region Newfoundland and Labrador, SW Canada
Labrador Basin 12 E3 var. Labrador Sea Basin. undersea basin Labrador Sea
Labrador Sea 60 A4 sea NW Atlantic Ocean
Labrador Sea Basin see Labrador Basin
Labudalin see Ergun
Labutta 115 A5 Ayeyarwady, SW Myanmar (Burma)
Laç 79 C6 var. Laci. Lezhë, C Albania
La Calera 42 B4 Valparaíso, C Chile
La Carolina 70 D4 Andalucía, S Spain
Laccadive Islands 110 A3 Eng. Laccadive Islands. island group India, N Indian Ocean
Laccadive Islands/Laccadive Minicoy and Amindivi Islands, the see Lakshadweep
La Ceiba 30 D2 Atlántida, N Honduras
Lachanás 82 B3 Kentrikí Makedonía, N Greece
La Chaux-de-Fonds 73 A7 Neuchâtel, W Switzerland
Lachlan River 127 C6 river New South Wales, SE Australia
Laci see Laç
la Ciotat 69 D6 anc. Citharista. Bouches-du-Rhône, SE France
Lacobriga see Lagos
La Concepción 31 E5 var. Concepción. Chiriquí, W Panama
La Concepción 36 C1 Zulia, NW Venezuela
La Condamine 69 C8 W Monaco
Laconia 19 G2 New Hampshire, NE USA
La Crosse 18 A2 Wisconsin, N USA
La Cruz 30 D4 Guanacaste, NW Costa Rica
Lake Ladoga 88 B3 Eng. Lake Ladoga, Fin. Laatokka. lake NW Russian Federation
Ladoga, Lake see Ladozhskoye, Ozero
Ladysmith 18 B2 Wisconsin, N USA
Lae 122 B3 Morobe, W Papua New Guinea
Læsø 63 B7 island N Denmark
La Esperanza 30 C2 Intibucá, SW Honduras
Lafayette 18 C4 Indiana, N USA
Lafayette 20 B3 Louisiana, S USA
La Fé 32 A2 Pinar del Río, W Cuba
Lafia 53 G4 Nassarawa, C Nigeria
la Flèche 68 B4 Sarthe, NW France
Lagdo, Lac de 54 B4 lake N Cameroon
Laghouat 48 D2 N Algeria
Lagos 53 F5 Lagos, SW Nigeria
Lagos 70 B5 anc. Lacobriga. Faro, S Portugal
Lagos de Moreno 29 E4 Jalisco, SW Mexico
Lagouira 48 A4 SW Western Sahara
La Grande 24 C3 Oregon, NW USA
La Guaira 44 B4 Distrito Federal, N Venezuela
Lagunas 42 B1 Tarapacá, N Chile
Lagunillas 39 G4 Santa Cruz, SE Bolivia
La Habana 32 B2 var. Havana. country capital Ciudad de La Habana, W Cuba
Lahat 116 B4 Sumatera, W Indonesia
La Haye see 's-Gravenhage
Laholm 63 B7 Halland, S Sweden
Lahore 112 D2 Punjab, NE Pakistan
Lahr 73 A6 Baden-Württemberg, S Germany
Lahti 63 D5 Swe. Lahtis. Etelä-Suomi, S Finland
Lahtis see Lahti
Laï 54 B4 prev. Behagle, De Behagle. Tandjilé, S Chad
Laibach see Ljubljana
Lai Châu 114 D3 Lai Châu, N Vietnam
Laila see Laylā
La Junta 22 D5 Colorado, C USA
Lake Charles 20 A3 Louisiana, S USA
Lake City 21 E3 Florida, SE USA
Lake District 67 C5 physical region NW England, United Kingdom
Lake Havasu City 26 A2 Arizona, SW USA
Lake Jackson 27 H4 Texas, SW USA
Lakeland 21 E4 Florida, SE USA
Lakeside 25 C8 California, W USA
Lake State see Michigan
Lakewood 22 D4 Colorado, C USA
Lakhnau see Lucknow
Lakonikós Kólpos 83 B7 gulf S Greece
Lakselv 62 D2 Lapp. Leavdnja. Finnmark, N Norway
la Laon see Laon
Lalibela 50 C4 Āmara, Ethiopia
La Libertad 30 B1 Petén, N Guatemala
La Ligua 42 B4 Valparaíso, C Chile
Lalín 70 C1 Galicia, NW Spain
Lalitpur 113 F3 Central, C Nepal
La Louvière 65 B6 Hainaut, S Belgium
la Maddalena 74 A4 Sardegna, Italy, C Mediterranean Sea
la Manche see English Channel
Lamar 22 D5 Colorado, C USA
La Marmora, Punta 75 A5 mountain Sardegna, Italy, C Mediterranean Sea
La Massana 69 A8 La Massana, W Andorra Europe
Lambaréné 55 A6 Moyen-Ogooué, W Gabon
Lamego 70 C2 Viseu, N Portugal
Lamesa 27 E3 Texas, SW USA
Lamezia Terme 75 D6 Calabria, SE Italy
Lamía 83 B5 Stereá Ellás, C Greece
Lamoni 23 F4 Iowa, C USA
Lampang 114 C4 var. Muang Lampang. Lampang, NW Thailand
Lámpeia 83 B6 Dytikí Ellás, S Greece
Lanbi Kyun 115 B6 prev. Sullivan Island. island Mergui Archipelago, S Myanmar (Burma)
Lancang Jiang see Mekong
Lancaster 67 D5 NW England, United Kingdom
Lancaster 25 C7 California, W USA
Lancaster 19 F4 Pennsylvania, NE USA
Lancaster Sound 15 F2 sound Nunavut, N Canada
Lan-chou/Lan-chow/Lanchow see Lanzhou
Landao see Lantau Island
Landen 65 C6 Vlaams Brabant, C Belgium
Lander 22 C3 Wyoming, C USA
Landerneau 68 A3 Finistère, NW France
Landes 69 B5 cultural region SW France
Land of Enchantment see New Mexico
The Land of Opportunity see Arkansas
Land of Steady Habits see Connecticut
Land of the Midnight Sun see Alaska
Landsberg see Gorzów Wielkopolski, Lubuskie, Poland
Landsberg an der Warthe see Gorzów Wielkopolski
Land's End 67 B8 headland SW England, United Kingdom
Landshut 73 C6 Bayern, SE Germany
Langar 101 E2 Rus. Lyangar. Navoiy Viloyati, C Uzbekistan
Langfang 106 D4 Hebei, E China
Langkawi, Pulau 115 B7 island Peninsular Malaysia
Langres 68 D4 Haute-Marne, N France
Langsa 116 A3 Sumatera, W Indonesia
Lang Shan 105 E3 mountain range N China
Lang Sơn 114 D3 var. Langson. Lang Sơn, N Vietnam
Langson see Lang Sơn
Lang Suan 115 B6 Chumphon, SW Thailand
Languedoc 69 C6 cultural region S France
Länkäran 95 H3 Rus. Lenkoran'. S Azerbaijan
Lansing 18 C3 state capital Michigan, N USA
Lanta, Ko 115 B7 island S Thailand
Lantau Island 106 A2 Cant. Tai Yue Shan, Chin. Landao. island Hong Kong, S China
Lan-ts'ang Chiang see Mekong
Lantung, Gulf of see Liaodong Wan
Lanzarote 48 B3 island Islas Canarias, Spain, NE Atlantic Ocean
Lanzhou 106 B4 var. Lan-chou, Lanchow, Lan-chow; prev. Kaolan. province capital Gansu, C China
Lao Cai 114 D3 Lao Cai, N Vietnam
Laodicea/Laodicea ad Mare see Al Lādhiqīyah
Laoet see Laut, Pulau
Laojunmiao 106 A3 prev. Yumen. Gansu, N China
Laon 68 D3 var. la Laon; anc. Laudunum. Aisne, N France
Lao People's Democratic Republic see Laos
La Orchila, Isla 36 D1 island N Venezuela
La Oroya 38 C3 Junín, C Peru
Laos 114 D4 off. Lao People's Democratic Republic. country SE Asia
La Palma 31 G5 Darién, SE Panama
La Palma 48 A3 island Islas Canarias, Spain, NE Atlantic Ocean
La Paz 39 F4 var. La Paz de Ayacucho. country capital La Paz, W Bolivia
La Paz 28 B3 Baja California Sur, NW Mexico
La Paz, Bahía de 28 B3 bay W Mexico
La Paz de Ayacucho see La Paz
La Perouse Strait 108 D1 Jap. Sōya-kaikyō, Rus. Proliv Laperuza. strait Japan/Russian Federation
Laperuza, Proliv see La Perouse Strait
Lápithos see Lapta
Lapland 62 D3 Fin. Lappi, Swe. Lappland. cultural region N Europe
La Plata 42 D4 Buenos Aires, E Argentina
La Plata see Sucre
Lappeenranta 63 E5 Swe. Villmanstrand. Etelä-Suomi, SE Finland
Lappi/Lappland see Lapland
Lappo see Lapua
Lapta 80 C5 Gk. Lápithos. NW Cyprus
Laptev Sea 93 E2 Eng. Laptev Sea. sea Arctic Ocean
Laptev Sea see Laptevykh, More
Lapua 63 D5 Swe. Lappo. Länsi-Suomi, W Finland
Lapurdum see Bayonne
Łapy 76 E3 Podlaskie, NE Poland
La Quiaca 42 C2 Jujuy, N Argentina
L'Aquila 74 C4 var. Aquila, Aquila degli Abruzzi. Abruzzo, C Italy
Laracha 70 B1 Galicia, NW Spain
Laramie 22 C4 Wyoming, C USA
Laramie Mountains 22 C3 mountain range Wyoming, C USA
Laredo 71 E1 Cantabria, N Spain
Laredo 27 F5 Texas, SW USA
La Réunion see Réunion
Largeau see Faya
Largo 21 E4 Florida, SE USA
Largo, Cayo 32 B2 island W Cuba
Lario see Como, Lago di
La Rioja 42 C3 La Rioja, NW Argentina
La Rioja 71 E2 autonomous community N Spain
Lárisa 82 B4 var. Larissa. Thessalía, C Greece
Larissa see Lárisa
Lārkāna 112 B3 var. Larkhana. Sind, SE Pakistan
Larkhana see Lārkāna
Larnaca see Lárnaka
Lárnaka 80 C5 var. Larnaca, Larnax. SE Cyprus
Larnax see Lárnaka
la Rochelle 68 B4 anc. Rupella. Charente-Maritime, W France
la Roche-sur-Yon 68 B4 prev. Bourbon Vendée, Napoléon-Vendée. Vendée, NW France
La Roda 71 E3 Castilla-La Mancha, C Spain
La Romana 33 E3 E Dominican Republic
Larvotto 69 C8 N Monaco Europe
La-sa see Lhasa
Las Cabezas de San Juan 70 C5 Andalucía, S Spain
Las Cruces 26 D3 New Mexico, SW USA
La See d'Urgel 71 G1 var. La Seu d'Urgell, Seo de Urgel. Cataluña, NE Spain
La Serena 42 B3 Coquimbo, C Chile
La Seu d'Urgell see La See d'Urgel
la Seyne-sur-Mer 69 D6 Var, SE France
Lashio 114 B3 Shan State, E Myanmar (Burma)
Lashkar Gāh 100 D5 var. Lash-Kar-Gar'. Helmand, S Afghanistan
Lash-Kar-Gar' see Lashkar Gāh
La Sila 75 D6 mountain range SW Italy
La Sirena 30 D3 Región Autónoma Atlántico Sur, E Nicaragua
Łask 76 C4 Łódzkie, C Poland
Las Lomitas 42 D2 Formosa, N Argentina
La Solana 71 E4 Castilla-La Mancha, C Spain
Las Palmas 48 A3 var. Las Palmas de Gran Canaria. Gran Canaria, Islas Canarias, Spain, NE Atlantic Ocean
Las Palmas de Gran Canaria see Las Palmas
La Spezia 74 B3 Liguria, NW Italy
Lassa see Lhasa
Las Tablas 31 F5 Los Santos, S Panama
Last Frontier, The see Alaska
Las Tunas 32 C2 var. Victoria de las Tunas. Las Tunas, E Cuba
La Suisse see Switzerland
Las Vegas 25 D7 Nevada, W USA
Latacunga 38 B1 Cotopaxi, C Ecuador
la Teste 69 B5 Gironde, SW France
Latina 75 C5 prev. Littoria. Lazio, C Italy
La Tortuga, Isla 37 E1 var. Isla Tortuga. island N Venezuela
La Tuque 17 E4 Québec, SE Canada
Latvia 84 C3 off. Republic of Latvia, Ger. Lettland, Latv. Latvija, Latvijas Republika; prev. Latvian SSR, Rus. Latviyskaya SSR. country NE Europe
Latvian SSR/Latvija/Latvijas Republika/ Latviyskaya SSR see Latvia
Latvia, Republic of see Latvia
Laudunum see Laon
Laudus see St-Lô
Lauenburg/Lauenburg in Pommern see Lębork
Lau Group 123 E4 island group E Fiji
Lauis see Lugano
Launceston 127 C8 Tasmania, SE Australia
La Unión 30 C2 Olancho, C Honduras
La Unión 71 F4 Murcia, SE Spain
Laurel 20 C3 Mississippi, S USA
Laurel 22 C2 Montana, NW USA
Laurentian Highlands see Laurentian Mountains
Laurentian Mountains 17 E3 var. Laurentian Highlands, Fr. Les Laurentides. plateau Newfoundland and Labrador/Québec, Canada
Laurentides, Les see Laurentian Mountains
Lauria 75 D6 Basilicata, S Italy
Laurinburg 21 F1 North Carolina, SE USA
Lauru see Choiseul
Lausanne 73 A7 It. Losanna. Vaud, SW Switzerland
Laut, Pulau 116 D4 prev. Laoet. island Borneo, C Indonesia
Laval 16 D4 Québec, SE Canada
Laval 68 B3 Mayenne, NW France
La Vall D'Uixó 71 F3 var. Vall D'Uxó. País Valenciano, E Spain
La Vega 33 E3 var. Concepción de la Vega. C Dominican Republic
La Vila Joíosa see Villajoyosa
Lávrio 83 C6 prev. Lávrion. Attikí, C Greece
Lávrion see Lávrio
Lawrence 19 G3 Massachusetts, NE USA
Lawrenceburg 20 C1 Tennessee, S USA
Lawton 27 F2 Oklahoma, C USA
Laylā 99 C5 var. Laila. Ar Riyāḍ, C Saudi Arabia
Lazarev Sea 132 B1 sea Antarctica
Lázaro Cárdenas 29 E5 Michoacán de Ocampo, SW Mexico
Leal see Lihula
Leamhcán see Lucan
Leamington 16 C5 Ontario, S Canada
Leavdnja see Lakselv
Lebak 117 E3 Mindanao, S Philippines
Lebanese Republic see Lebanon
Lebanon 23 G5 Missouri, C USA
Lebanon 19 G2 New Hampshire, NE USA
Lebanon 24 B3 Oregon, NW USA
Lebanon 96 A4 off. Lebanese Republic, Ar. Al Lubnān, Fr. Liban. country SW Asia
Lebanon, Mount see Liban, Jebel
Lebap 100 D2 Lebapskiy Velayat, NE Turkmenistan
Lebedin see Lebedyn
Lebedyn 87 F2 Rus. Lebedin. Sums'ka Oblast', NE Ukraine
Lębork 76 C2 var. Lębórk, Ger. Lauenburg, Lauenburg in Pommern. Pomorskie, N Poland
Lebrija 70 C5 Andalucía, S Spain
Lebu 43 A5 Bío Bío, C Chile
le Cannet 69 D6 Alpes-Maritimes, SE France
Le Cap see Cap-Haïtien
Lecce 75 E6 Puglia, SE Italy
Lechainá 83 B6 var. Lehena, Lekhainá. Dytikí Ellás, S Greece
Ledo Salinarius see Lons-le-Saunier
Leduc 15 E5 Alberta, SW Canada
Leech Lake 23 F2 lake Minnesota, N USA
Leeds 67 D5 N England, United Kingdom
Leek 64 E2 Groningen, NE Netherlands
Leer 72 A3 Niedersachsen, NW Germany
Leeuwarden 64 D1 Fris. Ljouwert. Friesland, N Netherlands
Leeuwin, Cape 120 A5 headland Western Australia
Leeward Islands 33 G3 island group E West Indies
Leeward Islands see Sotavento, Ilhas de
Lefkáda 83 A5 prev. Levkás. Lefkáda, Iónia Nisiá, Greece, C Mediterranean Sea
Lefkáda 83 A5 It. Santa Maura, prev. Levkás; anc. Leucas. island Iónia Nisiá, Greece, C Mediterranean Sea
Lefká Óri 83 C7 mountain range Kríti, Greece, E Mediterranean Sea
Lefkímmi 83 A5 var. Levkímmi. Kérkyra, Iónia Nisiá, Greece, C Mediterranean Sea
Lefkosía/Lefkoşa see Nicosia
Legaceaster see Chester
Legaspi see Legazpi City
Leghorn see Livorno
Legnica 76 B4 Ger. Liegnitz. Dolnośląskie, SW Poland
le Havre 68 B3 Eng. Havre; prev. le Havre-de-Grâce. Seine-Maritime, N France
le Havre-de-Grâce see le Havre
Lehena see Lechainá
Leicester 67 D6 Lat. Batae Coritanorum. C England, United Kingdom
Leiden 64 B3 prev. Leyden; anc. Lugdunum Batavorum. Zuid-Holland, W Netherlands
Leie 68 D2 Fr. Lys. river Belgium/France
Leinster 67 B6 Ir. Cúige Laighean. cultural region E Ireland
Leipsic see Leipzig
Leipsoí 83 E6 island Dodekánisa, Greece, Aegean Sea
Leipzig 72 C4 Pol. Lipsk, hist. Leipsic; anc. Lipsia. Sachsen, E Germany
Leiria 70 B3 anc. Collipo. Leiria, C Portugal
Leirvik 63 A6 Hordaland, S Norway
Lek 64 C4 river SW Netherlands
Lekhainá see Lechainá
Lekhchevo 82 C2 Montana, NW Bulgaria
Leksand 63 C5 Dalarna, C Sweden
Lel'chitsy see Lyel'chytsy
le Léman see Geneva, Lake
Lelystad 64 D3 Flevoland, C Netherlands
Léman, Lac see Geneva, Lake
le Mans 68 B3 Sarthe, NW France
Lemberg see L'viv
Lemesós 80 C5 var. Limassol. SW Cyprus
Lemhi Range 24 D3 mountain range Idaho, C USA North America
Lemnos see Límnos
Lemovices see Limoges
Lena 93 F3 river NE Russian Federation
Lena Tablemount 119 B7 seamount S Indian Ocean
Len Dao 106 C8 island S Spratly Islands
Lengshuitan see Yongzhou
Leninabad see Khujand
Leninakan see Gyumri
Lenine 87 G5 Rus. Lenino. Respublika Krym, S Ukraine
Leninogor see Ridder
Leningrad see Sankt-Peterburg
Leningradskaya 132 B4 Russian research station Antarctica
Lenino see Lenine, Ukraine
Leninobod see Khujand
Leninpol' 101 F2 Talasskaya Oblast', NW Kyrgyzstan
Lenin-Turkmenski see Türkmenabat
Lenkoran' see Länkäran
Lenti 77 B7 Zala, SW Hungary
Lentia see Linz
Leoben 73 E7 Steiermark, C Austria
León 29 E4 var. León de los Aldamas. Guanajuato, C Mexico
León 30 C3 León, NW Nicaragua
León 70 D1 Castilla-León, NW Spain
León de los Aldamas see León
Leonídio 83 B6 var. Leonídi. Pelopónnisos, S Greece
Leonídi see Leonídio
Léopold II, Lac see Mai-Ndombe, Lac
Léopoldville see Kinshasa
Lepe 70 C4 Andalucía, S Spain
Lepel' see Lyepyel'
le Portel 68 C2 Pas-de-Calais, N France
Le Puglie see Puglia
le Puy 69 C5 prev. le Puy-en-Velay, hist. Anicium, Podium Anicensis. Haute-Loire, C France
le Puy-en-Velay see le Puy
Léré 54 B4 Mayo-Kébbi, SW Chad
Lérida see Lleida
Lerma 70 D2 Castilla-León, N Spain
Leros 83 D6 island Dodekánisa, Greece, Aegean Sea
Lernayin Gharabakh see Nagorno-Karabakh
Lerwick 66 D1 NE Scotland, United Kingdom
Lesbos 94 A3 anc. Lesbos. island E Greece
Lesbos see Lésvos
Les Cayes see Cayes
Les Gonaïves see Gonaïves
Leshan 106 B5 Sichuan, C China
les Herbiers 68 B4 Vendée, NW France
Lesh/Leshi see Lezhë
Lesina see Hvar
Leskovac 79 E5 Serbia, SE Serbia
Lesnoy 92 C3 Sverdlovskaya Oblast', C Russian Federation
Lesotho 56 D4 off. Kingdom of Lesotho; prev. Basutoland. country S Africa
Lesotho, Kingdom of see Lesotho
les Sables-d'Olonne 68 B4 Vendée, NW France
Lesser Antarctica see West Antarctica
Lesser Antilles 33 G4 island group E West Indies
Lesser Caucasus 95 F2 Rus. Malyy Kavkaz. mountain range SW Asia
Lesser Khingan Range see Xiao Hinggan Ling
Lesser Sunda Islands 117 E5 Eng. Lesser Sunda Islands. island group C Indonesia
Lesser Sunda Islands see Nusa Tenggara
Leszno 76 B4 Ger. Lissa. Wielkopolskie, C Poland
Lethbridge 15 E5 Alberta, SW Canada
Lethem 37 F3 S Guyana
Leti, Kepulauan 117 F5 island group E Indonesia
Letpadan 114 B4 Bago, SW Myanmar (Burma)
Letsôk-aw Kyun 115 B6 var. Letsutan Island; prev. Domel Island. island Mergui Archipelago, S Myanmar (Burma)
Letsutan Island see Letsôk-aw Kyun
Lettland see Latvia
Lëtzebuerg see Luxembourg
Leucas see Lefkáda
Leuven 65 C6 Fr. Louvain, Ger. Löwen. Vlaams Brabant, C Belgium
Leuze see Leuze-en-Hainaut
Leuze-en-Hainaut 65 B6 var. Leuze. Hainaut, SW Belgium
Léva see Levice
Levanger 62 B4 Nord-Trøndelag, C Norway
Levelland 27 E2 Texas, SW USA
Leverkusen 72 A4 Nordrhein-Westfalen, W Germany
Levice 77 C6 Ger. Lewentz, Hung. Léva, Lewenz. Nitriansky Kraj, SW Slovakia
Levin 128 D4 Manawatu-Wanganui, North Island, New Zealand
Levkás see Lefkáda
Levkímmi see Lefkímmi
Lewentz/Lewenz see Levice
Lewis, Isle of 66 B2 island NW Scotland, United Kingdom
Lewis Range 22 B1 mountain range Montana, NW USA
Lewiston 24 C2 Idaho, NW USA
Lewiston 19 G2 Maine, NE USA
Lewistown 22 C1 Montana, NW USA
Lexington 18 C5 Kentucky, S USA
Lexington 23 E4 Nebraska, C USA
Leyden see Leiden
Leyte 117 F2 island C Philippines
Leżajsk 77 E5 Podkarpackie, SE Poland
Lezha see Lezhë
Lezhë 79 C6 var. Lezha; prev. Lesh, Leshi. Lezhë, NW Albania
Lhasa 104 C5 var. La-sa, Lassa. Xizang Zizhiqu, W China
Lhaviyani Atoll see Faadhippolhu Atoll
Lhazê 104 C5 var. Quxar. Xizang Zizhiqu, China E Asia
L'Hospitalet de Llobregat 71 G2 var. Hospitalet. Cataluña, NE Spain
Liancourt Rocks 109 A5 island group Japan/South Korea
Lianyungang 106 D4 var. Xinpu. Jiangsu, E China
Liao see Liaoning
Liaodong Wan 105 G3 Eng. Gulf of Lantung, Gulf of Liaotung. gulf NE China
Liao He 103 E1 river NE China
Liaoning 106 D3 var. Liao, Liaoning Sheng, Shengking, hist. Fengtien, Shenking. province NE China
Liaoning Sheng see Liaoning
Liaoyuan 107 E3 var. Dongliao, Shuang-liao, Jap. Chengchiatun. Jilin, NE China
Liard see Fort Liard
Liban see Lebanon
Liban, Jebel 96 B4 Ar. Jabal al Gharbt, Jabal Lubnān, Eng. Mount Lebanon. mountain range C Lebanon
Libau see Liepāja
Libby 22 A1 Montana, NW USA
Liberal 23 E5 Kansas, C USA
Liberalitas Julia see Évora
Liberec 76 B4 Ger. Reichenberg. Liberecký Kraj, N Czech Republic
Liberia 30 D4 Guanacaste, NW Costa Rica
Liberia 52 C5 off. Republic of Liberia. country W Africa
Liberia, Republic of see Liberia
Libian Desert see Libyan Desert
Lībīyah, Aş Şaḩrā' al see Libyan Desert
Libourne 69 B5 Gironde, SW France
Libreville 55 A5 country capital Estuaire, NW Gabon
Libya 49 F3 off. Great Socialist People's Libyan Arab Jamahiriya, Ar. Al Jamāhīrīyah al 'Arabīyah al Lībīyah ash Sha'bīyah al Ishtirākīy; prev. Libyan Arab Republic. country N Africa
Libyan Arab Republic see Libya
Libyan Desert 49 H4 var. Libian Desert, Ar. Aş Şaḩrā' al Lībīyah. desert N Africa
Libyan Plateau 81 F4 var. Aḍ Diffah. plateau Egypt/Libya
Lichtenfels 73 C5 Bayern, SE Germany
Lichtenvoorde 64 E4 Gelderland, E Netherlands

Lichuan – Ma'dabā

Lichuan *106 C5* Hubei, C China
Lida *85 B5* Hrodzyenskaya Voblasts', W Belarus
Lidhorikíon *see* Lidoríki
Lidköping *63 B6* Västra Götaland, S Sweden
Lidokhorikion *see* Lidoríki
Lidoríki *83 B5 prev.* Lidhorikíon, Lidokhorikion. Stereá Ellás, C Greece
Lidzbark Warmiński *76 D2 Ger.* Heilsberg. Olsztyn, N Poland
Liechtenstein *72 D1 off.* Principality of Liechtenstein. *country* C Europe
Liechtenstein, Principality of *see* Liechtenstein
Liège *65 D6 Dut.* Luik, *Ger.* Lüttich. Liège, E Belgium
Liegnitz *see* Legnica
Lienz *73 D7* Tirol, W Austria
Liepāja *84 B3 Ger.* Libau. Liepāja, W Latvia
Lietuva *see* Lithuania
Lievenhof *see* Līvāni
Liezen *73 D7* Steiermark, C Austria
Liffey *67 B6 river* Ireland
Lifou *122 D5 island* Îles Loyauté, E New Caledonia
Liger *see* Loire
Ligure, Appennino *74 A2 Eng.* Ligurian Mountains. *mountain range* NW Italy
Ligure, Mar *see* Ligurian Sea
Ligurian Mountains *see* Ligure, Appennino
Ligurian Sea *74 A3 Fr.* Mer Ligurienne, *It.* Mar Ligure. *sea* N Mediterranean Sea
Ligurienne, Mer *see* Ligurian Sea
Līhu'e *25 A7 var.* Lihue. Kaua'i, Hawaii, USA
Lihue *see* Līhu'e
Lihula *84 D2 Ger.* Leal. Läänemaa, W Estonia
Liivi Laht *see* Riga, Gulf of
Likasi *55 D7 prev.* Jadotville. Shaba, SE Dem. Rep. Congo
Liknes *63 A6* Vest-Agder, S Norway
Lille *68 C2 var.* l'Isle, *Dut.* Rijssel, *Flem.* Ryssel, *prev.* Lisle; *anc.* Insula. Nord, N France
Lillehammer *63 B5* Oppland, S Norway
Lillestrøm *63 B6* Akershus, S Norway
Lilongwe *57 E2 country capital* Central , W Malawi
Lilybaeum *see* Marsala
Lima *38 C4 country capital* Lima, W Peru
Limanowa *77 D5* Małopolskie, S Poland
Limassol *see* Lemesós
Limerick *67 A6 Ir.* Luimneach. Limerick, SW Ireland
Limín Vathéos *see* Sámos
Límnos *81 F3 anc.* Lemnos. *island* E Greece
Limoges *69 C5 anc.* Augustoritum Lemovicensium, Lemovices. Haute-Vienne, C France
Limón *31 E4 var.* Puerto Limón. Limón, E Costa Rica
Limón *30 D2* Colón, NE Honduras
Limonum *see* Poitiers
Limousin *69 C5 cultural region* C France
Limoux *69 C6* Aude, S France
Limpopo *56 D3 var.* Crocodile. *river* S Africa
Linares *42 B4* Maule, C Chile
Linares *29 E3* Nuevo León, NE Mexico
Linares *70 D4* Andalucía, S Spain
Lincoln *67 D5 anc.* Lindum, Lindum Colonia. E England, United Kingdom
Lincoln *19 H2* Maine, NE USA
Lincoln *23 F4 state capital* Nebraska, C USA
Lincoln Sea *12 D2 sea* Arctic Ocean
Linden *37 F3* E Guyana
Líndhos *see* Líndos
Lindi *51 D8* Lindi, SE Tanzania
Líndos *83 E7 var.* Líndhos. Ródos, Dodekánisa, Greece, Aegean Sea
Lindum/Lindum Colonia *see* Lincoln
Line Islands *123 G3 island group* E Kiribati
Lingeh *see* Bandar-e Lengeh
Lingen *72 A3 var.* Lingen an der Ems. Niedersachsen, NW Germany
Lingen an der Ems *see* Lingen
Lingga, Kepulauan *116 B4 island group* W Indonesia
Linköping *63 C6* Östergötland, S Sweden
Linz *73 D6 anc.* Lentia. Oberösterreich, N Austria
Lion, Gulf of *69 C7 Eng.* Gulf of Lion, Gulf of Lions; *anc.* Sinus Gallicus. *gulf* S France
Lion, Gulf of/Lions, Gulf of *see* Lion, Golfe du
Liozno *see* Lyozna
Lipari *75 D6 island* Isole Eolie, S Italy
Lipari Islands/Lipari, Isole *see* Eolie, Isole
Lipetsk *89 B5* Lipetskaya Oblast', W Russian Federation
Lipno *76 C3* Kujawsko-pomorskie, C Poland
Lipova *86 A4 Hung.* Lippa. Arad, W Romania
Lipovets *see* Lypovets'
Lippa *see* Lipova
Lipsia/Lipsk *see* Leipzig
Lira *51 B6* N Uganda
Lisala *55 C5* Equateur, N Dem. Rep. Congo
Lisboa *70 B4 Eng.* Lisbon; *anc.* Felicitas Julia, Olisipo. *country capital* Lisboa, W Portugal
Lisbon *see* Lisboa
Lisichansk *see* Lysychans'k
Lisieux *68 B3 anc.* Noviomagus. Calvados, N France
Liski *89 B6 prev.* Georgiu-Dezh. Voronezhskaya Oblast', W Russian Federation
Lisle/l'Isle *see* Lille
Lismore *127 E5* New South Wales, SE Australia
Lissa *see* Vis, Croatia
Lissa *see* Leszno, Poland
Lisse *64 C3* Zuid-Holland, W Netherlands
Litang *106 A5 var.* Gaocheng. Sichuan, C China
Līṭani, Nahr el *97 B5 var.* Nahr al Litant. *river* C Lebanon
Litant, Nahr al *see* Līṭani, Nahr el
Litauen *see* Lithuania
Lithgow *127 D6* New South Wales, SE Australia
Lithuania *84 B4 off.* Republic of Lithuania, *Ger.* Litauen, *Lith.* Lietuva, *Pol.* Litwa, *Rus.* Litva; *prev.* Lithuanian SSR, *Rus.* Litovskaya SSR. *country* NE Europe
Lithuanian SSR *see* Lithuania
Lithuania, Republic of *see* Lithuania
Litóchoro *82 B4 var.* Litohoro, Litókhoron. Kentrikí Makedonía, N Greece
Litohoro/Litókhoron *see* Litóchoro
Litovskaya SSR *see* Lithuania
Little Alföld *77 C6 Ger.* Kleines Ungarisches Tiefland, *Hung.* Kisalföld, *Slvk.* Podunajská Rovina. *plain* Hungary/Slovakia
Little Andaman *111 F2 island* Andaman Islands, India, NE Indian Ocean
Little Barrier Island *128 D2 island* N New Zealand
Little Bay *71 H5 bay* Alboran Sea, Mediterranean Sea
Little Cayman *32 B3 island* E Cayman Islands
Little Falls *23 F2* Minnesota, N USA
Littlefield *27 E2* Texas, SW USA
Little Inagua *32 D2 var.* Inagua Islands. *island* S Bahamas
Little Minch, The *66 B3 strait* NW Scotland, United Kingdom
Little Missouri River *22 D2 river* NW USA
Little Nicobar *111 G3 island* Nicobar Islands, India, NE Indian Ocean
Little Rhody *see* Rhode Island
Little Rock *20 B1 state capital* Arkansas, C USA
Little Saint Bernard Pass *69 D5 Fr.* Col du Petit St-Bernard, *It.* Colle del Piccolo San Bernardo. *pass* France/Italy
Little Sound *20 A5 bay* Bermuda, NW Atlantic Ocean
Littleton *22 D4* Colorado, C USA
Littoria *see* Latina
Litva/Litwa *see* Lithuania
Liu-chou/Liuchow *see* Liuzhou
Liuzhou *106 C6 var.* Liu-chou, Liuchow. Guangxi Zhuangzu Zizhiqu, S China
Livanátai *see* Livanátes
Livanátes *83 B5 prev.* Livanátai. Stereá Ellás, C Greece
Līvāni *84 D4 Ger.* Lievenhof. Preiļi, SE Latvia
Liverpool *17 F5* Nova Scotia, SE Canada
Liverpool *67 C5* NW England, United Kingdom
Livingston *22 B2* Montana, NW USA
Livingston *27 H3* Texas, SW USA
Livingstone *56 C3 var.* Maramba. Southern, S Zambia
Livingstone *27 H3 var.* Maramba. Southern, S Zambia
Livingstone Mountains *129 A7 mountain range* South Island, New Zealand
Livno *78 B4* Federicija Bosna I Hercegovina, SW Bosnia and Herzegovina
Livojoki *62 D4 river* C Finland
Livonia *18 D3* Michigan, N USA
Livorno *74 B3 Eng.* Leghorn. Toscana, C Italy
Lixian Jiang *see* Black River
Lixoúri *83 A5 prev.* Lixoúrion. Kefallinía, Iónia Nisiá, Greece, C Mediterranean Sea
Lixoúrion *see* Lixoúri
Lizarra *see* Estella
Ljouwert *see* Leeuwarden
Ljubelj *see* Loibl Pass
Ljubljana *73 D7 Ger.* Laibach, *It.* Lubiana; *anc.* Aemona, Emona. *country capital* C Slovenia
Ljungby *63 B7* Kronoberg, S Sweden
Ljusdal *63 C5* Gävleborg, C Sweden
Ljusnan *63 C5 river* C Sweden
Llanelli *67 C6 prev.* Llanelly. SW Wales, United Kingdom
Llanelly *see* Llanelli
Llanes *70 D1* Asturias, N Spain
Llanos *36 D2 physical region* Colombia/Venezuela
Lleida *71 F2 Cast.* Lérida; *anc.* Ilerda. Cataluña, NE Spain
Llucmajor *71 G3* Mallorca, Spain, W Mediterranean Sea
Loaita Island *106 C8 island* W Spratly Islands
Loanda *see* Luanda
Lobatse *56 C4 var.* Lobatsi. Kgatleng, SE Botswana
Lobatsi *see* Lobatse
Löbau *72 D4* Sachsen, E Germany
Lobito *56 B2* Benguela, W Angola
Lob Nor *see* Lop Nur
Lobositz *see* Lovosice
Loburi *see* Lop Buri
Locarno *73 B8 Ger.* Luggarus. Ticino, S Switzerland
Lochem *64 E3* Gelderland, E Netherlands
Lockport *19 E3* New York, NE USA
Lodja *55 D6* Kasai-Oriental, C Dem. Rep. Congo
Lodwar *51 C6* Rift Valley, NW Kenya
Łódź *76 D4 Rus.* Lodz. Łódź, C Poland
Loei *114 C4 var.* Loey, Muang Loei. Loei, C Thailand
Loey *see* Loei
Lofoten *62 B3 var.* Lofoten Islands. *island group* C Norway
Lofoten Islands *see* Lofoten
Logan *22 B3* Utah, W USA
Logan, Mount *14 D3 mountain* Yukon Territory, W Canada
Logroño *71 E1 anc.* Vareia, *Lat.* Juliobriga. La Rioja, N Spain
Loibl Pass *73 D7 Ger.* Loiblpass, *Slvn.* Ljubelj. *pass* Austria/Slovenia
Loiblpass *see* Loibl Pass
Loikaw *114 B4* Kayah State, C Myanmar (Burma)
Loire *68 B4 var.* Liger. *river* C France
Loja *38 B2* Loja, S Ecuador
Lokitaung *51 C5* Rift Valley, NW Kenya
Lokoja *53 G4* Kogi, C Nigeria
Loksa *84 E2 Ger.* Loxa. Harjumaa, NW Estonia
Lolland *63 B8 prev.* Laaland. *island* S Denmark
Lom *82 C1 prev.* Lom-Palanka. Montana, NW Bulgaria
Lomami *55 D6 river* C Dem. Rep. Congo
Lomas *38 D4* Arequipa, SW Peru
Lomas de Zamora *42 D4* Buenos Aires, E Argentina
Lombardia *74 B2 Eng.* Lombardy. *region* N Italy
Lombardy *see* Lombardia
Lombok, Pulau *116 D5 island* Nusa Tenggara, C Indonesia
Lomé *53 F5 country capital* S Togo
Lomela *55 D6* Kasai-Oriental, C Dem. Rep. Congo
Lommel *65 C5* Limburg, N Belgium
Lomond, Loch *66 B4 lake* C Scotland, United Kingdom
Lomonosov Ridge *133 B3 var.* Harris Ridge, *Rus.* Khrebet Homonsova. *undersea ridge* Arctic Ocean
Lomonsova, Khrebet *see* Lomonosov Ridge
Lom-Palanka *see* Lom
Lompoc *25 B7* California, W USA
Lom Sak *114 C4 var.* Muang Lom Sak. Phetchabun, C Thailand
Łomża *76 D3 Rus.* Lomzha. Podlaskie, NE Poland
Lomzha *see* Łomża
Loncoche *43 B5* Araucanía, C Chile
Londinium *see* London
London *67 A7 anc.* Augusta, *Lat.* Londinium. *country capital* SE England, United Kingdom
London *16 C5* Ontario, S Canada
London *18 C5* Kentucky, S USA
Londonderry *66 B4 var.* Derry, *Ir.* Doire. NW Northern Ireland, United Kingdom
Londonderry, Cape *124 C2 cape* Western Australia
Londrina *41 E4* Paraná, S Brazil
Lone Star State *see* Texas
Long Bay *21 F2 bay* W Jamaica
Long Beach *25 C7* California, W USA
Longford *67 B5 Ir.* An Longfort. Longford, C Ireland
Long Island *32 D2 island* C Bahamas
Long Island *19 G4 island* New York, NE USA
Longlac *16 C3* Ontario, S Canada
Longmont *22 D4* Colorado, C USA
Longreach *126 C4* Queensland, E Australia
Long Strait *93 G1 Eng.* Long Strait. *strait* NE Russian Federation
Long Strait *see* Longa, Proliv
Longview *27 H3* Texas, SW USA
Longview *24 B2* Washington, NW USA
Long Xuyên *115 D6 var.* Longxuyen. An Giang, S Vietnam
Longxuyen *see* Long Xuyên
Longyan *106 D6* Fujian, SE China
Longyearbyen *61 G2 dependent territory capital* Spitsbergen, W Svalbard
Lons-le-Saunier *68 D4 anc.* Ledo Salinarius. Jura, E France
Lop Buri *115 C5 var.* Loburi. Lop Buri, C Thailand
Lop Nor *see* Lop Nur
Lop Nur *104 C3 var.* Lob Nor, Lop Nor, Lo-pu Po. *seasonal lake* NW China
Loppersum *64 E1* Groningen, NE Netherlands
Lo-pu Po *see* Lop Nur
Lorca *71 E4 Ar.* Lurka; *anc.* Eliocroca, *Lat.* Illurco. Murcia, S Spain
Lord Howe Island *120 C4 island* E Australia
Lord Howe Rise *120 C4 undersea rise* SW Pacific Ocean
Loreto *28 B3* Baja California Sur, W Mexico
Lorient *68 A3 prev.* l'Orient. Morbihan, NW France
l'Orient *see* Lorient
Lorn, Firth of *66 B4 inlet* W Scotland, United Kingdom
Loro Sae *see* East Timor
Lörrach *73 A7* Baden-Württemberg, S Germany
Lorraine *68 D3 cultural region* NE France
Los Alamos *26 C1* New Mexico, SW USA
Los Amates *30 B2* Izabal, E Guatemala
Los Ángeles *43 B5* Bío Bío, C Chile
Los Angeles *25 C7* California, W USA
Losanna *see* Lausanne
Lošinj *78 A3 Ger.* Lussin, *It.* Lussino. *island* W Croatia
Loslau *see* Wodzisław Śląski
Los Mochis *28 C3* Sinaloa, C Mexico
Losonc/Losontz *see* Lučenec
Los Roques, Islas *36 D1 island group* N Venezuela
Lot *69 B5 cultural region* S France
Lot *69 B5 river* S France
Lotagipi Swamp *51 C5 wetland* Kenya/Sudan
Lötzen *see* Giżycko
Loualaba *see* Lualaba
Louangnamtha *114 C3 var.* Luong Nam Tha. Louang Namtha, N Laos
Louangphabang *102 D3 var.* Louangphrabang, Luang Prabang. Louangphabang, N Laos
Louangphrabang *see* Louangphabang
Loubomo *see* Dolisie
Loudéac *68 A3* Côtes d'Armor, NW France
Loudi *106 C5* Hunan, S China
Louga *52 B3* NW Senegal
Louisiade Archipelago *122 B4 island group* SE Papua New Guinea
Louisiana *20 A2 off.* State of Louisiana, *also known as* Creole State, Pelican State. *state* S USA
Louisville *18 C5* Kentucky, S USA
Louisville Ridge *121 E4 undersea ridge* S Pacific Ocean
Loup River *23 E4 river* Nebraska, C USA
Lourdes *69 B6* Hautes-Pyrénées, S France
Lourenço Marques *see* Maputo
Louth *67 E5* E England, United Kingdom
Loutrá *82 C4* Kentrikí Makedonía, N Greece
Louvain *see* Leuven
Louvain-la Neuve *65 C6* Walloon Brabant, C Belgium
Louviers *68 C3* Eure, N France
Lovech *82 C2* Lovech, N Bulgaria
Loveland *22 D4* Colorado, C USA
Lovosice *76 A4 Ger.* Lobositz. Ústecký Kraj, NW Czech Republic
Lóvua *56 C1* Moxico, E Angola
Lowell *19 G3* Massachusetts, NE USA
Löwen *see* Leuven
Lower California *26 A4 Eng.* Lower California. *peninsula* NW Mexico
Lower California *see* Baja California
Lower Hutt *129 D5* Wellington, North Island, New Zealand
Lower Lough Erne *67 A5 lake* SW Northern Ireland, United Kingdom
Lower Red Lake *23 F1 lake* Minnesota, N USA
Lower Rhine *see* Neder Rijn
Lower Tunguska *93 E3 Eng.* Lower Tunguska. *river* N Russian Federation
Lower Tunguska *see* Nizhnyaya Tunguska
Lowestoft *67 E6* E England, United Kingdom
Loxa *see* Loksa
Lo-yang *see* Luoyang
Loyauté, Îles *122 D5 island group* S New Caledonia
Loyev *see* Loyew
Loyew *85 D8 Rus.* Loyev. Homyel'skaya Voblasts', SE Belarus
Loznica *78 C3* Serbia, W Serbia
Lu *see* Shandong, China
Lualaba *55 D6 Fr.* Loualaba. *river* SE Dem. Rep. Congo
Luanda *56 A1 var.* Loanda, *Port.* São Paulo de Loanda. *country capital* Luanda, NW Angola
Luang Prabang *see* Louangphabang
Luang, Thale *115 C7 lagoon* S Thailand
Luangua, Rio *see* Luangwa
Luangwa *51 B8 var.* Aruângua, Rio Luangua. *river* Mozambique/Zambia
Luanshya *56 D2* Copperbelt, C Zambia
Luarca *70 C1* Asturias, N Spain
Lubaczów *77 E5 var.* Lúbaczów. Podkarpackie, SE Poland
L'uban' *76 B4* Leningradskaya Oblast', Russian Federation
Lubānas Ezers *see* Lubāns
Lubango *56 B2 Port.* Sá da Bandeira. Huíla, SW Angola
Lubāns *84 D4 var.* Lubānas Ezers. *lake* E Latvia
Lubao *55 D6* Kasai-Oriental, C Dem. Rep. Congo
Lübben *72 D4* Brandenburg, E Germany
Lübbenau *72 D4* Brandenburg, E Germany
Lubbock *27 E2* Texas, SW USA
Lübeck *72 C2* Schleswig-Holstein, N Germany
Lubelska, Wyżyna *76 E4 plateau* SE Poland
Lüben *see* Lubin
Lubiana *see* Ljubljana
Lubin *76 B4 Ger.* Lüben. Dolnośląskie, SW Poland
Lublin *76 E4 Rus.* Lyublin. Lubelskie, E Poland
Lubliniec *76 C4* Śląskie, S Poland
Lubnān, Jabal *see* Liban, Jebel
Lubny *87 F2* Poltavs'ka Oblast', NE Ukraine
Lubsko *76 B4 Ger.* Sommerfeld. Lubuskie, W Poland
Lubumbashi *55 E8 prev.* Élisabethville. Shaba, SE Dem. Rep. Congo
Lubutu *55 D6* Maniema, E Dem. Rep. Congo
Luca *see* Lucca
Lucan *67 B5 Ir.* Leamhcán. Dublin, E Ireland
Lucanian Mountains *see* Lucano, Appennino
Lucano, Appennino *75 D5 Eng.* Lucanian Mountains. *mountain range* S Italy
Lucapa *56 C1 var.* Lukapa. Lunda Norte, NE Angola
Lucca *74 B3 anc.* Luca. Toscana, C Italy
Lucea *32 A4* W Jamaica
Lucena *117 E1 off.* Lucena City. Luzon, N Philippines
Lucena *70 D4* Andalucía, S Spain
Lucena City *see* Lucena
Lučenec *77 D6 Ger.* Losontz, *Hung.* Losonc. Banskobystrický Kraj, C Slovakia
Lucentum *see* Alicante
Lucerna/Lucerne *see* Luzern
Luchow *see* Hefei
Łuck *see* Luts'k
Lucknow *113 E3 var.* Lakhnau. *state capital* Uttar Pradesh, N India
Lüda *see* Dalian
Luda Kamchiya *82 D2 river* E Bulgaria
Ludasch *see* Luduş
Lüderitz *56 B4 prev.* Angra Pequena. Karas, SW Namibia
Ludhiāna *112 D2* Punjab, N India
Ludington *18 C2* Michigan, N USA
Ludsan *see* Ludza
Luduş *86 B4 Ger.* Ludasch, *Hung.* Marosludas. Mureş, C Romania
Ludvika *63 C6* Dalarna, C Sweden
Ludwigsburg *73 B6* Baden-Württemberg, SW Germany
Lüdwigsfelde *72 D3* Brandenburg, NE Germany
Ludwigshafen *73 B5 var.* Ludwigshafen am Rhein. Rheinland-Pfalz, W Germany
Ludwigshafen am Rhein *see* Ludwigshafen
Ludwigslust *72 C3* Mecklenburg-Vorpommern, N Germany
Ludza *84 D4 Ger.* Ludsan. Ludza, E Latvia
Luebo *55 C6* Kasai-Occidental, SW Dem. Rep. Congo
Luena *56 C2 var.* Lwena, *Port.* Luso. Moxico, E Angola
Lufira *55 E7 river* SE Dem. Rep. Congo
Lufkin *27 H3* Texas, SW USA
Luga *88 A4* Leningradskaya Oblast', NW Russian Federation
Lugano *73 B8 Ger.* Lauis. Ticino, S Switzerland
Lugansk *see* Luhans'k
Lugdunum *see* Lyon
Lugdunum Batavorum *see* Leiden
Lugenda, Rio *57 E2 river* N Mozambique
Luggarus *see* Locarno
Lugh Ganana *see* Luuq
Lugo *70 C1 anc.* Lugus Augusti. Galicia, NW Spain
Lugoj *86 A4 Ger.* Lugosch, *Hung.* Lugos. Timiş, W Romania
Lugos/Lugosch *see* Lugoj
Lugus Augusti *see* Lugo
Luguvallium/Luguvallum *see* Carlisle
Luhans'k *87 H3 Rus.* Lugansk; *prev.* Voroshilovgrad. Luhans'ka Oblast', E Ukraine
Luimneach *see* Limerick
Lukapa *see* Lucapa
Lukenie *55 C6 river* C Dem. Rep. Congo
Lukovit *82 C2* Lovech, N Bulgaria
Łuków *76 E4 Ger.* Bogendorf. Lubelskie, E Poland
Lukuga *55 D7 river* SE Dem. Rep. Congo
Luleå *62 D4* Norrbotten, N Sweden
Luleälven *62 C3 river* N Sweden
Lulonga *55 C5 river* NW Dem. Rep. Congo
Lulua *55 D7 river* S Dem. Rep. Congo
Luluabourg *see* Kananga
Lumber State *see* Maine
Lumbo *57 F2* Nampula, NE Mozambique
Lumsden *129 A7* Southland, South Island, New Zealand
Lund *63 B7* Skåne, S Sweden
Lüneburg *72 C3* Niedersachsen, N Germany
Lunga, Isola *see* Dugi Otok
Lungkiang *see* Qiqihar
Lungué-Bungo *56 C2 var.* Lungwebungu. *river* Angola/Zambia
Lungwebungu *see* Lungué-Bungo
Luninets *see* Luninyets
Łuniniec *see* Luninyets
Luninyets *85 B7 Pol.* Łuniniec, *Rus.* Luninets. Brestskaya Voblasts', SW Belarus
Lunteren *64 D4* Gelderland, C Netherlands
Luong Nam Tha *see* Louangnamtha
Luoyang *106 C4 var.* Honan, Lo-yang. Henan, C China
Lupatia *see* Altamura
Lúrio *57 F2* Nampula, NE Mozambique
Lúrio, Rio *57 E2 river* NE Mozambique
Lurka *see* Lorca
Lusaka *56 D2 country capital* Lusaka, SE Zambia
Lushnja *see* Lushnjë
Lushnjë *79 C6 var.* Lushnja. Fier, C Albania
Luso *see* Luena
Lussin/Lussino *see* Lošinj
Lūt, Baḩrat/Lut, Bahret *see* Dead Sea
Lut, Dasht-e *98 D3 var.* Kavīr-e Lūt. *desert* E Iran
Lutetia/Lutetia Parisiorum *see* Paris
Lūt, Kavīr-e *see* Lūt, Dasht-e
Luton *67 D6* E England, United Kingdom
Łutselk'e *15 F4 prev.* Snowdrift. Northwest Territories, W Canada
Luts'k *86 C1 Pol.* Łuck, *Rus.* Lutsk. Volyns'ka Oblast', NW Ukraine
Lutsk *see* Luts'k
Lüttich *see* Liège
Lutzow-Holm Bay *132 C2 var.* Lutzow-Holm Bay. *bay* Antarctica
Lutzow-Holm Bay *see* Lützow Holmbukta
Luuq *51 D6 It.* Lugh Ganana. Gedo, SW Somalia
Luvua *55 D7 river* SE Dem. Rep. Congo
Luwego *51 C8 river* S Tanzania
Luxembourg *65 D8 country capital* Luxembourg, S Luxembourg
Luxembourg *65 D8 off.* Grand Duchy of Luxembourg, *var.* Lëtzebuerg, Luxemburg. *country* NW Europe
Luxemburg *see* Luxembourg
Luxor *50 B2 Ar.* Al Uqşur. E Egypt
Luza *88 C4* Kirovskaya Oblast', NW Russian Federation
Luz, Costa de la *70 C5 coastal region* SW Spain
Luzern *73 B7 Fr.* Lucerne, *It.* Lucerna. Luzern, C Switzerland
Luzon *117 E1 island* N Philippines
Luzon Strait *103 E3 strait* Philippines/Taiwan
L'viv *86 B2 Ger.* Lemberg, *Pol.* Lwów, *Rus.* L'vov. L'vivs'ka Oblast', W Ukraine
L'vov *see* L'viv
Lwena *see* Luena
Lwów *see* L'viv
Lyakhavichy *85 B6 Rus.* Lyakhovichi. Brestskaya Voblasts', SW Belarus
Lyakhovichi *see* Lyakhavichy
Lyallpur *see* Faisalābād
Lyangar *see* Langar
Lyck *see* Ełk
Lycksele *62 C4* Västerbotten, N Sweden
Lycopolis *see* Asyūţ
Lyel'chytsy *85 C7 Rus.* Lel'chitsy. Homyel'skaya Voblasts', SE Belarus
Lyepyel' *85 D5 Rus.* Lepel'. Vitsyebskaya Voblasts', N Belarus
Lyme Bay *67 C7 bay* S England, United Kingdom
Lynchburg *19 E5* Virginia, NE USA
Lynn *see* King's Lynn
Lynn Lake *15 F4* Manitoba, C Canada
Lynn Regis *see* King's Lynn
Lyon *69 D5 Eng.* Lyons; *anc.* Lugdunum. Rhône, E France
Lyons *see* Lyon
Lyozna *85 E6 Rus.* Liozno. Vitsyebskaya Voblasts', NE Belarus
Lypovets' *86 D2 Rus.* Lipovets. Vinnyts'ka Oblast', C Ukraine
Lys *see* Leie
Lysychans'k *87 H3 Rus.* Lisichansk. Luhans'ka Oblast', E Ukraine
Lyttelton *129 C6* South Island, New Zealand
Lyublin *see* Lublin
Lyubotin *see* Lyubotyn
Lyubotyn *87 G2 Rus.* Lyubotin. Kharkivs'ka Oblast', E Ukraine
Lyulyakovo *82 E2 prev.* Keremitlik. Burgas, E Bulgaria
Lyusina *85 B6 Rus.* Lyusino. Brestskaya Voblasts', SW Belarus
Lyusino *see* Lyusina

M

Maale *see* Male'
Ma'ān *97 B7* Ma'ān, SW Jordan
Maardu *84 D2 Ger.* Maart. Harjumaa, NW Estonia
Ma'aret-en-Nu'man *see* Ma'arrat an Nu'mān
Ma'arrat an Nu'mān *96 B3 var.* Ma'aret-en-Nu'man, *Fr.* Maarret enn Naamâne. Idlib, NW Syria
Maarret enn Naamâne *see* Ma'arrat an Nu'mān
Maart *see* Maardu
Maas *see* Meuse
Maaseik *65 D5 prev.* Maeseyck. Limburg, NE Belgium
Maastricht *65 D6 var.* Maestricht; *anc.* Traiectum ad Mosam, Traiectum Tungorum. Limburg, SE Netherlands
Macao *107 C6 Chin.* Aomen, *Port.* Macau. E Asia
Macapá *41 E1 state capital* Amapá, N Brazil
Macarsca *see* Makarska
Macassar *see* Makassar
Macău *see* Makó, Hungary
Macau *see* Macao
MacCluer Gulf *see* Berau, Teluk
Macdonnell Ranges *124 D4 mountain range* Northern Territory, C Australia
Macedonia *see* Macedonia, FYR
Macedonia, FYR *79 D6 off.* the Former Yugoslav Republic of Macedonia, *var.* Macedonia, *Mac.* Makedonija, *abbrev.* FYR Macedonia, FYROM. *country* SE Europe
Macedonia, the Former Yugoslav Republic of *see* Macedonia, FYR
Maceió *41 G3 state capital* Alagoas, E Brazil
Machachi *38 B1* Pichincha, C Ecuador
Machala *38 B2* El Oro, SW Ecuador
Machanga *57 E3* Sofala, E Mozambique
Machilīpatnam *110 D1 var.* Bandar Masulipatnam. Andhra Pradesh, E India
Machiques *36 C2* Zulia, NW Venezuela
Macías Nguema Biyogo *see* Bioco, Isla de
Măcin *86 D5* Tulcea, SE Romania
Mackay *126 D4* Queensland, NE Australia
Mackay, Lake *124 C4 salt lake* Northern Territory/Western Australia
Mackenzie *15 E3 river* Northwest Territories, NW Canada
Mackenzie Bay *132 D3 bay* Antarctica
Mackenzie Mountains *14 D3 mountain range* Northwest Territories, NW Canada
Macleod, Lake *124 A4 lake* Western Australia
Macomb *18 A4* Illinois, N USA
Macomer *75 A5* Sardegna, Italy, C Mediterranean Sea
Mâcon *69 D5 anc.* Matisco, Matisco Ædourum. Saône-et-Loire, C France
Macon *20 D2* Georgia, SE USA
Macon *23 G4* Missouri, C USA
Macquarie Ridge *132 C5 undersea ridge* SW Pacific Ocean
Macuspana *29 G4* Tabasco, SE Mexico
Ma'dabā *97 B6 var.* Mādabā, Madeba; *anc.* Medeba. Ma'dabā, NW Jordan

Mādabā – Masuku

Mādabā see Ma'dabā
Madagascar 57 F3 off. Democratic Republic of Madagascar, Malg. Madagasikara; prev. Malagasy Republic. country W Indian Ocean
Madagascar 57 F3 island W Indian Ocean
Madagascar Basin 47 E7 undersea basin W Indian Ocean
Madagascar, Democratic Republic of see Madagascar
Madagascar Plateau 47 E7 var. Madagascar Ridge, Madagascar Rise, Rus. Madagaskarskiy Khrebet. undersea plateau W Indian Ocean
Madagascar Rise/Madagascar Ridge see Madagascar Plateau
Madagasikara see Madagascar
Madagaskarskiy Khrebet see Madagascar Plateau
Madang 122 B3 Madang, N Papua New Guinea
Madanīyīn see Médenine
Madarska see Hungary
Made 64 C4 Noord-Brabant, S Netherlands
Madeba see Ma'dabā
Madeira 48 A2 var. Ilha de Madeira. island Madeira, Portugal, NE Atlantic Ocean
Madeira, Ilha de see Madeira
Madeira Plain 44 C3 abyssal plain E Atlantic Ocean
Madeira, Rio 40 D2 var. Río Madera. river Bolivia/Brazil
Madeleine, Îles de la 17 F4 Eng. Magdalen Islands. island group Québec, E Canada
Madera 25 B6 California, W USA
Madera, Río see Madeira, Rio
Madhya Pradesh 113 E4 prev. Central Provinces and Berar. cultural region C India
Madīnat ath Thawrah 96 C2 var. Ath Thawrah. Ar Raqqah, N Syria
Madioen see Madiun
Madison 23 F3 South Dakota, N USA
Madison 18 B3 state capital Wisconsin, N USA
Madiun 116 D5 prev. Madioen. Jawa, C Indonesia
Madoera see Madura, Pulau
Madona 84 D4 Ger. Modohn. Madona, E Latvia
Madras see Chennai
Madras see Tamil Nādu
Madre de Dios, Río 39 E3 river Bolivia/Peru
Madre del Sur, Sierra 29 E5 mountain range S Mexico
Madre, Laguna 29 F3 lagoon NE Mexico
Madre, Laguna 27 G5 lagoon Texas, SW USA
Madre Occidental, Sierra 28 C3 var. Western Sierra Madre. mountain range C Mexico
Madre Oriental, Sierra 29 E3 var. Eastern Sierra Madre. mountain range C Mexico
Madrid 70 D3 country capital Madrid, C Spain
Madura see Madurai
Madurai 110 C3 prev. Madura, Mathurai. Tamil Nādu, S India
Madura, Pulau 116 D5 prev. Madoera. island C Indonesia
Maebashi 109 D5 var. Maebasi, Mayebashi. Gunma, Honshū, S Japan
Maebasi see Maebashi
Mae Nam Khong see Mekong
Mae Nam Nan 114 C4 river NW Thailand
Mae Nam Yom 114 C4 river W Thailand
Maeseyck see Maaseik
Maestricht see Maastricht
Maéwo 122 D4 prev. Aurora. island C Vanuatu
Mafia 51 D7 island E Tanzania
Mafraq/Muḥāfaẓat al Mafraq see Al Mafraq
Magadan 93 G3 Magadanskaya Oblast', E Russian Federation
Magallanes see Punta Arenas
Magallanes, Estrecho de see Magellan, Strait of
Magangué 36 B2 Bolívar, N Colombia
Magdalena 39 F3 Beni, N Bolivia
Magdalena 28 B1 Sonora, NW Mexico
Isla Magdalena 28 B3 island W Mexico
Magdalena, Río 36 B2 river C Colombia
Magdalen Islands see Madeleine, Îles de la
Magdeburg 72 C4 Sachsen-Anhalt, C Germany
Magelang 116 C5 Jawa, C Indonesia
Magellan, Strait of 43 B8 Sp. Estrecho de Magallanes. strait Argentina/Chile
Magerøy see Magerøya
Magerøya 62 D1 var. Magerøy, Lapp. Máhkarávju. island N Norway
Maggiore, Lago see Maggiore, Lake
Maggiore, Lake 74 B1 It. Lago Maggiore. lake Italy/Switzerland
Maglaj 78 C3 Federacija Bosna I Hercegovina, N Bosnia and Herzegovina
Maglie 75 E6 Puglia, SE Italy
Magna 22 B4 Utah, W USA
Magnesia see Manisa
Magnitogorsk 92 B4 Chelyabinskaya Oblast', C Russian Federation
Magnolia State see Mississippi
Magta' Lahjar 52 C3 var. Magta Lahjar, Magta' Lahjar, Magtá Lahjar. Brakna, SW Mauritania
Magway 114 A3 var. Magwe. Magway, W Myanmar (Burma)
Magyar-Becse see Bečej
Magyarkanizsa see Kanjiža
Magyarország see Hungary
Mahajanga 57 F2 var. Majunga. Mahajanga, NW Madagascar
Mahakam, Sungai 116 D4 var. Koetai, Kutai. river Borneo, C Indonesia
Mahalapye 56 D3 var. Mahalatswe. Central, SE Botswana
Mahalatswe see Mahalapye
Māhān 98 D3 Kermān, E Iran
Mahānadi 113 F4 river E India
Mahārāshtra 112 D5 cultural region W India
Mahbés see El Mahbas
Mahbūbnagar 112 D5 Andhra Pradesh, C India
Mahdia 49 F2 var. Al Mahdīyah, Mehdia. NE Tunisia
Mahé 57 H1 island Inner Islands, NE Seychelles
Mahia Peninsula 128 E4 peninsula North Island, New Zealand
Mahilyow 85 D6 Rus. Mogilëv. Mahilyowskaya Voblasts', E Belarus
Máhkarávju see Magerøya
Mahmūd-e 'Erāqī see Maḥmūd-e Rāqī
Maḥmūd-e Rāqī 101 E4 var. Mahmūd-e 'Erāqī. Kāpīsā, NE Afghanistan
Mahón 71 H3 Cat. Maó, Eng. Port Mahon; anc. Portus Magonis. Menorca, Spain, W Mediterranean Sea
Mähren see Moravia
Mährisch-Weisskirchen see Hranice
Maicao 36 C1 La Guajira, N Colombia
Mai Ceu/Mai Chio see Maych'ew
Maidstone 67 E7 SE England, United Kingdom
Maiduguri 53 H4 Borno, NE Nigeria
Mailand see Milano
Maimāna see Meymaneh
Main 73 B5 river C Germany
Mai-Ndombe, Lac 55 C6 prev. Lac Léopold II. lake W Dem. Rep. Congo
Maine 19 G2 off. State of Maine, also known as Lumber State, Pine Tree State. state NE USA
Maine 68 B3 cultural region NW France
Maine, Gulf of 19 H2 gulf NE USA
Mainland 66 C2 island N Scotland, United Kingdom
Mainland 66 D1 island NE Scotland, United Kingdom
Mainz 73 B5 Fr. Mayence. Rheinland-Pfalz, SW Germany
Maio 52 A3 var. Mayo. island Ilhas de Sotavento, SE Cape Verde
Maisur see Mysore, India
Maisur see Karnātaka, India
Maizhokunggar 104 C5 Xizang Zizhiqu, W China
Majorca 71 G3 Eng. Majorca; anc. Baleares Major. island Islas Baleares, Spain, W Mediterranean Sea
Majorca see Mallorca
Mājro see Majuro Atoll
Majunga see Mahajanga
Majuro Atoll 122 D2 var. Mājro. atoll Ratak Chain, SE Marshall Islands
Makale see Mek'elē
Makarov Basin 133 B3 undersea basin Arctic Ocean
Makarska 78 B4 It. Macarsca. Split-Dalmacija, SE Croatia
Makasar see Makassar
Makasar, Selat see Makassar Straits
Makassar 117 E4 var. Macassar, Makasar; prev. Ujungpandang. Sulawesi, C Indonesia
Makassar Straits 116 D4 Ind. Makasar Selat. strait C Indonesia
Makay 57 F3 var. Massif du Makay. mountain range SW Madagascar
Makay, Massif du see Makay
Makedonija see Macedonia, FYR
Makeni 52 C4 C Sierra Leone
Makeyevka see Makiyivka
Makhachkala 92 A4 prev. Petrovsk-Port. Respublika Dagestan, SW Russian Federation
Makin 122 D2 prev. Pitt Island. atoll Tungaru, W Kiribati
Makira see San Cristobal
Makiyivka 87 G3 Rus. Makeyevka; prev. Dmitriyevsk. Donets'ka Oblast', E Ukraine
Makkah 99 A5 Eng. Mecca. Makkah, W Saudi Arabia
Makkovik 17 F2 Newfoundland and Labrador, NE Canada
Makó 77 D7 Rom. Macău. Csongrád, SE Hungary
Makoua 55 B5 Cuvette, C Congo
Makran Coast 98 E4 coastal region SE Iran
Makrany 85 A6 Rus. Mokrany. Brestskaya Voblasts', SW Belarus
Mākū 98 B2 Āžarbāyjān-e Gharbī, NW Iran
Makurdi 53 G4 Benue, C Nigeria
Mala see Malaita, Solomon Islands
Malabār Coast 110 B3 coast SW India
Malabo 55 A5 prev. Santa Isabel. country capital Isla de Bioco, NW Equatorial Guinea
Malaca see Málaga
Malacca, Strait of 116 B3 Ind. Selat Malaka. strait Indonesia/Malaysia
Malacka see Malacky
Malacky 77 C6 Hung. Malacka. Bratislavský Kraj, W Slovakia
Maladzyechna 85 C5 Pol. Molodeczno, Rus. Molodechno. Minskaya Voblasts', C Belarus
Málaga 70 D5 anc. Malaca. Andalucía, S Spain
Malagarasi River 51 B7 river W Tanzania Africa
Malagasy Republic see Madagascar
Malaita 122 C3 var. Mala. island N Solomon Islands
Malakal 51 B5 Upper Nile, S Sudan
Malakula see Malekula
Malang 116 D5 Jawa, C Indonesia
Malange see Malanje
Malanje 56 B1 var. Malange. Malanje, NW Angola
Mälaren 63 C6 lake C Sweden
Malatya 95 E4 anc. Melitene. Malatya, SE Turkey
Mala Vyska 87 E3 Rus. Malaya Viska. Kirovohrads'ka Oblast', S Ukraine
Malawi 57 E1 off. Republic of Malaŵi; prev. Nyasaland, Nyasaland Protectorate. country S Africa
Malawi, Lake see Nyasa, Lake
Malaŵi, Republic of see Malawi
Malaya Viska see Mala Vyska
Malay Peninsula 102 D4 peninsula Malaysia/Thailand
Malaysia 116 B3 off. Malaysia, var. Federation of Malaysia; prev. the separate territories of Federation of Malaya, Sarawak and Sabah (North Borneo) and Singapore. country SE Asia
Malaysia, Federation of see Malaysia
Malbork 76 C2 Ger. Marienburg, Marienburg in Westpreussen. Pomorskie, N Poland
Malchin 72 C3 Mecklenburg-Vorpommern, N Germany
Malden 23 H5 Missouri, C USA
Malden Island 123 G3 prev. Independence Island. atoll E Kiribati
Maldives 110 A4 off. Maldivian Divehi, Republic of Maldives. country N Indian Ocean
Maldives, Republic of see Maldives
Maldivian Divehi see Maldives
Male' 110 B4 Div. Maale. country capital Male' Atoll, C Maldives
Male' Atoll 110 B4 var. Kaafu Atoll. atoll C Maldives
Malekula 122 D4 var. Malakula; prev. Mallicolo. island W Vanuatu
Malesína 83 C5 Stereá Ellás, E Greece
Malheur Lake 24 C3 lake Oregon, NW USA
Mali 53 E3 off. Republic of Mali, Fr. République du Mali; prev. French Sudan, Sudanese Republic. country W Africa
Malik, Wadi al see Milk, Wadi el
Mali Kyun 115 B5 var. Tavoy Island. island Mergui Archipelago, S Myanmar (Burma)
Malin see Malyn
Malindi 51 D7 Coast, SE Kenya
Malines see Mechelen
Mali, Republic of see Mali
Mali, République du see Mali
Malkiye see Al Mālikīyah
Malko Tŭrnovo 82 E3 Burgas, E Bulgaria
Mallaig 66 B3 N Scotland, United Kingdom
Mallawī 50 B2 var. Mallawi. C Egypt
Mallawi see Mallawī
Mallicolo see Malekula
Malmberget 62 C3 Lapp. Malmivaara. Norrbotten, N Sweden
Malmédy 65 D6 Liège, E Belgium
Malmivaara see Malmberget
Malmö 63 B7 Skåne, S Sweden
Maļoeļap see Maloelap Atoll
Maloelap Atoll 122 D1 var. Maļoeļap. atoll E Marshall Islands
Małopolska, Wyżyna 76 D4 plateau S Poland
Malozemel'skaya Tundra 88 D3 physical region NW Russian Federation
Malta 84 D4 Rēzekne, SE Latvia
Malta 22 C1 Montana, NW USA
Malta 75 C8 off. Republic of Malta. country C Mediterranean Sea
Malta 75 C8 island Malta, C Mediterranean Sea
Malta, Canale di see Malta Channel
Malta Channel 75 C8 It. Canale di Malta. strait Italy/Malta
Malta, Republic of see Malta
Maluku, Laut see Molucca Sea
Malung 63 B6 Dalarna, C Sweden
Malventum see Benevento
Malvina, Isla Gran see West Falkland
Malvinas, Islas see Falkland Islands
Malyn 86 D2 Rus. Malin. Zhytomyrs'ka Oblast', N Ukraine
Malyy Kavkaz see Lesser Caucasus
Mamberamo, Sungai 117 H4 river Papua, E Indonesia
Mambij see Manbij
Mamonovo 84 A4 Ger. Heiligenbeil. Kaliningradskaya Oblast', W Russian Federation
Mamoré, Rio 39 F3 river Bolivia/Brazil
Mamou 52 C4 W Guinea
Mamoudzou 57 F2 dependent territory capital C Mayotte
Mamuno 56 C3 Ghanzi, W Botswana
Manacor 71 G3 Mallorca, Spain, W Mediterranean Sea
Manado 117 F3 prev. Menado. Sulawesi, C Indonesia
Managua 30 D3 country capital Managua, W Nicaragua
Managua, Lake 30 C3 var. Xolotlán. lake W Nicaragua
Manakara 57 G4 Fianarantsoa, SE Madagascar
Manama see Al Manāmah
Mananjary 57 G3 Fianarantsoa, SE Madagascar
Manáos see Manaus
Manapouri, Lake 129 A7 lake South Island, New Zealand
Manar see Mannar
Manas, Gora 101 E2 mountain Kyrgyzstan/Uzbekistan
Manaus 40 D2 prev. Manáos. state capital Amazonas, NW Brazil
Manavgat 94 B4 Antalya, SW Turkey
Manbij 96 C2 var. Mambij, Fr. Membidj. Ḥalab, N Syria
Manchester 67 D5 Lat. Mancunium. NW England, United Kingdom
Manchester 19 G3 New Hampshire, NE USA
Man-chou-li see Manzhouli
Manchurian Plain 103 E1 plain NE China
Máncio Lima see Japiim
Mancunium see Manchester
Mand see Mand, Rūd-e
Mandalay 114 B3 Mandalay, C Myanmar (Burma)
Mandan 23 E2 North Dakota, N USA
Mandeville 32 B5 C Jamaica
Mándra 83 C6 Attikí, C Greece
Rud-e Mand 98 D4 var. Mand. river S Iran
Mandurah 125 A6 Western Australia
Manduria 75 E5 Puglia, SE Italy
Mandya 110 C2 Karnātaka, C India
Manfredonia 75 D5 Puglia, SE Italy
Mangai 55 C6 Bandundu, W Dem. Rep. Congo
Mangaia 123 G5 island group S Cook Islands
Mangalia 86 D5 anc. Callatis. Constanța, SE Romania
Mangalmé 54 C3 Guéra, SE Chad
Mangalore 110 B2 Karnātaka, W India
Mangaung see Bloemfontein
Mango see Sansanné-Mango, Togo
Mangoky 57 F3 river W Madagascar
Manhattan 23 F4 Kansas, C USA
Manicouagan, Réservoir 16 D3 lake Québec, E Canada
Manihiki 123 G4 atoll N Cook Islands
Manihiki Plateau 121 E3 undersea plateau C Pacific Ocean
Maniitsoq 60 C3 var. Manītsoq, Dan. Sukkertoppen. Kitaa, S Greenland
Manila 117 E1 off. City of Manila. country capital Luzon, N Philippines
Manila, City of see Manila
Manisa 94 A3 var. Manissa, prev. Saruhan; anc. Magnesia. Manisa, W Turkey
Manissa see Manisa
Manitoba 15 F5 province S Canada
Manitoba, Lake 15 F5 lake Manitoba, S Canada
Manitoulin Island 16 C4 island Ontario, S Canada
Manītsoq see Maniitsoq
Manizales 36 B3 Caldas, W Colombia
Manjimup 125 A7 Western Australia
Mankato 23 F3 Minnesota, N USA
Manlleu 71 G2 Cataluña, NE Spain
Manly 126 E1 Iowa, C USA
Manmād 112 C5 Mahārāshtra, W India
Mannar 110 C3 var. Manar. Northern Province, NW Sri Lanka
Mannar, Gulf of 110 C3 gulf India/Sri Lanka
Mannheim 73 B5 Baden-Württemberg, SW Germany
Manono 55 E7 Shaba, SE Dem. Rep. Congo
Manosque 69 D6 Alpes-de-Haute-Provence, SE France
Manra 123 F3 prev. Sydney Island. atoll Phoenix Islands, C Kiribati
Mansa 56 D2 prev. Fort Rosebery. Luapula, N Zambia
Mansel Island 15 G3 island Nunavut, NE Canada
Mansfield 18 D4 Ohio, N USA
Manta 38 A2 Manabí, W Ecuador
Manteca 25 B6 California, W USA
Mantoue see Mantova
Mantova 74 B2 Eng. Mantua, Fr. Mantoue. Lombardia, NW Italy
Mantua see Mantova
Manuae 123 G4 island S Cook Islands
Manukau see Manurewa
Manurewa 128 D3 var. Manukau. Auckland, North Island, New Zealand
Manzanares 71 E3 Castilla-La Mancha, C Spain
Manzanillo 32 C3 Granma, E Cuba
Manzanillo 28 D4 Colima, SW Mexico
Manzhouli 105 F1 var. Man-chou-li. Nei Mongol Zizhiqu, N China
Mao 54 B3 Kanem, W Chad
Maó see Mahón
Maoke, Pegunungan 117 H4 Dut. Sneeuw-gebergte, Eng. Snow Mountains. mountain range Papua, E Indonesia
Maoming 106 C6 Guangdong, S China
Mapmaker Seamounts 103 H2 seamount range N Pacific Ocean
Maputo 56 D4 prev. Lourenço Marques. country capital Maputo, S Mozambique
Marabá 41 F2 Pará, NE Brazil
Maracaibo 36 C1 Zulia, NW Venezuela
Maracaibo, Gulf of see Venezuela, Golfo de
Maracaibo, Lake 36 C2 var. Lake Maracaibo. inlet NW Venezuela
Maracaibo, Lake see Maracaibo, Lago de
Maracay 36 D2 Aragua, N Venezuela
Marada see Marādah
Marādah 49 G3 var. Marada. N Libya
Maradi 53 G3 Maradi, S Niger
Maragha see Marāgheh
Marāgheh 98 C2 var. Maragha. Āžarbāyjān-e Khāvarī, NW Iran
Marajó, Baía de 41 F1 bay N Brazil
Marajó, Ilha de 41 E1 island N Brazil
Marakesh see Marrakech
Maramba see Livingstone
Maramba see Livingstone
Maranhão 41 F2 off. Estado do Maranhão. state E Brazil
Maranhão 41 F2 off. Estado do Maranhão. region E Brazil
Maranhão, Estado do see Maranhão
Marañón, Río 38 B2 river N Peru
Marathon 16 C4 Ontario, S Canada
Marathón see Marathónas
Marathónas 83 C5 prev. Marathón. Attikí, C Greece
Mārāzā 95 H2 Rus. Maraza. E Azerbaijan
Maraza see Mārāzā
Marbella 70 D5 Andalucía, S Spain
Marble Bar 124 B4 Western Australia
Marburg see Marburg an der Lahn, Germany
Marburg see Maribor, Slovenia
Marburg an der Lahn 72 B4 hist. Marburg. Hessen, W Germany
March see Morava
Marche 74 C3 Eng. Marches. region C Italy
Marche 69 C5 cultural region C France
Marche-en-Famenne 65 C7 Luxembourg, SE Belgium
Marchena, Isla 38 B5 var. Bindloe Island. island Galapagos Islands, Ecuador, E Pacific Ocean
Marches see Marche
Mar Chiquita, Laguna 42 C3 lake C Argentina
Marcounda see Markounda
Mardān 112 C1 North-West Frontier Province, N Pakistan
Mar del Plata 43 D5 Buenos Aires, E Argentina
Mardin 95 E4 Mardin, SE Turkey
Maré 122 D5 island Îles Loyauté, E New Caledonia
Marea Neagră see Black Sea
Mareeba 126 D3 Queensland, NE Australia
Marek see Dupnitsa
Marganets see Marhanets'
Margarita, Isla de 37 E1 island N Venezuela
Margate 67 E7 prev. Mergate. SE England, United Kingdom
Margherita see Jamaame
Margherita, Lake 51 C5 Eng. Lake Margherita, It. Abbaia. lake SW Ethiopia
Margherita, Lake see Ābaya Hāyk'
Marghita 86 B3 Hung. Margitta. Bihor, NW Romania
Margitta see Marghita
Marhanets' 87 F3 Rus. Marganets. Dnipropetrovs'ka Oblast', E Ukraine
María Cleofas, Isla 28 C4 island C Mexico
Maria Island 127 C8 island Tasmania, SE Australia
María Madre, Isla 28 C4 island C Mexico
María Magdalena, Isla 28 C4 island C Mexico
Mariana Trench 103 G4 var. Challenger Deep. trench W Pacific Ocean
Mariánské Lázně 77 A5 Ger. Marienbad. Karlovarský Kraj, W Czech Republic
Marías, Islas 28 C4 island group C Mexico
Maria-Theresiopel see Subotica
Maribor 73 E7 Ger. Marburg. NE Slovenia
Marica see Maritsa
Maridi 51 B5 Western Equatoria, SW Sudan
Marie Byrd Land 132 A3 physical region Antarctica
Marie-Galante 33 G4 var. Ceyre to the Caribs. island SE Guadeloupe
Marienbad see Mariánské Lázně
Marienburg see Alūksne, Latvia
Marienburg see Malbork, Poland
Marienburg in Westpreussen see Malbork
Marienhausen see Viļaka
Mariental 56 B4 Hardap, SW Namibia
Marienwerder see Kwidzyń
Mariestad 63 B6 Västra Götaland, S Sweden
Marietta 20 D2 Georgia, SE USA
Marijampolė 84 B4 prev. Kapsukas. Marijampolė, S Lithuania
Marília 41 E4 São Paulo, S Brazil
Marín 70 B1 Galicia, NW Spain
Mar'ina Gorka see Mar"ina Horka
Mar"ina Horka 85 C6 Rus. Mar'ina Gorka. Minskaya Voblasts', C Belarus
Maringá 41 E4 Paraná, S Brazil
Marion 23 G3 Iowa, C USA
Marion 18 D4 Ohio, N USA
Marion, Lake 21 E2 reservoir South Carolina, SE USA
Mariscal Estigarribia 42 D2 Boquerón, NW Paraguay
Maritsa 82 D3 var. Marica, Gk. Évros, Turk. Meriç; anc. Hebrus. river SW Europe
Maritzburg see Pietermaritzburg
Mariupol' 87 G4 prev. Zhdanov. Donets'ka Oblast', SE Ukraine
Marka 51 D6 var. Merca. Shabeellaha Hoose, S Somalia
Markham, Mount 132 B4 mountain Antarctica
Markounda 54 C4 var. Marcounda. Ouham, NW Central African Republic
Marktredwitz 73 C5 Bayern, E Germany
Marlborough 126 D4 Queensland, E Australia
Marmanda see Marmande
Marmande 69 B5 anc. Marmanda. Lot-et-Garonne, SW France
Sea of Marmara 94 A2 Eng. Sea of Marmara. sea NW Turkey
Marmara, Sea of see Marmara Denizi
Marmaris 94 A4 Muğla, SW Turkey
Marne 68 C3 cultural region N France
Marne 68 D3 river N France
Maro 54 C4 Moyen-Chari, S Chad
Maroantsetra 57 G2 Toamasina, NE Madagascar
Maromokotro 57 G2 mountain N Madagascar
Maroni 37 G3 Dut. Marowijne. river French Guiana/Suriname
Maroshevíz see Toplița
Marosludas see Luduș
Marosvásárhely see Târgu Mureș
Marotiri 121 F4 var. Îlots de Bass, Morotiri. island group Îles Australes, SW French Polynesia
Maroua 54 B3 Extrême-Nord, N Cameroon
Marowijne see Maroni
Marquesas Fracture Zone 131 E3 fracture zone E Pacific Ocean
Marquette 18 B1 Michigan, N USA
Marrakech 48 C2 var. Marakesh, Eng. Marrakesh; prev. Morocco. W Morocco
Marrakesh see Marrakech
Marrawah 127 C8 Tasmania, SE Australia
Marree 127 B5 South Australia
Marsá al Burayqah 49 G3 var. Al Burayqah. N Libya
Marsabit 51 C6 Eastern, N Kenya
Marsala 75 B7 anc. Lilybaeum. Sicilia, Italy, C Mediterranean Sea
Marsberg 72 B4 Nordrhein-Westfalen, W Germany
Marseille 69 D6 Eng. Marseilles; anc. Massilia. Bouches-du-Rhône, SE France
Marseilles see Marseille
Marshall 23 F2 Minnesota, N USA
Marshall 27 H2 Texas, SW USA
Marshall Islands 122 C1 off. Republic of the Marshall Islands. country W Pacific Ocean
Marshall Islands, Republic of the see Marshall Islands
Marshall Seamounts 103 H3 seamount range SW Pacific Ocean
Marsh Harbour 32 C1 Great Abaco, W Bahamas
Martaban 114 B4 var. Moktama. Mon State, S Myanmar (Burma)
Martha's Vineyard 19 G3 island Massachusetts, NE USA
Martigues 69 D6 Bouches-du-Rhône, SE France
Martin 77 C5 Ger. Sankt Martin, Hung. Turócszentmárton; prev. Turčianský Svätý Martin. Žilinský Kraj, N Slovakia
Martinique 33 G4 French overseas department E West Indies
Martinique Channel see Martinique Passage
Martinique Passage 33 G4 var. Dominica Channel, Martinique Channel. channel Dominica/Martinique
Marton 128 D4 Manawatu-Wanganui, North Island, New Zealand
Martos 70 D4 Andalucía, S Spain
Marungu 55 E7 mountain range SE Dem. Rep. Congo
Mary 100 D3 prev. Merv. Mary Welaýaty, S Turkmenistan
Maryborough 127 D4 Queensland, E Australia
Maryborough see Port Laoise
Mary Island see Kanton
Maryland 19 E5 off. State of Maryland, also known as America in Miniature, Cockade State, Free State, Old Line State. state NE USA
Maryland, State of see Maryland
Maryville 23 F4 Missouri, C USA
Maryville 20 D1 Tennessee, S USA
Masai Steppe 51 C7 grassland NW Tanzania
Masaka 51 B6 SW Uganda
Masallı 95 H3 Rus. Masally. S Azerbaijan
Masally see Masallı
Masasi 51 C8 Mtwara, SE Tanzania
Masawa/Massawa see Mits'iwa
Masaya 30 D3 Masaya, W Nicaragua
Mascarene Basin 119 B5 undersea basin W Indian Ocean
Mascarene Islands 57 H4 island group W Indian Ocean
Mascarene Plain 119 B5 abyssal plain W Indian Ocean
Mascarene Plateau 119 B5 undersea plateau W Indian Ocean
Maseru 56 D4 country capital W Lesotho
Mas-ha 97 D7 W West Bank Asia
Mashhad 98 E2 var. Meshed. Khorāsān-Razavī, NE Iran
Masindi 51 B6 W Uganda
Masīra see Maṣīrah, Jazīrat
Masira, Gulf of 99 E5 var. Gulf of Masira. bay E Oman
Masira, Gulf of see Maṣīrah, Khalīj
Maṣīrah, Jazīrat 99 E5 var. Masīra. island E Oman
Masis see Büyükağrı Dağı
Maskat see Masqaṭ
Mason City 23 F3 Iowa, C USA
Masqaṭ 99 E5 var. Maskat, Eng. Muscat. country capital NE Oman
Massa 74 B3 Toscana, C Italy
Massachusetts 19 G3 off. Commonwealth of Massachusetts, also known as Bay State, Old Bay State, Old Colony State. state NE USA
Massenya 54 B3 Chari-Baguirmi, SW Chad
Massif Central 69 C5 plateau C France
Massilia see Marseille
Massoukou see Franceville
Mastanli see Momchilgrad
Masterton 129 D5 Wellington, North Island, New Zealand
Masty 85 B5 Rus. Mosty. Hrodzyenskaya Voblasts', W Belarus
Masuda 109 B6 Shimane, Honshū, SW Japan
Masuku see Franceville

Masvingo – Mocuba

Masvingo *56 D3 prev.* Fort Victoria, Nyanda, Victoria. Masvingo, SE Zimbabwe
Maşyāf *96 B3 Fr.* Misiaf. Ḩamāh, C Syria
Matadi *55 B6* Bas-Congo, W Dem. Rep. Congo
Matagalpa *30 D3* Matagalpa, C Nicaragua
Matale *110 D3* Central Province, C Sri Lanka
Matam *52 C3* NE Senegal
Matamata *128 D3* Waikato, North Island, New Zealand
Matamoros *28 D3* Coahuila de Zaragoza, NE Mexico
Matamoros *29 E2* Tamaulipas, C Mexico
Matane *17 E4* Québec, SE Canada
Matanzas *32 B2* Matanzas, NW Cuba
Matara *110 D4* Southern Province, S Sri Lanka
Mataram *116 D5* Pulau Lombok, C Indonesia
Mataró *71 G2 anc.* Illuro. Cataluña, E Spain
Mataura *129 B7* Southland, South Island, New Zealand
Mataura *129 B7 river* South Island, New Zealand
Mata Uta *see* Matā'utu
Matā'utu *123 E4 var.* Mata Uta. *dependent territory capital* Île Uvea, Wallis and Futuna
Matera *75 E5* Basilicata, S Italy
Mathurai *see* Madurai
Matianus *see* Orūmīyeh, Daryācheh-ye
Matías Romero *29 F5* Oaxaca, SE Mexico
Matisco/Matisco Ædourum *see* Mâcon
Mato Grosso *41 E3 off.* Estado de Mato Grosso; *prev.* Matto Grosso. *state* W Brazil
Mato Grosso *41 E3 off.* Estado de Mato Grosso; *prev.* Matto Grosso. *region* W Brazil
Mato Grosso do Sul *41 E4 off.* Estado de Mato Grosso do Sul. *state* S Brazil
Mato Grosso do Sul *41 E4 off.* Estado de Mato Grosso do Sul. *region* S Brazil
Mato Grosso do Sul, Estado de *see* Mato Grosso do Sul
Mato Grosso, Estado de *see* Mato Grosso
Mato Grosso, Planalto de *34 C4 plateau* C Brazil
Matosinhos *70 B2 prev.* Matozinhos. Porto, NW Portugal
Matozinhos *see* Matosinhos
Matsue *109 B6 var.* Matsuye, Matue. Shimane, Honshū, SW Japan
Matsumoto *109 C5 var.* Matumoto. Nagano, Honshū, S Japan
Matsuyama *109 B7 var.* Matuyama. Ehime, Shikoku, SW Japan
Matsuye *see* Matsue
Matterhorn *73 A8 It.* Monte Cervino. *mountain* Italy/Switzerland
Matthews Ridge *37 F2* N Guyana
Matthew Town *32 D2* Great Inagua, S Bahamas
Matto Grosso *see* Mato Grosso
Matucana *38 C4* Lima, W Peru
Matue *see* Matsue
Matumoto *see* Matsumoto
Maturín *37 E2* Monagas, NE Venezuela
Matuyama *see* Matsuyama
Mau *113 E3 var.* Maunāth Bhanjan. Uttar Pradesh, N India
Maui *25 B8 island* Hawai'i, USA, C Pacific Ocean
Maun *56 C3* North-West, C Botswana
Maunāth Bhanjan *see* Mau
Mauren *72 E1* NE Liechtenstein Europe
Maurice *see* Mauritius
Mauritania *52 C2 off.* Islamic Republic of Mauritania, *Ar.* Mūrītānīyah. *country* W Africa
Mauritania, Islamic Republic of *see* Mauritania
Mauritius *57 H3 off.* Republic of Mauritius, *Fr.* Maurice. *country* W Indian Ocean
Mauritius *119 B5 island* W Indian Ocean
Mauritius, Republic of *see* Mauritius
Mawlamyaing *see* Mawlamyine
Mawlamyine *114 B4 var.* Mawlamyaing, Moulmein. Mon State, S Myanmar (Burma)
Mawson *132 D2 Australian research station* Antarctica
Mayadin *see* Al Mayādīn
Mayaguana *32 D2 island* SE Bahamas
Mayaguana Passage *32 D2 passage* SE Bahamas
Mayagüez *33 F3* W Puerto Rico
Mayamey *98 D2* Semnān, N Iran
Maya Mountains *30 B2 Sp.* Montañas Mayas. *mountain range* Belize/Guatemala
Mayas, Montañas *see* Maya Mountains
Maych'ew *50 C4 var.* Mai Chio, *It.* Mai Ceu. Tigray, N Ethiopia
Maydān Shahr *see* Meydān Shahr
Mayebashi *see* Maebashi
Mayence *see* Mainz
Mayfield *129 B6* Canterbury, South Island, New Zealand
Maykop *89 A7* Respublika Adygeya, SW Russian Federation
Maymana *see* Meymaneh
Maymyo *see* Pyin-Oo-Lwin
Mayo *see* Maio
Mayor Island *128 D3 island* NE New Zealand
Mayor Pablo Lagerenza *see* Capitán Pablo Lagerenza
Mayotte *57 F2 French territorial collectivity* E Africa
May Pen *32 B5* C Jamaica
Mayyit, Al Baḩr al *see* Dead Sea
Mazabuka *56 D2* Southern, S Zambia
Mazaca *see* Kayseri
Mazagan *see* El-Jadida
Mazār-e Sharīf *101 E3 var.* Mazār-i Sharif. Balkh, N Afghanistan
Mazār-i Sharif *see* Mazār-e Sharīf
Mazatlán *28 C3* Sinaloa, C Mexico
Mažeikiai *84 B3* Telšiai, NW Lithuania
Mazirbe *84 C2* Talsi, NW Latvia
Mazra'a *see* Al Mazra'ah
Mazury *76 D3 physical region* NE Poland
Mazyr *85 C7 Rus.* Mozyr'. Homyel'skaya Voblasts', SE Belarus
Mbabane *56 D4 country capital* NW Swaziland
Mbacké *see* Mbaké
Mbaïki *55 C5 var.* M'Baiki. Lobaye, SW Central African Republic
M'Baiki *see* Mbaïki
Mbaké *52 B3 var.* Mbacké. W Senegal
Mbala *56 D1 prev.* Abercorn. Northern, NE Zambia
Mbale *51 C6* E Uganda
Mbandaka *55 C5 prev.* Coquilhatville. Equateur, NW Dem. Rep. Congo
M'Banza Congo *56 B1 var.* Mbanza Congo; *prev.* São Salvador, São Salvador do Congo. Dem. Rep. Congo, NW Angola
Mbanza-Ngungu *55 B6* Bas-Congo, W Dem. Rep. Congo
Mbarara *51 B6* SW Uganda
Mbé *54 B4* Nord, N Cameroon
Mbeya *51 C7* Mbeya, SW Tanzania
Mbomou/M'Bomu/Mbomu *see* Bomu
Mbour *52 B3* W Senegal
Mbuji-Mayi *55 D7 prev.* Bakwanga. Kasai-Oriental, S Dem. Rep. Congo
McAlester *27 G2* Oklahoma, C USA
McAllen *27 G5* Texas, SW USA
McCamey *27 E3* Texas, SW USA
McClintock Channel *15 F2 channel* Nunavut, N Canada
McComb *20 B3* Mississippi, S USA
McCook *23 E4* Nebraska, C USA
McKean Island *123 E3 island* Phoenix Islands, C Kiribati
Mount McKinley *14 C3 var.* Denali. *mountain* Alaska, USA
McKinley Park *14 C3* Alaska, USA
McMinnville *24 B3* Oregon, NW USA
McMurdo *132 B4 US research station* Antarctica
McPherson *23 E5* Kansas, C USA
McPherson *see* Fort McPherson
Mdantsane *56 D5* Eastern Cape, SE South Africa
Mead, Lake *25 D6 reservoir* Arizona/Nevada, W USA
Mecca *see* Makkah
Mechelen *65 C5 Eng.* Mechlin, *Fr.* Malines. Antwerpen, C Belgium
Mechlin *see* Mechelen
Mecklenburger Bucht *72 C2 bay* N Germany
Mecsek *77 C7 mountain range* SW Hungary
Medan *116 B3* Sumatera, E Indonesia
Medeba *see* Ma'dabā
Medellín *36 B3* Antioquia, NW Colombia
Médenine *49 F2 var.* Madanīyīn. SE Tunisia
Medeshamstede *see* Peterborough
Medford *24 B4* Oregon, NW USA
Medgidia *86 D5* Constanța, SE Romania
Medgyes *see* Mediaș
Mediaș *86 B4 Ger.* Mediasch, *Hung.* Medgyes. Sibiu, C Romania
Mediasch *see* Mediaș
Medicine Hat *15 F5* Alberta, SW Canada
Medina *see* Al Madīnah
Medinaceli *71 E2* Castilla-León, N Spain
Medina del Campo *70 D2* Castilla-León, N Spain
Medinat Israel *see* Israel
Mediolanum *see* Saintes, France
Mediolanum *see* Milano, Italy
Mediomatrica *see* Metz
Mediterranean Sea *80 D3 Fr.* Mer Méditerranée. *sea* Africa/Asia/Europe
Méditerranée, Mer *see* Mediterranean Sea
Médoc *69 B5 cultural region* SW France
Medvezh'yegorsk *88 B3* Respublika Kareliya, NW Russian Federation
Meekatharra *125 B5* Western Australia
Meemu Atoll *see* Mulakatholhu
Meerssen *65 D6 var.* Mersen. Limburg, SE Netherlands
Meerut *112 D2* Uttar Pradesh, N India
Megáli Préspa, Límni *see* Prespa, Lake
Meghālaya *91 G3 cultural region* NE India
Mehdia *see* Mahdia
Meheso *see* Mī'ēso
Me Hka *see* Nmai Hka
Mehriz *98 D3* Yazd, C Iran
Mehtar Lām *101 F4 var.* Mehtarlām, Meterlam, Methariam, Metharlam. Laghmān, E Afghanistan
Mehtarlām *see* Mehtar Lām
Meiktila *114 B3* Mandalay, C Myanmar (Burma)
Méjico *see* Mexico
Mejillones *42 B2* Antofagasta, N Chile
Mek'elē *50 C4 var.* Makale. Tigray, N Ethiopia
Mékhé *52 B3* NW Senegal
Mekong *102 D3 var.* Lan-ts'ang Chiang, *Cam.* Mékôngk, *Chin.* Lancang Jiang, *Lao.* Mènam Khong, *Th.* Mae Nam Khong, *Tib.* Dza Chu, *Vtn.* Sông Tiên Giang. *river* SE Asia
Mékôngk *see* Mekong
Mekong, Mouths of the *115 E6 delta* S Vietnam
Melaka *116 B3 var.* Malacca. Melaka, Peninsular Malaysia
Melaka, Selat *see* Malacca, Strait of
Melanesia *122 D3 island group* W Pacific Ocean
Melanesian Basin *120 C2 undersea basin* W Pacific Ocean
Melbourne *127 C7 state capital* Victoria, SE Australia
Melbourne *21 E4* Florida, SE USA
Meleda *see* Mljet
Melghir, Chott *49 E2 var.* Chott Melrhir. *salt lake* E Algeria
Melilla *58 B5 anc.* Rusaddir, Russadir. Melilla, Spain, N Africa
Melilla *48 D2 enclave* Spain, N Africa
Melita *15 F5* Manitoba, S Canada
Melita *see* Mljet
Melitene *see* Malatya
Melitopol' *87 F4* Zaporiz'ka Oblast', SE Ukraine
Melle *65 B5* Oost-Vlaanderen, NW Belgium
Mellerud *63 B6* Västra Götaland, S Sweden
Mellieħa *80 B5* E Malta
Mellizo Sur, Cerro *43 A7 mountain* S Chile
Melo *42 E4* Cerro Largo, NE Uruguay
Melodunum *see* Melun
Melrhir, Chott *see* Melghir, Chott
Melsungen *72 B4* Hessen, C Germany
Melun *68 C3 anc.* Melodunum. Seine-et-Marne, N France
Melville Bay/Melville Bugt *see* Qimusseriarsuaq
Melville Island *124 D2 island* Northern Territory, N Australia
Melville Island *15 E2 island* Parry Islands, Northwest Territories, NW Canada
Melville, Lake *17 F2 lake* Newfoundland and Labrador, E Canada
Melville Peninsula *15 G3 peninsula* Nunavut, NE Canada
Melville Sound *see* Viscount Melville Sound
Membidj *see* Manbij
Memel *see* Neman, NE Europe
Memel *see* Klaipeda, Lithuania
Memmingen *73 B6* Bayern, S Germany
Memphis *20 C1* Tennessee, S USA
Menaam *see* Menaldum
Menado *see* Manado
Ménaka *53 F3* Goa, E Mali
Menaldum *64 D1 Fris.* Menaam. Friesland, N Netherlands
Mènam Khong *see* Mekong
Mendaña Fracture Zone *131 F4 fracture zone* E Pacific Ocean
Mende *69 C5 anc.* Mimatum. Lozère, S France
Mendeleyev Ridge *133 B2 undersea ridge* Arctic Ocean
Mendocino Fracture Zone *130 D2 fracture zone* NE Pacific Ocean
Mendoza *42 B4* Mendoza, W Argentina
Menemen *94 A3* İzmir, W Turkey
Menengiyn Tal *105 F2 plain* E Mongolia
Menongue *56 B2 var.* Vila Serpa Pinto, *Port.* Serpa Pinto. Cuando Cubango, C Angola
Mentawai, Kepulauan *116 A4 island group* W Indonesia
Meppel *64 D2* Drenthe, NE Netherlands
Meran *see* Merano
Merano *74 C1 Ger.* Meran. Trentino-Alto Adige, N Italy
Merca *see* Marka
Mercedes *42 D3* Corrientes, NE Argentina
Mercedes *42 D4* Soriano, SW Uruguay
Meredith, Lake *27 E1 reservoir* Texas, SW USA
Merefa *87 G2* Kharkivs'ka Oblast', E Ukraine
Mergate *see* Margate
Mergui *see* Myeik
Mergui Archipelago *115 B6 island group* S Myanmar (Burma)
Mérida *29 H3* Yucatán, SW Mexico
Mérida *70 C4 anc.* Augusta Emerita. Extremadura, W Spain
Mérida *36 C2* Mérida, W Venezuela
Meridian *20 C2* Mississippi, S USA
Mérignac *69 B5* Gironde, SW France
Merín, Laguna *see* Mirim Lagoon
Merkulovichi *see* Myerkulavichy
Merowe *50 B3* Northern, N Sudan
Merredin *125 B6* Western Australia
Mersen *see* Meerssen
Mersey *67 D5 river* NW England, United Kingdom
Mersin *94 C4 var.* İçel. İçel, S Turkey
Mērsrags *84 C3* Talsi, NW Latvia
Meru *51 C6* Eastern, C Kenya
Merv *see* Mary
Merzifon *94 D2* Amasya, N Turkey
Merzig *73 A5* Saarland, SW Germany
Mesa *26 B2* Arizona, SW USA
Meseritz *see* Międzyrzecz
Meshed *see* Mashhad
Mesopotamia *35 C5 var.* Mesopotamia Argentina. *physical region* NE Argentina
Mesopotamia Argentina *see* Mesopotamia
Messalo, Rio *57 E2 var.* Mualo. *river* NE Mozambique
Messana/Messene *see* Messina
Messina *75 D7 var.* Messana, Messene; *anc.* Zancle. Sicilia, Italy, C Mediterranean Sea
Messina *see* Musina
Messina, Strait of *75 D7 Eng.* Strait of Messina. *strait* SW Italy
Messina, Strait of *see* Messina, Stretto di
Messíni *83 B6* Pelopónnisos, S Greece
Mesta *see* Néstos
Mestghanem *see* Mostaganem
Mestia *95 F1 var.* Mestiya. N Georgia
Mestiya *see* Mestia
Mestre *74 C2* Veneto, NE Italy
Metairie *20 B3* Louisiana, S USA
Metán *42 C2* Salta, N Argentina
Metapán *30 B2* Santa Ana, NW El Salvador
Meta, Río *36 D3 river* Colombia/Venezuela
Meterlam *see* Mehtar Lām
Methariam/Metharlam *see* Mehtar Lām
Metis *see* Metz
Metković *78 B4* Dubrovnik-Neretva, SE Croatia
Métsovo *82 B4 prev.* Métsovon. Ípeiros, C Greece
Métsovon *see* Métsovo
Metz *68 D3 anc.* Divodurum Mediomatricum, Mediomatrica, Metis. Moselle, NE France
Meulaboh *116 A3* Sumatera, W Indonesia
Meuse *65 C6 Dut.* Maas. *river* W Europe
Mexcala, Río *see* Balsas, Río
Mexicali *28 A1* Baja California, NW Mexico
Mexicanos, Estados Unidos *see* Mexico
México *29 E4 var.* Ciudad de México, *Eng.* Mexico City. *country capital* México, C Mexico
Mexico *23 G4* Missouri, C USA
Mexico *28 C3 off.* United Mexican States, *var.* Méjico, México, *Sp.* Estados Unidos Mexicanos. *country* N Central America
México *see* Mexico
Mexico City *see* México
México, Golfo de *see* Mexico, Gulf of
Mexico, Gulf of *29 F2 Sp.* Golfo de México. *gulf* W Atlantic Ocean
Meyadine *see* Al Mayādīn
Meydān Shahr *101 E4 var.* Maydān Shahr. Vardak, E Afghanistan
Meymaneh *100 D3 var.* Maimāna, Maymana. Fāryāb, NW Afghanistan
Mezen' *88 D3 river* NW Russian Federation
Mezőtúr *77 D7* Jász-Nagykun-Szolnok, E Hungary
Mġarr *80 A5* Gozo, N Malta
Miadzioł Nowy *see* Myadzyel
Miahuatlán *29 F5 var.* Miahuatlán de Porfirio Díaz. Oaxaca, SE Mexico
Miahuatlán de Porfirio Díaz *see* Miahuatlán
Miami *21 F5* Florida, SE USA
Miami *27 G1* Oklahoma, C USA
Miami Beach *21 F5* Florida, SE USA
Miāneh *98 C2 var.* Miyāneh. Āẕarbāyjān-e Sharqī, NW Iran
Mianyang *106 B5* Sichuan, C China
Miastko *76 C2 Ger.* Rummelsburg in Pommern. Pomorskie, N Poland
Mi Chai *see* Nong Khai
Michalovce *77 E5 Ger.* Grossmichel, *Hung.* Nagymihály. Košický Kraj, E Slovakia
Michigan *18 C1 off.* State of Michigan, *also known as* Great Lakes State, Lake State, Wolverine State. *state* N USA
Michigan, Lake *18 C2 lake* N USA
Michurin *see* Tsarevo
Michurinsk *89 B5* Tambovskaya Oblast', W Russian Federation
Micoud *33 F2* SE Saint Lucia
Micronesia *122 B1 off.* Federated States of Micronesia. *country* W Pacific Ocean
Micronesia *122 C1 island group* W Pacific Ocean
Micronesia, Federated States of *see* Micronesia
Mid-Atlantic Cordillera *see* Mid-Atlantic Ridge
Mid-Atlantic Ridge *44 C3 var.* Mid-Atlantic Cordillera, Mid-Atlantic Rise, Mid-Atlantic Swell. *undersea ridge* Atlantic Ocean
Mid-Atlantic Rise/Mid-Atlantic Swell *see* Mid-Atlantic Ridge
Middelburg *65 B5* Zeeland, SW Netherlands
Middelharnis *64 B4* Zuid-Holland, SW Netherlands
Middelkerke *65 A5* West-Vlaanderen, W Belgium
Middle America Trench *13 B7 trench* E Pacific Ocean
Middle Andaman *111 F2 island* Andaman Islands, India, NE Indian Ocean
Middle Atlas *48 C2 Eng.* Middle Atlas. *mountain range* N Morocco
Middle Atlas *see* Moyen Atlas
Middleburg Island *see* 'Eua
Middle Congo *see* Congo (Republic of)
Middlesboro *18 C5* Kentucky, S USA
Middlesbrough *67 D5* N England, United Kingdom
Middletown *19 F4* New Jersey, NE USA
Middletown *19 F3* New York, NE USA
Mid-Indian Basin *119 C5 undersea basin* N Indian Ocean
Mid-Indian Ridge *119 C5 var.* Central Indian Ridge. *undersea ridge* C Indian Ocean
Midland *16 D5* Ontario, S Canada
Midland *18 C3* Michigan, N USA
Midland *27 E3* Texas, SW USA
Mid-Pacific Mountains *130 C2 var.* Mid-Pacific Seamounts. *seamount range* NW Pacific Ocean
Mid-Pacific Seamounts *see* Mid-Pacific Mountains
Midway Islands *130 D2 US territory* C Pacific Ocean
Miechów *77 D5* Małopolskie, S Poland
Międzyrzec Podlaski *76 E3* Lubelskie, E Poland
Międzyrzecz *76 B3 Ger.* Meseritz. Lubuskie, W Poland
Mielec *77 D5* Podkarpackie, SE Poland
Miercurea-Ciuc *86 C4 Ger.* Szeklerburg, *Hung.* Csíkszereda. Harghita, C Romania
Mieres del Camín *see* Mieres del Camino
Mieres del Camino *70 D1 var.* Mieres del Camín. Asturias, NW Spain
Mī'ēso *51 D5 var.* Meheso, Miesso. Oromīya, C Ethiopia
Miesso *see* Mī'ēso
Mifrats Hefa *97 A5 Eng.* Bay of Haifa; *prev.* MifrazHefa. *bay* N Israel
Miguel Asua *28 D3 var.* Miguel Auza. Zacatecas, C Mexico
Miguel Auza *see* Miguel Asua
Mijdrecht *64 C3* Utrecht, C Netherlands
Mikashevichi *see* Mikashevichy
Mikashevichy *85 C7 Pol.* Mikaszewicze, *Rus.* Mikashevichi. Brestskaya Voblasts', SW Belarus
Mikaszewicze *see* Mikashevichy
Mikhaylovgrad *see* Montana
Mikhaylovka *89 B6* Volgogradskaya Oblast', SW Russian Federation
Míkonos *see* Mýkonos
Mikre *82 C2* Lovech, N Bulgaria
Mikun' *88 D4* Respublika Komi, NW Russian Federation
Mikuni-sanmyaku *109 D5 mountain range* Honshū, N Japan Asia
Mikura-jima *109 D6 island* E Japan
Milagro *38 B2* Guayas, SW Ecuador
Milan *see* Milano
Milange *57 E2* Zambézia, NE Mozambique
Milano *74 B2 Eng.* Milan, *Ger.* Mailand; *anc.* Mediolanum. Lombardia, N Italy
Milas *94 A4* Muğla, SW Turkey
Milashavichy *85 C7 Rus.* Milashevichi. Homyel'skaya Voblasts', SE Belarus
Milashevichi *see* Milashavichy
Mildura *127 C6* Victoria, SE Australia
Mile *see* Mili Atoll
Miles *127 D5* Queensland, E Australia
Miles City *22 C2* Montana, NW USA
Milford *see* Milford Haven
Milford Haven *67 C6 prev.* Milford. SW Wales, United Kingdom
Milford Sound *129 A6* Southland, South Island, New Zealand
Milford Sound *129 A6 inlet* South Island, New Zealand
Milh, Bahr al *see* Razāzah, Buḩayrat ar
Mili Atoll *122 D2 var.* Mile. *atoll* Ratak Chain, SE Marshall Islands
Mil'kovo *93 H3* Kamchatskaya Oblast', E Russian Federation
Milk River *15 E5* Alberta, SW Canada
Milk River *22 C1 river* Montana, NW USA
Milk, Wadi el *66 B4 var.* Wadi al Malik. *river* C Sudan
Milledgeville *21 E2* Georgia, SE USA
Mille Lacs Lake *23 F2 lake* Minnesota, N USA
Millennium Island *121 F3 prev.* Caroline Island, Thornton Island. *atoll* Line Islands, E Kiribati
Millerovo *89 B6* Rostovskaya Oblast', SW Russian Federation
Mílos *83 C6 island* Kykládes, Greece, Aegean Sea
Mílos *83 C6 island* Kykládes, Greece, Aegean Sea
Mílos *83 C7 island* Kykládes, Greece, Aegean Sea
Milton *129 B7* Otago, South Island, New Zealand
Milton Keynes *67 D6* SE England, United Kingdom
Milwaukee *18 B3* Wisconsin, N USA
Mimatum *see* Mende
Min *see* Fujian
Mīnā' Qābūs *118 B3* NE Oman
Minas Gerais *41 F3 off.* Estado de Minas Gerais. *state* E Brazil
Minas Gerais *41 F3 off.* Estado de Minas Gerais. *region* E Brazil
Minas Gerais, Estado de *see* Minas Gerais
Minatitlán *29 F4* Veracruz-Llave, E Mexico
Minbu *114 A3* Magway, W Myanmar (Burma)
Minch, The *66 B3 var.* North Minch. *strait* NW Scotland, United Kingdom
Mindanao *117 F2 island* S Philippines
Mindanao Sea *see* Bohol Sea
Mindelheim *73 C6* Bayern, S Germany
Mindello *see* Mindelo
Mindelo *52 A2 var.* Mindello; *prev.* Porto Grande. São Vicente, N Cape Verde
Minden *72 B4 anc.* Minthun. Nordrhein-Westfalen, NW Germany
Mindoro *117 E2 island* N Philippines
Mindoro Strait *117 E2 strait* W Philippines
Mineral Wells *27 F2* Texas, SW USA
Mingäçevir *95 G2 Rus.* Mingechaur, Mingechevir. C Azerbaijan
Mingechaur/Mingechevir *see* Mingäçevir
Mingora *see* Saidu Sharif
Minho *70 B2 former province* N Portugal
Minho *70 B2 Sp.* Miño. *river* Portugal/Spain
Minho, Rio *see* Miño
Minicoy Island *110 B3 island* SW India
Minius *see* Miño
Minna *53 G4* Niger, C Nigeria
Minneapolis *23 F2* Minnesota, N USA
Minnesota *23 F2 off.* State of Minnesota, *also known as* Gopher State, New England of the West, North Star State. *state* N USA
Miño *70 B2 var.* Mino, Minius, *Port.* Rio Minho. *river* Portugal/Spain
Miño *see* Minho, Rio
Minorca *71 H3 Eng.* Minorca; *anc.* Balearis Minor. *island* Islas Baleares, Spain, W Mediterranean Sea
Minorca *see* Menorca
Minot *23 E1* North Dakota, N USA
Minsk *85 C6 country capital* Minskaya Voblasts', C Belarus
Minskaya Wzvyshsha *85 C6 mountain range* C Belarus
Mińsk Mazowiecki *76 D3 var.* Nowo-Minsk. Mazowieckie, C Poland
Minthun *see* Minden
Minto, Lac *16 D2 lake* Québec, C Canada
Minya *see* Al Minyā
Miraflores *28 C3* Baja California Sur, W Mexico
Miranda de Ebro *71 E1* La Rioja, N Spain
Mirgorod *see* Myrhorod
Miri *116 D3* Sarawak, East Malaysia
Mirim Lagoon *41 E5 var.* Lake Mirim, *Sp.* Laguna Merín. *lagoon* Brazil/Uruguay
Mirim, Lake *see* Mirim Lagoon
Mírina *see* Mýrina
Mīrjāveh *98 E4* Sīstān va Balūchestān, SE Iran
Mirny *132 C3 Russian research station* Antarctica
Mirnyy *93 F3* Respublika Sakha (Yakutiya), NE Russian Federation
Mīrpur Khās *112 B3* Sind, SE Pakistan
Mirtoan Sea *83 C6 Eng.* Mirtoan Sea; *anc.* Myrtoum Mare. *sea* S Greece
Mirtoan Sea *see* Mirtóo Pélagos
Misiaf *see* Maşyāf
Miskito Coast *see* La Mosquitia
Miskitos, Cayos *31 E2 island group* NE Nicaragua
Miskolc *77 D6* Borsod-Abaúj-Zemplén, NE Hungary
Misool, Pulau *117 F4 island* Maluku, E Indonesia
Mişrātah *49 F2 var.* Misurata. NW Libya
Mission *27 G5* Texas, SW USA
Mississippi *20 B2 off.* State of Mississippi, *also known as* Bayou State, Magnolia State. *state* SE USA
Mississippi Delta *20 B4 delta* Louisiana, S USA
Mississippi River *13 C6 river* C USA
Missoula *22 B1* Montana, NW USA
Missouri *23 F5 off.* State of Missouri, *also known as* Bullion State, Show Me State. *state* C USA
Missouri River *23 E3 river* C USA
Mistassini, Lac *16 D3 lake* Québec, SE Canada
Mistelbach an der Zaya *73 E6* Niederösterreich, NE Austria
Misti, Volcán *39 E4 volcano* S Peru
Misurata *see* Mişrātah
Mitau *see* Jelgava
Mitchell *127 D5* Queensland, E Australia
Mitchell *23 E3* South Dakota, N USA
Mitchell, Mount *21 E1 mountain* North Carolina, SE USA
Mitchell River *126 C2 river* Queensland, NE Australia
Mi Tho *see* My Tho
Mitilíni *see* Mytilíni
Mito *109 D5* Ibaraki, Honshū, S Japan
Mitrovica/Mitrovicë *see* Kosovska Mitrovica, Serbia
Mitrovica/Mitrowitz *see* Sremska Mitrovica, Serbia
Mitrovicë *79 D5 Serb.* Mitrovica, Kosovska Mitrovica, Titova Mitrovica. N Kosovo
Mits'iwa *50 C4 var.* Masawa, Massawa. E Eritrea
Mitspe Ramon *97 A7 prev.* Mizpe Ramon. Southern, S Israel
Mittelstadt *see* Baia Sprie
Mitú *36 C4* Vaupés, SE Colombia
Mitumba, Chaîne des/Mitumba Range *see* Mitumba, Monts
Mitumba Range *55 E7 var.* Chaîne des Mitumba, Mitumba Range. *mountain range* E Dem. Rep. Congo
Miueru Wantipa, Lake *55 E7 lake* N Zambia
Miyake-jima *109 D6 island* Sakishima-shotō, SW Japan
Miyako *108 D4* Iwate, Honshū, C Japan
Miyakonojō *109 B8 var.* Miyakonzyô. Miyazaki, Kyūshū, SW Japan
Miyakonzyô *see* Miyakonojō
Miyāneh *see* Miāneh
Miyazaki *109 B8* Miyazaki, Kyūshū, SW Japan
Mizil *86 C5* Prahova, SE Romania
Miziya *82 C1* Vratsa, NW Bulgaria
Mizpe Ramon *see* Mitspe Ramon
Mjøsa *63 B6 var.* Mjøsen. *lake* S Norway
Mjøsen *see* Mjøsa
Mladenovac *78 D4* Serbia, C Serbia
Mława *76 D3* Mazowieckie, C Poland
Mljet *79 B5 It.* Meleda; *anc.* Melita. *island* S Croatia
Mmabatho *56 C4* North-West, N South Africa
Moab *22 B5* Utah, W USA
Moa Island *126 C1 island* Queensland, NE Australia
Moanda *55 B6 var.* Mouanda. Haut-Ogooué, SE Gabon
Moba *55 E7* Katanga, E Dem. Rep. Congo
Mobay *see* Montego Bay
Mobaye *55 C5* Basse-Kotto, S Central African Republic
Moberly *23 G4* Missouri, C USA
Mobile *20 C3* Alabama, S USA
Mobutu Sese Seko, Lac *see* Albert, Lake
Moçâmedes *see* Namibe
Mochudi *56 C4* Kgatleng, SE Botswana
Mocímboa da Praia *57 F2 var.* Vila de Mocímboa da Praia. Cabo Delgado, N Mozambique
Môco *56 B2 var.* Morro de Môco. *mountain* W Angola
Mocoa *36 A4* Putumayo, SW Colombia
Môco, Morro de *see* Môco
Mocuba *57 E3* Zambézia, NE Mozambique

Modena – Nagyvárad

Modena 74 B3 anc. Mutina. Emilia-Romagna, N Italy
Modesto 25 B6 California, W USA
Modica 75 C7 anc. Motyca. Sicilia, Italy, C Mediterranean Sea
Modimolle 56 D4 prev. Nylstroom. Limpopo, NE South Africa
Modohn see Madona
Modriča 78 C3 Republika Srpska, N Bosnia and Herzegovina
Moe 127 C7 Victoria, SE Australia
Möen see Møn, Denmark
Moero, Lac see Mweru, Lake
Moeskroen see Mouscron
Mogadiscio/Mogadishu see Muqdisho
Mogador see Essaouira
Mogilëv see Mahilyow
Mogilev-Podol'skiy see Mohyliv-Podil's'kyy
Mogilno 76 C3 Kujawsko-pomorskie, C Poland
Moḩammadābād-e Rīgān 98 E4 Kermān, SE Iran
Mohammedia 48 C2 prev. Fédala. NW Morocco
Mohave, Lake 25 D7 reservoir Arizona/Nevada, W USA
Mohawk River 19 F3 river New York, NE USA
Mohéli see Mwali
Mohns Ridge 61 F3 undersea ridge Greenland Sea/Norwegian Sea
Moho 39 E4 Puno, SE Peru
Mohoro 51 C7 Pwani, E Tanzania
Mohyliv-Podil's'kyy 86 D3 Rus. Mogilev-Podol'skiy. Vinnyts'ka Oblast', C Ukraine
Moi 63 A6 Rogaland, S Norway
Moili see Mwali
Mo i Rana 62 C3 Nordland, C Norway
Mõisaküla 84 D3 Ger. Moiseküll. Viljandimaa, S Estonia
Moiseküll see Mõisaküla
Moissac 69 B6 Tarn-et-Garonne, S France
Mojácar 71 E5 Andalucía, S Spain
Mojave Desert 25 D7 plain California, W USA
Mokrany see Makrany
Moktama see Martaban
Mol 65 C5 prev. Moll. Antwerpen, N Belgium
Moldavia see Moldova
Moldavian SSR/Moldavskaya SSR see Moldova
Molde 63 A5 Møre og Romsdal, S Norway
Moldotau, Khrebet see Moldo-Too, Khrebet
Moldo-Too, Khrebet 101 G2 prev. Khrebet Moldotau. mountain range C Kyrgyzstan
Moldova 86 D3 off. Republic of Moldova, var. Moldavia; prev. Moldavian SSR, Rus. Moldavskaya SSR. country SE Europe
Moldova Nouă 86 A4 Ger. Neumoldowa, Hung. Újmoldova. Caraş-Severin, SW Romania
Moldova, Republic of see Moldova
Moldoveanul see Vârful Moldoveanu
Molfetta 75 E5 Puglia, SE Italy
Moll see Mol
Mollendo 39 E4 Arequipa, SW Peru
Mölndal 63 B7 Västra Götaland, S Sweden
Molochans'k 87 G4 Rus. Molochansk. Zaporiz'ka Oblast', SE Ukraine
Molodechno/Molodeczno see Maladzyechna
Molodezhnaya 132 C2 Russian research station Antarctica
Moloka'i 25 B8 var. Molokai. island Hawaiian Islands, Hawai'i, USA
Molokai Fracture Zone 131 E2 tectonic feature NE Pacific Ocean
Molopo 56 C4 seasonal river Botswana/South Africa
Mólos 83 B5 Stereá Ellás, C Greece
Molotov see Severodvinsk, Arkhangel'skaya Oblast', Russian Federation
Molotov see Perm', Permskaya Oblast', Russian Federation
Moluccas 117 F4 Dut. Molukken, Eng. Moluccas; prev. Spice Islands. island group E Indonesia
Moluccas see Maluku
Molucca Sea 117 F4 Ind. Laut Maluku. sea E Indonesia
Molukken see Maluku
Mombasa 51 D7 Coast, SE Kenya
Mombetsu see Monbetsu
Momchilgrad 82 D3 prev. Mastanli. Kŭrdzhali, S Bulgaria
Møn 63 B8 prev. Möen. island SE Denmark
Mona, Canal de la see Mona Passage
Monaco 69 C7 var. Monaco-Ville; anc. Monoecus. country capital S Monaco
Monaco 69 E6 off. Principality of Monaco. country W Europe
Monaco see München
Monaco, Port de 69 C8 bay S Monaco W Mediterranean Sea
Monaco, Principality of see Monaco
Monaco-Ville see Monaco
Monahans 27 E3 Texas, SW USA
Mona, Isla 33 E3 island W Puerto Rico
Mona Passage 33 E3 Sp. Canal de la Mona. channel Dominican Republic/Puerto Rico
Monastir see Bitola
Monbetsu 108 D2 var. Mombetsu, Monbetu. Hokkaidō, NE Japan
Monbetu see Monbetsu
Moncalieri 74 A2 Piemonte, NW Italy
Monchegorsk 88 C2 Murmanskaya Oblast', NW Russian Federation
Monclova 28 D2 Coahuila de Zaragoza, NE Mexico
Moncton 17 F4 New Brunswick, SE Canada
Mondovì 74 A2 Piemonte, NW Italy
Monfalcone 74 D2 Friuli-Venezia Giulia, NE Italy
Monforte de Lemos 70 C1 Galicia, NW Spain
Mongo 54 C3 Guéra, C Chad
Mongolia 104 C2 Mong. Mongol Uls. country E Asia
Mongolia, Plateau of 102 D1 plateau E Mongolia
Mongol Uls see Mongolia
Mongora see Saidu Sharif
Mongos, Chaîne des see Bongo, Massif des
Mongu 56 C2 Western, W Zambia
Monkchester see Newcastle upon Tyne
Monkey Bay 57 E2 Southern, SE Malawi
Monkey River see Monkey River Town
Monkey River Town 30 C2 var. Monkey River. Toledo, SE Belize
Monoecus see Monaco
Mono Lake 25 C6 lake California, W USA
Monostor see Beli Manastir
Monovar 71 F4 Cat. Monover. País Valenciano, E Spain
Monover see Monovar
Monroe 20 B2 Louisiana, S USA
Monrovia 52 C5 country capital W Liberia
Mons 65 B6 Dut. Bergen. Hainaut, S Belgium
Monselice 74 C2 Veneto, NE Italy
Montana 82 C2 prev. Ferdinand, Mikhaylovgrad. Montana, NW Bulgaria
Montana 22 B1 off. State of Montana, also known as Mountain State, Treasure State. state NW USA
Montargis 68 C4 Loiret, C France
Montauban 69 B6 Tarn-et-Garonne, S France
Montbéliard 68 D4 Doubs, E France
Mont Cenis, Col du 69 D5 pass E France
Mont-de-Marsan 69 B6 Landes, SW France
Monteagudo 39 G4 Chuquisaca, S Bolivia
Montecarlo 69 C8 Misiones, NE Argentina
Monte Caseros 42 D3 Corrientes, NE Argentina
Monte Cristi 32 D3 var. San Fernando de Monte Cristi. NW Dominican Republic
Monte Croce Carnico, Passo di see Plöcken Pass
Montegiardino 74 E2 SE San Marino
Montego Bay 32 A4 var. Mobay. W Jamaica
Montélimar 69 D5 anc. Acunum Acusio, Montilium Adhemari. Drôme, E France
Montemorelos 29 E3 Nuevo León, NE Mexico
Montenegro 79 C5 Serb. Crna Gora. country SW Europe
Monte Patria 42 B3 Coquimbo, N Chile
Monterey 25 B6 California, W USA
Monterey see Monterrey
Monterey Bay 25 A6 bay California, W USA
Montería 36 B2 Córdoba, NW Colombia
Montero 39 G4 Santa Cruz, C Bolivia
Monterrey 29 E3 var. Monterey. Nuevo León, NE Mexico
Montes Claros 41 F3 Minas Gerais, SE Brazil
Montevideo 42 D4 country capital Montevideo, S Uruguay
Montevideo 23 F2 Minnesota, N USA
Montgenèvre, Col de 69 D5 pass France/Italy
Montgomery 20 D2 state capital Alabama, S USA
Montgomery see Sāhīwāl
Monthey 73 A7 Valais, SW Switzerland
Montilium Adhemari see Montélimar
Montluçon 68 C4 Allier, C France
Montoro 70 D4 Andalucía, S Spain
Montpelier 19 G2 state capital Vermont, NE USA
Montpellier 69 C6 Hérault, S France
Montréal 17 E4 Eng. Montreal. Québec, SE Canada
Montrose 66 D3 E Scotland, United Kingdom
Montrose 22 C5 Colorado, C USA
Montserrat 33 G3 var. Emerald Isle. UK dependent territory E West Indies
Monywa 114 B3 Sagaing, C Myanmar (Burma)
Monza 74 B2 Lombardia, N Italy
Monze 56 D2 Southern, S Zambia
Monzón 71 F2 Aragón, NE Spain
Moonie 127 D5 Queensland, E Australia
Moon-Sund see Väinameri
Moora 125 A6 Western Australia
Moore 27 G1 Oklahoma, C USA
Moore, Lake 125 B6 lake Western Australia
Moorhead 23 F2 Minnesota, N USA
Moose 16 C3 river Ontario, S Canada
Moosehead Lake 19 G1 lake Maine, NE USA
Moosonee 16 C3 Ontario, SE Canada
Mopti 53 E3 Mopti, C Mali
Moquegua 39 E4 Moquegua, SE Peru
Mora 63 C5 Dalarna, C Sweden
Morales 30 C2 Izabal, E Guatemala
Morant Bay 32 B5 E Jamaica
Moratalla 71 E4 Murcia, SE Spain
Morava 77 C5 var. March. river C Europe
Morava see Moravia, Czech Republic
Morava see Velika Morava, Serbia
Moravia 77 B5 Cz. Morava, Ger. Mähren. cultural region E Czech Republic
Moray Firth 66 C3 inlet N Scotland, United Kingdom
Morea see Pelopónnisos
Moreau River 22 D2 river South Dakota, N USA
Moree 127 D5 New South Wales, SE Australia
Morelia 29 E4 Michoacán de Ocampo, S Mexico
Morena, Sierra 70 C4 mountain range S Spain
Moreni 86 C5 Dâmboviţa, S Romania
Morgan City 20 B3 Louisiana, S USA
Darya-ye Morghab 100 D3 Rus. Murgab, Murghab, Turkm. Murgap, Murgap Deryasy. river Afghanistan/Turkmenistan
Darya-ye Morghab 100 D3 Rus. Murgab, Murghab, Turkm. Murgap, Murgap Deryasy. river Afghanistan/Turkmenistan
Morghāb, Daryā-ye see Murgap
Morioka 108 D4 Iwate, Honshū, C Japan
Morlaix 68 A3 Finistère, NW France
Mormon State see Utah
Mornington Abyssal Plain 45 A7 abyssal plain SE Pacific Ocean
Mornington Island 126 B2 island Wellesley Islands, Queensland, N Australia
Morocco 48 B3 off. Kingdom of Morocco, Ar. Al Mamlakah. country N Africa
Morocco see Marrakech
Morocco, Kingdom of see Morocco
Morogoro 51 C7 Morogoro, E Tanzania
Moro Gulf 117 E3 gulf S Philippines
Morón 32 C2 Ciego de Ávila, C Cuba
Mörön 104 D2 Hövsgöl, N Mongolia
Morondava 57 F3 Toliara, W Madagascar
Moroni 57 F2 country capital Grande Comore, NW Comoros
Morotai, Pulau 117 F3 island Maluku, E Indonesia
Morotiri see Marotiri
Morphou see Güzelyurt
Morrinsville 128 D3 Waikato, North Island, New Zealand
Morris 23 F2 Minnesota, N USA
Morris Jesup, Kap 61 E1 headland N Greenland
Morvan 68 D4 physical region C France
Moscow 24 C2 Idaho, NW USA
Moscow see Moskva
Mosel 73 A5 Fr. Moselle. river W Europe
Mosel see Moselle
Moselle 65 E8 Ger. Mosel. river W Europe
Moselle see Mosel
Mosgiel 129 B7 Otago, South Island, New Zealand
Moshi 51 C7 Kilimanjaro, NE Tanzania
Mosjøen 62 B4 Nordland, C Norway
Moskovskiy see Moskva
Moskva 89 B5 Eng. Moscow. country capital Gorod Moskva, W Russian Federation
Moskva 101 E3 Rus. Moskovskiy; prev. Chubek. SW Tajikistan
Moson and Magyaróvár see Mosonmagyaróvár
Mosonmagyaróvár 77 C6 Ger. Wieselburg-Ungarisch-Altenburg; prev. Moson and Magyaróvár, Ger. Wieselburg and Ungarisch-Altenburg. Győr-Moson-Sopron, NW Hungary
Mosquito Coast 31 E3 var. Miskito Coast, Eng. Mosquito Coast. coastal region E Nicaragua
Mosquito Coast see La Mosquitia
Mosquito Gulf 31 F4 Eng. Mosquito Gulf. gulf N Panama
Mosquito Gulf see Mosquitos, Golfo de los
Moss 63 B6 Østfold, S Norway
Mossâmedes see Namibe
Mosselbaai 56 C5 var. Mosselbai, Eng. Mossel Bay. Western Cape, SW South Africa
Mosselbai/Mossel Bay see Mosselbaai
Mossendjo 55 B6 Niari, SW Congo
Mossoró 41 G2 Rio Grande do Norte, NE Brazil
Most 76 A4 Ger. Brüx. Ústecký Kraj, NW Czech Republic
Mosta 80 B5 var. Musta. C Malta
Mostaganem 48 D2 var. Mestghanem. NW Algeria
Mostar 78 C4 Federacija Bosna I Hercegovina, S Bosnia and Herzegovina
Mosty see Masty
Mosul see Al Mawşil
Mota del Cuervo 71 E3 Castilla-La Mancha, C Spain
Motagua, Río 30 B2 river Guatemala/Honduras
Mother of Presidents/Mother of States see Virginia
Motril 70 D5 Andalucía, S Spain
Motru 86 B4 Gorj, SW Romania
Motueka 129 C5 Tasman, South Island, New Zealand
Motul 29 H3 var. Motul de Felipe Carrillo Puerto. Yucatán, SE Mexico
Motul de Felipe Carrillo Puerto see Motul
Motyca see Modica
Mouanda see Moanda
Mouhoun see Black Volta
Mouila 55 A6 Ngounié, C Gabon
Moukden see Shenyang
Mould Bay 15 E2 Prince Patrick Island, Northwest Territories, N Canada
Moulins 68 C4 Allier, C France
Moulmein see Mawlamyine
Moundou 54 B4 Logone-Occidental, SW Chad
Moŭng Roessei 115 D5 Bătdâmbâng, W Cambodia
Moun Hou see Black Volta
Mountain Home 20 B1 Arkansas, C USA
Mountain State see Montana
Mountain State see West Virginia
Mount Cook 129 B6 Canterbury, South Island, New Zealand
Mount Desert Island 19 H2 island Maine, NE USA
Mount Gambier 127 B7 South Australia
Mount Isa 126 B3 Queensland, C Australia
Mount Magnet 125 B5 Western Australia
Mount Pleasant 23 G4 Iowa, C USA
Mount Pleasant 18 C3 Michigan, N USA
Mount Vernon 18 B5 Illinois, N USA
Mount Vernon 24 B1 Washington, NW USA
Mourdi, Dépression du 54 C2 desert lowland Chad/Sudan
Mouscron 65 A6 Dut. Moeskroen. Hainaut, W Belgium
Mouse River see Souris River
Moussoro 54 B3 Kanem, W Chad
Moyen-Congo see Congo (Republic of)
Mo'ynoq 100 C1 Rus. Muynak. Qoraqalpog'iston Respublikasi, NW Uzbekistan
Moyobamba 38 B2 San Martín, NW Peru
Moyu 104 B3 var. Karakax. Xinjiang Uygur Zizhiqu, NW China
Moyynkum, Peski 101 F1 Kaz. Moyynqum. desert S Kazakhstan
Moyynqum see Moyynkum, Peski
Mozambika, Lakandranon' i see Mozambique Channel
Mozambique 57 E3 off. Republic of Mozambique; prev. People's Republic of Mozambique, Portuguese East Africa. country S Africa
Mozambique Basin see Natal Basin
Mozambique, Canal de see Mozambique Channel
Mozambique Channel 57 E3 Fr. Canal de Mozambique, Mal. Lakandranon' i Mozambika. strait W Indian Ocean
Mozambique, People's Republic of see Mozambique
Mozambique Plateau 47 D7 var. Mozambique Rise. undersea plateau SW Indian Ocean
Mozambique, Republic of see Mozambique
Mozambique Rise see Mozambique Plateau
Mozyr' see Mazyr
Mpama 55 B6 river C Congo
Mpika 56 D2 Northern, NE Zambia
Mqinvartsveri see Kazbek
Mrągowo 76 D2 Ger. Sensburg. Warmińsko-Mazurskie, NE Poland
Mtkvari see Kura
Mtwara 51 D8 Mtwara, SE Tanzania
Mualo see Messalo, Rio
Muang Chiang Rai see Chiang Rai
Muang Kalasin see Kalasin
Muang Khammouan see Thakhèk
Muang Không 115 D5 Champasak, S Laos
Muang Khôngxédôn 115 D5 var. Khong Sedone. Salavan, S Laos
Muang Khon Kaen see Khon Kaen
Muang Lampang see Lampang
Muang Loei see Loei
Muang Lom Sak see Lom Sak
Muang Nakhon Sawan see Nakhon Sawan
Muang Namo 114 C3 Oudômxai, N Laos
Muang Nan see Nan
Muang Phalan 114 D4 var. Muang Phalane. Savannakhét, S Laos
Muang Phalane see Muang Phalan
Muang Phayao see Phayao
Muang Phitsanulok see Phitsanulok
Muang Phrae see Phrae
Muang Roi Et see Roi Et
Muang Sakon Nakhon see Sakon Nakhon
Muang Samut Prakan see Samut Prakan
Muang Sing 114 C3 Louang Namtha, N Laos
Muang Ubon see Ubon Ratchathani
Muang Xaignabouri see Xaignabouli
Muar 116 B3 var. Bandar Maharani. Johor, Peninsular Malaysia
Mucojo 57 F2 Cabo Delgado, N Mozambique
Mudanjiang 107 E3 var. Mu-tan-chiang. Heilongjiang, NE China
Mudon 115 B5 Mon State, S Myanmar (Burma)
Muenchen see München
Muenster see Münster
Mufulira 56 D2 Copperbelt, C Zambia
Mughla see Muğla
Muğla 94 A4 var. Mughla. Muğla, SW Turkey
Mūḩ, Sabkhat al 96 C3 lake C Syria
Muhu Väin see Väinameri
Muisne 38 A1 Esmeraldas, NW Ecuador
Mukacheve 86 B3 Hung. Munkács, Rus. Mukachevo. Zakarpats'ka Oblast', W Ukraine
Mukachevo see Mukacheve
Mukalla see Al Mukallā
Mukden see Shenyang
Mula 71 E4 Murcia, SE Spain
Mulakatholhu 110 B4 var. Meemu Atoll, Mulaku Atoll. atoll C Maldives
Mulaku Atoll see Mulakatholhu
Muleshoe 27 E2 Texas, SW USA
Mulhacén 71 E5 var. Cerro de Mulhacén. mountain S Spain
Mulhacén, Cerro de see Mulhacén
Mülhausen see Mulhouse
Mülheim 73 A6 var. Mulheim an der Ruhr. Nordrhein-Westfalen, W Germany
Mulheim an der Ruhr see Mülheim
Mulhouse 68 E4 Ger. Mülhausen. Haut-Rhin, NE France
Müller-gerbergte see Muller, Pegunungan
Muller, Pegunungan 116 D4 Dut. Müller-gerbergte. mountain range Borneo, C Indonesia
Mull, Isle of 66 B4 island W Scotland, United Kingdom
Mulongo 55 D7 Katanga, SE Dem. Rep. Congo
Multān 112 C2 Punjab, E Pakistan
Mumbai 112 C5 prev. Bombay. state capital Mahārāshtra, W India
Munamägi see Suur Munamägi
Münchberg 73 C5 Bayern, E Germany
München 73 C6 var. Muenchen, Eng. Munich, It. Monaco. Bayern, SE Germany
Muncie 18 C4 Indiana, N USA
Mungbere 55 E5 Orientale, NE Dem. Rep. Congo
Mu Nggava see Rennell
Munich see München
Munkács see Mukacheve
Münster 72 A4 var. Muenster, Münster in Westfalen. Nordrhein-Westfalen, W Germany
Munster 67 A6 Ir. Cúige Mumhan. cultural region S Ireland
Münster in Westfalen see Münster
Muong Xiang Ngeun 114 C4 var. Xieng Ngeun. Louangphabang, N Laos
Muonio 62 D3 Lappi, N Finland
Muonioälv/Muoniojoki see Muonionjoki
Muonionjoki 62 D3 var. Muoniojoki, Swe. Muonioälv. river Finland/Sweden
Muqāţ 97 C5 Al Mafraq, E Jordan
Muqdisho 51 D6 Eng. Mogadishu, It. Mogadiscio. country capital Banaadir, S Somalia
Mur 73 E7 SCr. Mura. river C Europe
Mura see Mur
Muradiye 95 F3 Van, E Turkey
Murapara see Murupara
Murata 74 E2 S San Marino
Murchison River 125 A5 river Western Australia
Murcia 71 F4 Murcia, SE Spain
Murcia 71 E4 autonomous community SE Spain
Mureş 86 A4 river Hungary/Romania
Murfreesboro 20 D1 Tennessee, S USA
Murgab see Morghāb, Daryā-ye/Murgap/Murghob
Murgab see Morghāb, Daryā-ye/Murgap/Murghob
Murgab see Murghob
Murgap 100 D3 Mary Welaýaty, S Turkmenistan
Murgap 100 D3 var. Deryasy Murgap, Murghab, Pash. Daryā-ye Morghāb, Rus. Murgab. river Afghanistan/Turkmenistan
Murgap see Morghāb, Daryā-ye
Murgap see Morghāb, Daryā-ye
Murgap Deryasy see Morghāb, Daryā-ye
Murgap Deryasy see Morghāb, Daryā-ye
Murghab see Morghāb, Daryā-ye
Murghab see Morghāb, Daryā-ye
Murghob 101 F3 Rus. Murgab. SE Tajikistan
Murgon 127 E5 Queensland, E Australia
Mūrītānīyah see Mauritania
Müritz 72 C3 var. Müritzee. lake NE Germany
Müritzee see Müritz
Murmansk 88 C2 Murmanskaya Oblast', NW Russian Federation
Murmashi 88 C2 Murmanskaya Oblast', NW Russian Federation
Murom 89 B5 Vladimirskaya Oblast', W Russian Federation
Muroran 108 D3 Hokkaidō, NE Japan
Muros 70 B1 Galicia, NW Spain
Murray Fracture Zone 131 E2 fracture zone NE Pacific Ocean
Murray Range see Murray Ridge
Murray Ridge 90 C5 var. Murray Range. undersea ridge N Arabian Sea
Murray River 127 B6 river SE Australia
Murrumbidgee River 127 C6 river New South Wales, SE Australia
Murska Sobota 73 E7 Ger. Olsnitz. NE Slovenia
Murupara 128 E3 var. Murapara. Bay of Plenty, North Island, New Zealand
Murviedro see Sagunto
Murwāra 113 E4 Madhya Pradesh, N India
Murwillumbah 127 E5 New South Wales, SE Australia
Murzuq, Edeyin see Murzuq, Idhān
Murzuq, Idhan 49 F4 var. Edeyin Murzuq. desert SW Libya
Mürzzuschlag 73 E7 Steiermark, E Austria
Muş 95 F3 var. Mush. Muş, E Turkey
Musa, Gebel 50 C2 var. Gebel Mûsa. mountain NE Egypt
Mûsa, Gebel see Mūsá, Jabal
Musala 82 B3 mountain W Bulgaria
Muscat see Masqaţ
Muscat and Oman see Oman
Muscatine 23 G3 Iowa, C USA
Musgrave Ranges 125 D5 mountain range South Australia
Musina 56 D3 prev. Messina. Limpopo, NE South Africa
Muskegon 18 C3 Michigan, N USA
Muskogean see Tallahassee
Muskogee 27 G1 Oklahoma, C USA
Musoma 51 C6 Mara, N Tanzania
Musta see Mosta
Mustafa-Pasha see Svilengrad
Musters, Lago 43 B6 lake S Argentina
Muswellbrook 127 D6 New South Wales, SE Australia
Mut 94 C4 İçel, S Turkey
Mu-tan-chiang see Mudanjiang
Mutare 56 D3 var. Mutari; prev. Umtali. Manicaland, E Zimbabwe
Mutari see Mutare
Mutina see Modena
Mutsu-wan 108 D3 bay N Japan
Muttonbird Islands 129 A8 island group SW New Zealand
Mu Us Shadi 105 E3 var. Ordos Desert; prev. Mu Us Shamo. desert N China
Mu Us Shamo see Mu Us Shadi
Muy Muy 30 D3 Matagalpa, C Nicaragua
Muynak see Mo'ynoq
Mužlja 78 D3 Hung. Felsőmuzslya; prev. Gornja Mužlja. Vojvodina, N Serbia
Mwali 57 F2 var. Moili, Fr. Mohéli. island S Comoros
Mwanza 51 B6 Mwanza, NW Tanzania
Mweka 55 C6 Kasai-Occidental, C Dem. Rep. Congo
Mwene-Ditu 55 D7 Kasai-Oriental, S Dem. Rep. Congo
Mweru, Lake 55 D7 var. Lac Moero. lake Dem. Rep. Congo/Zambia
Myadel' see Myadzyel
Myadzyel 85 C5 Pol. Miadzioł Nowy, Rus. Myadel'. Minskaya Voblasts', N Belarus
Myanaung 114 B4 Ayeyarwady, SW Myanmar (Burma)
Myaungmya 114 A4 Ayeyarwady, SW Myanmar (Burma)
Myaydo see Aunglan
Myeik 115 B6 var. Mergui. Tanintharyi, S Myanmar (Burma)
Myerkulavichy 85 D7 Rus. Merkulovichi. Homyel'skaya Voblasts', SE Belarus
Myingyan 114 B3 Mandalay, C Myanmar (Burma)
Myitkyina 114 B2 Kachin State, N Myanmar (Burma)
Mykolayiv 87 E4 Rus. Nikolayev. Mykolayivs'ka Oblast', S Ukraine
Mykonos 83 D6 var. Míkonos. island Kykládes, Greece, Aegean Sea
Myrhorod 87 F2 Rus. Mirgorod. Poltavs'ka Oblast', NE Ukraine
Mýrina 82 D4 var. Mírina. Límnos, SE Greece
Myrtle Beach 21 F2 South Carolina, SE USA
Mýrtos 83 D8 Kríti, Greece, E Mediterranean Sea
Myrtoum Mare see Mirtóo Pélagos
Myślibórz 76 B3 Zachodnio-pomorskie, NW Poland
Mysore 110 C2 var. Maisur. Karnātaka, W India
Mysore see Karnātaka
My Tho 115 E6 var. Mi Tho. Tiên Giang, S Vietnam
Mytilene see Mytilíni
Mytilíni 83 D5 var. Mitilíni; anc. Mytilene. Lésvos, E Greece
Mzuzu 57 E2 Northern, N Malawi

N

Naberezhnyye Chelny 89 D5 prev. Brezhnev. Respublika Tatarstan, W Russian Federation
Nablus 97 A6 var. Năbulus, Heb. Shekhem; anc. Neapolis, Bibl. Shechem. N West Bank
Năbulus see Nablus
Nacala 57 F2 Nampula, NE Mozambique
Na-Ch'ii see Nagqu
Nada see Danzhou
Nadi 123 E4 prev. Nandi. Viti Levu, W Fiji
Nadur 80 A5 Gozo, N Malta
Nadvirna 86 C3 Pol. Nadwórna, Rus. Nadvornaya. Ivano-Frankivs'ka Oblast', W Ukraine
Nadvoitsy 88 B3 Respublika Kareliya, NW Russian Federation
Nadvornaya/Nadwórna see Nadvirna
Nadym 92 C3 Yamalo-Nenetskiy Avtonomnyy Okrug, N Russian Federation
Náfpaktos 83 B5 var. Návpaktos. Dytikí Ellás, C Greece
Náfplio 83 B6 prev. Návplion. Pelopónnisos, S Greece
Naga 117 E2 off. Naga City; prev. Nueva Caceres. Luzon, N Philippines
Naga City see Naga
Nagano 109 C5 Nagano, Honshū, S Japan
Nagaoka 109 D5 Niigata, Honshū, C Japan
Nagara Pathom see Nakhon Pathom
Nagara Sridharmaraj see Nakhon Si Thammarat
Nagara Svarga see Nakhon Sawan
Nagasaki 109 A7 Nagasaki, Kyūshū, SW Japan
Nagato 109 A7 Yamaguchi, Honshū, SW Japan
Nāgercoil 110 C3 Tamil Nādu, SE India
Nagorno-Karabakh 95 G3 var. Nagorno-Karabakhskaya Avtonomnaya Oblast, Arm. Lerrnayin Gharabakh, Az. Dağliq Quarabağ, Rus. Nagornyy Karabakh. former autonomous region SW Azerbaijan
Nagorno- Karabakhskaya Avtonomnaya Oblast see Nagorno-Karabakh
Nagornyy Karabakh see Nagorno-Karabakh
Nagoya 109 C6 Aichi, Honshū, SW Japan
Nāgpur 112 D4 Mahārāshtra, C India
Nagqu 104 C5 Chin. Na-Ch'ii; prev. Hei-ho. Xizang Zizhiqu, W China
Nagybánya see Baia Mare
Nagybecskerek see Zrenjanin
Nagydisznód see Cisnădie
Nagyenyed see Aiud
Nagykálló 77 E6 Szabolcs-Szatmár-Bereg, E Hungary
Nagykanizsa 77 C7 Ger. Grosskanizsa. Zala, SW Hungary
Nagykároly see Carei
Nagykikinda see Kikinda
Nagykőrös 77 D7 Pest, C Hungary
Nagymihály see Michalovce
Nagysurány see Šurany
Nagyszalonta see Salonta
Nagyszeben see Sibiu
Nagyszentmiklós see Sânnicolau Mare
Nagyszöllös see Vynohradiv
Nagyszombat see Trnava
Nagytapolcsány see Topoľčany
Nagyvárad see Oradea

Naha – Nizhyn

Naha *108 A3* Okinawa, Okinawa, SW Japan
Nahariya *97 A5 prev.* Nahariyya. Northern, N Israel
Nahariyya *see* Nahariya
Nahuel Huapí, Lago *43 B5 lake* W Argentina
Nain *17 F2* Newfoundland and Labrador, NE Canada
Nā'īn *98 D3* Eşfahān, C Iran
Nairobi *47 E5 country capital* Nairobi Area, S Kenya
Nairobi *51 C6* Nairobi Area, S Kenya
Naissus *see* Niš
Najaf *see* An Najaf
Najima *see* Fukuoka
Najin *107 E3* NE North Korea
Najrān *99 B6 var.* Abā as Su'ūd. Najrān, S Saudi Arabia
Nakambé *see* White Volta
Nakamura *109 B7 var.* Shimanto. Kōchi, Shikoku, SW Japan
Nakatsugawa *109 C6 var.* Nakatugawa. Gifu, Honshū, SW Japan
Nakatugawa *see* Nakatsugawa
Nakhichevan' *see* Naxçıvan
Nakhodka *93 G5* Primorskiy Kray, SE Russian Federation
Nakhon Pathom *115 C5 var.* Nagara Pathom, Nakorn Pathom. Nakhon Pathom, W Thailand
Nakhon Ratchasima *115 C5 var.* Khorat, Korat. Nakhon Ratchasima, E Thailand
Nakhon Sawan *115 C5 var.* Muang Nakhon Sawan, Nagara Svarga. Nakhon Sawan, W Thailand
Nakhon Si Thammarat *115 C7 var.* Nagara Sridharmaraj, Nakhon Sithamnaraj. Nakhon Si Thammarat, SW Thailand
Nakhon Sithamnaraj *see* Nakhon Si Thammarat
Nakorn Pathom *see* Nakhon Pathom
Nakuru *51 C6* Rift Valley, SW Kenya
Nal'chik *89 B8* Kabardino-Balkarskaya Respublika, SW Russian Federation
Nālūt *49 F2* NW Libya
Namakan Lake *18 A1 lake* Canada/USA
Namangan *101 F2* Namangan Viloyati, E Uzbekistan
Nambala *56 D2* Central, C Zambia
Nam Co *104 C5 lake* W China
Nam Đinh *114 D3* Nam Ha, N Vietnam
Namib Desert *56 B3 desert* W Namibia
Namibe *56 A2 Port.* Moçâmedes, Mossâmedes. Namibe, SW Angola
Namibia *56 B3 off.* Republic of Namibia, *var.* South West Africa, *Afr.* Suidwes-Afrika, *Ger.* Deutsch-Südwestafrika; *prev.* German Southwest Africa, South-West Africa. *country* S Africa
Namibia, Republic of *see* Namibia
Namnetes *see* Nantes
Namo *see* Namu Atoll
Nam Ou *114 C3 river* N Laos
Nampa *24 D3* Idaho, NW USA
Nampula *57 E2* Nampula, NE Mozambique
Namsos *62 B4* Nord-Trøndelag, C Norway
Nam Tha *114 C4 river* N Laos
Namu Atoll *122 D2 var.* Namo. *atoll* Ralik Chain, C Marshall Islands
Namur *65 C6 Dut.* Namen. Namur, SE Belgium
Namyit Island *106 C8 island* S Spratly Islands
Nan *114 C4 var.* Muang Nan. Nan, NW Thailand
Nanaimo *14 D5* Vancouver Island, British Columbia, SW Canada
Nanchang *106 C5 var.* Nan-ch'ang, Nanch'ang-hsien. *province capital* Jiangxi, S China
Nan-ch'ang *see* Nanchang
Nanch'ang-hsien *see* Nanchang
Nan-ching *see* Nanjing
Nancy *68 D3* Meurthe-et-Moselle, NE France
Nandaime *30 D3* Granada, SW Nicaragua
Nānded *112 D5* Mahārāshtra, C India
Nandi *see* Nadi
Nándorhgy *see* Oţelu Roşu
Nandyāl *110 C1* Andhra Pradesh, E India
Nan Hai *see* South China Sea
Naniwa *see* Ōsaka
Nanjing *106 D5 var.* Nan-ching, Nanking; *prev.* Chianning, Chian-ning, Kiang-ning, Jiangsu. *province capital* Jiangsu, E China
Nanking *see* Nanjing
Nanning *106 B6 var.* Nan-ning; *prev.* Yung-ning. Guangxi Zhuangzu Zizhiqu, S China
Nan-ning *see* Nanning
Nanortalik *60 C5* Kitaa, S Greenland
Nanpan Jiang *114 D2 river* S China
Nanping *106 D6 var.* Nan-p'ing; *prev.* Yenping. Fujian, SE China
Nan-p'ing *see* Nanping
Nansei Syotō Trench *see* Ryukyu Trench
Nansen Basin *133 C4 undersea basin* Arctic Ocean
Nansen Cordillera *133 B3 var.* Arctic Mid Oceanic Ridge, Nansen Ridge. *seamount range* Arctic Ocean
Nansen Ridge *see* Nansen Cordillera
Nansha Qundao *see* Spratly Islands
Nanterre *68 D1* Hauts-de-Seine, N France
Nantes *68 B4 Bret.* Naoned; *anc.* Condivincum, Namnetes. Loire-Atlantique, NW France
Nantucket Island *19 G3 island* Massachusetts, NE USA
Nanumaga *123 E3 var.* Nanumanga. *atoll* NW Tuvalu
Nanumanga *see* Nanumaga
Nanumea Atoll *123 E3 atoll* NW Tuvalu
Nanyang *106 C5 var.* Nan-yang. Henan, C China
Nan-yang *see* Nanyang
Naoned *see* Nantes
Napa *25 B6* California, W USA
Napier *128 E4* Hawke's Bay, North Island, New Zealand
Naples *21 E5* Florida, SE USA
Naples *see* Napoli
Napo *34 A3 province* NE Ecuador
Napoléon-Vendée *see* la Roche-sur-Yon
Napoli *75 C5 Eng.* Naples, *Ger.* Neapel; *anc.* Neapolis. Campania, S Italy
Napo, Río *38 C1 river* Ecuador/Peru
Naracoorte *127 B7* South Australia
Naradhivas *see* Narathiwat
Narathiwat *115 C7 var.* Naradhivas. Narathiwat, SW Thailand
Narbada *see* Narmada
Narbo Martius *see* Narbonne
Narbonne *69 C6 anc.* Narbo Martius. Aude, S France
Narborough Island *see* Fernandina, Isla
Nares Abyssal Plain *see* Nares Plain
Nares Plain *13 E6 var.* Nares Abyssal Plain. *abyssal plain* NW Atlantic Ocean
Nares Stræde *see* Nares Strait
Nares Strait *60 D1 Dan.* Nares Stræde. *strait* Canada/Greenland
Narew *76 E3 river* E Poland
Narmada *102 B3 var.* Narbada. *river* C India
Narova *see* Narva
Narovlya *see* Narowlya
Narowlya *85 C8 Rus.* Narovlya. Homyel'skaya Voblasts', SE Belarus
Närpes *63 D5 Fin.* Närpiö. Länsi-Suomi, W Finland
Närpiö *see* Närpes
Narrabri *127 D6* New South Wales, SE Australia
Narrogin *125 B6* Western Australia
Narva *84 E2* Ida-Virumaa, NE Estonia
Narva *84 E2 prev.* Narova. *river* Estonia/Russian Federation
Narva Bay *84 E2 Est.* Narva Laht, *Ger.* Narwa-Bucht, *Rus.* Narvskiy Zaliv. *bay* Estonia/Russian Federation
Narva Laht *see* Narva Bay
Narva Reservoir *84 E2 Est.* Narva Veehoidla, *Rus.* Narvskoye Vodokhranilishche. *reservoir* Estonia/Russian Federation
Narva Veehoidla *see* Narva Reservoir
Narvik *62 C3* Nordland, C Norway
Narvskiy Zaliv *see* Narva Bay
Narvskoye Vodokhranilishche *see* Narva Reservoir
Narwa-Bucht *see* Narva Bay
Nar'yan-Mar *88 D3 prev.* Beloshchel'ye, Dzerzhinskiy. Nenetskiy Avtonomnyy Okrug, NW Russian Federation
Naryn *101 G2* Narynskaya Oblast', C Kyrgyzstan
Năsăud *86 B3 Ger.* Nussdorf, *Hung.* Naszód. Bistriţa-Năsăud, N Romania
Nase *see* Naze
Nāshik *112 C5 prev.* Nāsik. Mahārāshtra, W India
Nashua *19 G3* New Hampshire, NE USA
Nashville *20 C1 state capital* Tennessee, S USA
Näsijärvi *63 D5 lake* SW Finland
Nāsik *see* Nāshik
Nasir, Buhayrat/Nâşir,Buḥeiret *see* Nasser, Lake
Nāsiri *see* Ahvāz
Nasiriya *see* An Nāşirīyah
Nassau *32 C1 country capital* New Providence, N Bahamas
Nasser, Lake *50 B3 var.* Buhayrat Nasir, Buḥayrat Nāşir, Buḥeiret Nâşir. *lake* Egypt/Sudan
Naszód *see* Năsăud
Nata *56 C3* Central, NE Botswana
Natal *41 G2 state capital* Rio Grande do Norte, E Brazil
Natal Basin *119 A6 var.* Mozambique Basin. *undersea basin* W Indian Ocean
Natanya *see* Netanya
Natchez *20 B3* Mississippi, S USA
Natchitoches *20 A2* Louisiana, S USA
Nathanya *see* Netanya
Natitingou *53 F4* NW Benin
Natsrat *see* Natzrat
Natuna Islands *see* Natuna, Kepulauan
Natuna, Kepulauan *102 D4 var.* Natuna Islands. *island group* W Indonesia
Naturaliste Plateau *119 E6 undersea plateau* E Indian Ocean
Natzrat *97 A5 var.* Natsrat, *Ar.* En Nazira, *Eng.* Nazareth; *prev.* Nazerat. Northern, N Israel
Naugard *see* Nowogard
Naujamiestis *84 C4* Panevėžys, C Lithuania
Nauru *122 D2 off.* Republic of Nauru; *prev.* Pleasant Island. *country* W Pacific Ocean
Nauru, Republic of *see* Nauru
Nauta *38 C2* Loreto, N Peru
Navahrudak *85 C6 Pol.* Nowogródek, *Rus.* Novogrudok. Hrodzyenskaya Voblasts', W Belarus
Navanagar *see* Jāmnagar
Navapolatsk *85 D5 Rus.* Novopolotsk. Vitsyebskaya Voblasts', N Belarus
Navarra *71 E2 Eng./Fr.* Navarre. *autonomous community* N Spain
Navarre *see* Navarra
Navassa Island *32 C3 US unincorporated territory* C West Indies
Navoi *see* Navoiy
Navoiy *101 E2 Rus.* Navoi. Navoiy Viloyati, C Uzbekistan
Navojoa *28 C2* Sonora, NW Mexico
Navolat *see* Navolato
Navolato *28 C3 var.* Navolat. Sinaloa, C Mexico
Návpaktos *see* Náfpaktos
Návplion *see* Náfplio
Nawabashah *see* Nawābshāh
Nawābshāh *112 B3 var.* Nawabashah. Sind, S Pakistan
Naxçıvan *95 G3 Rus.* Nakhichevan'. SW Azerbaijan
Náxos *83 D6 var.* Naxos. Náxos, Kykládes, Greece, Aegean Sea
Náxos *83 D6 island* Kykládes, Greece, Aegean Sea
Nayoro *108 D2* Hokkaidō, NE Japan
Nay Pyi Taw *114 B4 country capital* Mandalay, C Myanmar (Burma)
Nazareth *see* Natzrat
Nazca *38 D4* Ica, S Peru
Nazca Ridge *35 A5 undersea ridge* E Pacific Ocean
Naze *108 B3 var.* Nase. Kagoshima, Amami-ōshima, SW Japan
Nazerat *see* Natzrat
Nazilli *94 A4* Aydın, SW Turkey
Nazrēt *51 C5 var.* Adama, Hadama. Oromīya, C Ethiopia
N'Dalatando *56 B1 Port.* Salazar, Vila Salazar. Cuanza Norte, NW Angola
Ndélé *54 C4* Bamingui-Bangoran, N Central African Republic
Ndendé *55 B6* Ngounié, S Gabon
Ndindi *55 A6* Nyanga, S Gabon
Ndjamena *54 B3 var.* N'Djamena; *prev.* Fort-Lamy. *country capital* Chari-Baguirmi, W Chad
N'Djamena *see* Ndjamena
Ndjolé *55 A5* Moyen-Ogooué, W Gabon
Ndola *56 D2* Copperbelt, C Zambia
Ndzouani *see* Anjouan
Neagh, Lough *67 B5 lake* E Northern Ireland, United Kingdom
Néa Moudanía *82 C4 var.* Néa Moudhaniá. Kentrikí Makedonía, N Greece
Néa Moudhaniá *see* Néa Moudanía
Neapel *see* Napoli
Neápoli *82 B4 prev.* Neápolis. Dytikí Makedonía, N Greece
Neápoli *83 D8* Kríti, Greece, E Mediterranean Sea
Neápoli *83 C7* Pelopónnisos, S Greece
Neápolis *see* Neápoli, Greece
Neapolis *see* Napoli, Italy
Neapolis *see* Nablus, West Bank
Near Islands *14 A2 island group* Aleutian Islands, Alaska, USA
Néa Zíchni *82 C3 var.* Néa Zíkhni; *prev.* Néa Zíkhna. Kentrikí Makedonía, NE Greece
Néa Zíkhna/Néa Zíkhni *see* Néa Zíchni
Nebaj *30 B2* Quiché, W Guatemala
Nebitdag *see* Balkanabat
Neblina, Pico da *40 C1 mountain* NW Brazil
Nebraska *22 D4 off.* State of Nebraska, *also known as* Blackwater State, Cornhusker State, Tree Planters State. *state* C USA
Nebraska City *23 F4* Nebraska, C USA
Neches River *27 H3 river* Texas, SW USA
Neckar *73 B6 river* SW Germany
Necochea *43 D5* Buenos Aires, E Argentina
Nederland *see* Netherlands
Neder Rijn *64 D4 Eng.* Lower Rhine. *river* C Netherlands
Nederweert *65 D5* Limburg, SE Netherlands
Neede *64 E3* Gelderland, E Netherlands
Neerpelt *65 D5* Limburg, NE Belgium
Neftekamsk *89 D5* Respublika Bashkortostan, W Russian Federation
Neftezavodsk *see* Seýdi
Negara Brunei Darussalam *see* Brunei
Negēlē *51 D5 var.* Negelli, *It.* Neghelli. Oromīya, C Ethiopia
Negelli *see* Negēlē
Negev *97 A7 Eng.* Negev. *desert* S Israel
Negev *see* HaNegev
Neghelli *see* Negēlē
Negomane *57 E2 var.* Negomano. Cabo Delgado, N Mozambique
Negomano *see* Negomane
Negombo *110 C3* Western Province, SW Sri Lanka
Negotin *78 E4* Serbia, E Serbia
Negra, Punta *38 A3 headland* NW Peru
Negreşti *see* Negreşti-Oaş
Negreşti-Oaş *86 B3 Hung.* Avasfelsőfalu; *prev.* Negreşti. Satu Mare, NE Romania
Negro, Río *43 C5 river* E Argentina
Negro, Río *40 D1 river* N South America
Negro, Río *42 D4 river* Brazil/Uruguay
Negros *117 E2 island* C Philippines
Nehbandān *98 E3* Khorāsān, E Iran
Neijiang *106 B5* Sichuan, C China
Neiva *36 B3* Huila, S Colombia
Nellore *110 D2* Andhra Pradesh, E India
Nelson *129 C5* Nelson, South Island, New Zealand
Nelson *15 G4 river* Manitoba, C Canada
Néma *52 D3* Hodh ech Chargui, SE Mauritania
Neman *84 B4 Ger.* Ragnit. Kaliningradskaya Oblast', W Russian Federation
Neman *84 A4 Bel.* Nyoman, *Ger.* Memel, *Lith.* Nemunas, *Pol.* Niemen. *river* NE Europe
Nemausus *see* Nîmes
Neméa *83 B6* Pelopónnisos, S Greece
Nemetocenna *see* Arras
Nemours *68 C3* Seine-et-Marne, N France
Nemunas *see* Neman
Nemuro *108 E2* Hokkaidō, NE Japan
Neochóri *83 B5* Dytikí Elláda, C Greece
Nepal *113 E3 off.* Nepal. *country* S Asia
Nepal *see* Nepal
Nereta *84 C4* Aizkraukle, S Latvia
Neretva *78 C4 river* Bosnia and Herzegovina/Croatia
Neris *85 C5 Bel.* Viliya, *Pol.* Wilia; *prev. Pol.* Wilja. *river* Belarus/Lithuania
Neris *see* Viliya
Nerva *70 C4* Andalucía, S Spain
Neryungri *93 F4* Respublika Sakha (Yakutiya), NE Russian Federation
Neskaupstadhur *61 E5* Austurland, E Iceland
Ness, Loch *66 C3 lake* N Scotland, United Kingdom
Nesterov *see* Zhovkva
Néstos *82 C3 Bul.* Mesta, *Turk.* Kara Su. *river* Bulgaria/Greece
Nesvizh *see* Nyasvizh
Netanya *97 A6 var.* Natanya, Nathanya. Central, C Israel
Netherlands *64 C3 off.* Kingdom of the Netherlands, *var.* Holland, *Dut.* Koninkrijk der Nederlanden, Nederland. *country* NW Europe
Netherlands Antilles *33 E5 prev.* Dutch West Indies. *Dutch autonomous region* S Caribbean Sea
Netherlands East Indies *see* Indonesia
Netherlands Guiana *see* Suriname
Netherlands, Kingdom of the *see* Netherlands
Netherlands New Guinea *see* Papua
Nettilling Lake *15 G3 lake* Baffin Island, Nunavut, N Canada
Netze *see* Noteć
Neu Amerika *see* Puławy
Neubrandenburg *72 D3* Mecklenburg-Vorpommern, NE Germany
Neuchâtel *73 A7 Ger.* Neuenburg. Neuchâtel, W Switzerland
Neuchâtel, Lac de *73 A7 Ger.* Neuenburger See. *lake* W Switzerland
Neuenburger See *see* Neuchâtel, Lac de
Neufchâteau *65 D8* Luxembourg, SE Belgium
Neugradisk *see* Nova Gradiška
Neuhof *see* Zgierz
Neukuhren *see* Pionerskiy
Neumarkt *see* Târgu Secuiesc, Covasna, Romania
Neumarkt *see* Târgu Mureş
Neumoldowa *see* Moldova Nouă
Neumünster *72 B2* Schleswig-Holstein, N Germany
Neunkirchen *73 A5* Saarland, SW Germany
Neuquén *43 B5* Neuquén, SE Argentina
Neuruppin *72 C3* Brandenburg, NE Germany
Neusalz an der Oder *see* Nowa Sól
Neu Sandec *see* Nowy Sącz
Neusatz *see* Novi Sad
Neusiedler See *73 E6 Hung.* Fertő. *lake* Austria/Hungary
Neusohl *see* Banská Bystrica
Neustadt *see* Baia Mare, Maramureş, Romania
Neustadt an der Haardt *see* Neustadt an der Weinstrasse
Neustadt an der Weinstrasse *73 B5 prev.* Neustadt an der Haardt, *hist.* Niewenstat; *anc.* Nova Civitas. Rheinland-Pfalz, SW Germany
Neustadtl *see* Novo mesto
Neustettin *see* Szczecinek
Neustrelitz *72 D3* Mecklenburg-Vorpommern, NE Germany
Neutra *see* Nitra
Neu-Ulm *73 B6* Bayern, S Germany
Neuwied *73 A5* Rheinland-Pfalz, W Germany
Neuzen *see* Terneuzen
Nevada *25 C5 off.* State of Nevada, *also known as* Battle Born State, Sagebrush State, Silver State. *state* W USA
Nevers *68 C4 anc.* Noviodunum. Nièvre, C France
Neves *54 E2* São Tomé, S Sao Tome and Principe, Africa
Nevinnomyssk *89 B7* Stavropol'skiy Kray, SW Russian Federation
Nevşehir *94 C3 var.* Nevshehr. Nevşehir, C Turkey
Newala *51 C8* Mtwara, SE Tanzania
New Albany *18 C5* Indiana, N USA
New Amsterdam *37 G3* E Guyana
Newark *19 F4* New Jersey, NE USA
New Bedford *19 G3* Massachusetts, NE USA
Newberg *24 B3* Oregon, NW USA
New Bern *21 F1* North Carolina, SE USA
New Braunfels *27 G4* Texas, SW USA
Newbridge *67 B6 Ir.* An Droichead Nua. Kildare, C Ireland
New Britain *122 B3 island* E Papua New Guinea
New Brunswick *17 E4 Fr.* Nouveau-Brunswick. *province* SE Canada
New Caledonia *122 D4 var.* Kanaky, *Fr.* Nouvelle-Calédonie. *French overseas territory* SW Pacific Ocean
New Caledonia *122 C5 island* SW Pacific Ocean
New Caledonia Basin *120 C4 undersea basin* W Pacific Ocean
Newcastle *127 D6* New South Wales, SE Australia
Newcastle *see* Newcastle upon Tyne
Newcastle upon Tyne *66 D4 var.* Newcastle, *hist.* Monkchester, *Lat.* Pons Aelii. NE England, United Kingdom
New Delhi *112 D3 country capital* Delhi, N India
New England of the West *see* Minnesota
Newfoundland *17 G3 Fr.* Terre-Neuve. *island* Newfoundland and Labrador, SE Canada
Newfoundland and Labrador *17 F2 Fr.* Terre Neuve. *province* E Canada
Newfoundland Basin *44 B3 undersea feature* NW Atlantic Ocean
New Georgia Islands *122 C3 island group* NW Solomon Islands
New Glasgow *17 F4* Nova Scotia, SE Canada
New Goa *see* Panaji
New Guinea *122 A3 Dut.* Nieuw Guinea, *Ind.* Irian. *island* Indonesia/Papua New Guinea
New Hampshire *19 F2 off.* State of New Hampshire, *also known as* Granite State. *state* NE USA
New Haven *19 G3* Connecticut, NE USA
New Hebrides *see* Vanuatu
New Iberia *20 B3* Louisiana, S USA
New Ireland *122 C3 island* NE Papua New Guinea
New Jersey *19 F4 off.* State of New Jersey, *also known as* The Garden State. *state* NE USA
Newman *124 B4* Western Australia
Newmarket *67 E6* E England, United Kingdom
New Mexico *26 C2 off.* State of New Mexico, *also known as* Land of Enchantment, Sunshine State. *state* SW USA
New Orleans *20 B3* Louisiana, S USA
New Plymouth *128 C4* Taranaki, North Island, New Zealand
Newport *67 D7* S England, United Kingdom
Newport *67 C7* SE Wales, United Kingdom
Newport *18 C4* Kentucky, S USA
Newport *19 G2* Vermont, NE USA
Newport News *19 F5* Virginia, NE USA
New Providence *32 C1 island* N Bahamas
Newquay *67 C7* SW England, United Kingdom
Newry *67 B5 Ir.* An tIúr. SE Northern Ireland, United Kingdom
New Sarum *see* Salisbury
New Siberian Islands *93 F1 Eng.* New Siberian Islands. *island group* N Russian Federation
New Siberian Islands *see* Novosibirskiye Ostrova
New South Wales *127 C6 state* SE Australia
Newton *23 G3* Iowa, C USA
Newton *23 F5* Kansas, C USA
Newtownabbey *67 B5 Ir.* Baile na Mainistreach. E Northern Ireland, United Kingdom
New Ulm *23 F2* Minnesota, N USA
New York *19 F4* New York, NE USA
New York *19 F3 state* NE USA
New Zealand *128 A4 country* SW Pacific Ocean
Neyveli *110 C2* Tamil Nādu, SE India
Nezhin *see* Nizhyn
Ngangze Co *104 B5 lake* W China
Ngaoundéré *54 B4 var.* N'Gaoundéré. Adamaoua, N Cameroon
N'Gaoundéré *see* Ngaoundéré
Ngazidja *57 F2 Fr.* Grande-Comore. *island* NW Comoros
N'Giva *56 B3 var.* Ondjiva, *Port.* Vila Pereira de Eça. Cunene, S Angola
Ngo *55 B6* Plateaux, SE Congo
Ngoko *55 B5 river* Cameroon/Congo
Ngourti *53 H3* Diffa, E Niger
Nguigmi *53 H3 var.* N'Guigmi. Diffa, SE Niger
N'Guigmi *see* Nguigmi
N'Gunza *see* Sumbe
Nguru *53 G3* Yobe, NE Nigeria
Nha Trang *115 E6* Khanh Hoa, S Vietnam
Niagara Falls *16 D5* Ontario, S Canada
Niagara Falls *19 E3* New York, NE USA
Niagara Falls *18 D3 waterfall* Canada/USA
Niamey *53 F3 country capital* Niamey, SW Niger
Niangay, Lac *53 E3 lake* E Mali
Nia-Nia *55 E5* Orientale, NE Dem. Rep. Congo
Nias, Pulau *116 A3 island* W Indonesia
Nicaea *see* Nice
Nicaragua *30 D3 off.* Republic of Nicaragua. *country* Central America
Lake Nicaragua *30 D4 var.* Cocibolca, Gran Lago, *Eng.* Lake Nicaragua. *lake* S Nicaragua
Nicaragua, Lake *see* Nicaragua, Lago de
Nicaragua, Republic of *see* Nicaragua
Nicaria *see* Ikaría
Nice *69 D6 It.* Nizza; *anc.* Nicaea. Alpes-Maritimes, SE France
Nicephorium *see* Ar Raqqah
Nicholas II Land *see* Severnaya Zemlya
Nicholls Town *32 C1* Andros Island, NW Bahamas
Nicobar Islands *102 B4 island group* India, E Indian Ocean
Nicosia *80 C5 Gk.* Lefkosía, *Turk.* Lefkoşa. *country capital* C Cyprus
Nicoya *30 D4* Guanacaste, W Costa Rica
Nicoya, Golfo de *30 D5 gulf* W Costa Rica
Nicoya, Península de *30 D4 peninsula* NW Costa Rica
Nida *84 A3 Ger.* Nidden. Klaipėda, SW Lithuania
Nidaros *see* Trondheim
Nidden *see* Nida
Nidzica *76 D3 Ger.* Niedenburg. Warmińsko-Mazurskie, NE Poland
Niedenburg *see* Nidzica
Niedere Tauern *77 A6 mountain range* C Austria
Niemen *see* Neman
Nieśwież *see* Nyasvizh
Nieuw Amsterdam *37 G3* Commewijne, NE Suriname
Nieuw-Bergen *64 D4* Limburg, SE Netherlands
Nieuwegein *64 C4* Utrecht, C Netherlands
Nieuw Guinea *see* New Guinea
Nieuw Nickerie *37 G3* Nickerie, NW Suriname
Niewenstat *see* Neustadt an der Weinstrasse
Niğde *94 C4* Niğde, C Turkey
Niger *53 F3 off.* Republic of Niger. *country* W Africa
Niger *53 F4 river* W Africa
Nigeria *53 F4 off.* Federal Republic of Nigeria. *country* W Africa
Nigeria, Federal Republic of *see* Nigeria
Niger, Mouths of the *53 F5 delta* S Nigeria
Niger, Republic of *see* Niger
Nihon *see* Japan
Niigata *109 D5* Niigata, Honshū, C Japan
Niihama *109 B7* Ehime, Shikoku, SW Japan
Ni'ihau *25 A7 var.* Niihau. *island* Hawai'i, USA, C Pacific Ocean
Nii-jima *109 D6 island* E Japan
Nijkerk *64 D3* Gelderland, C Netherlands
Nijlen *65 C5* Antwerpen, N Belgium
Nijmegen *64 D4 Ger.* Nimwegen; *anc.* Noviomagus. Gelderland, SE Netherlands
Nikaria *see* Ikaría
Nikel' *88 C2 Finn.* Kolosjoki. Murmanskaya Oblast', NW Russian Federation
Nikiniki *117 E5* Timor, S Indonesia
Niklasmarkt *see* Gheorgheni
Nikolainkaupunki *see* Vaasa
Nikolayev *see* Mykolayiv
Nikol'sk *see* Ussuriysk
Nikol'sk-Ussuriyskiy *see* Ussuriysk
Nikopol' *87 F3* Dnipropetrovs'ka Oblast', SE Ukraine
Nikšić *79 C5* C Montenegro
Nikumaroro *123 E3 ; prev.* Gardner Island. *atoll* Phoenix Islands, C Kiribati
Nikunau *123 E3 var.* Nukunau; *prev.* Byron Island. *atoll* Tungaru, W Kiribati
Nile *50 B2 former province* NW Uganda
Nile *46 D3 Ar.* Nahr an Nil. *river* N Africa
Nile Delta *50 B1 delta* N Egypt
Nîl, Nahr an *see* Nile
Nîmes *69 C6 anc.* Nemausus, Nismes. Gard, S France
Nimwegen *see* Nijmegen
Nine Degree Channel *110 B3 channel* India/Maldives
Ninetyeast Ridge *119 D5 undersea feature* E Indian Ocean
Ninety Mile Beach *128 C1 beach* North Island, New Zealand
Ningbo *106 D5 var.* Ning-po, Yin-hsien; *prev.* Ninghsien. Zhejiang, SE China
Ning-hsia *see* Ningxia
Ninghsien *see* Ningbo
Ning-po *see* Ningbo
Ningsia/Ningsia Hui/Ningsia Hui Autonomous Region *see* Ningxia
Ningxia *106 B4 off.* Ningxia Huizu Zizhiqu, *var.* Ning-hsia, Ningsia, *Eng.* Ningsia Hui, Ningsia Hui Autonomous Region. *autonomous region* N China
Ningxia Huizu Zizhiqu *see* Ningxia
Nio *see* Íos
Nio *see* Íos
Nio *see* Íos
Niobrara River *23 E3 river* Nebraska/Wyoming, C USA
Nioro *52 D3 var.* Nioro du Sahel. Kayes, W Mali
Nioro du Sahel *see* Nioro
Niort *68 B4* Deux-Sèvres, W France
Nipigon *16 B4* Ontario, S Canada
Nipigon, Lake *16 B3 lake* Ontario, S Canada
Nippon *see* Japan
Niš *79 E5 Eng.* Nish, *Ger.* Nisch; *anc.* Naissus. Serbia, SE Serbia
Nişab *98 B4* Al Ḥudūd ash Shamālīyah, N Saudi Arabia
Nisch/Nish *see* Niš
Nisibin *see* Nusaybin
Nisiros *see* Nísyros
Nisko *76 E4* Podkrapackie, SE Poland
Nismes *see* Nîmes
Nistru *see* Dniester
Nísyros *83 E7 var.* Nisiros. *island* Dodekánisa, Greece, Aegean Sea
Nitra *77 C6 Ger.* Neutra, *Hung.* Nyitra. Nitriansky Kraj, SW Slovakia
Nitra *77 C6 Ger.* Neutra, *Hung.* Nyitra. *river* W Slovakia
Niuatobutabu *see* Niuatoputapu
Niuatoputapu *123 E4 var.* Niuatobutabu; *prev.* Keppel Island. *island* N Tonga
Niue *123 F4 self-governing territory in free association with New Zealand* S Pacific Ocean
Niulakita *123 E3 var.* Nurakita. *atoll* S Tuvalu
Niutao *123 E3 atoll* NW Tuvalu
Nivernais *68 C4 cultural region* C France
Nizāmābād *112 D5* Andhra Pradesh, C India
Nizhnegorskiy *see* Nyzhn'ohirs'kyy
Nizhnekamsk *89 C5* Respublika Tatarstan, W Russian Federation
Nizhnevartovsk *92 D3* Khanty-Mansiyskiy Avtonomnyy Okrug-Yugra, C Russian Federation
Nizhniy Novgorod *89 C5 prev.* Gor'kiy. Nizhegorodskaya Oblast', W Russian Federation
Nizhniy Odes *88 D4* Respublika Komi, NW Russian Federation
Nizhyn *87 E1 Rus.* Nezhin. Chernihivs'ka Oblast', NE Ukraine

Nizza – Oppeln

Nizza *see* Nice
Njombe *51 C8* Iringa, S Tanzania
Nkayi *55 B6 prev.* Jacob. Bouenza, S Congo
Nkongsamba *54 A4 var.* N'Kongsamba. Littoral, W Cameroon
N'Kongsamba *see* Nkongsamba
Nmai Hka *114 B2 var.* Me Hka. *river* N Myanmar (Burma)
Nobeoka *109 B7* Miyazaki, Kyūshū, SW Japan
Noboribetsu *108 D3 var.* Noboribetu. Hokkaidō, NE Japan
Noboribetu *see* Noboribetsu
Nogales *28 B1* Sonora, NW Mexico
Nogales *26 B3* Arizona, SW USA
Nogal Valley *see* Dooxo Nugaaleed
Noire, Rivi`ere *see* Black River
Nokia *63 D5* Länsi-Suomi, W Finland
Nokou *54 B3* Kanem, W Chad
Nola *55 B5* Sangha-Mbaéré, SW Central African Republic
Nolinsk *89 C5* Kirovskaya Oblast', NW Russian Federation
Nongkaya *see* Nong Khai
Nong Khai *114 C4 var.* Mi Chai, Nongkaya. Nong Khai, E Thailand
Nonouti *122 D2 prev.* Sydenham Island. *atoll* Tungaru, W Kiribati
Noord-Beveland *64 B4 var.* North Beveland. *island* SW Netherlands
Noordwijk aan Zee *64 C3* Zuid-Holland, W Netherlands
Noordzee *see* North Sea
Nora *63 C6* Örebro, C Sweden
Norak *101 E3 Rus.* Nurek. W Tajikistan
Nord *61 F1* Avannaarsua, N Greenland
Nordaustlandet *61 G1 island* NE Svalbard
Norden *72 A3* Niedersachsen, NW Germany
Norderstedt *72 B3* Schleswig-Holstein, N Germany
Nordfriesische Inseln *see* North Frisian Islands
Nordhausen *72 C4* Thüringen, C Germany
Nordhorn *72 A3* Niedersachsen, NW Germany
Nord, Mer du *see* North Sea
Nord-Ouest, Territoires du *see* Northwest Territories
Nordsee/Nordsjøen/Nordsøen *see* North Sea
Norfolk *23 E3* Nebraska, C USA
Norfolk *19 F5* Virginia, NE USA
Norfolk Island *120 D4 Australian external territory* SW Pacific Ocean
Norfolk Ridge *120 D4 undersea feature* W Pacific Ocean
Norge *see* Norway
Norias *27 G5* Texas, SW USA
Noril'sk *92 D3* Taymyrskiy (Dolgano-Nenetskiy) Avtonomnyy Okrug, N Russian Federation
Norman *27 G1* Oklahoma, C USA
Normandes, Îles *see* Channel Islands
Normandie *68 B3 Eng.* Normandy. *cultural region* N France
Normandy *see* Normandie
Normanton *126 C3* Queensland, NE Australia
Norrköping *63 C6* Östergötland, S Sweden
Norrtälje *63 C6* Stockholm, C Sweden
Norseman *125 B6* Western Australia
Norske Havet *see* Norwegian Sea
North Albanian Alps *79 C5 Alb.* Bjeshkët e Namuna, *SCr.* Prokletije. *mountain range* SE Europe
Northallerton *67 D5* N England, United Kingdom
Northam *125 A6* Western Australia
North America *12 continent*
Northampton *67 D6* C England, United Kingdom
North Andaman *111 F2 island* Andaman Islands, India, NE Indian Ocean
North Australian Basin *119 E5 Fr.* Bassin Nord de l' Australie. *undersea feature* E Indian Ocean
North Bay *16 D4* Ontario, S Canada
North Beveland *see* Noord-Beveland
North Borneo *see* Sabah
North Cape *128 C1 headland* North Island, New Zealand
North Cape *62 D1 Eng.* North Cape. *headland* N Norway
North Cape *see* Nordkapp
North Carolina *21 E1 off.* State of North Carolina, *also known as* Old North State, Tar Heel State, Turpentine State. *state* SE USA
North Channel *18 D2 lake channel* Canada/USA
North Charleston *21 F2* South Carolina, SE USA
North Dakota *22 D2 off.* State of North Dakota, *also known as* Flickertail State, Peace Garden State, Sioux State. *state* N USA
North Devon Island *see* Devon Island
North East Frontier Agency/North East Frontier Agency of Assam *see* Arunāchal Pradesh
Northeast Providence Channel *32 C1 channel* N Bahamas
Northeim *72 B4* Niedersachsen, C Germany
Northern Cook Islands *123 F4 island group* N Cook Islands
Northern Dvina *88 C4 var.* Northern Dvina. *river* NW Russian Federation
Northern Dvina *see* Severnaya Dvina
Northern Ireland *66 B4 var.* The Six Counties. *cultural region* Northern Ireland, United Kingdom
Northern Mariana Islands *120 B1 US commonwealth territory* W Pacific Ocean
Northern Rhodesia *see* Zambia
Northern Sporades *83 C5 var.* Vóreioi Sporádes, Vórioi Sporádhes, *Eng.* Northern Sporades. *island group* E Greece
Northern Sporades *see* Vóreies Sporádes
Northern Territory *122 A5 territory* N Australia
North European Plain *59 E3 plain* N Europe
Northfield *23 F2* Minnesota, N USA
North Fiji Basin *120 D3 undersea feature* N Coral Sea
North Frisian Islands *72 B2 var.* Nordfriesische Inseln. *island group* N Germany
North Huvadhu Atoll *110 B5 var.* Gaafu Alifu Atoll. *atoll* S Maldives
North Island *128 B2 island* N New Zealand
North Korea *107 E3 off.* Democratic People's Republic of Korea, *Kor.* Chosŏn-minjujuŭi-inmin-kanghwaguk. *country* E Asia
North Little Rock *20 B1* Arkansas, C USA
North Minch *see* Minch, The
North Mole *71 G4 harbour wall* NW Gibraltar Europe
North Platte *23 E4* Nebraska, C USA
North Platte River *22 D4 river* C USA
North Pole *133 B3 pole* Arctic Ocean
North Saskatchewan *15 F5 river* Alberta/ Saskatchewan, S Canada
North Sea *58 D3 Dan.* Nordsøen, *Dut.* Noordzee, *Fr.* Mer du Nord, *Ger.* Nordsee, *Nor.* Nordsjøen; *prev.* German Ocean, *Lat.* Mare Germanicum. *sea* NW Europe
North Siberian Lowland *93 E2 var.* North Siberian Plain, *Eng.* North Siberian Lowland. *lowlands* N Russian Federation
North Siberian Lowland/North Siberian Plain *see* Severo-Sibirskaya Nizmennost'
North Star State *see* Minnesota
North Taranaki Bight *128 C3 gulf* North Island, New Zealand
North Uist *66 B3 island* NW Scotland, United Kingdom
Northwest Atlantic Mid-Ocean Canyon *12 E4 undersea feature* N Atlantic Ocean
North West Highlands *66 C3 mountain range* N Scotland, United Kingdom
Northwest Pacific Basin *91 G4 undersea feature* NW Pacific Ocean
Northwest Territories *15 E3 Fr.* Territoires du Nord-Ouest. *territory* NW Canada
Northwind Plain *133 B2 undersea feature* Arctic Ocean
Norton Sound *14 C2 inlet* Alaska, USA
Norway *63 A5 off.* Kingdom of Norway, *Nor.* Norge. *country* N Europe
Norway, Kingdom of *see* Norway
Norwegian Basin *61 F4 undersea feature* NW Norwegian Sea
Norwegian Sea *61 F4 var.* Norske Havet. *sea* NE Atlantic Ocean
Norwich *67 E6* E England, United Kingdom
Nösen *see* Bistriţa
Noshiro *108 D4 var.* Nosiro; *prev.* Noshirominato. Akita, Honshū, C Japan
Noshirominato/Nosiro *see* Noshiro
Nosivka *87 E1 Rus.* Nosovka. Chernihivs'ka Oblast', NE Ukraine
Nosovka *see* Nosivka
Noşratābād *98 E3* Sīstān va Balūchestān, E Iran
Nossob *56 C4 river* E Namibia
Noteć *76 C3 Ger.* Netze. *river* NW Poland
Nótiες Sporádes *see* Dodekánisa
Nottingham *67 D6* C England, United Kingdom
Nouâdhibou *52 B2 prev.* Port-Étienne. Dakhlet Nouâdhibou, W Mauritania
Nouakchott *52 B2 country capital* Nouakchott District, SW Mauritania
Nouméa *122 C5 dependent territory capital* Province Sud, S New Caledonia
Nouveau-Brunswick *see* New Brunswick
Nouvelle-Calédonie *see* New Caledonia
Nouvelle Écosse *see* Nova Scotia
Nova Civitas *see* Neustadt an der Weinstrasse
Nova Gorica *73 D8* W Slovenia
Nova Gradiška *78 C3 Ger.* Neugradisk, *Hung.* Újgradiska. Brod-Posavina, NE Croatia
Nova Iguaçu *41 F4* Rio de Janeiro, SE Brazil
Nova Lisboa *see* Huambo
Novara *74 B2 anc.* Novaria. Piemonte, NW Italy
Novaria *see* Novara
Nova Scotia *17 F4 Fr.* Nouvelle Écosse. *province* SE Canada
Nova Scotia *13 E5 physical region* SE Canada
Novaya Sibir', Ostrov *93 F1 island* Novosibirskiye Ostrova, NE Russian Federation
Novaya Zemlya *88 D1 island group* N Russian Federation
Novaya Zemlya Trough *see* East Novaya Zemlya Trough
Novgorod *see* Velikiy Novgorod
Novi Grad *see* Bosanski Novi
Novi Iskŭr *82 C2* Sofiya-Grad, W Bulgaria
Noviodunum *see* Nevers, Nièvre, France
Noviomagus *see* Lisieux, Calvados, France
Noviomagus *see* Nijmegen, Netherlands
Novi Pazar *79 D5 Turk.* Yenipazar. Serbia, S Serbia
Novi Sad *78 D3 Ger.* Neusatz, *Hung.* Újvidék. Vojvodina, N Serbia
Novoazovs'k *87 G4 Rus.* Novoazovsk. Donets'ka Oblast', E Ukraine
Novocheboksarsk *89 C5* Chuvashskaya Respublika, W Russian Federation
Novocherkassk *89 B7* Rostovskaya Oblast', SW Russian Federation
Novodvinsk *88 C3* Arkhangel'skaya Oblast', NW Russian Federation
Novograd-Volynskiy *see* Novohrad-Volyns'kyy
Novogrudok *see* Navahrudak
Novohrad-Volyns'kyy *86 D2 Rus.* Novograd-Volynskiy. Zhytomyrs'ka Oblast', N Ukraine
Novokazalinsk *see* Ayteke Bi
Novokuznetsk *92 D4 prev.* Stalinsk. Kemerovskaya Oblast', S Russian Federation
Novolazarevskaya *132 C2 Russian research station* Antarctica
Novo mesto *73 E8 Ger.* Rudolfswert; *prev. Ger.* Neustadtl. SE Slovenia
Novomoskovsk *89 B5* Tul'skaya Oblast', W Russian Federation
Novomoskovs'k *87 F3 Rus.* Novomoskovsk. Dnipropetrovs'ka Oblast', E Ukraine
Novopolotsk *see* Navapolatsk
Novoradomsk *see* Radomsko
Novo Redondo *see* Sumbe
Novorossiysk *89 A7* Krasnodarskiy Kray, SW Russian Federation
Novoshakhtinsk *89 B6* Rostovskaya Oblast', SW Russian Federation
Novosibirsk *92 D4* Novosibirskaya Oblast', C Russian Federation
Novotroitsk *89 D6* Orenburgskaya Oblast', W Russian Federation
Novotroitskoye *see* Novotroyits'ke, Ukraine
Novotroyits'ke *87 F4 Rus.* Novotroitskoye. Khersons'ka Oblast', S Ukraine
Novo-Urgench *see* Urganch
Novovolyns'k *86 C1 Rus.* Novovolynsk. Volyns'ka Oblast', NW Ukraine
Novy Dvor *85 B6 Rus.* Novyy Dvor. Hrodzyenskaya Voblasts', W Belarus
Novyy Bug *see* Novyy Buh
Novyy Buh *87 E3 Rus.* Novyy Bug. Mykolayivs'ka Oblast', S Ukraine
Novyy Dvor *see* Novy Dvor
Novyy Margilan *see* Farg'ona
Novyy Uzen' *see* Zhanaozen
Nowa Sól *76 B4 var.* Nowasól, *Ger.* Neusalz an der Oder. Lubuskie, W Poland
Nowasól *see* Nowa Sól
Nowogard *76 B2 var.* Nowógard, *Ger.* Naugard. Zachodnio-pomorskie, NW Poland
Nowogródek *see* Navahrudak
Nowo-Minsk *see* Mińsk Mazowiecki
Nowy Dwór Mazowiecki *76 D3* Mazowieckie, C Poland
Nowy Sącz *77 D5 Ger.* Neu Sandec. Małopolskie, S Poland
Nowy Tomyśl *76 B3 var.* Nowy Tomysl. Wielkopolskie, C Poland
Nowy Tomysl *see* Nowy Tomyśl
Noyon *68 C3* Oise, N France
Nsanje *57 E3* Southern, S Malawi
Nsawam *53 E5* SE Ghana
Ntomba, Lac *55 C6 var.* Lac Tumba. *lake* NW Dem. Rep. Congo
Nubian Desert *50 B3 desert* NE Sudan
Nu Chiang *see* Salween
Nu'eima *97 E7* E West Bank Asia
Nueva Caceres *see* Naga
Nueva Gerona *32 B2* Isla de la Juventud, S Cuba
Nueva Rosita *28 D2* Coahuila de Zaragoza, NE Mexico
Nuevitas *32 C2* Camagüey, E Cuba
Nuevo, Bajo *31 G1 island* NW Colombia South America
Nuevo Casas Grandes *28 C1* Chihuahua, N Mexico
Nuevo, Golfo *43 C6 gulf* S Argentina
Nuevo Laredo *29 E2* Tamaulipas, NE Mexico
Nui Atoll *123 E3 atoll* W Tuvalu
Nu Jiang *see* Salween
Nûk *see* Nuuk
Nukha *see* Şäki
Nuku'alofa *123 E5 country capital* Tongatapu, S Tonga
Nukufetau Atoll *123 E3 atoll* C Tuvalu
Nukulaelae Atoll *123 E3 var.* Nukulailai. *atoll* E Tuvalu
Nukulailai *see* Nukulaelae Atoll
Nukunau *see* Nikunau
Nukunonu Atoll *123 E3 island* C Tokelau
Nukus *100 C2* Qoraqalpog'iston Respublikasi, W Uzbekistan
Nullarbor Plain *125 C6 plateau* South Australia/ Western Australia
Nunap Isua *60 C5 var.* Uummannarsuaq, *Dan.* Kap Farvel, *Eng.* Cape Farewell. *cape* S Greenland
Nunavut *15 F3 territory* N Canada
Nuneaton *67 D6* C England, United Kingdom
Nunivak Island *14 B2 island* Alaska, USA
Nunspeet *64 D3* Gelderland, E Netherlands
Nuoro *75 A5* Sardegna, Italy, C Mediterranean Sea
Nuquí *36 A3* Chocó, W Colombia
Nurakita *see* Niulakita
Nurata *see* Nurota
Nurek *see* Norak
Nuremberg *see* Nürnberg
Nurmes *62 E4* Itä-Suomi, E Finland
Nürnberg *73 C5 Eng.* Nuremberg. Bayern, S Germany
Nurota *101 E2 Rus.* Nurata. Navoiy Viloyati, C Uzbekistan
Nusaybin *95 F4 var.* Nisibin. Manisa, SE Turkey
Nussdorf *see* Năsăud
Nutmeg State *see* Connecticut
Nuuk *60 C4 var.* Nûk, *Dan.* Godthaab, Godthåb. *dependent territory capital* Kitaa, SW Greenland
Nyagan' *92 C3* Khanty-Mansiyskiy Avtonomnyy Okrug-Yugra, N Russian Federation
Nyainqentanglha Shan *104 C5 mountain range* W China
Nyala *50 A4* Southern Darfur, W Sudan
Nyamapanda *56 D3* Mashonaland East, NE Zimbabwe
Nyamtumbo *51 C8* Ruvuma, S Tanzania
Nyanda *see* Masvingo
Nyandoma *88 C4* Arkhangel'skaya Oblast', NW Russian Federation
Nyantakara *51 B7* Kagera, NW Tanzania
Nyasa, Lake *57 E2 var.* Lake Malawi; *prev.* Lago Nyassa. *lake* E Africa
Nyasaland/Nyasaland Protectorate *see* Malawi
Nyassa, Lago *see* Nyasa, Lake
Nyasvizh *85 C6 Pol.* Nieśwież, *Rus.* Nesvizh. Minskaya Voblasts', C Belarus
Nyaunglebin *114 B4* Bago, SW Myanmar (Burma)
Nyeri *51 C6* Central, C Kenya
Nyíregyháza *77 D6* Szabolcs-Szatmár-Bereg, NE Hungary
Nyitra *see* Nitra
Nykøbing *63 B8* Storstrøm, SE Denmark
Nyköping *63 C6* Södermanland, S Sweden
Nylstroom *see* Modimolle
Nyngan *127 D6* New South Wales, SE Australia
Nyoman *see* Neman
Nyurba *93 F3* Respublika Sakha (Yakutiya), NE Russian Federation
Nyzhn'ohirs'kyy *87 F4 Rus.* Nizhnegorskiy. Respublika Krym, S Ukraine
NZ *see* New Zealand
Nzega *51 C7* Tabora, C Tanzania
Nzérékoré *52 D4* SE Guinea
Nzwani *see* Anjouan

O

Oa'hu *25 A7 var.* Oahu. *island* Hawai'ian Islands, Hawai'i, USA
Oak Harbor *24 B1* Washington, NW USA
Oakland *25 B6* California, W USA
Oamaru *129 B7* Otago, South Island, New Zealand
Oaxaca *29 F5 var.* Oaxaca de Juárez; *prev.* Antequera. Oaxaca, SE Mexico
Oaxaca de Juárez *see* Oaxaca
Ob' *90 C2 river* C Russian Federation
Obal' *85 D5 Rus.* Obol'. Vitsyebskaya Voblasts', N Belarus
Oban *66 C4* W Scotland, United Kingdom
Oban *see* Halfmoon Bay
Obando *see* Puerto Inírida
Obdorsk *see* Salekhard
Óbecse *see* Bečej
Obeliai *84 C4* Panevėžys, NE Lithuania
Oberhollabrunn *see* Tulln
Ob', Gulf of *92 D3 Eng.* Gulf of Ob. *gulf* N Russian Federation
Ob', Gulf of *see* Obskaya Guba
Obidovichi *see* Abidavichy
Obihiro *108 D2* Hokkaidō, NE Japan
Obo *54 D4* Haut-Mbomou, E Central African Republic
Obock *50 D4* E Djibouti
Obol' *see* Obal'
Oborniki *76 C3* Wielkolpolskie, W Poland
Obrovo *see* Abrova
Ob' Tablemount *119 B7 undersea feature* S Indian Ocean
Ocala *21 E4* Florida, SE USA
Ocaña *36 B2* Norte de Santander, N Colombia
Ocaña *70 D3* Castilla-La Mancha, C Spain
O Carballiño *70 C1 Cast.* Carballiño. Galicia, NW Spain
Occidental, Cordillera *39 E4 mountain range* Bolivia/Chile
Occidental, Cordillera *36 B2 mountain range* W Colombia
Ocean Falls *14 D5* British Columbia, SW Canada
Ocean Island *see* Banaba
Oceanside *25 C8* California, W USA
Ocean State *see* Rhode Island
Ochakiv *87 E4 Rus.* Ochakov. Mykolayivs'ka Oblast', S Ukraine
Ochakov *see* Ochakiv
Ochamchira *see* Och'amch'ire
Och'amch'ire *95 E2 Rus.* Ochamchira. W Georgia
Ocho Rios *32 B4* C Jamaica
Ochrida *see* Ohrid
Ochrida, Lake *see* Ohrid, Lake
Ocotal *30 D3* Nueva Segovia, NW Nicaragua
Ocozocuautla *29 G5* Chiapas, SE Mexico
October Revolution Island *93 E2 Eng.* October Revolution Island. *island* Severnaya Zemlya, N Russian Federation
October Revolution Island *see* Oktyabr'skoy Revolyutsii, Ostrov
Ocú *31 F5* Herrera, S Panama
Ōdate *108 D3* Akita, Honshū, C Japan
Oddur *see* Xuddur
Ödemiş *94 A4* İzmir, SW Turkey
Ödenburg *see* Sopron
Odenpäh *see* Otepää
Odense *63 B7* Fyn, C Denmark
Oder *76 B3 Cz./Pol.* Odra. *river* C Europe
Oderhaff *see* Szczeciński, Zalew
Odesa *87 E4 Rus.* Odessa. Odes'ka Oblast', SW Ukraine
Odessa *27 E3* Texas, SW USA
Odessa *see* Odesa
Odessus *see* Varna
Odienné *52 D4* NW Ivory Coast
Ôdôngk *115 D6* Kâmpóng Spoe, S Cambodia
Odoorn *64 E2* Drenthe, NE Netherlands
Odra *see* Oder
Oesel *see* Saaremaa
Of *95 E2* Trabzon, NE Turkey
Ofanto *75 D5 river* S Italy
Offenbach *73 B5 var.* Offenbach am Main. Hessen, W Germany
Offenbach am Main *see* Offenbach
Offenburg *73 B6* Baden-Württemberg, SW Germany
Ogaadeen *see* Ogaden
Ogaden *51 D5 Som.* Ogaadeen. *plateau* Ethiopia/ Somalia
Ōgaki *109 C6* Gifu, Honshū, SW Japan
Ogallala *22 D4* Nebraska, C USA
Ogbomosho *53 F4 var.* Ogmoboso. Oyo, W Nigeria
Ogden *22 B4* Utah, W USA
Ogdensburg *19 F2* New York, NE USA
Ogmoboso *see* Ogbomosho
Ogulin *78 A3* Karlovac, NW Croatia
Ohio *18 C4 off.* State of Ohio, *also known as* Buckeye State. *state* N USA
Ohio River *18 C4 river* N USA
Ohlau *see* Oława
Ohri *see* Ohrid
Ohrid *79 D6 Turk.* Ochrida, Ohri. SW FYR Macedonia
Ohrid, Lake *79 D6 var.* Lake Ochrida, *Alb.* Liqeni i Ohrit, *Mac.* Ohridsko Ezero. *lake* Albania/ FYR Macedonia
Ohridsko Ezero/Ohrit, Liqeni i *see* Ohrid, Lake
Ohura *128 D3* Manawatu-Wanganui, North Island, New Zealand
Oirschot *65 C5* Noord-Brabant, S Netherlands
Oise *68 C3 river* N France
Oistins *33 G2* S Barbados
Ōita *109 B7* Ōita, Kyūshū, SW Japan
Ojinaga *28 D2* Chihuahua, N Mexico
Ojos del Salado, Cerro *42 B3 mountain* W Argentina
Okaihau *128 C2* Northland, North Island, New Zealand
Ókanizsa *see* Kanjiža
Okāra *112 C2* Punjab, E Pakistan
Okavanggo *see* Cubango/Okavango
Okavango *see* Cubango
Okavango Delta *56 C3 wetland* N Botswana
Okayama *109 B6* Okayama, Honshū, SW Japan
Okazaki *109 C6* Aichi, Honshū, C Japan
Okeechobee, Lake *21 E4 lake* Florida, SE USA
Okefenokee Swamp *21 E3 wetland* Georgia, SE USA
Okhotsk *93 G3* Khabarovskiy Kray, E Russian Federation
Okhotsk, Sea of *91 F3 sea* NW Pacific Ocean
Okhtyrka *87 F2 Rus.* Akhtyrka. Sums'ka Oblast', NE Ukraine
Oki-guntō *see* Oki-shotō
Okinawa *108 A3 island* SW Japan
Okinawa-shoto *108 A3 island group* Nansei-shotō, SW Japan Asia
Oki-shoto *109 B6 var.* Oki-guntō. *island group* SW Japan
Oklahoma *27 F2 off.* State of Oklahoma, *also known as* The Sooner State. *state* C USA
Oklahoma City *27 G1 state capital* Oklahoma, C USA
Okmulgee *27 G1* Oklahoma, C USA
Oko, Wadi *50 C3 river* NE Sudan
Oktyabr'skiy *89 D6* Volgogradskaya Oblast', SW Russian Federation
Oktyabr'skiy *see* Aktsyabrski
Okulovka *88 B4 var.* Okulovka. Novgorodskaya Oblast', W Russian Federation
Okulovka *see* Okulovka
Okushiri-to *108 C3 var.* Okusiri Tô. *island* NE Japan
Okusiri Tô *see* Okushiri-tō
Oláh-Toplicza *see* Toplița
Öland *63 C7 island* S Sweden
Olavarría *43 D5* Buenos Aires, E Argentina
Oława *76 C4 Ger.* Ohlau. Dolnośląskie, SW Poland
Olbia *75 A5 prev.* Terranova Pausania. Sardegna, Italy, C Mediterranean Sea
Old Bay State/Old Colony State *see* Massachusetts
Old Dominion *see* Virginia
Oldebroek *64 D3* Gelderland, E Netherlands
Oldenburg *72 B3* Niedersachsen, NW Germany
Oldenburg *72 C2 var.* Oldenburg in Holstein. Schleswig-Holstein, N Germany
Oldenburg in Holstein *see* Oldenburg
Oldenzaal *64 E3* Overijssel, E Netherlands
Old Harbour *32 B5* C Jamaica
Old Line State *see* Maryland
Old North State *see* North Carolina
Olëkma *93 F4 river* C Russian Federation
Olëkminsk *93 F3* Respublika Sakha (Yakutiya), NE Russian Federation
Oleksandrivka *87 E3 Rus.* Aleksandrovka. Kirovohrads'ka Oblast', C Ukraine
Oleksandriya *87 F3 Rus.* Aleksandriya. Kirovohrads'ka Oblast', C Ukraine
Olenegorsk *88 C2* Murmanskaya Oblast', NW Russian Federation
Olenëk *93 E3* Respublika Sakha (Yakutiya), NE Russian Federation
Olenëk *93 E3 river* NE Russian Federation
Oléron, Île d' *69 A5 island* W France
Olevs'k *86 D1 Rus.* Olevsk. Zhytomyrs'ka Oblast', N Ukraine
Olevsk *see* Olevs'k
Ölgiy *104 C2* Bayan-Ölgiy, W Mongolia
Olhão *70 B5* Faro, S Portugal
Olifa *56 B3* Kunene, NW Namibia
Ólimbos *see* Ólympos
Olimpo *see* Fuerte Olimpo
Olisipo *see* Lisboa
Olita *see* Alytus
Oliva *71 F4* País Valenciano, E Spain
Olivet *68 C4* Loiret, C France
Olmaliq *101 E2 Rus.* Almalyk. Toshkent Viloyati, E Uzbekistan
Olmütz *see* Olomouc
Olomouc *77 C5 Ger.* Olmütz, *Pol.* Ołomuniec. Olomoucký Kraj, E Czech Republic
Ołomuniec *see* Olomouc
Olonets *88 B3* Respublika Kareliya, NW Russian Federation
Olovyannaya *93 F4* Chitinskaya Oblast', S Russian Federation
Olpe *72 B4* Nordrhein-Westfalen, W Germany
Olshanka *see* Vil'shanka
Olsnitz *see* Murska Sobota
Olsztyn *76 D2 Ger.* Allenstein. Warmińsko-Mazurskie, N Poland
Olt *86 B5 var.* Oltul, *Ger.* Alt. *river* S Romania
Olteniţa *86 C5 prev. Eng.* Oltenitsa; *anc.* Constantiola. Călăraşi, SE Romania
Oltenitsa *see* Olteniţa
Oltul *see* Olt
Olvera *70 D5* Andalucía, S Spain
Ol'viopol' *see* Pervomays'k
Olympia *24 B2 state capital* Washington, NW USA
Olympic Mountains *24 A2 mountain range* Washington, NW USA
Olympus, Mount *82 B4 var.* Ólimbos, *Eng.* Mount Olympus. *mountain* N Greece
Omagh *67 B5 Ir.* An Ómaigh. W Northern Ireland, United Kingdom
Omaha *23 F4* Nebraska, C USA
Oman *99 D6 off.* Sultanate of Oman, *Ar.* Salṭanat 'Umān; *prev.* Muscat and Oman. *country* SW Asia
Oman, Gulf of *98 E4 Ar.* Khalīj 'Umān. *gulf* N Arabian Sea
Oman, Sultanate of *see* Oman
Omboué *55 A6* Ogooué-Maritime, W Gabon
Omdurman *50 B4 var.* Umm Durmān. Khartoum, C Sudan
Ometepe, Isla de *30 D4 island* S Nicaragua
Ommen *64 E3* Overijssel, E Netherlands
Omsk *92 C4* Omskaya Oblast', C Russian Federation
Ōmuta *109 A7* Fukuoka, Kyūshū, SW Japan
Onda *71 F3* País Valenciano, E Spain
Ondjiva *see* N'Giva
Öndörhaan *105 E2 var.* Undur Khan; *prev.* Tsetsen Khan. Hentiy, E Mongolia
Onega *88 C3* Arkhangel'skaya Oblast', NW Russian Federation
Onega *88 B4 river* NW Russian Federation
Lake Onega *88 B4 Eng.* Lake Onega. *lake* NW Russian Federation
Onega, Lake *see* Onezhskoye Ozero
Onex *73 A7* Genève, SW Switzerland
Ongole *110 D1* Andhra Pradesh, E India
Onitsha *53 G5* Anambra, S Nigeria
Onon Gol *105 E2 river* N Mongolia
Onslow *124 A4* Western Australia
Onslow Bay *21 F1 bay* North Carolina, E USA
Ontario *16 B3 province* S Canada
Ontario, Lake *19 E3 lake* Canada/USA
Onteniente *see* Ontinyent
Ontinyent *71 F4 var.* Onteniente. País Valenciano, E Spain
Ontong Java Rise *103 H4 undersea feature* W Pacific Ocean
Onuba *see* Huelva
Oodeypore *see* Udaipur
Oos-Londen *see* East London
Oostakker *65 B5* Oost-Vlaanderen, NW Belgium
Oostburg *65 B5* Zeeland, SW Netherlands
Oostende *65 A5 Eng.* Ostend, *Fr.* Ostende. West-Vlaanderen, NW Belgium
Oosterbeek *64 D4* Gelderland, SE Netherlands
Oosterhout *64 C4* Noord-Brabant, S Netherlands
Opatija *78 A2 It.* Abbazia. Primorje-Gorski Kotar, NW Croatia
Opava *77 C5 Ger.* Troppau. Moravskoslezský Kraj, E Czech Republic
Ópazova *see* Stara Pazova
Opelika *20 D2* Alabama, S USA
Opelousas *20 B3* Louisiana, S USA
Ophiusa *see* Formentera
Opmeer *64 C2* Noord-Holland, NW Netherlands
Opochka *88 A4* Pskovskaya Oblast', W Russian Federation
Opole *76 C4 Ger.* Oppeln. Opolskie, S Poland
Oporto *see* Porto
Opotiki *128 E3* Bay of Plenty, North Island, New Zealand
Oppeln *see* Opole

Oppidum Ubiorum – Pátra

Oppidum Ubiorum see Köln
Oqtosh 101 E2 Rus. Aktash. Samarqand Viloyati, C Uzbekistan
Oradea 86 B3 prev. Oradea Mare, Ger. Grosswardein, Hung. Nagyvárad. Bihor, NW Romania
Oradea Mare see Oradea
Orahovac see Rahovec
Oral see Ural'sk
Oran 48 D2 var. Ouahran, Wahran. NW Algeria
Orange 127 D6 New South Wales, SE Australia
Orange 69 D6 anc. Arausio. Vaucluse, SE France
Orangeburg 21 E2 South Carolina, SE USA
Orange Cone see Orange Fan
Orange Fan 47 C7 var. Orange Cone. undersea feature SW Indian Ocean
Orange Mouth/Orangemund see Oranjemund
Orange River 56 B4 Afr. Oranjerivier. river S Africa
Orange Walk 30 C1 Orange Walk, N Belize
Oranienburg 72 D3 Brandenburg, NE Germany
Oranjemund 56 B4 var. Orangemund; prev. Orange Mouth. Karas, SW Namibia
Oranjerivier see Orange River
Oranjestad 33 E5 dependent territory capital W Aruba
Orany see Varėna
Orașul Stalin see Brașov
Oravicabánya see Oravița
Oravița 86 A4 Ger. Orawitza, Hung. Oravicabánya. Caraș-Severin, SW Romania
Orawitza see Oravița
Orbetello 74 B4 Toscana, C Italy
Orcadas 132 A1 Argentinian research station South Orkney Islands, Antarctica
Orchard Homes 22 B1 Montana, NW USA
Ordino 69 A8 Ordino, NW Andorra Europe
Ordos Desert see Mu Us Shadi
Ordu 94 D2 anc. Cotyora. Ordu, N Turkey
Ordzhonikidze 87 F3 Dnipropetrovs'ka Oblast', E Ukraine
Ordzhonikidze see Vladikavkaz, Russian Federation
Ordzhonikidze see Yenakiyeve, Ukraine
Orealla 37 G3 E Guyana
Örebro 63 C6 Örebro, C Sweden
Oregon 24 B3 off. State of Oregon, also known as Beaver State, Sunset State, Valentine State, Webfoot State. state NW USA
Oregon City 24 B3 Oregon, NW USA
Oregon, State of see Oregon
Orekhov see Orikhiv
Orël 89 B5 Orlovskaya Oblast', W Russian Federation
Orem 22 B4 Utah, W USA
Ore Mountains 73 C5 Cz. Krušné Hory, Eng. Ore Mountains. mountain range Czech Republic/Germany
Ore Mountains see Erzgebirge/Krušné Hory
Orenburg 89 D6 prev. Chkalov. Orenburgskaya Oblast', W Russian Federation
Orense see Ourense
Oreor see Koror
Orestiáda 82 D3 prev. Orestiás. Anatolikí Makedonía kai Thráki, NE Greece
Orestiás see Orestiáda
Organ Peak 26 D3 mountain New Mexico, SW USA
Orgeyev see Orhei
Orhei 86 D3 var. Orheiu, Rus. Orgeyev. N Moldova
Orheiu see Orhei
Oriental, Cordillera 38 D3 mountain range Bolivia/Peru
Oriental, Cordillera 36 B3 mountain range C Colombia
Orihuela 71 F4 País Valenciano, E Spain
Orikhiv 87 G3 Rus. Orekhov. Zaporiz'ka Oblast', SE Ukraine
Orinoco, Río 37 E2 river Colombia/Venezuela
Orissa 113 F4 cultural region NE India
Orissaare see Orissaare
Orissaare 84 C2 Ger. Orissaar. Saaremaa, W Estonia
Oristano 75 A5 Sardegna, Italy, C Mediterranean Sea
Orito 36 A4 Putumayo, SW Colombia
Orizaba, Volcán Pico de 13 C7 var. Citlaltépetl. mountain S Mexico
Orkney see Orkney Islands
Orkney Islands 66 C2 var. Orkney, Orkneys. island group N Scotland, United Kingdom
Orkneys see Orkney Islands
Orlando 21 E4 Florida, SE USA
Orléanais 68 C4 cultural region C France
Orléans 68 C4 anc. Aurelianum. Loiret, C France
Orléansville see Chlef
Orly 68 E2 international airport Essonne, N France
Orlya 85 B6 Hrodzyenskaya Voblasts', W Belarus
Ormsö see Vormsi
Ormuz, Strait of see Hormuz, Strait of
Örnsköldsvik 63 C5 Västernorrland, C Sweden
Orolaunum see Arlon
Orol Dengizi see Aral Sea
Oromocto 17 F4 New Brunswick, SE Canada
Orona 123 F3 prev. Hull Island. atoll Phoenix Islands, C Kiribati
Oropeza see Cochabamba
Orosirá Rodhópis see Rhodope Mountains
Orpington 67 B8 United Kingdom
Orschowa see Orșova
Orsha 85 E6 Vitsyebskaya Voblasts', NE Belarus
Orsk 92 B4 Orenburgskaya Oblast', W Russian Federation
Orșova 86 A4 Ger. Orschowa, Hung. Orsova. Mehedinți, SW Romania
Ortelsburg see Szczytno
Orthez 69 B6 Pyrénées-Atlantiques, SW France
Ortona 74 D4 Abruzzo, C Italy
Oruba see Aruba
Oruro 39 F4 Oruro, W Bolivia
Oryokko see Yalu
Ōsaka 109 C6 hist. Naniwa. Ōsaka, Honshū, SW Japan
Ōsaki see Furukawa
Osa, Península de 31 E5 peninsula S Costa Rica
Osborn Plateau 119 D5 undersea feature E Indian Ocean
Osca see Huesca
Ösel see Saaremaa
Osh 101 F2 Oshskaya Oblast', SW Kyrgyzstan
Oshawa 16 D5 Ontario, SE Canada
Oshikango 56 B3 Ohangwena, N Namibia
O-shima 109 D6 island S Japan
Oshkosh 18 B2 Wisconsin, N USA
Oshmyany see Ashmyany
Osiek see Osijek
Osijek 78 C3 prev. Osiek, Osjek, Ger. Esseg, Hung. Eszék. Osijek-Baranja, E Croatia
Osipenko see Berdyans'k
Osipovichi see Asipovichy
Osjek see Osijek
Oskaloosa 23 G4 Iowa, C USA
Oskarshamn 63 C7 Kalmar, S Sweden
Öskemen see Ust'-Kamenogorsk
Oskil 87 G2 Rus. Oskil. river Russian Federation/Ukraine
Oskil see Oskil
Oslo 63 B6 prev. Christiania, Kristiania. country capital Oslo, S Norway
Osmaniye 94 D4 Osmaniye, S Turkey
Osnabrück 72 A3 Niedersachsen, NW Germany
Osogov Mountains 82 B3 var. Osogovske Planine, Osogovski Planina, Mac. Osogovski Planini. mountain range Bulgaria/FYR Macedonia
Osogovske Planine/Osogovski Planina/Osogovski Planini see Osogov Mountains
Oșorhei see Târgu Mureș
Osorno 43 B5 Los Lagos, C Chile
Oss 64 D4 Noord-Brabant, S Netherlands
Ossa, Serra d' 70 C4 mountain range SE Portugal
Ossora 93 H2 Koryakskiy Avtonomnyy Okrug, E Russian Federation
Ostee see Baltic Sea
Ostend/Ostende see Oostende
Oster 87 E1 Chernihivs'ka Oblast', N Ukraine
Östermyra see Seinäjoki
Osterode/Osterode in Ostpreussen see Ostróda
Österreich see Austria
Östersund 63 C5 Jämtland, C Sweden
Ostia Aterni see Pescara
Ostiglia 74 C2 Lombardia, N Italy
Ostrava 77 C5 Moravskoslezský Kraj, E Czech Republic
Ostróda 76 D3 Ger. Osterode, Osterode in Ostpreussen. Warmińsko-Mazurskie, NE Poland
Ostrołęka 76 D3 Ger. Wiesenhof, Rus. Ostrolenka. Mazowieckie, C Poland
Ostrolenka see Ostrołęka
Ostrov 88 A4 Latv. Austrava. Pskovskaya Oblast', W Russian Federation
Ostrovets see Ostrowiec Świętokrzyski
Ostrovnoy 88 C2 Murmanskaya Oblast', NW Russian Federation
Ostrów see Ostrów Wielkopolski
Ostrowiec see Ostrowiec Świętokrzyski
Ostrowiec Świętokrzyski 76 D4 var. Ostrowiec, Rus. Ostrovets. Świętokrzyskie, C Poland
Ostrów Mazowiecka 76 D3 var. Ostrów Mazowiecki. Mazowieckie, NE Poland
Ostrów Mazowiecki see Ostrów Mazowiecka
Ostrowo see Ostrów Wielkopolski
Ostrów Wielkopolski 76 C4 var. Ostrów, Ger. Ostrowo. Wielkopolskie, C Poland
Ostyako-Voguls'k see Khanty-Mansiysk
Osum see Osumit, Lumi i
Ōsumi-shotō 109 A8 island group Kagoshima, Nansei-shotō, SW Japan Asia East China Sea Pacific Ocean
Osumit, Lumi i 79 D7 var. Osum. river SE Albania
Osuna 70 D4 Andalucía, S Spain
Oswego 19 F2 New York, NE USA
Otago Peninsula 129 B7 peninsula South Island, New Zealand
Otaki 128 D4 Wellington, North Island, New Zealand
Otaru 108 C2 Hokkaidō, NE Japan
Otavalo 38 B1 Imbabura, N Ecuador
Otavi 56 B3 Otjozondjupa, N Namibia
Oțelu Roșu 86 B4 Ger. Ferdinandsberg, Hung. Nándorhgy. Caraș-Severin, SW Romania
Otepää 84 D3 Ger. Odenpäh. Valgamaa, SE Estonia
Oti 53 E4 river N Togo
Otira 129 C6 West Coast, South Island, New Zealand
Otjiwarongo 56 B3 Otjozondjupa, N Namibia
Otorohanga 128 D3 Waikato, North Island, New Zealand
Otranto, Canale d' see Otranto, Strait of
Otranto, Strait of 79 C6 It. Canale d'Otranto. strait Albania/Italy
Otrokovice 77 C5 Ger. Otrokowitz. Zlínský Kraj, E Czech Republic
Otrokowitz see Otrokovice
Ōtsu 109 C6 var. Ōtu. Shiga, Honshū, SW Japan
Ottawa 16 D5 country capital Ontario, SE Canada
Ottawa 18 B3 Illinois, N USA
Ottawa 23 F5 Kansas, C USA
Ottawa 19 E2 Fr. Outaouais. river Ontario/Québec, SE Canada
Ottawa Islands 16 C1 island group Nunavut, C Canada
Ottignies 65 C6 Wallon Brabant, C Belgium
Ottumwa 23 G4 Iowa, C USA
Ōtu see Ōtsu
Ouachita Mountains 20 A1 mountain range Arkansas/Oklahoma, C USA
Ouachita River 20 B2 river Arkansas/Louisiana, C USA
Ouagadougou 53 E4 var. Wagadugu. country capital C Burkina
Ouahigouya 53 E3 NW Burkina
Ouahran see Oran
Oualâta 52 D3 var. Oualata. Hodh ech Chargui, SE Mauritania
Ouanary 37 H3 E French Guiana
Ouanda Djallé 54 D4 Vakaga, NE Central African Republic
Ouarâne 52 D2 desert C Mauritania
Ouargla 49 E2 var. Wargla. NE Algeria
Ouarzazate 48 C3 S Morocco
Oubangui 55 C5 Fr. Oubangui. river C Africa
Oubangui see Ubangi
Oubangui-Chari see Central African Republic
Oubangui-Chari, Territoire de l' see Central African Republic
Oudjda see Oujda
Ouessant, Île d' 68 A3 Eng. Ushant. island NW France
Ouésso 55 B5 Sangha, NW Congo
Oujda 48 D2 Ar. Oudjda, Ujda. NE Morocco
Oujeft 52 C2 Adrar, C Mauritania
Oulu 62 D4 Swe. Uleåborg. Oulu, C Finland
Oulujärvi 62 D4 Swe. Uleträsk. lake C Finland
Oulujoki 62 D4 Swe. Uleälv. river C Finland
Ounasjoki 62 D3 river N Finland
Ounianga Kébir 54 C2 Borkou-Ennedi-Tibesti, N Chad
Oup see Auob
Oupeye 65 D6 Liège, E Belgium
Our 65 D6 river NW Europe
Ourense 70 C1 Cast. Orense, Lat. Aurium. Galicia, NW Spain
Ourique 70 B4 Beja, S Portugal
Ours, Grand Lac de l' see Great Bear Lake
Ourthe 65 D7 river E Belgium
Ouse 67 D5 river N England, United Kingdom
Outaouais see Ottawa
Outer Hebrides 66 B3 var. Western Isles. island group NW Scotland, United Kingdom
Outer Islands 57 G1 island group SW Seychelles Africa W Indian Ocean
Outes 70 B1 Galicia, NW Spain
Ouvéa 122 D5 island Îles Loyauté, NE New Caledonia
Ouyen 127 C6 Victoria, SE Australia
Ovalle 42 B3 Coquimbo, N Chile
Ovar 70 B2 Aveiro, N Portugal
Overflakkee 64 B4 island SW Netherlands
Overijse 65 C6 Vlaams Brabant, C Belgium
Oviedo 70 C1 anc. Asturias. Asturias, NW Spain
Ovilava see Wels
Ovruch 86 D1 Zhytomyrs'ka Oblast', N Ukraine
Owando 55 B5 prev. Fort Rousset. Cuvette, C Congo
Owase 109 C6 Mie, Honshū, SW Japan
Owatonna 23 F3 Minnesota, N USA
Owen Fracture Zone 118 B4 tectonic feature W Arabian Sea
Owen, Mount 129 C5 mountain South Island, New Zealand
Owensboro 18 B5 Kentucky, S USA
Owen Stanley Range 122 B3 mountain range S Papua New Guinea
Owerri 53 G5 Imo, S Nigeria
Owo 53 F5 Ondo, SW Nigeria
Owyhee River 24 C4 river Idaho/Oregon, NW USA
Oxford 129 C6 Canterbury, South Island, New Zealand
Oxford 67 D6 Lat. Oxonia. S England, United Kingdom
Oxkutzcab 29 H4 Yucatán, SE Mexico
Oxnard 25 B7 California, W USA
Oxonia see Oxford
Oxus see Amu Darya
Oyama 109 D5 Tochigi, Honshū, S Japan
Oyem 55 B5 Woleu-Ntem, N Gabon
Oyo 55 B6 Cuvette, C Congo
Oyo 53 F4 Oyo, W Nigeria
Ozark 20 D3 Alabama, S USA
Ozark Plateau 23 G5 plain Arkansas/Missouri, C USA
Ozarks, Lake of the 23 F5 reservoir Missouri, C USA
Ozbourn Seamount 130 D4 undersea feature W Pacific Ocean
Ózd 77 D6 Borsod-Abaúj-Zemplén, NE Hungary
Ozieri 75 A5 Sardegna, Italy, C Mediterranean Sea

P

Paamiut 60 B4 var. Pâmiut, Dan. Frederikshåb. S Greenland
Pa-an see Hpa-an
Pabianice 76 C4 Łódzski, Poland
Pabna 113 G4 Rajshahi, W Bangladesh
Pacaraima, Sierra/Pacaraim, Serra see Pakaraima Mountains
Pachuca 29 E4 var. Pachuca de Soto. Hidalgo, C Mexico
Pachuca de Soto see Pachuca
Pacific-Antarctic Ridge 132 B5 undersea feature S Pacific Ocean
Pacific Ocean 130 D3 ocean
Padalung see Phatthalung
Padang 116 B4 Sumatera, W Indonesia
Paderborn 72 B4 Nordrhein-Westfalen, NW Germany
Padma see Brahmaputra
Padma see Ganges
Padova 74 C2 Eng. Padua; anc. Patavium. Veneto, NE Italy
Padre Island 27 G5 island Texas, SW USA
Padua see Padova
Paducah 18 B5 Kentucky, S USA
Paeroa 128 D3 Waikato, North Island, New Zealand
Páfos 80 C5 var. Paphos. W Cyprus
Pag 78 A3 It. Pago. island Zadar, C Croatia
Page 26 B1 Arizona, SW USA
Pago see Pag
Pago Pago 123 F4 dependent territory capital Tutuila, W American Samoa
Pahiatua 128 D4 Manawatu-Wanganui, North Island, New Zealand
Pahsien see Chongqing
Paide 84 D2 Ger. Weissenstein. Järvamaa, N Estonia
Paihia 128 D2 Northland, North Island, New Zealand
Päijänne 63 D5 lake S Finland
Paine, Cerro 43 A7 mountain S Chile
Painted Desert 26 B1 desert Arizona, SW USA
Paisance see Piacenza
Paisley 66 C4 W Scotland, United Kingdom
País Valenciano 71 F3 var. Valencia, Cat. València; anc. Valentia. autonomous community NE Spain
País Vasco 71 E1 cultural region N Spain
Paita 38 B3 Piura, NW Peru
Pakanbaru see Pekanbaru
Pakaraima Mountains 37 E3 var. Serra Pacaraim, Sierra Pacaraima. mountain range N South America
Pakistan 112 A2 off. Islamic Republic of Pakistan, var. Islami Jamhuriya e Pakistan. country S Asia
Pakistan, Islamic Republic of see Pakistan
Pakistan, Islami Jamhuriya e see Pakistan
Paknam see Samut Prakan
Pakokku 114 A3 Magway, C Myanmar (Burma)
Pak Phanang 115 C7 var. Ban Pak Phanang. Nakhon Si Thammarat, SW Thailand
Pakruojis 84 C4 Šiaulai, N Lithuania
Paks 77 C7 Tolna, S Hungary
Paksé see Pakxé
Pakxé 115 D5 var. Paksé. Champasak, S Laos
Palafrugell 71 G2 Cataluña, NE Spain
Palagruža 79 B5 It. Pelagosa. island SW Croatia
Palaiá Epídavros 83 C6 Pelopónnisos, S Greece
Palaiseau 68 D2 Essonne, N France
Palamós 71 G2 Cataluña, NE Spain
Palamuse 84 E2 Ger. Sankt-Bartholomäi. Jõgevamaa, E Estonia
Palanka see Bačka Palanka
Pālanpur 112 C4 Gujarāt, W India
Palantia see Palencia
Palapye 56 D3 Central, SE Botswana
Palau 122 A2 var. Belau. country W Pacific Ocean
Palawan 117 E2 island W Philippines
Palawan Passage 116 D2 passage W Philippines
Paldiski 84 D2 prev. Baltiski, Eng. Baltic Port, Ger. Baltischport. Harjumaa, NW Estonia
Palembang 116 B4 Sumatera, W Indonesia
Palencia 70 D2 anc. Palantia, Pallantia. Castilla-León, NW Spain
Palerme see Palermo
Palermo 75 C7 Fr. Palerme; anc. Panhormus, Panormus. Sicilia, Italy, C Mediterranean Sea
Pāli 112 C3 Rājasthān, N India
Palikir 122 C2 country capital Pohnpei, E Micronesia
Palimé see Kpalimé
Palioúri, Akrotírio 82 C4 var. Akrotírio Kanestron. headland N Greece
Palk Strait 110 C3 strait India/Sri Lanka
Pallantia see Palencia
Palliser, Cape 129 D5 headland North Island, New Zealand
Palma 71 G3 var. Palma de Mallorca. Mallorca, Spain, W Mediterranean Sea
Palma del Río 70 D4 Andalucía, S Spain
Palma de Mallorca see Palma
Palmar Sur 31 E5 Puntarenas, SE Costa Rica
Palma Soriano 32 C3 Santiago de Cuba, E Cuba
Palm Beach 126 E1 New South Wales, E Australia
Palmer 132 A2 US research station Antarctica
Palmer Land 132 A3 physical region Antarctica
Palmerston 123 F4 island S Cook Islands
Palmerston see Darwin
Palmerston North 128 D4 Manawatu-Wanganui, North Island, New Zealand
The Palmetto State see South Carolina
Palmi 75 D7 Calabria, SW Italy
Palmira 36 B3 Valle del Cauca, W Colombia
Palm Springs 25 D7 California, W USA
Palmyra see Tudmur
Palmyra Atoll 123 G2 US privately owned unincorporated territory C Pacific Ocean
Palo Alto 25 B6 California, W USA
Paloe see Denpasar, Bali, C Indonesia
Paloe see Palu
Palu 117 E4 prev. Paloe. Sulawesi, C Indonesia
Pamiers 69 B6 Ariège, S France
Pamir 101 F3 var. Daryā-ye Pāmīr, Taj. Dar"yoi Pomir. river Afghanistan/Tajikistan
Pāmīr, Daryā-ye see Pamir
Pamir/Pāmīr, Daryā-ye see Pamirs
Pamirs 101 F3 Pash. Daryā-ye Pāmīr, Rus. Pamir. mountain range C Asia
Pâmiut see Paamiut
Pamlico Sound 21 G1 sound North Carolina, SE USA
Pampa 27 E1 Texas, SW USA
Pampa Aullagas, Lago see Poopó, Lago
Pampas 42 C4 plain C Argentina
Pampeluna see Pamplona
Pamplona 36 C2 Norte de Santander, N Colombia
Pamplona 71 E1 Basq. Iruña, prev. Pampeluna; anc. Pompaelo. Navarra, N Spain
Panaji 110 B1 var. Pangim, Panjim, New Goa. state capital Goa, W India
Panamá 31 G4 var. Ciudad de Panama, Eng. Panama City. country capital Panamá, C Panama
Panama 31 G5 off. Republic of Panama. country Central America
Panama Basin 13 C8 undersea feature E Pacific Ocean
Panama Canal 31 F4 canal E Panama
Panama City 20 D3 Florida, SE USA
Panama City see Panamá
Gulf of Panama 31 G5 var. Gulf of Panama. gulf S Panama
Panama, Gulf of see Panamá, Golfo de
Isthmus of Panama 31 G4 Eng. Isthmus of Panama; prev. Isthmus of Darien. isthmus E Panama
Panama, Isthmus of see Panama, Istmo de
Panama, Republic of see Panama
Panay Island 117 E2 island C Philippines
Pančevo 78 D3 Ger. Pantschowa, Hung. Pancsova. Vojvodina, N Serbia
Pancsova see Pančevo
Paneas see Bāniyās
Panevėžys 84 C4 Panevėžys, C Lithuania
Pangim see Panaji
Pangkalpinang 116 C4 Pulau Bangka, W Indonesia
Pang-Nga see Phang-Nga
Panhormus see Palermo
Panjim see Panaji
Panopolis see Akhmīm
Pánormos 83 C7 Kríti, Greece, E Mediterranean Sea
Panormus see Palermo
Pantanal 41 E3 var. Pantanalmato-Grossense. swamp SW Brazil
Pantanalmato-Grossense see Pantanal
Pantelleria, Isola di 75 B7 island SW Italy
Pantschowa see Pančevo
Pánuco 29 E3 Veracruz-Llave, E Mexico
Pao-chi/Paoki see Baoji
Paola 80 B5 E Malta
Pao-shan see Baoshan
Pao-t'ou/Paotow see Baotou
Papagayo, Golfo de 30 C4 gulf NW Costa Rica
Papakura 128 D3 Auckland, North Island, New Zealand
Papantla 29 F4 var. Papantla de Olarte. Veracruz-Llave, E Mexico
Papantla de Olarte see Papantla
Papeete 123 H4 dependent territory capital Tahiti, W French Polynesia
Paphos see Páfos
Papilė 84 B3 Šiaulai, NW Lithuania
Papillion 23 F4 Nebraska, C USA
Papua 117 H4 var. Irian Barat, West Irian, West New Guinea, West Papua; prev. Dutch New Guinea, Irian Jaya, Netherlands New Guinea. province E Indonesia
Papua and New Guinea, Territory of see Papua New Guinea
Papua, Gulf of 122 B3 gulf S Papua New Guinea
Papua New Guinea 122 B3 off. Independent State of Papua New Guinea; prev. Territory of Papua and New Guinea. country NW Melanesia
Papua New Guinea, Independent State of see Papua New Guinea
Papuk 78 C3 mountain range NE Croatia
Pará 41 E2 off. Estado do Pará. state NE Brazil
Pará 41 E2 off. Estado do Pará. region NE Brazil
Pará see Belém
Paracel Islands 103 E3 disputed territory SE Asia
Paraćin 78 D4 Serbia, C Serbia
Paradise of the Pacific see Hawai'i
Pará, Estado do see Pará
Paragua, Río 37 E3 river SE Venezuela
Paraguay 42 C2 country C South America
Paraguay 42 D2 var. Río Paraguay. river C South America
Paraguay, Río see Paraguay
Parahiba/Parahyba see Paraíba
Paraíba 41 G2 off. Estado da Paraíba; prev. Parahiba, Parahyba. state E Brazil
Paraíba 41 G2 off. Estado da Paraíba; prev. Parahiba, Parahyba. region E Brazil
Paraíba see João Pessoa
Paraíba, Estado da see Paraíba
Parakou 53 F4 C Benin
Paramaribo 37 G3 country capital Paramaribo, N Suriname
Paramushir, Ostrov 93 H3 island SE Russian Federation
Paraná 41 E4 Entre Ríos, E Argentina
Paraná 41 E5 off. Estado do Paraná. region S Brazil
Paraná 41 E5 off. Estado do Paraná. state S Brazil
Paraná 35 C5 var. Alto Paraná. river C South America
Paraná, Estado do see Paraná
Paranésti 82 C3 var. Paranestio. Anatolikí Makedonía kai Thráki, NE Greece
Paranestio see Paranésti
Paraparaumu 129 D5 Wellington, North Island, New Zealand
Parchim 72 C3 Mecklenburg-Vorpommern, N Germany
Parczew 76 E4 Lubelskie, E Poland
Pardubice 77 B5 Ger. Pardubitz. Pardubický Kraj, C Czech Republic
Pardubitz see Pardubice
Parechcha 85 B5 Pol. Porzecze, Rus. Porech'ye. Hrodzyenskaya Voblasts', W Belarus
Parecis, Chapada dos 40 D3 var. Serra dos Parecis. mountain range W Brazil
Parecis, Serra dos see Parecis, Chapada dos
Parenzo see Poreč
Parepare 117 E4 Sulawesi, C Indonesia
Párga 83 A5 Ípeiros, W Greece
Paria, Golfo de see Paria, Gulf of
Paria, Gulf of 37 E1 var. Golfo de Paria. gulf Trinidad and Tobago/Venezuela
Parika 37 F2 NE Guyana
Paris 68 D1 anc. Lutetia, Lutetia Parisiorum, Parisii. country capital Paris, N France
Paris 27 G2 Texas, SW USA
Parisii see Paris
Parkersburg 18 D4 West Virginia, NE USA
Parkes 127 D6 New South Wales, SE Australia
Parkhar see Farkhor
Parma 74 B2 Emilia-Romagna, N Italy
Parnahyba see Parnaíba
Parnaíba 41 F2 var. Parnahyba. Piauí, E Brazil
Pärnu 84 D2 Ger. Pernau, Latv. Pērnava; prev. Rus. Pernov. Pärnumaa, SW Estonia
Pärnu 84 D2 var. Parnu Jõgi, Ger. Pernau. river SW Estonia
Pärnu-Jaagupi 84 D2 Ger. Sankt-Jakobi. Pärnumaa, SW Estonia
Parnu Jõgi see Pärnu
Pärnu Laht 84 D2 Ger. Pernauer Bucht. bay SW Estonia
Paropamisus Range see Sefīd Kūh, Selseleh-ye
Páros 83 D6 island Kykládes, Greece, Aegean Sea
Páros 83 D6 island Kykládes, Greece, Aegean Sea
Páros 83 C6 island Kykládes, Greece, Aegean Sea
Parral 42 B4 Maule, C Chile
Parral see Hidalgo del Parral
Parramatta 126 D1 New South Wales, SE Australia
Parras 28 D3 var. Parras de la Fuente. Coahuila de Zaragoza, NE Mexico
Parras de la Fuente see Parras
Parsons 23 F5 Kansas, C USA
Pasadena 25 C7 California, W USA
Pasadena 27 H4 Texas, SW USA
Pașcani 86 C3 Hung. Páskán. Iași, NE Romania
Pasco 24 C2 Washington, NW USA
Pasewalk 72 D3 Mecklenburg-Vorpommern, NE Germany
Pashkeni see Bolyarovo
Pasinler 95 F3 Erzurum, NE Turkey
Páskán see Pașcani
Pasłęk 76 D2 Ger. Preußisch Holland. Warmińsko-Mazurskie, NE Poland
Pasni 112 A3 Baluchistān, SW Pakistan
Paso de Indios 43 B6 Chubut, S Argentina
Passarowitz see Požarevac
Passau 73 D6 Bayern, SE Germany
Passo Fundo 41 E5 Rio Grande do Sul, S Brazil
Pastavy 85 C5 Pol. Postawy, Rus. Postavy. Vitsyebskaya Voblasts', NW Belarus
Pastaza, Río 38 B2 river Ecuador/Peru
Pasto 36 A4 Nariño, SW Colombia
Pasvalys 84 C4 Panevėžys, N Lithuania
Patagonia 35 B7 physical region Argentina/Chile
Patalung see Phatthalung
Patani see Pattani
Patavium see Padova
Patea 128 D4 Taranaki, North Island, New Zealand
Paterson 19 F3 New Jersey, NE USA
Pathein 114 A4 var. Bassein. Ayeyarwady, SW Myanmar (Burma)
Pátmos 83 D6 island Dodekánisa, Greece, Aegean Sea
Patna 113 F3 var. Azimabad. state capital Bihār, N India
Patnos 95 F3 Ağrı, E Turkey
Patos, Lagoa dos 41 E5 lagoon S Brazil
Pátra 83 B5 Eng. Patras; prev. Pátrai. Dytikí Ellás, S Greece

Pátrai/Patras – Port An Dúnáin

Pátrai/Patras see Pátra
Pattani 115 C7 var. Patani. Pattani, SW Thailand
Pattaya 115 C5 Chon Buri, S Thailand
Patuca, Río 30 D2 river E Honduras
Pau 69 B6 Pyrénées-Atlantiques, SW France
Paulatuk 15 E3 Northwest Territories, NW Canada
Paungde 114 B4 Bago, C Myanmar (Burma)
Pautalia see Kyustendil
Pavia 74 B2 anc. Ticinum. Lombardia, N Italy
Pāvilosta 84 B3 Liepāja, W Latvia
Pavlikeni 82 D2 Veliko Tŭrnovo, N Bulgaria
Pavlodar 92 C4 Pavlodar, NE Kazakhstan
Pavlograd see Pavlohrad
Pavlohrad 87 G3 Rus. Pavlograd. Dnipropetrovs'ka Oblast', E Ukraine
Pawai, Pulau 116 A2 island SW Singapore Asia
Pawn 114 B3 river C Myanmar (Burma)
Pax Augusta see Badajoz
Pax Julia see Beja
Paxoí 83 A5 island Iónia Nisiá, Greece, C Mediterranean Sea
Payo Obispo see Chetumal
Paysandú 42 D4 Paysandú, W Uruguay
Pazar 95 E2 Rize, NE Turkey
Pazardzhik 82 C3 prev. Tatar Pazardzhik. Pazardzhik, SW Bulgaria
Peace Garden State see North Dakota
Peach State see Georgia
Pearl Islands 31 G5 Eng. Pearl Islands. island group SE Panama
Pearl Islands see Perlas, Archipiélago de las
Pearl Lagoon 31 E3 Eng. Pearl Lagoon. lagoon E Nicaragua
Pearl Lagoon see Perlas, Laguna de
Pearl River 20 B3 river Louisiana/Mississippi, S USA
Pearsall 27 F4 Texas, SW USA
Peawanuk 16 C2 prev. Winisk. Ontario, C Canada
Peawanuk 16 C2 river Ontario, S Canada
Peć see Pejë
Pechora 88 D3 Respublika Komi, NW Russian Federation
Pechora 88 D3 river NW Russian Federation
Pechora Sea 88 D2 Eng. Pechora Sea. sea NW Russian Federation
Pechora Sea see Pechorskoye More
Pecos 27 E3 Texas, SW USA
Pecos River 27 E3 river New Mexico/Texas, SW USA
Pécs 77 C7 Ger. Fünfkirchen, Lat. Sopianae. Baranya, SW Hungary
Pedra Lume 52 A3 Sal, NE Cape Verde
Pedro Cays 32 C3 island group Greater Antilles, S Jamaica North America N Caribbean Sea W Atlantic Ocean
Pedro Juan Caballero 42 D2 Amambay, E Paraguay
Peer 65 D5 Limburg, NE Belgium
Pegasus Bay 129 C6 bay South Island, New Zealand
Pegu see Bago
Pehuajó 42 C4 Buenos Aires, E Argentina
Pei-ching see Beijing/Beijing Shi
Peine 72 B3 Niedersachsen, C Germany
Pei-p'ing see Beijing/Beijing Shi
Peipsi Järv/Peipus-See see Peipus, Lake
Peipus, Lake 84 E3 Est. Peipsi Järv, Ger. Peipus-See, Rus. Chudskoye Ozero. lake Estonia/Russian Federation
Peiraías 83 C6 prev. Piraiévs, Eng. Piraeus. Attikí, C Greece
Pejë 79 D5 Serb. Peć. W Kosovo
Pèk 114 D4 var. Xieng Khouang; prev. Xiangkhoang. Xiangkhoang, N Laos
Pekalongan 116 C4 Jawa, C Indonesia
Pekanbaru 116 B3 var. Pakanbaru. Sumatera, W Indonesia
Pekin 18 B4 Illinois, N USA
Peking see Beijing/Beijing Shi
Pelagie 75 B8 island group SW Italy
Pelagosa see Palagruža
Pelican State see Louisiana
Pelly Bay see Kugaaruk
Pélmonostor see Beli Manastir
Peloponnese 83 B6 var. Morea, Eng. Peloponnese; anc. Peloponnesus. peninsula S Greece
Peloponnese/Peloponnesus see Pelopónnisos
Pematangsiantar 116 B3 Sumatera, W Indonesia
Pemba 57 F2 prev. Port Amelia, Porto Amélia. Cabo Delgado, NE Mozambique
Pemba 51 D7 island E Tanzania
Pembroke 16 D4 Ontario, SE Canada
Penang see George Town
Penang see Pinang, Pulau, Peninsular Malaysia
Penas, Golfo de 43 A7 gulf S Chile
Penderma see Bandırma
Pendleton 24 C3 Oregon, NW USA
Pend Oreille, Lake 24 D2 lake Idaho, NW USA
Peneius see Pineiós
Peng-pu see Bengbu
Penibético, Sistema see Béticos, Sistemas
Peniche 70 B3 Leiria, W Portugal
Peninsular State see Florida
Penninae, Alpes/Pennine, Alpi see Pennine Alps
Pennine Alps 73 A8 Fr. Alpes Pennines, It. Alpi Pennine, Lat. Alpes Penninae. mountain range Italy/Switzerland
Pennine Chain see Pennines
Pennines 67 D5 var. Pennine Chain. mountain range N England, United Kingdom
Pennines, Alpes see Pennine Alps
Pennsylvania 19 E4 off. Commonwealth of Pennsylvania, also known as Keystone State. state NE USA
Penobscot River 19 G2 river Maine, NE USA
Penong 127 A6 South Australia
Penonomé 31 F5 Coclé, C Panama
Penrhyn 123 G3 atoll N Cook Islands
Penrhyn Basin 121 F3 undersea feature C Pacific Ocean
Penrith 126 D1 New South Wales, SE Australia
Penrith 67 D5 NW England, United Kingdom
Pensacola 20 C3 Florida, SE USA
Pentecost 122 D4 Fr. Pentecôte. island C Vanuatu
Pentecôte see Pentecost
Penza 89 C6 Penzenskaya Oblast', W Russian Federation
Penzance 67 C7 SW England, United Kingdom
Peoria 18 B4 Illinois, N USA
Perchtoldsdorf 73 E6 Niederösterreich, NE Austria
Percival Lakes 124 C4 lakes Western Australia
Perdido, Monte 71 F1 mountain NE Spain
Perece Vela Basin see West Mariana Basin
Pereira 36 B3 Risaralda, W Colombia
Peremyshl see Przemyśl
Pergamino 42 C4 Buenos Aires, E Argentina
Périgueux 69 C5 anc. Vesuna. Dordogne, SW France
Perito Moreno 43 B6 Santa Cruz, S Argentina
Perleberg 72 C3 Brandenburg, N Germany
Perlepe see Prilep
Perm' 92 C3 prev. Molotov. Permskaya Oblast', NW Russian Federation
Pernambuco 41 G2 off. Estado de Pernambuco. region E Brazil
Pernambuco 41 G2 off. Estado de Pernambuco. state E Brazil
Pernambuco see Recife
Pernambuco Abyssal Plain see Pernambuco Plain
Pernambuco, Estado de see Pernambuco
Pernambuco Plain 45 C5 var. Pernambuco Abyssal Plain. undersea feature E Atlantic Ocean
Pernau see Pärnu
Pernauer Bucht see Pärnu Laht
Pērnava see Pärnu
Pernik 82 B2 prev. Dimitrovo. Pernik, W Bulgaria
Pernov see Pärnu
Perote 29 F4 Veracruz-Llave, E Mexico
Pérouse see Perugia
Perovsk see Kyzylorda
Perpignan 69 C6 Pyrénées-Orientales, S France
Perryton 27 F1 Texas, SW USA
Perryville 23 H5 Missouri, C USA
Persia see Iran
Perth 125 A6 state capital Western Australia
Perth 66 C4 C Scotland, United Kingdom
Perth Basin 119 E6 undersea feature SE Indian Ocean
Peru 38 C3 off. Republic of Peru. country W South America
Peru see Beru
Peru Basin 45 A5 undersea feature E Pacific Ocean
Peru-Chile Trench 34 A4 undersea feature E Pacific Ocean
Perugia 74 C4 Fr. Pérouse; anc. Perusia. Umbria, C Italy
Perugia, Lake of see Trasimeno, Lago
Peru, Republic of see Peru
Perusia see Perugia
Péruwelz 65 B6 Hainaut, SW Belgium
Pervomays'k 87 E3 prev. Ol'viopol'. Mykolayivs'ka Oblast', S Ukraine
Pervyy Kuril'skiy Proliv 93 H3 strait E Russian Federation
Pesaro 74 C3 anc. Pisaurum. Marche, C Italy
Pescara 74 D4 anc. Aternum, Ostia Aterni. Abruzzo, C Italy
Peshāwar 112 C1 North-West Frontier Province, N Pakistan
Peshkopi 79 C6 var. Peshkopia, Peshkopija. Dibër, NE Albania
Peshkopia/Peshkopija see Peshkopi
Pessac 69 B5 Gironde, SW France
Petach-Tikva see Petah Tikva
Petah Tikva 97 A6 var. Petach-Tikva, Petah Tiqva, Petakh Tikva; prev. Petah Tiqwa. Tel Aviv, C Israel
Petah Tiqwa see Petah Tikva
Petakh Tikva/Petah Tiqva see Petah Tikva
Pétange 65 D8 Luxembourg, SW Luxembourg
Petchaburi see Phetchaburi
Peterborough 127 B6 South Australia
Peterborough 16 D5 Ontario, SE Canada
Peterborough 67 E6 prev. Medeshamstede. E England, United Kingdom
Peterhead 66 D3 NE Scotland, United Kingdom
Peter I Øy 132 A3 Norwegian dependency Antarctica
Petermann Bjerg 61 E3 mountain C Greenland
Petersburg 19 E5 Virginia, NE USA
Peters Mine 37 F3 var. Peter's Mine. N Guyana
Petit St-Bernard, Col du see Little Saint Bernard Pass
Peto 29 H4 Yucatán, SE Mexico
Petoskey 18 C2 Michigan, N USA
Petra see Wādī Mūsā
Petrich 82 C3 Blagoevgrad, SW Bulgaria
Petrikau see Piotrków Trybunalski
Petrikov see Pyetrykaw
Petrinja 78 B3 Sisak-Moslavina, C Croatia
Petroaleksandrovsk see To'rtkok'l
Petrodvorets 88 A4 Fin. Pietarhovi. Leningradskaya Oblast', NW Russian Federation
Petrograd see Sankt-Peterburg
Petrokov see Piotrków Trybunalski
Petropavl see Petropavlovsk
Petropavlovsk 92 C4 Kaz. Petropavl. Severnyy Kazakhstan, N Kazakhstan
Petropavlovsk-Kamchatskiy 93 H3 Kamchatskaya Oblast', E Russian Federation
Petroșani 86 B4 var. Petroșeni, Ger. Petroschen, Hung. Petrozsény. Hunedoara, W Romania
Petroschen/Petroșeni see Petroșani
Petroskoi see Petrozavodsk
Petrovgrad see Zrenjanin
Petrovsk-Port see Makhachkala
Petrozavodsk 92 B2 Fin. Petroskoi. Respublika Kareliya, NW Russian Federation
Petrozsény see Petroșani
Pettau see Ptuj
Pevek 93 G1 Chukotskiy Avtonomnyy Okrug, NE Russian Federation
Pezinok 77 C6 Ger. Bösing, Hung. Bazin. Bratislavský Kraj, W Slovakia
Pforzheim 73 B6 Baden-Württemberg, SW Germany
Pfungstadt 73 B5 Hessen, W Germany
Phangan, Ko 115 C6 island SW Thailand
Phang-Nga 115 B7 var. Pang-Nga, Phangnga. Phangnga, SW Thailand
Phangnga see Phang-Nga
Phan Rang/Phanrang see Phan Rang-Thap Cham
Phan Rang-Thap Cham 115 E6 var. Phanrang, Phan Rang, Phan Rang Thap Cham. Ninh Thuân, S Vietnam
Phan Thiêt 115 E6 Binh Thuân, S Vietnam
Pharnacia see Giresun
Pharus see Hvar
Phatthalung 115 C7 var. Padalung, Patalung. Phatthalung, SW Thailand
Phayao 114 C4 var. Muang Phayao. Phayao, NW Thailand
Phenix City 20 D2 Alabama, S USA
Phet Buri see Phetchaburi
Phetchaburi 115 C5 var. Bejraburi, Petchaburi, Phet Buri. Phetchaburi, SW Thailand
Philadelphia 19 F4 Pennsylvania, NE USA
Philadelphia see 'Ammān
Philippine Basin 103 F3 undersea feature W Pacific Ocean
Philippine Islands 117 E1 island group W Pacific Ocean
Philippines 117 E1 off. Republic of the Philippines. country SE Asia
Philippine Sea 103 F3 sea W Pacific Ocean
Philippines, Republic of the see Philippines
Philippine Trench 120 A1 undersea feature W Philippine Sea
Philippopolis see Plovdiv
Phitsanulok 114 C4 var. Bisnulok, Muang Phitsanulok, Pitsanulok. Phitsanulok, C Thailand
Phlórina see Flórina
Phnom Penh see Phnum Penh
Phnum Penh 115 D6 var. Phnom Penh. country capital Phnum Penh, S Cambodia
Phoenix 26 B2 state capital Arizona, SW USA
Phoenix Islands 123 E3 island group C Kiribati
Phôngsali 114 C3 var. Phong Saly. Phôngsali, N Laos
Phong Saly see Phôngsali
Phrae 114 C4 var. Muang Phrae, Prae. Phrae, NW Thailand
Phra Nakhon Si Ayutthaya see Ayutthaya
Phra Thong, Ko 115 B6 island SW Thailand
Phuket 115 B7 var. Bhuket, Puket, Mal. Ujung Salang; prev. Junkseylon, Salang. Phuket, SW Thailand
Phuket, Ko 115 B7 island SW Thailand
Phumĭ Kâmpóng Trâbêk 115 D5 prev. Phum Kompong Trabek. Kâmpóng Thum, C Cambodia
Phumĭ Sâmraông 115 D5 prev. Phum Samrong. Siĕmréab, NW Cambodia
Phum Kompong Trabek see Phumĭ Kâmpóng Trâbêk
Phum Samrong see Phumĭ Sâmraông
Phu Vinh see Tra Vinh
Phyu 114 B4 var. Hpyu, Pyu. Bago, C Myanmar (Burma)
Piacenza 74 B2 Fr. Paisance; anc. Placentia. Emilia-Romagna, N Italy
Piatra-Neamț 86 C4 Hung. Karácsonkő. Neamț, NE Romania
Piauhy see Piauí
Piauí 41 F2 off. Estado do Piauí; prev. Piauhy. state E Brazil
Piauí 41 F2 off. Estado do Piauí; prev. Piauhy. region E Brazil
Piauí, Estado do see Piauí
Picardie 68 C3 Eng. Picardy. cultural region N France
Picardy see Picardie
Piccolo San Bernardo, Colle di see Little Saint Bernard Pass
Pichilemu 42 B4 Libertador, C Chile
Pico 70 A5 var. Ilha do Pico. island Azores, Portugal, NE Atlantic Ocean
Pico, Ilha do see Pico
Picos 41 F2 Piauí, E Brazil
Picton 129 C5 Marlborough, South Island, New Zealand
Piedmont see Piemonte
Piedras Negras 29 E2 var. Ciudad Porfirio Díaz. Coahuila de Zaragoza, NE Mexico
Pielavesi 62 D4 lake C Finland
Pielinen 62 E4 var. Pielisjärvi. lake E Finland
Pielisjärvi see Pielinen
Piemonte 74 A2 Eng. Piedmont. region NW Italy
Pierre 23 E3 state capital South Dakota, N USA
Piešťany 77 C6 Ger. Pistyan, Hung. Pöstyén. Tranavský Kraj, W Slovakia
Pietarhovi see Petrodvorets
Pietari see Sankt-Peterburg
Pietarsaari see Jakobstad
Pietermaritzburg 56 C5 var. Maritzburg. KwaZulu/Natal, E South Africa
Pietersburg see Polokwane
Bay of Pigs 32 B2 Eng. Bay of Pigs. bay SE Cuba
Pigs, Bay of see Cochinos, Bahía de
Pihkva Järv see Pskov, Lake
Pijijiapan 29 G5 Chiapas, SE Mexico
Pikes Peak 22 C5 mountain Colorado, C USA
Pikeville 18 D5 Kentucky, S USA
Pikinni see Bikini Atoll
Piła 76 B3 Ger. Schneidemühl. Wielkopolskie, C Poland
Pilar 42 D3 var. Villa del Pilar. Ñeembucú, S Paraguay
Pilcomayo, Rio 35 C5 river C South America
Pilos see Pýlos
Pilsen see Plzeň
Pilzno see Plzeň
Pinang see Pinang, Pulau, Peninsular Malaysia
Pinang see George Town
Pinang, Pulau 116 B3 var. Penang, Pinang; prev. Prince of Wales Island. island Peninsular Malaysia
Pinar del Río 32 A2 Pinar del Río, W Cuba
Píndhos/Píndhos Óros see Píndos
Pindus Mountains 82 A4 var. Píndhos Óros, Eng. Pindus Mountains; prev. Píndhos. mountain range C Greece
Pindus Mountains see Píndos
Pine Bluff 20 B2 Arkansas, C USA
Pine Creek 124 D2 Northern Territory, N Australia
Pinega 88 C3 river NW Russian Federation
Pineiós 82 B4 var. Piniós; anc. Peneius. river C Greece
Pineland 27 H3 Texas, SW USA
Pínes, Akrotírio 82 C4 var. Akrotírio Pínnes. headland N Greece
Pines, The Isle of the see Juventud, Isla de la
Pine Tree State see Maine
Pingdingshan 106 C4 Henan, C China
Pingkiang see Harbin
Ping, Mae Nam 114 B4 river W Thailand
Piniós see Pineiós
Pinkiang see Harbin
Pínnes, Akrotírio see Pínes, Akrotírio
Pinos, Isla de see Juventud, Isla de la
Pinotepa Nacional 29 F5 var. Santiago Pinotepa Nacional. Oaxaca, SE Mexico
Pinsk 85 B7 Pol. Pińsk. Brestskaya Voblasts', SW Belarus
Pinta, Isla 38 A5 var. Abingdon. island Galapagos Islands, Ecuador, E Pacific Ocean
Piombino 74 B3 Toscana, C Italy
Pioneer Mountains 24 D3 mountain range Montana, N USA North America
Pionerskiy 84 A4 Ger. Neukuhren. Kaliningradskaya Oblast', W Russian Federation
Piotrków Trybunalski 76 D4 Ger. Petrikau, Rus. Petrokov. Łodzkie, C Poland
Piraeus/Piraiévs see Peiraías
Pírgos see Pýrgos
Pirineos see Pyrenees
Piripiri 41 F2 Piauí, E Brazil
Pirna 72 D4 Sachsen, E Germany
Pirot 79 E5 Serbia, SE Serbia
Piryatin see Pyryatyn
Pisa 74 B3 var. Pisae. Toscana, C Italy
Pisae see Pisa
Pisaurum see Pesaro
Pisco 38 D4 Ica, SW Peru
Písek 77 A5 Budějovický Kraj, S Czech Republic
Pishan 104 A3 var. Guma. Xinjiang Uygur Zizhiqu, NW China
Pishpek see Bishkek
Pistoia 74 B3 anc. Pistoria, Pistoriæ. Toscana, C Italy
Pistoria/Pistoriæ see Pistoia
Pistyan see Piešťany
Pisz 76 D3 Ger. Johannisburg. Warmińsko-Mazurskie, NE Poland
Pita 52 C4 NW Guinea
Pitalito 36 B4 Huila, S Colombia
Pitcairn Island 121 G4 island S Pitcairn Islands
Pitcairn Islands 121 G4 UK dependent territory C Pacific Ocean
Piteå 62 D4 Norrbotten, N Sweden
Pitești 86 B5 Argeș, S Romania
Pitsanulok see Phitsanulok
Pitt Island see Makin
Pittsburg 23 F5 Kansas, C USA
Pittsburgh 19 E4 Pennsylvania, NE USA
Pittsfield 19 F3 Massachusetts, NE USA
Piura 38 B2 Piura, NW Peru
Pivdennyy Buh 87 E3 Rus. Yuzhnyy Bug. river S Ukraine
Placentia see Piacenza
Placetas 32 B2 Villa Clara, C Cuba
Plainview 27 E2 Texas, SW USA
Planeta Rica 36 B2 Córdoba, NW Colombia
Planken 72 E1 C Liechtenstein Europe
Plano 27 G2 Texas, SW USA
Plasencia 70 C3 Extremadura, W Spain
Plate, River 42 D4 var. River Plate. estuary Argentina/Uruguay
Plate, River see Plata, Río de la
Platinum 14 C3 Alaska, USA
Plattensee see Balaton
Platte River 23 E4 river Nebraska, C USA
Plattsburgh 19 F2 New York, NE USA
Plauen 73 C5 var. Plauen im Vogtland. Sachsen, E Germany
Plauen im Vogtland see Plauen
Pļaviņas 84 D4 Ger. Stockmannshof. Aizkraukle, S Latvia
Plây Cu 115 E5 var. Pleiku. Gia Lai, C Vietnam
Pleasant Island see Nauru
Pleiku see Plây Cu
Plenty, Bay of 128 E3 bay North Island, New Zealand
Plérin 68 A3 Côtes d'Armor, NW France
Plesetsk 88 C3 Arkhangel'skaya Oblast', NW Russian Federation
Pleshchenitsy see Plyeshchanitsy
Pleskau see Pskov
Pleskauer See see Pskov, Lake
Pleskava see Pskov
Pleszew 76 C4 Wielkopolskie, C Poland
Pleven 82 C2 prev. Plevna. Pleven, N Bulgaria
Plevlja/Plevlje see Pljevlja
Plevna see Pleven
Pljevlja 78 C4 prev. Plevlja, Plevlje. N Montenegro
Plocce see Ploče
Ploče 78 B4 It. Plocce; prev. Kardeljevo. Dubrovnik-Neretva, SE Croatia
Płock 76 D3 Ger. Plozk. Mazowieckie, C Poland
Plöcken Pass 73 C7 Ger. Plöckenpass, It. Passo di Monte Croce Carnico. pass SW Austria
Plöckenpass see Plöcken Pass
Ploești see Ploiești
Ploiești 86 C5 prev. Ploești. Prahova, SE Romania
Plomári 83 D5 prev. Plomárion. Lésvos, E Greece
Plomárion see Plomári
Płońsk 76 D3 Mazowieckie, C Poland
Plovdiv 82 C3 prev. Eumolpias; anc. Evmolpia, Philippopolis, Lat. Trimontium. Plovdiv, C Bulgaria
Plozk see Płock
Plungė 84 B3 Telšiai, W Lithuania
Plyeshchanitsy 85 D5 Rus. Pleshchenitsy. Minskaya Voblasts', N Belarus
Plymouth 33 G3 dependent territory capital SW Montserrat
Plymouth 67 C7 SW England, United Kingdom
Plzeň 77 A5 Ger. Pilsen, Pol. Pilzno. Plzeňský Kraj, W Czech Republic
Po 58 D4 river N Italy
Pobedy, Pik 104 B3 Chin. Tomür Feng. mountain China/Kyrgyzstan
Po, Bocche del see Po, Foci del
Pocahontas 20 B1 Arkansas, C USA
Pocatello 24 E4 Idaho, NW USA
Pochinok 89 A5 Smolenskaya Oblast', W Russian Federation
Pocking 73 D6 Bayern, SE Germany
Poděbrady 77 B5 Ger. Podiebrad. Středočeský Kraj, C Czech Republic
Podgorica 79 C5 prev. Titograd. country capital S Montenegro
Podiebrad see Poděbrady
Podil's'ka Vysochina 86 D3 plateau W Ukraine
Podium Anicensis see le Puy
Podol'sk 89 B5 Moskovskaya Oblast', W Russian Federation
Podravska Slatina see Slatina
Podujevë 79 D5 Serb. Podujevo. N Kosovo
Podujevo see Podujevë
Podunajská Rovina see Little Alföld
Poetovio see Ptuj
Pogradec 79 D6 var. Pogradeci. Korçë, SE Albania
Pogradeci see Pogradec
Pohjanlahti see Bothnia, Gulf of
Pohnpei 122 C2 prev. Ponape Ascension Island. island E Micronesia
Poictiers see Poitiers
Poinsett, Cape 132 D4 headland Antarctica
Point de Galle see Galle
Pointe-à-Pitre 33 G3 Grande Terre, C Guadeloupe
Pointe-Noire 55 B6 Kouilou, S Congo
Point Lay 14 C2 Alaska, USA
Poitiers 68 B4 prev. Poictiers; anc. Limonum. Vienne, W France
Poitou 68 B4 cultural region W France
Pokharā 113 E3 Western, C Nepal
Pokrovka see Kyzyl-Suu
Pokrovs'ke 87 G3 Rus. Pokrovskoye. Dnipropetrovs'ka Oblast', E Ukraine
Pokrovskoye see Pokrovs'ke
Pola see Pula
Pola de Lena 70 D1 Asturias, N Spain
Poland 76 B4 off. Republic of Poland, var. Polish Republic, Pol. Polska, Rzeczpospolita Polska; prev. Pol. Polska Rzeczpospolita Ludowa, The Polish People's Republic. country C Europe
Poland, Republic of see Poland
Polatlı 94 C3 Ankara, C Turkey
Polatsk 85 D5 Rus. Polotsk. Vitsyebskaya Voblasts', N Belarus
Pol-e Khomrī 101 E4 var. Pul-i-Khumri. Baghlān, NE Afghanistan
Poli see Pólis
Polikastro/Políkastron see Polýkastro
Polikrayshte 82 D2 Veliko Tŭrnovo, N Bulgaria
Pólis 80 C5 var. Poli. W Cyprus
Polish People's Republic, The see Poland
Polish Republic see Poland
Polkowice 76 B4 Ger. Heerwegen. Dolnośląskie, W Poland
Pollença 71 G3 Mallorca, Spain, W Mediterranean Sea
Pologi see Polohy
Polohy 87 G3 Rus. Pologi. Zaporiz'ka Oblast', SE Ukraine
Polokwane 56 D4 prev. Pietersburg. Limpopo, NE South Africa
Polonne 86 D2 Rus. Polonnoye. Khmel'nyts'ka Oblast', NW Ukraine
Polonnoye see Polonne
Polotsk see Polatsk
Polska/Polska, Rzeczpospolita/Polska Rzeczpospolita Ludowa see Poland
Polsko Kosovo 82 D2 Ruse, N Bulgaria
Poltava 87 F2 Poltavs'ka Oblast', NE Ukraine
Poltoratsk see Aşgabat
Põlva 84 E3 Ger. Pölwe. Põlvamaa, SE Estonia
Pölwe see Põlva
Polyarnyy 88 C2 Murmanskaya Oblast', NW Russian Federation
Polýkastro 82 B3 var. Polikastro; prev. Políkastron. Kentrikí Makedonía, N Greece
Polynesia 121 F4 island group C Pacific Ocean
Pomeranian Bay 72 D2 Ger. Pommersche Bucht, Pol. Zatoka Pomorska. bay Germany/Poland
Pomir, Dar"yoi see Pamir/Pāmīr, Daryā-ye
Pommersche Bucht see Pomeranian Bay
Pomorska, Zatoka see Pomeranian Bay
Pomorskiy Proliv 88 D2 strait NW Russian Federation
Po, Mouth of the 74 C2 var. Bocche del Po. river NE Italy
Pompaelo see Pamplona
Pompano Beach 21 F5 Florida, SE USA
Ponape Ascension Island see Pohnpei
Ponca City 27 G1 Oklahoma, C USA
Ponce 33 F3 C Puerto Rico
Pondicherry 110 C2 var. Puduchcheri, Fr. Pondichéry. Pondicherry, SE India
Ponferrada 70 C1 Castilla-León, NW Spain
Poniatowa 76 E4 Lubelskie, E Poland
Pons Aelii see Newcastle upon Tyne
Pons Vetus see Pontevedra
Ponta Delgada 70 B5 São Miguel, Azores, Portugal, NE Atlantic Ocean
Ponta Grossa 41 E4 Paraná, S Brazil
Pontarlier 68 D4 Doubs, E France
Ponteareas 70 B2 Galicia, NW Spain
Ponte da Barca 70 B2 Viana do Castelo, N Portugal
Pontevedra 70 B1 anc. Pons Vetus. Galicia, NW Spain
Pontiac 18 D3 Michigan, N USA
Pontianak 116 C4 Borneo, C Indonesia
Pontisarae see Pontoise
Pontivy 68 A3 Morbihan, NW France
Pontoise 68 C3 anc. Briva Isarae, Cergy-Pontoise, Pontisarae. Val-d'Oise, N France
Ponziane Island 75 C5 island C Italy
Poole 67 D7 S England, United Kingdom
Poona see Pune
Poopó, Lago 39 F4 var. Lago Pampa Aullagas. lake W Bolivia
Popayán 36 B4 Cauca, SW Colombia
Poperinge 65 A6 West-Vlaanderen, W Belgium
Poplar Bluff 23 G5 Missouri, C USA
Popocatépetl 29 E4 volcano S Mexico
Popper see Poprad
Poprad 77 D5 Ger. Deutschendorf, Hung. Poprád. Prešovský Kraj, E Slovakia
Poprád 77 D5 Ger. Popper, Hung. Poprád. river Poland/Slovakia
Porbandar 112 B4 Gujarāt, W India
Porcupine Plain 58 B3 undersea feature E Atlantic Ocean
Pordenone 74 C2 anc. Portenau. Friuli-Venezia Giulia, NE Italy
Poreč 78 A2 It. Parenzo. Istra, NW Croatia
Porech'ye see Parechcha
Pori 63 D5 Swe. Björneborg. Länsi-Suomi, SW Finland
Porirua 129 D5 Wellington, North Island, New Zealand
Porkhov 88 A4 Pskovskaya Oblast', W Russian Federation
Porlamar 37 E1 Nueva Esparta, NE Venezuela
Póros 83 C6 Póros, S Greece
Póros 83 A5 Kefallinía, Iónia Nisiá, Greece, C Mediterranean Sea
Pors see Porsangenfijorden
Porsangenfijorden 62 D2 Lapp. Pors. fjord N Norway
Porsgrunn 63 B6 Telemark, S Norway
Portachuelo 39 G4 Santa Cruz, C Bolivia
Portadown 67 B5 Ir. Port An Dúnáin. S Northern Ireland, United Kingdom
Portalegre 70 C3 anc. Ammaia, Amoea. Portalegre, E Portugal
Port Alexander 14 D4 Baranof Island, Alaska, USA
Port Alfred 56 D5 Eastern Cape, S South Africa
Port Amelia see Pemba
Port An Dúnáin see Portadown

Rudzyensk – San Marino

Rudzyensk 85 C6 Rus. Rudensk. Minskaya Voblasts', C Belarus
Rufiji 51 C7 river E Tanzania
Rufino 42 C4 Santa Fe, C Argentina
Rugāji 84 D4 Balvi, E Latvia
Rügen 72 D2 headland NE Germany
Ruggell 72 E1 N Liechtenstein Europe
Ruhja see Rūjiena
Ruhnu 84 C2 var. Ruhnu Saar, Swe. Runö. island SW Estonia
Ruhnu Saar see Ruhnu
Rujen see Rūjiena
Rūjiena 84 D3 Est. Ruhja, Ger. Rujen. Valmiera, N Latvia
Rukwa, Lake 51 B7 lake SE Tanzania
Rum see Rhum
Ruma 78 D3 Vojvodina, N Serbia
Rumadiya see Ar Ramādī
Rumania/Rumänien see Romania
Rumbek 51 B5 El Buhayrat, S Sudan
Rum Cay 32 D2 island C Bahamas
Rumia 76 C2 Pomorskie, N Poland
Rummah, Wādī ar see Rimah, Wādī ar
Rummelsburg in Pommern see Miastko
Rumuniya/Rumŭniya/Rumunjska see Romania
Runanga 129 B5 West Coast, South Island, New Zealand
Rundu 56 C3 var. Runtu. Okavango, NE Namibia
Runö see Ruhnu
Runtu see Rundu
Ruoqiang 104 C3 var. Jo-ch'iang, Uigh. Charkhlik, Charkhliq, Qarkilik. Xinjiang Uygur Zizhiqu, NW China
Rupea 86 C4 Ger. Reps, Hung. Kőhalom; prev. Cohalm. Braşov, C Romania
Rupel 65 B5 river N Belgium
Rupella see la Rochelle
Rupert, Rivière de 16 D3 river Québec, C Canada
Rusaddir see Melilla
Ruschuk/Rusçuk see Ruse
Ruse 82 D1 var. Ruschuk, Rustchuk, Turk. Rusçuk. Ruse, N Bulgaria
Russadir see Melilla
Russellville 20 A1 Arkansas, C USA
Russia see Russian Federation
Russian America see Alaska
Russian Federation 90 D2 off. Russian Federation, var. Russia, Latv. Krievija, Rus. Rossiyskaya Federatsiya. country Asia/Europe
Russian Federation see Russian Federation
Rustaq see Ar Rustāq
Rust'avi 95 G2 SE Georgia
Rustchuk see Ruse
Ruston 20 B2 Louisiana, S USA
Rutanzige, Lake see Edward, Lake
Rutba see Ar Ruṭbah
Rutlam see Ratlām
Rutland 19 F2 Vermont, NE USA
Rutog 104 A4 var. Rutög, Rutok. Xizang Zizhiqu, W China
Rutok see Rutog
Ruvuma 47 E5 var. Rio Rovuma. river Mozambique/Tanzania
Ruvuma see Rovuma, Rio
Ruwenzori 55 E5 mountain range Dem. Rep. Congo/Uganda
Ruzhany 85 B6 Brestskaya Voblasts', SW Belarus
Ružomberok 77 C5 Ger. Rosenberg, Hung. Rózsahegy. Žilinský Kraj, N Slovakia
Rwanda 51 B6 off. Rwandese Republic; prev. Ruanda. country C Africa
Rwandese Republic see Rwanda
Ryazan' 89 B5 Ryazanskaya Oblast', W Russian Federation
Rybach'ye see Balykchy
Rybinsk 88 B4 prev. Andropov. Yaroslavskaya Oblast', W Russian Federation
Rybnik 77 C5 Śląskie, S Poland
Rybnitsa see Ribniţa
Ryde 126 E1 United Kingdom
Ryki 76 D4 Lubelskie, E Poland
Rykovo see Yenakiyeve
Rypin 76 C3 Kujawsko-pomorskie, C Poland
Ryssel see Lille
Rysy 77 C5 mountain S Poland
Ryukyu Islands 103 E3 Eng. Ryukyu Islands. island group SW Japan
Ryukyu Islands 108 A2 Eng. Ryukyu Islands. island group SW Japan
Ryukyu Islands see Nansei-shotō
Ryukyu Islands see Nansei-shotō
Ryukyu Trench 103 F3 var. Nansei Syotō Trench. trench S East China Sea
Rzeszów 77 E5 Podkarpackie, SE Poland
Rzhev 88 B4 Tverskaya Oblast', W Russian Federation

S

Saale 72 C4 river C Germany
Saalfeld 73 C5 var. Saalfeld an der Saale. Thüringen, C Germany
Saalfeld an der Saale see Saalfeld
Saarbrücken 73 A6 Fr. Sarrebruck. Saarland, SW Germany
Sääre 84 C2 var. Sjar. Saaremaa, W Estonia
Saare see Saaremaa
Saaremaa 84 C2 Ger. Oesel, Ösel; prev. Saare. island W Estonia
Saariselkä 62 D2 Lapp. Suoločielgi. Lappi, N Finland
Sab' Ābār 96 C4 var. Sab'a Biyar, Sa'b Bi'ār. Ḥimṣ, C Syria
Sab'a Biyar see Sab' Ābār
Šabac 78 D3 Serbia, W Serbia
Sabadell 71 G2 Cataluña, E Spain
Sabah 116 D3 prev. British North Borneo, North Borneo. state East Malaysia
Sabanalarga 36 B1 Atlántico, N Colombia
Sabaneta 36 C1 Falcón, N Venezuela
Sabaria see Szombathely
Sab'atayn, Ramlat as 99 C6 desert C Yemen
Sabaya 39 F4 Oruro, S Bolivia
Sa'b Bi'ār see Sab' Ābār
Saberi, Hamun-e 100 C5 var. Daryācheh-ye Hāmun, Daryācheh-ye Sīstān. lake Afghanistan/Iran
Sabhā 49 F3 C Libya
Sabi see Save
Sabinas 29 E2 Coahuila de Zaragoza, NE Mexico
Sabinas Hidalgo 29 E2 Nuevo León, NE Mexico
Sabine River 27 H3 river Louisiana/Texas, SW USA
Sabkha see As Sabkhah
Sable, Cape 21 E5 headland Florida, SE USA
Sable Island 17 G4 island Nova Scotia, SE Canada
Şabyā 99 B6 Jīzān, SW Saudi Arabia
Sabzawar see Sabzevār
Sabzevār 98 D2 var. Sabzawar. Khorāsān-Razavī, NE Iran
Sachsen 72 D4 Eng. Saxony, Fr. Saxe. state E Germany
Sachs Harbour 15 E2 var. Ikaahuk. Banks Island, Northwest Territories, N Canada
Sächsisch-Reen/Sächsisch-Regen see Reghin
Sacramento 25 B5 state capital California, W USA
Sacramento Mountains 26 D2 mountain range New Mexico, SW USA
Sacramento River 25 B5 river California, W USA
Sacramento Valley 25 B5 valley California, W USA
Sá da Bandeira see Lubango
Şa'dah 99 B6 NW Yemen
Sado 109 C5 var. Sadoga-shima. island C Japan
Sadoga-shima see Sado
Saena Julia see Siena
Safad see Tsefat
Şafāqis see Sfax
Şafāshahr 98 D3 var. Deh Bīd. Fārs, C Iran
Safed see Tsefat
Säffle 63 B6 Värmland, C Sweden
Safford 26 C3 Arizona, SW USA
Safi 48 B2 W Morocco
Selseleh-ye Safīd Kuh 100 D4 Eng. Paropamisus Range. mountain range W Afghanistan
Sagaing 114 B3 Sagaing, C Myanmar (Burma)
Sagami-nada 109 D6 inlet SW Japan
Sagan see Żagań
Sāgar 112 D4 prev. Saugor. Madhya Pradesh, C India
Sagarmāthā see Everest, Mount
Sagebrush State see Nevada
Saghez see Saqqez
Saginaw 18 C3 Michigan, N USA
Saginaw Bay 18 D2 lake bay Michigan, N USA
Sagua la Grande 32 B2 Villa Clara, C Cuba
Sagunto 71 F3 Cat. Sagunt, Ar. Murviedro; anc. Saguntum. País Valenciano, E Spain
Sagunt/Saguntum see Sagunto
Sahara 46 B3 desert Libya/Algeria
Sahara el Gharbiya see Şaḥrā' al Gharbīyah
Saharan Atlas 48 D2 var. Saharan Atlas. mountain range Algeria/Morocco
Saharan Atlas see Atlas Saharien
Sahel 52 D3 physical region C Africa
Sāḥilīyah, Jibāl as 96 B3 mountain range NW Syria
Sāhīwāl 112 C2 prev. Montgomery. Punjab, E Pakistan
Saïda 97 A5 var. Şaydā, Sayida; anc. Sidon. W Lebanon
Sa'īdābād see Sīrjān
Saidpur 113 G3 var. Syedpur. Rajshahi, NW Bangladesh
Saidu Sharif 112 C1 var. Mingora, Mongora. North-West Frontier Province, N Pakistan
Saigon see Hô Chi Minh
Saimaa 63 E5 lake SE Finland
St Albans 67 E6 anc. Verulamium. E England, United Kingdom
Saint Albans 18 D5 West Virginia, NE USA
St Andrews 66 C4 E Scotland, United Kingdom
Saint Anna Trough see Svyataya Anna Trough
St. Ann's Bay 32 B4 C Jamaica
St. Anthony 17 G3 Newfoundland and Labrador, SE Canada
Saint Augustine 21 E3 Florida, SE USA
St Austell 67 C7 SW England, United Kingdom
St.Botolph's Town see Boston
St-Brieuc 68 A3 Côtes d'Armor, NW France
St. Catharines 16 D5 Ontario, S Canada
St-Chamond 69 D5 Loire, E France
Saint Christopher and Nevis, Federation of see Saint Kitts and Nevis
Saint Christopher-Nevis see Saint Kitts and Nevis
Saint Clair, Lake 18 D3 var. Lac à L'Eau Claire. lake Canada/USA
St-Claude 69 D5 anc. Condate. Jura, E France
Saint Cloud 23 F2 Minnesota, N USA
Saint Croix 33 F3 island S Virgin Islands (US)
Saint Croix River 18 A2 river Minnesota/Wisconsin, N USA
St David's Island 20 B5 island E Bermuda
St-Denis 57 G4 dependent territory capital NW Réunion
St-Dié 68 E4 Vosges, NE France
St-Egrève 69 D5 Isère, E France
Sainte Marie, Cap see Vohimena, Tanjona
Saintes 69 B5 anc. Mediolanum. Charente-Maritime, W France
St-Étienne 69 D5 Loire, E France
St-Flour 69 C5 Cantal, C France
St-Gall/Saint Gall/St. Gallen see Sankt Gallen
St-Gaudens 69 B6 Haute-Garonne, S France
Saint George 127 D5 Queensland, E Australia
St George 20 B4 N Bermuda
Saint George 22 A5 Utah, W USA
St. George's 33 G5 country capital SW Grenada
St-Georges 17 E4 Québec, SE Canada
St-Georges 37 H3 E French Guiana
Saint George's Channel 67 B6 channel Ireland/Wales, United Kingdom
St George's Island 20 B4 island E Bermuda
Saint Helena 47 B6 UK dependent territory C Atlantic Ocean
St. Helena Bay 56 B5 bay SW South Africa
St Helier 67 D8 dependent territory capital S Jersey, Channel Islands
St.Iago de la Vega see Spanish Town
Saint Ignace 18 C2 Michigan, N USA
St-Jean, Lac 17 E4 lake Québec, SE Canada
Saint Joe River 24 D2 river Idaho, NW USA
St. John 17 F4 New Brunswick, SE Canada
Saint-John see Saint John
Saint John River 19 H1 Fr. Saint-John. river Canada/USA
St John's 33 G3 country capital Antigua, Antigua and Barbuda
St. John's 17 H3 province capital Newfoundland and Labrador, E Canada
Saint Joseph 23 F4 Missouri, C USA
St Julian's 80 B5 N Malta
St Kilda 66 A3 island NW Scotland, United Kingdom
Saint Kitts and Nevis 33 F3 off. Federation of Saint Christopher and Nevis, var. Saint Christopher-Nevis. country E West Indies
St-Laurent see St-Laurent-du-Maroni
St-Laurent-du-Maroni 37 H3 var. St-Laurent. NW French Guiana
St-Laurent, Fleuve see St. Lawrence
St. Lawrence 17 E4 Fr. Fleuve St-Laurent. river Canada/USA
St. Lawrence, Gulf of 17 F3 gulf NW Atlantic Ocean
Saint Lawrence Island 14 B2 island Alaska, USA
St-Lô 68 B3 anc. Briovera, Laudus. Manche, N France
St-Louis 68 E4 Haut-Rhin, NE France
Saint Louis 52 B3 NW Senegal
Saint Louis 23 G4 Missouri, C USA
Saint Lucia 33 E1 country SE West Indies
Saint Lucia Channel 33 H4 channel Martinique/Saint Lucia
St-Malo 68 B3 Ille-et-Vilaine, NW France
St-Malo, Golfe de 68 A3 gulf NW France
Saint Martin see Sint Maarten
St.Matthew's Island see Zadetkyi Kyun
St. Matthias Group 122 B3 island group NE Papua New Guinea
St-Maur-des-Fossés 68 E2 Val-de-Marne, Île-de-France, N France Europe
St. Moritz 73 B7 Ger. Sankt Moritz, Rmsch. San Murezzan. Graubünden, SE Switzerland
St-Nazaire 68 A4 Loire-Atlantique, NW France
Saint Nicholas see São Nicolau
Saint-Nicolas see Sint-Niklaas
St-Omer 68 C2 Pas-de-Calais, N France
Saint Paul 23 F2 state capital Minnesota, N USA
St-Paul, Île 119 C6 island Île St-Paul, NE French Southern and Antarctic Territories Antarctica Indian Ocea
St Peter Port 67 D8 dependent territory capital C Guernsey, Channel Islands
Saint Petersburg 21 E4 Florida, SE USA
Saint Petersburg see Sankt-Peterburg
St-Pierre and Miquelon 17 G4 Fr. Îles St-Pierre et Miquelon. French territorial collectivity NE North America
St-Quentin 68 C3 Aisne, N France
Saint Thomas see São Tomé, Sao Tome and Principe
Saint Thomas see Charlotte Amalie, Virgin Islands (US)
Saint Ubes see Setúbal
Saint Vincent 33 G4 island N Saint Vincent and the Grenadines
Saint Vincent see São Vicente
Saint Vincent and the Grenadines 33 H4 country SE West Indies
Saint Vincent, Cape see São Vicente, Cabo de
Saint Vincent Passage 33 H4 passage Saint Lucia/Saint Vincent and the Grenadines
Saint Yves see Setúbal
Saipan 120 B1 island/country capital S Northern Mariana Islands
Saishū see Cheju-do
Sajama, Nevado 39 F4 mountain W Bolivia
Sajószentpéter 77 D6 Borsod-Abaúj-Zemplén, NE Hungary
Sakākah 98 B4 Al Jawf, NW Saudi Arabia
Sakakawea, Lake 22 D1 reservoir North Dakota, N USA
Sak'art'velo see Georgia
Sakata 108 D4 Yamagata, Honshū, C Japan
Sakhalin 93 G4 var. Sakhalin. island SE Russian Federation
Sakhalin see Sakhalin, Ostrov
Sakhon Nakhon see Sakon Nakhon
Şäki 95 G2 Rus. Sheki; prev. Nukha. NW Azerbaijan
Saki see Saky
Sakishima-shoto 108 A3 var. Sakisima Syotô. island group SW Japan
Sakisima Syotô see Sakishima-shotō
Sakiz see Saqqez
Sakiz-Adasi see Chíos
Sakon Nakhon 114 D4 var. Muang Sakon Nakhon, Sakhon Nakhon. Sakon Nakhon, E Thailand
Saky 87 F5 Rus. Saki. Respublika Krym, S Ukraine
Sal 52 A3 island Ilhas de Barlavento, NE Cape Verde
Sala 63 C6 Västmanland, C Sweden
Salacgrīva 84 C3 Est. Salatsi. Limbaži, N Latvia
Sala Consilina 75 D5 Campania, S Italy
Salado, Río 40 D5 river E Argentina
Salado, Río 42 C3 river C Argentina
Şalālah 99 D6 SW Oman
Salamá 30 B2 Baja Verapaz, C Guatemala
Salamanca 42 B4 Coquimbo, C Chile
Salamanca 70 D2 anc. Helmantica, Salmantica. Castilla-León, NW Spain
Salamīyah 96 B3 var. As Salamīyah. Ḥamāh, W Syria
Salang see Phuket
Salantai 84 B3 Klaipėda, NW Lithuania
Salatsi see Salacgrīva
Salavan 115 D5 var. Saravan, Saravane. Salavan, S Laos
Salavat 89 D6 Respublika Bashkortostan, W Russian Federation
Sala y Gomez 131 F4 island Chile, E Pacific Ocean
Sala y Gomez Fracture Zone see Sala y Gomez Ridge
Sala y Gomez Ridge 131 G4 var. Sala y Gomez Fracture Zone. fracture zone SE Pacific Ocean
Salazar see N'Dalatando
Šalčininkai 85 C5 Vilnius, SE Lithuania
Saldubа see Zaragoza
Saldus 84 B3 Ger. Frauenburg. Saldus, W Latvia
Sale 127 C7 Victoria, SE Australia
Salé 48 C2 NW Morocco
Salekhard 92 D3 prev. Obdorsk. Yamalo-Nenetskiy Avtonomnyy Okrug, N Russian Federation
Salem 110 C2 Tamil Nādu, SE India
Salem 24 B3 state capital Oregon, NW USA
Salerno 75 D5 anc. Salernum. Campania, S Italy
Salerno, Gulf of 75 C5 Eng. Gulf of Salerno. gulf S Italy
Salerno, Gulf of see Salerno, Golfo di
Salernum see Salerno
Salihorsk 85 C7 Rus. Soligorsk. Minskaya Voblasts', S Belarus
Salima 57 E2 Central, C Malawi
Salina 23 E5 Kansas, C USA
Salina Cruz 29 F5 Oaxaca, SE Mexico
Salinas 38 A2 Guayas, W Ecuador
Salinas 25 B6 California, W USA
Salisbury 67 D7 var. New Sarum. S England, United Kingdom
Salisbury see Harare
Sállan see Sørøya
Sallyana see Şalyan
Salmantica see Salamanca
Salmon River 24 D3 river Idaho, NW USA
Salmon River Mountains 24 D3 mountain range Idaho, NW USA
Salo 63 D6 Länsi-Suomi, SW Finland
Salon-de-Provence 69 D6 Bouches-du-Rhône, SE France
Salonica/Salonika see Thessaloníki
Salonta 86 A3 Hung. Nagyszalonta. Bihor, W Romania
Sal'sk 89 B7 Rostovskaya Oblast', SW Russian Federation
Salt see As Salṭ
Salta 42 C2 Salta, NW Argentina
Saltash 67 C7 SW England, United Kingdom
Saltillo 29 E3 Coahuila de Zaragoza, NE Mexico
Salt Lake City 22 B4 state capital Utah, W USA
Salto 42 D4 Salto, N Uruguay
Salton Sea 25 D8 lake California, W USA
Salvador 41 G3 prev. São Salvador. state capital Bahia, E Brazil
Salween 102 C2 Bur. Thanlwin, Chin. Nu Chiang, Nu Jiang. river SE Asia
Şalyan 113 E3 var. Sallyana. Mid Western, W Nepal
Salzburg 73 D6 anc. Juvavum. Salzburg, N Austria
Salzgitter 72 C4 prev. Watenstedt-Salzgitter. Niedersachsen, C Germany
Salzwedel 72 C3 Sachsen-Anhalt, N Germany
Šamac see Bosanski Šamac
Samakhixai 115 E5 var. Attapu, Attopeu. Attapu, S Laos
Samalayuca 28 C1 Chihuahua, N Mexico
Samar 117 F2 island C Philippines
Samara 92 B3 prev. Kuybyshev. Samarskaya Oblast', W Russian Federation
Samarang see Semarang
Samarinda 116 D4 Borneo, C Indonesia
Samarkand see Samarqand
Samarkandski/Samarkandskoye see Temirtau
Samarobriva see Amiens
Samarqand 101 E2 Rus. Samarkand. Samarqand Viloyati, C Uzbekistan
Samawa see As Samāwah
Sambalpur 113 F4 Orissa, E India
Sambava 57 G2 Antsiranana, NE Madagascar
Sambir 86 B2 Rus. Sambor. L'vivs'ka Oblast', NW Ukraine
Sambor see Sambir
Sambre 68 D2 river Belgium/France
Samfya 56 D2 Luapula, N Zambia
Saminatal 72 E2 valley Austria/Liechtenstein Europe
Samnān see Semnān
Sam Neua see Xam Nua
Samoa 123 E4 off. Independent State of Western Samoa, var. Sāmoa; prev. Western Samoa. country W Polynesia
Sāmoa see Samoa
Samoa Basin 121 E3 undersea basin W Pacific Ocean
Samobor 78 A2 Zagreb, N Croatia
Sámos 83 E6 prev. Limín Vathéos. Sámos, Dodekánisa, Greece, Aegean Sea
Sámos 83 D6 island Dodekánisa, Greece, Aegean Sea
Samothrace see Samothráki
Samothráki 82 D4 Samothráki, NE Greece
Samothráki 82 C4 anc. Samothrace. island NE Greece
Sampit 116 C4 Borneo, C Indonesia
Samsun 94 D2 anc. Amisus. Samsun, N Turkey
Samtredia 95 F2 W Georgia
Samui, Ko 115 C6 island SW Thailand
Samut Prakan 115 C5 var. Muang Samut Prakan, Paknam. Samut Prakan, C Thailand
San 52 D3 Ségou, C Mali
San 77 E5 river SE Poland
San'ā' 99 B6 Eng. Sana. country capital W Yemen
Sana 78 B3 river NW Bosnia and Herzegovina
Sanae 132 B2 South African research station Antarctica
Sanaga 55 B5 river C Cameroon
San Ambrosio, Isla 35 A5 Eng. San Ambrosio Island. island W Chile
San Ambrosio Island see San Ambrosio, Isla
Sanandaj 98 C3 prev. Sinneh. Kordestān, W Iran
San Andrés, Isla de 31 F3 island NW Colombia, Caribbean Sea
San Andrés Tuxtla 29 F4 var. Tuxtla. Veracruz-Llave, E Mexico
San Angelo 27 F3 Texas, SW USA
San Antonio 30 B2 Toledo, S Belize
San Antonio 42 B4 Valparaíso, C Chile
San Antonio 27 F4 Texas, SW USA
San Antonio Oeste 43 C5 Río Negro, E Argentina
San Antonio River 27 G4 river Texas, SW USA
Sanāw 99 C6 var. Sanaw. NE Yemen
San Benedicto, Isla 28 B4 island W Mexico
San Benito 30 B1 Petén, N Guatemala
San Benito 27 G5 Texas, SW USA
San Bernardino 25 C7 California, W USA
San Blas 28 C3 Sinaloa, C Mexico
San Blas, Cape 20 D3 headland Florida, SE USA
San Blas, Cordillera de 31 G4 mountain range NE Panama
San Carlos 30 D4 Río San Juan, S Nicaragua
San Carlos 26 B2 Arizona, SW USA
San Carlos see Quesada, Costa Rica
San Carlos de Ancud see Ancud
San Carlos de Bariloche 43 B5 Río Negro, SW Argentina
San Carlos del Zulia 36 C2 Zulia, W Venezuela
San Clemente Island 25 B8 island Channel Islands, California, W USA
San Cristóbal 36 C2 Táchira, W Venezuela
San Cristobal 122 C4 var. Makira. island SE Solomon Islands
San Cristóbal see San Cristóbal de Las Casas
San Cristóbal de Las Casas 29 G5 var. San Cristóbal. Chiapas, SE Mexico
San Cristóbal, Isla 38 B5 var. Chatham Island. island Galapagos Islands, Ecuador, E Pacific Ocean
Sancti Spíritus 32 B2 Sancti Spíritus, C Cuba
Sandakan 116 D3 Sabah, East Malaysia
Sandalwood Island see Sumba, Pulau
Sandanski 82 C3 prev. Sveti Vrach. Blagoevgrad, SW Bulgaria
Sanday 66 D2 island NE Scotland, United Kingdom
Sanders 26 C2 Arizona, SW USA
Sand Hills 22 D3 mountain range Nebraska, C USA
San Diego 25 C8 California, W USA
Sandnes 63 A6 Rogaland, S Norway
Sandomierz 76 D4 Rus. Sandomir. Świętokrzyskie, C Poland
Sandomir see Sandomierz
Sandoway see Thandwe
Sandpoint 24 C1 Idaho, NW USA
Sand Springs 27 G1 Oklahoma, C USA
Sandusky 18 D3 Ohio, N USA
Sandvika 63 A6 Akershus, S Norway
Sandviken 63 C6 Gävleborg, C Sweden
Sandwich Island see Éfaté
Sandwich Islands see Hawaiian Islands
Sandy Bay 71 H5 Saskatchewan, C Canada
Sandy City 22 B4 Utah, W USA
Sandy Lake 16 B3 lake Ontario, C Canada
San Esteban 30 D2 Olancho, C Honduras
San Eugenio/San Eugenio del Cuareim see Artigas
San Felipe 36 D1 Yaracuy, NW Venezuela
San Felipe de Puerto Plata see Puerto Plata
San Félix, Isla 35 A5 Eng. San Felix Island. island W Chile
San Felix Island see San Félix, Isla
San Fernando 70 C5 prev. Isla de León. Andalucía, S Spain
San Fernando 33 H5 Trinidad, Trinidad and Tobago
San Fernando 24 D1 California, W USA
San Fernando 36 D2 var. San Fernando de Apure. Apure, C Venezuela
San Fernando de Apure see San Fernando
San Fernando del Valle de Catamarca 42 C3 var. Catamarca. Catamarca, NW Argentina
San Fernando de Monte Cristi see Monte Cristi
San Francisco 25 B6 California, W USA
San Francisco del Oro 28 C2 Chihuahua, N Mexico
San Francisco de Macorís 33 E3 C Dominican Republic
San Fructuoso see Tacuarembó
San Gabriel 38 B1 Carchi, N Ecuador
San Gabriel Mountains 24 E1 mountain range California, USA
Sangihe, Kepulauan see Sangir, Kepulauan
Sangir, Kepulauan 117 F3 var. Kepulauan Sangihe. island group N Indonesia
Sāngli 110 B1 Mahārāshtra, W India
Sangmélima 55 B5 Sud, S Cameroon
Sangre de Cristo Mountains 26 D1 mountain range Colorado/New Mexico, C USA
San Ignacio 30 B1 prev. Cayo, El Cayo. Cayo, W Belize
San Ignacio 39 F3 Beni, N Bolivia
San Ignacio 28 B2 Baja California Sur, W Mexico
San Joaquin Valley 25 B7 valley California, W USA
San Jorge, Gulf of 43 C6 var. Gulf of San Jorge. gulf S Argentina
San Jorge, Gulf of see San Jorge, Golfo
San José 31 E4 country capital San José, C Costa Rica
San José 39 G3 var. San José de Chiquitos. Santa Cruz, E Bolivia
San José 30 B3 var. Puerto San José. Escuintla, S Guatemala
San Jose 25 B6 California, W USA
San José see San José del Guaviare, Colombia
San José de Chiquitos see San José
San José de Cúcuta see Cúcuta
San José del Guaviare 36 C4 var. San José. Guaviare, S Colombia
San Juan 42 B4 San Juan, W Argentina
San Juan 33 F3 dependent territory capital NE Puerto Rico
San Juan see San Juan de los Morros
San Juan Bautista 42 D3 Misiones, S Paraguay
San Juan Bautista see Villahermosa
San Juan Bautista Tuxtepec see Tuxtepec
San Juan de Alicante 71 F4 País Valenciano, E Spain
San Juan del Norte 31 E4 var. Greytown. Río San Juan, SE Nicaragua
San Juan de los Morros 36 D2 var. San Juan. Guárico, N Venezuela
San Juanito, Isla 28 C4 island C Mexico
San Juan Mountains 26 D1 mountain range Colorado, C USA
San Juan, Río 31 E4 river Costa Rica/Nicaragua
San Juan River 26 C1 river Colorado/Utah, W USA
San Julián see Puerto San Julián
Sankt-Bartholomäi see Palamuse
Sankt Gallen 73 B7 var. St. Gallen, Eng. Saint Gall, Fr. St-Gall. Sankt Gallen, NE Switzerland
Sankt-Georgen see Sfântu Gheorghe
Sankt-Jakobi see Pärnu-Jaagupi, Pärnumaa, Estonia
Sankt Martin see Martin
Sankt Moritz see St. Moritz
Sankt-Peterburg 88 B4 prev. Leningrad, Petrograd, Eng. Saint Petersburg, Fin. Pietari. Leningradskaya Oblast', NW Russian Federation
Sankt Pölten 73 E6 Niederösterreich, N Austria
Sankt Veit am Flaum see Rijeka
Sankuru 55 D6 river C Dem. Rep. Congo
Şanlıurfa 95 E4 prev. Sanli Urfa, Urfa; anc. Edessa. şanlıurfa, S Turkey
Sanli Urfa see Şanlıurfa
San Lorenzo 39 G5 Tarija, S Bolivia
San Lorenzo 38 A1 Esmeraldas, N Ecuador
San Lorenzo, Isla 38 C4 island W Peru
Sanlúcar de Barrameda 70 C5 Andalucía, S Spain
San Luis 42 C4 San Luis, C Argentina
San Luis 30 B2 Petén, NE Guatemala
San Luis 28 A1 var. San Luis Río Colorado. Sonora, NW Mexico
San Luis Obispo 25 B7 California, W USA
San Luis Potosí 29 E3 San Luis Potosí, C Mexico
San Luis Río Colorado see San Luis
San Marcos 30 A2 San Marcos, W Guatemala
San Marcos 27 G4 Texas, SW USA
San Marcos de Arica see Arica
San Marino 74 E1 country capital C San Marino

San Marino – Shaddādī

San Marino 74 D1 off. Republic of San Marino. country S Europe
San Marino, Republic of see San Marino
San Martín 132 A2 Argentinian research station Antarctica
San Mateo 37 E2 Anzoátegui, NE Venezuela
San Matías 39 H3 Santa Cruz, E Bolivia
San Matías, Gulf of 43 C5 var. Gulf of San Matías. gulf E Argentina
San Matías, Gulf of see San Matías, Golfo
Sanmenxia 106 C4 var. Shan Xian. Henan, C China
Sânmiclăuş Mare see Sânnicolau Mare
San Miguel 30 C3 San Miguel, SE El Salvador
San Miguel 28 D2 Coahuila de Zaragoza, N Mexico
San Miguel de Ibarra see Ibarra
San Miguel de Tucumán 42 C3 var. Tucumán. Tucumán, N Argentina
San Miguelito 31 G4 Panamá, C Panama
San Miguel, Río 39 G3 river E Bolivia
San Murezzan see St. Moritz
Sannār see Sennar
Sânnicolaul-Mare see Sânnicolau Mare
Sânnicolau Mare 86 A4 var. Sânnicolaul-Mare, Hung. Nagyszentmiklós; prev. Sânmiclăuş Mare, Sinnicolau Mare. Timiş, W Romania
Sanok 77 E5 Podkarpackie, SE Poland
San Pablo 39 F5 Potosí, S Bolivia
San Pedro 30 C1 Corozal, NE Belize
San-Pédro 52 D5 S Ivory Coast
San Pedro 28 D3 var. San Pedro de las Colonias. Coahuila de Zaragoza, NE Mexico
San Pedro de la Cueva 28 C2 Sonora, NW Mexico
San Pedro de las Colonias see San Pedro
San Pedro de Lloc 38 B3 La Libertad, NW Peru
San Pedro Mártir, Sierra 28 A1 mountain range NW Mexico
San Pedro Sula 30 C2 Cortés, NW Honduras
San Rafael 42 B4 Mendoza, W Argentina
San Rafael Mountains 25 C7 mountain range California, W USA
San Ramón de la Nueva Orán 42 C2 Salta, N Argentina
San Remo 74 A3 Liguria, NW Italy
San Salvador 30 B3 country capital San Salvador, SW El Salvador
San Salvador 32 D2 prev. Watlings Island. island E Bahamas
San Salvador de Jujuy 42 C2 var. Jujuy. Jujuy, N Argentina
San Salvador, Isla 38 A4 island Ecuador
Sansanné-Mango 53 E4 var. Mango. N Togo
Sansepolcro 74 C3 Toscana, C Italy
San Severo 75 D5 Puglia, SE Italy
Santa Ana 39 F3 Beni, N Bolivia
Santa Ana 30 B3 Santa Ana, NW El Salvador
Santa Ana 24 D2 California, W USA
Santa Ana de Coro see Coro
Santa Ana Mountains 24 E2 mountain range California, W USA
Santa Barbara 28 C2 Chihuahua, N Mexico
Santa Barbara 25 C7 California, W USA
Santa Catalina Island 25 B8 island Channel Islands, California, W USA
Santa Catarina 41 E5 off. Estado de Santa Catarina. state S Brazil
Santa Catarina 41 E5 off. Estado de Santa Catarina. region S Brazil
Santa Catarina, Estado de see Santa Catarina
Santa Clara 32 B2 Villa Clara, C Cuba
Santa Clarita 24 D1 California, USA
Santa Comba 70 B1 Galicia, NW Spain
Santa Cruz 54 E2 São Tomé, S Sao Tome and Principe, Africa
Santa Cruz 25 B6 California, W USA
Santa Cruz 39 G4 department E Bolivia
Santa Cruz Barillas see Barillas
Santa Cruz del Quiché 30 B2 Quiché, W Guatemala
Santa Cruz de Tenerife 48 A3 Tenerife, Islas Canarias, Spain, NE Atlantic Ocean
Santa Cruz, Isla 38 B5 var. Indefatigable Island, Isla Chávez. island Galapagos Islands, Ecuador, E Pacific Ocean
Santa Cruz Islands 122 D3 island group E Solomon Islands
Santa Cruz, Río 43 B7 river S Argentina
Santa Elena 30 B1 Cayo, W Belize
Santa Fe 42 C4 Santa Fe, C Argentina
Santa Fe 26 D1 state capital New Mexico, SW USA
Santa Fe see Bogotá
Santa Fe de Bogotá see Bogotá
Santa Genoveva 28 B3 mountain W Mexico
Santa Isabel 122 C3 var. Bughotu. island N Solomon Islands
Santa Isabel see Malabo
Santa Lucia Range 25 B7 mountain range California, W USA
Santa Margarita, Isla 28 B3 island W Mexico
Santa Maria 41 E5 Rio Grande do Sul, S Brazil
Santa Maria 25 B7 California, USA
Santa Maria 70 A5 island Azores, Portugal, NE Atlantic Ocean
Santa María del Buen Aire see Buenos Aires
Santa María, Isla 38 A5 var. Isla Floreana, Charles Island. island Galapagos Islands, Ecuador, E Pacific Ocean
Santa Marta 36 B1 Magdalena, N Colombia
Santa Maura see Lefkáda
Santa Monica 24 D1 California, W USA
Santana 54 E2 São Tomé, C Sao Tome and Principe, Africa
Santander 70 D1 Cantabria, N Spain
Santarém 41 E2 Pará, N Brazil
Santarém 70 B3 anc. Scalabis. Santarém, W Portugal
Santa Rosa 42 C4 La Pampa, C Argentina
Santa Rosa see Santa Rosa de Copán
Santa Rosa de Copán 30 C2 var. Santa Rosa. Copán, W Honduras
Santa Rosa Island 25 B8 island California, W USA
Sant Carles de la Rápida see Sant Carles de la Ràpita
Sant Carles de la Ràpita 71 F3 var. Sant Carles de la Rápida. Cataluña, NE Spain
Santiago 42 B4 var. Gran Santiago. country capital Santiago, C Chile
Santiago 33 E3 var. Santiago de los Caballeros. N Dominican Republic
Santiago 31 F5 Veraguas, S Panama
Santiago 70 B1 var. Santiago de Compostela, Eng. Compostella; anc. Campus Stellae. Galicia, NW Spain
Santiago 52 A3 var. São Tiago. island Ilhas de Sotavento, S Cape Verde
Santiago see Santiago de Cuba, Cuba
Santiago de Compostela see Santiago
Santiago de Cuba 32 C3 var. Santiago. Santiago de Cuba, E Cuba
Santiago de Guayaquil see Guayaquil
Santiago del Estero 42 C3 Santiago del Estero, C Argentina
Santiago de los Caballeros see Santiago, Dominican Republic
Santiago de los Caballeros see Ciudad de Guatemala, Guatemala
Santiago Pinotepa Nacional see Pinotepa Nacional
Santiago, Río 38 B2 river N Peru
Santi Quaranta see Sarandë
Santissima Trinidad see Chilung
Sant Julià de Lòria 69 A8 Sant Julià de Lòria, SW Andorra Europe
Santo see Espiritu Santo
Santo Antão 52 A2 island Ilhas de Barlavento, N Cape Verde
Santo António 54 E1 Príncipe, N Sao Tome and Principe, Africa
Santo Domingo 33 D3 prev. Ciudad Trujillo. country capital SE Dominican Republic
Santo Domingo de los Colorados 38 B1 Pichincha, NW Ecuador
Santo Domingo Tehuantepec see Tehuantepec
San Tomé de Guayana see Ciudad Guayana
Santos 41 F4 São Paulo, S Brazil
Santos Plateau 35 D5 undersea plateau SW Atlantic Ocean
Santo Tomé 42 D3 Corrientes, NE Argentina
Santo Tomé de Guayana see Ciudad Guayana
San Valentín, Cerro 43 A6 mountain S Chile
San Vicente 30 C3 San Vicente, C El Salvador
São Francisco, Rio 41 F3 river E Brazil
Sao Hill 51 C7 Iringa, S Tanzania
São João da Madeira 70 B2 Aveiro, N Portugal
São Jorge 70 A5 island Azores, Portugal, NE Atlantic Ocean
São Luís 41 F2 state capital Maranhão, NE Brazil
São Mandol see São Manuel, Rio
São Manuel, Rio 41 E3 var. São Mandol, Teles Pirés. river C Brazil
São Marcos, Baía de 41 F1 bay N Brazil
São Miguel 70 A5 island Azores, Portugal, NE Atlantic Ocean
Saona, Isla 33 E3 island SE Dominican Republic
Saône 69 D5 river E France
São Nicolau 52 A3 Eng. Saint Nicholas. island Ilhas de Barlavento, N Cape Verde
São Paulo 41 E4 state capital São Paulo, S Brazil
São Paulo 41 E4 off. Estado de São Paulo. state S Brazil
São Paulo 41 E4 off. Estado de São Paulo. region S Brazil
São Paulo de Loanda see Luanda
São Paulo, Estado de see São Paulo
São Pedro do Rio Grande do Sul see Rio Grande
São Roque, Cabo de 41 G2 headland E Brazil
São Salvador see Salvador, Brazil
São Salvador/São Salvador do Congo see M'Banza Congo, Angola
São Tiago see Santiago
São Tomé 55 A5 country capital São Tomé, S Sao Tome and Principe
São Tomé 54 E2 Eng. Saint Thomas. island S Sao Tome and Principe
Sao Tome and Principe 54 D1 off. Democratic Republic of Sao Tome and Principe. country E Atlantic Ocean
Sao Tome and Principe, Democratic Republic of see Sao Tome and Principe
São Tomé, Pico de 54 D2 mountain São Tomé, C Sao Tome and Principe, Africa
São Vicente 52 A3 Eng. Saint Vincent. island Ilhas de Barlavento, N Cape Verde
São Vicente, Cabo de 70 B5 Eng. Cape Saint Vincent, Port. Cabo de São Vicente. cape S Portugal
São Vicente, Cabo de see São Vicente, Cabo de
Sápai see Sápes
Sapele 53 F5 Delta, S Nigeria
Sápes 82 D3 var. Sápai. Anatolikí Makedonía kai Thráki, NE Greece
Sapir 97 B7 prev. Sappir. Southern, S Israel
Sa Pobla 71 G3 Mallorca, Spain, W Mediterranean Sea
Sappir see Sapir
Sapporo 108 D2 Hokkaidō, NE Japan
Sapri 75 D6 Campania, S Italy
Sapulpa 27 G1 Oklahoma, C USA
Saqqez 98 C2 var. Saghez, Sakiz, Saqqiz. Kordestān, NW Iran
Saqqiz see Saqqez
Sara Buri 115 C5 var. Saraburi. Saraburi, C Thailand
Saraburi see Sara Buri
Saragossa see Zaragoza
Saragt see Sarahs
Saraguro 38 B2 Loja, S Ecuador
Sarahs 100 D3 var. Saragt, Rus. Serakhs. Ahal Welaýaty, S Turkmenistan
Sarajevo 78 C4 country capital Federacija Bosna I Hercegovina, SE Bosnia and Herzegovina
Sarakhs 98 E2 Khorāsān-Razavī, NE Iran
Saraktash 89 D6 Orenburgskaya Oblast', W Russian Federation
Saran' 92 C4 Kaz. Saran. Karaganda, C Kazakhstan
Saranda see Sarandë
Sarandë 79 C7 var. Saranda, It. Porto Edda; prev. Santi Quaranta. Vlorë, S Albania
Saransk 89 C5 Respublika Mordoviya, W Russian Federation
Sarasota 21 E4 Florida, SE USA
Saratov 92 B3 Saratovskaya Oblast', W Russian Federation
Saravan/Saravane see Salavan
Sarawak 116 D3 state East Malaysia
Sarawak see Kuching
Sarcelles 68 D1 Val-d'Oise, Île-de-France, N France Europe
Sardinia 75 A5 Eng. Sardinia. island Italy, C Mediterranean Sea
Sardinia see Sardegna
Sarera, Teluk see Cenderawasih, Teluk
Sargasso Sea 44 B4 sea W Atlantic Ocean
Sargodha 112 C2 Punjab, NE Pakistan
Sarh 54 C4 prev. Fort-Archambault. Moyen-Chari, S Chad
Sārī 98 D2 var. Sari, Sāri. Māzandarān, N Iran
Saría 83 E7 island SE Greece
Sarıkamış 95 F3 Kars, NE Turkey
Sarikol Range 101 G3 Rus. Sarykol'skiy Khrebet. mountain range China/Tajikistan
Sark 67 D8 Fr. Sercq. island Channel Islands
Şarkışla 94 D3 Sivas, C Turkey
Sarmiento 43 B6 Chubut, S Argentina
Sarnia 16 C5 Ontario, S Canada
Sarny 86 C1 Rivnens'ka Oblast', NW Ukraine
Sarochyna 85 D5 Rus. Sorochino. Vitsyebskaya Voblasts', N Belarus
Sarov 89 C5 prev. Sarova. Respublika Mordoviya, SW Russian Federation
Sarova see Sarov
Sarpsborg 63 B6 Østfold, S Norway
Sarrebruck see Saarbrücken
Sartène 69 E7 Corse, France, C Mediterranean Sea
Sarthe 68 B4 river N France
Sárti 82 C4 Kentrikí Makedonía, N Greece
Saruhan see Manisa
Saryarqa see Kazakhskiy Melkosopochnik
Sarykol'skiy Khrebet see Sarikol Range
Sary-Tash 101 F2 Oshskaya Oblast', SW Kyrgyzstan
Saryyesik-Atyrau, Peski 101 G1 desert E Kazakhstan
Sasebo 109 A7 Nagasaki, Kyūshū, SW Japan
Saskatchewan 15 F5 province SW Canada
Saskatchewan 15 F5 river Manitoba/ Saskatchewan, C Canada
Saskatoon 15 F5 Saskatchewan, S Canada
Sasovo 89 B5 Ryazanskaya Oblast', W Russian Federation
Sassandra 52 D5 S Ivory Coast
Sassandra 52 D5 var. Ibo, Sassandra Fleuve. river S Ivory Coast
Sassandra Fleuve see Sassandra
Sassari 75 A5 Sardegna, Italy, C Mediterranean Sea
Sassenheim 64 C3 Zuid-Holland, W Netherlands
Sassnitz 72 D2 Mecklenburg-Vorpommern, NE Germany
Sathmar see Satu Mare
Sátoraljaújhely 77 D6 Borsod-Abaúj-Zemplén, NE Hungary
Satpura Range 112 D4 mountain range C India
Satsuma-Sendai see Sendai
Satsunan-shoto 108 A3 island group Nansei-shotō, SW Japan Asia
Sattanen 62 D3 Lappi, NE Finland
Satu Mare 86 B3 Ger. Sathmar, Hung. Szatmárnémeti. Satu Mare, NW Romania
Sau see Sava
Saudi Arabia 99 B5 off. Kingdom of Saudi Arabia, Al 'Arabīyah as Su'ūdīyah, Ar. Al Mamlakah al 'Arabīyah as Su'ūdīyah. country SW Asia
Saudi Arabia, Kingdom of see Saudi Arabia
Sauer see Sûre
Saugor see Sāgar
Saulkrasti 84 C3 Rīga, C Latvia
Sault Sainte Marie 18 C1 Michigan, N USA
Sault Sainte Marie 16 C4 Michigan, N USA
Sault Ste. Marie 16 C4 Ontario, S Canada
Saumur 68 B4 Maine-et-Loire, NW France
Saurimo 56 C1 Port. Henrique de Carvalho, Vila Henrique de Carvalho. Lunda Sul, NE Angola
Sava 85 E6 Mahilyowskaya Voblasts', E Belarus
Savá 30 D2 Colón, N Honduras
Savai'i 123 E4 island NW Samoa
Savannah 21 E2 Georgia, SE USA
Savannah River 21 E2 river Georgia/South Carolina, SE USA
Savannakhét see Khanthabouli
Savanna-La-Mar 32 A5 W Jamaica
Savaria see Szombathely
Save 78 B3 Eng. Save, Ger. Sau, Hung. Száva. river SE Europe
Save see Sava
Save, Rio 57 E3 var. Sabi. river Mozambique/ Zimbabwe
Saverne 68 E3 var. Zabern; anc. Tres Tabernae. Bas-Rhin, NE France
Savigliano 74 A2 Piemonte, NW Italy
Savigsivik see Savissivik
Savinski see Savinskiy
Savinskiy 88 C3 var. Savinski. Arkhangel'skaya Oblast', NW Russian Federation
Savissivik 60 D1 var. Savigsivik. Avannaarsua, N Greenland
Savoie 69 D5 cultural region E France
Savona 74 A2 Liguria, NW Italy
Savu Sea 117 E5 Ind. Laut Sawu. sea S Indonesia
Sawakin see Suakin
Sawdirī see Sodiri
Sawhāj 50 B2 var. Sawhāj var. Sohâg, Suliag. C Egypt
Sawhāj see Sawhāj
Şawqirah 99 D6 var. Suqrah. S Oman
Sawu, Laut see Savu Sea
Saxe see Sachsen
Saxony see Sachsen
Sayaboury see Xaignabouli
Sayanskiy Khrebet 90 D3 mountain range S Russian Federation
Saýat 100 D3 Rus. Sayat. Lebap Welaýaty, E Turkmenistan
Sayaxché 30 B2 Petén, N Guatemala
Şaydā/Sayida see Saïda
Sayhūt 99 D6 E Yemen
Saynshand 105 E2 Dornogovĭ, SE Mongolia
Sayre 19 E3 Pennsylvania, NE USA
Say'ūn 99 C6 var. Saywūn. C Yemen
Saywūn see Say'ūn
Scalabis see Santarém
Scandinavia 44 D2 geophysical region NW Europe
Scarborough 67 D5 N England, United Kingdom
Scarpanto see Kárpathos
Scebeli see Shebeli
Schaan 72 E1 W Liechtenstein Europe
Schaerbeek 65 C6 Brussels, C Belgium
Schaffhausen 73 B7 Fr. Schaffhouse. Schaffhausen, N Switzerland
Schaffhouse see Schaffhausen
Schagen 64 C2 Noord-Holland, NW Netherlands
Schaulen see Šiauliai
Schebschi Mountains see Shebshi Mountains
Scheessel 72 B3 Niedersachsen, NW Germany
Schefferville 17 E2 Québec, E Canada
Schelde see Scheldt
Scheldt 65 B5 Dut. Schelde, Fr. Escaut. river W Europe
Schell Creek Range 25 D5 mountain range Nevada, W USA
Schenectady 19 F3 New York, NE USA
Schertz 27 G4 Texas, SW USA
Schiermonnikoog 64 D1 Fris. Skiermûntseach. island Waddeneilanden, N Netherlands
Schijndel 64 D4 Noord-Brabant, S Netherlands
Schil see Jiu
Schiltigheim 68 E3 Bas-Rhin, NE France
Schivelbein see Świdwin
Schleswig 72 B2 Schleswig-Holstein, N Germany
Schleswig-Holstein 72 B2 state N Germany
Schlettstadt see Sélestat
Schlochau see Człuchów
Schneekoppe see Sněžka
Schneidemühl see Piła
Schoden see Skuodas
Schönebeck 72 C4 Sachsen-Anhalt, C Germany
Schönlanke see Trzcianka
Schooten see Schoten
Schoten 65 C5 var. Schooten. Antwerpen, N Belgium
Schouwen 64 B4 island SW Netherlands
Schwabenalb see Schwäbische Alb
Schwäbische Alb 73 B6 var. Schwabenalb, Eng. Swabian Jura. mountain range S Germany
Schwandorf 73 C5 Bayern, SE Germany
Schwaz 73 C7 Tirol, W Austria
Schweidnitz see Świdnica
Schweinfurt 73 B5 Bayern, SE Germany
Schweiz see Switzerland
Schwerin 72 C3 Mecklenburg-Vorpommern, N Germany
Schwertberg see Świecie
Schwiebus see Świebodzin
Schwyz 73 B7 var. Schwiz. Schwyz, C Switzerland
Schyl see Jiu
Scio see Chíos
Scoresby Sound/Scoresbysund see Ittoqqortoormiit
Scoresby Sund see Kangertittivaq
Scotia Sea 35 C8 sea SW Atlantic Ocean
Scotland 66 C3 cultural region Scotland, U K
Scott Base 132 B4 NZ research station Antarctica
Scott Island 132 B5 island Antarctica
Scottsbluff 22 D3 Nebraska, C USA
Scottsboro 20 D1 Alabama, S USA
Scottsdale 26 B2 Arizona, SW USA
Scranton 19 F3 Pennsylvania, NE USA
Scrobesbyrig' see Shrewsbury
Scupi see Skopje
Scutari see Shkodër
Scutari, Lake 79 C5 Alb. Liqeni i Shkodrës, SCr. Skadarsko Jezero. lake Albania/Montenegro
Scyros see Skýros
Searcy 20 B1 Arkansas, C USA
Seattle 24 B2 Washington, NW USA
Sébaco 30 D3 Matagalpa, W Nicaragua
Sebaste/Sebastia see Sivas
Sebastían Vizcaíno, Bahía 28 A2 bay NW Mexico
Sebastopol see Sevastopol'
Sebenico see Šibenik
Sechura, Bahía de 38 A3 bay NW Peru
Secunderābād 112 D5 var. Sikandarabad. Andhra Pradesh, C India
Sedan 68 D3 Ardennes, N France
Seddon 129 D5 Marlborough, South Island, New Zealand
Seddonville 129 C5 West Coast, South Island, New Zealand
Sédhiou 52 B3 SW Senegal
Sedlez see Siedlce
Sedona 26 B2 Arizona, SW USA
Sedunum see Sion
Seeland see Sjælland
Seenu Atoll see Addu Atoll
Seesen 72 B4 Niedersachsen, C Germany
Segestica see Sisak
Segezha 88 B3 Respublika Kareliya, NW Russian Federation
Seghedin see Szeged
Segna see Senj
Segodunum see Rodez
Ségou 52 D3 var. Segu. Ségou, C Mali
Segovia 70 D2 Castilla-León, C Spain
Segoviao Wangkí see Coco, Río
Segu see Ségou
Séguédine 53 H2 Agadez, NE Niger
Seguin 27 G4 Texas, SW USA
Segura 71 E4 river S Spain
Seinäjoki 63 D5 Swe. Östermyra. Länsi-Suomi, W Finland
Seine 68 D1 river N France
Seine, Baie de la 68 B3 bay N France
Sekondi see Sekondi-Takoradi
Sekondi-Takoradi 53 E5 var. Sekondi. S Ghana
Selānik see Thessaloníki
Selenga 105 E1 Mong. Selenge Mörön. river Mongolia/Russian Federation
Selenge Mörön see Selenga
Sélestat 68 E4 Ger. Schlettstadt. Bas-Rhin, NE France
Seleucia see Silifke
Selfoss 61 E5 Sudhurland, SW Iceland
Sélibabi 52 C3 var. Sélibaby. Guidimaka, S Mauritania
Sélibaby see Sélibabi
Selma 25 C6 California, W USA
Selway River 24 D2 river Idaho, NW USA North America
Selwyn Range 126 B3 mountain range Queensland, C Australia
Selzaete see Zelzate
Semarang 116 C5 var. Samarang. Jawa, C Indonesia
Sembé 55 B5 Sangha, NW Congo
Semendria see Smederevo
Semey see Semipalatinsk
Semezhevo see Syemyezhava
Seminole 27 E3 Texas, SW USA
Seminole, Lake 20 D3 reservoir Florida/Georgia, SE USA
Semipalatinsk 92 D4 Kaz. Semey. Vostochnyy Kazakhstan, E Kazakhstan
Semnān 98 D3 var. Samnān. Semnān, N Iran
Semois 65 C8 river SE Belgium
Sendai 109 A8 var. Satsuma-Sendai. Kagoshima, Kyūshū, SW Japan
Sendai 108 D4 Miyagi, Honshū, C Japan
Sendai-wan 108 D4 bay E Japan
Senec 77 C6 Ger. Wartberg, Hung. Szenc; prev. Szempcz. Bratislavský Kraj, W Slovakia
Senegal 52 B3 off. Republic of Senegal, Fr. Sénégal. country W Africa
Senegal 52 C3 Fr. Sénégal. river W Africa
Senegal, Republic of see Senegal
Senftenberg 72 D4 Brandenburg, E Germany
Senia see Senj
Senica 77 C6 Ger. Senitz, Hung. Szenice. Trnavský Kraj, W Slovakia
Seniça see Sjenica
Senitz see Senica
Senj 78 A3 Ger. Zengg, It. Segna; anc. Senia. Lika-Senj, NW Croatia
Senja 62 C2 prev. Senjen. island N Norway
Senjen see Senja
Senkaku-shoto 108 A3 island group SW Japan
Senlis 68 C3 Oise, N France
Sennar 50 C4 var. Sannār. Sinnar, C Sudan
Senones see Sens
Sens 68 C3 anc. Agendicum, Senones. Yonne, C France
Sensburg see Mrągowo
Sên, Stœng 115 D5 river C Cambodia
Senta 78 D3 Hung. Zenta. Vojvodina, N Serbia
Seo de Urgel see La See d'Urgel
Seoul see Sŏul
Şepşi-Sângeorz/Sepsiszentgyőrgy see Sfântu Gheorghe
Sept-Îles 17 E3 Québec, SE Canada
Seraing 65 D6 Liège, E Belgium
Serakhs see Sarahs
Seram, Laut see Ceram Sea
Pulau Seram 117 F4 var. Serang, Eng. Ceram. island Maluku, E Indonesia
Serang 116 C5 Jawa, C Indonesia
Serang see Seram, Pulau
Serasan, Selat 116 C3 strait Indonesia/Malaysia
Serbia 78 D4 off. Federal Republic of Serbia; prev. Yugoslavia, SCr. Jugoslavija. country SE Europe
Serbia, Federal Republic of see Serbia
Sercq see Sark
Serdar 100 C2 prev. Rus. Gyzyrlabat, Kizyl-Arvat. Balkan Welaýaty, W Turkmenistan
Serdica see Sofiya
Serdobol' see Sortavala
Serenje 56 D2 Central, E Zambia
Seres see Sérres
Seret/Sereth see Siret
Serhetabat 100 D4 prev. Rus. Gushgy, Kushka. Mary Welaýaty, S Turkmenistan
Sérifos 83 C6 anc. Seriphos. island Kykládes, Greece, Aegean Sea
Seriphos see Sérifos
Serov 92 C3 Sverdlovskaya Oblast', C Russian Federation
Serowe 56 D3 Central, SE Botswana
Serpa Pinto see Menongue
Serpent's Mouth, The 37 F2 Sp. Boca de la Serpiente. strait Trinidad and Tobago/Venezuela
Serpiente, Boca de la see Serpent's Mouth, The
Serpukhov 89 B5 Moskovskaya Oblast', W Russian Federation
Sérrai see Sérres
Serrana, Cayo de 31 F2 island group NW Colombia South America
Serranilla, Cayo de 31 F2 island group NW Colombia South America Caribbean Sea
Serravalle 74 E1 N San Marino
Sérres 82 C3 var. Seres; prev. Sérrai. Kentrikí Makedonía, NE Greece
Sesdlets see Siedlce
Sesto San Giovanni 74 B2 Lombardia, N Italy
Sesvete 78 B2 Zagreb, N Croatia
Setabis see Xàtiva
Sète 69 C6 prev. Cette. Hérault, S France
Setesdal 63 A6 valley S Norway
Sétif 49 E2 var. Stif. N Algeria
Setté Cama 55 A6 Ogooué-Maritime, SW Gabon
Setúbal 70 B4 Eng. Saint Ubes, Saint Yves. Setúbal, W Portugal
Setúbal, Baía de 70 B4 bay W Portugal
Seul, Lac 16 B3 lake Ontario, S Canada
Sevan 95 G2 C Armenia
Sevan, Lake 95 G3 Eng. Lake Sevan, Rus. Ozero Sevan. lake E Armenia
Sevan, Lake/Sevan, Ozero see Sevana Lich
Sevastopol' 87 F5 Eng. Sebastopol. Respublika Krym, S Ukraine
Severn 16 B2 river Ontario, S Canada
Severn 67 D6 Wel. Hafren. river England/Wales, United Kingdom
Severnaya Zemlya 93 E2 var. Nicholas II Land. island group N Russian Federation
Severnyy 88 E3 Respublika Komi, NW Russian Federation
Severodonetsk see Syeverodonets'k
Severodvinsk 88 C3 prev. Molotov, Sudostroy. Arkhangel'skaya Oblast', NW Russian Federation
Severomorsk 88 C2 Murmanskaya Oblast', NW Russian Federation
Seversk 92 D4 Tomskaya Oblast', C Russian Federation
Sevier Lake 22 A4 lake Utah, W USA
Sevilla 70 C4 Eng. Seville; anc. Hispalis. Andalucía, SW Spain
Seville see Sevilla
Sevlievo 82 D2 Gabrovo, N Bulgaria
Sevluš/Sevlyush see Vynohradiv
Seward's Folly see Alaska
Seychelles 57 G1 off. Republic of Seychelles. country W Indian Ocean
Seychelles, Republic of see Seychelles
Seydhisfjördhur 61 E5 Austurland, E Iceland
Seýdi 100 D2 Rus. Seydi; prev. Neftezavodsk. Lebap Welaýaty, E Turkmenistan
Seyhan see Adana
Sfákia see Chóra Sfakíon
Sfântu Gheorghe 86 C4 Ger. Sankt-Georgen, Hung. Sepsiszentgyőrgy; prev. Şepşi-Sângeorz, Sfîntu Gheorghe. Covasna, C Romania
Sfax 49 F2 Ar. Şafāqis. E Tunisia
Sfîntu Gheorghe see Sfântu Gheorghe
's-Gravenhage 64 B4 var. Den Haag, Eng. The Hague, Fr. La Haye. country capital Zuid-Holland, W Netherlands
's-Gravenzande 64 B4 Zuid-Holland, W Netherlands
Shaan/Shaanxi Sheng see Shaanxi
Shaanxi 106 B5 var. Shaan, Shaanxi Sheng, Shan-hsi, Shenshi, Shensi. province C China
Shabani see Zvishavane
Shabeelle, Webi see Shebeli
Shache 104 A3 var. Yarkant. Xinjiang Uygur Zizhiqu, NW China
Shacheng see Huailai
Shackleton Ice Shelf 132 D3 ice shelf Antarctica
Shaddādi see Ash Shadādah

Shāhābād – Soltau

Shāhābād see Eslāmābād
Sha Hi see Orūmīyeh, Daryācheh-ye
Shahjahanabad see Delhi
Shahr-e Kord 98 C3 var. Shahr Kord. Chahār Maḩall va Bakhtīārī, C Iran
Shahr Kord see Shahr-e Kord
Shāhrūd 98 D2 prev. Emāmrūd, Emāmshahr. Semnān, N Iran
Shalkar 92 B4 var. Chelkar. Aktyubinsk, W Kazakhstan
Shām, Bādiyat ash see Syrian Desert
Shana see Kuril'sk
Shandī see Shendi
Shandong 106 D4 var. Lu, Shandong Sheng, Shantung. province E China
Shandong Sheng see Shandong
Shanghai 106 D5 var. Shang-hai. Shanghai Shi, E China
Shangrao 106 D5 Jiangxi, S China
Shan-hsi see Shaanxi, China
Shan-hsi see Shanxi, China
Shannon 67 A6 Ir. An tSionainn. river W Ireland
Shan Plateau 114 B3 plateau E Myanmar (Burma)
Shansi see Shanxi
Shantar Islands see Shantarskiye Ostrova
Shantarskiye Ostrova 93 G3 Eng. Shantar Islands. island group E Russian Federation
Shantou 106 D6 var. Shan-t'ou, Swatow. Guangdong, S China
Shan-t'ou see Shantou
Shantung see Shandong
Shanxi 106 C4 var. Jin, Shan-hsi, Shansi, Shanxi Sheng. province C China
Shan Xian see Sanmenxia
Shanxi Sheng see Shanxi
Shaoguan 106 C6 var. Shao-kuan, Cant. Kukong; prev. Ch'u-chiang. Guangdong, S China
Shao-kuan see Shaoguan
Shaqrā' 98 B4 Ar Riyāḑ, C Saudi Arabia
Shaqrā see Shuqrah
Shar 92 D5 var. Charsk. Vostochnyy Kazakhstan, E Kazakhstan
Shari 108 D2 Hokkaidō, NE Japan
Shari see Chari
Sharjah see Ash Shāriqah
Shark Bay 125 A5 bay Western Australia
Sharqī, Al Jabal ash/Sharqi, Jebel esh see Anti-Lebanon
Shashe 56 D3 var. Shashi. river Botswana/Zimbabwe
Shashi see Shashe
Shatskiy Rise 103 G1 undersea rise N Pacific Ocean
Shawnee 27 G1 Oklahoma, C USA
Shaykh, Jabal ash see Hermon, Mount
Shchadryn 85 D7 Rus. Shchedrin. Homyel'skaya Voblasts', SE Belarus
Shchedrin see Shchadryn
Shcheglovsk see Kemerovo
Shchëkino 89 B5 Tul'skaya Oblast', W Russian Federation
Shchors 87 E1 Chernihivs'ka Oblast', N Ukraine
Shchuchin see Shchuchyn
Shchuchinsk 92 C4 prev. Shchuchye. Akmola, N Kazakhstan
Shchuchye see Shchuchinsk
Shchuchyn 85 B5 Pol. Szczuczyn Nowogródzki, Rus. Shchuchin. Hrodzyenskaya Voblasts', W Belarus
Shebekino 89 A6 Belgorodskaya Oblast', W Russian Federation
Shebelē Wenz, Wabē see Shebeli
Shebeli 51 D5 Amh. Wabē Shebelē Wenz, It. Scebeli, Som. Webi Shabeelle. river Ethiopia/Somalia
Sheberghān 101 E3 var. Shibarghān, Shiberghan, Shiberghān. Jowzjān, N Afghanistan
Sheboygan 18 B2 Wisconsin, N USA
Shebshi Mountains 54 A4 var. Schebschi Mountains. mountain range E Nigeria
Shechem see Nablus
Shedadi see Ash Shadādah
Sheffield 67 D5 N England, United Kingdom
Shekhem see Nablus
Sheki see Şäki
Shelby 22 B1 Montana, NW USA
Sheldon 23 F3 Iowa, C USA
Shelekhov Gulf 93 G2 Eng. Shelekhov Gulf. gulf E Russian Federation
Shelekhov Gulf see Shelikhova, Zaliv
Shendi 50 C4 var. Shandī. River Nile, NE Sudan
Shengking see Liaoning
Shenking see Liaoning
Shenshi/Shensi see Shaanxi
Shenyang 106 D3 Chin. Shen-yang, Eng. Moukden, Mukden; prev. Fengtien. province capital Liaoning, NE China
Shen-yang see Shenyang
Shepetivka 86 D2 Rus. Shepetovka. Khmel'nyts'ka Oblast', NW Ukraine
Shepetovka see Shepetivka
Shepparton 127 C7 Victoria, SE Australia
Sherbrooke 17 E4 Québec, SE Canada
Shereik 50 C3 River Nile, N Sudan
Sheridan 22 C2 Wyoming, C USA
Sherman 27 G2 Texas, SW USA
's-Hertogenbosch 64 C4 Fr. Bois-le-Duc, Ger. Herzogenbusch. Noord-Brabant, S Netherlands
Shetland Islands 66 D1 island group NE Scotland, United Kingdom
Shevchenko see Aktau
Shibarghān see Sheberghān
Shiberghan/Shiberghān see Sheberghān
Shibetsu 108 D2 var. Sibetu. Hokkaidō, NE Japan
Shibh Jazirat Sīnā' see Sinai
Shibushi-wan 109 B8 bay SW Japan
Shigatse see Xigazê
Shih-chia-chuang/Shihmen see Shijiazhuang
Shihezi 104 C2 Xinjiang Uygur Zizhiqu, NW China
Shiichi see Shyichy
Shijiazhuang 106 C4 var. Shih-chia-chuang; prev. Shihmen. province capital Hebei, E China
Shikārpur 112 B3 Sind, S Pakistan
Shikoku 109 C7 var. Sikoku. island SW Japan
Shikoku Basin 103 F2 var. Sikoku Basin. undersea basin N Philippine Sea
Shikotan, Ostrov 108 E2 Jap. Shikotan-tō. island NE Russian Federation
Shikotan-tō see Shikotan, Ostrov
Shilabo 51 D5 Sumalē, E Ethiopia
Shiliguri 113 F3 prev. Siliguri. West Bengal, NE India
Shilka 93 F4 river S Russian Federation
Shillong 113 G3 state capital Meghālaya, NE India
Shimanto see Nakamura
Shimbir Berris see Shimbiris
Shimbiris 50 E4 var. Shimbir Berris. mountain N Somalia
Shimoga 110 C2 Karnātaka, W India
Shimonoseki 109 A7 var. Simonoseki, hist. Akamagaseki, Bakan. Yamaguchi, Honshū, SW Japan
Shinano-gawa 109 C5 var. Sinano Gawa. river Honshū, C Japan
Shīndand 100 D4 Herāt, W Afghanistan
Shingū 109 C6 var. Singû. Wakayama, Honshū, SW Japan
Shinjō 108 D4 var. Sinzyô. Yamagata, Honshū, C Japan
Shinyanga 51 C7 Shinyanga, NW Tanzania
Shiprock 26 C1 New Mexico, SW USA
Shīrāz 98 D4 var. Shīrāz. Fārs, S Iran
Shishchitsy see Shyshchytsy
Shivpuri 112 D3 Madhya Pradesh, C India
Shizugawa 108 D4 Miyagi, Honshū, NE Japan
Shizuoka 109 D6 var. Sizuoka. Shizuoka, Honshū, S Japan
Shklov see Shklow
Shklow 85 D6 Rus. Shklov. Mahilyowskaya Voblasts', E Belarus
Shkodër 79 C5 var. Shkodra, It. Scutari, SCr. Skadar. Shkodër, NW Albania
Shkodra see Shkodër
Shkodrës, Liqeni i see Scutari, Lake
Shkumbinit, Lumi i 79 C6 var. Shkumbî, Shkumbin. river C Albania
Shkumbî/Shkumbin see Shkumbinit, Lumi i
Sholāpur see Solāpur
Shostka 87 F1 Sums'ka Oblast', NE Ukraine
Show Low 26 B2 Arizona, SW USA
Show Me State see Missouri
Shpola 87 E3 Cherkas'ka Oblast', N Ukraine
Shqipëria/Shqipërisë, Republika e see Albania
Shreveport 20 A2 Louisiana, S USA
Shrewsbury 67 D6 hist. Scrobesbyrig'. W England, United Kingdom
Shu 92 C5 Kaz. Shū. Zhambyl, SE Kazakhstan
Shuang-liao see Liaoyuan
Shū, Kazakhstan see Shu
Shumagin Islands 14 B3 island group Alaska, USA
Shumen 82 D2 Shumen, NE Bulgaria
Shumilina 85 E5 Rus. Shumilino. Vitsyebskaya Voblasts', NE Belarus
Shumilino see Shumilina
Shunsen see Ch'unch'ŏn
Shuqrah 99 B7 var. Shaqrā. SW Yemen
Shwebo 114 B3 Sagaing, C Myanmar (Burma)
Shyichy 85 C7 Rus. Shiichi. Homyel'skaya Voblasts', SE Belarus
Shymkent 92 B5 prev. Chimkent. Yuzhnyy Kazakhstan, S Kazakhstan
Shyshchytsy 85 C6 Rus. Shishchitsy. Minskaya Voblasts', C Belarus
Siam see Thailand
Siam, Gulf of see Thailand, Gulf of
Sian see Xi'an
Siang see Brahmaputra
Siangtan see Xiangtan
Šiauliai 84 B4 Ger. Schaulen. Šiauliai, N Lithuania
Siazan' see Siyäzän
Sibay 89 D6 Respublika Bashkortostan, W Russian Federation
Šibenik 78 B4 It. Sebenico. Šibenik-Knin, S Croatia
Siberia 93 E3 var. Siberia. physical region NE Russian Federation
Siberia see Sibir'
Siberoet see Siberut, Pulau
Siberut, Pulau 116 A4 prev. Siberoet. island Kepulauan Mentawai, W Indonesia
Sibi 112 B2 Baluchistān, SW Pakistan
Sibiti 55 B6 Lékoumou, S Congo
Sibiu 86 B4 Ger. Hermannstadt, Hung. Nagyszeben. Sibiu, C Romania
Sibolga 116 B3 Sumatera, W Indonesia
Sibu 116 D3 Sarawak, East Malaysia
Sibut 54 C4 prev. Fort-Sibut. Kémo, S Central African Republic
Sibuyan Sea 117 E2 sea W Pacific Ocean
Sichon 115 C6 var. Ban Sichon, Si Chon. Nakhon Si Thammarat, SW Thailand
Si Chon see Sichon
Sichuan 106 B5 var. Chuan, Sichuan Sheng, Ssu-ch'uan, Szechuan, Szechwan. province C China
Sichuan Pendi 106 B5 basin C China
Sichuan Sheng see Sichuan
Sicilian Channel see Sicily, Strait of
Sicily 75 C7 Eng. Sicily; anc. Trinacria. island Italy, C Mediterranean Sea
Sicily, Strait of 75 B7 var. Sicilian Channel. strait C Mediterranean Sea
Sicuani 39 E4 Cusco, S Peru
Sidári 82 A4 Kérkyra, Iónia Nisiá, Greece, C Mediterranean Sea
Sidas 116 C4 Borneo, C Indonesia
Siderno 75 D7 Calabria, SW Italy
Sidhirókastron see Sidirókastro
Sidi Barrâni 50 A1 NW Egypt
Sidi Bel Abbès 48 D2 var. Sidi bel Abbès, Sidi-Bel-Abbès. NW Algeria
Sidirókastro 82 C3 prev. Sidhirókastron. Kentrikí Makedonía, NE Greece
Sidley, Mount 132 B4 mountain Antarctica
Sidney 22 D1 Montana, NW USA
Sidney 22 D4 Nebraska, C USA
Sidney 18 C4 Ohio, N USA
Sidon see Saïda
Sidra see Surt
Sidra/Sidra, Gulf of see Surt, Khalīj, N Libya
Siebenbürgen see Transylvania
Siedlce 76 E3 Ger. Sedlez, Rus. Sesdlets. Mazowieckie, C Poland
Siegen 72 B4 Nordrhein-Westfalen, W Germany
Siemiatycze 76 E3 Podlaskie, NE Poland
Siena 74 B3 Fr. Sienne; anc. Saena Julia. Toscana, C Italy
Sienne see Siena
Sieradz 76 C4 Sieradz, C Poland
Sierpc 76 D3 Mazowieckie, C Poland
Sierra Leone 52 C4 off. Republic of Sierra Leone. country W Africa
Sierra Leone Basin 44 C4 undersea basin E Atlantic Ocean
Sierra Leone, Republic of see Sierra Leone
Sierra Leone Ridge see Sierra Leone Rise
Sierra Leone Rise 44 C4 var. Sierra Leone Ridge, Sierra Leone Schwelle. undersea rise E Atlantic Ocean
Sierra Leone Schwelle see Sierra Leone Rise
Sierra Madre 30 B2 var. Sierra de Soconusco. mountain range Guatemala/Mexico
Sierra Nevada 70 D5 mountain range S Spain
Sierra Nevada 25 C6 mountain range W USA
Sierra Vieja 26 D3 mountain range Texas, SW USA
Sierra Vista 26 B3 Arizona, SW USA
Sífnos 83 C6 anc. Siphnos. island Kykládes, Greece, Aegean Sea
Sigli 116 A3 Sumatera, W Indonesia
Siglufjördhur 61 E4 Nordhurland Vestra, N Iceland
Signal Peak 26 A2 mountain Arizona, SW USA
Signan see Xi'an
Signy 132 A2 UK research station South Orkney Islands, Antarctica
Siguatepeque 30 C2 Comayagua, W Honduras
Siguiri 52 D4 NE Guinea
Sihanoukville see Kâmpóng Saôm
Siilinjärvi 62 E4 Itä-Suomi, C Finland
Siirt 95 F4 var. Sert; anc. Tigranocerta. Siirt, SE Turkey
Sikandarabad see Secunderābād
Sikasso 52 D4 Sikasso, S Mali
Sikeston 23 H5 Missouri, C USA
Sikhote-Alin', Khrebet 93 G4 mountain range SE Russian Federation
Siking see Xi'an
Siklós 77 C7 Baranya, SW Hungary
Sikoku see Shikoku
Sikoku Basin see Shikoku Basin
Šilalė 84 B4 Tauragė, W Lithuania
Silchar 113 G3 Assam, NE India
Silesia 76 B4 physical region SW Poland
Silifke 94 C4 anc. Seleucia. İçel, S Turkey
Siliguri see Shiliguri
Siling Co 104 C5 lake W China
Silinhot see Xilinhot
Silistra 82 E1 var. Silistria; anc. Durostorum. Silistra, NE Bulgaria
Silistria see Silistra
Sillamäe 84 E2 Ger. Sillamäggi. Ida-Virumaa, NE Estonia
Sillamäggi see Sillamäe
Sillein see Žilina
Šilutė 84 B4 Ger. Heydekrug. Klaipėda, W Lithuania
Silvan 95 E4 Dıyarbakır, SE Turkey
Silva Porto see Kuito
Silver State see Colorado
Silver State see Nevada
Simanichy 85 C7 Rus. Simonichi. Homyel'skaya Voblasts', SE Belarus
Simav 94 B3 Kütahya, W Turkey
Simav Çayı 94 A3 river NW Turkey
Simbirsk see Ul'yanovsk
Simeto 75 C7 river Sicilia, Italy, C Mediterranean Sea
Simeulue, Pulau 116 A3 island NW Indonesia
Simferopol' 87 F5 Respublika Krym, S Ukraine
Simitla 82 C3 Blagoevgrad, SW Bulgaria
Şimlăul Silvaniei/Şimleul Silvaniei see Şimleu Silvaniei
Şimleu Silvaniei 86 B3 Hung. Szilágysomlyó; prev. Şimlăul Silvaniei, Şimleul Silvaniei. Sălaj, NW Romania
Simonichi see Simanichy
Simonoseki see Shimonoseki
Simpelveld 65 D6 Limburg, SE Netherlands
Simplon Pass 73 B8 pass S Switzerland
Simpson see Fort Simpson
Simpson Desert 126 B4 desert Northern Territory/South Australia
Sinai 50 C2 var. Sinai Peninsula, Ar. Shibh Jazirat Sīnā', Sînâ. physical region NE Egypt
Sinaia 86 C4 Prahova, SE Romania
Sinano Gawa see Shinano-gawa
Sînâ/Sinai Peninsula see Sinai
Sincelejo 36 B2 Sucre, NW Colombia
Sind 112 B3 var. Sindh. province SE Pakistan
Sindelfingen 73 B6 Baden-Württemberg, SW Germany
Sindh see Sind
Sindi 84 D2 Ger. Zintenhof. Pärnumaa, SW Estonia
Sines 70 B4 Setúbal, S Portugal
Singan see Xi'an
Singapore 116 B3 country capital S Singapore
Singapore 116 A1 off. Republic of Singapore. country SE Asia
Singapore, Republic of see Singapore
Singen 73 B6 Baden-Württemberg, S Germany
Singida 51 C7 Singida, C Tanzania
Singkang 117 E4 Sulawesi, C Indonesia
Singkawang 116 C3 Borneo, C Indonesia
Singora see Songkhla
Singû see Shingū
Sining see Xining
Siniscola 75 A5 Sardegna, Italy, C Mediterranean Sea
Sinj 78 B4 Split-Dalmacija, SE Croatia
Sinkiang/Sinkiang Uighur Autonomous Region see Xinjiang Uygur Zizhiqu
Sinnamarie see Sinnamary
Sinnamary 37 H3 var. Sinnamarie. N French Guiana
Sinneh see Sanandaj
Sînnicolau Mare see Sânnicolau Mare
Sinoe, Lacul see Sinoie, Lacul
Sinoie, Lacul 86 D5 prev. Lacul Sinoe. lagoon SE Romania
Sinop 94 D2 anc. Sinope. Sinop, N Turkey
Sinope see Sinop
Sinsheim 73 B6 Baden-Württemberg, SW Germany
Sint Maarten 33 G3 Eng. Saint Martin. island N Netherlands Antilles
Sint-Michielsgestel 64 C4 Noord-Brabant, S Netherlands
Sîn-Miclăuş see Gheorgheni
Sint-Niklaas 65 B5 Fr. Saint-Nicolas. Oost-Vlaanderen, N Belgium
Sint-Pieters-Leeuw 65 B6 Vlaams Brabant, C Belgium
Sintra 70 B3 prev. Cintra. Lisboa, W Portugal
Sinujiif 51 E5 Nugaal, NE Somalia
Sinus Aelaniticus see Aqaba, Gulf of
Sinus Gallicus see Lion, Golfe du
Sinyang see Xinyang
Sinzyô see Shinjō
Sion 73 A7 Ger. Sitten; anc. Sedunum. Valais, SW Switzerland
Sioux City 23 F3 Iowa, C USA
Sioux Falls 23 F3 South Dakota, N USA
Sioux State see North Dakota
Siphnos see Sífnos
Siping 106 D3 var. Ssu-p'ing, Szeping; prev. Ssu-p'ing-chieh. Jilin, NE China
Siple, Mount 132 A4 mountain Siple Island, Antarctica
Siquirres 31 E4 Limón, E Costa Rica
Siracusa 75 D7 Eng. Syracuse. Sicilia, Italy, C Mediterranean Sea
Sir Edward Pellew Group 126 B2 island group Northern Territory, NE Australia
Siret 86 C3 var. Siretul, Ger. Sereth, Rus. Seret. river Romania/Ukraine
Siretul see Siret
Siria see Syria
Sirikit Reservoir 114 C4 lake N Thailand
Sīrjān 98 D4 prev. Sa'īdābād. Kermān, S Iran
Sirna see Sýrna
Şırnak 95 F4 Şırnak, SE Turkey
Síros see Sýros
Sirte see Surt
Sirte, Gulf of 49 F2 Eng. Gulf of Sidra, Gulf of Sirti, Sidra. gulf N Libya
Sirti, Gulf of see Sirte, Gulf of
Sisak 78 B3 var. Siscia, Ger. Sissek, Hung. Sziszek; anc. Segestica. Sisak-Moslavina, C Croatia
Siscia see Sisak
Sisimiut 60 C3 var. Holsteinborg, Holsteinsborg, Holstenborg, Holstensborg. Kitaa, S Greenland
Sissek see Sisak
Sīstān, Daryācheh-ye see Şāberī, Hāmūn-e
Sitaş Cristuru see Cristuru Secuiesc
Siteía 83 D8 var. Sitía. Kríti, Greece, E Mediterranean Sea
Sitges 71 G2 Cataluña, NE Spain
Sitía see Siteía
Sittang see Sittoung
Sittard 65 D5 Limburg, SE Netherlands
Sitten see Sion
Sittoung 114 B4 var. Sittang. river S Myanmar (Burma)
Sittwe 114 A3 var. Akyab. Rakhine State, W Myanmar (Burma)
Siuna 30 D3 Región Autónoma Atlántico Norte, NE Nicaragua
Siut see Asyūţ
Sivas 94 D3 anc. Sebastia, Sebaste. Sivas, C Turkey
Siverek 95 E4 Şanlıurfa, S Turkey
Siwa see Sīwah
Sīwah 50 A2 var. Siwa. NW Egypt
Six Counties, The see Northern Ireland
Six-Fours-les-Plages 69 D6 Var, SE France
Siyäzän 95 H2 Rus. Siazan'. NE Azerbaijan
Sjar see Sääre
Sjenica 79 D5 Turk. Seniça. Serbia, SW Serbia
Skadar see Shkodër
Skadarsko Jezero see Scutari, Lake
Skagerak see Skagerrak
Skagerrak 63 A6 var. Skagerak. channel N Europe
Skagit River 24 B1 river Washington, NW USA
Skalka 62 C3 lake N Sweden
Skarżysko-Kamienna 76 D4 Świętokrzyskie, C Poland
Skaudvilė 84 B4 Tauragė, SW Lithuania
Skegness 67 E6 E England, United Kingdom
Skellefteå 62 D4 Västerbotten, N Sweden
Skellefteälven 62 C4 river N Sweden
Ski 63 B6 Akershus, S Norway
Skíathos 83 C5 Skíathos, Vóreies Sporádes, Greece, Aegean Sea
Skidal' 85 B5 Rus. Skidel'. Hrodzyenskaya Voblasts', W Belarus
Skidel' see Skidal'
Skiermûntseach see Schiermonnikoog
Skierniewice 76 D3 Łódzkie, C Poland
Skiftet 84 C1 strait Finland Atlantic Ocean Baltic Sea Gulf of Bothnia/Gulf of Finland
Skíros see Skýros
Skópelos 83 C5 Skópelos, Vóreies Sporádes, Greece, Aegean Sea
Skopje 79 D6 var. Üsküb, Turk. Üsküp, prev. Skoplje; anc. Scupi. country capital N FYR Macedonia
Skoplje see Skopje
Skovorodino 93 F4 Amurskaya Oblast', SE Russian Federation
Skuodas 84 B3 Ger. Schoden, Pol. Szkudy. Klaipėda, NW Lithuania
Skye, Isle of 66 B3 island NW Scotland, United Kingdom
Skylge see Terschelling
Skýros 83 C5 var. Skíros. Skýros, Vóreies Sporádes, Greece, Aegean Sea
Skýros 83 C5 var. Skíros; anc. Scyros. island Vóreies Sporádes, Greece, Aegean Sea
Slagelse 63 B7 Vestsjælland, E Denmark
Slatina 78 C3 Hung. Szlatina; prev. Podravska Slatina. Virovitica-Podravina, NE Croatia
Slatina 86 B5 Olt, S Romania
Slavgorod see Slawharad
Slavonska Požega see Požega
Slavonski Brod 78 C3 Ger. Brod, Hung. Bród; prev. Brod, Brod na Savi. Brod-Posavina, NE Croatia
Slavuta 86 C2 Khmel'nyts'ka Oblast', NW Ukraine
Slavyansk see Slov"yans'k
Slawharad 85 E7 Rus. Slavgorod. Mahilyowskaya Voblasts', E Belarus
Sławno 76 C2 Zachodnio-pomorskie, NW Poland
Slēmānī see As Sulaymānīyah
Sliema 80 B5 N Malta
Sligo 67 A5 Ir. Sligeach. Sligo, NW Ireland
Sliven 82 D2 var. Slivno. Sliven, C Bulgaria
Slivnitsa 82 B2 Sofiya, W Bulgaria
Slivno see Sliven
Slobozia 86 C5 Ialomiţa, SE Romania
Slonim 85 B6 Pol. Słonim. Hrodzyenskaya Voblasts', W Belarus
Słonim see Slonim
Slovakia 77 C6 off. Slovenská Republika, Ger. Slowakei, Hung. Szlovákia, Slvk. Slovensko. country C Europe
Slovak Ore Mountains see Slovenské rudohorie
Slovenia 73 D8 off. Republic of Slovenia, Ger. Slowenien, Slvn. Slovenija. country SE Europe
Slovenia, Republic of see Slovenia
Slovenija see Slovenia
Slovenská Republika see Slovakia
Slovenské rudohorie 77 D6 Eng. Slovak Ore Mountains, Ger. Slowakisches Erzgebirge, Ungarisches Erzgebirge. mountain range C Slovakia
Slovensko see Slovakia
Slov"yans'k 87 G3 Rus. Slavyansk. Donets'ka Oblast', E Ukraine
Slowakei see Slovakia
Slowakisches Erzgebirge see Slovenské rudohorie
Slowenien see Slovenia
Słubice 76 B3 Ger. Frankfurt. Lubuskie, W Poland
Sluch 86 D1 river NW Ukraine
Słupsk 76 C2 Ger. Stolp. Pomorskie, N Poland
Slutsk 85 C6 Minskaya Voblasts', S Belarus
Smallwood Reservoir 17 F2 lake Newfoundland and Labrador, S Canada
Smara 48 B3 var. Es Semara. N Western Sahara
Smarhon' 85 C5 Pol. Smorgonie, Rus. Smorgon'. Hrodzyenskaya Voblasts', W Belarus
Smederevo 78 D4 Ger. Semendria. Serbia, N Serbia
Smederevska Palanka 78 D4 Serbia, C Serbia
Smela see Smila
Smila 87 E2 Rus. Smela. Cherkas'ka Oblast', C Ukraine
Smilten see Smiltene
Smiltene 84 D3 Ger. Smilten. Valka, N Latvia
Smøla 62 A4 island W Norway
Smolensk 89 A5 Smolenskaya Oblast', W Russian Federation
Smorgon'/Smorgonie see Smarhon'
Smyrna see İzmir
Snake 12 B4 river Yukon Territory, NW Canada
Snake River 24 C3 river NW USA
Snake River Plain 24 D4 plain Idaho, NW USA
Sneek 64 D2 Friesland, N Netherlands
Sneeuw-gebergte see Maoke, Pegunungan
Sněžka 76 B4 Ger. Schneekoppe, Pol. Śnieżka. mountain N Czech Republic/Poland
Śniardwy, Jezioro 76 D2 Ger. Spirdingsee. lake NE Poland
Sniečkus see Visaginas
Śnieżka see Sněžka
Snina 77 E5 Hung. Szinna. Prešovský Kraj, E Slovakia
Snowdonia 67 C6 mountain range NW Wales, United Kingdom
Snowdrift see Łutselk'e
Snow Mountains see Maoke, Pegunungan
Snyder 27 F3 Texas, SW USA
Sobradinho, Barragem de see Sobradinho, Represa de
Sobradinho, Represa de 41 F2 var. Barragem de Sobradinho. reservoir E Brazil
Sochi 89 A7 Krasnodarskiy Kray, SW Russian Federation
Société, Îles de la/Society Islands see Société, Archipel de la
Society Islands 123 G4 var. Archipel de Tahiti, Îles de la Société, Eng. Society Islands. island group W French Polynesia
Soconusco, Sierra de see Sierra Madre
Socorro 26 D2 New Mexico, SW USA
Socorro, Isla 28 B5 island W Mexico
Socotra 99 C7 var. Sokotra, Eng. Socotra. island SE Yemen
Socotra see Suquṭrā
Soc Trăng 115 D6 var. Khanh Hung. Soc Trăng, S Vietnam
Socuéllamos 71 E3 Castilla-La Mancha, C Spain
Sodankylä 62 D3 Lappi, N Finland
Sodari see Sodiri
Söderhamn 63 C5 Gävleborg, C Sweden
Södertälje 63 C6 Stockholm, C Sweden
Sodiri 50 B4 var. Sawdirī, Sodari. Northern Kordofan, C Sudan
Soekaboemi see Sukabumi
Soemba see Sumba, Pulau
Soengaipenoeh see Sungaipenuh
Soerabaja see Surabaya
Soerakarta see Surakarta
Sofia see Sofiya
Sofiya 82 C2 var. Sophia, Eng. Sofia, Lat. Serdica. country capital Sofiya-Grad, W Bulgaria
Sogamoso 36 B3 Boyacá, C Colombia
Sognefjorden 63 A5 fjord NE North Sea
Soḩāg see Sawhāj
Sohar see Şuḩār
Sohm Plain 44 B3 abyssal plain NW Atlantic Ocean
Sohrau see Żory
Sokal' 86 C2 Rus. Sokal. L'vivs'ka Oblast', NW Ukraine
Söke 94 A4 Aydın, SW Turkey
Sokhumi 95 E1 Rus. Sukhumi. NW Georgia
Sokodé 53 F4 C Togo
Sokol 88 C4 Vologodskaya Oblast', NW Russian Federation
Sokółka 76 E3 Podlaskie, NE Poland
Sokolov 77 A5 Ger. Falkenau an der Eger; prev. Falknov nad Ohří. Karlovarský Kraj, W Czech Republic
Sokone 52 B3 W Senegal
Sokoto 53 F3 Sokoto, NW Nigeria
Sokoto 53 F4 river NW Nigeria
Sokotra see Suquṭrā
Solāpur 102 B3 var. Sholāpur. Mahārāshtra, W India
Solca 86 C3 Ger. Solka. Suceava, N Romania
Sol, Costa del 70 D5 coastal region S Spain
Soldeu 69 B7 NE Andorra Europe
Solec Kujawski 76 C3 Kujawsko-pomorskie, C Poland
Soledad 36 B1 Atlántico, N Colombia
Isla Soledad see East Falkland
Soligorsk see Salihorsk
Solikamsk 92 C3 Permskaya Oblast', NW Russian Federation
Sol'-Iletsk 89 D6 Orenburgskaya Oblast', W Russian Federation
Solingen 72 A4 Nordrhein-Westfalen, W Germany
Solka see Solca
Sollentuna 63 C6 Stockholm, C Sweden
Solo see Surakarta
Solok 116 B4 Sumatera, W Indonesia
Solomon Islands 122 C3 prev. British Solomon Islands Protectorate. country W Solomon Islands N Melanesia W Pacific Ocean
Solomon Islands 122 C3 island group Papua New Guinea/Solomon Islands
Solomon Sea 122 B3 sea W Pacific Ocean
Soltau 72 B3 Niedersachsen, NW Germany

Sol'tsy – Sydney

Sol'tsy *88 A4* Novgorodskaya Oblast', W Russian Federation
Solun *see* Thessaloníki
Solwezi *56 D2* North Western, NW Zambia
Sōma *108 D4* Fukushima, Honshū, C Japan
Somalia *51 D5 off.* Somali Democratic Republic, *Som.* Jamuuriyada Demuqraadiga Soomaaliyeed, Soomaaliya; *prev.* Italian Somaliland, Somaliland Protectorate. *country* E Africa
Somali Basin *47 E5 undersea basin* W Indian Ocean
Somali Democratic Republic *see* Somalia
Somaliland *51 D5 disputed territory* N Somalia
Somaliland Protectorate *see* Somalia
Sombor *78 C3 Hung.* Zombor. Vojvodina, NW Serbia
Someren *65 D5* Noord-Brabant, SE Netherlands
Somerset *20 A5 var.* Somerset Village. W Bermuda
Somerset *18 C5* Kentucky, S USA
Somerset Island *20 A5 island* W Bermuda
Somerset Island *15 F2 island* Queen Elizabeth Islands, Nunavut, NW Canada
Somerset Village *see* Somerset
Somers Islands *see* Bermuda
Somerton *26 A2* Arizona, SW USA
Someş *86 B3 river* Hungary/Romania Europe
Somme *68 C2 river* N France
Sommerfeld *see* Lubsko
Somotillo *30 C3* Chinandega, NW Nicaragua
Somoto *30 D3* Madriz, NW Nicaragua
Songea *51 C8* Ruvuma, S Tanzania
Sŏngjin *see* Kimch'aek
Songkhla *115 C7 var.* Songkla, *Mal.* Singora. Songkhla, SW Thailand
Songkla *see* Songkhla
Sonoran Desert *26 A3 var.* Desierto de Altar. *desert* Mexico/USA
Sonsonate *30 B3* Sonsonate, W El Salvador
Soochow *see* Suzhou
Soomaaliya/Soomaaliyeed, Jamuuriyada Demuqraadiga *see* Somalia
Soome Laht *see* Finland, Gulf of
Sop Hao *114 D3* Houaphan, N Laos
Sophia *see* Sofiya
Sopianae *see* Pécs
Sopot *76 C2 Ger.* Zoppot. Pomorskie, N Poland
Sopron *77 B6 Ger.* Ödenburg. Győr-Moson-Sopron, NW Hungary
Sorau/Sorau in der Niederlausitz *see* Żary
Sorgues *69 D6* Vaucluse, SE France
Sorgun *94 D3* Yozgat, C Turkey
Soria *71 E2* Castilla-León, N Spain
Soroca *86 D3 Rus.* Soroki. N Moldova
Sorochino *see* Sarochyna
Soroki *see* Soroca
Sorong *117 F4* Papua, E Indonesia
Sørøy *see* Sørøya
Sørøya *62 C2 var.* Sørøy, *Lapp.* Sállan. *island* N Norway
Sortavala *88 B3 prev.* Serdobol'. Respublika Kareliya, NW Russian Federation
Sotavento, Ilhas de *52 A3 var.* Leeward Islands. *island group* S Cape Verde
Sotkamo *62 E4* Oulu, C Finland
Souanké *55 B5* Sangha, NW Congo
Soueida *see* As Suwaydā'
Souflí *82 D3 prev.* Souflíon. Anatolikí Makedonía kai Thráki, NE Greece
Souflíon *see* Souflí
Soufrière *33 F2* W Saint Lucia
Soukhné *see* As Sukhnah
Sŏul *107 E4 off.* Sŏul-t'ŭkpyŏlsi, *Eng.* Seoul, *Jap.* Keijō; *prev.* Kyŏngsŏng. *country capital* NW South Korea
Sŏul-t'ŭkpyŏlsi *see* Sŏul
Soûr *97 A5 var.* Şūr; *anc.* Tyre. SW Lebanon
Souris River *23 E1 var.* Mouse River. *river* Canada/USA
Soúrpi *83 B5* Thessalía, C Greece
Sousse *49 F2 var.* Süsah. NE Tunisia
South Africa *56 C4 off.* Republic of South Africa, *Afr.* Suid-Afrika. *country* S Africa
South Africa, Republic of *see* South Africa
South America *34 continent*
Southampton *67 D7 hist.* Hamwih, *Lat.* Clausentum. S England, United Kingdom
Southampton Island *15 G3 island* Nunavut, NE Canada
South Andaman *111 F2 island* Andaman Islands, India, NE Indian Ocean
South Australia *127 A5 state* S Australia
South Australian Basin *120 B5 undersea basin* SW Indian Ocean
South Bend *18 C3* Indiana, N USA
South Beveland *see* Zuid-Beveland
South Bruny Island *127 C8 island* Tasmania, SE Australia
South Carolina *21 E2 off.* State of South Carolina, *also known as* The Palmetto State. *state* SE USA
South Carpathians *see* Carpaţii Meridionali
South China Basin *103 E4 undersea basin* SE South China Sea
South China Sea *103 E4 Chin.* Nan Hai, *Ind.* Laut Cina Selatan, *Vtn.* Biên Đông. *sea* SE Asia
South Dakota *22 D2 off.* State of South Dakota, *also known as* The Coyote State, Sunshine State. *state* N USA
Southeast Indian Ridge *119 D7 undersea ridge* Indian Ocean/Pacific Ocean
Southeast Pacific Basin *131 E5 var.* Belling Hausen Mulde. *undersea basin* SE Pacific Ocean
South East Point *127 C7 headland* Victoria, S Australia
Southend-on-Sea *67 E6* E England, United Kingdom
Southern Alps *129 B6 mountain range* South Island, New Zealand
Southern Cook Islands *123 F4 island group* S Cook Islands
Southern Cross *125 B6* Western Australia
Southern Indian Lake *15 F4 lake* Manitoba, C Canada
Southern Ocean *45 B7 ocean* Atlantic Ocean/Indian Ocean/Pacific Ocean
Southern Uplands *66 C4 mountain range* S Scotland, United Kingdom
South Fiji Basin *120 D4 undersea basin* S Pacific Ocean
South Geomagnetic Pole *132 B3 pole* Antarctica
South Georgia *35 D8 island* South Georgia and the South Sandwich Islands, SW Atlantic Ocean
South Goulburn Island *124 E2 island* Northern Territory, N Australia
South Huvadhu Atoll *110 A5 atoll* S Maldives
South Indian Basin *119 D7 undersea basin* Indian Ocean/Pacific Ocean
South Island *129 C6 island* S New Zealand
South Korea *107 E4 off.* Republic of Korea, *Kor.* Taehan Min'guk. *country* E Asia
South Lake Tahoe *25 C5* California, W USA
South Orkney Islands *132 A2 island group* Antarctica
South Ossetia *95 F2 former autonomous region* SW Georgia
South Pacific Basin *see* Southwest Pacific Basin
South Platte River *22 D4 river* Colorado/Nebraska, C USA
South Pole *132 B3 pole* Antarctica
South Sandwich Islands *35 D8 island group* SW Atlantic Ocean
South Sandwich Trench *35 E8 trench* SW Atlantic Ocean
South Shetland Islands *132 A2 island group* Antarctica
South Shields *66 D4* NE England, United Kingdom
South Sioux City *23 F3* Nebraska, C USA
South Taranaki Bight *128 C4 bight* SE Tasman Sea
South Tasmania Plateau *see* Tasman Plateau
South Uist *66 B3 island* NW Scotland, United Kingdom
South-West Africa/South West Africa *see* Namibia
South West Cape *129 A8 headland* Stewart Island, New Zealand
Southwest Indian Ocean Ridge *see* Southwest Indian Ridge
Southwest Indian Ridge *119 B6 var.* Southwest Indian Ocean Ridge. *undersea ridge* SW Indian Ocean
Southwest Pacific Basin *121 E4 var.* South Pacific Basin. *undersea basin* SE Pacific Ocean
Sovereign Base Area *80 C5 uk military installation* S Cyprus
Soweto *56 D4* Gauteng, NE South Africa
Sōya-kaikyō *see* La Perouse Strait
Spain *70 D3 off.* Kingdom of Spain, *Sp.* España; *anc.* Hispania, Iberia, *Lat.* Hispana. *country* SW Europe
Spain, Kingdom of *see* Spain
Spalato *see* Split
Spanish Town *32 B5 hist.* St.Iago de la Vega. C Jamaica
Sparks *25 C5* Nevada, W USA
Sparta *see* Spárti
Spartanburg *21 E1* South Carolina, SE USA
Spárti *83 B6 Eng.* Sparta. Pelopónnisos, S Greece
Spearfish *22 D2* South Dakota, N USA
Speightstown *33 G1* NW Barbados
Spencer *23 F3* Iowa, C USA
Spencer Gulf *127 B6 gulf* South Australia
Spey *66 C3 river* NE Scotland, United Kingdom
Spice Islands *see* Maluku
Spiess Seamount *45 C7 seamount* S Atlantic Ocean
Spijkenisse *64 B4* Zuid-Holland, SW Netherlands
Spíli *83 C8* Kríti, Greece, E Mediterranean Sea
Spīn Būldak *101 E5* Kandahār, S Afghanistan
Spirdingsee *see* Śniardwy, Jezioro
Spitsbergen *61 F2 island* NW Svalbard
Split *78 B4 It.* Spalato. Split-Dalmacija, S Croatia
Špoģi *84 D4* Daugvapils, SE Latvia
Spokane *24 C2* Washington, NW USA
Spratly Islands *116 B2 Chin.* Nansha Qundao. *disputed territory* SE Asia
Spree *72 D4 river* E Germany
Springfield *18 B4 state capital* Illinois, N USA
Springfield *19 G3* Massachusetts, NE USA
Springfield *23 G5* Missouri, C USA
Springfield *18 C4* Ohio, N USA
Springfield *24 B3* Oregon, NW USA
Spring Garden *37 F2* NE Guyana
Spring Hill *21 E4* Florida, SE USA
Springs Junction *129 C5* West Coast, South Island, New Zealand
Springsure *126 D4* Queensland, E Australia
Sprottau *see* Szprotawa
Spruce Knob *19 E4 mountain* West Virginia, NE USA
Srbinje *see* Foča
Srbobran *78 D3 var.* Bácsszenttamás, *Hung.* Szenttamás. Vojvodina, N Serbia
Srebrenica *78 C4* Republika Srpska, E Bosnia and Herzegovina
Sredets *82 D2 prev.* Syulemeshlii. Stara Zagora, C Bulgaria
Sredets *82 E2 prev.* Grudovo. Burgas, E Bulgaria
Sremska Mitrovica *78 C3 prev.* Mitrovica, *Ger.* Mitrowitz. Vojvodina, NW Serbia
Srepok, Sông *see* Srêpôk, Tônle
Srêpôk, Tônle *115 E5 var.* Sông Srepok. *river* Cambodia/Vietnam
Sri Aman *116 C3* Sarawak, East Malaysia
Sri Jayawardanapura *see* Sri Jayewardanapura Kotte
Sri Jayewardanapura Kotte *110 D3 var.* Sri Jayawardanapura. Western Province, W Sri Lanka
Srīkākulam *113 F5* Andhra Pradesh, E India
Sri Lanka *110 D3 off.* Democratic Socialist Republic of Sri Lanka; *prev.* Ceylon. *country* S Asia
Sri Lanka, Democratic Socialist Republic of *see* Sri Lanka
Srinagarind Reservoir *115 C5 lake* W Thailand
Srpska, Republika *78 B3 republic* Bosnia and Herzegovina
Ssu-ch'uan *see* Sichuan
Ssu-p'ing/Ssu-p'ing-chieh *see* Siping
Stabroek *65 B5* Antwerpen, N Belgium
Stade *72 B3* Niedersachsen, NW Germany
Stadskanaal *64 E2* Groningen, NE Netherlands
Stafford *67 D6* C England, United Kingdom
Staicele *84 D3* Limbaži, N Latvia
Ştaierdorf-Anina *see* Anina
Stájerlakanina *see* Anina
Stakhanov *87 H3* Luhans'ka Oblast', E Ukraine
Stalin *see* Varna
Stalinabad *see* Dushanbe
Stalingrad *see* Volgograd
Stalino *see* Donets'k
Stalinobod *see* Dushanbe
Stalinsk *see* Novokuznetsk
Stalinski Zaliv *see* Varnenski Zaliv
Stalin, Yazovir *see* Iskŭr, Yazovir
Stalowa Wola *76 E4* Podkarpackie, SE Poland
Stamford *19 F3* Connecticut, NE USA
Stampalia *see* Astypálaia
Stanislau *see* Ivano-Frankivs'k
Stanislav *see* Ivano-Frankivs'k
Stanisławów *see* Ivano-Frankivs'k
Stanke Dimitrov *see* Dupnitsa
Stanley *43 D7 var.* Port Stanley, Puerto Argentino. *dependent territory capital* East Falkland, Falkland Islands
Stanleyville *see* Kisangani
Stann Creek *see* Dangriga
Stanovoy Khrebet *91 E3 mountain range* SE Russian Federation
Stanthorpe *127 D5* Queensland, E Australia
Staphorst *64 D2* Overijssel, E Netherlands
Starachowice *76 D4* Świętokrzyskie, C Poland
Stara Kanjiža *see* Kanjiža
Stara Pazova *78 D3 Ger.* Altpasua, *Hung.* Ópazova. Vojvodina, N Serbia
Stara Planina *see* Balkan Mountains
Stara Zagora *82 D2 Lat.* Augusta Trajana. Stara Zagora, C Bulgaria
Starbuck Island *123 G3 prev.* Volunteer Island. *island* E Kiribati
Stargard in Pommern *see* Stargard Szczeciński
Stargard Szczeciński *76 B3 Ger.* Stargard in Pommern. Zachodnio-pomorskie, NW Poland
Stari Bečej *see* Bečej
Starobel'sk *see* Starobil's'k
Starobil's'k *87 H2 Rus.* Starobel'sk. Luhans'ka Oblast', E Ukraine
Starobin *85 C7 var.* Starobyn. Minskaya Voblasts', S Belarus
Starobyn *see* Starobin
Starogard Gdański *76 C2 Ger.* Preussisch-Stargard. Pomorskie, N Poland
Starokonstantinov *see* Starokostyantyniv
Starokostyantyniv *86 D2 Rus.* Starokonstantinov. Khmel'nyts'ka Oblast', NW Ukraine
Starominskaya *89 A7* Krasnodarskiy Kray, SW Russian Federation
Staryya Darohi *85 C6 Rus.* Staryye Dorogi. Minskaya Voblasts', S Belarus
Staryye Dorogi *see* Staryya Darohi
Staryy Oskol *89 B6* Belgorodskaya Oblast', W Russian Federation
State College *19 E4* Pennsylvania, NE USA
Staten Island *see* Estados, Isla de los
Statesboro *21 E2* Georgia, SE USA
States, The *see* United States of America
Staunton *19 E5* Virginia, NE USA
Stavanger *63 A6* Rogaland, S Norway
Stavers Island *see* Vostok Island
Stavropol' *89 B7 prev.* Voroshilovsk. Stavropol'skiy Kray, SW Russian Federation
Stavropol' *see* Tol'yatti
Steamboat Springs *22 C4* Colorado, C USA
Steenwijk *64 D2* Overijssel, N Netherlands
Steier *see* Steyr
Steierdorf/Steierdorf-Anina *see* Anina
Steinamanger *see* Szombathely
Steinkjer *62 B4* Nord-Trøndelag, C Norway
Stejarul *see* Karapelit
Stendal *72 C3* Sachsen-Anhalt, C Germany
Stepanakert *see* Xankändi
Stephenville *27 F3* Texas, SW USA
Sterling *22 D4* Colorado, C USA
Sterling *18 B3* Illinois, N USA
Sterlitamak *92 B3* Respublika Bashkortostan, W Russian Federation
Stettin *see* Szczecin
Stettiner Haff *see* Szczeciński, Zalew
Stevenage *67 E6* E England, United Kingdom
Stevens Point *18 B2* Wisconsin, N USA
Stewart Island *129 A8 island* S New Zealand
Steyerlak-Anina *see* Anina
Steyr *73 D6 var.* Steier. Oberösterreich, N Austria
Stif *see* Sétif
Stillwater *27 G1* Oklahoma, C USA
Štip *79 E6* E FYR Macedonia
Stirling *66 C4* C Scotland, United Kingdom
Stjørdalshalsen *62 B4* Nord-Trøndelag, C Norway
Stockach *73 B6* Baden-Württemberg, S Germany
Stockholm *63 C6 country capital* Stockholm, C Sweden
Stockmannshof *see* Pļaviņas
Stockton *25 B6* California, W USA
Stockton Plateau *27 E4 plain* Texas, SW USA
Stœng Trêng *115 D5 prev.* Stung Treng. Stœng Trêng, NE Cambodia
Stoke *see* Stoke-on-Trent
Stoke-on-Trent *67 D6 var.* Stoke. C England, United Kingdom
Stolbce *see* Stowbtsy
Stolbtsy *see* Stowbtsy
Stolp *see* Słupsk
Stolpmünde *see* Ustka
Stómio *82 B4* Thessalía, C Greece
Store Bælt *see* Storebælt
Storebælt *see* Storebælt
Støren *63 B5* Sør-Trøndelag, S Norway
Storfjorden *61 G2 fjord* S Norway
Storhammer *see* Hamar
Stornoway *66 B2* NW Scotland, United Kingdom
Storsjön *63 B5 lake* C Sweden
Storuman *62 C4* Västerbotten, N Sweden
Storuman *62 C4 lake* N Sweden
Stowbtsy *85 C6 Pol.* Stolbce, *Rus.* Stolbtsy. Minskaya Voblasts', C Belarus
Strabane *67 B5 Ir.* An Srath Bán. W Northern Ireland, United Kingdom
Strakonice *77 A5 Ger.* Strakonitz. Jihočeský Kraj, S Czech Republic
Strakonitz *see* Strakonice
Stralsund *72 D2* Mecklenburg-Vorpommern, NE Germany
Stranraer *67 C5* S Scotland, United Kingdom
Strasbourg *68 E3 Ger.* Strassburg; *anc.* Argentoratum. Bas-Rhin, NE France
Străşeni *86 D3 var.* Strasheny. C Moldova
Strasheny *see* Străşeni
Strassburg *see* Strasbourg, France
Strassburg *see* Aiud, Romania
Stratford *128 D4* Taranaki, North Island, New Zealand
Strathfield *126 E2* New South Wales, E Australia
Straubing *73 C6* Bayern, SE Germany
Strehaia *86 B5* Mehedinţi, SW Romania
Strelka *92 D4* Krasnoyarskiy Kray, C Russian Federation
Strigonium *see* Esztergom
Strofilia *see* Strofyliá
Strofyliá *83 C5 var.* Strofilia. Évvoia, C Greece
Stromboli *75 D6 island* Isole Eolie, S Italy
Stromeferry *66 C3* N Scotland, United Kingdom
Strömstad *63 B6* Västra Götaland, S Sweden
Strömsund *62 C4* Jämtland, C Sweden
Struga *79 D6* SW FYR Macedonia
Struma *see* Strymónas
Strumica *79 E6* E FYR Macedonia
Strumyani *82 C3* Blagoevgrad, SW Bulgaria
Strymónas *82 C3 Bul.* Struma. *river* Bulgaria/Greece
Stryy *86 B2* L'vivs'ka Oblast', NW Ukraine
Studholme *129 B6* Canterbury, South Island, New Zealand
Stuhlweissenberg *see* Székesfehérvár
Stung Treng *see* Stœng Trêng
Sturgis *22 D3* South Dakota, N USA
Stuttgart *73 B6* Baden-Württemberg, SW Germany
Stykkishólmur *61 E4* Vesturland, W Iceland
Styr *86 C1 Rus.* Styr'. *river* Belarus/Ukraine
Su *see* Jiangsu
Suakin *50 C3 var.* Sawakin. Red Sea, NE Sudan
Subačius *84 C4* Panevėžys, NE Lithuania
Subaykhān *96 E3* Dayr az Zawr, E Syria
Subotica *78 D2 Ger.* Maria-Theresiopel, *Hung.* Szabadka. Vojvodina, N Serbia
Suceava *86 C3 Ger.* Suczawa, *Hung.* Szucsava. Suceava, NE Romania
Su-chou *see* Suzhou
Suchow *see* Xuzhou, Jiangsu, China
Suchow *see* Suzhou, Jiangsu, China
Sucker State *see* Illinois
Sucre *39 F4 hist.* Chuquisaca, La Plata. *country capital* Chuquisaca, S Bolivia
Suczawa *see* Suceava
Sudan *50 A4 off.* Republic of Sudan, *Ar.* Jumhuriyat as-Sudan; *prev.* Anglo-Egyptian Sudan. *country* N Africa
Sudanese Republic *see* Mali
Sudan, Jumhuriyat as- *see* Sudan
Sudan, Republic of *see* Sudan
Sudbury *16 C4* Ontario, S Canada
Sudd *51 B5 swamp region* S Sudan
Sudeten *76 B4 var.* Sudetes, Sudetic Mountains, *Cz./Pol.* Sudety. *mountain range* Czech Republic/Poland
Sudetes/Sudetic Mountains/Sudety *see* Sudeten
Südkarpaten *see* Carpaţii Meridionali
Südliche Morava *see* Južna Morava
Sudong, Pulau *116 A2 island* SW Singapore Asia
Sudostroy *see* Severodvinsk
Sue *51 B5 river* S Sudan
Sueca *71 F3* País Valenciano, E Spain
Sue Wood Bay *20 B5 bay* W Bermuda North America W Atlantic Ocean
Suez *50 B1 Ar.* As Suways, El Suweis. NE Egypt
Suez Canal *50 B1 Ar.* Qanāt as Suways. *canal* NE Egypt
Suez, Gulf of *see* Khalīj as Suways
Suğla Gölü *94 C4 lake* SW Turkey
Şuḩār *99 D5 var.* Sohar. N Oman
Sühbaatar *105 E1* Selenge, N Mongolia
Suhl *73 C5* Thüringen, C Germany
Suicheng *see* Suixi
Suid-Afrika *see* South Africa
Suidwes-Afrika *see* Namibia
Suixi *106 C6 var.* Suicheng. Guangdong, S China
Sujāwal *112 B3* Sind, SE Pakistan
Sukabumi *116 C5 prev.* Soekaboemi. Jawa, C Indonesia
Sukagawa *109 D5* Fukushima, Honshū, C Japan
Sukarnapura *see* Jayapura
Sukarno, Puntjak *see* Jaya, Puncak
Sukhne *see* As Sukhnah
Sukhona *88 C4 var.* Tot'ma. *river* NW Russian Federation
Sukhumi *see* Sokhumi
Sukkertoppen *see* Maniitsoq
Sukkur *112 B3* Sind, SE Pakistan
Sukumo *109 B7* Kōchi, Shikoku, SW Japan
Sulaimaniya *see* As Sulaymānīyah
Sulaiman Range *112 C2 mountain range* C Pakistan
Sula, Kepulauan *117 E4 island group* C Indonesia
Sulawesi, Laut *see* Celebes Sea
Sulechów *76 B3 Ger.* Züllichau. Lubuskie, W Poland
Suliag *see* Sawhāj
Sullana *38 B2* Piura, NW Peru
Sullivan Island *see* Lanbi Kyun
Sulphur Springs *27 G2* Texas, SW USA
Sultānābād *see* Arāk
Sulu Archipelago *117 E3 island group* SW Philippines
Sülüktü *see* Sulyukta
Sulu, Laut *see* Sulu Sea
Sulu Sea *117 E2 var.* Laut Sulu. *sea* SW Philippines
Sulyukta *101 E2 Kir.* Sülüktü. Batkenskaya Oblast', SW Kyrgyzstan
Sumatera *115 B8 Eng.* Sumatra. *island* W Indonesia
Sumatra *see* Sumatera
Šumava *see* Bohemian Forest
Sumba, Pulau *117 E5 Eng.* Sandalwood Island; *prev.* Soemba. *island* Nusa Tenggara, C Indonesia
Sumba, Selat *117 E5 strait* Nusa Tenggara, S Indonesia
Sumbawanga *51 B7* Rukwa, W Tanzania
Sumbe *56 B2 var.* N'Gunza, *Port.* Novo Redondo. Cuanza Sul, W Angola
Sumeih *51 B5* Southern Darfur, S Sudan
Sumgait *see* Sumqayıt, Azerbaijan
Summer Lake *24 B4 lake* Oregon, NW USA
Summit *71 H5* Alaska, USA
Sumqayıt *95 H2 Rus.* Sumgait. E Azerbaijan
Sumy *87 F2* Sums'ka Oblast', NE Ukraine
Sunbury *127 C7* Victoria, SE Australia
Sunda Islands *see* Greater Sunda Islands
Sunda, Selat *116 B5 strait* Jawa/Sumatera, SW Indonesia
Sunda Trench *see* Java Trench
Sunderland *66 D4 var.* Wearmouth. NE England, United Kingdom
Sundsvall *63 C5* Västernorrland, C Sweden
Sunflower State *see* Kansas
Sungaipenuh *116 B4 prev.* Soengaipenoeh. Sumatera, W Indonesia
Sunnyvale *25 A6* California, W USA
Sunset State *see* Oregon
Sunshine State *see* Florida
Sunshine State *see* New Mexico
Sunshine State *see* South Dakota
Suntar *93 F3* Respublika Sakha (Yakutiya), NE Russian Federation
Sunyani *53 E5* W Ghana
Suoločielgi *see* Saariselkä
Suomenlahti *see* Finland, Gulf of
Suomen Tasavalta/Suomi *see* Finland
Suomussalmi *62 E4* Oulu, E Finland
Suŏng *115 D6* Kâmpóng Cham, C Cambodia
Suoyarvi *88 B3* Respublika Kareliya, NW Russian Federation
Supe *38 C3* Lima, W Peru
Supérieur, Lac *see* Superior, Lake
Superior *18 A1* Wisconsin, N USA
Superior, Lake *18 B1 Fr.* Lac Supérieur. *lake* Canada/USA
Suqrah *see* Şawqirah
Şūr *99 E5* NE Oman
Şūr *see* Soûr
Surabaja *see* Surabaya
Surabaya *116 D5 prev.* Surabaja, Soerabaja. Jawa, C Indonesia
Surakarta *116 C5 Eng.* Solo; *prev.* Soerakarta. Jawa, S Indonesia
Šurany *77 C6 Hung.* Nagysurány. Nitriansky Kraj, SW Slovakia
Sūrat *112 C4* Gujarāt, W India
Suratdhani *see* Surat Thani
Surat Thani *115 C6 var.* Suratdhani. Surat Thani, SW Thailand
Surazh *85 E5* Vitsyebskaya Voblasts', NE Belarus
Surdulica *79 E5* Serbia, SE Serbia
Sûre *65 D7 var.* Sauer. *river* W Europe
Surendranagar *112 C4* Gujarāt, W India
Surfers Paradise *127 E5* Queensland, E Australia
Surgut *92 D3* Khanty-Mansiyskiy Avtonomnyy Okrug-Yugra, C Russian Federation
Surin *115 D5* Surin, E Thailand
Surinam *see* Suriname
Suriname *37 G3 off.* Republic of Suriname, *var.* Surinam; *prev.* Dutch Guiana, Netherlands Guiana. *country* N South America
Suriname, Republic of *see* Suriname
Sūrīya/Sūrīyah, Al-Jumhūrīyah al-'Arabīyah as- *see* Syria
Surkhab, Darya-i- *see* Kahmard, Daryā-ye
Surkhob *101 F3 river* C Tajikistan
Surt *49 G2 var.* Sidra, Sirte. N Libya
Surtsey *61 E5 island* S Iceland
Suruga-wan *109 D6 bay* SE Japan
Susa *74 A2* Piemonte, NE Italy
Sūsah *see* Sousse
Susanville *25 B5* California, W USA
Susitna *14 C3* Alaska, USA
Susteren *65 D5* Limburg, SE Netherlands
Susuman *93 G3* Magadanskaya Oblast', E Russian Federation
Sutlej *112 C2 river* India/Pakistan
Suur Munamägi *84 D3 var.* Munamägi, *Ger.* Eier-Berg. *mountain* SE Estonia
Suur Väin *84 C2 Ger.* Grosser Sund. *strait* W Estonia
Suva *123 E4 country capital* Viti Levu, W Fiji
Suvalkai/Suvalki *see* Suwałki
Suwałki *76 E2 Lith.* Suvalkai, *Rus.* Suvalki. Podlaskie, NE Poland
Şuwār *see* Aş Şuwār
Suways, Qanāt as *see* Suez Canal
Suweida *see* As Suwaydā'
Suzhou *106 D5 var.* Soochow, Su-chou, Suchow; *prev.* Wuhsien. Jiangsu, E China
Svalbard *61 E1 Norwegian dependency* Arctic Ocean
Svartisen *62 C3 glacier* C Norway
Svay Riĕng *115 D6* Svay Riĕng, S Cambodia
Sveg *63 B5* Jämtland, C Sweden
Svenstavik *63 C5* Jämtland, C Sweden
Sverdlovsk *see* Yekaterinburg
Sverige *see* Sweden
Sveti Vrach *see* Sandanski
Svetlogorsk *see* Svyetlahorsk
Svetlograd *89 B7* Stavropol'skiy Kray, SW Russian Federation
Svetlovodsk *see* Svitlovods'k
Svetozarevo *see* Jagodina
Svilengrad *82 D3 prev.* Mustafa-Pasha. Khaskovo, S Bulgaria
Svitlovods'k *87 F3 Rus.* Svetlovodsk. Kirovohrads'ka Oblast', C Ukraine
Svizzera *see* Switzerland
Svobodnyy *93 G4* Amurskaya Oblast', SE Russian Federation
Svyataya Anna Trough *133 C4 var.* Saint Anna Trough. *trough* N Kara Sea
Svyetlahorsk *85 D7 Rus.* Svetlogorsk. Homyel'skaya Voblasts', SE Belarus
Swabian Jura *see* Schwäbische Alb
Swakopmund *56 B3* Erongo, W Namibia
Swan Islands *31 E1 island group* NE Honduras North America
Swansea *67 C7 Wel.* Abertawe. S Wales, United Kingdom
Swarzędz *76 C3* Poznań, W Poland
Swatow *see* Shantou
Swaziland *56 D4 off.* Kingdom of Swaziland. *country* S Africa
Swaziland, Kingdom of *see* Swaziland
Sweden *62 B4 off.* Kingdom of Sweden, *Swe.* Sverige. *country* N Europe
Sweden, Kingdom of *see* Sweden
Sweetwater *27 F3* Texas, SW USA
Świdnica *76 B4 Ger.* Schweidnitz. Wałbrzych, SW Poland
Świdwin *76 B2 Ger.* Schivelbein. Zachodnio-pomorskie, NW Poland
Świebodzice *76 B4 Ger.* Freiburg in Schlesien, Swiebodzice. Walbrzych, SW Poland
Świebodzin *76 B3 Ger.* Schwiebus. Lubuskie, W Poland
Świecie *76 C3 Ger.* Schwertberg. Kujawsko-pomorskie, C Poland
Swindon *67 D7* S England, United Kingdom
Swinemünde *see* Świnoujście
Świnoujście *76 B2 Ger.* Swinemünde. Zachodnio-pomorskie, NW Poland
Swiss Confederation *see* Switzerland
Switzerland *73 A7 off.* Swiss Confederation, *Fr.* La Suisse, *Ger.* Schweiz, *It.* Svizzera; *anc.* Helvetia. *country* C Europe
Sycaminum *see* Hefa
Sydenham Island *see* Nonouti
Sydney *126 D1 state capital* New South Wales, SE Australia

Sydney – Therezina

Sydney 17 G4 Cape Breton Island, Nova Scotia, SE Canada
Sydney Island see Manra
Syedpur see Saidpur
Syemyezhava 85 C6 Rus. Semezhevo. Minskaya Voblasts', C Belarus
Syene see Aswân
Syeverodonets'k 87 H3 Rus. Severodonetsk. Luhans'ka Oblast', E Ukraine
Syktyvkar 88 D4 prev. Ust'-Sysol'sk. Respublika Komi, NW Russian Federation
Sylhet 113 G3 Sylhet, NE Bangladesh
Synel'nykove 87 G3 Dnipropetrovs'ka Oblast', E Ukraine
Syowa 132 C2 Japanese research station Antarctica
Syracuse 19 E3 New York, NE USA
Syracuse see Siracusa
Syrdar'ya 92 B4 Sirdaryo Viloyati, E Uzbekistan
Syria 96 B3 off. Syrian Arab Republic, var. Siria, Syrie, Ar. Al-Jumhūrīyah al-'Arabīyah as-Sūrīyah, Sūrīya. country SW Asia
Syrian Arab Republic see Syria
Syrian Desert 97 D5 Ar. Al Hamad, Bādiyat ash Shām. desert SW Asia
Syrie see Syria
Sýrna 83 E7 var. Sirna. island Kykládes, Greece, Aegean Sea
Sýros 83 C6 var. Síros. island Kykládes, Greece, Aegean Sea
Syulemeshlii see Sredets
Syvash, Zaliv see Syvash, Zatoka
Syvash, Zatoka 87 F4 Rus. Zaliv Syvash. inlet S Ukraine
Syzran' 89 C6 Samarskaya Oblast', W Russian Federation
Szabadka see Subotica
Szamotuły 76 B3 Poznań, W Poland
Szászrégen see Reghin
Szatmárrnémeti see Satu Mare
Száva see Sava
Szczecin 76 B3 Eng./Ger. Stettin. Zachodnio-pomorskie, NW Poland
Szczecinek 76 B2 Ger. Neustettin. Zachodnio-pomorskie, NW Poland
Szczeciński, Zalew 76 A2 var. Stettiner Haff, Ger. Oderhaff. bay Germany/Poland
Szczuczyn Nowogródzki see Shchuchyn
Szczytno 76 D3 Ger. Ortelsburg. Warmińsko-Mazurskie, NE Poland
Szechuan/Szechwan see Sichuan
Szeged 77 D7 Ger. Szegedin, Rom. Seghedin. Csongrád, SE Hungary
Szegedin see Szeged
Székelykeresztúr see Cristuru Secuiesc
Székesfehérvár 77 C6 Ger. Stuhlweissenberg; anc. Alba Regia. Fejér, W Hungary
Szeklerburg see Miercurea-Ciuc
Szekler Neumarkt see Târgu Secuiesc
Szekszárd 77 C7 Tolna, S Hungary
Szempcz/Szenc see Senec
Szenice see Senica
Szenttamás see Srbobran
Szeping see Siping
Szilágysomlyó see Şimleu Silvaniei
Szinna see Snina
Sziszek see Sisak
Szitás-Keresztúr see Cristuru Secuiesc
Szkudy see Skuodas
Szlatina see Slatina
Szlovákia see Slovakia
Szolnok 77 D6 Jász-Nagykun-Szolnok, C Hungary
Szombathely 77 B6 Ger. Steinamanger; anc. Sabaria, Savaria. Vas, W Hungary
Szprotawa 76 B4 Ger. Sprottau. Lubuskie, W Poland
Sztálinváros see Dunaújváros
Szucsava see Suceava

T

Tabariya, Bahrat see Tiberias, Lake
Table Rock Lake 27 G1 reservoir Arkansas/Missouri, C USA
Tábor 77 B5 Jihočeský Kraj, S Czech Republic
Tabora 51 B7 Tabora, W Tanzania
Tabrīz 98 C2 var. Tebriz; anc. Tauris. Āžarbāyjān-e Sharqī, NW Iran
Tabuaeran 123 G2 prev. Fanning Island. atoll Line Islands, E Kiribati
Tabūk 98 A4 Tabūk, NW Saudi Arabia
Täby 63 C6 Stockholm, C Sweden
Tachau see Tachov
Tachov 77 A5 Ger. Tachau. Plveňský Kraj, W Czech Republic
Tacloban 117 F2 off. Tacloban City. Leyte, C Philippines
Tacloban City see Tacloban
Tacna 39 E4 Tacna, SE Peru
Tacoma 24 B2 Washington, NW USA
Tacuarembó 42 D4 prev. San Fructuoso. Tacuarembó, C Uruguay
Tademaït, Plateau du 48 D3 plateau C Algeria
Tadmor/Tadmur see Tudmur
Tādpatri 110 C2 Andhra Pradesh, E India
Tadzhikistan see Tajikistan
Taegu 107 E4 off. Taegu-gwangyŏksi, var. Daegu, Jap. Taikyū. SE South Korea
Taegu-gwangyŏksi see Taegu
Taehan-haehyŏp see Korea Strait
Taehan Min'guk see South Korea
Taejŏn 107 E4 off. Taejŏn-gwangyŏksi, Jap. Taiden. C South Korea
Taejŏn-gwangyŏksi see Taejŏn
Tafassâsset, Ténéré du 53 G2 desert N Niger
Tafila/Ţafīlah, Muḩāfaẓat aţ see Aţ Ţafīlah
Taganrog 89 A7 Rostovskaya Oblast', SW Russian Federation
Taganrog, Gulf of 87 G4 Rus. Taganrogskiy Zaliv, Ukr. Tahanroz'ka Zatoka. gulf Russian Federation/Ukraine
Taganrogskiy Zaliv see Taganrog, Gulf of
Taguatinga 41 F3 Tocantins, C Brazil
Tagus 70 C3 Port. Rio Tejo, Sp. Río Tajo. river Portugal/Spain
Tagus Plain 58 A4 abyssal plain E Atlantic Ocean
Tahanroz'ka Zatoka see Taganrog, Gulf of
Tahat 49 E4 mountain SE Algeria
Tahiti 123 H4 island Îles du Vent, W French Polynesia
Tahiti, Archipel de see Société, Archipel de la
Tahlequah 27 G1 Oklahoma, C USA
Tahoe, Lake 25 B5 lake California/Nevada, W USA
Tahoua 53 F3 Tahoua, W Niger
Taichū see T'aichung
T'aichung 106 D6 Jap. Taichū; prev. Taiwan. C Taiwan
Taiden see Taejŏn
Taieri 129 B7 river South Island, New Zealand
Taihape 128 D4 Manawatu-Wanganui, North Island, New Zealand
Taihoku see T'aipei
Taikyū see Taegu
Tailem Bend 127 B7 South Australia
T'ainan 106 D6 Jap. Tainan; prev. Dainan. S Taiwan
T'aipei 106 D6 Jap. Taihoku; prev. Daihoku. country capital N Taiwan
Taiping 116 B3 Perak, Peninsular Malaysia
Taiwan 106 D6 off. Republic of China, var. Formosa, Formo'sa. country E Asia
Taiwan see T'aichung
T'aiwan Haihsia/Taiwan Haixia see Taiwan Strait
Taiwan Strait 106 D6 var. Formosa Strait, Chin. T'aiwan Haihsia, Taiwan Haixia. strait China/Taiwan
Taiyuan 106 C4 var. T'ai-yuan, T'ai-yüan; prev. Yangku. province capital Shanxi, C China
T'ai-yuan/T'ai-yüan see Taiyuan
Ta'izz 99 B7 SW Yemen
Tajikistan 101 E3 off. Republic of Tajikistan, Rus. Tadzhikistan, Taj. Jumhurii Tojikiston; prev. Tajik S.S.R. country C Asia
Tajikistan, Republic of see Tajikistan
Tajik S.S.R see Tajikistan
Tajo, Río see Tagus
Tak 114 C4 var. Rahaeng. Tak, W Thailand
Takao see Kaohsiung
Takaoka 109 C5 Toyama, Honshū, SW Japan
Takapuna 128 D2 Auckland, North Island, New Zealand
Takhiatash see Takiatosh
Takhtakupyr see Taxtako'pir
Takikawa 108 D2 Hokkaidō, NE Japan
Takla Makan Desert 104 B3 Eng. Takla Makan Desert. desert NW China
Takla Makan Desert see Taklimakan Shamo
Takow see Kaohsiung
Takutea 123 G4 island S Cook Islands
Talabriga see Aveiro, Portugal
Talabriga see Talavera de la Reina, Spain
Talachyn 85 D6 Rus. Tolochin. Vitsyebskaya Voblasts', NE Belarus
Talamanca, Cordillera de 31 E5 mountain range S Costa Rica
Talara 38 B2 Piura, NW Peru
Talas 101 F2 Talasskaya Oblast', NW Kyrgyzstan
Talaud, Kepulauan 117 F3 island group E Indonesia
Talavera de la Reina 70 D3 anc. Caesarobriga, Talabriga. Castilla-La Mancha, C Spain
Talca 42 B4 Maule, C Chile
Talcahuano 43 B5 Bío Bío, C Chile
Taldykorgan 92 C5 Kaz. Taldyqorghan; prev. Taldy-Kurgan. Taldykorgan, SE Kazakhstan
Taldy-Kurgan/Taldyqorghan see Taldykorgan
Ta-lien see Dalian
Taliq-an see Tāloqān
Tal'ka 85 C6 Minskaya Voblasts', C Belarus
Talkhof see Puurmani
Tallahassee 20 D3 prev. Muskogean. state capital Florida, SE USA
Tall al Abyaḑ see At Tall al Abyaḑ
Tallin see Tallinn
Tallinn 84 D2 Ger. Reval, Rus. Tallin; prev. Revel. country capital Harjumaa, NW Estonia
Tall Kalakh 96 B4 var. Tell Kalakh. Ḩimş, C Syria
Tallulah 20 B2 Louisiana, S USA
Talnakh 92 D3 Taymyrskiy (Dolgano-Nenetskiy) Avtonomnyy Okrug, N Russian Federation
Tal'ne 87 E3 Rus. Tal'noye. Cherkas'ka Oblast', C Ukraine
Tal'noye see Tal'ne
Taloga 27 F1 Oklahoma, C USA
Tāloqān 101 E3 var. Taliq-an. Takhār, NE Afghanistan
Talsen see Talsi
Talsi 84 C3 Ger. Talsen. Talsi, NW Latvia
Taltal 42 B2 Antofagasta, N Chile
Talvik 62 D2 Finnmark, N Norway
Tamabo, Banjaran 116 D3 mountain range East Malaysia
Tamale 53 E4 C Ghana
Tamana 123 E3 prev. Rotcher Island. atoll Tungaru, W Kiribati
Tamanrasset 49 E4 var. Tamenghest. S Algeria
Tamar 67 C7 river SW England, United Kingdom
Tamar see Tudmur
Tamatave see Toamasina
Tamazunchale 29 E4 San Luis Potosí, C Mexico
Tambacounda 52 C3 SE Senegal
Tambov 89 B6 Tambovskaya Oblast', W Russian Federation
Tambura 51 B5 Western Equatoria, SW Sudan
Tamchaket see Tâmchekket
Tâmchekket 52 C3 var. Tamchaket. Hodh el Gharbi, S Mauritania
Tamenghest see Tamanrasset
Tamiahua, Laguna de 29 F4 lagoon Veracruz-Llave, Mexico
Tamil Nādu 110 C3 prev. Madras. cultural region SE India
Tam Ky 115 E5 Quang Nam-ƒa Nāng, C Vietnam
Tammerfors see Tampere
Tampa 21 E4 Florida, SE USA
Tampa Bay 21 E4 bay Florida, SE USA
Tampere 63 D5 Swe. Tammerfors. Länsi-Suomi, W Finland
Tampico 29 E3 Tamaulipas, C Mexico
Tamworth 127 D6 New South Wales, SE Australia
Tanabe 109 C7 Wakayama, Honshū, SW Japan
Tana Bru 62 D2 Finnmark, N Norway
Tanais see Don
Lake Tana 50 C4 var. Lake Tana. lake NW Ethiopia
Tana, Lake see T'ana Hāyk'
Tanami Desert 124 D3 desert Northern Territory, N Australia
Tananarive see Antananarivo
Ţăndărei 86 D5 Ialomiţa, SE Romania
Tandil 43 D5 Buenos Aires, E Argentina
Tandjoengkarang see Bandar Lampung
Tanega-shima 109 B8 island Nansei-shotō, SW Japan
Tanen Taunggyi see Tane Range
Tane Range 114 B4 Bur. Tanen Taunggyi. mountain range W Thailand
Tanezrouft 48 D4 desert Algeria/Mali
Ţanf, Jabal aţ 96 D4 mountain SE Syria
Tanga 51 C7 Tanga, E Tanzania
Tanganyika and Zanzibar see Tanzania
Tanganyika, Lake 51 B7 lake E Africa
Tanger 48 C2 var. Tangiers, Tangier, Fr./Ger. Tangerk, Sp. Tánger; anc. Tingis. NW Morocco
Tangerk see Tanger
Tanggula Shan 104 C4 mountain W China
Tangier see Tanger
Tangiers see Tanger
Tangra Yumco 104 B5 var. Tangro Tso. lake W China
Tangro Tso see Tangra Yumco
Tangshan 106 D3 var. T'ang-shan. Hebei, E China
T'ang-shan see Tangshan
Tanimbar, Kepulauan 117 F5 island group Maluku, E Indonesia
Tanjungkarang/Tanjungkarang-Telukbetung see Bandar Lampung
Tanna 122 D4 island S Vanuatu
Tannenhof see Krynica
Tan-Tan 48 B3 SW Morocco
Tan-tung see Dandong
Tanzania 51 C7 off. United Republic of Tanzania, Swa. Jamhuri ya Muungano wa Tanzania; prev. German East Africa, Tanganyika and Zanzibar. country E Africa
Tanzania, Jamhuri ya Muungano wa see Tanzania
Tanzania, United Republic of see Tanzania
Taoudenit see Taoudenni
Taoudenni 53 E2 var. Taoudenit. Tombouctou, N Mali
Tapa 84 E2 Ger. Taps. Lääne-Virumaa, NE Estonia
Tapachula 29 G5 Chiapas, SE Mexico
Tapaiu see Gvardeysk
Tapajós, Rio 41 E2 var. Tapajóz. river NW Brazil
Tapajóz see Tapajós, Rio
Taps see Tapa
Ţarābulus 49 F2 var. Ţarābulus al Gharb, Eng. Tripoli. country capital NW Libya
Ţarābulus al Gharb see Ţarābulus
Ţarābulus/Ţarābulus ash Shām see Tripoli
Taraclia 86 D4 Rus. Tarakilya. S Moldova
Tarakilya see Taraclia
Mount Taranaki 128 C4 var. Egmont. volcano North Island, New Zealand
Tarancón 71 E3 Castilla-La Mancha, C Spain
Taranto 75 E5 var. Tarentum. Puglia, SE Italy
Taranto, Gulf of 75 E6 Eng. Gulf of Taranto. gulf S Italy
Taranto, Gulf of see Taranto, Golfo di
Tarapoto 38 C2 San Martín, N Peru
Tarare 69 D5 Rhône, E France
Tarascon 69 D6 Bouches-du-Rhône, SE France
Tarawa 122 D2 atoll Tungaru, W Kiribati
Taraz 92 C5 prev. Aulie Ata, Auliye-Ata, Dzhambul, Zhambyl. Zhambyl, S Kazakhstan
Tarazona 71 E2 Aragón, NE Spain
Tarbes 69 B6 anc. Bigorra. Hautes-Pyrénées, S France
Tarcoola 127 A6 South Australia
Taree 127 D6 New South Wales, SE Australia
Tarentum see Taranto
Târgovişte 86 C5 prev. Tîrgovişte. Dâmboviţa, S Romania
Targu Jiu 86 B4 prev. Tîrgu Jiu. Gorj, W Romania
Târgul-Neamţ see Târgu-Neamţ
Târgul-Săcuiesc see Târgu Secuiesc
Târgu Mureş 86 B4 prev. Oşorhei, Tîrgu Mures, Ger. Neumarkt, Hung. Marosvásárhely. Mureş, C Romania
Târgu-Neamţ 86 C3 var. Târgul-Neamţ; prev. Tîrgu-Neamţ. Neamţ, NE Romania
Târgu Ocna 86 C4 Hung. Aknavásár; prev. Tîrgu Ocna. Bacău, E Romania
Târgu Secuiesc 86 C4 Ger. Neumarkt, Szekler Neumarkt, Hung. Kezdivásárhely; prev. Chezdi-Oşorheiu, Târgul-Săcuiesc, Tîrgu Secuiesc. Covasna, E Romania
Tar Heel State see North Carolina
Tarija 39 G5 Tarija, S Bolivia
Tarim 99 C6 C Yemen
Tarim Basin 102 C2 Eng. Tarim Basin. basin NW China
Tarim Basin see Tarim Pendi
Tarim He 104 B3 river NW China
Tarma 38 C3 Junín, C Peru
Tarn 69 C6 cultural region S France
Tarn 69 C6 river S France
Tarnobrzeg 76 D4 Podkarpackie, SE Poland
Tarnopol see Ternopil'
Tarnów 77 D5 Małopolskie, S Poland
Tarraco see Tarragona
Tarragona 71 G2 anc. Tarraco. Cataluña, E Spain
Tarrasa see Terrassa
Tàrrega 71 F2 var. Tarrega. Cataluña, NE Spain
Tarsatica see Rijeka
Tarsus 94 C4 İçel, S Turkey
Tartous/Tartouss see Ţarţūs
Tartu 84 D3 Ger. Dorpat; prev. Rus. Yurev, Yury'ev. Tartumaa, SE Estonia
Ţarţūs 96 A3 off. Muḩāfaẓat Ţarţūs, var. Tartous, Tartus. governorate W Syria
Ţarţūs, Muḩāfaẓat see Ţarţūs
Ta Ru Tao, Ko 115 B7 island S Thailand Asia
Tarvisio 74 D2 Friuli-Venezia Giulia, NE Italy
Tarvisium see Treviso
Tashauz see Daşoguz
Tashi Chho Dzong see Thimphu
Tashkent see Toshkent
Tash-Kömür see Tash-Kumyr
Tash-Kumyr 101 F2 Kir. Tash-Kömür. Dzhalal-Abadskaya Oblast', W Kyrgyzstan
Tashqurghan see Kholm
Tasikmalaja see Tasikmalaya
Tasikmalaya 116 C5 prev. Tasikmalaja. Jawa, C Indonesia
Tasman Basin 120 C5 var. East Australian Basin. undersea basin S Tasman Sea
Tasman Bay 129 C5 inlet South Island, New Zealand
Tasmania 127 B8 prev. Van Diemen's Land. state SE Australia
Tasmania 130 B4 island SE Australia
Tasman Plateau 120 C5 var. South Tasmania Plateau. undersea plateau SW Tasman Sea
Tasman Sea 120 C5 sea SW Pacific Ocean
Tassili-n-Ajjer 49 E4 plateau E Algeria
Tatabánya 77 C6 Komárom-Esztergom, NW Hungary
Tatar Pazardzhik see Pazardzhik
Tathlīth 99 B5 'Asīr, S Saudi Arabia
Tatra Mountains 77 D5 Ger. Tatra, Hung. Tátra, Pol./Slvk. Tatry. mountain range Poland/Slovakia
Tatra/Tátra see Tatra Mountains
Tatry see Tatra Mountains
Ta-t'ung/Tatung see Datong
Tatvan 95 F3 Bitlis, SE Turkey
Ta'ū 123 F4 var. Tau. island Manua Islands, E American Samoa
Taukum, Peski 101 G1 desert SE Kazakhstan
Taumarunui 128 D4 Manawatu-Wanganui, North Island, New Zealand
Taungdwingyi 114 B3 Magway, C Myanmar (Burma)
Taunggyi 114 B3 Shan State, C Myanmar (Burma)
Taungoo 114 B4 Bago, C Myanmar (Burma)
Taunton 67 C7 SW England, United Kingdom
Taupo 128 D3 Waikato, North Island, New Zealand
Taupo, Lake 128 D3 lake North Island, New Zealand
Tauragė 84 B4 Ger. Tauroggen. Tauragė, SW Lithuania
Tauranga 128 D3 Bay of Plenty, North Island, New Zealand
Tauris see Tabrīz
Tauroggen see Tauragė
Taurus Mountains 94 C4 Eng. Taurus Mountains. mountain range S Turkey
Taurus Mountains see Toros Dağları
Tavas 94 B4 Denizli, SW Turkey
Tavastehus see Hämeenlinna
Tavira 70 C5 Faro, S Portugal
Tavoy see Dawei
Tavoy Island see Mali Kyun
Ta Waewae Bay 129 A7 bay South Island, New Zealand
Tawakoni, Lake 27 G2 reservoir Texas, SW USA
Tawau 116 D3 Sabah, East Malaysia
Ţawkar see Tokar
Tawzar see Tozeur
Taxco 29 E4 var. Taxco de Alarcón. Guerrero, S Mexico
Taxco de Alarcón see Taxco
Takiatosh 100 C2 Rus. Takhiatash. Qoraqalpog'iston Respublikasi, W Uzbekistan
Taxtako'pir 100 D1 Rus. Takhtakupyr. Qoraqalpog'iston Respublikasi, NW Uzbekistan
Tay 66 C3 river C Scotland, United Kingdom
Taylor 27 G3 Texas, SW USA
Taymā' 98 A4 Tabūk, NW Saudi Arabia
Taymyr, Ozero 93 E2 lake N Russian Federation
Taymyr, Poluostrov 93 E2 peninsula N Russian Federation
Taz 92 D3 river N Russian Federation
T'bilisi 95 G2 Eng. Tiflis. country capital SE Georgia
Tchad see Chad
Tchad, Lac see Chad, Lake
Tchien see Zwedru
Tchongking see Chongqing
Tczew 76 C2 Ger. Dirschau. Pomorskie, N Poland
Te Anau 129 A7 Southland, South Island, New Zealand
Te Anau, Lake 129 A7 lake South Island, New Zealand
Teapa 29 G4 Tabasco, SE Mexico
Teate see Chieti
Tebingtinggi 116 B3 Sumatera, N Indonesia
Tebriz see Tabrīz
Techirghiol 86 D5 Constanţa, SE Romania
Tecomán 28 D4 Colima, SW Mexico
Tecpan 29 E5 var. Tecpan de Galeana. Guerrero, S Mexico
Tecpan de Galeana see Tecpan
Tecuci 86 C4 Galaţi, E Romania
Tedzhen see Harīrūd/Tejen
Tedzhen see Tejen
Tees 67 D5 river N England, United Kingdom
Tefé 40 D2 Amazonas, N Brazil
Tegal 116 C4 Jawa, C Indonesia
Tegelen 65 D5 Limburg, SE Netherlands
Tegucigalpa 30 C3 country capital Francisco Morazán, SW Honduras
Teheran see Tehrān
Tehrān 98 C3 var. Teheran. country capital Tehrān, N Iran
Tehuacán 29 F4 Puebla, S Mexico
Tehuantepec 29 F5 var. Santo Domingo Tehuantepec. Oaxaca, SE Mexico
Gulf of Tehuantepec 29 F5 var. Gulf of Tehuantepec. gulf S Mexico
Tehuantepec, Gulf of see Tehuantepec, Golfo de
Isthmus of Tehuantepec 29 F5 var. Isthmus of Tehuantepec. isthmus SE Mexico
Tehuantepec, Isthmus of see Tehuantepec, Istmo de
Tejen 100 C3 Rus. Tedzhen. Ahal Welaýaty, S Turkmenistan
Tejen see Harīrūd
Tejo, Rio see Tagus
Te Kao 128 C1 Northland, North Island, New Zealand
Tekax 29 H4 var. Tekax de Álvaro Obregón. Yucatán, SE Mexico
Tekax de Álvaro Obregón see Tekax
Tekeli 92 C5 Almaty, SE Kazakhstan
Tekirdağ 94 A2 It. Rodosto; anc. Bisanthe, Raidestos, Rhaedestus. Tekirdağ, NW Turkey
Te Kuiti 128 D3 Waikato, North Island, New Zealand
Tela 30 C2 Atlántida, NW Honduras
Telanaipura see Jambi
Tel Aviv-Jaffa see Tel Aviv-Yafo
Tel Aviv-Yafo 97 A6 var. Tel Aviv-Jaffa. Tel Aviv, C Israel
Teles Pirés see São Manuel, Rio
Telish 82 C2 prev. Azizie. Pleven, N Bulgaria
Tell Abiad/Tell Abyad see At Tall al Abyaḑ
Tell Kalakh see Tall Kalakh
Tell Shedadi see Ash Shadādah
Tel'man/Tel'mansk see Gubadag
Teloekbetoeng see Bandar Lampung
Telo Martius see Toulon
Telschen see Telšiai
Telšiai 84 B3 Ger. Telschen. Telšiai, NW Lithuania
Telukbetung see Bandar Lampung
Temerin 78 D3 Vojvodina, N Serbia
Temeschburg/Temeschwar see Timişoara
Temesvár/Temeswar see Timişoara
Temirtau 92 C4 prev. Samarkandski, Samarkandskoye. Karaganda, C Kazakhstan
Tempio Pausania 75 A5 Sardegna, Italy, C Mediterranean Sea
Temple 27 G3 Texas, SW USA
Temuco 43 B5 Araucanía, C Chile
Temuka 129 B6 Canterbury, South Island, New Zealand
Tenasserim 115 B6 Tanintharyi, S Myanmar (Burma)
Ténenkou 52 D3 Mopti, C Mali
Ténéré 53 G3 physical region C Niger
Tenerife 48 A3 island Islas Canarias, Spain, NE Atlantic Ocean
Tengger Shamo 105 E3 desert N China
Tengréla 52 D4 var. Tingréla. N Ivory Coast
Tenkodogo 53 E4 S Burkina
Tennant Creek 126 A3 Northern Territory, C Australia
Tennessee 20 C1 off. State of Tennessee, also known as The Volunteer State. state SE USA
Tennessee River 20 C1 river S USA
Tenos see Tínos
Tepelena see Tepelenë
Tepelenë 79 C7 var. Tepelena, It. Tepeleni. Gjirokastër, S Albania
Tepeleni see Tepelenë
Tepic 28 D4 Nayarit, C Mexico
Teplice 76 A4 Ger. Teplitz; prev. Teplice-Šanov, Teplitz-Schönau. Ustecký Kraj, NW Czech Republic
Teplice-Šanov/Teplitz/Teplitz-Schönau see Teplice
Tequila 28 D4 Jalisco, SW Mexico
Teraina 123 G2 prev. Washington Island. atoll Line Islands, E Kiribati
Teramo 74 C4 anc. Interamna. Abruzzi, C Italy
Tercan 95 E3 Erzincan, NE Turkey
Terceira 70 A5 var. Ilha Terceira. island Azores, Portugal, NE Atlantic Ocean
Terceira, Ilha see Terceira
Terekhovka see Tsyerakhowka
Teresina 41 F2 var. Therezina. state capital Piauí, NE Brazil
Termez see Termiz
Termia see Kýthnos
Términos, Laguna de 29 G4 lagoon SE Mexico
Termiz 101 E3 Rus. Termez. Surkhondaryo Viloyati, S Uzbekistan
Termoli 74 D4 Molise, C Italy
Terneuzen 65 B5 var. Neuzen. Zeeland, SW Netherlands
Terni 74 C4 anc. Interamna Nahars. Umbria, C Italy
Ternopil' 86 C2 Pol. Tarnopol, Rus. Ternopol'. Ternopil's'ka Oblast', W Ukraine
Ternopol' see Ternopil'
Terracina 75 C5 Lazio, C Italy
Terranova di Sicilia see Gela
Terranova Pausania see Olbia
Terrassa 71 G2 Cast. Tarrasa. Cataluña, E Spain
Terre Adélie 132 C4 physical region Antarctica
Terre Haute 18 B4 Indiana, N USA
Terre Neuve see Newfoundland and Labrador
Terschelling 64 C1 Fris. Skylge. island Waddeneilanden, N Netherlands
Teruel 71 F3 anc. Turba. Aragón, E Spain
Tervel 82 E1 prev. Kurtbunar, Rom. Curtbunar. Dobrich, NE Bulgaria
Tervueren see Tervuren
Tervuren 65 C6 var. Tervueren. Vlaams Brabant, C Belgium
Teseney 50 C4 var. Tessenei. W Eritrea
Tessalit 53 E2 Kidal, NE Mali
Tessaoua 53 G3 Maradi, S Niger
Tessenderlo 65 C5 Limburg, NE Belgium
Tessenei see Teseney
Testigos, Islas los 37 E1 island group N Venezuela
Tete 57 E2 Tete, NW Mozambique
Teterow 72 C3 Mecklenburg-Vorpommern, NE Germany
Tétouan 48 C2 var. Tetouan, Tetuán. N Morocco
Tetovo 79 D5 Razgrad, N Bulgaria
Tetschen see Děčín
Tetuán see Tétouan
Teverya see Tverya
Te Waewae Bay 129 A7 bay South Island, New Zealand
Texarkana 20 A2 Arkansas, C USA
Texarkana 27 H2 Texas, SW USA
Texas 27 F3 off. State of Texas, also known as Lone Star State. state S USA
Texas City 27 H4 Texas, SW USA
Texel 64 C2 island Waddeneilanden, NW Netherlands
Texoma, Lake 27 G2 reservoir Oklahoma/Texas, C USA
Teziutlán 29 F4 Puebla, S Mexico
Thaa Atoll see Kolhumadulu
Thai, Ao see Thailand, Gulf of
Thai Binh 114 D3 Thai Binh, N Vietnam
Thailand 115 C5 off. Kingdom of Thailand, Th. Prathet Thai; prev. Siam. country SE Asia
Thailand, Gulf of 115 C6 var. Gulf of Siam, Th. Ao Thai, Vtn. Vinh Thai Lan. gulf SE Asia
Thailand, Kingdom of see Thailand
Thai Lan, Vinh see Thailand, Gulf of
Thai Nguyên 114 D3 Bắc Thai, N Vietnam
Thakhèk 114 D4 var. Muang Khammouan. Khammouan, C Laos
Thamarīd see Thamarīt
Thamarīt 99 D6 var. Thamarīd, Thumrayt. SW Oman
Thames 128 D3 Waikato, North Island, New Zealand
Thames 67 B8 river S England, United Kingdom
Thandwe 114 A4 var. Sandoway. Rakhine State, W Myanmar (Burma)
Thanh Hoa 114 D3 Thanh Hoa, N Vietnam
Thanintari Taungdan see Bilauktaung Range
Thanlwin see Salween
Thar Desert 112 C3 var. Great Indian Desert, Indian Desert. desert India/Pakistan
Tharthar, Buhayrat ath 98 B3 lake C Iraq
Thásos 82 C4 Thásos, E Greece
Thásos 82 C4 island E Greece
Thaton 114 B4 Mon State, S Myanmar (Burma)
Thayetmyo 114 A4 Magway, C Myanmar (Burma)
The Crane 33 H2 var. Crane. S Barbados
The Dalles 24 B3 Oregon, NW USA
The Flatts Village see Flatts Village
The Hague see 's-Gravenhage
Theodosia see Feodosiya
The Pas 15 F5 Manitoba, C Canada
Therezina see Teresina

Tubuai, Îles/Tubuai Islands – Vatican City

Tubuai, Îles/Tubuai Islands *see* Australes, Îles
Tucker's Town *20 B5* E Bermuda
Tuckum *see* Tukums
Tucson *26 B3* Arizona, SW USA
Tucumán *see* San Miguel de Tucumán
Tucumcari *27 E2* New Mexico, SW USA
Tucupita *37 E2* Delta Amacuro, NE Venezuela
Tucuruí, Represa de *41 F2 reservoir* NE Brazil
Tudela *71 E2 Basq.* Tutera; *anc.* Tutela. Navarra, N Spain
Tudmur *96 C3 var.* Tadmur, Tamar, *Gk.* Palmyra, *Bibl.* Tadmor. Ḩimş, C Syria
Tuguegarao *117 E1* Luzon, N Philippines
Tuktoyaktuk *15 E3* Northwest Territories, NW Canada
Tukums *84 C3 Ger.* Tuckum. Tukums, W Latvia
Tula *89 B5* Tul'skaya Oblast', W Russian Federation
Tulancingo *29 E4* Hidalgo, C Mexico
Tulare Lake Bed *25 C7 salt flat* California, W USA
Tulcán *38 B1* Carchi, N Ecuador
Tulcea *86 D5* Tulcea, E Romania
Tul'chin *see* Tul'chyn
Tul'chyn *86 D3 Rus.* Tul'chin. Vinnyts'ka Oblast', C Ukraine
Tuléar *see* Toliara
Tulia *27 E2* Texas, SW USA
Tūlkarm *97 D7* West Bank, Israel
Tulle *69 C5 anc.* Tutela. Corrèze, C France
Tulln *73 E6 var.* Oberhollabrunn. Niederösterreich, NE Austria
Tully *126 D3* Queensland, NE Australia
Tulsa *27 G1* Oklahoma, C USA
Tuluá *36 B3* Valle del Cauca, W Colombia
Tulun *93 E4* Irkutskaya Oblast', S Russian Federation
Tumaco *36 A4* Nariño, SW Colombia
Tumba, Lac *see* Ntomba, Lac
Tumbes *38 A2* Tumbes, NW Peru
Tumkūr *110 C2* Karnātaka, W India
Tumuc-Humac Mountains *41 E1 var.* Serra Tumucumaque. *mountain range* N South America
Tumucumaque, Serra *see* Tumuc-Humac Mountains
Tunca Nehri *see* Tundzha
Tunduru *51 C8* Ruvuma, S Tanzania
Tundzha *82 D3 Turk.* Tunca Nehri. *river* Bulgaria/Turkey
Tungabhadra Reservoir *110 C2 lake* S India
Tungaru *123 E2 prev.* Gilbert Islands. *island group* W Kiribati
T'ung-shan *see* Xuzhou
Tungsten *14 D4* Northwest Territories, W Canada
Tung-t'ing Hu *see* Dongting Hu
Tunis *49 E1 var.* Tūnis. *country capital* NE Tunisia
Tunis, Golfe de *80 D3 Ar.* Khalīj Tūnis. *gulf* NE Tunisia
Tunisia *49 F2 off.* Tunisian Republic, *Ar.* Al Jumhūrīyah at Tūnisīyah, *Fr.* République Tunisienne. *country* N Africa
Tunisian Republic *see* Tunisia
Tunisienne, République *see* Tunisia
Tūnisīyah, Al Jumhūrīyah at *see* Tunisia
Tūnis, Khalīj *see* Tunis, Golfe de
Tunja *36 B3* Boyacá, C Colombia
Tuong Buong *see* Tương Đương
Tương Đương *114 D4 var.* Tuong Buong. Nghê An, N Vietnam
Tüp *see* Tyup
Tupelo *20 C2* Mississippi, S USA
Tupiza *39 G5* Potosí, S Bolivia
Turabah *99 B5* Makkah, W Saudi Arabia
Turangi *128 D4* Waikato, North Island, New Zealand
Turan Lowland *100 C2 var.* Turan Plain, *Kaz.* Turan Oypaty, *Rus.* Turanskaya Nizmennost', *Turk.* Turan Pesligi, *Uzb.* Turan Pasttekisligi. *plain* C Asia
Turan Oypaty/Turan Pesligi/Turan Plain/Turanskaya Nizmennost' *see* Turan Lowland
Turan Pasttekisligi *see* Turan Lowland
Ţurayf *98 A3* Al Ḩudūd ash Shamālīyah, NW Saudi Arabia
Turba *see* Teruel
Turbat *112 A3* Baluchistān, SW Pakistan
Turčianský Svätý Martin *see* Martin
Turda *86 B4 Ger.* Thorenburg, *Hung.* Torda. Cluj, NW Romania
Turek *76 C3* Wielkopolskie, C Poland
Turfan *see* Turpan
Turin *see* Torino
Turkana, Lake *51 C6 var.* Lake Rudolf. *lake* N Kenya
Turkestan *92 B5 Kaz.* Türkistan. Yuzhnyy Kazakhstan, S Kazakhstan
Turkey *94 B3 off.* Republic of Turkey, *Turk.* Türkiye Cumhuriyeti. *country* SW Asia
Turkey, Republic of *see* Turkey
Turkish Republic of Northern Cyprus *80 D5 disputed territory* Cyprus
Türkistan *see* Turkestan
Türkiye Cumhuriyeti *see* Turkey
Türkmenabat *100 D3 prev. Rus.* Chardzhev, Chardzhou, Chardzhui, Lenin-Turkmenski, *Turkm.* Chärjew. Lebap Welaýaty, E Turkmenistan
Türkmen Aylagy *100 B2 Rus.* Turkmenskiy Zaliv. *lake gulf* W Turkmenistan
Turkmenbashi *see* Türkmenbaşy
Türkmenbaşy *100 B2 Rus.* Turkmenbashi; *prev.* Krasnovodsk. Balkan Welaýaty, W Turkmenistan
Türkmenbasy Aylagy *100 A2 prev. Rus.* Krasnovodskiy Zaliv, *Turkm.* Krasnowodsk Aylagy. *lake Gulf* W Turkmenistan
Turkmenistan *100 B2* ; *prev.* Turkmenskaya Soviet Socialist Republic. *country* C Asia
Turkmenskaya Soviet Socialist Republic *see* Turkmenistan
Turkmenskiy Zaliv *see* Türkmen Aylagy
Turks and Caicos Islands *33 E2 UK dependent territory* N West Indies
Turku *63 D6 Swe.* Åbo. Länsi-Suomi, SW Finland
Turlock *25 B6* California, W USA
Turnagain, Cape *128 D4 headland* North Island, New Zealand
Turnau *see* Turnov
Turnhout *65 C5* Antwerpen, N Belgium
Turnov *76 B4 Ger.* Turnau. Liberecký Kraj, N Czech Republic
Tŭrnovo *see* Veliko Tŭrnovo
Turnu Măgurele *86 B5 var.* Turnu-Măgurele. Teleorman, S Romania
Turnu Severin *see* Drobeta-Turnu Severin
Turócszentmárton *see* Martin
Turoni *see* Tours
Turpan *104 C3 var.* Turfan. Xinjiang Uygur Zizhiqu, NW China
Turpan Depression *see* Turpan Pendi
Turpan Pendi *104 C3 Eng.* Turpan Depression. *depression* NW China
Turpentine State *see* North Carolina
Türtkŭl/Turtkul' *see* To'rtkok'l
Turuga *see* Tsuruga
Turuoka *see* Tsuruoka
Tuscaloosa *20 C2* Alabama, S USA
Tuscan Archipelago *see* Toscano, Arcipelago
Tuscany *see* Toscana
Tusima *see* Tsushima
Tutela *see* Tulle, France
Tutela *see* Tudela, Spain
Tutera *see* Tudela
Tuticorin *110 C3* Tamil Nādu, SE India
Tutrakan *82 D1* Silistra, NE Bulgaria
Tutuila *123 F4 island* W American Samoa
Tuvalu *123 E3 prev.* Ellice Islands. *country* SW Pacific Ocean
Tuwayq, Jabal *99 C5 mountain range* C Saudi Arabia
Tuxpan *28 D4* Jalisco, C Mexico
Tuxpan *28 D4* Nayarit, C Mexico
Tuxpán *29 F4 var.* Tuxpán de Rodríguez Cano. Veracruz-Llave, E Mexico
Tuxpán de Rodríguez Cano *see* Tuxpán
Tuxtepec *29 F4 var.* San Juan Bautista Tuxtepec. Oaxaca, S Mexico
Tuxtla *29 G5 var.* Tuxtla Gutiérrez. Chiapas, SE Mexico
Tuxtla *see* San Andrés Tuxtla
Tuxtla Gutiérrez *see* Tuxtla
Tuy Hoa *115 E5* Phu Yên, S Vietnam
Tuz, Lake *94 C3 lake* C Turkey
Tver' *88 B4 prev.* Kalinin. Tverskaya Oblast', W Russian Federation
Tverya *97 B5 var.* Tiberias; *prev.* Teverya. Northern, N Israel
Twin Falls *24 D4* Idaho, NW USA
Tyan'-Shan' *see* Tien Shan
Tychy *77 D5 Ger.* Tichau. Śląskie, S Poland
Tyler *27 G3* Texas, SW USA
Tylos *see* Bahrain
Tympáki *83 C8 var.* Timbaki; *prev.* Timbákion. Kríti, Greece, E Mediterranean Sea
Tynda *93 F4* Amurskaya Oblast', SE Russian Federation
Tyne *66 D4 river* N England, United Kingdom
Tyôsi *see* Chōshi
Tyras *see* Dniester
Tyre *see* Soûr
Tyrnau *see* Trnava
Týrnavos *82 B4 var.* Tírnavos. Thessalía, C Greece
Tyrol *see* Tirol
Tyros *see* Bahrain
Tyrrhenian Sea *75 B6 It.* Mare Tirreno. *sea* N Mediterranean Sea
Tyumen' *92 C3* Tyumenskaya Oblast', C Russian Federation
Tyup *101 G2 Kir.* Tüp. Issyk-Kul'skaya Oblast', NE Kyrgyzstan
Tywyn *67 C6* W Wales, United Kingdom
Tzekung *see* Zigong
Tziá *83 C6 prev.* Kéa, Kéos; *anc.* Ceos. *island* Kykládes, Greece, Aegean Sea

U

UAE *see* United Arab Emirates
Uanle Uen *see* Wanlaweyn
Uaupés, Rio *see* Vaupés, Río
Ubangi-Shari *see* Central African Republic
Ube *109 B7* Yamaguchi, Honshū, SW Japan
Ubeda *71 E4* Andalucía, S Spain
Uberaba *41 F4* Minas Gerais, SE Brazil
Uberlândia *41 F4* Minas Gerais, SE Brazil
Ubol Rajadhani/Ubol Ratchathani *see* Ubon Ratchathani
Ubon Ratchathani *115 D5 var.* Muang Ubon, Ubol Rajadhani, Ubol Ratchathani, Udon Ratchathani. Ubon Ratchathani, E Thailand
Ubrique *70 D5* Andalucía, S Spain
Ubsu-Nur, Ozero *see* Uvs Nuur
Ucayali, Río *38 D3 river* C Peru
Uchiura-wan *108 D3 bay* NW Pacific Ocean
Uchkuduk *see* Uchquduq
Uchquduq *100 D2 Rus.* Uchkuduk. Navoiy Viloyati, N Uzbekistan
Uchtagan Gumy/Uchtagan, Peski *see* Uçtagan Gumy
Uçtagan Gumy *100 C2 var.* Uchtagan Gumy, *Rus.* Peski Uchtagan. *desert* NW Turkmenistan
Udaipur *112 C3 prev.* Oodeypore. Rājasthān, N India
Uddevalla *63 B6* Västra Götaland, S Sweden
Udine *74 D2 anc.* Utina. Friuli-Venezia Giulia, NE Italy
Udintsev Fracture Zone *132 A5 tectonic feature* S Pacific Ocean
Udipi *see* Udupi
Udon Ratchathani *see* Ubon Ratchathani
Udon Thani *114 C4 var.* Ban Mak Khaeng, Udorndhani. Udon Thani, N Thailand
Udorndhani *see* Udon Thani
Udupi *110 B2 var.* Udipi. Karnātaka, SW India
Uele *55 D5 var.* Welle. *river* NE Dem. Rep. Congo
Uelzen *72 C3* Niedersachsen, N Germany
Ufa *89 D6* Respublika Bashkortostan, W Russian Federation
Ugāle *84 C2* Ventspils, NW Latvia
Uganda *51 B6 off.* Republic of Uganda. *country* E Africa
Uganda, Republic of *see* Uganda
Uhorshchyna *see* Hungary
Uhuru Peak *see* Kilimanjaro
Uíge *56 B1 Port.* Carmona, Vila Marechal Carmona. Uíge, NW Angola
Uinta Mountains *22 B4 mountain range* Utah, W USA
Uitenhage *56 C5* Eastern Cape, S South Africa
Uithoorn *64 C3* Noord-Holland, C Netherlands
Ujda *see* Oujda
Ujelang Atoll *122 C1 var.* Wujlān. *atoll* Ralik Chain, W Marshall Islands
Újgradiska *see* Nova Gradiška
Újmoldova *see* Moldova Nouă
Ujungpandang *see* Makassar
Ujung Salang *see* Phuket
Újvidék *see* Novi Sad
UK *see* United Kingdom
Ukhta *92 C3* Respublika Komi, NW Russian Federation
Ukiah *25 B5* California, W USA
Ukmergė *84 C4 Pol.* Wiłkomierz. Vilnius, C Lithuania
Ukraina *see* Ukraine
Ukraine *86 C2 off.* Ukraine, *Rus.* Ukraina, *Ukr.* Ukrayina; *prev.* Ukrainian Soviet Socialist Republic, Ukrainskay S.S.R. *country* SE Europe
Ukraine *see* Ukraine
Ukrainian Soviet Socialist Republic *see* Ukraine
Ukrainskay S.S.R/Ukrayina *see* Ukraine
Ulaanbaatar *105 E2 Eng.* Ulan Bator; *prev.* Urga. *country capital* Töv, C Mongolia
Ulaangom *104 C2* Uvs, NW Mongolia
Ulan Bator *see* Ulaanbaatar
Ulanhad *see* Chifeng
Ulan-Ude *93 E4 prev.* Verkhneudinsk. Respublika Buryatiya, S Russian Federation
Uleälv *see* Oulujoki
Uleträsk *see* Oulujärvi
Ulft *64 E4* Gelderland, E Netherlands
Ullapool *66 C3* N Scotland, United Kingdom
Ulm *73 B6* Baden-Württemberg, S Germany
Ulsan *107 E4 Jap.* Urusan. SE South Korea
Ulster *67 B5 province* Northern Ireland, United Kingdom/Ireland
Ulungur Hu *104 B2 lake* NW China
Uluru *125 D5 var.* Ayers Rock. *monolith* Northern Territory, C Australia
Ulyanivka *87 E3 Rus.* Ul'yanovka. Kirovohrads'ka Oblast', C Ukraine
Ul'yanovka *see* Ulyanivka
Ul'yanovsk *89 C5 prev.* Simbirsk. Ul'yanovskaya Oblast', W Russian Federation
Umán *29 H3* Yucatán, SE Mexico
Uman' *87 E3 Rus.* Uman. Cherkas'ka Oblast', C Ukraine
Uman *see* Uman'
Umanak/Umanaq *see* Uummannaq
'Umān, Khalīj *see* Oman, Gulf of
'Umān, Salṭanat *see* Oman
Umbrian-Machigian Mountains *see* Umbro-Marchigiano, Appennino
Umbro-Marchigiano, Appennino *74 C3 Eng.* Umbrian-Machigian Mountains. *mountain range* C Italy
Umeå *62 C4* Västerbotten, N Sweden
Umeälven *62 C4 river* N Sweden
Umiat *14 D2* Alaska, USA
Umm Buru *50 A4* Western Darfur, W Sudan
Umm Durmān *see* Omdurman
Umm Ruwaba *50 C4 var.* Umm Ruwābah, Um Ruwāba. Northern Kordofan, C Sudan
Umm Ruwābah *see* Umm Ruwaba
Umnak Island *14 A3 island* Aleutian Islands, Alaska, USA
Um Ruwāba *see* Umm Ruwaba
Umtali *see* Mutare
Umtata *56 D5* Eastern Cape, SE South Africa
Una *78 B3 river* Bosnia and Herzegovina/Croatia
Unac *78 B3 river* W Bosnia and Herzegovina
Unalaska Island *14 A3 island* Aleutian Islands, Alaska, USA
'Unayzah *98 B4 var.* Anaiza. Al Qaşīm, C Saudi Arabia
Unci *see* Almería
Uncía *39 F4* Potosí, C Bolivia
Uncompahgre Peak *22 B5 mountain* Colorado, C USA
Undur Khan *see* Öndörhaan
Ungaria *see* Hungary
Ungarisches Erzgebirge *see* Slovenské rudohorie
Ungarn *see* Hungary
Ungava Bay *17 E1 bay* Québec, E Canada
Ungava Peninsula *16 D1 peninsula* Québec, SE Canada
Ungeny *see* Ungheni
Ungheni *86 D3 Rus.* Ungeny. W Moldova
Unguja *see* Zanzibar
Üngüz Angyrsyndaky Garagum *100 C2 Rus.* Zaunguzskiye Garagumy. *desert* N Turkmenistan
Ungvár *see* Uzhhorod
Unimak Island *14 B3 island* Aleutian Islands, Alaska, USA
Union *21 E1* South Carolina, SE USA
Union City *20 C1* Tennessee, S USA
Union of Myanmar *see* Burma
United Arab Emirates *99 C5 Ar.* Al Imārāt al 'Arabīyah al Muttaḩidah, *abbrev.* UAE; *prev.* Trucial States. *country* SW Asia
United Arab Republic *see* Egypt
United Kingdom *67 B5 off.* United Kingdom of Great Britain and Northern Ireland, *abbrev.* UK. *country* NW Europe
United Kingdom of Great Britain and Northern Ireland *see* United Kingdom
United Mexican States *see* Mexico
United Provinces *see* Uttar Pradesh
United States of America *13 B5 off.* United States of America, *var.* America, The States, *abbrev.* U.S., USA. *country* North America
United States of America *see* United States of America
Unst *66 D1 island* NE Scotland, United Kingdom
Ünye *94 D2* Ordu, W Turkey
Upala *30 D4* Alajuela, NW Costa Rica
Upata *37 E2* Bolívar, E Venezuela
Upemba, Lac *55 D7 lake* SE Dem. Rep. Congo
Upernavik *60 C2 var.* Upernivik. Kitaa, C Greenland
Upernivik *see* Upernavik
Upington *56 C4* Northern Cape, W South Africa
'Upolu *123 F4 island* SE Samoa
Upper Klamath Lake *24 A4 lake* Oregon, NW USA
Upper Lough Erne *67 A5 lake* SW Northern Ireland, United Kingdom
Upper Red Lake *23 F1 lake* Minnesota, N USA
Upper Volta *see* Burkina
Uppsala *63 C6* Uppsala, C Sweden
Uqsuqtuuq *see* Gjoa Haven
Ural *90 B3 Kaz.* Zayyq. *river* Kazakhstan/Russian Federation
Ural Mountains *92 C3 var.* Ural'skiy Khrebet, *Eng.* Ural Mountains. *mountain range* Kazakhstan/Russian Federation
Ural Mountains *see* Ural'skiye Gory
Ural'sk *92 B3 Kaz.* Oral. Zapadnyy Kazakhstan, NW Kazakhstan
Ural'skiy Khrebet *see* Ural'skiye Gory
Uraricoera *40 D1* Roraima, N Brazil
Ura-Tyube *see* Ŭroteppa
Urbandale *23 F3* Iowa, C USA
Urdunn *see* Jordan
Uren' *89 C5* Nizhegorodskaya Oblast', W Russian Federation
Urga *see* Ulaanbaatar
Urganch *100 D2 Rus.* Urgench; *prev.* Novo-Urgench. Xorazm Viloyati, W Uzbekistan
Urgench *see* Urganch
Urgut *101 E3* Samarqand Viloyati, C Uzbekistan
Lake Urmia *99 C2 var.* Matianus, Sha Hi, Urumi Yeh, *Eng.* Lake Urmia; *prev.* Daryācheh-ye Reẕā'īyeh. *lake* NW Iran
Urmia, Lake *see* Orūmīyeh, Daryācheh-ye
Uroševac *see* Ferizaj
Ŭroteppa *101 E2 Rus.* Ura-Tyube. NW Tajikistan
Uruapan *29 E4 var.* Uruapan del Progreso. Michoacán de Ocampo, SW Mexico
Uruapan del Progreso *see* Uruapan
Uruguai, Rio *see* Uruguay
Uruguay *42 D4 off.* Oriental Republic of Uruguay; *prev.* La Banda Oriental. *country* E South America
Uruguay *42 D3 var.* Rio Uruguai, Río Uruguay. *river* E South America
Uruguay, Oriental Republic of *see* Uruguay
Uruguay, Río *see* Uruguay
Urumchi *see* Ürümqi
Urumi Yeh *see* Orūmīyeh, Daryācheh-ye
Ürümqi *104 C3 var.* Tihwa, Urumchi, Urumqi, Urumtsi, Wu-lu-k'o-mu-shi, Wu-lu-mu-ch'i; *prev.* Ti-hua. Xinjiang Uygur Zizhiqu, NW China
Urumtsi *see* Ürümqi
Urundi *see* Burundi
Urup, Ostrov *93 H4 island* Kuril'skiye Ostrova, SE Russian Federation
Urusan *see* Ulsan
Urziceni *86 C5* Ialomiţa, SE Romania
Usa *88 E3 river* NW Russian Federation
Uşak *94 B3 prev.* Ushak. Uşak, W Turkey
Ushak *see* Uşak
Ushant *see* Ouessant, Île d'
Ushuaia *43 B8* Tierra del Fuego, S Argentina
Usinsk *88 E3* Respublika Komi, NW Russian Federation
Üsküb/Üsküp *see* Skopje
Usmas Ezers *84 B3 lake* NW Latvia
Usol'ye-Sibirskoye *93 E4* Irkutskaya Oblast', C Russian Federation
Ussel *69 C5* Corrèze, C France
Ussuriysk *93 G5 prev.* Nikol'sk, Nikol'sk-Ussuriyskiy, Voroshilov. Primorskiy Kray, SE Russian Federation
Ustica *75 B6 island* S Italy
Ust'-Ilimsk *93 E4* Irkutskaya Oblast', C Russian Federation
Ústí nad Labem *76 A4 Ger.* Aussig. Ústecký Kraj, NW Czech Republic
Ustinov *see* Izhevsk
Ustka *76 C2 Ger.* Stolpmünde. Pomorskie, N Poland
Ust'-Kamchatsk *93 H2* Kamchatskaya Oblast', E Russian Federation
Ust'-Kamenogorsk *92 D5 Kaz.* Öskemen. Vostochnyy Kazakhstan, E Kazakhstan
Ust'-Kut *93 E4* Irkutskaya Oblast', C Russian Federation
Ust'-Olenëk *93 E3* Respublika Sakha (Yakutiya), NE Russian Federation
Ustrzyki Dolne *77 E5* Podkarpackie, SE Poland
Ust'-Sysol'sk *see* Syktyvkar
Ust Urt *see* Ustyurt Plateau
Ustyurt Plateau *100 B1 var.* Ust Urt, *Uzb.* Ustyurt Platosi. *plateau* Kazakhstan/Uzbekistan
Ustyurt Platosi *see* Ustyurt Plateau
Usulután *30 C3* Usulután, SE El Salvador
Usumacinta, Río *30 B1 river* Guatemala/Mexico
Usumbura *see* Bujumbura
U.S./USA *see* United States of America
Utah *22 B4 off.* State of Utah, *also known as* Beehive State, Mormon State. *state* W USA
Utah Lake *22 B4 lake* Utah, W USA
Utena *84 C4* Utena, E Lithuania
Utica *19 F3* New York, NE USA
Utina *see* Udine
Utrecht *64 C4 Lat.* Trajectum ad Rhenum. Utrecht, C Netherlands
Utsunomiya *109 D5 var.* Utunomiya. Tochigi, Honshū, S Japan
Uttarakhand *113 E2 cultural region* N India
Uttar Pradesh *113 E3 prev.* United Provinces, United Provinces of Agra and Oudh. *cultural region* N India
Utunomiya *see* Utsunomiya
Uulu *84 D2* Pärnumaa, SW Estonia
Uummannaq *60 C3 var.* Umanak, Umanaq. Kitaa, C Greenland
Uummannarsuaq *see* Nunap Isua
Uvalde *27 F4* Texas, SW USA
Uvaravichy *85 D7 Rus.* Uvarovichi. Homyel'skaya Voblasts', SE Belarus
Uvarovichi *see* Uvaravichy
Uvea, Île *123 E4 island* N Wallis and Futuna
Uvs Nuur *104 C1 var.* Ozero Ubsu-Nur. *lake* Mongolia/Russian Federation
'Uwaynāt, Jabal al *50 A3 var.* Jebel Uweinat. *mountain* Libya/Sudan
Uweinat, Jebel *see* 'Uwaynāt, Jabal al
Uyo *53 G5* Akwa Ibom, S Nigeria
Uyuni *39 F5* Potosí, W Bolivia
Uzbekistan *100 D2 off.* Republic of Uzbekistan. *country* C Asia
Uzbekistan, Republic of *see* Uzbekistan
Uzhgorod *see* Uzhhorod
Uzhhorod *86 B2 Rus.* Uzhgorod; *prev.* Ungvár. Zakarpats'ka Oblast', W Ukraine
Užice *78 D4 prev.* Titovo Užice. Serbia, W Serbia

V

Vaal *56 D4 river* C South Africa
Vaals *65 D6* Limburg, SE Netherlands
Vaasa *63 D5 Swe.* Vasa; *prev.* Nikolainkaupunki. Länsi-Suomi, W Finland
Vaassen *64 D3* Gelderland, E Netherlands
Vác *77 C6 Ger.* Waitzen. Pest, N Hungary
Vadodara *112 C4 prev.* Baroda. Gujarāt, W India
Vaduz *72 E2 country capital* W Liechtenstein
Vág *see* Váh
Vágbeszterce *see* Považská Bystrica
Váh *77 C5 Ger.* Waag, *Hung.* Vág. *river* W Slovakia
Váhtjer *see* Gällivare
Väinameri *84 C2 prev.* Muhu Väin, *Ger.* Moon-Sund. *sea* E Baltic Sea
Vajdahunyad *see* Hunedoara
Valachia *see* Wallachia
Valday *88 B4* Novgorodskaya Oblast', W Russian Federation
Valdecañas, Embalse de *70 D3 reservoir* W Spain
Valdepeñas *71 E4* Castilla-La Mancha, C Spain
Valdés, Península *43 C6 peninsula* SE Argentina
Valdez *14 C3* Alaska, USA
Valdia *see* Weldiya
Valdivia *43 B5* Los Lagos, C Chile
Val-d'Or *16 D4* Québec, SE Canada
Valdosta *21 E3* Georgia, SE USA
Valence *69 D5 anc.* Valentia, Valentia Julia, Ventia. Drôme, E France
Valencia *71 F3* País Valenciano, E Spain
Valencia *24 D1* California, USA
Valencia *36 D1* Carabobo, N Venezuela
Valencia, Gulf of *71 F3 var.* Gulf of Valencia. *gulf* E Spain
Valencia, Gulf of *see* Valencia, Golfo de
Valencia/València *see* País Valenciano
Valenciennes *68 D2* Nord, N France
Valentia *see* Valence, France
Valentia *see* País Valenciano
Valentia Julia *see* Valence
Valentine State *see* Oregon
Valera *36 C2* Trujillo, NW Venezuela
Valetta *see* Valletta
Valga *84 D3 Ger.* Walk, *Latv.* Valka. Valgamaa, S Estonia
Valira *69 A8 river* Andorra/Spain Europe
Valjevo *78 C4* Serbia, W Serbia
Valjok *see* Válljohka
Valka *84 D3 Ger.* Walk. Valka, N Latvia
Valka *see* Valga
Valkenswaard *65 D5* Noord-Brabant, S Netherlands
Valladolid *29 H3* Yucatán, SE Mexico
Valladolid *70 D2* Castilla-León, NW Spain
Vall D'Uxó *see* La Vall D'Uixó
Valle de La Pascua *36 D2* Guárico, N Venezuela
Valledupar *36 B1* Cesar, N Colombia
Vallejo *25 B6* California, W USA
Vallenar *42 B3* Atacama, N Chile
Valletta *75 C8 prev.* Valetta. *country capital* E Malta
Valley City *23 E2* North Dakota, N USA
Válljohka *62 D2 var.* Valjok. Finnmark, N Norway
Valls *71 G2* Cataluña, NE Spain
Valmiera *84 D3 Est.* Volmari, *Ger.* Wolmar. Valmiera, N Latvia
Valona *see* Vlorë
Valozhyn *85 C5 Pol.* Wołożyn, *Rus.* Volozhin. Minskaya Voblasts', C Belarus
Valparaíso *42 B4* Valparaíso, C Chile
Valparaiso *18 C3* Indiana, N USA
Valverde del Camino *70 C4* Andalucía, S Spain
Van *95 F3* Van, E Turkey
Vanadzor *95 F2 prev.* Kirovakan. N Armenia
Vancouver *14 D5* British Columbia, SW Canada
Vancouver *24 B3* Washington, NW USA
Vancouver Island *14 D5 island* British Columbia, SW Canada
Vanda *see* Vantaa
Van Diemen Gulf *124 D2 gulf* Northern Territory, N Australia
Van Diemen's Land *see* Tasmania
Vaner, Lake *see* Vänern
Vänern *63 B6 Eng.* Lake Vaner; *prev.* Lake Vener. *lake* S Sweden
Vangaindrano *57 G4* Fianarantsoa, SE Madagascar
Van Horn *26 D3* Texas, SW USA
Lake Van *95 F3 Eng.* Lake Van; *anc.* Thospitis. *salt lake* E Turkey
Van, Lake *see* Van Gölü
Vannes *68 A3 anc.* Dariorigum. Morbihan, NW France
Vantaa *63 D6 Swe.* Vanda. Etelä-Suomi, S Finland
Vanua Levu *123 E4 island* N Fiji
Vanuatu *122 C4 off.* Republic of Vanuatu; *prev.* New Hebrides. *country* SW Pacific Ocean
Vanuatu, Republic of *see* Vanuatu
Van Wert *18 C4* Ohio, N USA
Vapincum *see* Gap
Varakļāni *84 D4* Madona, C Latvia
Vārānasi *113 E3 prev.* Banaras, Benares, *hist.* Kasi. Uttar Pradesh, N India
Varangerfjorden *62 E2 Lapp.* Várjjatvuotna. *fjord* N Norway
Varangerhalvøya *62 D2 Lapp.* Várnjárga. *peninsula* N Norway
Varannó *see* Vranov nad Topl'ou
Varasd *see* Varaždin
Varaždin *78 B2 Ger.* Warasdin, *Hung.* Varasd. Varaždin, N Croatia
Varberg *63 B7* Halland, S Sweden
Vardar *79 E6 Gk.* Axiós. *river* FYR Macedonia/Greece
Varde *63 A7* Ribe, W Denmark
Vareia *see* Logroño
Varėna *85 B5 Pol.* Orany. Alytus, S Lithuania
Varese *74 B2* Lombardia, N Italy
Vârful Moldoveanu *86 B4 var.* Moldoveanul; *prev.* Vîrful Moldoveanu. *mountain* C Romania
Várjjatvuotna *see* Varangerfjorden
Varkaus *63 E5* Itä-Suomi, C Finland
Varna *82 E2 prev.* Stalin; *anc.* Odessus. Varna, E Bulgaria
Varnenski Zaliv *82 E2 prev.* Stalinski Zaliv. *bay* E Bulgaria
Várnjárga *see* Varangerhalvøya
Varshava *see* Warszawa
Vasa *see* Vaasa
Vasilikí *83 A5* Lefkáda, Iónia Nisiá, Greece, C Mediterranean Sea
Vasilishki *85 B5 Pol.* Wasiliszki. Hrodzyenskaya Voblasts', W Belarus
Vasil'kov *see* Vasyl'kiv
Vaslui *86 D4* Vaslui, C Romania
Västerås *63 C6* Västmanland, C Sweden
Vasyl'kiv *87 E2 var.* Vasil'kov. Kyyivs'ka Oblast', N Ukraine
Vaté *see* Éfaté
Vatican City *75 A7 off.* Vatican City. *country* S Europe
Vatican City *see* Vatican City

Waterville – Yorkton

Waterville *19 G2* Maine, NE USA
Watford *67 A7* E England, United Kingdom
Watlings Island *see* San Salvador
Watsa *55 E5* Orientale, NE Dem. Rep. Congo
Watts Bar Lake *20 D1 reservoir* Tennessee, S USA
Wau *51 B5 var.* Wāw. Western Bahr el Ghazal, S Sudan
Waukegan *18 B3* Illinois, N USA
Waukesha *18 B3* Wisconsin, N USA
Wausau *18 B2* Wisconsin, N USA
Waverly *23 G3* Iowa, C USA
Wavre *65 C6* Walloon Brabant, C Belgium
Wāw *see* Wau
Wawa *16 C4* Ontario, S Canada
Waycross *21 E3* Georgia, SE USA
Wearmouth *see* Sunderland
Webfoot State *see* Oregon
Webster City *23 F3* Iowa, C USA
Weddell Plain *132 A2 abyssal plain* SW Atlantic Ocean
Weddell Sea *132 A2 sea* SW Atlantic Ocean
Weener *72 A3* Niedersachsen, NW Germany
Weert *65 D5* Limburg, SE Netherlands
Weesp *64 C3* Noord-Holland, C Netherlands
Węgorzewo *76 D2 Ger.* Angerburg. Warmińsko-Mazurskie, NE Poland
Weichsel *see* Wisła
Weimar *72 C4* Thüringen, C Germany
Weissenburg *see* Alba Iulia, Romania
Weissenburg in Bayern *73 C6* Bayern, SE Germany
Weissenstein *see* Paide
Weisskirchen *see* Bela Crkva
Weiswampach *65 D7* Diekirch, N Luxembourg
Wejherowo *76 C2* Pomorskie, NW Poland
Welchman Hall *33 G1* C Barbados
Weldiya *50 C4 var.* Waldia, *It.* Valdia. Āmara, N Ethiopia
Welkom *56 D4* Free State, C South Africa
Welle *see* Uele
Wellesley Islands *126 B2 island group* Queensland, N Australia
Wellington *129 D5 country capital* Wellington, North Island, New Zealand
Wellington *23 F5* Kansas, C USA
Wellington *see* Wellington, Isla
Wellington, Isla *43 A7 var.* Wellington. *island* S Chile
Wells *24 D4* Nevada, W USA
Wellsford *128 D2* Auckland, North Island, New Zealand
Wells, Lake *125 C5 lake* Western Australia
Wels *73 D6 anc.* Ovilava. Oberösterreich, N Austria
Wembley *67 A8* Alberta, W Canada
Wemmel *65 B6* Vlaams Brabant, C Belgium
Wenatchee *24 B2* Washington, NW USA
Wenchi *53 E4* W Ghana
Wen-chou/Wenchow *see* Wenzhou
Wendau *see* Võnnu
Wenden *see* Cēsis
Wenzhou *106 D5 var.* Wen-chou, Wenchow. Zhejiang, SE China
Werda *56 C4* Kgalagadi, S Botswana
Werder *see* Virtsu
Werenów *see* Voranava
Werkendam *64 C4* Noord-Brabant, S Netherlands
Werowitz *see* Virovitica
Werro *see* Võru
Werschetz *see* Vršac
Wesenberg *see* Rakvere
Weser *72 B3 river* NW Germany
Wessel Islands *126 B1 island group* Northern Territory, N Australia
West Antarctica *132 A3 var.* Lesser Antarctica. *physical region* Antarctica
West Australian Basin *see* Wharton Basin
West Bank *97 A6 disputed region* SW Asia
West Bend *18 B3* Wisconsin, N USA
West Bengal *113 F4 cultural region* NE India
West Cape *129 A7 headland* South Island, New Zealand
West Des Moines *23 F3* Iowa, C USA
Westerland *72 B2* Schleswig-Holstein, N Germany
Western Australia *124 B4 state* W Australia
Western Bug *see* Bug
Western Carpathians *77 E7 mountain range* W Romania Europe
Western Desert *50 B2 var.* Sahara el Gharbîya, *Eng.* Western Desert. *desert* C Egypt
Western Desert *see* Şaḩrā' al Gharbīyah
Western Dvina *63 E7 Bel.* Dzvina, *Ger.* Düna, *Latv.* Daugava, *Rus.* Zapadnaya Dvina. *river* W Europe
Western Ghats *112 C5 mountain range* SW India
Western Isles *see* Outer Hebrides
Western Punjab *see* Punjab
Western Sahara *48 B3 disputed territory* N Africa
Western Samoa *see* Samoa
Western Samoa, Independent State of *see* Samoa
Western Sayans *92 D4 Eng.* Western Sayans. *mountain range* S Russian Federation
Western Sayans *see* Zapadnyy Sayan
Western Scheldt *65 B5 Eng.* Western Scheldt; *prev.* Honte. *inlet* S North Sea
Western Scheldt *see* Westerschelde
Western Sierra Madre *see* Madre Occidental, Sierra
West Falkland *43 C7 var.* Gran Malvina, Isla Gran Malvina. *island* W Falkland Islands
West Fargo *23 F2* North Dakota, N USA
West Frisian Islands *64 C1 Eng.* West Frisian Islands. *island group* N Netherlands
West Frisian Islands *see* Waddeneilanden
West Irian *see* Papua
Westliche Morava *see* Zapadna Morava
West Mariana Basin *120 B1 var.* Perece Vela Basin. *undersea feature* W Pacific Ocean
West Memphis *20 B1* Arkansas, C USA
West New Guinea *see* Papua
Weston-super-Mare *67 D7* SW England, United Kingdom
West Palm Beach *21 F4* Florida, SE USA
West Papua *see* Papua
Westport *129 C5* West Coast, South Island, New Zealand
West Punjab *see* Punjab
West River *see* Xi Jiang
West Siberian Plain *92 C3 Eng.* West Siberian Plain. *plain* C Russian Federation
West Siberian Plain *see* Zapadno-Sibirskaya Ravnina
West Virginia *18 D4 off.* State of West Virginia, *also known as* Mountain State. *state* NE USA
Wetar, Pulau *117 F5 island* Kepulauan Damar, E Indonesia
Wetzlar *73 B5* Hessen, W Germany
Wevok *14 C2 var.* Wewuk. Alaska, USA
Wewuk *see* Wevok
Wexford *67 B6 Ir.* Loch Garman. SE Ireland
Weyburn *15 F5* Saskatchewan, S Canada
Weymouth *67 D7* S England, United Kingdom
Wezep *64 D3* Gelderland, E Netherlands
Whakatane *128 E3* Bay of Plenty, North Island, New Zealand
Whale Cove *15 G3* Nunavut, C Canada
Whangarei *128 D2* Northland, North Island, New Zealand
Wharton Basin *119 D5 var.* West Australian Basin. *undersea feature* E Indian Ocean
Whataroa *129 B6* West Coast, South Island, New Zealand
Wheatland *22 D3* Wyoming, C USA
Wheeler Peak *26 D1 mountain* New Mexico, SW USA
Wheeling *18 D4* West Virginia, NE USA
Whitby *67 D5* N England, United Kingdom
Whitefish *22 B1* Montana, NW USA
Whitehaven *67 C5* NW England, United Kingdom
Whitehorse *14 D4 territory capital* Yukon Territory, W Canada
White Nile *50 B4 var.* Bahr el Jebel. *river* S Sudan
White Nile *50 B4 Ar.* Al Baḩr al Abyaḑ, An Nil al Abyaḑ, Bahr el Jebel. *river* SE Sudan
White River *22 D3 river* South Dakota, N USA
White Sea *88 C3 Eng.* White Sea. *sea* NW Russian Federation
White Sea *see* Beloye More
White Volta *53 E4 var.* Nakambé, *Fr.* Volta Blanche. *river* Burkina/Ghana
Whitianga *128 D2* Waikato, North Island, New Zealand
Whitney, Mount *25 C6 mountain* California, W USA
Whitsunday Group *126 D3 island group* Queensland, E Australia
Whyalla *127 B6* South Australia
Wichita *23 F5* Kansas, C USA
Wichita Falls *27 F2* Texas, SW USA
Wichita River *27 F2 river* Texas, SW USA
Wickenburg *26 B2* Arizona, SW USA
Wicklow *67 B6 Ir.* Cill Mhantáin. *county* E Ireland
Wicklow Mountains *67 B6 Ir.* Sléibhte Chill Mhantáin. *mountain range* E Ireland
Wieliczka *77 D5* Małopolskie, S Poland
Wieluń *76 C4* Sieradz, C Poland
Wien *73 E6 Eng.* Vienna, *Hung.* Bécs, *Slvk.* Vídeň, *Slvn.* Dunaj; *anc.* Vindobona. *country capital* Wien, NE Austria
Wiener Neustadt *73 E6* Niederösterreich, E Austria
Wierden *64 E3* Overijssel, E Netherlands
Wiesbaden *73 B5* Hessen, W Germany
Wieselburg and Ungarisch-Altenburg/ Wieselburg-Ungarisch-Altenburg *see* Mosonmagyaróvár
Wiesenhof *see* Ostrołęka
Wight, Isle of *67 D7 island* United Kingdom
Wigorna Ceaster *see* Worcester
Wijchen *64 D4* Gelderland, SE Netherlands
Wijk bij Duurstede *64 D4* Utrecht, C Netherlands
Wilcannia *127 C6* New South Wales, SE Australia
Wilejka *see* Vilyeyka
Wilhelm, Mount *122 B3 mountain* C Papua New Guinea
Wilhelm-Pieck-Stadt *see* Guben
Wilhelmshaven *72 B3* Niedersachsen, NW Germany
Wilia/Wilja *see* Neris
Wilkes Barre *19 F3* Pennsylvania, NE USA
Wilkes Land *132 C4 physical region* Antarctica
Wilkomierz *see* Ukmergė
Willard *26 D2* New Mexico, SW USA
Willcox *26 C3* Arizona, SW USA
Willebroek *65 B5* Antwerpen, C Belgium
Willemstad *33 E5 dependent territory capital* Curaçao, Netherlands Antilles
Williston *22 D1* North Dakota, N USA
Wilmington *19 F4* Delaware, NE USA
Wilmington *21 F2* North Carolina, SE USA
Wilmington *18 C4* Ohio, N USA
Wilna/Wilno *see* Vilnius
Wilrijk *65 C5* Antwerpen, N Belgium
Winchester *67 D7 hist.* Wintanceaster, *Lat.* Venta Belgarum. S England, United Kingdom
Winchester *19 E4* Virginia, NE USA
Windau *see* Ventspils, Latvia
Windau *see* Venta, Latvia/Lithuania
Windhoek *56 B3 Ger.* Windhuk. *country capital* Khomas, C Namibia
Windhuk *see* Windhoek
Windorah *126 C4* Queensland, C Australia
Windsor *16 C5* Ontario, S Canada
Windsor *67 D7* S England, United Kingdom
Windsor *19 G3* Connecticut, NE USA
Windward Islands *33 H4 island group* E West Indies
Windward Islands *see* Barlavento, Ilhas de, Cape Verde
Windward Passage *32 D3 Sp.* Paso de los Vientos. *channel* Cuba/Haiti
Winisk *see* Peawanuk
Winkowitz *see* Vinkovci
Winnebago, Lake *18 B2 lake* Wisconsin, N USA
Winnemucca *25 C5* Nevada, W USA
Winnipeg *15 G5 province capital* Manitoba, S Canada
Winnipeg, Lake *15 G5 lake* Manitoba, C Canada
Winnipegosis, Lake *16 A3 lake* Manitoba, C Canada
Winona *23 G3* Minnesota, N USA
Winschoten *64 E2* Groningen, NE Netherlands
Winsen *72 B3* Niedersachsen, N Germany
Winston Salem *21 E1* North Carolina, SE USA
Winsum *64 D1* Groningen, NE Netherlands
Wintanceaster *see* Winchester
Winterswijk *64 E4* Gelderland, E Netherlands
Winterthur *73 B7* Zürich, NE Switzerland
Winton *126 C4* Queensland, E Australia
Winton *129 A7* Southland, South Island, New Zealand
Wisby *see* Visby
Wisconsin *18 A2 off.* State of Wisconsin, *also known as* Badger State. *state* N USA
Wisconsin Rapids *18 B2* Wisconsin, N USA
Wisconsin River *18 B3 river* Wisconsin, N USA
Wiślany, Zalew *see* Vistula Lagoon
Wismar *72 C2* Mecklenburg-Vorpommern, N Germany
Wittenberge *72 C3* Brandenburg, N Germany
Wittlich *73 A5* Rheinland-Pfalz, SW Germany
Wittstock *72 C3* Brandenburg, NE Germany
W. J. van Blommesteinmeer *37 G3 reservoir* E Suriname
Władysławowo *76 C2* Pomorskie, N Poland
Włocławek *76 C3 Ger./Rus.* Vlotslavsk. Kujawsko-pomorskie, C Poland
Włodawa *76 E4 Rus.* Vlodava. Lubelskie, SE Poland
Włodzimierz *see* Volodymyr-Volyns'kyy
Wlotzkasbaken *56 B3* Erongo, W Namibia
Wodonga *127 C7* Victoria, SE Australia
Wodzisław Śląski *77 C5 Ger.* Loslau. Śląskie, S Poland
Wojerecy *see* Hoyerswerda
Wōjjā *see* Wotje Atoll
Wojwodina *see* Vojvodina
Woking *67 D7* SE England, United Kingdom
Wolf, Isla *38 A4 island* Galápagos, Galapagos Islands, W Ecuador South America
Wolfsberg *73 D7* Kärnten, SE Austria
Wolfsburg *72 C3* Niedersachsen, N Germany
Wolgast *72 D2* Mecklenburg-Vorpommern, NE Germany
Wołkowysk *see* Vawkavysk
Wöllan *see* Velenje
Wollaston Lake *15 F4* Saskatchewan, C Canada
Wollongong *127 D6* New South Wales, SE Australia
Wolmar *see* Valmiera
Wołożyn *see* Valozhyn
Wolvega *64 D2 Fris.* Wolvegea. Friesland, N Netherlands
Wolvegea *see* Wolvega
Wolverhampton *67 D6* C England, United Kingdom
Wolverine State *see* Michigan
Wŏnsan *107 E3* SE North Korea
Woodburn *24 B3* Oregon, NW USA
Woodland *25 B5* California, W USA
Woodruff *18 B2* Wisconsin, N USA
Woods, Lake of the *16 A3 Fr.* Lac des Bois. *lake* Canada/USA
Woodville *128 D4* Manawatu-Wanganui, North Island, New Zealand
Woodward *27 F1* Oklahoma, C USA
Worcester *56 C5* Western Cape, SW South Africa
Worcester *67 D6 hist.* Wigorna Ceaster. W England, United Kingdom
Worcester *19 G3* Massachusetts, NE USA
Workington *67 C5* NW England, United Kingdom
Worland *22 C3* Wyoming, C USA
Wormatia *see* Worms
Worms *73 B5 anc.* Augusta Vangionum, Borbetomagus, Wormatia. Rheinland-Pfalz, SW Germany
Worms *see* Vormsi
Worthington *23 F3* Minnesota, N USA
Wotje Atoll *122 D1 var.* Wōjjā. *atoll* Ratak Chain, E Marshall Islands
Woudrichem *64 C4* Noord-Brabant, S Netherlands
Wrangel Island *93 F1 Eng.* Wrangel Island. *island* NE Russian Federation
Wrangel Island *see* Vrangelya, Ostrov
Wrangel Plain *133 B2 undersea feature* Arctic Ocean
Wrocław *76 C4 Eng./Ger.* Breslau. Dolnośląskie, SW Poland
Września *76 C3* Wielkopolskie, C Poland
Wsetin *see* Vsetín
Wuchang *see* Wuhan
Wuday'ah *99 C6 spring/well* S Saudi Arabia
Wuhai *105 E3 var.* Haibowan. Nei Mongol Zizhiqu, N China
Wuhan *106 C5 var.* Han-kou, Han-k'ou, Hanyang, Wuchang, Wu-han; *prev.* Hankow. *province capital* Hubei, C China
Wu-han *see* Wuhan
Wuhsien *see* Suzhou
Wuhsi/Wu-his *see* Wuxi
Wuhu *106 D5 var.* Wu-na-mu. Anhui, E China
Wujlān *see* Ujelang Atoll
Wukari *53 G4* Taraba, E Nigeria
Wuliang Shan *106 A6 mountain range* SW China
Wu-lu-k'o-mu-shi/Wu-lu-mu-ch'i *see* Ürümqi
Wu-na-mu *see* Wuhu
Wuppertal *72 A4 prev.* Barmen-Elberfeld. Nordrhein-Westfalen, W Germany
Würzburg *73 B5* Bayern, SW Germany
Wusih *see* Wuxi
Wuxi *106 D5 var.* Wuhsi, Wu-hsi, Wusih. Jiangsu, E China
Wuyi Shan *103 E3 mountain range* SE China
Wye *67 C6 Wel.* Gwy. *river* England/Wales, United Kingdom
Wyłkowyszki *see* Vilkaviškis
Wyndham *124 D3* Western Australia
Wyoming *18 C3* Michigan, N USA
Wyoming *22 B3 off.* State of Wyoming, *also known as* Equality State. *state* C USA
Wyszków *76 D3 Ger.* Probstberg. Mazowieckie, NE Poland

X

Xaafuun, Raas *50 E4 var.* Ras Hafun. *cape* NE Somalia
Xaçmaz *95 H2 Rus.* Khachmas. N Azerbaijan
Xaignabouli *114 C4 prev.* Muang Xaignabouri, *Fr.* Sayaboury. Xaignabouli, N Laos
Xai-Xai *57 E4 prev.* João Belo, Vila de João Belo. Gaza, S Mozambique
Xalapa *29 F4* Veracruz-Llave, Mexico
Xam Nua *114 D3 var.* Sam Neua. Houaphan, N Laos
Xankändi *95 G3 Rus.* Khankendi; *prev.* Stepanakert. SW Azerbaijan
Xánthi *82 C3* Anatolikí Makedonía kai Thráki, NE Greece
Xàtiva *71 F3 Cas.* Xátiva; *anc.* Setabis, *var.* Jativa. País Valenciano, E Spain
Xauen *see* Chefchaouen
Xäzär Dänizi *see* Caspian Sea
Xeres *see* Jeréz de la Frontera
Xiaguan *see* Dali
Xiamen *106 D6 var.* Hsia-men; *prev.* Amoy. Fujian, SE China
Xi'an *106 C4 var.* Changan, Sian, Signan, Siking, Singan, Xian. *province capital* Shaanxi, C China
Xiang *see* Hunan
Xianggang *see* Hong Kong
Xiangkhoang *see* Pèk
Xiangtan *106 C5 var.* Hsiang-t'an, Siangtan. Hunan, S China
Xiao Hinggan Ling *106 D2 Eng.* Lesser Khingan Range. *mountain range* NE China
Xichang *106 B5* Sichuan, C China
Xieng Khouang *see* Pèk
Xieng Ngeun *see* Muong Xiang Ngeun
Xigazê *104 C5 var.* Jih-k'a-tse, Shigatse, Xigaze. Xizang Zizhiqu, W China
Xi Jiang *102 D3 var.* Hsi Chiang, *Eng.* West River. *river* S China
Xilinhot *105 F2 var.* Silinhot. Nei Mongol Zizhiqu, N China
Xilokastro *see* Xylókastro
Xin *see* Xinjiang Uygur Zizhiqu
Xingkai Hu *see* Khanka, Lake
Xingu, Rio *41 E2 river* C Brazil
Xingxingxia *104 D3* Xinjiang Uygur Zizhiqu, NW China
Xining *105 E4 var.* Hsining, Hsi-ning, Sining. *province capital* Qinghai, C China
Xinjiang *see* Xinjiang Uygur Zizhiqu
Xinjiang Uygur Zizhiqu *104 B3 var.* Sinkiang, Sinkiang Uighur Autonomous Region, Xin, Xinjiang. *autonomous region* NW China
Xinpu *see* Lianyungang
Xinxiang *106 C4* Henan, C China
Xinyang *106 C5 var.* Hsin-yang, Sinyang. Henan, C China
Xinzo de Limia *70 C2* Galicia, NW Spain
Xiqing Shan *102 D2 mountain range* C China
Xiva *100 D2 Rus.* Khiva, Khiwa. Xorazm Viloyati, W Uzbekistan
Xixón *see* Gijón
Xizang *see* Xizang Zizhiqu
Xizang Gaoyuan *see* Qingzang Gaoyuan
Xizang Zizhiqu *104 B4 var.* Thibet, Tibetan Autonomous Region, Xizang, *Eng.* Tibet. *autonomous region* W China
Xolotlán *see* Managua, Lago de
Xucheng *see* Xuwen
Xuddur *51 D5 var.* Hudur, *It.* Oddur. Bakool, SW Somalia
Xuwen *106 C7 var.* Xucheng. Guangdong, S China
Xuzhou *106 D4 var.* Hsu-chou, Suchow, Tongshan; *prev.* T'ung-shan. Jiangsu, E China
Xylókastro *83 B5 var.* Xilokastro. Pelopónnisos, S Greece

Y

Ya'an *106 B5 var.* Yaan. Sichuan, C China
Yabēlo *51 C5* Oromīya, C Ethiopia
Yablis *31 E2* Región Autónoma Atlántico Norte, NE Nicaragua
Yablonovyy Khrebet *93 F4 mountain range* S Russian Federation
Yabrai Shan *105 E3 mountain range* NE China
Yafran *49 F2* NW Libya
Yaghan Basin *45 B7 undersea feature* SE Pacific Ocean
Yagotin *see* Yahotyn
Yahotyn *87 E2 Rus.* Yagotin. Kyyivs'ka Oblast', N Ukraine
Yahualica *28 D4* Jalisco, SW Mexico
Yakima *24 B2* Washington, NW USA
Yakima River *24 B2 river* Washington, NW USA
Yakoruda *82 C3* Blagoevgrad, SW Bulgaria
Yaku-shima *109 B8 island* Nansei-shotō, SW Japan
Yakutat *14 D4* Alaska, USA
Yakutsk *93 F3* Respublika Sakha (Yakutiya), NE Russian Federation
Yala *115 C7* Yala, SW Thailand
Yalizava *85 D6 Rus.* Yelizovo. Mahilyowskaya Voblasts', E Belarus
Yalong Jiang *106 A5 river* C China
Yalova *94 B3* Yalova, NW Turkey
Yalpug, Ozero *see* Yalpuh, Ozero
Yalpuh, Ozero *86 D4 Rus.* Ozero Yalpug. *lake* SW Ukraine
Yalta *87 F5* Respublika Krym, S Ukraine
Yalu *103 E2 Chin.* Yalu Jiang, *Jap.* Oryokko, *Kor.* Amnok-kang. *river* China/North Korea
Yalu Jiang *see* Yalu
Yamaguchi *109 B7 var.* Yamaguti. Yamaguchi, Honshū, SW Japan
Yamal, Poluostrov *92 D2 peninsula* N Russian Federation
Yamaniyah, Al Jumhūrīyah al *see* Yemen
Yambio *51 B5 var.* Yambiyo. Western Equatoria, S Sudan
Yambiyo *see* Yambio
Yambol *82 D2 Turk.* Yanboli. Yambol, E Bulgaria
Yamdena, Pulau *117 G5 prev.* Jamdena. *island* Kepulauan Tanimbar, E Indonesia
Yamoussoukro *52 D5 country capital* C Ivory Coast
Yamuna *112 D3 prev.* Jumna. *river* N India
Yana *93 F2 river* NE Russian Federation
Yanboli *see* Yambol
Yanbu 'al Baḩr *99 A5* Al Madīnah, W Saudi Arabia
Yangambi *55 D5* Orientale, N Dem. Rep. Congo
Yangchow *see* Yangzhou
Yangiyo'l *101 E2 Rus.* Yangiyul'. Toshkent Viloyati, E Uzbekistan
Yangiyul' *see* Yangiyo'l
Yangku *see* Taiyuan
Yangon *114 B4 Eng.* Rangoon. Yangon, S Myanmar (Burma)
Yangtze *106 B5 var.* Yangtze Kiang, *Eng.* Yangtze. *river* C China
Yangtze *see* Chang Jiang/Jinsha Jiang
Yangtze *see* Jinsha Jiang
Yangtze Kiang *see* Chang Jiang
Yangzhou *106 D5 var.* Yangchow. Jiangsu, E China
Yankton *23 E3* South Dakota, N USA
Yannina *see* Ioánnina
Yanskiy Zaliv *91 F2 bay* N Russian Federation
Yantai *106 D4 var.* Yan-t'ai; *prev.* Chefoo, Chih-fu. Shandong, E China
Yaoundé *55 B5 var.* Yaunde. *country capital* Centre, S Cameroon
Yap *122 A1 island* Caroline Islands, W Micronesia
Yapanskoye More East Sea/Japan, Sea of
Yapen, Pulau *117 G4 prev.* Japen. *island* E Indonesia
Yap Trench *120 B2 var.* Yap Trough. *undersea feature* SE Philippine Sea
Yap Trough *see* Yap Trench
Yapurá *see* Caquetá, Río, Brazil/Colombia
Yapurá *see* Japurá, Rio, Brazil/Colombia
Yaqui, Río *28 C2 river* NW Mexico
Yaransk *89 C5* Kirovskaya Oblast', NW Russian Federation
Yarega *88 D4* Respublika Komi, NW Russian Federation
Yarkant *see* Shache
Yarlung Zangbo Jiang *see* Brahmaputra
Yarmouth *17 F5* Nova Scotia, SE Canada
Yarmouth *see* Great Yarmouth
Yaroslav *see* Jarosław
Yaroslavl' *88 B4* Yaroslavskaya Oblast', W Russian Federation
Yarumal *36 B2* Antioquia, NW Colombia
Yasyel'da *85 B7 river* Brestskaya Voblasts', SW Belarus Europe
Yatsushiro *109 A7 var.* Yatusiro. Kumamoto, Kyūshū, SW Japan
Yatusiro *see* Yatsushiro
Yaunde *see* Yaoundé
Yavarí *see* Javari, Rio
Rio Yavari *40 C2 var.* Yavarí. *river* Brazil/Peru
Yaviza *31 H5* Darién, SE Panama
Yavoriv *86 B2 Pol.* Jaworów, *Rus.* Yavorov. L'vivs'ka Oblast', NW Ukraine
Yavorov *see* Yavoriv
Yazd *98 D3 var.* Yezd. Yazd, C Iran
Yazoo City *20 B2* Mississippi, S USA
Yding Skovhøj *63 A7 hill* C Denmark
Ýdra *83 C6 var.* Ídhra. *island* Ýdra, S Greece
Ye *115 B5* Mon State, S Myanmar (Burma)
Yecheng *104 A3 var.* Kargilik. Xinjiang Uygur Zizhiqu, NW China
Yefremov *89 B5* Tul'skaya Oblast', W Russian Federation
Yekaterinburg *92 C3 prev.* Sverdlovsk. Sverdlovskaya Oblast', C Russian Federation
Yekaterinodar *see* Krasnodar
Yekaterinoslav *see* Dnipropetrovs'k
Yelets *89 B5* Lipetskaya Oblast', W Russian Federation
Yelisavetpol *see* Gäncä
Yelizavetgrad *see* Kirovohrad
Yelizovo *see* Yalizava
Yell *66 D1 island* NE Scotland, United Kingdom
Yellowhammer State *see* Alabama
Yellowknife *15 E4 territory capital* Northwest Territories, W Canada
Yellow River *106 C4 var.* Yellow River. *river* C China
Yellow River *see* Huang He
Yellow Sea *106 D4 Chin.* Huang Hai, *Kor.* Hwang-Hae. *sea* E Asia
Yellowstone River *22 C2 river* Montana/ Wyoming, NW USA
Yel'sk *85 C7* Homyel'skaya Voblasts', SE Belarus
Yelwa *53 F4* Kebbi, W Nigeria
Yemen *99 C7 off.* Republic of Yemen, *Ar.* Al Jumhuriyah al Yamaniyah, Al Yaman. *country* SW Asia
Yemen, Republic of *see* Yemen
Yemva *88 D4 prev.* Zheleznodorozhnyy. Respublika Komi, NW Russian Federation
Yenakiyeve *87 G3 Rus.* Yenakiyevo; *prev.* Ordzhonikidze, Rykovo. Donets'ka Oblast', E Ukraine
Yenakiyevo *see* Yenakiyeve
Yenangyaung *114 A3* Magway, W Myanmar (Burma)
Yendi *53 E4* NE Ghana
Yengisar *104 A3* Xinjiang Uygur Zizhiqu, NW China
Yenierenköy *80 D4 var.* Yialousa, *Gk.* Agialoúsa. NE Cyprus
Yenipazar *see* Novi Pazar
Yenisey *92 D3 river* Mongolia/Russian Federation
Yenping *see* Nanping
Yeovil *67 D7* SW England, United Kingdom
Yeppoon *126 D4* Queensland, E Australia
Yerevan *95 F3 Eng.* Erivan. *country capital* C Armenia
Yeriho *see* Jericho
Yerushalayim *see* Jerusalem
Yeso *see* Hokkaidō
Yeu, Île d' *68 A4 island* NW France
Yevlakh *see* Yevlax
Yevlax *95 G2 Rus.* Yevlakh. C Azerbaijan
Yevpatoriya *87 F5* Respublika Krym, S Ukraine
Yeya *87 H4 river* SW Russian Federation
Yezerishche *see* Yezyaryshcha
Yezo *see* Hokkaidō
Yezyaryshcha *85 E5 Rus.* Yezerishche. Vitsyebskaya Voblasts', NE Belarus
Yialousa *see* Yenierenköy
Yiannitsá *see* Giannitsá
Yichang *106 C5* Hubei, C China
Yıldızeli *94 D3* Sivas, N Turkey
Yinchuan *106 B4 var.* Yinch'uan, Yin-ch'uan, Yinchwan. *province capital* Ningxia, N China
Yinchwan *see* Yinchuan
Yindu He *see* Indus
Yin-hsien *see* Ningbo
Yining *104 B2 var.* I-ning, *Uigh.* Gulja, Kuldja. Xinjiang Uygur Zizhiqu, NW China
Yin-tu Ho *see* Indus
Yisrael/Yisra'el *see* Israel
Yíthion *see* Gýtheio
Yogyakarta *116 C5 prev.* Djokjakarta, Jogjakarta, Jokyakarta. Jawa, C Indonesia
Yokohama *109 D5* Aomori, Honshū, C Japan
Yokohama *108 A2* Kanagawa, Honshū, S Japan
Yokote *108 D4* Akita, Honshū, C Japan
Yola *53 H4* Adamawa, E Nigeria
Yonago *109 B6* Tottori, Honshū, SW Japan
Yong'an *106 D6 var.* Yongan. Fujian, SE China
Yongzhou *107 C6 var.* Lengshuitan. Hunan, S China
Yonkers *19 F3* New York, NE USA
Yonne *68 C4 river* C France
Yopal *36 C3 var.* El Yopal. Casanare, C Colombia
York *67 D5 anc.* Eboracum, Eburacum. N England, United Kingdom
York *23 E4* Nebraska, C USA
York, Cape *126 C1 headland* Queensland, NE Australia
York, Kap *see* Innaanganeq
Yorkton *15 F5* Saskatchewan, S Canada